# The
# Diana
## Chronicles

Tina Brown was twenty-five when she became editor-in-chief of *Tatler*, reviving the nearly defunct 270-year-old magazine. She went on to become editor-in-chief of *Vanity Fair*, and in 1992 she became the first female editor of *The New Yorker*. In 2000, Tina Brown was awarded a C.B.E. She is married to Sir Harold Evans and has two children. They reside in New York.

# The
# Diana
# Chronicles

# Tina Brown

arrow books

5 7 9 10 8 6 4

Arrow Books
20 Vauxhall Bridge Road
London SW1V 2SA

Century is part of the Penguin Random House
group of companies whose addresses can be found at
global.penguinrandomhouse.com.

First published in 2007 by Century
First published in paperback in 2008 by Arrow Books
This edition published by Arrow Books in 2017

www.penguin.co.uk

A CIP catalogue record for this book
is available from the British Library.

ISBN 9781784758868

Typeset in 9.68/11.94 pt Goudy Old Style BT by Jouve (UK), Milton Keynes
Printed and bound in Great Britain by Clays Ltd, Elcograf S.p.A.

Penguin Random House is committed to a sustainable future
for our business, our readers and our planet. This book is made
from Forest Stewardship Council® certified paper.

*For Harry, always*

# Contents

# Acknowledgements

One of the nice things for me about writing this book has been the chance to spend so much time in London, after twenty-two years of living in New York and only visiting my mother country as what Diana used to call a July American. It allowed me to reactivate friendships from my years at *Tatler* magazine in the early 1980s, when we covered the rise of the nineteen-year-old Lady Diana Spencer with obsessive interest, and also to make numerous new friends among people who, over the years, were either involved with the Princess or wrote interestingly about her, or both.

In the last eighteen months, I have interviewed over 250 men and women – members of Diana's intimate circle, associates in her public life and partners in her philanthropy – and I am indebted to them all for their recollections and insights. I name and acknowledge these individuals separately below, with the regrettable exception of those who spoke on the basis of anonymity. They know who they are and they have my appreciation.

It was gracious of Prime Minister Tony Blair to see me and share his reflections on Diana. I thank, too, his associates Jonathan Powell and Alastair Campbell. I was fortunate in that the timing of my enquiries into the controversies surrounding Diana's death coincided with the formal investigations by Lord Stevens, former Commissioner, Metropolitan Police, culminating in the publication of the Operation Paget Inquiry report at the end of 2006. I am grateful to Lord Stevens for his enlightening interview and his colleague Mike Hargadon for staying in touch throughout. The Operation Paget Inquiry report is a formidable piece of work to which all future Diana chroniclers will be likewise indebted.

No document, however detailed, can substitute for seeing things for yourself. One of the most fruitful days of research I spent was an excursion to Paris on a detailed walk-through of the crash in the Pont d'Alma tunnel with Jean-Michel Caradec'h, formerly a senior reporter and a war reporter with *Paris Match* and *L'Express*. M. Caradec'h's 2006 book about the last hours of the Princess, *Lady Diana: L'enquête criminelle*, is a superb analysis of the French investigation which ended in 1999. I am indebted to him for many points he helped illuminate, as I am to the punctilious reporting of Martyn Gregory's *Diana: The Last Days*.

I struck gold when Sally Bedell Smith, who wrote an authoritative biography, *Diana: In Search of Herself*, in 1999, steered me to Jacqueline Williams. Ms Williams, a British researcher of outstanding quality and an associate producer of television documentaries, has worked with such distinguished authors as Robert Lacey, Ted Morgan and Peter Evans. She combines intellectual rigour with journalistic tenacity and an editor's eye for the telling detail. She is also an organisational powerhouse. Working with me on what was my maiden foray into long-form non-fiction, she set a standard of excellence it was inspiring to try to keep up with. Jackie, I am forever grateful for your contributions to this book, for all you have taught me, and for the pleasure of your company.

I struck gold again when Brian Hitchen, the former editor of the *Daily Star* and the *Sunday Express*, introduced me to Philippa Kennedy. As an experienced newspaper reporter and the former editor of the *Press Gazette* in London from December 1999 to November 2002, she was indispensable to my understanding of the Diana years of British journalism especially after I no longer worked in the UK. I was fortunate again to be able to raid Mr Hitchen's voluminous Rolodex of talent for the royal expertise of the former *Daily Express* journalist Ashley Walton. His email answers to my questions were usually back before I'd had a chance to get my morning cappuccino from Starbucks. At various times along the way I received interesting research from Sallyann Kleibel, Robert Pursley, Rosie Atkinson and the indefatigable Andrew Kirk. The investigative labours of journalist and researcher Garrick Alder on the Web about the Squidgygate tapes stimulated me to look more into this bizarre episode in royal snooping. I thank him for giving me access to the longer unpublished version of his findings. As I delved into the mysteries, communications expert John Nelson, the managing director of Crew Green Consulting Ltd, was extremely forbearing with my technical illiteracy.

More generous leads: Jacqueline Williams's second career as a documentary researcher for Atlantic Productions led me to Atlantic's

CEO and Executive Producer, Anthony Geffen, whose prior work on a Diana project guided me to many interesting avenues. Another talented documentary maker, Phil Craig, producer of *Diana: Story of a Princess*, was generous with his contacts and transcripts. The book Mr Craig co-authored with Tim Clayton, based on the TV series, is full of excellent material.

My favourite excursion after Paris was a visit to Scotland's Blairquhan Castle in Ayrshire to observe Stephen Frears, who was in the process of directing the memorable movie *The Queen*, as he worked with his cast and production team to bring to life Peter Morgan's brilliant screenplay about the aftermath of the death of the Princess of Wales. During the course of their research for the film, they had garnered many unusual insights they shared with me. Watching Dame Helen Mirren morphing back and forth between takes from the irreverent contemporary actress to the emotionally veiled monarch only increased my awe of her Oscar-winning gifts. 'England was built on shoes like these,' she commented as she slid her feet into some monarchical walking brogues.

Our knowledge of Diana owes much to the writings of Andrew Morton, whose *Diana: Her True Story* – and the verbatim version, *Diana: Her True Story – In Her Own Words* remains one of the great publishing scoops ever. He has been most helpful to me. So has Patrick Jephson. *Shadows of a Princess*, his memoir of his eight years as Diana's equerry and then private secretary, is replete with intriguing observations as well as an insider's perspective on what it takes to run a princess who becomes a global phenomenon. Ken Wharfe MVO, Diana's former personal protection officer, was generous with his time, and I referred often to his robust memoir, *Diana: A Closely Guarded Secret*. Paul Burrell's two memoirs, too, have much touching detail to commend them.

Royal biographers seem to be an extremely collegial breed. I had help and encouragement from such titans of the genre as Robert Lacey, Anthony Holden, Kenneth Rose CBE, Hugo Vickers, Jonathan Dimbleby and Ingrid Seward. Gyles Brandreth's biography, *Charles & Camilla: Portrait of a Love Affair*, was valuable as much for its humour as for the store of information it provides. There have been so many books about Diana that it was a relief towards the end of my research to turn to the sound judgements of Sarah Bradford's biography, *Diana*. I thoroughly recommend Charles Spencer's *The Spencers: A Personal History of an English Family* and *Althorp: The Story of an English House* which combine his personal knowledge of the Spencer family's history with a historian's scholarship and a felicitous style. For a sympathetic portrait of Frances Shand Kydd there is none more informative than *Frances: The Remarkable Story of Princess Diana's Mother* by Max Riddington and Gavan Naden. A full list of the books that have enriched this one can be found on pages 431–4.

I am grateful to India Hicks for allowing me to quote from a private letter written to her uncle Lord Brabourne recalling the awful day her grandfather Earl Mountbatten was murdered. Lady Sarah Berry was generous with her help on the period before Diana was born. Andrew Tilberis kindly allowed me to quote from a letter Diana wrote to his late wife, *Harper's Bazaar*'s legendary editor Liz Tilberis. Some of the material in *The Diana Chronicles* has appeared in columns about the royals written for the *Washington Post* Style section (2003–5). I thank my editor there, Deborah Heard, and the *Washington Post* for permission to include it.

I was greatly helped by having been a Condé Nast editor for eighteen years in London and New York. I warmly thank former colleagues Stephen Schiff, Bob Colacello, John Lahr, Brenda Phipps, Caroline Graham, Adam Gopnik, Simon Schama, Christina Garrett, Jane Sarkin and Wayne Lawson. My former *Tatler* colleague, Nicholas Coleridge, who has become both a bestselling novelist and managing director of Condé Nast UK, and Geordie Greig, the current editor of *Tatler*, were wonderfully forthcoming with phone numbers and email addresses it would have otherwise taken for ever to find, as well as with their observations. Some of the material for Chapter 12 first appeared in *Vanity Fair* in the article I wrote in October 1985 'The Mouse That Roared', and I appreciate the permission to quote it here. My former *Vanity Fair* partner in crime, the gifted photographer Annie Leibovitz, with her usual generosity insisted on taking the portrait the publisher required for my book jacket. I thank her for her time and her talent.

A non-fiction book that is researched mainly in another country is an expensive and awkward proposition, and my trips to London would not have been half as comfortable, centrally located and fashionably cool if Ian Schrager had not made a room available every time I hit town at his fabulous Sanderson Hotel in Berners Street. The young staff there operates with New York energy and London manners, a helpful combination for a demanding writer with a moody computer. Speaking of which, I lost count of the number of times that my computer gurus Chris and Ryan Cuddihy showed up at the Evans-Brown ménage in

# Acknowledgements

Quogue, Long Island, at unusual hours of the night to perform some miracle to a frozen machine. I thank them both profusely.

I would like to thank the librarians and staff of the British Library, the New York Public Library and the British Library Newspapers on Colindale Avenue. I drew constantly on that jewel of a resource, the Hans Tasiemka Archives, assembled by Edda Tasiemka (aka the Human Google) and her late husband Hans. Edda is helped now by her assiduous assistant Heidi Raj.

Throughout the conception and writing of *The Diana Chronicles*, I received much valuable counsel from my dear friend and literary agent Ed Victor. His support of a writer does not stop when contracts have been exchanged. I am grateful to Gail Rebuck, Chief Executive of Random House, for her immediate enthusiasm, and to Publishing Director Mark Booth so ably supported by Charlotte Haycock, Assistant Editor. It has been a pleasure, too, to work with them and with the fastidious copy-editing of Katherine Fry.

It's pathetic how much writers depend on encouragement. At moments when I was especially racked with misgivings I was grateful to my friend the British biographer Julie Kavanagh for her supportive critique, to Gabé Doppelt, LA Bureau chief of *W* magazine, and to Sir Peter Stothard, who was editor of *The Times* during the nineties, Craig Raine, the literary editor and poet, and Hendrik Hertzberg, my old (but surprisingly youthful!) *New Yorker* consigliere. My brother, Chris Brown, chose exactly the right moment to show up from Australia and give the manuscript a reading that helped me lick an earlier draft into shape. The legendary former Simon & Schuster editor and author Michael Korda was kind enough to offer his experienced critique at a time when I needed an objective eye, and I am indebted to his kindness at a time when he was on deadline himself.

I seem to be blessed with an incomparable claque of supportive girlfriends who provided pep talks whenever I was flagging and I thank here each and every one. I humbly salute my two children, George and Izzy, not only for their merry boosterism but also for their forbearance. I promise never again to lock myself in a hotel room for an entire family vacation.

I cannot be effusive enough in my gratitude to Kara Simonetti, my dedicated, tireless and superbly organised executive assistant, who slaved over every page of this manuscript in its many vexing incarnations and subjected each fact and detail to perfectionist scrutiny.

Lastly – no, firstly – no, from first to last and back again – this book would never have got past word one without the help, sustenance, affection, and Christlike patience of my husband, Harry Evans. If only poor Princess Diana could have experienced such love at home.

With thanks and appreciation to: Professor Michael Adler, Barry Allsop, Charles Anson, Lady Elizabeth Anson, Dickie Arbiter LVO, Joe Armstrong, Harry Arnold, Margaret Aro, Jacques Azagury, Ann Barr, Andrew Barrow, Mikhail Baryshnikov, Tony Benn, Edward Berry, Lord Birt, Michael Birt, Manolo Blahnik, Sir Ian Blair and Lady Blair, Amy Bloom, Chris Boffey, Mark Bolland, Noel Botham, Hamish Bowles, Lord Bragg, Stephen Brasher, Pat Breen, Marie Brenner, Tom Brokaw, Danae Brook, Joan Juliet Buck, William F. Buckley, Major Colin Burgess, Charlie Campbell, Duncan Campbell, Professor David Cannadine, Cindy Cathcart, Miles Chapman, Jimmy Choo, Mary Clarke, Wensley Clarkson, Max Clifford, Michael Cole, Dr James Colthurst, Richard Compton Miller, Chris Connelly, Jasper Conran, Shirley Conran, Alison Croose, Tessa Dahl, Phil Dampier, the Earl of Dartmouth, Alain de Botton, Maxine de Brunner, Anne de Courcy, The Rt Hon. Lord Deedes, Nigel Dempster, Lord Donoughue, Diana Donovan, Sue Douglas, Ervin Duggan, Mike Dunlea, Nell Dunn, Dominick Dunne, Victor Edelstein, Arthur Edwards, Robert Edwards, Michael Eisner, Elizabeth Emanuel, Sally Emerson, Nikki English, Robin Esser, Meredith Etherington-Smith, Joanna Farrell, Mohamed Al Fayed, Anna Fels, Bert Fields, Oliver Foot, Amanda Foreman, Teddy Forstmann, Chris Fortunato, Grainne Fox, James Fox, Debbie Frank, Sarah Frank, Lady Antonia Fraser, Lady Fiona Fraser, Jason Fraser, Sir David Frost OBE, Stephen Fry, Charlotte Gerard, Garth Gibbs, Emma Gilbey, Sarah Giles, Barbara Gilmour, Lady Anne Glenconner, Lord Glenconner, Clive Goodman, Lord Gould, Eileen Graham, John Graham, Tim Graham, Roy Greenslade, Sir Jeremy Greenstock KCMG, Betty Greif, Sir Ronald Grierson, David Griffin RVM, Pamela Gross, Jennifer Guerini-Maraldi, Barbara Guggenheim, Sabrina Guinness, Ali Gunn, Graeme Hall, Tony Hall, Alan Hamilton, Belinda Harley, Colleen Harris, Robert Harris, Paddy Harverson, Nicky Haslam, Selina Hastings, Veronica Hearst, Marie Helvin, Reinaldo Herrera, Nicola Hewitt, Robert Higdon, John Hockenberry, Warren Hoge, Sandra Horley, The Rt Hon. Sir Robin Janvrin KCVO CB, the Rt Hon. Lady Jay, Simon Jenkins, Paul Johnson, Dafydd Jones, Tessa Jowell, Dmitri Kasterine, Sean Kavanagh-Dowset, Richard Kay, Douglas Keay, Sara Keene, Alan Keyes, Mary Killen, Jeremy King, Dr

Acknowledgements

Henry Kissinger, Andrew Knight, Phillip Knightley, Cynthia Knights, Steve Kroft, Dominic Lawson, Leon LeCash, Jeffrey Leeds, Ken Lennox, the 5th Earl of Lichfield, Marguerite Littman, Sir Nicholas Lloyd, Brian MacArthur, Ross MacGibbon, Colonel Allan Mallinson, Karyn Marcus, Jon Marder, Aretha Marinzeck, Candice Marks, Bob Marshall, Frederic Martel, Victoria Mather, Ghislaine Maxwell, Cynthia McFadden, Peter McKay, Susan Mercandetti, Jon Michaud, George Milburn, Edward Mirzoeff, the Hon Rosa Monckton, Derry Moore, Patrea More Nesbitt, Peter Morgan, Piers Morgan, Susan Nagel, Andrew Neil, Louise Nicholson, Jamie Niven, John Norman, Katherine O'Hearn, Bruce Oldfield, Susie Orbach, John Overton, Harry Page, Lord and Lady Palumbo, Vivienne Parry, Nicky Perry, Holly Peterson, Tom Petrie, Maggie Phillips, Erin Pizzey, Amanda Platell, Shaun Plunket, David Pogson, Eve Pollard, Gerald Posner, General Colin L. Powell, USA (Ret), Lord and Lady Puttnam, Cindy Quillinan, Maggie Ray, Lord Rees-Mogg, James Reginato, Lynda Resnick, Sebastian Rich, Andrew Roberts, Edward Roberts, Geoffrey Robertson QC, Mary Robertson, Ruth Rogers, Dr Isadore Rosenfeld, Lord Rothschild OM GBE FBA, Penny Russell-Smith, Marcus Rutherford, Carol Ryan, Zoe Sallis, Hitesh Shah, William Shand Kydd, Alice Shaw, Michael Shea CVO, Beverly Sills, Simone Simmons, Sir Roger Singleton CBE, Wayne Sleep, Liz Smith, Jon Snow, Emma Soames, Jesper Soeresen, Raine, Countess Spencer, Robert Spencer, Lady Stevens, Sir Jocelyn Stevens CVO, Richard Stott, Alice Straw, Chris Sullivan, Ben Summerskill, Janice Sutherland, Mimi Swartz, Camilla Swift, Hugo Swire, Andre Leon Talley, William Tallon RVM, David Tang, Colin Tebbutt MVO, Ian Telford, Mario Testino, Barbara Timms, Steve Torrington, John Travolta, Professor Donald Trelford, Brittany Trevenen, Linda Van, Marjatta van Boeschoten, Lucia van der Post, Kate Waddington, Judy Wade, Simon Walker, Christine Ward, Lord Weidenfeld, Lady Weinberg, the Earl of Westmorland, James Whitaker, Michael White, John Whitehead, Kim Willsher, Steve Wood, Mervyn Wycherley, Hassan Yassin, Lucy Yeomans, Peter York, the Biography Channel, Christie's Auction House, ITN Factual, ITV, Metropolitan Police Public Access Office, Vintage Magazine Shop and Women's Entertainment Network.

# Introduction by Andrew Marr

The death of Diana, Princess of Wales undoubtedly shook the British in a way no other royal event in modern times has done. Equally certainly, she was the first genuine royal celebrity. Her divorce and then her violent death were among the worst events the House of Windsor has ever faced. So twenty years on, what does she mean?

Diana's Britain already seems a lost, different country. Tony Blair was only a few months into his first premiership – young, brightly smiling, charismatic and relatively untarnished. The country was getting used to unfamiliar politicians such as Gordon Brown and David Blunkett. Enthusiasm for the EU was widespread across most of the political spectrum; New Labour cabinet ministers would tell anyone prepared to listen that Britain would shortly join the euro.

The first generation of the iPhone was still a decade in the future. Victoria Adams had just been dubbed 'Posh Spice' and her group were at their zenith; she would not marry a certain well-known footballer for another two years. Two Californian geeks were about to register a strange name for their proposed search engine – Google. But Internet use was still relatively uncommon in Britain – just 7.5% of people were merrily clicking away, compared to more than 90% now.

By contrast, the newspapers were much more powerful – well before the forced closure of the News of the World and rising public worries about entrapment and eavesdropping, this was the last roar of tabloid Britain. If anything epitomised this last hurrah it was Diana's tumultuous love affair with the camera and the tabloids. Briefly a victim, she was drawn into a vortex of exploitation before blossoming from puppet into puppeteer.

One of Tina Brown's advantages as a biographer is that she also inhabited this fame-hungry, fast-moving world of 1980s and 1990s journalism that Diana basked in. If we want to relive that strange era at the end of the twentieth century, when hair was big and shoulders were padded, and the celebrity stories were gigantic and multicoloured, then we need a guide who was there at the time and remembers it clearly. Tina's status in New York also turns out to be useful; had Diana lived, then it's a reasonable assumption that she would have ended up living in the United States, a place where she found rather more air to breathe than in class-bound, tabloid-stalked London.

Still, twenty years on we are *such* different people. I think we were more innocent, naive then, like oddly youthful family members in old video footage. We had bought into the Diana story in ways that wouldn't be repeated by any other figure later on. The shock of Diana's death was so sharp because so many of us had lived our lives by proxy through her. We had talked about class and Peter York's 'Sloane Rangers' because of that demure, embarrassed, gawky young aristo first pursued by snappers through West London. Royalists celebrated her marriage as a great moment of rejuvenation for the Windsors; republicans scurried off abroad and bristled with despair about the state of the national debate. The ups and downs of Diana's marriage, its miseries and triumphs, were discussed and refracted back in our own relationships. We learned about bulimia because of her. Our jaws dropped at those salacious tape revelations. We sat at home transfixed by the *Panorama* interview and for days talked about nothing else. We debated the propriety or otherwise of her later boyfriends and we divided across dinner tables about Prince Charles's behaviour.

So by the time she died, Diana had become truly nestled inside the imaginations of most of us. We felt she represented something we British were becoming in general – more open about our emotions, more liberal, perhaps even kinder. She hugged and kissed her sons in public. She took up righteous if unpopular causes, from Aids to landmines, an unapologetically political (small p) campaigner we hadn't seen in royal circles before. Her death was felt not just as the shocking death of a young mother in a motor accident, but as a punch to the solar plexus of tens of millions of people she had never met – something meaningful in the national story.

This was why, no doubt, so many people were desperate to believe that there was a sinister conspiracy behind her death, with senior members of the royal family and/or the security services pulling the strings to prevent an embarrassing second marriage. This was why, also, there was that strange mutinous mood in central London when the Queen and the Duke of Edinburgh declined to hurry straight down from Balmoral and join the exhibition of public grief, leaving only the sinister sound of the wind rustling through the plastic wrapping of thousands of bundles of decaying flowers at the gates of the palace.

Back in the present, it seems so long ago, and so hysterical. Because of the royal connection and her own high-wattage charisma, Diana came to mean something to millions of people that was – to be blunt – silly and unreasonable. No fallible human being should ever have been the glossy receptacle of so much panting expectation. Any real person subjected to the hot adoration of tens of millions, and the frantic insistence that 'you understand me' would melt into a puddle of exhaustion or a cloud of hysterical laughter. Some of what happened was the fault of the public. We treated her as a Botticelli heroine, as a painted representative of ideal womanhood – mocked, rejected, damaged and yet rising from the waves to forgive us. Or even, perhaps, like a secular Virgin Mary, eternally loving and innocent, walking through the evil and corruption of everyday life. The midsummer hysteria of 1997 had very little to do with the woman who loved and lost, who became a cunning user of others, who learned to be an excellent mother, and who was then killed in a random, meaningless accident in a Paris underpass. We had projected onto her our hopes and our anger, so that when she died we felt properly bereaved. How childish we were.

For the royal family, her death was a crisis, yes – but they got through it quickly and relatively easily in contrast to the public. After making her public acknowledgement of Diana's power, the Queen herself became more popular than ever. So far as the royal establishment is concerned, individuals learned to be Diana-like – to express their emotions and to smile more, and to play the newspaper game bravely – but beyond that, nothing really changed. In fact, soon that sunlit, naively enthusiastically pro-European and leftish Britain of 1997 would be buried itself – by the Iraq War, by the 2008 financial crash, and because of its own ageing and exhaustion.

After Diana's death, memorialists came up with books – this one being the best – as well as walks, fountains, playgrounds, statues and innumerable domestic objects. The clever, damaged, haunted young woman behind the photographs emerged and became truly immortalised in the people's hearts. Ten years later, her sons raised money with a huge pop concert, and today, Diana's name and face continue to be used by many charities, hospitals and other public concerns.

Yet her most potent and impressive memorial is the behaviour of her two sons, then the teenagers Wills and Harry, now the Duke of Cambridge and Prince Henry of Wales. When we saw them, aged fifteen and twelve, walking white-faced and shocked behind their mother's coffin, they looked like ultimate victims. The offspring of a ruined marriage, surrounded and snapped at by a piously intrusive media, and without their devoted mother – how could they possibly grow up to be happy and useful people?

But they did. Both sons, growing up, put the occasional foot wrong and fell foul of censorious newspaper editors. But each of them seemed to emerge as emotionally mature, serious-minded and attractive men in whose hands the Windsor dynasty seems, for the moment, pretty safe.

Much of the credit must go to the warm way that Diana brought them up, but much must also go to the much less popular figure of Prince Charles. He was seen in the aftermath of his divorce as chilly to the point of cruelty. Having been sent unhappily away to school himself, detesting much of his own upbringing, how could he learn the modern empathetic parenting skills we are taught to admire? Well, his evident success as a parent suggests that the public view of him was wide of the mark; for he is a father adored by his children – and there can be no greater happiness than that.

In the end, the life and death of Diana was a family story – the story of the Windsor family – and families (most of them, not all) are remarkably resilient. Again and again, despite the pessimism of Philip Larkin, one generation learns from the mistakes of the previous one. Feuds are forgotten; hatchets are buried. Parents leave you with the strengths they had. Again and again, the damaged and the angry discover for themselves the necessity of forgiveness and love. Every day, individuals die, and every day their families go on; and this is also the Windsor story.

But perhaps the legacy that Diana has given us is that we as a nation have become, since her life and death, a little less hysterical. When Kate Middleton married Diana's older son, there seemed a danger that she would suffer just the same intolerable burden of projection. Indeed, she's popular. People talk about what she wears, and seem to like pictures of her toddlers too. She takes her charity work admirably seriously.

Yet she isn't Diana. Partly, of course, she isn't tortured by the experience of becoming a leading member of the royal household, as Diana was. She is calmer and more level-headed. And while the younger royals still face a self-righteous and aggressive media – Prince Harry above all at the moment – things aren't quite as overheated as they used to be. Could it be that, back in the strange summer of 1997, we exhausted some of our frantic over-enthusiasm and projected emotion? That we, as it were, were bled out?

If so, then the legacy of that extraordinary year is unexpectedly positive: the royal family survived and became more popular, and the rest of us – well, we grew up.

Andrew Marr
March 2017

# Foreword

In June 2006, nearly nine years after Diana's death, I attended a ball – hosted, improbably, by *Tatler* magazine and Mikhail Gorbachev – at Althorp, the ancestral home of the Spencer family in Northamptonshire. I looked up at the glowing windows from which Diana, during an unhappy visit with Prince Charles soon after their marriage, had gazed moodily at the rolling, moonlit grounds. The crowd partying in the tent that night was her crowd – the London demi-monde of fashion and café society and media. She would have lit up the gathering with her radiance and charm. It seemed all wrong for her to lie buried on that lonely island in the lake. All wrong for the laughter and the voices not to include hers. As the band played on and the summer night dwindled, I kept waiting for her to come down and join us and the last nine years to disappear.

Diana would have been fifty in July 2011. What would she have been like? Still great-looking: that's a given. Her mother, Frances Shand Kydd, with her cornflower-blue eyes and well-turned legs, was a handsome woman to the very end. Fashion-wise, Diana would have gone the J. Crew and Galliano route in the same vein as Michelle Obama, always knowing how to mix the casual with the glam. There is no doubt she would have kept her chin taut with strategic Botox shots and her bare arms buff from the gym.

Remarriage? At least two, I suspect, on both sides of the Atlantic. Always so professional herself, she would have soon grown exasperated with Dodi Fayed's hopeless unpunctuality (though staying on good terms with his father, Mohamed, who could still be relied on to cough up for a table or two at a charity dinner). After the break-up with Dodi she would have probably moved to New York, where I picture her spending a few cocooned years married to a super-rich hedge fund guy. Eventually, having wearied of the boredom of weekends in his big tasteless house in upstate New York, she would have shed him too, and might have drifted into undercover trysts with someone more exciting – a former American president with a country place nearby, for example, or a globetrotting French finance wizard destined for the Elysée. Gliding sleekly into her forties, she'd have developed a taste for men of power over boys of play, international movers and shakers who'd invite her not just on extended trips floating off the Côte d'Azur but to brainy summits at Ditchley or private sessions at Davos. I suspect she would have retained a weakness for men in uniform, and a yen for dashing Muslim men. (A two-year fling with a Pakistani general rumoured to have links to the ISI would have been a particular headache for the Foreign Office.)

Diana would have been well pleased with the scandal at Rupert Murdoch's *News of the World* – the one that revealed that for years the British tabloids had been hacking into the phones of celebrities and royals and publishing the illicit skimmings. She would have sued for sure, and her collected damages would have broken all records. Is it possible that even Squidgygate, the embarrassingly steamy phone call between Diana and her lover James Gilbey in December of 1989, was really one of the earliest examples of press malfeasance? I never believed the bizarre explanation, investigated at length here in *The Diana Chronicles*, that a radio ham named Cyril Reenan had picked up this call and offered it to the *Sun*. Was Reenan, who later spoke of 'being set up by a sinister conspiracy' and died in 2004, really a cover for a nefarious phone hacker? If so, Diana's obsession about eavesdroppers in the last days of her life – often mocked as paranoia – was simply the sound intuition of a careful student of the folkways of Fleet Street.

Politically, Diana would have soon parted company with Tony Blair, stung by his failure to use her, as she had hoped, for big peacemaking missions overseas. He would have tried to woo her back each election cycle, but Diana was shrewd when it came to the conducting of feuds. While I suspect she would have been reconciled with her mother, I doubt she would have ever forgiven her brother, Earl Spencer, for abruptly withdrawing the refuge of a house on Althorp's grounds at the time she needed it most. Diana was too wounded in childhood and in marriage to forgive the people who let her down. Perhaps the Earl understood that, and guilt was the impetus for his fiery repudiation of the royals at her funeral (and also for his insistence that she should be enshrined at Althorp for ever). I believe her best male friend in later years would have been, poignantly, her reviled first husband. She and Charles had begun to reach a delicate understanding towards the end of her life. She would no longer have been impatient of Charles's causes. Rather she would have empathised and asked his advice about hers. After so many loves and losses she might have even given up hating Camilla. The Duchess's galleon-sized Lady Bracknell hat at William's wedding would have offered satisfaction enough.

And Kate, the newly minted Duchess of Cambridge? How would Diana have handled her son's steadfast affection for a woman other than herself? The rising public adoration of Kate would have afforded Diana some tricky moments. Pleased, yes. But, like Frances Shand Kydd – who, days before Diana's wedding, suddenly burst out, 'I have good long legs – like my daughter' – Diana would have had to adjust to a broadening of the limelight. Her edge over Kate, of course, was the epic of her princessly suffering, which would always make Diana's story more interesting. ('Happily ever after' will never have the same allure to the press as 'It all went wrong') But she would have loved being a firm defender of the Middletons against the Palace snobs and ostentatiously made Kate's dynamic mother, Carole Middleton, her new BFF. To William's slight irritation she would also have begun to see his in-laws' comfortable, relaxed house in Berkshire as a haven for herself, casting Kate's solid, dependable father, Michael, as yet another shoulder to lean on. Diana was always searching for the kind of supportive family that she never had.

Would our heroine by now have found peace? Yes, I believe she would. Sustained by the two things she cared about most: her children and her work.

In July 1997, Diana told me she'd been discussing the idea of making television films to further promote her work on behalf of the victims of landmines, leprosy, and HIV/Aids. As the years rolled by, her foundation would have become one of the most prestigious in the world. For a woman whose private life was so ruled by her heart, Diana was a surprisingly good executive. She knew how to make things happen. She knew how to run a team. She had a galvanic focus when her compassionate feelings were stirred. Her Princess Diana Foundation, fuelled by a steady pipeline of Fayed and Forstman millions (her ex-boyfriend, billionaire Theodore Forstman, stayed in close touch), might have rivalled the Clinton Global Initiative by now. In the world disasters of the last few years – 9/11, the tsunamis, the Pakistan earthquake, Hurricane Katrina, the Japanese nuclear catastrophe – you know Diana would have been first at the scene in a hard hat with a camera crew (and, by now, ten million followers on Twitter). She would have kept her spotlight trained on individual sufferers whom she'd continued to visit and care for and touch. At a time when the world has disaster fatigue, I miss the generosity of her star power and what it could accomplish.

'One day I will get you back your HRH,' fourteen-year-old William told his mother at the time of her divorce. And in many ways he already has. He made considerable efforts to include the memory of his mother in the most important day of his life. The engagement ring he placed on Kate's finger belonged to his mother. In the days before the ceremony there was a sacred trip with his fiancée to Diana's grave on the island in the lake. The opening hymn at the wedding, 'Guide Me, O Thou Great Redeemer', was one of Diana's favourites, chosen by William and Harry to close her funeral service and the memorial service to mark the tenth anniversary of her death.

The way William has matured has reflected so much of Diana's tender messaging to him as a child. It made him sure and steady in his choice of the woman he loved after years of considered courtship. Like his scampish heart-throb younger brother, William is relaxed with the media and informal in his presentation to the public. When the couple drove out of Buckingham Palace in his father's 41-year-old open-topped Aston Martin DB6 Volante, the gesture showed all his mother's theatrical flair. Those huge blue eyes of Diana's, gazing out from under an elegant but fashion-forward 'fascinator', in the front row of Westminister Abbey, would have shone with pride.

Indeed, so much of William's current happiness could not have happened without the mother who fought for a different way of royal life. Thanks to the discreet Palace self-examination after the turbulent scenes before Diana's funeral, the Queen, too, has profoundly changed. She is far more available to her people. Her advisers today are much more media-savvy, much less 'top drawer' than the crusty enforcers of tradition who cramped the life of the Princess of Wales. At Easter this year, the Queen was photographed riding in the woods at Windsor with her two youngest grandchildren, one of whom was attached to her by a leading rein. When she saw the picture, the Queen liked it so much she told the Palace to release it to the press. That would never have happened ten years ago, let alone twenty. It was a private moment that told a story: the Queen as Granny.

The picture, like the wedding, was a pure Diana moment.

# Chapter 1

# A Tunnel in Paris

'If I had Diana with me I would take her to the jungle, not the Ritz.'

— Dodi Fayed's uncle, Hassan Yassin, 2006

Paris, 31 August 1997. The car that sped into the Pont d'Alma tunnel at twenty-three minutes past midnight was carrying the most famous woman in the world. The icon of blondeness whose long legs were crossed in the back seat of the black Mercedes was at the end of a chaotic night out and her mood was sour. You could see her displeasure in the tight expression caught by the closed-circuit security camera as she pushed quickly through the revolving doors of the Ritz hotel's front entrance on the Place Vendôme.

Arthur Edwards, the dean of royal photographers, knew that look well. It still bothers him when he thinks of it. For sixteen years there hadn't been a mood of the Princess that wasn't caught, logged, pored over, blown up and flashed to every news desk on the planet, and Edwards, the rumpled, balding cockney from the *Sun* had been witness to most of them. He had taken the very first stolen picture of Lady Diana Spencer at a polo match in Sussex one year before she married Prince Charles and he was one of the first of the British royal photographers to arrive at the gates of Pitié-Salpêtrière in Paris where she died. He says the last time he had seen that troubled expression was during a visit to Great Ormond Street Hospital for Children in February 1992. Her downcast mood had had a sad result for the waiting rat pack: she refused to look at the camera on her way out. Edwards and his colleagues were rewarded only when a construction worker gave the Princess a wolf whistle and she couldn't help responding and lifting her head. *Snap.* Like every other photographer in Fleet Street throughout the eighties and nineties, Edwards lived for — and on — Diana's smile.

On that last night in Paris with Dodi Fayed the Princess knew things were out of control. So Edwards recalls today in a bar in London. He was a genuine favourite of Diana's. His avuncular face is creased with regret, as if had he been there he could have done something about it. 'She wanted to get home. She wanted to see the boys. She wasn't a pop star. She was a princess. She was used to the front door, a red carpet. That whole Dodi thing – decoy cars, back entrances – that wasn't Diana's style.'[1]

Edwards is wrong about that. The chaos of her last night was increasingly Diana's style ever since the divorce which had transformed her from a protected royal princess into a free-floating global celebrity. The fact that she was rattling around Paris with a haphazard playboy like Dodi at the end of August was proof of it. The British Ambassador didn't even know she was in town. Nor did the French authorities. In August most upscale Parisians head north to Deauville for the polo and the racing or to the cool woods of their country estates in the Loire or Bordeaux. Dodi had use of a lavish apartment in a building belonging to his father on the Rue Arsène-Houssaye overlooking the Champs-Elysées, so what need did they have of a hotel suite? They were at the Ritz that night only because Dodi was intent on showing off his father's wealth, dispatching hotel flunkeys on yet more shopping expeditions. No one pursued by paparazzi would otherwise choose this venue as a hideout. Paris's most prestigious hotel at that time of the year is crawling with camera-toting tourists and rubber-neckers. At the end of the seasonal exit from town even the more exclusive areas of the hotel – such as its restaurant, L'Espadon – have a louche air of rootless extravagance. South American call girls with hirsute operators from emerging markets and rich old ladies with predatory nephews can be seen poring over the wine list under the *trompe d'oeil* of its opulent ceiling. Dinner for two sets you back £400.

The ambience this place typifies was exactly the kind Diana couldn't stand. She had just auctioned off all the grand and glittering dresses of her old life for charity at Christie's in New York to prove it. When she crossed the Atlantic for the opening preview in July 1997, Anna Wintour, the editor-in-chief of *Vogue*, and I had lunch with her at the Four Seasons, the Park Avenue restaurant that served as an unofficial canteen for Condé Nast executives. 'I've kept a few things,' Diana said about the upcoming auction, 'but you know that Catherine Walker with all the bugle beads? People in England don't wear those kind of clothes any more.'[2]

What struck me at lunch was how much celebrity itself had transformed Diana's appearance. I have come to think that being looked at obsessively by people you don't know actually changes the way your face and body are assembled – not just in the obvious ways of enhanced fashion sense or tricks of charm and self-possession but in the illusion of size. The heads of world-class celebrities literally seem to enlarge. Hillary Clinton's, for instance, has grown enormously since she was the mere wife of the Governor of Arkansas. It nods when she talks to you like a balloon float in a Thanksgiving Day parade. The years of limelight so inflated the circumference of Jackie O's cranium, it seemed her real face must be concealed by an oversized Halloween mask. If you looked into her eyes you could see her in there somewhere, screaming.

In the case of Diana, it was as if everything had been elongated and hand-coloured. The tall, soft-cheeked English rose I first met at the American Embassy in 1981, when she was a new bride, had become as phosphorescent as a cartoon. Striding on three-inch heels across the high-ceilinged grill room of the Four Seasons, she towered like Barbarella. Her Chanel suit was a sharp, animated green, her tan as flawless as if it had been airbrushed on. The gently flushed skin of her face wasn't just peachy; it was softer than a child's velveteen rabbit. No wonder she made such an impact at the bedsides of sick children. Arriving in a flashing cone of artificial light, she must have seemed to them like a glowing angel come to soothe the sorrows of our world below. Her instinct to move to America was spot on. She would only ever feel at home now in the culture that invented fame the size of hers. 'You can feel the energy go up when the Americans arrive in July for Wimbledon,' she told me wistfully.

Diana was already worrying at lunch about where she might go in August. Putting out a deckchair in her spacious garden at Kensington Palace was not a conceivable option for someone with an aversion to books. Besides, it would be lonely. 'It will be so difficult,' she said, 'without the boys.' For a divorced princess, the month when glamour appearances are on hold only magnified the yawning empty nest inflicted by the upper-class pedagogical custom of sending children away to boarding school at the age of eight. For her two sons, William and Harry, August meant Balmoral with their father and deluxe vagrancy for their mother. Everyone from her old life had withdrawn to spartan family lodges in the Scottish heather or rambling villas in Tuscany where they played Monopoly with their kids and read Frederick Forsyth novels. Diana, no longer HRH, was not so welcome in such circles now that she had cut her ties with the royal family. The moneyed social players of her newer London circle didn't rush to ask her to stay in August either. Who could face the palaver? It would be worse than having Madonna as a house guest. Not because Diana herself was spoilt or demanding. On the contrary, her notion of hedonism was to iron her own and her hostesses' clothes herself. ('I've finished my ironing. Would you like me to do yours?' she called downstairs to Lady Annabel Goldsmith and Jemima Khan when she went with them on private visit to Pakistan in February 1996.)[3] It was one thing to enjoy the lustre of having the Princess of Wales to dinner in London, quite another to put up with her house-guest requirements for longer than a weekend. At this point it needed a fortress as secure as Colditz to keep the press and the loonies at bay. Then there was the aftermath of having the tabloids scavenge through your garbage for newsworthy evidence. Only Dodi's father, Mohamed Al Fayed, was keen enough and rich enough to take on the aggravation. The Egyptian merchant, who in 1985 had bought the Mecca of London shopping, Harrods, in the hope of storming the British Establishment, still dreamed about royal connections. His yacht, his cliffside compound in the South of France, his Ritz hotel in Paris were Diana's new castles in the air. 'He has all the toys,' she told a friend.[4]

The result was that her last two weeks with Dodi had been like a made-for-TV version of her honeymoon with Prince Charles in 1981. Instead of the royal yacht *Britannia* with its Royal Marine bands and crew of 220, it was Mohamed Al Fayed's feverishly refurbished *Jonikal*, acquired for £12 million one month before to impress her, complete with the piped-in music of Julio Iglesias. Instead of a black-tie dinner on board *Britannia* in honour of Egyptian President Anwar Sadat and his wife Jihan with the private secretary Francis Cornish in attendance, it was smooching with Egyptian lounge lizard Dodi Fayed over caviar and candles, waited on by the star-struck butler René Delorm. Instead of the disciplined, floating privacy of a closely guarded royal destination, it was a pestered cruise of the Mediterranean's highest profile resorts in a shark pond of paparazzi. Their telephoto lenses were trained on the *Jonikal*'s windows as the vacationing couple ate and slept.

There were also similarities between the first and last men in her life. Both were cowed by powerful fathers. The heir to Harrods, like the Prince of Wales, pursued Diana primarily because his father encouraged him to. Even the two bodyguards on the trip, Trevor Rees-

Jones and Alexander 'Kez' Wingfield, reported not to Dodi but his dad. 'If Dodi did something that was contravening what his father wanted, I had to report it to his father,' Rees-Jones said.[5] Dodi had been all set to marry a Calvin Klein model named Kelly Fisher on 9 August 1997 until – on Bastille Day, 14 July – his father summoned him from Paris to join the first holiday with the Princess and made wooing her an urgent imperative. The baffled Fisher was kept out of sight in St Tropez on board Al Fayed's B-list boat, a former US Coastguard cutter, the *Cujo*. Dodi visited her at night in secret until she wised up to the subterfuge and tried to sue for breach of contract.

The difference on this neo-honeymoon cruise was that it didn't matter to Diana if Dodi was his father's puppet as long as he picked up the tab and was nice to her. She told one of her confidantes, Lady Elsa Bowker, cosmopolitan glamour granny and widow of the British diplomat Sir James Bowker, that with Dodi, she felt so 'taken care of'.[6] Diana needed that. In July, Prince Charles had held a very public coming-out party for the fiftieth birthday of his mistress of twenty-four years, Camilla Parker Bowles at, of all places, Highgrove in Gloucestershire, the former marital home he'd shared with Diana. The same month the Princess's lover of two years, the Pakistani heart surgeon Hasnat Khan, dashed her hopes by making it clear he didn't want to go public. After these two hits Dodi was the perfect antidote: charming, sexually attentive, intellectually unthreatening – and temporary. 'He doesn't demand anything from me,' Diana explained happily to her friend, the dress designer Lana Marks.[7] Another Diana friend, the Labour peeress Margaret Jay, summed up the romance to me with this offering of female wisdom: 'We've all had our Dodi Fayeds.'[8]

In August of 1997 Diana was seeking to replace what she had possessed as a still-married princess with a superstar's version of the same, a life of guarded insulation. She had swapped the stiff upper rictus of courtiers and servants for the Hollywood equivalent, the celebrity servant class of healing therapists, astrologers, acupuncturists, hairdressers, colonic irrigationists, aromatherapists, shoe designers and fashion stylists who these days lead boldface lives of their own that enable them to hobnob as their clients' equals. They filled Diana's time in between the psychic ministrations of a consoling possé of surrogate mothers. Even her £17 million divorce settlement could feel strained by this ever expanding support network. She sometimes had as many as four therapy treatments a day at £200 a throw. Paul Burrell, her butler at Kensington Palace, and his wife Maria were among the few in her old court who made the transition to her new one. Previously confined to a respectful distance by his training in the Queen's household, Burrell eagerly morphed after Diana's divorce from royal servant to celebrity handler.

There was a powerful difference in the two roles. A servant glides away; a handler lingers. A servant is instructed; a handler shares. Burrell didn't just bring in the breakfast tray and open the door for Diana's friends. He tsk-tsked over her choice in clothes, determining the 'wow factor'. He doled out tissues during weepy videos with her when they were alone in the Palace.[9] He acted as a go-between in her secret love affair with Khan. He also eavesdropped on her calls, whispered about his colleagues, promoted himself to the press as the man Diana called 'my rock'. ('What she actually said to him was, "You're wearing my frock,"'[10] cracked an exasperated former member of the Queen Mother's staff about Burrell's vaunted role in the Princess's life.)

The problem for Diana now was that her new court could preserve her ego but not her person. Because she stubbornly refused to retain the royal security detail, seeing them as spies for the enemy camp, she was doomed to seek protection from the paranoid rich. 'From the day she was divorced,' said her driver, the former royal protection officer Colin Tebbutt, 'we lost the official car. That was the worst day's work the government ever did.'[11] The holiday offer with Dodi seemed a watertight solution for her protection. Mohamed Al Fayed has always supported a costly apparatus of bodyguards, surveillance cameras and informers. On his own trips to Paris he travelled with a retinue of eight bodyguards and was transported from the Le Bourget airport in a bulletproof Mercedes with a medically equipped backup car. Dodi, it seems, had inherited his father's obsession. A former girlfriend of his, the Hawaiian-born model Marie Helvin, used to be both irked and amused by the fact that a night out with Dodi always featured security goons with pockets stuffed with 'bungs', as they called the wads of cash they were handed to buy off any trouble, alerting each other on walkie-talkies of Dodi's imminent arrivals and departures as if he was a head of state with a list of dangerous enemies instead of an affable, slightly hopeless party boy with a wide circle of maternal female admirers. For Diana the hunted, this apparatus of security was a powerful attraction. So was the bonhomous atmosphere of the Fayeds' extended family. Alienated from her own, she was relaxed by the warmth as much as the wealth.

For women over thirty-five, glamour has three Stations of the Cross: denial, disguise and compromise. As she entered her thirty-seventh year Diana told herself she was looking for love. But what she was really seeking was a guy with a Gulfstream. Her needs at this juncture had more in common with those of second-act sirens like Elizabeth Hurley than with those of anyone currently residing in Balmoral. She was reaching the point at which she could no longer kid herself that men of large seriousness and modest means – like Dr Hasnat Khan, or even her earlier swain, handsome Guards officer James Hewitt – would be able to spirit her away from her fame to a life of low-key normality. She had enjoyed escapist idylls with both men that worked only when and because they were secret. Hewitt used to whisk her off to Devon, where she'd help his mother do the dishes in her snug cottage. Khan, hidden under a blanket in Paul Burrell's car, would arrive at Kensington Palace with Kentucky Fried Chicken for dinner *à deux* with the Princess. When he took her on a date she wore a black wig and glasses and thrilled to the excitement of standing undetected in a line at Ronnie Scott's jazz club. She called her 'healing therapist' Simone Simmons from outside the club once and said how much she loved standing in the queue, admitting she'd never had to wait in line for anything before. 'I'm queuing!' she crowed happily into her mobile phone. 'It's wonderful! You meet so many different people in a queue!'[12] Diana saw this as the cosy index of her future life with Khan. But, as Khan himself recognised, it was Marie Antoinette stuff, a daydream that would have exploded when it collided with reality. In the multimedia age downsizing was unfeasible. Besides, she would have died of boredom.

And so Diana, like her role model Jackie, who tried to re-create the fortress of the presidency with the playthings of Aristotle Onassis, was scouring in her last days for a new kind of prince, one who could underwrite the needs of global celebrity. Aboard the *Jonikal*, where she was supposed to be wrapped in dreams of becoming Mrs Fayed, Diana was thinking about the future, appraising the CVs of suitors with better long-term prospects than the affable Dodi, who had to go cap in hand to his father for everything. She still called Khan's uncle to assure him that she and Dodi were just friends, but she also kept other possibilities on the boil, such as the New York financier Theodore Forstmann who owned not only a Gulfstream aircraft but the company that manufactured it. From the boat she was deep in discussions with her friend the Chinese entrepreneur David Tang, who was helping her make plans for a three-day visit to Hong Kong in September. Tang, known as 'Tango' to his friends, an ebullient social catalyst of the London scene, was arranging her charity appearances there and meetings with government officials. Tang was not a boyfriend, but Diana's new interest in China was also stoked by Gulu Lalvani. The fifty-eight-year-old Hong Kong-based electronics entrepreneur was founder and CEO of Binatone, a company that was valued in 2003 at some £300 million. The Monday before the accident the Princess made plans from the *Jonikal* to see Lalvani on her return to London. They had celebrated together the night of Tony Blair's election win in May 1997 and had been seeing each other a couple of times a week. 'There was nothing she wouldn't confide in me or I wouldn't confide in her,' Lalvani said in the December after her death.[13] It was Lalvani's appearance in her life in January that caused Diana's last breach in the spring of 1997 with her mother, who exploded on the phone about her daughter's 'relationships with Muslim men'. Lalvani was actually a Punjabi Sikh, but as far as Mrs Shand Kydd was concerned he was still unacceptably brown. Friends called him 'the Crater of Tranquillity' because of his cool disposition and pitted complexion.[14] In June Diana took Lalvani dancing at Annabel's, the Berkeley Square nightclub, in the hopes of making Hasnat jealous. She did not understand that it was just this kind of exposure that her medical heart-throb most derided and dreaded. If she had understood that, it might have been the man she really loved on a sundeck with her, not his ersatz replacement. The deluge of trashy images from the *Jonikal* must have filled the earnest Khan less with regret than with relief that he was not a part of the madness. It was the prospect of just such career-trivialising photo ops that had made him so wary of becoming formally attached to Diana's searing exposure.

To Diana, the forty-two-year-old Dodi Fayed seemed perfectly cast for a romance of retaliation against both her ex-lover and her ex-husband. 'She just wanted to make the people at Balmoral as angry as possible,' her friend Lord Palumbo, the multimillionaire art collector, told me.[15] Her choice of agent provocateur was actually a gentle soul whose childhood in Egypt and expensive European boarding schools had been as lonely as Prince Charles's. Dodi's parents were divorced when he was two, with Al Fayed winning custody, but the father was almost never home. 'He spoiled Dodi, which is not the same as being there for him,' said the film producer and now Labour peer David Puttnam.[16] Dodi was the kind of loner who is always surrounded by people. He loved to cook Middle Eastern dishes with his butler, perfume his apartment with scented lilac candles, listen intently at the feet of movie stars, and do lines of cocaine. When he was twenty-four years old, Fayed set him up in a film company called Allied Stars, which meant he could date actresses and call himself an executive producer. He got lucky with his very first project, Puttnam's Oscar-winning *Chariots of Fire*, in which his father invested £2 million. It gave him the right to hang around the set until Puttnam threw him off for handing out coke to the cast. Not much success followed that, but the indeterminate nature of the movie business suited his amorphous temperament. Dodi's house in Beverly Hills was party central, a magnet for freeloaders, gold diggers and deal jockeys exploiting his childlike generosity. He threw, on average, four parties a week. 'He was good at being rich,' Marie Helvin said fondly. 'He was always sending me long-stemmed roses and boxes of mangoes.'[17] In the course of Dodi's six-week relationship with Diana he showered her with a multi-stranded seed pearl bracelet fastened with jewel-encrusted dragons' heads, a rectangular Jaeger-LeCoultre wristwatch studded with diamonds, a silver photo frame with a romantic inscription, and a gold dress ring with pavé diamonds that was on her finger at the time of the accident.

Dodi's cash came from his father, not from business success. Like many coke users, he was terminally indecisive. His butler, René Delorm, once waited three months in an apartment in Switzerland for Dodi to decide whether he wanted to live in Paris, London or Gstaad. Girlfriends would sit all day packed and ready for Dodi to show up to take them to LA on the private plane. This infuriated Marie Helvin, as did his cavalier treatment of London's hostesses. When it came to dinner parties, Dodi had restaurant manners: he had a habit of cancelling at the last minute, as if the invitation was a booking at the local bistro. One of Fayed's minders explained to Diana's driver, Colin Tebbutt, 'What you've got to remember is there are three times round here: English time, Arab time and Dodi time.'[18] On vacation with the two of them, Dodi's bodyguards Kez Wingfield and Trevor Rees-Jones found his ever more erratic movements a source of rising consternation. Working for Dodi was a nightmare at the best of times. 'He'd be sitting in a traffic jam in the middle of the rush hour,' Rees-Jones said, 'and it would be, "Why have you gone this way?" He hated sitting in traffic, always wanted to push through, jump lanes, to try to get somewhere more quickly. He'd order me to speed up when I knew a speed camera was coming.'[19] There had been a chaotic evening ashore in Monte Carlo when Dodi suddenly decided to send for the tender and take the

Princess for a walk, then got her lost after a long pant up a hill trying to evade the paparazzi. The targets of every tabloid photographer in the world huddled alone at a bus stop trying to figure out where they were. Rees-Jones began to feel sorry for the Princess; he believed she deserved better. On the first Al Fayed vacation at his St Tropez estate in July with William and Harry in tow, Rees-Jones had been touched at how carefree and warm she was wandering around a funfair and going on the rides with her kids until the press ruined it for them. 'She was lovely,' he reflected. 'And her children were fantastic . . . She could do miles better than this guy, for Christ's sake.'[20]

Prince William shared Rees-Jones's view. He felt mounting dismay at his mother's relationship with Dodi and was uncomfortable with the Al Fayed displays of conspicuous consumption. He told friends he had felt as if he was being 'tested' on the July vacation. 'Suddenly a group of people he barely knew were acting like a sort of substitute family.'[21] The pictures of her frolicking aboard the *Jonikal* in August led to a blow-up on the phone with his mother. The fifteen-year-old Prince was dreading the commentary from schoolmates when he returned to Eton for the autumn term. It's doubtful whether Dodi could have long withstood William's disapproval. Nor would Diana herself have withstood any indication of Dodi's renewed drug abuse, which she abhorred. Unreliability of any kind annoyed her. In her role as Princess she was crisply decisive and punctilious in obligation.

What happened to that other Diana on this extended summer folly? When we had lunched together in New York in July she was so self-possessed, so exhilaratingly focused. She saw Tony Blair's election as Prime Minister as a new broom that would sweep her old life away and entrust her with a humanitarian mission. Blair told me he had Diana in mind to boost the Africa initiative on overseas aid and debt cancellation that became the millennium campaign. He and Cherie had invited Diana and William to lunch at Chequers, and they had played football on the lawn. Only months before the *Jonikal* left on its pleasure cruise Diana had undertaken the most courageous mission of her life – to campaign against anti-personnel mines.

As recently as 8 August she had flown to Bosnia–Herzegovina with Lord Deedes, the venerable former editor of the *Daily Telegraph*, who was impressed by her 'silent stillness, how good she was at hearing and dealing with grief, simply stretching out a hand to touch, applying her own brand of soothing tranquillity'.[22] Again and again, Diana turned around sceptical members of the press corps by her porous quality of empathy. In January, the *Sunday Times* war reporter Christina Lamb, was exposed to her up close visiting landmine victims in Angola and was struck by how she never turned her head away from injuries so gruesome she herself could not look at them despite years of Third World reporting. 'She had something I'd only ever seen before from Nelson Mandela,' Lamb wrote, 'a kind of aura that made people want to be with her and a completely natural, straight-from-the-heart sense of how to bring hope to those who seemed to have little to live for.'[23]

Now, just three weeks after her stellar performance in Bosnia, here she was on a hot night in August, revelling in high-life flash, pursued by the farting motorbikes of the international press. Ever since 3.20 p.m. that afternoon, the moment Fayed's Gulfstream 4 had landed at Le Bourget airport after the ninety-minute flight from Sardinia, seven of the paparazzi had been on the tail of Diana and Dodi's two-vehicle mini-motorcade (the Mercedes and a backup Range Rover for the luggage). To shake them off, Dodi ordered his driver to put the pedal to the metal and take them not to the Ritz as planned but to another Fayed trophy, the former home in the Bois de Boulogne of the Duke and Duchess of Windsor. Showing girls this house was one of Dodi's standard romantic ploys. He had taken Kelly Fisher there only the month before.

The house, a fourteen-room, nineteenth-century villa with a tree-filled garden, was part of Mohamed Al Fayed's endless obeisance to royal myth. Raised in Alexandria, the son of a school inspector when Egypt was still under British rule, the stocky, pugilistic Al Fayed, was always obsessed with finding ways to live out his childhood fantasies of imperial glory. His striving to be accepted by the Establishment in London held up a mirror to the British upper class that was as unflattering to them as to him, maybe more so – a reminder of how snobbery and colonial racism can twist the psyches of its perpetrators and its victims alike. Doubtless he dreamed of some day being elevated to the House of Lords, and in return much of the elite took an almost sadistic pleasure in rejecting him. (*Private Eye* mocked him as 'the Phoney Pharaoh'.)

Over the years Al Fayed reacted to such rejections, first with disillusionment and then with anger. He took satisfaction in either acquiring gilt-edged British institutions or holding them rudely accountable for the standards he expected of them, whether it was Harrods, the venerable humour magazine *Punch* or the royal family. (When QC Geoffrey Robertson advanced this theory of Al Fayed's motivation to the man himself, he beamed, 'Ah! You have understood my idealism.')[24] In October 1994 Al Fayed exploded a news-bomb under John Major's Tory government with what became known as the cash-for-questions scandal. He brazenly revealed that in his takeover battle for Harrods in 1985 he had paid Members of Parliament, including Neil Hamilton, junior minister at the Department of Trade and Industry, to ask questions in Parliament on his behalf. Lobbyist Ian Greer, who was hired by Al Fayed to plant questions, allegedly told Al Fayed, 'You rent a taxi, a London taxi, you rent an MP.'[25] Al Fayed used the left-leaning *Guardian* newspaper to fanfare his allegations of corruption, well timed to follow Major's pledge to the House of Commons that he would root out corruption. Al Fayed's motive was revenge. He felt the Conservative government had betrayed him when it ordered the Department of Trade and Industry to investigate the financial underpinnings for his purchase of Harrods. The fact that three years later he still held out hope for redemptive royal connections would be touching if he had not pursued his social aspirations with such transparent manipulation. The DTI inquiry revealed he had lied about his assets, his background, and even the date of his birth.

The acquisition of the Villa Windsor lease in Paris was meant to be another of Al Fayed's sackings and pillagings of an establishment redoubt, but as usual he got it critically wrong. Le Bois, which the exiled Duke and Duchess of Windsor moved to in 1953, was a symbol not of royal style but of ostracism and failure. Perhaps Al Fayed subliminally identified with the pariah status of Mrs Simpson. The villa's tasteful rooms are haunted by memories of what the Duke gave up when he abandoned his duty – dignity, family, the country he loved. Contrary to what Al Fayed's spokesman, former BBC Court correspondent, Michael Cole, told two American journalists working for *Time* magazine, Diana, on 30 August, could hardly have had time to meet an unnamed Italian designer and go round the house with him inspecting every room and cupboard because the log shows she was only there for 31 minutes.[26] It cut too close to the bone for her to linger at a place of royal exile while her boys were nestling in the bosom of the Windsor family at Balmoral and she was floating, Wallis Simpson-like, around the pleasure spots of the Mediterranean. Diana found it 'spooky' and stayed for only thirty minutes. The ghosts of the Windsor house tour only contributed to Diana's longing to get the hell out of Paris and go home.

The evening, however, was about to descend to its last act of bedlam and myth. Diana was being propelled towards a posthumous charade of eternal betrothal to Dodi Fayed. While she recovered from the revving paparazzi pursuit with a soothing blow-dry in the Ritz's Imperial Suite, Dodi was off on another errand to impress her: the purchase of more rocks from the fancy jewellers, Repossi, across from the hotel in the Place Vendôme. The boss of this august joint, Alberto Repossi himself, and his wife Angela were ready to receive him. In Mohamed Al Fayed's fairy story, Diana and Dodi had spied an engagement ring, from a range archly entitled 'Tell Me Yes', in Repossi's Monte Carlo branch with the intention of having it sized and collected in Paris. In fact, the perennially vague Dodi didn't know what he wanted. He seemed to have had an unclear idea about a ring that he and Diana had glimpsed in the window of the Monte Carlo store, though the bodyguards later remembered no such visit. The eager Repossis laid out, for his delectation, a shiny array of watches, rings and bracelets, but nothing caught Dodi's fancy. Grabbing a brochure of other goodies that Diana might like, he was out of there in a record seven minutes, twenty-seven seconds.[27] So where was the engagement ring of legendary repute that was to plight his troth with the Princess? It was on the finger of the enterprising Angela Repossi. Within thirty minutes of Dodi leaving, the Ritz's acting manager, Claude Roulet, returned to pick up the edited jewellery selection and noticed that Mrs Repossi was herself sporting a ring that looked better to Roulet than anything Dodi had been offered. At his request she removed the ring, cleaned it and Roulet took it for Dodi on approval – the first time Dodi knew of the existence of any 'Tell Me Yes' engagement ring.[28]

It may have been Dodi's intention to pop the question – his butler René Delorm said it was – but it is unlikely that Diana would so quickly have reversed the position she had separately rehearsed with both Paul Burrell and Rosa Monckton before Dodi presented her a Bulgari band aboard the *Jonikal*. She told her friend Rosa: 'He's given me a bracelet. He's given me a watch. I know that the next thing will be a ring.' Then she laughed and said: 'Rosa, that's going firmly on the fourth finger of my right hand,'[29] an evasion of commitment Burrell endorses with his own version in his book, *The Way We Were*. It is unlikely, too, that Mohamed Al Fayed (who was paying) and M. Repossi between them would have let Dodi propose to the Princess with an eleven thousand dollar ring purchased in such an ad hoc fashion. A Diana engagement ring to be photographed by every media outlet in the world would surely have been a more extravagant item featuring a diamond as big as – well, as big as the Ritz. At her tearful press conference on 14 August 1997 in

Los Angeles, Kelly Fisher displayed a sapphire and diamond engagement ring from Dodi, valued at £118,000. Was the Princess worth less than Dodi's dumped fiancée? Then there is the question of the all-important one-upmanship with the Windsors. Even the famously thrifty Queen Elizabeth II had forked out more than £28,500 to the royal jeweller Garrard for the sapphire and diamond ring Charles gave Diana on their engagement. Does anyone think Al Fayed would have allowed himself to be outshone in a retail matter? Besides, M. Repossi himself, in the first interview he gave to TV producer Martyn Gregory, said the ring he sold to Dodi that night was not an engagement ring.[30] Only later did he change his story to insist that it was – and it must be remembered that clients of the Ritz hotel were some of Repossi's best customers.

Today the engagement ring that wasn't can be viewed in the display cabinet of the Dodi and Diana memorial at Harrods, along with a champagne glass from the Imperial Suite, a splashing fountain, and two suspended cameos of the couple flanked by eternally flickering white candles. The fact that the ring in the Harrods display case does not match Repossi's description of what he said Dodi bought for Diana is just one more of the mysteries in Mohamed Al Fayed's obfuscating world of commerce and make-believe.

Diana never wore it anyway as we know. What followed its purchase was the night's crescendo of motion madness. Was Dodi back to the old coke habit that had got him ejected from David Puttnam's film set? Diana's friends have said she had begun to be suspicious of his trips to the bathroom.[31] But no traces of cocaine were found in the blood test conducted on Dodi (or Diana) by the pathologist at the 1997 post-mortem in London. Dodi's agitation and erratic insructions that night were simply that of a man hopelessly out of his depth, panicked by the burden of becoming the worlds most high profile Romeo. Thierry Rocher, the Ritz's night-manager told the French police '. . . he was at the end of his tether . . . and, in my opinion . . . this could have changed Mr Paul's behaviour whilst he was at the wheel.'[32]

The countdown to disaster unfolds like a speeded-up movie. Consider the sequence.

7 p.m. In a swarm of paparazzi, the two lovers take off from the Ritz to Dodi's apartment on the Rue Arsène-Houssaye. The Princess is upset by the shouting and shoving of the photographers outside. But do the couple stay inside murmuring sweet nothings? No.

9.35 p.m. They come out into the mob scene to go out for a dinner they could have easily had served at home. They take off down the Champs-Elysées at the head of a buzzing convoy of press. The body-guards in the backup car are furious – not with the journalists in pursuit, but with their own charge. They are hired to protect Dodi and Diana but have been offered no clue where they are going. Dodi tells his driver to head for Chez Benoit, a chic bistro near the Pompidou Centre. He has sent M. Roulet of the Ritz ahead to make sure they will have a five-star welcome. The chasing bikes and scooters stick to the Mercedes 'like real devils', in the words of a witness. Diana is used to their persistence, but it panics Dodi. He cannot handle real aggravation, only the pretend kind. What rattles his cage is that paparazzi are coming at them from all sides, not just behind them. Now he wants to forget Chez Benoit, never mind M. Roulet and the fuss he is choreographing for their arrival.

9.45 p.m. He tells the driver to go back to the Ritz – they'll dine there instead. This is bad news for the maître d' of L'Espadon, the Ritz's restaurant. The place is packed and in the fifteen minutes he has been given by Dodi, it's a nightmare to rustle up a table. The son of the owner and the Princess of Wales are in danger of having no place to sit!

9.53 p.m. Diana enters the hotel followed by Dodi. The couple are dropped not at the more discreet Rue Cambon back entrance but at the unavoidably public front. The night security officer, François Tendil, is so alarmed by the gathering photographers he summons from off duty the Ritz's acting head of security, Henri Paul. Meanwhile, two snappers emerge from nowhere and hassle Diana. Dodi loses it with M. Tendil – the whole thing, he yells, is 'a fuck-up'. The couple head for the dining room. Dodi berates Kez Wingfield with what Wingfield remembers as 'the mother of all bollockings' for not having gone ahead of them to clear the street and run interference – an impossible feat for the bodyguard for whom the whole night has been a magical mystery tour.[33] Seated at the hastily prepared table in the dining room Diana loses it, too. One of the most poignant images of her last hours is of a beautiful woman quietly weeping in full view of the clientèle of the L'Espadon restaurant.

10.03 p.m. The couple, having ordered dinner, never stay to eat it. They retreat from the embarrassing stares and ask for their meal to be sent up to the Imperial Suite they vacated three hours earlier. While they dine, their two bodyguards wait for them in the hotel's Bar Vendôme where Henri Paul joins them. Paul knocks back two yellow drinks thought by the bodyguards to be pineapple cordial but later identified as the alcoholic pastis Ricard, a favourite of the French. Outside, the hotel front entrance is now under siege. Alerted by TV reports that Diana is inside, hundreds of curious fans have augmented the battalion of paparazzi. Every time a blonde goes in or out of the hotel, a raucous cheer goes up, like Oscar night on the red carpet. That Diana and Dodi didn't just remain closeted in their suite from the start for a quiet romantic evening – and that, now back in that haven, they don't stay the night rather than plunge themselves again into the vortex of media aggravation for a third time as they are about to do – suggests an almost compulsive need to be seen.

It was a need they seemed to share. One of Dodi's uncles, the Saudi businessman Hassan Yassin, happened to be in Paris. Dodi had invited him to meet Diana and have a drink with them in the bar. Yassin was late, and by the time he arrived the couple had left again for Dodi's apartment on their last journey. Yassin's opinion today: 'Both of them had the publicity bug. If I had Diana with me I would take her to the jungle, not the Ritz.'[34]

But would she have gone? That's the question. Dodi was a novice at the media game, but Diana was the most artful practitioner alive. She was way ahead of her contemporaries in foreseeing a world where celebrity was, so to speak, the coin of the realm. Today we are used to the phenomenon of movie stars commanding the airwaves to opine about Darfur or the environment. Journalists, artists and foreign-policy mavens get in line for the patronage of a Brad Pitt or a George Clooney if they want to have their ideas taken seriously by power, just as their seventeenth-century equivalents waited around for the patronage of the Earl of Southampton. An aristocrat herself, Diana knew that the aristocracy of birth was now irrelevant. All that counted was the aristocracy of exposure.

The trouble was that, through muddles of the heart, she abused that exposure. The camera was Diana's fatal attraction. She had a sixth sense about when it was trained on her even when she couldn't see it. It had created the image that had given her so much power and she was addicted to its magic, even when it hurt. Her life's obsession was how to control the genie she had released. All through the holiday she had been doing a dangerous dance with the press. When she learned about Charles's birthday party for Camilla at Highgrove she said to Lady Bowker: 'Elsa, you know what I thought the other day? What a wonderful idea if I were to put on my bathing suit and hide under the birthday cake and suddenly just jump out!'[35] She more or less did. The 'snap' of her long legs and arched body in a pale blue one-piece about to execute an elegant dive from the *Jonikal* had gladdened the hearts of newspaper editors all over the world. After her death it was revealed that the most sensational images of her final summer – for example, the famous front page of the *Sunday Mirror*, headlined 'THE KISS' and featuring a shot of her in a clinch with the bare-chested Dodi off the coast of Corsica, for which the paper paid the photographer, Mario Brenna, a quarter of a million pounds – were the direct result of tips from Diana herself. When they appeared, the Princess called the photographer, Jason Fraser, who worked in cahoots with Brenna – not to protest but to ask why they were so grainy.[36] On her last night in Paris, she reached Richard Kay, her confidant at the *Daily Mail*, on his mobile phone shopping in Knightsbridge to find out what was going on in the press and said how much she dreaded the Sunday papers coming out.[37] It did not occur to her to ignore them.

What she underestimated was Mohamed Al Fayed's own appetite for the spotlight. All through the holiday it had puzzled Diana that the press always knew their whereabouts. She suspected Al Fayed was leaking information, she told Kay, and indeed he was.[38] Al Fayed had hired a publicist, Max Clifford, to brief the gossip columnists and tout the holiday fling as the romance of the century. The additional hype proved incendiary.

So thoroughly have Diana's last hours been refracted through the prism of competing recriminations, it is easy to forget why she accepted the invitation to go on holiday with the Fayeds in the first place: she believed they offered protection. Yet it seems that she died because the men in Al Fayed's empire weren't looking after her. Not Dodi, whose plans were as chaotic as he was; not Al Fayed, if he approved his son's cockamamie notion of using the Ritz's acting head of security, Henri Paul, to drive them instead of a qualified chauffeur*; not Henri Paul himself, who was found to be have imbibed a cocktail of prescription drugs and showed a blood alcohol three times the legal limit. Little wonder that Mohamed Al Fayed's storm of grief at the loss of his son has been so volcanic in its repercussions of blame.

Six minutes past midnight. The lovers leave the Imperial Suite and make their way to the service elevator on the first floor. Even here Diana can feel the presence of an observer – the closed-circuit TV lens – instinctively, as she and Dodi descend to the service entrance, she looks up at the hidden camera and, for the last time, smiles.[39] I think of Diana in that last hour in her trim blazer, cropped white summer trousers and high-heeled Versace shoes as she scurries through the Ritz's corridor of boutique display cases. She hardly glances at the gleaming windows of Hermès scarves and spangled watches and seductive lingerie and flashy brooches that advertise the luxe life of Eurotrash leisure. She moves at a clip with Dodi and the bodyguards through the grand salon that leads to the swanky Hemingway Bar and the elegant nightspot, the Ritz Club. On the pavement near the hotel's back entrance in the Rue Cambon, where the carpark attendant has brought round Henri Paul's black Mercedes, the heavyset man his colleagues call *triste et solitaire* has arrived to drive her away through celebrity's electric storm. Does she think then of her sons, asleep in a Scottish castle? As she slides quickly into the back seat of the Mercedes on that close Parisian night, does she suddenly miss the cool English rain?

It has often been said that by the summer of 1997 Diana was in a spiral of self-destruction. I prefer to think of her last exhibitionist weeks as a relapse, a wounded and wounding gesture triggered by the ruin once again of all her romantic hopes. It is one of the saddest ironies of her life that just when she was on the point of casting off the most toxic elements of celebrity culture and using her fame as collateral for daring social activism she should be locked by death in a freeze-frame of deadly glitz.

The car jockey Frédéric Lucard handed Henri Paul the keys to the Mercedes. Before he got into the car, the chauffeur paused before he got into the car to taunt the jostling photographers with a show of bravado. 'Don't try to follow us, in case you won't catch us.'[40]

Now the low buzz of assembling bikes reveals that the paparazzi have spotted the subterfuge of the back exit. At 12.20 a.m., with Henri Paul at the wheel, the Mercedes pulls away from the kerb and with a screech of rubber, takes off, pursued by the furies, for Dodi's apartment in the Rue Arsène-Houssaye by way of the Pont d'Alma tunnel.

# Chapter 2

# A Slide Show

'Dear Mummy and Daddy, I went to bed with a candle in my room.'

– Diana to her parents, 1966

Once upon a time she wasn't famous. Once upon a time she was the little fair-haired girl you see in the pencil sketch on display at Althorp, her ancestral home in Northamptonshire, sitting on a nursery chair in a grey pleated skirt, nursing her dolly. The life of Diana, Princess of Wales, blazed so early that the remnants of her childhood have a peculiar tenderness. Behind the glass cases at Althorp are such artefacts as her early album of pressed flowers. The white wicker shelf from her bedroom supporting the humdrum collection of little china animals she loved. A big white juvenile book titled *Learning to Swim and Dive*. Her tap shoes. The boxed set of a miniature 'nutshell' library. The small red school blazer with the red-and-yellow uniform scarf. The school trunk marked D. SPENCER with the photo of her as a gangly nine-year-old about to load it into the open boot of the car to go with her to school at Riddlesworth. You can hear the scrunch of the gravel, the busy slamming of doors, the running back into the house to find a missing lacrosse stick, all the bustle of boarding school returns.

The childish, undistinguished letters resonate through the years. 'Dear Mummy and Daddy,' reads an early one from Park House in 1966, 'I hope you had a nice journey and that you are enjoying your holiday. We had a power cut on Monday and I went to bed with a candle in my room.'[1] Why does this sound lonely? Perhaps because we know that there will soon be heartache behind Mummy's absence from home.

Diana's parents' marriage began to unravel two years before she was born in July 1961, though it did not publicly come apart until she was six. Her father, Johnnie, the 8th Earl Spencer and her mother, Frances Fermoy, had been married for fourteen years when Frances walked out and, in a bitter divorce, lost custody of Diana and her three siblings. Today, the amateur movies and still photographs Earl Spencer took of his family reflect none of that drama. How faithfully the Earl documented the uneventful surfaces of their lives at Park House, Sandringham, the solid Victorian mansion on the grounds of the Queen's estate. The Spencer family lived there for eighteen years before Diana's father inherited the grand estate of Althorp. Diana grew up associating the camera with love.

After years of tabloid narratives everything about Diana's childhood has been rewritten as prelude either to disaster or to certain fame, but no one close to the family remembers it that way. To them it was just a life like all the others, traditional, sheltered, full of the same casual privilege taking place in all the other Victorian piles and turreted mansions of England in the 1960s. The reels of Johnnie Spencer's films wind and rewind in an endless loop in the stable block that houses the exhibit of 'Diana: A Celebration' at Althorp. Members of the public pause in the darkened screening room, hypnotised by the flickering scenes of a family's vanished moments.

*Newborn Diana:* A country christening at the Sandringham church of St Mary Magdalene, 30 August 1961. Posh-looking Spencers and Fermoys, and assorted Northampton dignitaries mill around outside being sociable. Before Mary Quant and Biba changed it all, young married women still dressed like their mothers. Twenty-five-year-old Frances, far too young to be already the mother of three, looks flawlessly put together and crisp in her coiffed blonde ripples. She wears a pale blue matching suit and hat, a string of fat, creamy pearls and gazes down with a proud smile into the big blue eyes of the gurgling baby Diana – the last mother you would expect to throw it all over for a *coup de foudre*.

*Diana circa nine months:* The protective older sister Jane with a bow on one side of her hair and summer shorts, lifting her into the high, old-fashioned pram under the tree in the Park House garden. Diana's first memory was of the smell of the warm plastic of her pram hood.[2] Jane was always the sensible one, responsible, quiet and bookish with brown-haired, unremarkable looks. Sarah, the oldest sister, was the firecracker of the trio, sparky, untidy, as much of a temperamental redhead as her nephew Prince Harry is today.

*Diana at two:* Wispily blonde and adventurous scrambling around with her siblings on the plastic garden slide, or tearing across the grass in adorable red boots. A tea party set up on the lawn with paper cups and plates and a jug of lemonade for a bunch of unruly toddlers is Winnie-the-Pooh perfect. Johnnie Spencer always loved giving parties for his children. Their birthdays were famous in the county for the profusion of pony rides, children's zoos and miniature golf. He was equally generous with the next generation. At one memorable kiddie fest William and Harry attended, he arranged for little stores made by Harrods to be set up in the garden and the children were given bags of chocolate money to spend on toys.

*Diana at five:* The idyll moves to the seaside with the four children making sandcastles. The Spencers had a little beach hut in Brancaster on the north coast of Norfolk, about twenty minutes' drive away. In summer holidays the family often picnicked there on the broad white sands. Frances, still with her perfect platinum hair, lies on her back in shorts that display her long willowy legs. Diana gives a silent-movie squeal as she balances precariously on the shaky platform of her mother's feet.

*Diana at nine:* The long limbs are now Diana's. Frances is nowhere to be seen. The nannies have got prettier. In America a Kennedy would be sleeping with help that looked as good as this.

*Diana at eleven:* She poses against a garden fence in a swimsuit with her head thrown self-admiringly back like a model. Her catwalk stance shows off her legs that now seem to extend up to her ears like Bambi. She dances jubilantly with a red towel, making theatrical matador moves. Look at me! The old film from the early 1970s whirrs eerily in the silent screening room as the young beauty executes a cool, kingfisher dive into the Park House swimming pool.

Where are the signs in those early frames we know must be there, of a marriage about to disintegrate, of a bereft little girl living out events that would lead to an iconic future and a mutinous wound? Diana's friend Rosa Monckton reflected that 'children swing from happiness to unhappiness in a moment, because what they ultimately want to do is survive'.[3]

Diana found her own way of surviving.

# Chapter 3

# Difficult Women

'Worse thing happen at sea, my little sailors.'
– Diana's grandmother, Lady Fermoy, to her grandchildren, 1967

Lady Diana Spencer came from the last batch of privileged British girls boarded out in agreeable, undemanding schools and allowed to leave qualified for nothing beyond the quest for a suitable husband. But in that speciality she read deeply. Her real education was sentimental and consisted of total teenage immersion in the rustling bubble bath of fragrant romantic fiction, the literary equivalent of afternoon soap operas. More than any others, the books that enraptured her young mind, saturating it with sugar, were those of the queen of swoons, Barbara Cartland. Famous for her heightened colour, her penchant for pink, her meringue coiffure and false eyelashes the size of a couple of condors, Cartland was capable, when agitated, of pecking a critic to death – a handy skill to have, since she was also the author of 723 romantic fantasies dictated from a chaise longue, with a total of a billion readers, not all of whom will admit to having read them.[1] No such reticence from the unworldly Diana: the first time the former Tory MP Gyles Brandreth met the Princess, in the early nineties, they began by talking about her teenage devotion to Cartland's fiction. She told him, 'In those stories was everyone I dreamed of, everything I hoped for.'[2]

A Cartland rescue fantasy follows an unchanging formula: brave, hard and dashing (yet ultimately tender) alpha man meets sweet, easy-to-overlook girl who, at bedtime, 'lets her hair loose at a single shake'. The hero cannot be bald, ginger, short or German. (The Second World War, in which Cartland lost two brothers, weighed heavily on her.) The heroine must be of childbearing age, usually between twenty-two and thirty-four; may be allowed one illegitimate child (through no fault of her own!); cannot be the man's social, intellectual or financial superior;

and must have an offbeat Graeco-fake-o name like Novella, Udda or Sita. At the end of the story, the shy, overlooked girl wins the heart and fortune of the Prince or Prince equivalent. One of Diana's favourites was *Bride to the King*: 'There was tenderness in his voice which made her press her cheek against his shoulder . . . Then he said, "Tonight, my darling, you are only a child and not yet a woman, and that is why I want you to think that I am the Prince of your heart, just as you are the Queen of mine." "I love you," she whispered as her head fell back on the soft pillows.' In short, prose that rots the brain.

Children faced with grave emotional distress often cling to a fantasy figure, or a magical friend. It took a fantasy village to sustain Diana. Her addiction to romance novels became a diabetes of the soul, leaving her spiritual bloodstream permanently polluted with saccharine. She might have been the reader-at-risk that George Eliot targeted in her 1856 essay, 'Silly Novels by Lady Novelists'. She clung so tenaciously to her dreams that they became a wilful act of unknowing. In the cad-about-town James Hewitt she saw only the Dashing Cavalry Officer; in the serious and private cardiologist Hasnat Khan, she saw the Heart-throb Doctor who would be at her side in Florence Nightingale missions; in the coked-out playboy Dodi Fayed she saw the liquid-eyed Arab Sheikh who would whisk her away on a magic carpet.

An early mentor who could compensate for her distracted parents might have grounded Diana's dreams and given her a head rinse. But there was no secure female role model anywhere in Diana's childhood to make up for the exit of her mother. The best of the bunch was her adored Spencer grandmother, Lady Cynthia, one of the sweetest women in Northamptonshire, but as her acquaintance Lord Glenconner put it, she was 'jellied' by the bullying of Diana's grandfather, the misanthropic 7th Earl Spencer. That left Diana her Fermoy grandmother, Ruth, who was a manipulative, self-absorbed snob and her stepmother, Raine, formerly Lady Dartmouth, whom Diana saw only as a hated usurper. It is ironic that Raine was the daughter of Barbara Cartland. Fate was giving Diana the inside track on the perversion of her own fairy story.

Many an aristocratic girl or boy with absent parents has been comforted by the warm bosom of the faithful family nanny who stayed long past adolescence. (If you slapped an Edwardian-style picture hat on the head of Camilla Parker Bowles you would be struck by her resemblance to Prince Charles's adored nanny, Mabel Anderson.) Diana's nannies unfortunately gave up on her all too fast. It is not surprising. She worked off her displaced rage at her mother's exit by tormenting them. Tactics included locking one irate young woman in the bathroom and throwing another's underwear out of the window amid screams of hyena laughter. She once laced a nanny's cushion with pins so that when she sat down the unfortunate woman leapt back up shrieking. And in a truly fiendish act, she tossed another's engagement ring down the drain.[3] Nanny Janet Thompson, who managed to tough it out for four years, said Diana could not be called a difficult child, but she could be obstinate – 'simply obstinate. She just would not co-operate. I think she may have seen how her elder sister, Sarah, was behaving and copied her.'[4] Sarah was the last one able to offer guidance to Diana. She was recklessly badly behaved, if lots of fun: she once rode her horse into the living room at Park House just to irritate the stuck-up Lady Fermoy. Sarah was thrown out of boarding school for getting drunk and in her teens developed severe anorexia. Only Mary Clarke, a sane and forthright Norfolk girl selected by Diana's father in an exhaustive Mary Poppins-like interview process, provided some ballast amid the emotional turmoil. But Mary left after two years with the family when Diana's younger brother Charles went to boarding school.

There was plenty of precedent for turbulence in Diana's family. 'The Spencers are difficult,' the Queen Mother once observed to a friend, using a word freighted with the semiotics of class.[5] She meant the men were bad-tempered, eccentric and choleric and the women were out of control. The erratic temperament went with their high colour, the 'red' in the Edwardian Red Earl's flowing beard (he died of apoplexy), and the scarlet blush in Diana Spencer's rounded cheeks. The Queen Mother might have added that the Fermoys were just as 'difficult' as the Spencers, producing women of implacable will and fierce desires. By marrying each other the family that sounded so good on paper as a royal alliance was almost continuously at war with itself and everybody else.

Diana's mother, Frances Roche, was imperious if you defied her. 'When she fixed you with those bright blue eyes she was more royal than the royals,' one of Prince Charles's former staffers said of her. She got away with it because she was so good-looking. 'She was not beautiful strictly speaking,' says her school friend Barbara Gilmour, 'but she was very attractive and blonde and sexy with such *joie de vivre* and fun about her.'[6] If she failed as a mother to Diana it was as much to do with her own parenting as it was to do with character. Her capacity to nurture was deformed by the prerogatives of class and expectation and her attempts to flee from both.

The Fermoys were less socially grounded than the ancient Spencer family, but they had more money. Frances's father, Maurice, was raised in New York by his American heiress mother who had been abandoned by her husband, the ne'er-do-well second son of the Irish peer Baron Fermoy. Maurice expected to continue leading his life as a Park Avenue American when he returned from France after the First World War, but a series of providential deaths left him the startled heir to the Fermoy title. In 1921 with a Harvard degree and a large American fortune, he sailed to England to claim the barony.

The new Lord Fermoy was an ebullient man, with an American openness and lack of pretension that went over surprisingly well in the stuffy realms of British aristocratic life. He won three elections as a Conservative MP for the Norfolk seat of King's Lynn. He was also an excellent shot and became a favoured house guest of King George V's younger son, the quiet Duke of York, joining shooting parties at their Norfolk home, Sandringham. His incorrigible roving eye was a thorn in the side of the woman he was to marry, Ruth Gill, the daughter of a moralistic Scottish colonel from Aberdeen. 'Maurice was a terrible bottom pincher,' Lady Glenconner remembers. 'I rather dreaded him.'[7] During his twenty-six-year marriage to Ruth, Maurice maintained at least one mistress who produced a love child in the neighbouring village of Sandringham and also fathered a daughter out of wedlock with a woman named Edith Travis whom he had met on a train to San Francisco in 1917 and continued to see on trips to America. The American daughter, Edith Howitt Hodgins, in her mid-eighties and living in Marin County, California, went public about her mother's lifelong devotion to the philandering peer in a 2004 book, *Lilac Days*, which the Spencer and Fermoy families today thunderously ignore. Edith's last affectionate letters to Fermoy piled up unopened for four months after his death before being bundled into a sack and burned on the instructions of Ruth. A secretary then dispatched a terse three-line letter to Marin County to tell his old mistress her beloved Maurice had died.[8]

British upper-class women of the pre-war generation were tough as old boots. They had used the word 'obey' in their marriage ceremonies which meant putting up with a lot. Raised in freezing country seats, given a second-class education, always playing second fiddle to their brothers, they cultivated resourcefulness and the ability to live in private worlds. It prepared them for a life of low emotional expectations, and husbands who were focused on being inattentive. Social activities after marriage revolved around male sporting events so wives spent their weekends hanging about in the rain at race meets or being left at home all day during shooting parties although you were still expected to change for lunch, tea and dinner. 'The men never noticed but the women still changed,' an elderly peer told me. It was the 'not being noticed' which shrivelled female sympathies, their aggressive beaky look comes from years of catering to oblivious men.

In Lady Fermoy's case, she had a gift for music to console her. Her wide, heart-shaped face and astonishing, copper-gold hair had first caught the eye of the portly forty-six-year-old Fermoy in Paris when she was twenty years old, studying classical piano at the Conservatoire under the great maestro Alfred Cortot. She was dating Fermoy's twin brother Frank but Ruth's high-mindedness was only equalled by a flinty desire to rise in the world. She homed in on Maurice as soon as she learned he was the older twin with the title. 'She was a woman of enormous confidence,' said her daughter Frances, 'unswerving in believing she was always right, which was very daunting.'[9] Marriage to a committed philanderer meant Ruth had to grow an impervious second skin, a charming, resilient mask. She never understood why her grand-daughter Diana was so childishly unwilling to live with a marriage that was no more an arrangement than hers had been.

Fermoy's womanising gave Ruth's social aspirations their spur. It chafed at her that Maurice's title came without a landed estate, but his friendship with the Duke of York paid dividends. The Duke persuaded his father, King George V, to let the Fermoys pick up the lease of their guest house on the Sandringham estate. In 1935 they moved into Park House, a handsome grey-stone mansion nestling behind the august oak, beech and fir trees on the fringe of the royal acres with glorious views of the royal parklands and cricket ground. Ruth gave birth there to a second daughter, Frances, the night that George V died. (A son and heir, Edmund, followed three years later.)

Great English families rise and fall because of their proximity either to the throne or to the heart of politics. The Fermoys' biggest social break was the abdication crisis of 1936. When George V's eldest son, Edward VIII, renounced the throne to marry the American divorcee Wallis Simpson, Maurice Fermoy's shy shooting friend, Bertie, and his wife Elizabeth were suddenly the new King and Queen of England. The bond between the couples had deepened during the abdication dramas.

Maurice Fermoy was a calm private sounding board for the agonised Duke of York and the two women were united in disgust at Edward and Mrs Simpson.

Once the Fermoys were established in royal circles, Lady Fermoy had only one priority, marrying off her two daughters, Frances and her elder sister Mary, to the best-connected men in the kingdom. Beneath the elegance of their façades, the drive for upper-class women in the fifties and early sixties to land a titled husband, preferably one with an estate, was a cut-throat business managed with quiet, heartless tenacity by their mothers. The wheeling and dealing for a marriage partner went on between the sixteen weeks of late March to early July when the London Season was in full bloom. This ritual of corralling upper-class girls and boys from approved lists and plunging them into a marathon of balls, parties and race meetings used to begin every year with a presentation at court to the monarch. Debutantes wore silk afternoon dresses, plumed hats and white gloves. As a deb entered the royal presence, she dropped a deep curtsy and began a delicate and complex piece of choreography – a painstakingly rehearsed backwards walk requiring her to look steadfastly ahead while nonchalantly manoeuvring back to her appointed place (a metaphor perhaps for the social machinations to get a husband that followed). The last debutante presentation at court was in 1958. 'We had to put a stop to it,' Princess Margaret said. 'Every tart in London was getting in.'[10]

Nobody was more tenacious in the social marriage market than Ruth Fermoy. Before Frances was even out of school Ruth went into action like a high-voltage Mrs Bennet in *Pride and Prejudice*. Realising that the less attractive older daughter Mary (described by one dance partner as 'immensely tall, bosomy and goggle-eyed') would be a tougher sell she fixed her hopes on the prospects of Frances and delayed Mary's coming-out dance until she could do a double whammy with the added value of both.

There was no greater catch in the early 1950s than Diana's father, Johnnie. The image of the 8th Earl Spencer will forever be defined by the truncheon-faced old buffer who squired his daughter with laboured pride up the aisle of St Paul's Cathedral. But when Frances Roche first laid eyes on Johnnie Spencer, he was tall, debonair and desirable. As Viscount Althorp, eldest son of the 7th Earl, he was the presumptive heir to Althorp House, a 121-room stately home with 14,000 acres of rolling Northamptonshire, Warwickshire and Norfolk farmland, complete with cottages, farms and villages. The family was older by 250 years than that Hanoverian import of the eighteenth century, King George I, whose descendants are today's House of Windsor. The Spencers could trace themselves back to 1469, when they were a respected clan of prospering sheep farmers in Warwickshire, already in a position to lend money to the monarchy. In 1603, James I repaid the royal debts with the traditional Get Out of Jail Free card – a barony, conferred on the prosperous Robert Spencer, which forty years later included the earldom of Sunderland.

In 1699, the Spencers entwined their illustrious family tree with that of the Churchill family when the daughter of the first Duke of Marlborough, hero-general of the Battle of Blenheim, married Charles Spencer. The result was a celebrated branch of the family – the Spencer-Churchills, who were residents of one of England's most spectacular stately homes, Blenheim Palace. The Spencers' glory days were the eighteenth century. They became powerful forces in the Whig Party, dedicated to restraining the power of the monarchy and supporters of the Protestant succession; in the nineteenth century they became parliamentary Liberals, rivals to the Tories. They were behind-the-scenes power brokers. They helped smooth the ascension to the throne of the Hanoverian Prince who became King George I. There was no paradox in the fact that seven or eight generations of Spencers were loyal courtiers and servants of the Crown. They were servants of the monarchy *they chose*. They saw themselves not as courtiers but – literally – as kingmakers, in touch with the populace but aloof from the merely rich. In 1765 George III upgraded their barony to an earldom.

Althorp House evolved from the red-bricked, moated redoubt of the first Earl into a princely power house with a superb collection of eighteenth-century furniture, a world-famous library and a picture gallery hung with masterpieces by Sir Joshua Reynolds, Thomas Gainsborough, Sir Anthony Van Dyck, Sir Peter Paul Rubens and George Stubbs. In the words of a leading historian of the aristocracy, David Cannadine, 'The Spencers were the very embodiment of glamour and grandeur, high rank and high living.'[11]

At Diana's funeral, when her brother Charles Spencer, the current Earl, spoke unforgettably from the pulpit of Westminster Abbey about Diana's sons needing their 'blood family' in the future, it was, to the stunned Windsors in the congregation, a chilling whiff of Whig arrogance from the past.

As the heir to the Spencer titles and Althorp, Johnnie's eligibility was already unassailable but his charms were further polished by Eton,

Sandhurst, his Second World War service in Europe in the Royal Scots Greys, plus his three years as an aide-de-camp to the Governor of South Australia. Better yet, he served as an equerry to King George VI and for two years to the young Queen Elizabeth. 'He was very good-looking then,' testifies a friend of Frances. 'He had a casual, unfocused charm.'[12] Lord Glenconner used to join him in club crawling for pretty girls, ending up at the Gargoyle in Mayfair, a fashionable place frequented by Lucian Freud and Cyril Connolly where, as Glenconner put it, 'you could see intellectuals shouting at each other'.[13] Johnnie may have played the field, but in the marriage market, he was spoken for. He was unofficially engaged to Lady Anne Coke, now Lady Glenconner, the nineteen-year-old slim, blonde and witty daughter of the Earl of Leicester, a Norfolk neighbour at the palatial Holkham Hall and friend of the Fermoys, whose violin recitals Ruth accompanied on the piano. A formal announcement was expected any minute.

Neither this fact, nor her friendship with Anne's parents, stopped Lady Fermoy in her naked pursuit of the future Earl Spencer for her own daughter, Frances. As Lady Glenconner told it to me, in the spring season of 1952, while she was a guest of Frances's older sister Mary in the Fermoys' Wilton Crescent house, Lady Fermoy encouraged her to invite her 'young man' round for drinks. When Johnnie Spencer arrived, Ruth was all over him with her expert charm and seemed very eager to know when he would call on his fiancée again. The next time Johnnie visited Anne at Wilton Crescent that year, Lady Fermoy announced that her teenage daughter Frances was unexpectedly home from boarding school and would be joining them.

*WHOOMPH!* That was the word Frances used to Barbara Gilmour when she described the immediate attraction she felt for Johnnie Spencer. Gilmour remembers it clearly because Frances used it again fifteen years later when Frances fell madly in love with the heir to a wallpaper fortune Peter Shand Kydd. At fifteen Frances was in that appealing transition age between schoolgirl and socialite, but her height made her seem much older. 'And suddenly,' Anne recalled, 'I could see that Lady Fermoy was pushing Frances like mad. "Do you like tennis, Johnnie? Oh, Frances adores tennis, don't you, Frances? Do you like swimming? Oh, Frances just *adores* swimming, don't you, Frances?" and Frances just stood there and simpered. Afterwards Johnnie said to me, "What a simply marvellous girl Frances is!" and I thought no more about it. But the next time I saw him he said, "The most beautiful pair of stockings arrived for me knitted by Frances at school!" You can guess whose idea that was!' Soon Anne started to perceive coolness in her fiancé. 'I was devastated when Johnnie dropped me,' she admitted. 'I was sent off on the *QE* to America ostensibly to sell Holkham pottery, but really to get over it. I sometimes wonder if I wasn't rich enough.'[14]

Frances's private income was an attraction, but Johnnie was infatuated. To court her officially, he had to wait two years until she was seventeen (when she had 'come out'), but the romance flourished privately. A friend who was in the same dorm with Frances at finishing school remembers her slipping out to make numerous steamy telephone calls to Johnnie 'with a lot of writhing around'. 'She was always a very sexy girl,' her friend says. 'Johnnie, of course, was over the moon.' Anne Coke couldn't compete with phone sex.

Lady Fermoy was well satisfied by her actions in sabotaging the Coke/Spencer romance. Beneath its frivolity the 'Season' was business, an elaborate, ritualistic parade of power, wealth, manners, beauty, possessions and suitability; designed to show off not just the girls' manners and breeding, but the more material assets of the family's antique furniture, portraits, silver and jewellery. The goal of the Fermoys' coming-out ball for Frances and Mary the following year was to clinch marriage proposals. On 21 May 1953 they entertained 450 guests in the splendour of Londonderry House. 'By two o'clock,' reported the *Standard*, 'eightsome reels and foursomes had made the ballroom bounce. By three o'clock the lights in the ballroom were switched off and guests danced in the darkness, illuminated only by the lights outside.' Lord Fermoy, in white tie and tails, opened the ball partnering the Queen Mother to the music of 'It's a Lovely Day Today'. When the tiny royal personage entered the ballroom at 11.15 p.m. wearing a pink-and-silver leaf-patterned organza gown and diamond tiara, the music stopped and all the women present dipped in a low, rustling curtsy.[15] The glamour of it all was a deal-closer for the rising courtier Johnnie Spencer, who danced the night away with Frances in her white organza ball gown scattered with rhinestones. For him, there was no greater aphrodisiac than royal connections.

The social forces that brought Diana's parents to the altar foreshadow much of what happened to her as Princess of Wales. In an echo of her daughter's predicament thirty years later Frances said, 'When you meet someone at the age of 15 and get engaged just five months out of school at 17, you can look back and ask "Was I adult?" I sure thought I was at the time.'[16]

*

Unfortunately, for Frances young Viscount Althorp was not the confident man about town he seemed. Like Prince Charles he was dominated by his father and made to wait for ever for his inheritance. His commanding officer considered him 'never the brightest of people. It was all squashed out of him by a domineering father.'[17] The old Earl, Jack Spencer, had 'a very peculiar temperament', according to his own sister, Lady Margaret Douglas-Home. 'He didn't see the point of ordinary people.'[18] Diana's younger brother, Charles, remembers their grandfather as 'a figure of awe. His moustache bristled. His stomach bulged under outsized trousers and he had the uncompromising air of a man who had no time whatever for fools.'[19] He was so relentlessly taciturn he outlawed small talk; on one occasion relished by the staff, he instructed the chauffeur of his Rolls to stop so he could get out and relieve himself behind a tree. The wind slammed the car door and the chauffeur assumed that as usual His Lordship was once again glowering in the back seat. He drove off without a backward look, leaving his irate employer stranded on the A40.

The Earl ridiculed his son Johnnie's intellect and kept him on an embarrassingly small allowance. By the 1950s, most of the Spencer wealth was on the walls rather than in the bank. Unlike many of his contemporaries, the old boy was too proud and too possessive of his treasures to open his ancestral seat to the public, the route taken by the 'showbiz' peers at other great houses like Beaulieu, Longleat and Woburn, who kept their estates afloat by turning them into aristocratic theme parks. Jack Spencer's solution was miserly, fastidious thrift. He hand-rinsed the china, dusted the books in the library, and relaxed at night by working on needlepoint seat covers for the chairs.

As it happened, the finest of his possessions was his wife and Johnnie's mother, Lady Cynthia, daughter of the Duke of Abercorn. When you come upon her portrait at Althorp, you might feel you are gazing on the rosy cheeks and candid blue eyes of her celebrated granddaughter. The likeness to Diana did not end there. Cynthia was famous in Northamptonshire for her compassion, scurrying round the county in her beat-up little Morris to visit the needy. Diana saw her as a figure of divine kindness. When, her favourite grandmother died, part of eleven-year-old Diana's sustaining network of fantasy was the belief that Lady Cynthia looked after her in the spirit world. Unfortunately, this saintly woman could not look after herself, let alone Diana. Her capitulation to the Earl's fierce will was a horrible example of female subservience. She escaped her husband's meanness by working for a few days as lady of the bedchamber to the Queen. I am told one of the many small unpleasantnesses the Earl used to like to inflict was to cancel his wife's instructions to the chauffeur to meet her at Northampton station when she returned from her Palace duties, just for the pleasure of making her telephone again and wait around. 'She looked like a washed-out emerald that had lost its colour,' says Lord Glenconner.[20]

Such abject subjugation of his mother gave Johnnie a complicated outlook on the opposite sex. He was attracted to women who fought back – and minded dreadfully when they did. It had been dinned into him by his father that producing an heir was his first priority. His young bride was expected to go through six pregnancies in nine years until she gave birth to a son. The first child, Sarah, was born in 1955, a honeymoon baby. On the death of Frances's father the same year, Lady Fermoy offered the young marrieds the lease of Park House, a generous act that got them away from the tyranny of Jack, but carried the seeds of marital tension since it reminded Johnnie of his dependency on Frances and her private income. In their new home, Frances gave birth to her second daughter, Jane. Inga Crane, a nurserymaid said Frances seemed a fulfilled and happy young mother at Park House: Lady Althorp was 'always laughing. They did a lot of entertaining and the house was full of lights and warmth and people in the evenings.'[21]

All that was missing was the Spencer heir. In 1960, Frances thought she had achieved the pinnacle of happiness with the birth of baby John Spencer. Her delight did not last. The doctors delivered a baby in serious trouble. In a cruel repression of feeling, which reflected the paternalistic nature of obstetrics at the time, Viscount Althorp decreed his wife must not be allowed to view or hold her son. Years later Frances recalled the chilling scene of how she struggled out of bed and banged frantically on the locked door. 'It was something that no human should be forced to endure. My baby was taken from me and I never saw his face. Not in life. Nor in death. No one ever mentioned what had happened.'[22] It was not till much later that Frances learned what was written on the baby's death certificate: 'Extensive malformation.'[23]

The blow of the boy's death seemed to strike at his father's *amour propre* and Frances's capacity to love him. At each of Frances's successive confinements the old Earl had built bonfires at Althorp ready to celebrate the impending birth of an heir. When she conceived again and miscarried, she concealed it from her husband. The birth of a third daughter after this was as much an agony as a blessing.

Diana Frances Spencer was born at 7.45 p.m. at Park House on 1 July 1961, in the same bedroom where her grandmother Lady Fermoy had given birth to her mother. She arrived with swiftness and ease on that warm July evening just as a great cheer resounded around Sandringham Cricket Club. The local speed cop had scored a century. 'I thought that was rather nice,' her mother recalled, 'that she came into the world with a clap of hands.'[24] But in the family there was no applause for the mother of a third girl. Diana's parents didn't get round to bestowing a name on their new daughter for a week and broke the news of her birth in *The Times* with nine words that could hardly be a more perfunctory expression of joy. 'Viscountess Althorp gave birth to a daughter on Saturday.'[25] The baptism ceremonies of her two elder sisters, Sarah and Jane, were awash in illustrious godparents. The Queen Mother was one of Sarah's and the Duke of Kent was Jane's, but only the esteemed wife of the Lord Lieutenant of Norfolk and assorted county neighbours were pictured in Johnnie's films of the christening of the future Princess of Wales.[26]

The months after Diana's birth were some of the worst in the Spencers' marriage. Johnnie turned into Henry VIII on a bad day, insisting Frances visit a succession of fertility doctors who subjected her to a humiliating battery of tests to discover why she produced only girls. It was as if the affable side of Johnnie was now in retreat and he pursued his obsession to produce an heir with the same cold insensitivity that the 7th Earl had inflicted on his mother. It was not till 1964 that the Althorp bonfires blazed at last. Charles Edward Maurice, the future 9th Earl Spencer, was born and later christened in the noble grandeur of the Henry VII Chapel in Westminster Abbey with the Queen Elizabeth II herself as his godmother.[27] Frances was off the hook, allowing the Spencer marriage to drift into an uneasy holding pattern.

The oblivious early days of Diana's childhood were a paean to gentle traditionalism – feeding trout in the lake in the royal park, hunting pigeons' eggs, climbing trees or hosing each other round the pool. Her father became Diana's first conquest. He found her his most responsive photographic subject, always looking back at him fetchingly as she dug her sandcastles or smiling under fluttery lashes as she wobbled around the lawn on her tricycle. On rambling walks with their nanny or on the pathways pushing baby Charles in his huge cavernous pram, the Spencer children sometimes encountered the Queen out riding when she was in residence at Sandringham and she would pause and chat to them. They were occasionally invited to the Big House to play. Prince

Andrew, the Queen's second son, was always supposed to be the one earmarked for Diana. 'I'm saving myself for him,' Diana joked to the butler, Mr Pendrey.[28] Nanny Janet Thompson tells of peeking into the Sandringham drawing room and seeing the Queen in a game of hide-and-seek with six-year-old Andrew and a cheery five-year-old Diana. In her account, Prince Charles, then seventeen, walked in at teatime and asked, 'Everything all right? It looks like a good party to me'[29] – a cameo appearance that seems rather poignant now, conjuring up as it does the young heir to the throne's large well-meaning ears, his fogeyish big brother concern, and his tiny future wife giggling behind a heavy silk curtain.

Frances, however, was as restive as she was resentful after her years as a brood mare. 'I'm so bloody bored with opening village fetes,' she told a friend soon after the birth of Jane in 1957.[30] She wanted to get to town more, go to concerts, head up some philanthropic cause. Even women in the shires were not immune to the restless currents that burst forth in the women's liberation movements of the sixties. Increasingly, there were spats with Johnnie about her London jaunts. The ageing Viscount Althorp was losing his looks and had acquired jolting cheeks and an increasingly ponderous delivery. He longed to move into Althorp but Frances now dreaded the day. On visits there, she felt she was locked in a museum after closing time. 'It was always a great fear to me. That house appears to hold enormous sadness.'[31] Perhaps Frances's trepidation also derived from watching Johnnie's mother shrivel under the old Earl's harsh treatment.

Once the two elder girls were in school, Frances started to please herself and go to town when she wanted. Her family income gave her independence and at only twenty-eight she was even more attractive than as a young bride – more self-assured, more conversationally amusing and more open for adventure. She wanted a taste of swinging London and there were plenty of prospects. She had arrived at the sexual heyday of all the other aristocratic Desperate Housewives, alert for long lunches at the Causerie in Claridge's and the offer of a diverting afternoon. It was inevitable perhaps that she fell in love. In the summer of 1966, her dinner partner at a London party she attended with Johnnie was the funny, rumpled charmer, Peter Shand Kydd, forty-one, who was there with his wife, Janet, an interior decorator. He had inherited a reasonable fortune from the sale of his family's wallpaper business and for the last few years had lived the life of a romantic wanderer, sheep farming in Australia. The two couples hit if off so well they went on a skiing holiday together in Courchevel in the French Alps.

*Whoomph!* The sparks that flew between Peter and Frances on that holiday in February 1967 were an explosive subtext hard to conceal on scenic chairlifts and intimate fondue evenings. Yet for the next five months Johnnie seemed or preferred not to notice. Or as Frances put it bitterly, he 'had so little interest in the heifer who had produced the prize calf'.[32] By April, Frances and Peter had embarked on a secret, escalating affair in a rented flat. By September, when the two elder girls left for boarding school, Johnnie confronted Frances with his suspicions of an affair and she stunned him by asking for a trial separation.

'It was a bolt out of the blue and knocked him flat,' Johnnie's friend Sir Julian Loyd has said.[33] Frances had acted in a way that was utterly incomprehensible to the son of the obedient Lady Cynthia and her stoic generation. Johnnie edited out the validity of his wife's discontent. 'How many of those years were happy?' he said later. 'I thought all of them, until the moment that we parted.'[34] He was so bemused he acquiesced in her taking Diana and Charles with her to a rented flat in Cadogan Square, and enrolling them in a London day school.

Lady Fermoy was incensed. Frances's unfortunate need to confess was, to Ruth, as appalling as the fact of the affair itself. She felt that the future Countess Spencer, soon to be the chatelaine of one of the most prestigious stately homes in England, would have surely been better advised to conduct her post-procreation amours in private, and keep her marriage alive in name at least. Plus, she adored Johnnie. 'I always thought she was a bit in love with him herself,' Lady Glenconner reflected.[35]

Egged on by his increasingly assertive mother-in-law, the usually dithery Viscount made a decisive move. He obtained court approval for Norfolk to be regarded as the permanent home of Diana and Charles, and sprang it on Frances at the end of a fraught family Christmas holiday together at Park House in 1967. The courts were closed for Christmas and Frances could do nothing. Not that it would have made any difference. Johnnie's rank and title would have prevailed. He had already enrolled Diana and Charles at Silfield School in King's Lynn. When the distraught Frances left without them after Christmas, the children were told she was soon coming back. It was the first of the big emotional lies that undermined Diana's faith in the empirical world. Diana later told her friend Cosima Somerset that her mother's exit was 'the most painful thing in her life, that the children weren't told why she was leaving permanently'.[36] Charles Spencer remains equally disturbed by the deception. On the day his mother's maid, Violet Collison, was suddenly very busy. Diana told him she came across Mrs Collison and their mother packing all her dresses and their mother said 'I'll be back very soon!'[37] To Andrew Morton, she recounted that her six-year-old self 'sat quietly at the bottom of the cold stone stairs at her Norfolk home, clutching the wrought iron banisters while all around her there was a determined bustle. She could hear her father loading suitcases into the boot of the car, then Frances, crunching across the gravel forecourt, the clunk of the car door being shut and the sound of a car engine revving and then slowly fading as her mother drove through the gates of Park House and out of her life.'[38] Diana sat on the steps week after week forlornly imagining her mother's return to live with them again.

Frances had rolled the dice and lost. 'It was so wrong to call Frances "The Bolter",' said Barbara Gilmour. 'She never expected to lose her children.'[39] Once the crusty skin of the aristocratic marital façade was peeled away, Frances's vulnerability as a woman was terrifyingly exposed. When she went back to Park House in the new year to renew her efforts to collect Diana and Charles, 'the door was shut in my face, I screamed at the butler to let me in . . . The house was so huge the children couldn't hear me from inside calling out for them. I think it was a long time before they realised the truth, that I hadn't abandoned them.'[40] Her fate as a mother was determined in April 1968 when Shand Kydd's wife, Janet Shand Kydd, won a divorce from Peter on the grounds of his adultery. Frances was now incontrovertibly the guilty party. In December 1968 she filed for divorce herself, enraging Johnnie by citing cruelty. He denied those charges and countersued on the grounds of her adultery. Whether there was anything to Frances's charge is still a source of debate. The Spencer family has no desire to air the sealed testimony of the court hearings that detail her case. The current Earl Spencer is said to vehemently reject his mother's cruelty charges as a ploy at the time to strengthen her plea for custody. My own view is that Johnnie became a bully not a batterer. Johnnie's conduct, as observed by others, suggests rather the kind of table-banging outbursts and small social cruelties practised by limited men who fear the spirited intelligence of their wives. Lady Sarah Spencer-Churchill remembers a dinner party at Park House at which Johnnie was so offensive towards Frances she was 'outraged and humiliated she stormed off swearing she'd had enough'.[41]

Diana, acutely attuned to the radar of disaster, later recalled listening, at the age of five, from her hiding place behind the door of the drawing room at Park House to the distressing sounds of a violent parental row. Her elder sister Sarah used to turn up the record player to drown the shouting matches.[42] I suspect the escalation into physical violence was Diana's secret childhood fear. During her marriage to Prince Charles she was always listening at doors, as she had as a child, seeking confirmation of the worst.

Viscount Althorp was granted a decree nisi on 15 April 1969,[43] and a month later Frances married Shand Kydd in a quiet registry office wedding, a century away from the sparkling, society-crammed Wedding of the Year to Viscount Althorp at Westminster Abbey fifteen years before. Johnnie was granted custody of the children. It was the shattering surprise witness to Johnnie's superior parenting claims that swung the verdict against Frances – her own mother Ruth, Lady Fermoy. 'Her mother's testimony was a bitter hurt, a deep wound. She was deeply angry as well as hurt,' said Barbara Gilmour.[44] Explaining Lady Fermoy's disavowal of her daughter, a family friend, Brodrick Haldane, takes the view that if Frances had 'left Johnnie for the Duke of Rutland that would have been all right, but to leave him for Mr Shand Kydd was more than she could endure'.[45] One of Ruth's fears, he said, was that Shand Kydd, having lost custody of his own three children, would take the Spencer children off to live on a ranch in Australia and they could come home with unfortunate Aussie accents.[46] Unfair perhaps, but it is hard not to conclude that Ruth was driven by the same ruthless social politics that had caused her to propel Frances into Johnnie's arms in the first place. Divorce was such anathema at Court, after the reverberations of Mrs Simpson, that Ruth felt impelled to sell out her daughter to preserve the high ground. Aspects of her testimony against Frances were gratuitously invasive. I am told that part of Frances's complaint was that Johnnie didn't satisfy her sexually. Ruth asserted that, on the contrary, Frances had always said she was sexually satisfied in the marriage.

The rift between Frances and her mother caused by the custody hearing never healed. It also planted in Diana a potent ambivalence about the Establishment. Her mother was now on the out list in royal circles, thanks in part to Lady Fermoy's influence. It sent the message that membership of the club required the sacrifice of all the ties of feeling. Now the young Diana kicked and screamed when her father announced she and her brother had been invited to the Big House by the Queen to join Prince Andrew and Prince Edward and others for a party. The chagrined Johnnie had the embarrassing job of telephoning Sandringham to decline the Queen's invitation. Lady Fermoy, who was unamused by such tantrums, told a friend that a school report had called the six-year-old Diana Spencer 'the most scheming little girl' the teacher had ever met.[47]

On the children's allotted weekend visits, Frances was always fraught. 'Every Saturday night, standard procedure she would start crying,' Diana remembered. ' "What's the matter, Mummy?" "Oh, I don't want you to leave tomorrow!" '[48] Diana was always gloomy and conflicted after these exchanges. Mary Clarke came to dread the hand-over at Liverpool Street station from the imposingly patrician mother, who was glacial in her resentment of the nanny usurper. 'Their mother had very little to say,' she recalled, 'and it was spoken to me via Diana.'[49] Nothing needling, but cold instructions economical as acupuncture. The most telling line about their childhood in Charles Spencer's funeral address was how Diana had not changed since the days when she 'endured those long train journeys between our parents' homes with me at weekends'.[50] The journeys soon got longer. After the final custody battle, the Shand Kydds moved far from the unforgiving eyes of Norfolk and the whisperings of London society to a thousand-acre farm on the windswept isle of Seil on the west coast of Scotland. For Diana it was another loss. 'Cheer up and grin and bear,' Lady Fermoy told her bereft grandchildren. 'Worse things happen at sea, my little sailors.'[51]

Not as far as the two youngest Spencers were concerned. The spirit of gaiety was gone from Park House along with Frances's furniture. Johnnie Spencer's abandonment was reminiscent of the hopeless Tony Last in Evelyn Waugh's novel *A Handful of Dust*. Englishmen play this role better than anyone else. The forty-three-year-old Viscount incarcerated himself in his study, speaking in words of one syllable to his chauffeur and his gamekeeper and sitting morosely for hours staring out of the window. He sought solace in the arms of women friends in London, but none of them seemed to click. Short of cash, locked into his interminable wait for his inheritance, the once so eligible Viscount Althorp was developing what Lord Glenconner terms 'an unfortunate raw sausage look'.[52]

He did his best. Being a single father in the upper classes in 1969 made Johnnie something of a curio. Each morning he dropped Diana and Charles at Silfield and each afternoon he picked them up. He made noises about the whereabouts of their wellington boots and their raincoats. He looked in on them in the nursery as they ate a bedtime snack of jam sandwiches and a glass of milk. Even so, he wasn't cut out to be a jolly New Age dad. His own formal childhood had moored him irrevocably to the detached parenting style of the aristocracy. Diana and Charles always took their meals with the nanny in the nursery while he supped in solitary grandeur in the dining room. 'I don't know anyone who brings up children like that any more,' Charles Spencer has observed.[53]

Journalists later rhapsodised about Diana's 'grand upbringing', but life for the children at Park House was desperately limited, timidly local. There was a reason why, as Princess of Wales, Diana never used her position, as Jacqueline Kennedy Onassis did, to invite an interesting mix of people to dinner parties. Socially, she felt inadequate. Her father fraternised with the dullest of landed gentry, whose children offered her a narrow range of friends. Her absentee mother could provide care-free sailing holidays on the coast but not much else in the way of expanding her children's horizons or building their confidence. Her highbrow grandmother, Lady Fermoy, was hardly diligent – as her friend the Queen Mother was with her own grandson Prince Charles – about exposing the Spencer children to stimulating ideas and people or offering warm encouragement to their developing interests.

Diana had drawn the short straw in this family melodrama. With her two older sisters at boarding school, she felt required to be her father's comforting angel. When she wasn't tormenting the nannies who were her mother's replacement, she trailed after her father, making him cups of tea and offering to bake him a cake. Her more robust sisters would often tell neighbours when asked where Diana was, 'Oh, Di's with Daddy. She likes staying at home to help him.'[54] 'Helping' was the way she expressed her longing to be loved, just as the Earl's way was to photograph her. Her cousin, the former army officer Robert Spencer, was impressed by how tender she was in her treatment of Charles. 'She was always the prettiest of the girls,' he says, 'but what made it a real joy to stay with them was what a wonderful older sister she was.'[55] At night she used to lie in bed listening to the pitiful sounds down the hall of her brother crying, 'I want my mummy.' She wanted to go and comfort him, but dreaded the creepiness of the corridor and stayed in bed, feeling guilty and sad.[56] Perhaps because at home she was always trying to pretend things were better than they were, at school Diana developed a reputation for making things up and creating dramas out of nothing. She had learned to get her way. For things she wanted, she batted her eyelids at her father and guilt-tripped her mother with tears.

Her dreams were of traditional marriage and happy families. Nanny Mary Clarke, meeting Diana for the first time, found her talkative and friendly, but obsessed with the idea of romance. 'I remember her saying, "I shall only get married when I am sure I am in love so that we will never be divorced," and this became something of a theme for her.'[57] Today Mary Clarke lives in a tiny doll's-house-like cottage in Winterton-on-Sea, Norfolk. She is a private, matter-of-fact blonde whose private life revolves round her dogs and her horse riding. She seems very sad still about how Diana's life turned out and angry with the royal family for turning the practical, warm little girl she looked after into a basket case and then rewriting her early life history to justify it.

Nothing was further from Diana's romantic dreams than the way her father came to satisfy his. The woman who surged into their father's life – 'supposedly incognito',[58] in Diana's words – was Raine Legge, the wife of the 9th Earl of Dartmouth. Even to her closest friends Raine came off as overblown and something of a preposterous figure – the gratingly posh voice, the red, drumming fingernails, the aerodynamic hair coiffed into an immobile bouffant helmet, the stuck-up insistence on changing three times a day for lunch, tea and formal dinner. Raine herself had had to survive parenting hell. Her mother, Barbara Cartland, may have been the author of the potboilers Diana devoured, but she had long been a leading player in the tabloids' theatre of embarrassment. Cartland dressed like a Belgravia version of Dame Edna Everage, with trailing clouds of pink chiffon and layers of recklessly applied fuchsia lipstick. Posses of small, yapping poodles in rhinestone collars followed her everywhere she went. She was a firm believer in alternative medicines and home-made cosmetic surgery achieved by hoisting her jowls aloft with sticky tape.

Raine's father, Alexander McCorquodale, was the heavy-drinking son of a printing tycoon who took a mistress and bolted the family. The divorce was acrimonious, leaving Cartland short of money and madly keeping up appearances. Absurdly snobbish, Cartland raised Raine as a social monster baby, thrusting her into the limelight from the moment she could wave a rattle. One especially awful moment in 1947 was a 'gramophone dance' given by Cartland at home in South Street, Mayfair, one of three coming-out parties for Raine. Cartland invited to the dinner beforehand only eligible, titled men who might be suitable husbands for her daughter. One of these admirers was the future Lord Glenconner. He arrived at the Cartland address for the party but got no further than the foot of the stairs. The Earl of Dartmouth, it seems, had just proposed. 'At the top of the staircase was Raine's mother in an aquamarine evening gown,' he told me. 'She called down, "Don't come up! Raine's engaged to be married!" '[59]

Given the theatrics of her mother, it's surprising that Raine didn't go under. But she turned out to have a ruthless discipline that persists to this day. She was intelligent and dynamic and absolutely dedicated to her own personal crusades. A Lady Who Can Get Things Done was Raine's stock-in-trade.

At the age of twenty-four Raine was already an admired member of Westminster City Council. On her way to Paris in November 1954, she made headlines by declaring, after a visit to the airport café at London's Heathrow, 'I have never seen such filth in my life.'[60] The remark caused enough of a furore that questions were asked in Parliament. Raine returned to Heathrow twelve days later for a triumphant photo op surveying the improvements wrought by her publicity. 'Everything is clean and nice,' she announced. 'I must congratulate everyone,' thus ending the nation's airport hygiene crisis.[61]

From early on, Raine's combination of energy and flattery was remarkably persuasive to the opposite sex. 'She was the only woman we knew who had a secretary and went to meetings,' an elderly peer told me admiringly.[62] In 1970, art historian and museum director Sir Roy Strong felt indebted to her help in getting the National Portrait Gallery listed as a historic building to protect it from demolition. 'I couldn't at the time reconcile this diamond-bespangled fashion plate with anyone remotely effective,' he wrote in his diary. 'In that I was to be proved immediately wrong.'[63]

Perhaps Raine's extreme persona was the distortion of a woman forced to channel her natural intelligence and leadership skills through the hoity-toity limitations of her era and class. Had she gone to Oxford instead of two hundred debutante balls she might have been Margaret Thatcher (whom she more than a little resembled, not least in her imperiousness). Instead, she has made Being Impossible her brand. Lord Glenconner remembers with affection Raine joining a house party in the seventies at Glen, his home in Scotland, when she was still Lady Dartmouth. On discovering that the cupboard in her bedroom was too short for her long evening dress she summoned the estate carpenter to come and dismantle the inside so she could hang it up without a crease.[64]

Her terrifying effectiveness also seems to have extended to sex. 'Johnnie was always terribly interested in sex, and so was Raine,' a mutual friend recalled. 'Raine used to scream, "Oh, you are wonderful! You are sexy!" When she was married to the Earl of Dartmouth she used to say coyly, "Gerald must have his rights."'[65] The affair took off when they collaborated on a pamphlet published in 1975 for the Historic Buildings Board, of which she was chairman. Its title was 'What About Our Heritage?'. Raine flattered Johnnie's idea of himself as a photographer by asking him to take the pictures. This gave her an opportunity to visit Althorp and charm the old Earl when he was still in residence. On that first visit, she committed the gaffe of sitting on a favourite needlepoint chair seat cover. 'You can't sit there,' he barked.[66] But she soon made up for it by appearing fascinated with the history of Althorp, plying him with chocolates, for which he had a weakness, and assiduously searching out new walking sticks for his collection.[67] The conquest of the father was a major victory. Soon the son was hopelessly in love.

Johnnie was a wilting fifty-one, and Diana thirteen when, on 9 June 1975, the old Earl Spencer died of pneumonia at the age of eighty-three. It was a decisive turning point in the saga of the Spencer family, not least because of the change it wrought in their father. Sad-sack Johnnie, Viscount Althorp, was suddenly the 8th Earl Spencer. (An earl's title, without the 'of', carries far more prestige than one with, e.g., Raine's husband, the Earl of Dartmouth, was diminished by his 'of'.) And what the owner of a stately home the size of Althorp needs is a chatelaine. It had always grieved Raine that her first husband, a charming but put-upon figure with whom Raine had four children, had a title but no stately home to go with it. After twenty-eight years of marriage to Dartmouth, Raine saw her chance. 'She wanted to marry Daddy,' Diana said to Andrew Morton. 'That was her target and that was it.'[68]

For the four children, accustomed to having their father entirely to themselves any new girlfriend was a nightmare – but this one was beyond belief. Aristocratic kids are almost aggressively laid-back in their style. From their parents they absorb the inverted snobbery of their class, which is calculated to put social interlopers off the scent and frustrate their attempts to penetrate. The grander you are, the more you underplay it. It was inconceivable to them that their low-key, old-shoe father should now so admire a woman who seemed to break all the restraining rules of entry. Their loathing of her was instantaneous. 'She used to sort of join us, accidentally find us in places and come and sit down and pour us with presents,' Diana said, 'and we all hated her so much because we thought she was going to take Daddy away from us.'[69] Sarah Spencer was now living in London, working as an assistant to Barbara Timms, the features editor at *Vogue*. Sarah's ear was to the gossip mill and she passed the dish about her father's new girlfriend on to her younger siblings. Diana grilled Mary Clarke, and the whole tribe was primed when Raine first arrived for lunch at Park House. Sarah broke through the cut-glass attempts at conversation by letting forth a loud burp. A shocked Lord Althorp reprimanded her with a sharp 'Sarah!' to which she replied, 'In the Arab countries it is recognised as a sign of appreciation.' Diana dissolved into giggles. Spencer was so appalled, he told Sarah to leave the table. A stunned silence fell across the room as Sarah abruptly pushed back her chair and walked out. Her father angrily cut off Diana when she tried to defend her sister.[70]

Diana was hurt, deeply, by the change in her father when Raine arrived. Her sisters were now aged nineteen and seventeen so she and Charles were hit the hardest. Whatever his deficiencies as a depressed single dad had been, he was there, providing Diana's everyday security. She wrote to him faithfully from boarding school. Now that he was away a lot in London, she pined for him when she was home, worried about him, worried about his absences. It was probably fear of Diana's reaction – at the highly emotional and vulnerable age of fifteen – that made her father commit an unforgivable act of parental cowardice, one that left an active wound. On 14 July 1976, six weeks after her divorce from the Earl of Dartmouth, Earl Spencer married Raine at a small ceremony at Caxton Hall without first notifying his daughters and son.

Charles Spencer learned of the marriage from his prep school headmaster the evening after it happened. He was flabbergasted. Diana and her sisters read about it in the newspapers. 'We weren't invited. "Not grand enough,"' Sarah Spencer commented to a reporter.[71] The Earl and the new Countess Spencer celebrated with a glittering ball for about a thousand people at Althorp. Again, the children were not invited. Significantly, they decided among themselves that it would be Diana who would exact punishment on their father. Even then, it must have been clear that their blushing, affectionate younger sister had the appropriate reservoirs of rage to pull off a suitably vindictive display of collective reprisal. She confronted their father at Althorp. The Earl thought his youngest and favourite daughter Diana was advancing towards him for a kiss, but she drew back her hand and slapped him hard across the face. 'That's from all of us, for hurting us,' she hurled at him. Then she stalked out of the room and slammed the door behind her. Her father flushed with rage and followed her. He took her by the wrist and spun her round: 'Don't you ever talk to me like that again,' he told her, shaking. 'Well, don't you ever do that to us again,' Diana replied and walked away.[72]

Diana's campaign against the ascendancy of the new Countess Althorp was a replay of her guerrilla warfare against her first nannies. She got a school friend to write Raine a poisonous letter. She made harassing telephone calls, hanging up if Raine answered. According to the butler, Mr Pendrey, because she wasn't allowed to use a stereo record system in the house, Diana pulled up the floorboards and disconnected the wiring so no one could use it.[73] It was perilous to hurt her. All through Diana's life, the vindictiveness of her spite when it was aroused went beyond the tantrum of a spoilt child. The historian and commentator Kenneth Rose found the atmosphere at Althorp 'awful' when he was a house guest in 1977: 'It was the first time I had met Diana. She was extraordinarily beautiful I thought. Huge soulful blue eyes and a beautiful complexion. On this occasion all three daughters were there and you could cut the atmosphere with a knife between Raine and the children. They joined us for a meal. I said to Jane, "Do you come here often?" and she said, "When I am asked." They never addressed a word to Raine. Johnnie was obviously uncomfortable. He'd lived in turmoil of family conflict – almost disinherited by his father, banished to Norfolk, then all the Frances acrimony.'[74]

A lot of Johnnie's old county friends in Northamptonshire melted away in the Raine era. One of the neighbours was asked if he was going to a big ball Raine was giving at Althorp. He replied, 'We don't recognise Raine,' as if she were an illegal government or a rogue state.[75]

What Johnnie's grand Norfolk friends and relations didn't recognise was that Raine's glitz was putting the Spencer family on the map again. Northamptonshire has always been a strangely isolated swathe of the lower Midlands. The unappealing eccentricities of Diana's grandfather, the 7th Earl, marginalised the family further still. Until Raine moved in, the old Earl haunted Johnnie's psyche and that of Althorp staff. It was unsettling for Johnnie to find them still bowing and scraping to his father's ghost. He had more substantial worries – specifically two and a half million pounds in death duties, not to mention eighty thousand pounds a year just to run the place. To save money the old Earl had been willing to live without modern conveniences. 'When I first stayed there it was like any country house,' Kenneth Rose said. 'A footman brought you a can of tepid water. There was some primitive central heating that gurgled all night.'[76] Raine turned her formidable energies to saving Althorp. She persuaded Johnnie to open the house to the public for the first time. The staff was pared to the bone; the cook, the footman and the land agent all got the sack. As part of opening the house to paying visitors, the limestone stable block was turned into a handsome tea and gift shop. This was enlightened and necessary but, being Raine, she went one step further, bringing in her own designers and painters to impose her individual style upon the house. Unfortunately, that style was at variance with Althorp's classical atmosphere and appearance. 'She stippled the library paint, instead of painting it ivory or white as it should have been,' a guest recalled. 'They had beautiful wooden floors with Persian rugs and she had it covered in wall to wall carpeting. Partridge, the Bond Street antique dealer, helped her with selling off a lot of the stuff.'[77] Going, going, gone were several portraits by Gainsborough, Georgian furniture and snuff boxes, seventeenth-century Marlborough gold wine coolers, over forty cottages on the Spencer estate and family papers. Raine's transgressions were especially rich coming from the author of 'What About Our Heritage?'. But that of course must have been part of the fun for her husband. It doesn't take Sigmund Freud to see his passivity in the face of her renovations and plunderings as Johnnie's sullen rebellion at last against the taste tyranny of his father. And one more thing: for the first time ever, the house was comfortable.

There were beaming pictures of Johnnie with Raine against the backdrop of the newly fashionable Althorp in every glossy magazine and gossip column. And Johnnie, far from hiding from the limelight, loved it. The worst aspect of his dependence on Raine as far as his children were concerned was the very thing he had a right to expect them to be pleased about: how happy he was. Raine boosted his confidence. She made him laugh. The Spencer children were outraged at what was being done to their heritage just when they had finally got to know it. 'They minded terribly what she did to Althorp,' a Spencer cousin said. 'It was so overpolished and overgilded and overshiny. She ruled his life and spent his money.'[78]

How could Diana's beloved father allow it? Her childhood had offered her a gallery of men as disappointing as the women: a vindictive, control-freak grandfather, a needy younger brother, and now the adored father had suddenly shown himself to be a henpecked coward. No wonder her mother had gone. Luckily, Diana knew in her heart a dashing prince on a white horse would sweep her up and rescue her. She was determined to make it happen. As Lady Glenconner noted, Diana inherited from Lady Cynthia Spencer her sweetness but from Lady Fermoy her slyness and steel.

## Chapter 4

# The Super Sloane

'Thick as a plank, that's me!'

– A Diana catchphrase

It's not cool any more for upper-class girls to be as directionless as Diana was in the 1970s. Of the four Spencer children – Sarah, Jane, Diana and Charles – Charles alone had first-rate education, attending Eton and Oxford. Diana's modern counterparts head for the top universities of Britain. Her son Prince William met his first steady girlfriend, Kate Middleton, as a fellow undergraduate at St Andrews University where she studied art history. The Sloane Rangers, as Diana's set was known in the 1980s, because they all lived and partied around London's Sloane Square, now seems as much part of ancient history as the pouffe dress.

Diana's formal education followed a template that would be almost inconceivable today. But as late as the 1970s it was routine for the rich daughter of an earl to leave school at sixteen to work as a nanny and a cleaner as Diana did, with no academic qualifications at all unless you count hamster husbandry. In this respect Diana's path hardly differed from her mother's and replicated exactly the course of her two elder sisters. The difference was that in her case virtually nothing of what little was offered in those genteel classrooms seemed to penetrate. It didn't help that her mother had been an all-round star at school and both her elder sisters had been academically bright. Sarah, when behaving herself,[1] was also an accomplished pianist and equestrian; Jane a school leader. Her three siblings were in the habit of shouting Diana down if the conversation strayed into brainier waters. She was defensive about her low intellectual wattage and made jokes about it. 'Thick as a plank, that's me!' she was oft heard to shriek. But as it happened, her inferiority complex became one of her greatest assets.

Diana was nine when Earl Spencer dispatched her to her first boarding school, Riddlesworth Hall, a small genial establishment for ninety girls near Diss, in Norfolk, two hours from Park House. Here there was a lot of flower arranging and an emphasis on arts and crafts and 'friendliness'. The jolly atmosphere seems to have been almost entirely due to the personality of the principal, Elizabeth Ridsdale, famed for her huge floral displays, who swept the girls up in her nurturing bosom. It was one of the happiest periods of Diana's life. She won all the swimming and diving cups, and the nice-girl trophy, the Leggat prize for Helpfulness. She also won perhaps the most endearing airhead award ever: the prize for best-kept guinea pig. At school, the surrogate family of twenty stuffed animals she kept on her bed at Park House had to be reduced to one, a green hippo whose eyes she painted with luminous paint so he could look out for her in the night.[2]

At twelve, she was still a nondescript schoolgirl with a slight tendency to chubbiness, but a discerning eye could see an evolving beauty. Her bachelor cousin Robert Spencer recalls 'her clear skin, and unforgettable smile and such fine teeth' when they met shortly after her twelfth birthday in 1973. 'It was obvious by now that she was going to be a stunning woman. She'd reached that age when she was very inquisitive about her elder sister, Sarah, going to dances.'[3] Sarah Spencer's debutante dance that year had been an extravagant bash at Castle Rising in Norfolk, a one-time seaport guarded by a rugged Norman fort. The guests arrived in carriages and alighted at a path lit by blazing torches. Johnnie Spencer was uneasily kitted out as Henry VIII and Sarah was glammed to the hilt in an Anne Boleyn costume that Raine – before the Spencer children knew she was more than just a friend of their father – had moved heaven, earth and Hollywood to procure from the makers of the film *Anne of a Thousand Days*.[4] Thus attired, the older Spencer gel danced the night away then made a splashy exit roaring off in her father's birthday present, a British Racing Green MGB GT sports car.

Diana followed Sarah and Jane to West Heath, a boarding school in Kent. It was a small, friendly refuge for daughters of the Scottish and English gentry, housed in a handsome eighteenth-century house in thirty-two acres of parkland. *The Good Schools Guide* described it as 'a haven for daughters of well-born conventional parents for whom the social result is more important than the academic', and the brochure-speak was accurate. At the age of seventeen its alumnae drifted off to work on the front desk at Sotheby's or as the posh voice at the end of a

Belgravia estate agent's telephone. Everyone seems to have been up front about the school's modest goals and the torpor of its academic ambition. The only admissions requirement was 'neat handwriting'. Even West Heath noted Diana's absence of rigour and intellectual curiosity. 'The groundwork wasn't there,' said Ruth Rudge, the head teacher. 'As with anyone with other things on her mind, she would go off in daydreams.'[5]

Diana channelled her enthusiasms into swimming and ballet. In the outdoor pool she wore the obligatory rubber bathing cap that made her look as bald as a department store mannequin – the nearest she'd ever come to being an egghead. Her one-piece suit with its Lycra modesty panel to occlude the crotch was designed to avoid exciting the boys from the school in Sevenoaks. Her swimming quickly won cups for her house. Growing too tall for ballet, she joined the handful of girls taking weekly half-hour tap lessons, won two cups and was judged the favourite of the society world's most famous ballet teacher, Madame Vacani, whose Pekinese she dutifully cherished, taking it for walkies around the extensive lawns.

Her West Heath peers viewed Diana as a helpful sort of person who was 'awfully sweet' to her hamsters Little Black Muff and Little Black Puff.[6] She was popular and fun which compensated for the fact that academically she was a big zero. The escalating divorce rate of the seventies parked plenty of single-parent children in the school's bucolic surroundings, so Diana didn't feel out of place. On the Sundays when outings were allowed, the tea hall was often scattered with girls whose families hadn't come to take them out. She made a lifelong friend of Carolyn Pride, who had the dorm bed next to hers and whose parents were also divorced. 'It wasn't a great trial to us and we didn't sit sobbing in a corner about it,' said Carolyn, briskly.[7] The matron Violet Allen commented: 'Most of the girls from a divorced family would come and have a little weep . . . I never saw her cry. She probably kept a lot to herself.'[8] She did. Her private remedy for her sadness at home was to sneak down to the big hall at night, put on her music and dance for hours on her own, lost in her fantasy world. 'It always released tremendous tension in my head' she told Andrew Morton.[9]

Geordie Greig (now editor of *Tatler*) was at Eton when the teenager from West Heath came to visit a fellow Etonian, James Bone. 'There was an ordinariness about her,' Greig told me. 'She was like any girl who gave spaghetti suppers in Fulham.'[10] Her father's inheritance of his earldom in June 1975 meant that the ordinary girl became Lady Diana

Spencer and the resident of a stately home (her sisters became Lady Sarah and Lady Jane, and her brother Charles, the son and heir, inherited the title of Viscount Althorp of Great Brington). The morning Diana heard the news, she rushed along the corridor at West Heath with her dressing gown billowing out behind her, saying, 'I'M A LADY! I'm *Lady* Diana now!'[11]

Today when we think of Diana, we tend to conjure up the nineties iteration of her personality – global, glitzy, a woman of world media. But being a Spencer, more perhaps than being a princess and more than being a global celebrity, was a formative factor of Diana's life. Althorp was a place of romantic aspiration. You leave the twenty-first century as soon as you pass from the encroaching suburbia of Great Brington village and turn into the long, tree-lined avenue to the great house. There is an immediate sense of pastoral harmony. Even the sheep are dotted through the park with pleasing asymmetry, like the reverie from a Regency window. Diana's life had been afflicted with the chaos and impermanence of modern social mores but in every treasure-crammed room of the Spencer family seat, she inhaled the hierarchical values of the past.

Because of Johnnie Spencer's war with his father, the children rarely visited the big house as a family when the old Earl was alive. Growing up, they knew almost nothing about their heritage – about the history of the treasures on display at Althorp, the books that were the glory of its library, the spectacular pictures that were leaning from its walls in their chains. 'I didn't even know I had any kind of title until I started getting these letters saying "The Honourable Charles Spencer"', Diana's brother has recalled.[12] Diana now fully understood her family's grandeur – and how that grandeur had shrunk. Her father's anxiety about money bred in her the sense that there was a Spencer glory that needed to be rescued.

With the two elder Spencer girls launched on their own lives in London, Diana, fourteen, and Charles, eleven, together roamed the unfamiliar halls of Althorp, chilly even in midsummer. Diana liked to hang out in the kitchens, chatting and snacking and listening to gossip. Betty Andrews, a cleaner at Althorp in 1975, recalled: 'Diana even used to cook for the staff. She loved to make bread-and-butter pudding for us and rice or milk pudding for herself.' She also did her brother's laundry: 'She would put his things in the washing machine and then iron them for him.'[13] As Princess of Wales, she was too ready to confide marital secrets to her Palace staff and servants because that is what she was accustomed to at home where there were few other friendly faces to talk to. Instead, there were the daunting faces of the Spencers' past.

In the picture gallery, so long that many an Althorp lady of bygone years used it for her morning power walk, her ancestors and their contemporaries stared down at Diana from their wide gilt frames. So many arched, moist-eyed beauties offering to please the egos of the Spencer males, so many self-assured political operators under the luxuriant periwigs of self-confident men. At one end there's a bevy of Charles II's mistresses painted by the court artist Sir Peter Lely, their heavy-lidded eyes and welcoming cleavages ready to remind Diana that power might be the domain of men but could still be achieved by other means. There is something unsettling about the uniform vivacity of the mistresses and chatelaines on the wall. Diana's seventeenth-century ancestress Sarah, the impetuous Duchess of Marlborough, was forever scheming for the career advancement of her husband, the first Duke (victor of the Battle of Blenheim), and her own position at court as the favourite of the (probably gay) monarch Queen Anne. In the upstairs dining room is a portrait she commissioned of herself holding in one hand the shorn-off tresses of her long auburn hair. As she wrote, she was in a mood of 'spiteful anger' after a row with the Duke when she took a pair of scissors to the copper coils he loved. Later, she was touched to find he'd saved the locks of hair in a box of his most treasured possessions.

Diana's other celebrated ancestress, Georgiana Spencer, daughter of the 1st Earl Spencer, married one of England's most eligible bachelors, the fifth Duke of Devonshire, and became politically influential as a campaigner for the Whig Party. Unfortunately, her high-born husband was one of the few men in England not in love with her. He moved his mistress, Lady Elizabeth Foster (who also happened to be Georgiana's best friend), into Chatsworth, their Derbyshire stately home, where they all lived in a tense *ménage à trois* for many years. Like Diana, Georgiana transformed herself from a shy ingénue into a social star and arbiter of fashion. She possessed a unique magnetism said to light up a room. Her disarming directness won hearts everywhere, but her feelings of neglect led her to become addicted to gambling, dissolute company and the unstable influence of hairdressers, costumiers and quacks. For Lady Diana Spencer, Althorp was full of prescient family ghosts. To escape them, she took to obsessively practising her dancing alone in the black-and-white entrance lobby.

Looming large in her romantic haze was the face she had framed in her school dormitory, a real Prince Charming, the 'Action Man' whose daring exploits on the polo field and the ski slopes, or intrepidly parachuting out of combat planes she could see on television or read about in the papers – the face of the most eligible bachelor in the whole United Kingdom, the twenty-first Prince of Wales. Every royalist schoolchild had joined the millions watching the glorious pageant of his 1969 investiture at the thirteenth-century Caernarvon Castle. How gracefully had her hero, the twenty-year-old heir to the throne, bowed his head to receive from the Queen the royal insignia of gold crown, mantle, ring, rod and sword in a ceremony echoing back to the Black Prince!

It was her sister Sarah who brought the real Charles into her life. In the summer of 1977, six months after he left the Royal Navy, Prince Charles met Sarah during the annual Royal Ascot house party at Windsor. Sarah was still suffering from the shock of being dumped two years earlier by Gerald Grosvenor, the outlandishly rich heir to the Dukedom of Westminster, which owns three hundred acres of the most exclusive commercial and residential property in London (including the land on which the American Embassy stands in Grosvenor Square). Coming so soon after her father's marriage to Raine, it was too much for Sarah. She had stopped eating, and was still anorexic.

It is curious in retrospect that Charles, who was to be so exasperated by Diana's bulimia, was very sympathetic to Sarah in her anorexic distress. The fact that he was now squiring her around was a pleasing consolation prize for Sarah after the Grosvenor heartbreak. She received a flattering stream of invitations to Windsor and Balmoral. In November of that year Sarah felt confident enough to invite the Prince to shoot with her father at Althorp. Schoolgirl Diana was there. She registered on Charles's radar only as a 'jolly' and 'bouncy'[14] (or 'binecy' as he would pronounce it) younger sister of Sarah, but for the sixteen-year-old Diana, seeing Prince Charles for the first time since her childhood was a 'whoomph' moment of her own. Once she had caught sight of the number-one royal bachelor striding with his Labrador through a ploughed field with the guns and beaters and dogs, there was no other rival for her heart but twenty-eight-year-old Charles Philip Arthur George, HRH the Prince of Wales, Earl of Chester, Duke of Cornwall, Duke of Rothesay, Earl of Carrick, Baron Renfrew, Lord of the Isles and Prince and Great Steward of Scotland – or 'Arthur' as he likes to be called when he climaxes (according to his ex Colombian hottie Cristabel Barria Borsage).[15]

After the shooting day, Diana could not forget this thrilling multiple presence. How could she? The royals had been embedded in the Spencers' idea of themselves for centuries. They were raised up by kings. The source of their wealth and influence was propinquity to the Crown. Diana may have disliked her childhood visits to Sandringham, but her imagination still revolved round the magical rescue power of princes. Even fifteen years later, in September of 1992, in videotapes made by her speech coach Peter Settelen, she still seemed able to savour her triumph over Sarah. The Prince turned to her – not her sister – to show him the treasures of the Althorp picture gallery, irritating Sarah so much she told Diana to get lost. 'I remember,' Diana tells Settelen, 'feeling desperately sorry for him [Charles] that my sister was wrapped around his neck because she's quite a tough old thing.'[16] Miaow.

Diana came back from that shooting-party weekend at Althorp in November 1977 incandescent with excitement. 'I've met him!' she exclaimed to the piano teacher Penny Walker. 'I've met him, I've met him at last!'[17] To Sarah's great irritation, her Cinderella sister was included in the invitation to Prince Charles's thirtieth birthday ball in November 1978. It was one of the most illustrious private parties the royal family had thrown since the 1930s, when the then Prince of Wales, the future Edward VIII, had been in his partying prime. The Argentine rake Luis Basualdo, a polo-playing friend of Charles, accompanied Diana into the picture gallery to watch the cabaret by the Three Degrees, the all-female vocal group from Philadelphia (whose big hit, back in 1974, had been 'When Will I See You Again'). Basualdo thought she was 'very shy, very naive but rather nice'.[18] Diana gazed down from the picture gallery at the thrilling sight of the elegant Prince dancing the night away, sometimes with Sarah, sometimes with the other lovely, sophisticated girls in his life, all of them more self-possessed and more accomplished than she: Lady Leonora Lichfield, Gerald Grosvenor's beautiful sister; Lady Jane Wellesley, the cool daughter of the Duke of Wellington; the curvaceous screen actress Susan George; Lady Tryon, glamour-girl Australian spouse of Charles's shooting friend Anthony; and one especially intimate-looking dance partner, the confident, laughing blonde, Camilla Parker Bowles.

It seemed to Diana she could hardly compete in this company. She had left West Heath in December 1977 having failed every one of her O-level exams not once but twice. How could she win Charles's heart with so few accomplishments? Turning over the examination papers turned her over inside; she just found herself unable to recall anything she had learned. Penny Junor reports that Diana's friends also blamed her sheer laziness – but neither was she ever pushed.

She did, in fact, have a talent that West Heath had already noticed. She had emotional intelligence. Whether it was inherited from her Spencer grandmother's instinctive compassion or her Fermoy grandfather's gift of spontaneous intimacy, Diana made her warmth available to anyone regardless of race, creed or nationality. An invisible thread of kindliness drew her to people who expected the least and needed the most. The distinguished historian Paul Johnson believes that Diana's empathy was a unique gift. 'She thought she knew nothing and was very stupid,' he told me. 'She made it impossible to criticise her, because she'd say, "I am very thick and uneducated," and I'd say, "I don't think you are thick at all," because, although she didn't know much, she had something that very few people possess. She had extraordinary intuition and could see people who were nice, and warm to them and sympathise with them . . . Very few people compare to what she had.'[19]

The Sevenoaks Voluntary Service recruited schools to visit Darenth Park, a large hospital for the mentally and physically handicapped in Dartford. Muriel Stevens, the hospital manager, organised the visits for West Heath. Every Tuesday and Thursday a minibus carried a group of bubbly teenagers to the hospital. It quickly took the fizz out of them – a daunting place, a huge, bleak Victorian Gothic building surrounded by the high walls necessary to confine some very disturbed people. Most of the girls, including Diana's sister, Sarah, considered the visits an ordeal. 'I remember them opening enormous wooden doors like in a medieval castle – you know the ones you'd have had to take a battering ram to,' said Sarah. 'It smelt of disinfectant and pee . . . You saw this sea of ill people just coming towards you.'[20]

The patients would be waiting for the West Heath girls under bright lights in a high-ceilinged hall with acoustics that made the echo of voices deafening.[21] The girls were supposed to dance with the patients. In Sarah's words, 'You tried to dance in a circle and all the men wanted to do was to dance with you close up . . . they were all people with mental problems, serious mental problems. We had never seen places like this: we were all sheltered little girlies.'[22] Muriel Stevens too, was aware how scary the experience could be and what she said about Diana's visits is worth quoting at length.

'It was intimidating to walk into that huge place with the level of noise and to see some of the very severely handicapped people . . . Some of them would be in wheelchairs. Some of them would be sitting on chairs and needed encouragement to move to get off them . . . because they were just so delighted to see these young people they would rush up and of course they would touch their hair, grab their hands. And if you're actually not used to it, that can be very frightening. Diana was never frightened. She was extremely relaxed in that setting which, for a young person of her age, was incredible.'[23]

What has stayed in Stevens's memory all these years is a sound fairly rarely heard in a mental hospital, the sweet sane laughter of companionship as Diana made jokes among her new friends. 'That tremendous laugh! That joyous sound! And it was wonderful because you wouldn't actually know what she was laughing at, or have any idea at all what had amused her, but at the sound alone you would find yourself smiling, and as you got closer and you heard it more, you'd find yourself laughing. It was a terrific sound . . .'[24]

There was a memorably touching sight, too. The hospital encouraged the teenage girls to relate to the wheelchair patients by bending down to their level and holding their hands. They could not rise to dance, but they liked to be moved to music. Most of the volunteers just pushed from behind as rhythmically as they could – not easy with awkward wheelchairs. Diana's lithe body and ballet training gave her an edge – and an idea. She stood facing the chair, leaned down to grasp the front handles and then danced *backwards*, the wheelchair and patient gliding in a circuit with her. 'Now that is incredibly agile and clever and there are not many people who could maintain their balance. And she kept an extremely good rhythm.'[25]

Diana flowered in the presence of the disabled or ill. In later life she could switch in a second from fractious or self-absorbed Princess to another level of deep connection to people who showed their need, or their involvement with the needy.

'It was an indefinable quality, something very rare and rather beautiful,' one of her relatives said. 'I was not surprised years later when she emerged as a great communicator. Even as a young child she had a strange way of getting through to people.'[26] Diana's genius as Princess of Wales was that she was able to 'channel' ordinary people while actually having less and less real exposure to them. Therapist, Simone Simmons, happened to live above a Tesco supermarket in Hendon in north London. She found Diana was as fascinated by her description of life 'out on the streets'[27] as if it were life on Mars. Princess Margaret had the same curiosity. Her fantasy was to travel incognito on a London double-decker bus.[28] The difference was that when Diana did leave her own world for the hospital ward or the homeless shelter it was never royal condescension. In her last interview before her death she told *Le Monde*, 'I'm much closer to the people at the bottom than the people at the top.'[29]

It never occurred to Diana, or anyone else at the time, that this empathy she had could be as powerful a force as intellect. Clever middle-class girls in England had been going to university for several generations but few in Diana's circle considered it. Nobody would have dreamed of suggesting to Diana that she might study for professional social work. In Diana's circles, the career choices after school would likely have been little different if she'd left with a hatful of scholastic prizes. Her brainy older sister Jane led a life after school that was not very different from the one ordained for Diana as a matter of course, which in Jane's case meant a lightweight job at *Vogue* where 'trustafarians', traditionally hired by Condé Nast magazines for their connections, could tread water until the right country squire came along. (Jane would snag the equable Robert Fellowes, later the Queen's private secretary, who was the son of the Spencers' trusty neighbour down the road from Park House, the Sandringham land agent Sir William Fellowes.) Sarah flitted around between her job at *Vogue*, one at an estate agent's, and a part-time position with Universal Aunts, a posh babysitting and ferrying service for children, which allowed her plenty of time for long weekends of partying. In May 1980, at the age of twenty-five, she married the Lincolnshire farmer Neil Edmund McCorquodale.

Earl Spencer dispatched the sixteen-year-old Diana in 1978 to the Swiss finishing school, the Institut Alpin Videmanette, in Gstaad, a patina-buffing academy similar to the ones that had groomed the manners of her mother and sisters. She was expected to come back fluent in French with husband-tempting cordon bleu cooking diplomas, but Diana was too self-conscious about her language skills to speak French and spent most of her time skiing and writing homesick letters. After three months, she was finished with her finishing school. She immediately went back for a visit with her old friends at West Heath where the matron Violet Allen observed she had lost a lot of weight.[30]

When Diana turned eighteen in 1979, the social climate was so changed that the last thing she wanted was a grand ball like Sarah's extravaganza six years before. She was emerging at the end of a genteel female social world that had almost entirely faded. 'Coming out' had already started to have other modern connotations than the traditional ritual of titled girls spending their eighteenth year attending balls, parties and race meets. By the seventies only New Money eager to crash into 'society' would think of self-advertising that they were 'doing the Season'. A few girls, whose mothers were insistent they stick with the old ritual, told their friends they were attending functions 'strictly for camp', and arrived at charity balls on motorbikes in a blaze of spiky punk hairdos. A recession was raging which would soon upend Labour and bring Mrs Thatcher to Downing Street. The landed gentry, always alert to provoking class warfare, were even less in the mood than usual for displays of their wealth. The vogue instead was for gang-bang multi-generational balls – a fashion started by the Queen in 1970 when in a dazzle of inspirational economy she spot-welded the seventieth birthdays of the Queen Mother, Lord Mountbatten, Princess Alice of Athlone and the Duke of Beaufort in a party for eight hundred guests at Windsor Castle. The Duke of Marlborough followed suit in 1976 with a similar group blowout ball that summer at Blenheim Palace, wrapping up in one package his own fiftieth birthday, his son's twenty-first and his daughter Henrietta's coming out. With such pretext in triplicate, when the band struck up, £20 million worth of jewels could take the floor with a clear conscience.

Diana was restive, not emancipated enough to challenge ladylike patterns that were increasingly obsolete but modern enough to want inchoately to escape them. She came across an article in the *Daily Telegraph*, which seemed to speak directly to her, about academic failures who later become roaring successes in life. Diana, the third girl who should have been a boy, the blonde dimwit who was always the butt of her sharper siblings' gentle condescension, secretly longed to show the world she was a star. Beneath the timid conventionality there were signs of gathering conviction. She clipped out the *Telegraph* story, slipped it under her father's door and began to pester him about moving from Northamptonshire to London.[31] Three months later she left a temporary job nannying for friends in the countryside and moved to London herself, staying in her mother's Knightsbridge apartment with two flatmates.[32]

The next step was to secure a menial job, the more menial the better. Slumming it was part of the inverted cachet of the Sloane Ranger world, since it also announced you didn't depend on your job for either money or status. To be cool, the job had to be manifestly silly. *Tatler*, the house magazine for the upper classes, ran a feature in 1984 under the title 'Nobs With Yob Jobs', chronicling all the Lucindas and

Henriettas currently dog walking or working as singing telegrams. The only 'must have' for a position was flexible hours. Diana's mother, still fretting over the lack of cooking skills her daughter had acquired at finishing school, prodded her to sign up for a three-month course in the art of fine cuisine. That Frances kept pushing Diana towards the same life that had bored her to death when she was married to Earl Spencer is a measure of how inexorable the social momentum of the past remained.

Diana travelled every day by Tube from Sloane Square to the Wimbledon home of a genial relic of seasons past named Elizabeth Russell who schooled the daughters of nobility in the correct consistency of sauces, the levity of soufflés and the lost art of a light jam sponge.[33] Diana stuck it out at Russell's for the whole three months, leaving with a diploma and quite a bit of additional poundage. The culinary brush-up was supposed to lead to a year or two of 'Cooking for Directors', a favoured career ruse to throw marriageable girls at money men in the City, though for Diana it led only to a few gigs providing canapés for her friends' cocktail parties.

'My fingers were always in the saucepans,' she recalled.[34] 'Slightly pudgy' was how she seemed to James Whitaker, then the society reporter for the Daily Star, when she bounced up to him at her sister Jane's wedding to Robert Fellowes in April 1978 at the Guards Chapel in London. She was 'in an unlovely pink dress' but he noted the 'flash of her cobalt blue eyes' when she rather smartly observed: 'I know you – you're the wicked Mr Whitaker, aren't you? I'm Diana.'[35] The pre-bulimic Diana adored food without the complication of, as Prince Charles once uncharitably put it, 'reappearing later'.[36] When she was feeling tense she was known to dash across the street to 'tuck into a good-sized chicken portion'.[37] Her friend Rory Scott once saw Diana gobble a one-pound bag of sweets while playing bridge.[38] 'Diana never had any early instability or eating disorder,' Mary Clarke attests. 'She loved good food, sweets, chocolates and biscuits. But that's because she was a nice country girl.'[39]

There is something oddly affecting about these conspicuously inconspicuous years of Diana, the 'country girl' lost in an apparently aimless drift in SW1. Knowing her destiny as we do we can see that interlude as she eventually saw it, as the last dreamy lull before the blaze of her future. The historian of the aristocracy David Cannadine has noted that aristocrats, having seen the endless supply of cheap labour vanish, turned instead to their own daughters to fill the gap. Diana spent her eighteenth and nineteenth years as a Trust Fund Cinderella, drifting through temporary work – low-stress, undemanding jobs that drew on her agreeable demeanour such as house-cleaning and child-care. Her life after West Heath was simply an extension of her cloistered existence during her schooldays. Flatmates and other friends were from boarding school or Norfolk; they shared the same taste in unpretentious Italian restaurants, mainstream pop music like the Police and Abba and clothing (tweed skirts and cardigans, Laura Ashley shirts with a pie-crust frill, low court shoes, shiny, natural-hued hair). As defined by Peter York, *Harpers & Queen* magazine's social barometer, 'Diana was pure state-of-the-art Sloane.'[40]

Diana's insistence that she was intellectually inadequate was consistent with the Sloane affect of determinedly 'not showing off'. The whole stance of 'silly me' was the effect of a demographic anxious to maintain low expectations as a way of avoiding envy. In today's celebrity culture – where even peers of the realm are supposed to strut their stuff – it sounds like the lost language of cranes. 'These girls are much more questy now,' in the judgement of York who should know, having written their bible, *The Official Sloane Ranger Handbook*. 'Even the most benighted Sloane today thinks there is something over the hill – even if it's Primrose Hill.'[41] Far from being 'questy', Diana's social life was built on the premise of unbroken familiarity. New encounters usually began with an extended name exchange. Aren't you a cousin of Henry Hambledon's? Wasn't your brother at school with my cousin Billie? And weren't we all at that silly firework party ten years ago when the Butler-Warings' dog had a heart attack?

Her circle of girlfriends spoke in the same voice, a clipped, unmelodic, vowel-swallowing patois that titled kids of the new millennium reject in favour of class-disguising fake-football lingo. House then was 'hice'. Yes was 'yah'. Prince Charles was 'Pris Chos'. Boring people were 'heavy furniture'; an old boring person was a 'real Horlicks'; parties where people might risk discussing politics and world affairs were described as 'terribly grown-up'. The weekend was spent in counties not towns: always 'I'm going to Wiltshire this Friday', never 'I'm going to West Stowell'. The Sloanes were never angry, they were 'absolutely livid', but not about anything important. A show of genuine feeling, especially in an argument would be met with the surprised: 'Sorry. I didn't know you cared so much.'

Diana's uneventful CV offers occasional tiny intriguing mysteries that are the low-wattage equivalent of George Bush's lost months in the

National Guard – in her case the question of what happened to a career teaching dance. In January 1979, again at her mother's suggestion, she signed on for a three-year training course as an apprentice teacher at the Kensington studio run by Madame Vacani, the grande dame she had impressed with her dancing at West Heath. In her new job, Diana was supposed to coach more than a dozen two-year-olds in pliés and pirouettes. In theory it was an ideal situation, combining Diana's love of ballet with her affinity with small children, but she hoped, too, that Madame Vacani would again recognise her star quality and put her on a fast track to success. Three months into the job, she just failed to show up. There was no explanation; she just stopped going. One account has Diana tearing all the tendons in a skiing accident. Another version has her with a minor leg injury. She explained her absence from the Vacani studio by saying she had hurt her foot and could no longer teach dance. The likely truth is that Cinderella was sick of waiting for the glass coach and lost interest. Instead, she drifted again, abandoning the visions of stardom for trance-like domestic subservience.

In July 1979 she nested at 60 Coleherne Court, a mansion block in the refined but unflashy area of South Kensington (closer to Earls Court than the heartland of fashionable South Ken), with mahogany lifts and a communal garden. Sarah found the three-bedroom flat for her while working at the estate agent's Savills and she shared it with three other Sloanes: Carolyn Pride, Virginia Pitman and Anne Bolton. Its purchase was funded with £50,000 from the bequest in the will of her rich American great-grandmother, Lord Fermoy's mother, Fanny Work.[42] Talking to a tabloid reporter about her flatmates, Diana said, 'They rent it from me.' Her apparent artlessness still allowed it to be known that she was a landlady, not a fellow tenant.[43] The writer and broadcaster Danae Brook, who lived on the floor below Diana, describes Coleherne Court as 'the sort of place where parents would feel their young daughters would be safe. There used to be a waiting list for flats. It was almost like a club.' Debs' mothers used to put their daughters there while they were learning how to do shorthand or work in a nursery before getting married. In these dying days of that social system, said Brooke, Diana was just another one of those upper-class girls who came and went.[44]

Diana kept a low profile at Coleherne Court. She put herself in charge of clean-up duty, and was known to rise before a meal was finished to clear the table rather than endure the sight of dirty dishes. The photographer Dmitri Kasterine went to dinner there at the invitation of one of the flatmates and halfway through Diana wandered in from a date. 'I thought what an odd girl she was. She had this sly, shy way of looking at you – she could hardly stand up straight – and even though she hadn't joined us for dinner went straight to the sink and started doing all the washing-up. She was totally undistinguished.'[45] Diana loved to take on the washing and ironing of shirts for friends. In a withering act of big-sister condescension, Sarah Spencer employed her for a pound an hour to clean the apartment she shared with another girl about town, Lucinda Craig Harvey. When Diana got engaged to Prince Charles, she responded to Lucinda's letter of congratulation: 'Gone are the days of Jif and dusters. Oh, dear, will I ever see them again?'[46]

In the autumn of 1979, Diana found one of the two part-time positions that would be the last she would ever take – assistant teacher at the Young England Kindergarten in Pimlico that was run by Kay Seth-Smith, an older graduate of West Heath. The kindergarten was set in a modest church hall with an out-of-tune piano, but it was the favoured preschool of such privileged tykes as former Prime Minister Harold Macmillan's great-grandson or the then Agriculture Minister Peter Walker's little boy. Across the street was the Pimlico state school where working-class pupils would occasionally pause to thumb their noses at the fluttering nannies and purring Bentleys lined up outside the tiny kindergarten opposite.[47] Six months later Diana signed on with the Occasional and Permanent Nannies agency in Beauchamp Place to do two days a week of nannying on the understanding that she would not venture into foreign territory, meaning outside the green zone of Sloane Square/Belgrave Square. Other stipulations were that she would never babysit in the evenings and weekends had to be kept free for socialising. She was taken on by an American family, the Robertsons.

'When she turned up on my doorstep in Belgrave Square I thought she was very pretty but plump or rather well padded, thick hair and very good make-up,' said Mrs Robertson who came to lunch with me in New York from the upstate, upscale town of Millbrook, where she now lives.[48] She is the kind of solid, bright executive mum, now retired, who was a different species from any of the women in the Spencers' sheltered circle. The Robertsons' nine-month-old son Patrick bonded with Diana instantly. 'She was so superior to all the other girls who applied – a standout for a nanny. Loved children, spoke beautifully, well turned out. She was so down to earth, happy to run out and do errands, do the dishes. She seemed to actually like housework. She always thought of herself as a dumb-bell.'[49] Within minutes of meeting Patrick, Diana got down on the floor with him and played with him in a warm, easy way that sent his high-powered mother off to work with a light heart.

When she hired her, Mrs Robertson had no idea Diana was an earl's daughter or that her sister Jane Fellowes, thanks to her husband Robert's job as assistant private secretary to the Queen, lived in a grace-and-favour apartment at Kensington Palace and had use of a holiday cottage on the Balmoral estate. 'She never told us where she was going for the weekends. Diana would say, "I am taking Patrick to my sister who lives in Kensington," but at no time did she say "who lives at Kensington Palace". She was very private. Never asked me personal questions either.'[50] Mrs Robertson had no idea either that when she said she was going to Scotland to stay with her sister she was visiting the Balmoral estate and would be included in royal activities with Prince Charles.

'Diana's routine with Patrick consisted of playtime on the floor with his toys and blocks . . . and lots of long walks in the fresh air . . . She always greeted him with a cuddle in the morning and snuggled with him before saying goodbye in the evening . . . She fed him breakfast and lunch, either baby food in jars . . . or yogurt or scrambled eggs until he was able to chew. He seldom took a nap . . .' Patrick loved to be read to, so Mary established a routine that Diana followed. 'She would read or sing the rhymes to him and then ask him, "Where's the bunny?" or "Where's the dog . . . tree . . . house . . . cat?" or whatever. He would give his wonderful smile and point to the correct figure on the page.'[51] Mrs Robertson's only run-in with the perfect nanny was over food for dinner. In one of her furtive acts of nervous wolfing, Diana picked out and ate all the meat in the stew that had been left to simmer on the stove for dinner. Robertson thought it 'a little bizarre' and left a note of complaint.[52] As she recalled it, 'I told her that it was no problem . . . she was more than welcome to anything in the house, but would she please let me know if she had finished any particular item so I could replace it before the stores closed.' Diana, 'ever polite and agreeable', replied: '"Yes, of course, Mrs Robertson, so sorry to have inconvenienced you."'[53] Soon afterwards, Robertson discovered in the sofa a loose cheque from one of London's most exclusive banks, Coutts, with *Lady Diana Spencer* in the lower right-hand corner. Nice. That was Diana declaring to her boss she wasn't, after all, just the 'help'.[54]

Mrs Robertson waited a week or two before saying casually, 'Well, well, well, so I saw who you are on the cheque.'[55] Diana smiled, gestured with a toss of her right hand, and said, 'Oh that.'[56] Once status is assured, you can pretend that it's meaningless. When Mrs Robertson expressed an interest in going to see Althorp, Diana surprised her with the snotty comment that it now looked like a bordello. Raine had become more powerful in Earl Spencer's affections than ever; he credited her with saving his life after a cerebral haemorrhage in September 1978. Amid bitter rows with his children at the hospital, she took over, using her formidable Rolodex to secure a wonder drug not yet released on the market. Emboldened by his gratitude, she had given up putting a polite gloss on the feud with his tiresome children. 'I'm absolutely sick of the Wicked Stepmother lark,' she told Jean Rook of the *Express*. 'You're never going to make me sound like a human being because people like to think I'm Dracula's mother.'

Having become aware of Diana's pedigree, Mrs Robertson found her willingness to do her domestic job so cheerfully admirable but puzzling. In Diana there was no hint of the kind of rebellion Robertson would have expected to see in her own country in those post-feminist years. As an American, she was amazed at 'how behind us' British women were – a generation behind, in Robertson's view. 'There were no women officers at the bank I worked at. Diana was doing such unbelievably menial things. The irony is that nannying for me was a step up from cleaning flats for Sarah's friends.'[57]

Around the time Diana moved into Coleherne Court, I moved into the editor's office at *Tatler*, charged, at the age of twenty-five, with reviving the fortunes of what had once been the *Hello!* magazine of Gosford Park. In the summer of 1980 the *Tatler* team were on a search for ravishing redheads for a fashion shoot and assumed, because of Lady Sarah Spencer's flaming carrot locks, her younger sister Diana would be a redhead too. *Tatler*'s fashion assistant Gabé Doppelt, now Los Angeles bureau chief of *W* magazine, still has her research notes. Beside Diana Spencer's name and address in Coleherne Court, Doppelt has written, 'No. Actually blonde & said to be shy.'[58]

At *Tatler*, we would be just as intrigued as Mrs Robertson that Diana seemed such a sociological throwback. Until she came into view our editorial staff were busy chronicling the rise of her opposite – the metropolitan anti-debs, girls from the same backgrounds as their country-mouse cousins but more mobile, more media-savvy, more driven towards a career.

All the girls spotlighted in *Tatler* at that time seemed to be doing bit parts in art movies or taking off to Sri Lanka for a gap year before Oxford or Cambridge or modelling for Andy Warhol's *Interview*. The definitive end-of-decade social event of the seventies was the riotously eclectic fancy dress party in Hampshire to celebrate the fortieth birthday of Nicky Haslam, the fashionable decorator. Haslam, dressed in white silk as an Indian raja, greeted guests who ranged from ancient society legends like Lady Diana Cooper and Sir Cecil Beaton to celebrities like Mick Jagger, Rupert Everett and Joan Collins. Camilla Parker Bowles's brother, Mark Shand, and a bunch of their cousins came in the white make-up and bowler hats sported by Malcolm McDowell in *A Clockwork Orange*. Lady Lambton, wife of the Tory peer who lost his job in the Cabinet in May 1973 for S and M activities with a prostitute, was a frog princess in a rubber diving suit. 'You can always tell a gentleman by the quality of his drugs,' an exuberant Lord Hesketh told me as we stood in line for the buffet. No sign of Lady Diana Spencer or her ilk there.

The tameness of her set was captured in a double-page spread in *Tatler* just before the engagement to Prince Charles: 'There are still a few girls left in Britain,' we wrote, 'who haven't been to bed with Jasper Guinness or Prince Stash Klossowski [two men about town of the period] and all of them are friends of Lady Diana Spencer.' Splashed beneath were the faces and mini bios of Lady Di's flatmates and pals. Twenty-one-year-old Virginia Pitman, a discreetly smiling country-bumpkin with short wavy chestnut hair: 'since leaving Hatherop Castle [school], a spell behind the counter at Asprey's has been followed by a Cordon Bleu cooking course and Cooking for Directors in the City', her bio read. 'She is about to embark on a china-mending course. Her goldfish Battersea, which is cosseted between plastic weeds from Harrods, is a perennial conversation piece.' Thumbnails of other Diana confidantes included Caroline Harbord-Hammond, twenty, with info about her 'skiing trips to Mirabelle . . . and six months "temping – I can't remember where"'; wine-family scion Simon Berry, twenty-three, 'celebrated at Eton for his precocious production of A. A. Milne's "Winnie the Pooh"'; Mary Ann Stewart-Richardson, twenty, 'most relaxed trotting along the East Anglian fens on a pony from her parents' country house, Creake Abbey'; and Sophie Kimball, who 'divides time between hunting from Great Easton Manor, strolling the moors from Altnaharra, Lairg, and window-shopping down Sloane Avenue'.[59] Our captions had the quiet snigger of satire but the girls in the pictures were oblivious. *Tatler* was their favourite magazine and the *Daily Express* photographer Steve Wood later used his freelancing for us as a calling card at Coleherne Court. On one occasion he slyly turned up with the gift of glossy pictures of the flatmates in the hopes of snapping Di. He was told she was too distressed to come out – Battersea the goldfish had died and she was 'in floods'.[60]

Mary Robertson saw no signs of a special boyfriend in her nanny's life, but was Diana really as wholesome and chaste as she appeared? Lady Colin Campbell, in her steamy book *The Real Diana*, cited a couple of unnamed bedmates who speak of Diana being an enthusiastic sex partner, big on post-coital cuddling, but no one has made a convincing, on-the-record claim to have been there before Charles. I am inclined to think that Diana had built a protective shield around her Prince Charming fantasy in which she had deposited her reserves of love and hurt. She mostly dated the kind of boys the comedian Harry Enfield used to call 'Tim Nice-but-Dim', garnered from childhood circles.[61] 'I never heard any evidence Diana had sex before marriage, which was as rare as rocking-horse shit,' said a long-time male friend.[62] Another admirer, Rory Scott, a lieutenant in the Life Guards, found Diana at the time 'sexually attractive and the relationship was not a platonic one as far as I was concerned, but it remained that way . . . You always felt that there was a lot you would never know about her.'[63] One thing Scott didn't get to know was something the Park House nannies had learned – that it was dangerous to scorn Diana. James Gilbey, the handsome and muscular heir to a gin fortune, paid the price for standing her up on a date. Diana's revenge was to mix a flour and egg paste with the help of flatmate Carolyn Pride and pour it over his Alfa Romeo.[64] As far as Gilbey was concerned, that was the end of Lady Diana Spencer until he met her again in 1989 at the house of her friend Julia Samuel.[65] Diana's marriage was in free fall by then and she was on the prowl, willing to complete unfinished business.

She did forge an enduring friendship with a convivial medical student, James Colthurst, second son of an Irish baronet whose family seat is the repository of the magical Blarney stone (and he seems to have inherited its gabby charms). She met him at a skiing party in a chalet in Val Claret in the French Alps where he was in a group with Simon Berry and a bunch of his Etonian friends. When she hurt her leg in that mysterious injury and had to stay on a week, Diana chalet-hopped and spent the week going on larky excursions to discos with them all and sleeping on their sofa bed. The skiers came back from the slopes to find Diana serving tea and cakes. 'I think the leg "injury" was just an excuse for her to get out of skiing,' Colthurst said with a smile.[66]

Back in London, Colthurst became a regular visitor to Coleherne

Court dinner parties and escorted Diana to the theatre. 'I took her to see *My Fair Lady* and she was totally enraptured. All she wanted to do after that was see the real Covent Garden and so a bunch of us tiptoed out at four o'clock in the morning and came back with a box of oranges.'[67] Four o'clock in the morning? Sorry, no, it is not a pointer to a sexy sleepover. Today Dr Colthurst is emphatic that he did not himself have any physical relationship with Diana, though he played a consigliere role in her life after the marriage to Prince Charles. He was the go-between when Diana needed a confidant to whom she would dictate the story of her marriage for a book by Andrew Morton. Dr Colthurst could think of no explanation why, despite the closeness of his friendship, he was excluded from Diana's wedding to Prince Charles in St Paul's Cathedral; the Coleherne Court flatmates, all of whom were on the guest list, invited him to their after-party.

Other members of that Val Claret ski party recalled how she surprised them one evening, piping up that one day she was going to marry Prince Charles – 'not "I want to" or "I'd like to" but "I am going to".' The assertion was all the more remarkable given that she had then met him only in the ploughed field at Althorp. Teased about how she could be so sure, Diana responded, 'he's the one man on the planet who is not allowed to divorce me'.[68] Simon Berry says that, back in London, he would sometimes take her for a nocturnal drive. 'One time we went past Buckingham Palace. I remember her saying, "Just drive round a few more times." It was late at night. She said, "What do you think? What do you think? Do you think I stand a chance?" I said, "It's much more likely you become a dancer." She said, "It could be quite fun. It would be like Anne Boleyn or Guinevere!" I said "I bloody hope not."'[69]

Dr Colthurst reflects that Diana was always, as he puts it, on the dream path. 'She was swept along by the force of it and then when the machinery of the press and Palace took over and made it into this big fairy story she could give into it, give over responsibility to it. It was bigger than her.'[70]

Diana did not confide her visions of marrying the heir to the throne to Mrs Robertson, but it was obvious she was fascinated by him. In September 1980, after she had first been photographed with the Prince, Mrs Robertson asked if anything was going to develop. 'Not really,' Diana replied. 'After all, he's thirty-one, and I'm only nineteen. He'd never look seriously at me.'[71] Robertson, not convinced by Diana's evasion, was prescient enough to see in Diana's reading tastes the omens of a mismatch. When Diana turned up at work with a Barbara

Cartland romance tucked under her arm, Robertson hoped it did not represent her only reading interests. How would this fit with Charles, wondered Robertson, a man famed for his taste for weighty authors such as Carl Jung and the mystical travel guru Laurens van der Post? Mrs Robertson tactfully suggested that Diana upgrade her reading and perhaps even 'scan *The Times* or the *Daily Telegraph* each day to learn a bit about current events if you want to keep up with Prince Charles'.[72] Robertson was worried that Diana's infatuation with 'wonderful, perfect' Charles was 'based on her romantic image of him, not on the man himself'.

In 1993, when she was ninety-two, Barbara Cartland herself put it this way: 'The only books she ever read were mine and they weren't awfully good for her.'[73]

## Chapter 5

# The Rise of the Beast

'You've just done something extremely stupid.'
– Prince Charles to Lady Sarah Spencer, March 1978

Just before Diana Spencer began to emerge so vividly into public life, a kind of journalistic global warming was altering the eco-balance between the British press and the British royal family. The sunshine of publicity in which Diana would at first be happy to bask, posing and smiling for the cameras, grew steadily hotter and harsher. As the superheated imperatives of an invasive press bumped up increasingly against the milder human necessity of privacy, scattered rains gave way to drenching gales and then to spectacular and finally lethal hurricanes. The ultimate tragedy of the disaster in the Paris tunnel in 1997 was that Diana herself had accelerated the climate change that ended up making her life literally impossible.

For Americans used to bland local newspapers homogenised by the stingy monopolies of big chains and no national newspapers except the bland *USA Today*, the staid national edition of the *New York Times* and the staid *Wall Street Journal*, the volume and variety of the British print press feels bewilderingly promiscuous. In 1980 there were ten national daily newspapers selling twenty million copies, more per capita than in any other country in the world. Their relative positions along the spectrum of sensation have remained consistent, but the entire spectrum has shifted sharply towards the garish, a trend accelerated by the resort to chequebook journalism – a practice of buying sources routinely denounced and routinely embraced. Despite the advent of the Web, the Brits remain voracious newspaper readers often buying more than one paper. That fact plus the country's compactness and news-stand culture make it impossible to ignore the daily blizzard of headlines, picked up immediately by television. When all the papers are on a rampage against some public figure, which nowadays is always, they invade your life. They are billboarded at every news-stand. They leap across your screen. They buzz around in your head all day like a low-grade fever. Paradoxically, it is the flair of the British tabloid press, its superb professional élan, that makes it so feared by its subjects and targets. So much good writing and theatrical presentation goes into mounting the daily crucifixions. So much competitive professional pride goes into finding just the right killer adjective.

The royal family used to be exempt from routine abuse. But in thirty years the tabloid view of royalty moved from the benign to the malign without a pause for magnanimity in between.

On 2 June 1953, the day the young Queen Elizabeth was crowned, the popular and serious press hailed a new Elizabethan age, a joyous rebirth of Britain's greatness. Her enthronement, the first ever televised, took place simultaneously with the news that a British team had conquered the unconquerable Everest and the Union Jack flew on the summit (and soon afterwards Roger Bannister broke the four-minute mile). After the austerity of the war years food rationing was over by 1954, prices were low, staff was cheap and the economy was on the mend. In 1950 the Labour majority in Parliament dropped to five seats and nineteen months later the ageing but still heroic Winston Churchill became Prime Minister again with a Tory majority. The mourning period for the death of King George VI was followed by the bursting forth of pent-up national exuberance, of which the new Queen Elizabeth II was the beneficiary. Her coronation year was a blast of joy, with street parties in the East End and serial glittering balls in Mayfair. The debutantes who came out that season participated in a breakneck bacchanalia of gulls' eggs in nests of straw, champagne breakfasts at dawn and four-foot-high gateaux alight with silver electric candles. In today's gift-bag culture of instant celebrities in borrowed jewels tramping up the red carpet past a heckling zoo of cursing, thrusting paparazzi, it's hard to conceive an era of glamour so elite or so unsecretively private. The absence of any media coverage that wasn't positive brought a spontaneity not possible now. The press at these extravagant parties was handpicked and always fulsome, allowing reporters from social diaries like the *Evening Standard*'s the kind of access they would kill for today. There were no worries about security and no worries of press betrayal.

Young, fashionable royalty went all over town with extraordinary freedom. They were not hunted, bodyguarded or misquoted. At any top-drawer event you attended in coronation year you could spot the vivacious Queen Mother (still only fifty-one) in a diamond tiara. 'She always seemed to be on tiptoe,' former deb's delight Shaun Plunket told me. 'Her presence was totally natural, even in her most dressed-up jewels, she had the ability to be herself, not someone whose body she got into for a grand occasion.' Or there was the luscious twenty-two-year-old Princess Margaret in white tulle, or more thrilling still, her elder sister, the glowing, serious, self-possessed young Queen herself, waltzing in iridescent satin with Prince Philip. 'All eyes were on Her Majesty,' said Plunket. 'She was so young and it was so long since we'd had a queen on the throne. Fifty years! And the only things we had ever read about her were positive.'[1]

That's the point. No royal since has had his or her mystique left so thoroughly intact. Is there anything we don't know about Prince Charles, including his desire to return to this life as a Tampax? The Queen then could do no wrong, and with her, the royal family. Intense was the rage visited on a Tory historian, Lord Altrincham, when in an obscure publication he suggested that Her Majesty was too attached to the upper classes, that she was a woman who came across as 'a captain of the hockey team, prefect and a recent candidate for confirmation'.[2] The Duke of Argyll urged that Altrincham should be hanged, drawn and quartered; the BBC exacted the modern equivalent by promptly dropping Altrincham from *Any Questions*, its iconic forum for public debate. He was slapped in the street. Club members moved to the other side of the coffee room when he came in. Altrincham, who soon afterwards transformed himself into the commoner John Grigg, observed: 'There was this atmosphere of almost cringing acceptance on the part of everybody in positions of authority whether politicians, churchmen, people running the press, people at the top in business. They all had this sort of attitude of uncritical acceptance of everything that was done by the Royal Family.'[3]

The notorious Altrincham – who actually believed very much in the monarchy as an institution – badly shook the establishment, but it was a member of the royal family who made the first dent in the mass culture of deference. The loose cannon was Princess Margaret, the Queen's younger saucier sister. Distraught at her father's death, she sought solace not only in prayer at St Paul's Church, Knightsbridge, but also in the company of someone who had been her father's Comptroller of the Household, a Battle of Britain war hero, a man seventeen years her senior she had met when she was twenty-one: Group Captain Peter

Townsend. The perfect romance? Alas, no. Marriage was out of the question. Townsend was divorced (like Wallis Simpson) and, perhaps worse, a member of staff. Under the Royal Marriages Act of 1772, no royal prince or princess could marry before the age of twenty-five without the permission of the Monarch and Parliament.

Margaret and Townsend were spotted together in an intimate exchange at the coronation of Queen Elizabeth by an eagle-eyed *Sunday Mirror* reporter, Audrey Whiting. Her editor refused to print anything about it. He didn't want to 'upset the ladies' day'.[4] The protectiveness people felt then towards members of the royal family is manifest in the fact that rumours about Margaret's new love affair had been bubbling away in the European and American press for weeks without a word making it into the British papers or broadcasting. But it was the *Daily Mirror*, whose feisty Welsh editorial director, Hugh Cudlipp, who decided to override his editors and had the impudence – outrage! – to turn the issue of Margaret's love life into a populist crusade. *The Times* had already assumed its lofty role of speaking for Britain, declaring that the royal family were a national symbol of family life and it would damage the monarchy for the Queen's sister to marry a divorced man. But Cudlipp saw his paper as representing the brave new Briton who had been through two world wars and who no longer cared to 'know his place in the social pecking order'. His *Daily Mirror* ran a poll on whether Margaret and Townsend should marry, addressing royalty in the vernacular of the street: 'COME ON MARGARET, MAKE UP YOUR MIND!'[5]

Such intrusion into the private life of a member of the royal family was considered deeply offensive, a rustle of mob rule in democratic rags. It provoked the first complaint to the newly created Press Council, a body of the great and the good set up to discipline press misconduct by moral force, and the Press Council duly censured the *Daily Mirror*. To invade privacy in this manner, it declared, was 'contrary to the best traditions of British journalism'.[6]

The Princess made her decision after a family summit when Prince Philip, sarcastic about where the beleaguered couple might live once cast out of Buckingham Palace, commented, 'It's not impossible to buy a house these days.' This was hardly fair to a princess of the blood who had been on the road shaking hands in villages in England and the Commonwealth since she was sixteen. But she went to the Archbishop of Canterbury to say she would not now be needing his spiritual counselling after all. 'Mindful of the Church's teachings that Christian

marriage is indissoluble, and conscious of my duty to the Commonwealth,' she declared, 'I have resolved to put these considerations
before any others.' She gave up the love of her life. 'What a wonderful
person the Holy Spirit is,' the Archbishop replied.[7] Margaret made her
own comment on the spirits against her years later when she saw Sir
Alan (Tommy) Lascelles, the Queen's private secretary, shuffling by to
post a letter from his Kensington Palace lodgings. According to her
chauffeur, she commanded him to run the brute down![8]

The powers that be – or that were – should have let Margaret marry
Townsend. He was, after all, a war veteran, a gentleman, a genial, well-
mannered stiff who would have made a perfectly agreeable addition to
the royal line-up. The *scandale*, though unprecedented, would have
been mild by the standards of a generation later. Perhaps it would have
acted as a vaccine, sparing the Windsors (and the rest of us) the rapid
frenzies of the Di years. At a minimum, Margaret would not have gone
on to enter a marriage that itself ended in divorce. Her sacrifice for
Queen and country turned out to be pointless. It gave her an unhappy
life and cut her no breaks with the press. Indeed, the circulation boost
of her troubles gave the tabloids their first scent of blood.

So did the unexpected whiff of sexuality around royalty, something
that Margaret, with her Elizabeth Taylor curves and wide movie-star
mouth, offered in abundance. Like Diana, Margaret was catnip to
glamour-hunting photographers; also like Diana, she at once colluded
with them and hid from their attention.

Without much to do except go out and about, Margaret was
escorted at night by a parade of glossy men about town. She was
photographed emerging from the chic Les Ambassadeurs Club at dawn
in mink coat and diamonds. She smoked from a long, sophisticated
cigarette holder. Where her parents had always been careful to holiday
in the country estates of their own kingdom, Margaret took jet-set
holidays in the Caribbean and came back with a suntan. She mixed
with a non-horsey set of actors, writers, dancers and playwrights. She
was news. When, seven years after the break with Townsend, she
married the swinging London photographer Anthony Armstrong-
Jones (ennobled as the 1st Earl of Snowdon a year after the wedding),
her plunge deeper into his café society world moved the royal family
decisively from regal seclusion towards showbiz availability. Press
boundaries were being trampled as much by the flamboyance and glitz
of Margaret herself as by press licence – a fact she did not like to
acknowledge. ('Fashion writers insist on treating her as they did me –

as if we were unreal figures straight from *Dynasty*,' she said of Diana twenty-five years later.)[9]

The culture of deference was beginning to crumble. John Lahr, the theatre critic, remembers his surprise on arriving in London in 1963 that at the end of a play nobody could bolt for the exit because the audience stood reverently for the playing of 'God Save the Queen'. Then one night he went to Spike Milligan's *The Bedsitting Room*. He told me: 'When we all stood for the national anthem, nothing happened. But from the wing, on a kazoo, we heard the recognisable rhythm of the hymn. Milligan stepped in front of the audience and said, "If you stand for that you'll stand for anything." The audience fell about.'[10]

The tempo of the tremors increased with the arrival in London in 1969 of the young (he was thirty-eight) and iconoclastic Rupert Murdoch. Riding in from Australia, he defeated Robert Maxwell to buy the biggest of the Sunday papers, the prurient *News of the World* ('All human life is here'). Murdoch upset the better sort from the outset. His first act was to exhume the ruinous affair between the call girl Christine Keeler and the Secretary of State for War John Profumo. Murdoch's purchase of Keeler's memoirs for serialisation in the *News of the World* was seen as a staggering breach of the British sense of fair play. Profumo had spent the previous six years in redemptive charity work, so Murdoch found himself a pariah overnight, condemned by the Press Council and fricasséed, to his great displeasure, on London Weekend Television by a relentless David Frost. (When Murdoch left the studio, says Frost, he told a reporter, 'London Weekend Television has made a powerful enemy tonight.')[11]

The great thing about being a pariah, however, is that it sets you free. If everybody is already pissed off, what does it matter if you piss off everybody even more? A year after he bought the *News of the World*, Murdoch snapped up a faltering broadsheet called the *Sun* – the sad descendant of the *Daily Herald*, once the crusading voice of the Labour Party – and relaunched it as a rollicking, up-yours tabloid featuring bare-breasted pin-ups every day. And he let his editors know that when it came to coverage of the circulation-building royals, the gloves were off. It was a reporter from the *Sun*, Harry Arnold, who followed up rumours of trouble in Princess Margaret's marriage in the early seventies. There were whispers that she was holidaying in Mustique with the much younger socialite Roddy Llewellyn. Recalling his scoop, Arnold said nostalgically, 'I took him [Roddy] for a coffee and for the price of about twenty pence, he told me the whole story of himself and Margaret.' There was shock, shock when Murdoch's *News of the World* published pictures of the two of them cavorting together in swimsuits. 'It was just amazing,' said Arnold. 'At that time and in that era the royals were still very pure and they behaved themselves and they weren't unfaithful and they didn't have affairs. And then along came this – well, he wasn't much short of a beatnik.'[12] Actually Roddy was a sweet, affectionate, slightly hopeless ageing hippy, a talented landscape gardener who offered kindness to Margaret at a time when her husband, Lord Snowdon, was largely indifferent to her. Her press narrative, however, was already sealed: she was irresponsible, flashy and, worse, a serial seasonal escapee of English weather.

Lady Diana Spencer took her bow at the nexus of a national malaise brought about by a sclerotic social-welfarism that had lost its way and an ever hotter press competition for royal stories. The plebeian tabloids – the *Sun*, the *Mirror* and the *Star* – no longer had the field to themselves. Under a swashbuckling editor, David English, the *Daily Mail* converted itself to a tabloid format in 1971 and quickly eclipsed a wilting *Daily Express* as the enduring bible of Middle England; English's successor, Paul Dacre, has only increased its power. (By 2006 the *Mail* was selling more than two million copies a day.)[13] The magic formula of the *Mail* was a combination of curtain-twitching class envy and strident rightist politics, with the added spice of the most waspish gossip columnist in London, Nigel Dempster, whose scoops from the highest circles of the establishment were read at every upper-class breakfast table like a ransom note. Dempster had a thirty-year reign of terror until he was felled by ill health. He was a miniaturist in tabloid takedowns. His demonic social energy seemed to take him everywhere at once; in a car he always drove at a hundred miles an hour with the horn blaring (as I discovered on a breakneck death ride with him once to the Derby). He was dapper, fiendishly well connected, dazzlingly anecdotal and blessed with total recall.

The *Mail* thrived on the national malaise and day after day stoked it with outrage. By the end of the 1970s faith in British institutions had nose-dived like the pound sterling. Prime Minister James Callaghan's Labour government was falling apart, beset by belligerent strikers in 1979's 'winter of discontent'. Whenever you turned on the TV some fat trade union boss was leaving No. 10 Downing Street making veiled threats about needing to talk to his fellow 'execker-tives' to decide whether or not you could get a train or bus to work the next day

– or read a newspaper. *The Times* and *Sunday Times* were shut down and did not publish for a whole year, with their new computer terminals hooded and draped pending union acceptance of what was laughingly called new technology.

At Oxford, where I was a student, the fashion throughout the seventies was for sarcastic embracing of national decline. 'SITUATION DESPERATE BUT NOT SERIOUS' is a headline that could summarise what it felt like to be English then. *Let's not make too much of a fuss, but we all appear to be going to hell on a sledge*. The Oxford Union proposed the debate motion that: This House believes the British Isles are sinking into the sea.

Everything about England increasingly seemed a joke, a disaster, a cock-up. That's why we all loved *Monty Python's Flying Circus*, with its 'Upper Class Twit of the Year' contests, its wheedling shopkeepers and tacky game-show hosts, and its 'Ministry of Silly Walks'. In the post-Python BBC sitcom *Fawlty Towers*, John Cleese's Basil Fawlty, the officiously clueless hotelier, perfectly nailed the cultural mood: a gigantic man, threatening but ineffectual, full of the postures and shibboleths of Empire, its pompous diction, manners and attitudes – and always betrayed by them. He was typical of the times because he was failing *and* furious.

But Cleese and his fellow Pythons represented a high-flown Oxbridgian take on the New British Impotence. Down in the streets, something else was happening. The unemployment rate among England's youth was at an all-time high, and nothing in the culture could speak to their explosive rage – not the creaky blunderbusses that the British film industry was producing (*Death on the Nile* or *A Bridge Too Far*) nor the foppish contrivances of David Bowie and Roxy Music. It took an inspired neo-Marxist entrepreneur named Malcolm McLaren to scoop up an unemployed (and musically inept) construction worker named John Lydon, rechristen him Johnny Rotten and launch the Sex Pistols – a cynically manufactured but profoundly apt expression of the emerging British self-hatred. Unlike the punk movement that was simultaneously emerging in America, British punk wasn't arty, apolitical and cool. It was anti-cool, anti-art and above all anti-British. 'God Save the Queen' was transmuted into a belligerent anthem, and, love it or hate it, everyone in Little England got the message.

A gossip industry flowered on the nation's decay of self-esteem. The apotheosis of the British style and mood was the fortnightly *Private Eye*. Originally a schoolboy bad-taste joke book published as a samizdat sheet in the sixties, it took that decade's appetite for late-night satire and hardened its edge. Its photo-fumetti covers mockingly put words in the mouths of the famous, it used acid for ink, and the derogatory nicknames it pinned on people in the news were so comically apt they became the semiotics of cool conversation. Sir James Goldsmith was Goldenballs, Prime Minister Harold Wilson was Prime Minister Wislon and Lyndon Johnson was Loony Bins Johnson.

The *Eye* unravelled the royal family's mystique by chronicling their lives as a weekly soap. It wasn't that they especially targeted the royals. They just treated them like everybody else, which was a change in itself. The Queen was Brenda, Prince Philip was Keith, Princess Margaret was Yvonne, Charles was Brian, and the married girlfriend with whom he was always on the phone was Venetia Barkworth Smythe. The 'Grovel' column, written by Nigel Dempster and Peter McKay, trafficked in the rumours, exposés and inflammatory unsubstantiated items that could never make it into the mainstream press. It worked both ways. Often stories originating from anonymous notes to 'Grovel' were test-run there for future life in the more 'respectable' outlets. And the *Eye*'s tone migrated along with the stories. It instructed British journalists on the attitude of seeing establishment figures as essentially comic material and any kind of aspirational sentiment as pretentious or absurd.

Thanks to Dempster and his pals at *Private Eye*, no longer were social diaries in newspapers a daily accounting of fashionable persons at fashionable gatherings the night before, but a poison-dart paragraph war between the tabs. 'In the old days, the status of the person who featured in the story was the most important aspect of the story,' Peter Tory, the journalist behind the William Hickey column in the *Daily Express* told me in 1979. 'Status is still important but only in so far as there is a genuine story.'[14] What was a genuine story? Anything bad or embarrassing that happened to the titled or rich. As Dempster himself put it, 'There is a holiday in my heart when I discover another marriage breakup.'[15]

Dempster's exposés in both 'Grovel' and the *Daily Mail* had a lasting effect on the sexual mores of the upper classes. For instance, Lady Antonia Fraser, the beautiful blonde author of prize-winning historical biographies had long enjoyed a complacent marriage with the Scottish aristocrat Sir Hugh Fraser, but it was index of the new press lore in England when Dempster published a list of the various famous lovers who had populated her extramarital life, including the apocryphal anecdote of how she rebuffed the Australian critic Clive James with 'I only sleep with the first eleven'.[16] Dempster's later revelation in the *Daily Mail* in April 1975 that Lady Antonia was now having an affair with the also married playwright Harold Pinter effectively brought an end to both marriages.

Older socialites whose lives spanned both eras were bewildered by the disrespect with which they suddenly were perceived. 'They're so vindictive, so ungallant today,' the ageing Duchess of Argyll told me in 1979, mournfully pointing at a mountain of scrapbooks filled with loving celebrations of her draculine good looks. 'Why can't they leave me alone? They are sick little men.'[17]

With all these tumbrils rolling, it's hardly surprising that by the end of the decade the aristocracy were in one of their periodic ostrich modes. Death duties, added to gift tax, were wreaking havoc. As Diana's father Earl Spencer had discovered when he inherited the bottomless pit of Althorp, survival depended on the ability of owners of stately homes to maintain these ancient piles. In the face of the merciless new gossip press seriously grand personages had to hide from the pervasive influence of envy. Everyone was startled when the Duke of Argyll burst into print with a defensive announcement about the number of kilts he had (only one kilt for morning and one for evening wear, he defiantly alleged). Or when the Earl of Warwick went so far as to flee his ancient family seat of Warwick Castle for an apartment in New York, taking with him a cache of Old Masters that the nation expected to stay right where they were. 'The castle stinks of old shoes, old socks and wet mackintoshes,' Warwick proclaimed from exile with rather admirable candour. 'How we dispose of the contents is entirely a personal affair.'[18]

The royal family didn't want or need any controversy like this. Ever since the abdication fiasco it had been much safer for the monarchy to be boring, and the Queen was striving to keep it that way. Her own social life was always carefully unadventurous. Childhood friends, horsey folk, courtier families. No one could really envy those royal picnics in the rain at Balmoral, those disaffected corgis, those draughty evenings working on enormous jigsaw puzzles or playing tiddlywinks after a brisk day slaughtering wildlife.

The trouble with all the discretion was that in a racier media age it made them look old hat. The monarchy was acquiring the stale, curdled taste of a British Rail cheese sandwich. Pictures of a middle-aged Princess Margaret churning grandly around the dance floor in her kaftan in Mustique hardly moved product. There was nothing scurrilous yet to say about Princess Anne and her currently placid marriage to the Army officer Captain Mark Phillips (of whom Lady Diana Cooper said, 'He is a perfect example of krishnamurti, cleansed of all thought').[19] Prince Andrew was just some grinning fellow in the Navy and Prince Edward was too young. The bachelor Prince Charles was the only game in town.

When the Queen set off on one of her royal tours an unthinkable thing happened: no one went to cover it. No television, no newspapers, not even the Press Association wire service (which no longer had a regular court reporter). The Palace saw this as a worrying sign, on the basis that the only one thing worse than having yourself exposed, is not being bothered about at all. Richard Stott, then editor of the Daily Mirror, expressed the underlying anxiety: 'If the Royal Family is not being reported on, it becomes irrelevant, and if it becomes irrelevant it will die.'[20]

Throughout the seventies, the guessing game of the Prince of Wales's love life was the sole excitement for the media. A bevy of royal sleuths, who were to play a major part in Diana's life, were poised to follow any scent in pursuit of the girl they referred to as 'The One', wherever it led without regard to any of the conventional boundaries. In the process they became stars themselves with their own moniker, 'The Rat Pack'. 'To the royals and the courtiers,' says Ashley Walton of the Daily Express, 'we were simply reptiles or scum. We got to calling ourselves "la crème de la scum".' They were welcomed by the royal machine on official foreign tours but less welcome when they chased holidaying members of the family down the pistes of Davos and Klosters, hid under coconut palms for sneaky long-range photographs or, festooned in field glasses and fishing rods, adopted Clouseau-like countrymen disguises for trespassing at Sandringham and Balmoral. They were a hardy, irreverent band of warring mates, royal groupies at heart. Among them, Harry Arnold was the Sun's most tenacious instrument. Always neatly groomed in a top-of-the-range Burton kind of way, he was as sharp as a ferret and unfazed by royal pomp and circumstance. (He retired in 2003 and latterly sports Spanish hidalgo-style side whiskers.) Reporter Arnold was teamed with the jovial photographer Arthur Edwards, who approached royal scoops like a general plotting a siege. At Sandringham, Prince Philip once greeted Edwards's cheery 'Happy New Year' with a succinct 'Bollocks!'[21]

The Sun's team was matched against the portly James Whitaker and photographer Ken Lennox at the Daily Star. Whitaker was a crack royal mercenary who had soldiered for every tabloid in Fleet Street. 'Mr Whitaker', as Diana was always careful to call him, had a posh enough education to have passed muster as a younger scion of the landed gentry. He played it to the max with Savile Row shirts and Windsor-knotted ties. He once appeared on the slopes in a red ski suit, earning from Diana the nickname Big Fat Tomato. Today he lives in Spain off the proceeds of his royal memoirs and, after a stint on the reality TV show *Celebrity Fit Club* (sometimes known as *Celebrity Fat Club*), is more svelte than in the past. The Diana years were his glory days. In the November after her death in 1997, when *Mirror* editor Piers Morgan told him he should now give up royal reporting, he burst into tears.[22] What Whitaker loved most was the chase, crawling through the under-growth of some royal playground with his photographic sidekick Lennox, a tough and wiry Scotsman who perfected the art of the undetected 'snatch' photo using a miniature Leica hidden under his jacket.

The formative moment in Diana's media education was when the gentlemen of the press put paid to Princes Charles's relationship with her elder sister, Sarah. At the height of their romance in February 1978, Sarah had accompanied Charles on a ski trip to Klosters. The rat pack staked them out, which Sarah, silly girl, thought was rather fun. Back in London, she made the killer mistake of lunching with two of the new friends she'd met on the slopes, Nigel Nelson of the *Daily Mail* and James Whitaker, thus ensuring that her kamikaze remarks would be published simultaneously. She blithely babbled on to them about her drinking at school: 'I would drink anything, whisky, Cointreau, gin, sherry or, most often, vodka, because the staff couldn't smell that. I was not the only sinner!' She elaborated on her expulsion from West Heath and her battles with anorexia nervosa: 'I bust up with my boyfriend within a month of returning from Australia and then just stopped eating. I would toy with a couple of pieces of lettuce and if I forced a meal down I would just bring it up again.'[23] In a pre-Oprah age, this was way too much information.

Sarah herself realised her mistake as soon as the words were out of her mouth. She muddled things more by trying some damage control, suggesting that Whitaker's interview had been obtained by foul means. This did not play well. Fleet Street hacks, even the scrappiest among them, close ranks when they feel their fraternity is unfairly assailed. Within days, Whitaker, under one of his many pseudonyms, Jeremy Slazenger, produced an expanded, unabridged version of his Sarah exclusive for *Woman's Own*. 'There is no chance of my marrying Prince Charles. He is a fabulous person but I am not in love with him,' Whitaker aka Slazenger quoted Sarah as saying. 'And I wouldn't marry anyone I didn't love, whether he were the dustman or the King of England. If he asked me I would turn him down. Prince Charles is a romantic who falls in love easily. But I can assure you that if there were to be any engagement between Prince Charles and me it would have happened by now. I am a whirlwind sort of lady, not a person who goes in for a long, slow courtship. Our relationship is totally platonic.'[24] Wow. The 'dustman' remark was especially unfortunate. Who did Sarah think she was? Eliza Doolittle? Knowing that *Woman's Own* was about to publish, she attempted to patch things up in advance by alerting Prince Charles to what was coming.

Cutting people off is one of the things the royal family does best. They love calibrating their responses from cordial forthcomingness to subtle, freezing withdrawal if you overstep the mark. An ill-judged remark, a whiff of familiarity and the pleasantly greeted social perpetrator no longer exists. Princess Margaret enjoyed destabilising her guests by flipping around in seconds from encouraging racy talk at the dinner table to suddenly pulling rank. If someone unguardedly referred to 'your father', she admonished, 'You mean, His Majesty the King.'

The best royal cuts, though, were subtle. They occurred with a swift, unspoken unanimity coordinated among their various households, and they were permanent. When Lady Sarah Spencer told Prince Charles she had given an interview to the press about their relationship there was a pause and he replied with deadly coldness, 'You've just done something extremely stupid.'[25] Within hours the drawbridge was up at Windsor Castle.

## Chapter 6

# The Quest for a Virgin Bride

'That's a fine animal you have there, sir.'
  – Camilla Shand to Prince Charles, summer of 1971

From a twenty-first-century perspective, the late-1970s search for a suitable virgin to marry Prince Charles feels now as anachronistic and misogynistic as the African practice of clitorectomy. It felt nearly as bizarre at the time. Only someone as retro as the eighteen-year-old Lady Diana Spencer could have said, 'I knew I had to keep myself tidy for what lay ahead.'[1]

Tidy? This was the post-pill, pre-Aids era of pre-marital sex – rampant, frequent, adventurous, and not necessarily all that selective. With girls going braless under their gypsy blouses, boys in tight jeans flaunting long Byronic curls, the Stones on the stereo and frontal nudity routine at the local Odeon, there was hardly a sentient Brit (or American or European) between the ages of twelve and fifty who didn't have sex on the brain. People were doing plenty of fantasising, but very little of it was about staying chaste for a marriage to Prince Charming. Countess Mountbatten, who was a lady-in-waiting at court, observed that Charles 'was unlucky to strike a period of history when girls, women in general had become so liberated and had led such free lives'.

Unlucky? Well, not entirely. In the Prince's own upper-class circle the girls were as fast as the cars. They were happy to repair to his rooms at Buckingham Palace after a late-night supper or be spirited down the M3 in his Aston Martin coupé for a discreet weekend tryst at Broadlands, the Hampshire home of Lord Louis Mountbatten, Prince Philip's uncle and Prince Charles's devoted great-uncle and mentor, known within the family as 'Uncle Dickie'.

The Prince has always been more glamorous in person than in pictures, where the flyaway ears tend to dominate. It's the grooming

that gives him lift-off, the knife-edged nature of the trouser crease, the
Savile Row tailoring of his manly shoulders, the crispness of his
Turnbull and Asser cuffs. There is usually a light, sporting tan from
riding or skiing that makes his eyes bluer than you expect. In any kind
of ceremonial attire the effect is more intense, especially when followed
by the obsequious rustle of attendant courtiers and sturdy Scotland
Yard detail. I saw the effect at a small concert at the Ashmolean
Museum in Oxford in the early nineties when he swept into the
auditorium wearing his scarlet academic gown and an expression of
sexy hauteur rather than the quizzical frown of red-carpet
conversations. He has to endure so many of those, his expertise at small
talk is flawless. He understands the definition of manners as the ability
to put someone else at their ease. (His friend, the actor and comedian
Stephen Fry, believes the knack of royal conversation with total
strangers is based on an ability to turn any answer into another
question. For example, 'So, Mr Doe, where are you living these days?'
'In America, Sir.' 'In America? That's the other side of the Atlantic
Ocean. When did you arrive?' 'In 1986, sir.' '1986? That's two years
after 1984,' etc.)[2] Unlike the other royals, Charles looks rich, which he
is. His annual income from the Duchy of Cornwall is around £14
million a year before expenditure and tax.[3] The Duchy of Cornwall
consists of about 54,850 hectares of land, most of it in the south-west
of the country.

During his years at Cambridge and in the navy, the Prince dated
actresses, models, socialites, colonial fly-bys, Peace Corps types, saucy
female grooms, and daughters of his parents' friends, but there wasn't a
virgin among them. Pillars of the British establishment were his sexual
enablers. He lost his own virginity courtesy of the Master of Trinity
College, Cambridge, 'Rab' Butler, the distinguished former Chancellor,
Foreign Secretary and Home Secretary who slipped a key to a side
entrance of the Master's lodge to his beautiful researcher, Lucia Santa
Cruz, daughter of the Chilean Ambassador at the court of St James, so
that the Prince could meet up with her in private.[4] 'Uncle Dickie'
Mountbatten kept a slush fund for paying off any potentially trouble-
some conquests. According to Nigel Dempster, the fund was in the
Bahamas and administered by a British lawyer through a private bank
in Nassau. Two, possibly three, six-figure dollar contracts were said to
have been signed between December 1974 and July 1979.[5]

The buzz among the exes was that the Prince was not a great lover –
'not even a very good one', blabbed a model who lived with one of his

occasional 'boffs' in the 1970s. 'He was excruciatingly shy and could only do it in the missionary position with the lights out.'⁶ He preferred bedmates who were free spirits, because they knew how to jolly him past his inhibitions. The ideal targets of his lust were girls like the all-American blonde Laura Jo Watkins, daughter of an admiral he encountered when his ship docked in San Diego; or, more seriously, the vibrant Davina Sheffield, daughter of an army major, who worked in an orphanage in Vietnam right up to the Vietcong entry into the city.

How much was all this glamour dating of Prince Charles a real interest in the women concerned? One of his aides believes that much of it was ritualistic gallantry: 'I always believed the boss was a non-marryer,' the aide said. 'He was the complete bachelor. Hunting, shooting and writing endless letters. There was a lot of gift buying and sending flowers but how much else I am not sure.'⁷ Charles, the aide felt, was more of a lost soul than he let on, always in search of the kind of highly charged emotional life than that he did not experience at home.

Queen Elizabeth II, consumed by her duty to the nation, was formal and frequently absent as a mother or deep in her 'red boxes', the endless flow of government dispatches concerning affairs of state. Acceding to the throne when she was only twenty-five was an impossible burden for a young married woman whose first child, Charles, was three at the time. She is fated to be defined for ever as a mother by the photograph of her returning from her royal tour of the Commonwealth in 1954 and shaking her five-year-old son gravely by the hand. There is not much room for spontaneity when parenting can only happen by appointment. A footman recounted to the author Brian Hoey how Prince Andrew would say to him, 'I want to see the Queen, never "my mother". Would you find out if she is available? And they had to dress properly before they saw their parents even if it was only going to be for a few minutes.'⁸ The unique loneliness of the monarch's position was compounded by her own stoic reserve. Margaret Rhodes, the Queen's cousin, believes the Queen's ability to express emotions has been frozen by marriage to Philip, rather than duty. 'Perhaps having married someone who is like Philip, it is difficult to go on expressing emotion to an unemotional person,' she has said. 'You find, in time, you can't express love any more.'⁹ There is no doubt the Queen has always been mad about her husband since the day in 1939 when she was thirteen-year-old 'Lillibet', King George VI's eldest's daughter, and escorted around the Royal Naval College at Dartmouth by the dashing eighteen-year-old Viking, a prince of Greece and Denmark. But being the Viking's wife – or his son – was not an easy assignment.

The Duke's intimidating height, vigorous self-assurance, and strong, interrogatory nose are a source of alarm to braver men than Prince Charles. Philip was raised in the harsh, Germanic tradition that considered culture decadent (he once referred to a Henry Moore sculpture as a 'monkey's gallstone') and always saw his sensitive eldest son as a project to whack into shape. As one former private secretary put it, 'Philip is a very bright man, but without the benefit of an education there is no discipline to balance the arrogance that goes with the intelligence. He quickly reaches prejudiced positions without the information to do so and can't be persuaded to change his mind.'[10] Another informed member of the royal household once politely raised questions in private about Philip's hostile assessment of Australia's Labour Prime Minister Gough Whitlam, controversially sacked by the Governor General in 1975, and was taken aback by how quickly Philip's voice became raised and irate. The Duke loudly informed the questioner he was 'a socialist arsehole' whom he never wished to speak to again.[11] Actually Philip never seemed to be at his best in Commonwealth territory. In Canada in 1969, he exclaimed, 'We don't come here for our health. We can think of other ways of enjoying ourselves.'[12]

Philip gives his boorish stereotyping plenty of ammunition but he's a deeper man than his public persona reveals. And he has mellowed a lot in the years since Diana died. But he bears the scars of a bruising childhood as a displaced Prince of Greece bounced into wandering exile when he was barely a year old: first to Italy arriving penniless, followed by London and Paris. His father, Prince Andrew, abandoned him to go off and live with his mistress in Monaco. His mother, Princess Alice, had a nervous breakdown and withdrew to Switzerland and later became a nun on the Greek island of Tinos. Philip never had a home until he married Elizabeth Windsor. Once he did, without whingeing, he sacrificed his own successful career in the navy and some would suggest his masculinity in having always to walk two paces behind his wife in public. He found a way to divert his energies to some serious passions of his own for the larger good. His energetic 46 year involvement in the World Wildlife Fund stems from a genuine environmental concern he passed on to his eldest son. The Queen's former press secretary, Michael Shea, tells how a Kuwaiti prince introduced himself to the Duke on a Gulf tour with the words, 'I am the Minister of the

Environment,' only to hear Philip reply, 'You've killed every bloody animal in Kuwait,' and walk away.[13] Most of the Duke's staff respect him because he's as loyal as he is direct. He was upset when the head of the Royal Protection Squad, Commander Michael Trestrail, had to resign after an exposé about Trestrail's private life with a gay hustler marked him as a security risk. The Duke went so far as to write to the Tory minister William Whitelaw with a blistering protest. Thereafter, Philip always saw to it that Trestrail continued to be invited to Palace social events. The Queen rarely takes any serious decision without his input. 'What does my husband think?' she will ask her private secretary, and if he does not know, she holds off until she finds out. Philip has spent his life running interference for the sovereign ('Don't jostle the Queen!' he barks at press who get too close), but his curtness can even now embarrass her. 'Sometimes, her technique when Philip's rude to her is to put up a smoke screen,' a palace official said to *Daily Telegraph* writer Graham Turner. 'She'll change the subject and start talking in riddles. Then, he's diverted, trying to find out what the hell she's talking about.'[14]

What frustrated Prince Charles was not so much the absence of feeling in his parents but that so little feeling was allowed to be shown – an important nuance that for a child amounts to the same thing. The only real warmth he experienced was from his grandmother, the Queen Mother, who had him to stay at her Scottish home, Birkhall, and encouraged him to talk to her about books and music and theatre. 'Now do have another buttery,' she would say over tea – plying her grandson with Scotland's answer to the croissant.[15] The Queen Mother was violently opposed to Philip's insistence on sending Charles to the boot camp boarding school Gordonstoun on the north-east coast of Scotland, rather than the more arts-based Eton. Just as she feared, Charles was friendless in a school where stuffing a fellow's head down the toilet was considered a mildly prankish act. Anyone remotely nice to the Prince was seen as trying to curry favour. When he complained, his father told him not to be so 'bloody wet'. BBC anchorman Jeremy Paxman was amazed during a stay with Prince Charles and Camilla at Sandringham that a guest getting up from her seat to fetch another cup of tea elicited from Charles the response, 'Oh don't go! It's happened all the time, from school onwards, people moving away from me, because they don't want to be seen as sucking up.'[16] Gordonstoun passed into folklore as Philip's most hard-bitten decision, but the Duke's motives at the time were not so unsound. He believed that at

Eton, a stone's throw from Windsor Castle, the heir to the throne would only meet the children of people he knew, whereas at Gordonstoun, far away from the nannying of the court – and insulated from Fleet Street – Charles had more of a chance to develop as a self-reliant man. Given what transpired in his private life, the Duke's dread of his eldest son becoming a pampered fop looks, from a distance, less eccentric.

Charles turned to Mountbatten for the male mentoring he could never receive from his father. The Prince hero-worshipped Uncle Dickie for his dashing, adventurous life and elegant self-confidence. Mountbatten's career had been an unstoppable rise – command of the destroyer HMS *Kelly* in the Second World War, Supreme Allied Commander of the South-East Asia battleground, overseeing the recapture of Burma from the Japanese, celebrated Viceroy of India in charge of its birth as an independent nation in 1948, and landing in 1959 at the very top of the navy as First Sea Lord. None of this made him a stuffed shirt. Mountbatten's marriage to the restlessly brilliant and very rich beauty Countess Edwina Mountbatten (née Ashley) had been scandalously open, both of them having, in today's terminology, 'lots of shag mates'. Edwina was as indefatigable in passion as she was in philanthropy – one of her multitudinous lovers, or at any rate admirers, was Pandit Nehru – whereas Dickie had the distinction of having male as well as female lovers, one of them being Noel Coward. *Private Eye* added to Mountbatten's list of titles by dubbing him 'Mountbottom of the Fleet'. He revelled in his influence over Charles, much to the irritation of Prince Philip and the Queen Mother who saw him as an ambitious social meddler, which he was. In one of his many avuncular letters to Charles in February 1974, Mountbatten advised: 'I believe, in a case like yours, the man should sow his wild oats and have as many affairs as he can before settling down . . .'

His counsel was taken too literally by the young Prince of Wales. The combination of wealth, royalty and sycophancy was in danger of making Charles as dangerously spoilt as his father had always feared. Despite his sensitivity on other matters the Prince expected his girlfriends to wait around all day for his attentions like groupies while he was exercising himself or his horse or otherwise engaged. Women were all over England's most eligible bachelor and it wasn't improving his character. He dismissed one of his fancies, Jane Ward, the former wife of an Hussars officer and assistant manager of the Guards Polo Club, by sending a detective over to her on the polo field with a peremptory message. An early girlfriend, Georgiana Russell, the strikingly attractive daughter of British Ambassador Sir John Russell, was vocal in her discontent after joining Charles at Balmoral for a romantic weekend and ending up sitting on a riverbank in the cold all day watching him fish. Charles was big on arriving at an event with one girl and leaving with a second, occasionally with both at once. After dancing together for hours at a ball in June 1977, he invited the exotic Colombian beauty Cristabel Barria Borsage to drive back with him to London while his date, Diana's sister Sarah, was crammed, fuming, into the back seat of his Aston Martin coupé.[17]

Husbands as well as mentors were the Prince's sexual enablers. All through the seventies Charles supplemented bachelor girls and bimbos with a willing cadre of married women. Their husbands rolled over for the same reasons their wives did, not *droit de seigneur*, but something at once medieval and modern: status. The reflected honour of royalty's trust outweighed such déclassé emotions as jealousy, humiliation or a sense of proprietorship. A willing romp was Australian blonde Dale Tryon, married to one of the Prince's closest sporting friends, Lord Tryon. She was a woman of confidential smiles and warm reassuring squeezes of the hand. The Prince loved her breezy, colonial frankness and often dropped in unannounced at the Tryons' London home in Walton Street or joined them as a holiday guest at their fishing lodge in Iceland. Married women were appealing to Charles because the need for secrecy made them 'safe'. Any girlfriend of Charles was the immediate subject of press harassment from the rat pack. 'In those days we were all so un-media savvy and the Royals didn't protect you at all,' Sabrina Guinness, daughter of the merchant banker James Guinness, told me of a Balmoral weekend she spent with Charles in September 1979. 'They just blamed you if you were caught by the press. When I was invited up to Balmoral, somebody leaked it. Not me. I didn't want anyone to know because I knew how much they hated that. But when I got to the airport in Scotland I was immediately surrounded. The family was furious with me. They behaved as if it was my fault. Prince Charles was just embarrassed.'[18]

Almost every week the press threw a new name into the hat as the next Queen of England. They scoured the lists of European royalty for a suitable bride for Charles as if they were sixteenth-century couriers for Good Queen Bess looking for allies against imperial Spain. Princess Caroline of Monaco was top of the list (she had been secretly fancied by Charles when she was just fifteen), but she had become too racy and café society for his rural tastes. The *Daily Express* invented a romance with Princess Marie Astrid of Luxembourg, then rubbished their own story on the grounds that the Prince of Wales could never marry a Roman Catholic.

There was an attempt to whip up a special relationship angle with Tricia Nixon, younger daughter of disgraced President Richard Nixon. On a White House visit in 2005, Charles, noting recent speculation that Lauren Bush, the president's attractive niece, might make a fitting bride for Prince William, ruminated that rumours of this sort were 'an entirely hereditary feature'.[19]

The press game was to first hype a girl as the next Queen of England and then discover the skeleton in the closet that would disqualify her. Fiona Watson, the curvaceous daughter of a landowner, was a prospect until a raunchy set of pictures in *Penthouse* turned her glass coach into a pumpkin. Hacks chased the lovely Davina Sheffield into the ladies' room at Heathrow looking for a quote about the kiss-and-tell memoir of her ex-boyfriend, James Beard, a powerboat racer and designer. The coolness of Lady Jane Wellesley, the Duke of Wellington's brainy daughter, defeated them. In 1974, when reporters camped outside her home in Fulham and asked her if she was to become the Princess of Wales, she replied pertly, 'I don't want another title – I've already got one.'[20] In the lulls between girlfriends, a staple newspaper space-filler on a foreign tour was paying some friendly cheesecake model to leap out of the surf and kiss the heir apparent.

The vulgarity of the bridal beauty contest and the noise of press speculation was increasingly irksome to the senior members of the royal family. The Queen Mother's views on the subject of Prince Charles's future bride matched those of the Queen: a virgin and soon. The Queen Mother believed that she was better qualified than anyone else to prescribe what was required in a Queen in Waiting. (When she heard of the engagement of the beauteous and very rich Lady Leonora Grosvenor and Lord Lichfield in 1975 she said, 'what a shame – we had been saving her for Prince Charles'.)[21] As Elizabeth Bowes-Lyon, the youngest daughter of a Scottish peer, the 14th Earl of Strathmore, the Queen Mother had been a virtuous young thing like Diana when she married the shy, unexciting Prince Albert, Duke of York (aka 'Bertie'), in 1923. Her wifely support, after the shocking abdication of his elder brother Edward, was the crucial factor in helping the stammering Duke evolve into the dignified monarch George VI, who led the British nation through the trauma of the Second World War. She saw in

Charles many of the recessive characteristics of George VI, and believed he was desperately in need of a wife strong enough both to handle the pressures of royal life and stiffen his backbone. 'Some plants need watering. [They] need to be forced.'[22] That was said to be her line on her Princely grandson.

Her opinion was crucial. Behind her creamy, adorable façade, the Queen Mother was a woman of steel when it came to matters of state and moral deportment – 'a marshmallow made on a welding machine', Cecil Beaton once called her.[23] No one had a longer memory for grievances. As soon as she became Queen, she permanently blacklisted Lady Emerald Cunard, the American heiress and great London society hostess, for having regularly entertained Wallis Simpson and Edward VIII before his abdication. Her energy for maintaining her profile was exhausting. ('For thirty-six hours, barely a minute to draw breath,' was Roy Strong's comment about the hectic social pace of one weekend as the Queen Mother's guest.)[24] Members of her household were encouraged never to retire, to their chagrin. As Hugo Vickers commented, she took the 'commendable but tough attitude that you were either alive or dead and if you were alive then you were working'.[25] She subtly dominated her devoted daughter. A senior courtier told Douglas Keay that the Queen's refrain was always: 'It's Mummy that matters. We mustn't do anything that hurts Mummy's feelings.'[26]

The Queen Mother's feelings were certainly aroused by what she viewed as Uncle Dickie's unseemly machinations to marry off Prince Charles to his granddaughter, Amanda Knatchbull, and she started actively to seek another candidate. Mountbatten, the last great-grandson of Queen Victoria, was related to most of the European royal families and had dynastic ambitions of his own. The Queen Mother, with her elephant's memory for slights, had never forgiven him for being the best friend of the former Duke of Windsor, whom he accompanied on a tour of India in 1922 – though he supported her husband in the crisis. She blamed Mountbatten for encouraging Charles to play the field for so long and thereby develop a taste for irresponsibility. In his 'wild oats' letter, Mountbatten had gone on to say that 'for a wife you [Charles] should choose a suitable and a sweet-charactered girl before she meets anyone else she might fall for'.[27] The formula fitted his granddaughter Amanda to a T. She was nine years younger than Charles and past-free as far as anyone could tell.

The Queen Mother was set on subverting this romance, seeing it not as a love match but a stratagem to aggrandise the Mountbatten family.

They gave themselves such airs these Mountbattens! Why, on the marriage of his nephew Philip Mountbatten to Elizabeth, he had even tried to get the Royal House of Windsor to change its name to the Royal House of Mountbatten! She was apprehensive of both his appetite and his abilities. As the Viceroy of India, sent out by the Labour government to confer independence, he had charmed the Indian Princes to yield to the new states of India and Pakistan. Now she learned he was hatching a plan to accompany the Prince on Charles's first tour of India in early 1979 and throw him together with the blossoming Amanda when they got there. This made the need for another name even more pressing.

Charles was doing his best to feel strongly about Amanda. After a holiday on Eleuthera in the Bahamas with Mountbatten and his daughter and son-in-law, Patricia and John Brabourne, around the time that Camilla was getting married, Charles had confessed to Mountbatten that he had begun to find Amanda, who was fifteen at the time, 'most disturbing'.[28]

In recent months, now that she was twenty, there had been more and more dates and warm exchanges. Amanda's parents smartly refused to let her go to India – fearing that she'd be eaten alive afterwards by the press – but Mountbatten, accustomed to disposing of the fate of millions, did not give up presuming the destiny of Charles and Amanda was his to decide. He stepped up his alarmist homilies to Charles, blasting him with a note in April 1979 that said he was becoming 'unkind and thoughtless'.[29] Another testy letter about the Prince's moral deportment, written earlier, veiled the real source of Uncle Dickie's irritation – that the Prince should get on with proposing marriage to Amanda. He was even sufficiently frustrated to use the dreaded D word to Charles, conjuring up the spectre of feckless 'Uncle David' (Edward VIII). 'I thought you were beginning on the downward slope which wrecked your Uncle David's life and led to his disgraceful abdication and his futile life ever after,' he railed.[30] In April 1979, Charles wrote to a friend, with a stifled yawn, 'I am becoming rather worried by all this talk about being self-centred and getting worse every year. I'm told that marriage is the only cure for me – and maybe it is! The media will simply not take me seriously until I do get married and apparently become responsible.'[31]

In mid-August 1979 the Prince of Wales finally psyched himself up to propose to Amanda Knatchbull. The two were aboard the royal yacht *Britannia* on the royal family's annual cruise of the Western Isles of Scotland. Much to his supposed chagrin (and probably to his secret relief), the admirable young woman turned him down. As with Jane Wellesley, her own privileged access was a deterrent. The girls who were most appropriate as future brides for Charles knew too much about the burdens and boredom of royal life and weren't impressed enough with the perks of princesshood to angle for the role. Amanda's mother gave another reason: 'No spark.'[32] Perhaps Miss Knatchbull knew too much about where Charles's real affections lay.

It was hardly a secret. Ever since he first met her in the early summer of 1971, Charles had found Camilla Shand – the magnetic blonde with an easy laugh and relaxed sense of humour – the one girlfriend he could never forget. Women who love horses usually love sex. It is no accident that, for girls, the onset of puberty is often marked by an obsession with horseflesh. Hunting, Charles's other favourite recreational activity, has always been an aphrodisiac. The adrenalin, the fresh air, and the tally-ho exhilaration are all big libido boosters, to say nothing of all that throbbing, galloping animal vitality between one's thighs. Women who hunt love risk as much as men do. And, as a rule, husbands and wives rarely hunt together. There is no set time to come home before dark, so the sporting day can extend erotically into twilight with alibi still intact.

Camilla Shand loved horses all right. A member of the Beaufort Hunt described her as ruthless on horseback. 'You often hear her screaming as you approach a fence. "Bloody hell, get out of the fucking way!"'[33] She was the daughter of a dashing war hero, Major Bruce Shand, and a high-toned society charmer, the Honourable Rosalind Cubitt. The Shand family was as warm and close as the Windsor family were not. Camilla was the eldest of three children. (With her sister Annabel and her brother Mark, the three attractive siblings were known as the Sexy Shands.) She grew up in an ambience both sporting and appreciative of the arts. The aura of her great-grandmother, Alice Keppel, favourite mistress of King Edward VII, contributed to the sexual haze around Camilla. Sir Harold Acton wrote of Mrs Keppel, 'None could compete with her glamour as a hostess. She could have impersonated *Britannia* in a *tableau vivant* and done that lady credit.'[34]

But Camilla's preferred way of life had little in common with that of the metropolitan Alice. While Keppel moved between her suite at the Ritz and L'Ombrellino, a fabulous villa in the hills outside Florence, Camilla was English countryside through and through. She never cared about clothes or make-up or shopping. She came from the grubby-knickers school of British grooming, with static-flying hedgerow hair and fingernails used to rooting around in the vegetable garden. She pulled her appearance together only when she rode to hounds, showing off her whip-cracking mastery of the sport in tight jodhpurs, frothing white stock and elegant black net snood. Marie Helvin, who, before hooking up with Dodi Fayed, dated Camilla's brother Mark Shand, remembers Camilla's earthy appeal at country weekends. 'She used to come in in these big muddy boots with her hair all blown around and good skin and she just looked great somehow.'[35]

Men have always loved Camilla. Hers is one of those direct, country-house personalities that specialise in instant candour. Being candid is not the same as being confessional (that dreaded word, with all its shuddery connotations for the royal family of Diana's BBC heart-to-heart with Martin Bashir). And being candid is not at all the same as being obvious. Every tabloid account of the history of their romance would have you believe that Camilla's opening gambit to the Prince was to say to him, 'You know, sir, my great-grandmother was the mistress of your great-great-grandfather – so how about it?'[36] This is somewhere between extremely improbable and utterly inconceivable. For a girl as socially savvy as Camilla Shand it would have been totally non-U to whip out her pedigree within seconds of meeting the heir to the British throne. Prince Charles would have known perfectly well who the Shands and the Cubitts were – and 'how about it?' is about as upper class a locution as 'cor blimey!'

What Camilla actually said that day spoke more deeply – and more arousingly – to Prince Charles than that oft-quoted and apocryphal come-on. Sizing up his horse with an expert eye, she told the Prince in her warm baritone, 'That's a fine animal you have there, sir.'[37] The fine animal in Charles responded with a leap of intimate recognition. Camilla Shand, later Parker Bowles, became the love of his life.

It was no secret that Camilla had already indulged in a couple of lusty post-debutante affairs. Her experience helped guide Charles to relax more in bed, as when she urged him to 'pretend I am a rocking horse'.[38] (Royal men never quite escape from the nursery.) But that same experience constrained the Prince from popping the question to, or even discussing the question with, the girl he fancied to distraction.

Instead, after a blissful six months of shared country pursuits, of dancing groin to groin at Annabel's, the Mayfair nightclub, and enjoying sex-charged suppers after the opera, Charles set sail on the naval frigate HMS *Minerva* for eight lonely months, hoping somehow

Camilla would wait. In an intense valedictory weekend with her at Broadlands, in December 1972, he declared his love for her but not his hand.

The late John Brabourne told Gyles Brandreth that Charles 'misjudged it' when he didn't propose that weekend, but Brabourne's widow, Patricia Mountbatten, believes it would have made no difference. 'He wouldn't have got anywhere anyway,' she said. Marriage to Camilla in 1973 'wouldn't have been possible, not then. Camilla had "a history" – and you didn't want a past that hung about. And she was a subject. And nobody marries a subject.'[39]

A more interesting question, however, is whether she would have married him if he'd asked. My own view is that the love of Camilla's life was not Prince Charles but the man she married first – Andrew Parker Bowles. He was a self-confident thirty-three-year-old major in the Blues and Royals, a prestigious regiment of the Household Cavalry and the son of the Queen Mother's close friend, the landowner and High Sheriff of Berkshire, Derek Parker Bowles. He seems to have been (and still is) one of those men who has the gift of bringing out the delicious worst in every woman he meets. His father was the same. 'In that world,' Minette Marrin wrote of the Parker Bowles household, 'drink flowed astonishingly freely, the language was often blue and the conversation earthy.'[40] Andrew adored women. He relished the chase and, his friends testify, the chase was rarely far from his mind. Also like his father, he was a royal groupie. One of his earlier diversions was a torrid affair with the young Princess Anne, who, in her stern way, has always enjoyed a roll in the hay. There was a romantic re-enactment of *La Ronde* on the dance floor at Annabel's one night in 1971 when it was clear that Princess Anne was in love with Andrew Parker Bowles, Camilla was in love with him too, and Charles was in love with Camilla.[41]

It took six years of persistence for Camilla to get Andrew to the altar. They were married at the Guards Chapel at Wellington Barracks, London on 4 July 1973, a mere five months after Charles sailed on the *Minerva*. The bride was thirteen days short of her twenty-sixth birthday. It was an all-out society wedding. The Queen Mother and Princess Anne both came to the service, and Princess Margaret joined the reception at St James's Palace.

Prince Charles was distraught when, in April 1973, he went ashore on Antigua and learned what was coming. In a private letter of 27 April to a friend, the Prince lamented how 'such a blissful, peaceful and mutually happy relationship' had been decreed by fate to only last 'a mere six months . . . I suppose the feeling of emptiness will pass eventually.'[42]

He was still at sea when the ceremony took place. It was just as well; he would have had to see how happy Camilla looked and how dazzling she was in a gown of white silk organdie with lashings of tulle held in place by a diamond tiara, and attended by six bridesmaids and ten pages.

It had taken Camilla so long to reel Andrew in because he was such an inveterate Don Juan, dedicated to playing the field. Lord Wyatt, the journalist and social fixer, records in his diary of the Queen Mother's cousin John Bowes-Lyon telling him that when Andrew was still hesitating about marriage, Camilla's parents were so keen they get on with it they suddenly put a notice in *The Times* announcing their engagement. Andrew thought that as it had been publicly announced, he could not go back on it.

Her dalliance with Charles had been fun, flattering, and sexy but her friends knew all along that her consuming passion was Andrew. It was the reason, really, she could handle Charles so well. As every woman knows, playing the game is so much easier when you're holding an ace.

The amazing thing about the Parker Bowleses' twenty-two-year marriage is how faithless it was right from the start – and not even primarily on Camilla's side. Andrew had had affairs throughout their courtship, and he didn't stop after the wedding. Camilla once described to a girlfriend, Carolyn Benson, a Bridget Jones moment when she let herself into Andrew's apartment with her key and discovered her lover 'distinctly uncomfortable'. A quick search of the flat revealed a married beauty 'crouched behind a sofa, quietly sobbing'.[43] In 2004, Lucian Freud painted a telling full-length portrait of Andrew Parker Bowles titled *The Brigadier* (as he became) which features him seated heavily in a padded leather chair wearing a dark blue, medal-festooned uniform with scarlet-and-gold cuffs and stripe up the leg. His expanding middle-aged girth spills out of the loosened jacket, but the expression on his fleshy face is of grand indifference rather than disarray.

Andrew's conquests always seemed to forgive him, and Camilla was no exception. He may have spent the week in London flagrantly chasing after one of her friends, but if you called at the Parker Bowleses' on Sunday morning at their manor house in Wiltshire, you'd find Andrew cooking breakfast and Camilla padding contentedly around the kitchen in an oversized man's shirt, or sitting on his lap affectionately messing with his hair. On country weekends with them at the end of the seventies, Marie Helvin noted how 'tight' the Parker Bowleses were as a couple. When they entertained at their vibrant dinner parties, they would often talk animatedly across the guests to each other. Helvin could never figure out how either Andrew's well-known womanising or the Prince Charles factor impacted on their marriage. She and Mark Shand and Camilla and Andrew would sometimes be staying at the same time with the Shand parents, Major Bruce and Rosalind, at their house in Sussex. All the Sunday papers would be spread out on the breakfast tables, a habitual in country-house parties. Throughout the Diana years, more often than not, there would be something suggestive about Charles and Camilla, but no one would acknowledge it. 'Sometimes, you would see Rosalind stiffen at the table as she read an article,' Helvin said, 'but no discussion. Ever.'[44]

In the early years of Camilla's marriage, when her husband was off during the week playing around in London, it was doubtless an agreeable boost for his wife that the Prince of Wales telephoned her so often and continued to confide in her about his ongoing bachelor affairs. A former member of the Queen's staff says that throughout Camilla's marriage to Parker Bowles, it was Charles's intensity of feeling that drove the sustained romantic friendship.[45] Camilla took the Prince's devotion for granted while at the same time making sure no newcomer usurped her. A friend of Camilla's believes the bond would have lapsed on Camilla's side if Charles had not been the Prince of Wales.[46] On weekends the Prince often showed up in the Parker Bowleses' kitchen in need of tea and sympathy. In return, Camilla could share her rueful stories of Andrew's wandering eye. One of her earlier flames, Rupert Hambro, remembered the masochistic glee Camilla took in telling him about the tricky situations Andrew's love life sometimes caused. 'She often saw the funny side of things afterwards,' said Hambro.[47]

Or pretended she did. Camilla's marital compromises had the effect of making adultery part of her way of life. Parker Bowles initiated her. Somehow, the pain his betrayals inflicted on her had to be minimised and laughed away.

It was the death of Charles's beloved Uncle Dickie on 27 August 1979 that threw Prince Charles's emotional life into chaos and revived his affair with Camilla. The murder was an appallingly brutal crime. Mountbatten's affection for his Irish neighbours around his holiday home, Classiebawn Castle at Mullaghmore in County Sligo on the west coast of Ireland, and theirs for him, created an opportunity for the assassination. Mountbatten's little fishing boat *Shadow V* was left unguarded. He had just sailed out of the harbour when a bomb concealed on board was detonated by remote control. His fifteen-year-old grandson Nicholas Knatchbull, who was also Prince Charles's godson, and the fifteen-year-old boatman Paul Maxwell were killed too. His daughter and son-in-law, Lord and Lady Brabourne, and Nicholas's twin brother Timothy were seriously injured. The Dowager Lady Brabourne, aged eighty-two, died the following morning from her wounds at Sligo hospital.

Prince Charles was in Iceland on a fishing holiday with Lord and Lady Tryon at the time of the murder and was met, ashen, at Heathrow by his valet Stephen Barry. From Heathrow they were driven to Windsor where Charles sat miserably in the garden, stunned and silent, trying to absorb the tragedy. In his journal, on 27 August 1979, he wrote: 'A mixture of desperate emotions swept over me – agony, disbelief, a kind of wretched numbness, closely followed by fierce and violent determination to see that something was done about the IRA.'[48]

The shock of that terrible morning still reverberates in the mind of Mountbatten's granddaughter India Hicks. Twenty-six years after the murder, in 2005 she returned for the first time to the scene of the events and wrote afterwards to her uncle Lord Brabourne:

Suddenly on those dunes in that startling Irish sunlight a memory leapt out and grabbed me by the throat. I was suddenly eleven years old and a bomb had gone off . . .

I had been shrimping with Grandpapa the day before. 'Decibel,' he would command (do you remember as the youngest of ten grandchildren I tended to talk a little loudly?), 'bring the nets!' and over slippery rocks I would inch forward to where he was.

Monday 27th August was a bright and sunny day that called for the usual fishing excursion, but having spent so much time in the water the previous day I opted to stay behind hoping for a trip to buy sweets. Grandpapa came into the hall and called to me 'look after my dog' and went down to the harbour. I was watching Laurel and Hardy with Ashley in the library when we heard the bang. For years after I would jump unnecessarily when a door slammed or a balloon burst. The police who had been following the boat on land came screeching up the drive. 'Just collecting our binoculars, to look at the pretty view,' they said. But we knew then, Ashley and I, I'm sure of it.

Valium pills and detective interviews followed. I was so confused. Grandpapa was dead, Nicky was missing in the sea and everyone else was being rushed to hospital in Sligo. Why was I on my own being 'interviewed' by a policeman, with Ashley and Edwina waiting outside for their turn, and where was Grandpapa's dog? I had to look after him.

I hid down by the sea on the rocks for a while. Someone found me and I can't remember who. I was eleven years old and I had never heard of a political assassination before. And then it all becomes a fuzz, funeral after funeral, nightmare after nightmare, a part of my childhood had been raped. Edwina, Ashley and I were helicoptered out by the British Army to Barons Court a few days later, or even a day later, again I can't remember. But I had Grandpapa's dog with me so that was OK and I remember trying to put the headphones over his ears instead of my own and a soldier gently replacing them.[49]

The Queen never wrote to express her condolences to Mountbatten's two daughters – Patricia, 2nd Countess Mountbatten and Lady Pamela Hicks, India's mother. But this was not, surely, because the Queen felt nothing but because she felt too much. It was more bearable for her to show her concern through official channels. A Palace staff member that weekend, whose job it was to tell the Queen that Mountbatten had been assassinated recalls: 'She said nothing except "Thank you very much", but later that night, about 9 p.m., she phoned me and said, "You have had a very difficult day. You really ought to go to bed" – which was unusual, because she's not a person who shows affection or gratitude.'[50]

What Charles needed now was not Windsor stoicism but Camilla's husky empathy on the other end of the phone. She had called him at Broadlands, where he was staying, to offer her support, and he poured out his confusion and pain to her. It was fortuitous for him that four months after the murder of Mountbatten, Lieutenant Colonel Andrew Parker Bowles left for Rhodesia with Lord Soames, the last British Governor. Parker Bowles was away for four months helping to oversee the transition to independence, leaving Camilla behind with their two children in Wiltshire. When word reached her via the grapevine that the rampant Lieutenant Colonel was now developing a warm friendship with Soames's daughter Charlotte, she knew how she could console herself.

You have to hand it to Camilla that she always knew how to stage her sexual reprisals. Or, as a male friend remarked, 'Only Camilla Parker Bowles could find a way to reheat a soufflé.'[51]

In April of 1980, when the Prince travelled to southern Africa to preside over the Independence Day celebrations that formalised Rhodesia's transmutation into Zimbabwe, Camilla travelled with Charles – not with Andrew, who had been in England briefly some days before. At Buckingham Palace there was consternation at press reports that Charles was taking 'his old flame' Camilla Parker Bowles to Zimbabwe as his official escort. The fact that Andrew Parker Bowles was now back in Zimbabwe only made the matter stickier and created a 'paradox' that had to be explained away with a briefing. 'Buckingham Palace have always been happier to see Charles in the company of happily married women because such sightings cannot give rise to rumour'[52] – that was the ingenious official gloss. On the plane to Zimbabwe, Charles and Camilla remained closeted, while the crew did its uncomfortable best to ignore the jollifications allegedly transpiring in the not quite soundproof royal cabin. At the dinner at Government House on 16 April, Charles, in full view of Andrew Parker Bowles, was flirting with Camilla so obviously that his private secretary Edward Adeane walked out.[53]

*Whoomph.* The sparks between Charles and Camilla blew into the open at the Cirencester Polo Club ball at Stowell Park at the end of June 1980. The Prince was there with his latest girlfriend, the beautiful twenty-five-year-old blonde spitfire, Anna Wallace, a Scottish landowner's daughter. Charles was for a time deeply infatuated with Wallace and had even been rumoured to have proposed. James Whitaker, on patrol on the banks of the River Dee in Scotland where Charles fished, caught him with Wallace in flagrante on a rug. 'Moments before the royal wick was lit,' guffawed Whitaker, 'he spotted us crawling on our bellies with cameras and binoculars. He jumped up and ran to hide in the bushes, ungallantly leaving poor Anna to cover herself up.'[54] Whitaker didn't print the story (a favour he was no doubt planning to call in), nor did any of the other members of the rat pack. But the more aggressive jungle beast Nigel Dempster gave warning that if pushed, he would not be so forbearing. 'Just in case Charles does get panicked into a formal proposal,' Dempster wrote in the *Daily Mail*, 'I have chilling news for him. There is a risqué picture of Anna in circulation – and I have a copy of it.'[55] Anna might have been tarnished as a bride, but she could still supplant Camilla as premier mistress.

Anna was nicknamed 'Whiplash Wallace' for her prowess on the hunting field, and Camilla knew exactly what that meant. The Prince's long-term lover needed to demonstrate, in public as well as in private, that she had the power to get the Prince of Wales back at her pleasure, and make that point to her philandering husband. When Charles asked Camilla to dance, the two of them were lip-locked half the night. 'On and on they went . . . kissing each other, French kissing, dance after dance. It was completely beyond the pale,' a guest recalled.[56] In a fury, the abandoned Anna took the hostess's car and drove away.

Such brazen exhibitionism on Camilla's part looks like pure triumphalism. Even Camilla's mother, who was present at the ball, was perturbed at the effect of such a display of flagrantly adulterous feeling, especially with Andrew present. But that was at least half the point, presumably – that Andrew *was* there, pretending, in the couple's endless marital games, to be impervious to his wife's making out in front of him with the heir to the throne. 'HRH is very fond of my wife . . . And she appears to be very fond of him,' Andrew drawled to a guest as he watched Camilla's performance with the Prince.[57]

The Lieutenant Colonel did not seem unhappy, as some men might have been, that his wife retained the attentions of the Prince of Wales. In 1987 he was promoted to Commanding Officer of the Household Cavalry Mounted Regiment, a signal honour that carried an apt ceremonial title: Silver-Stick-in-Waiting to Her Majesty Queen Elizabeth II. In April 2005 at the wedding of Charles and Camilla he could be seen beaming away in his pew like the mother of the bride.

For the royal family, Charles's obsession with Camilla had gone from being an acceptable dalliance to a serious roadblock to matrimony. Plus, it was causing unsavoury chatter. The Queen's private secretary had already come to inform her that there was dismay among senior officers in the Household Cavalry that the Prince of Wales was having a very public affair with a brother officer's wife. The Queen said nothing, but she absorbed the implications and did not like them. It was clear now that there were deeper emotional reasons why the slipper never seemed to fit. It went beyond the question of availability or pedigree. The awkward fact was that the heir to the throne, like his uncle, Edward VIII, was tenaciously in love with a married woman. Charles was now thirty-one, past the age he always promised he would marry. A bride must be found and fast. But who? They were running out of names of single girls plausibly *intacta*. Any woman near Charles's own age who was still a virgin could only be found in a sitcom. With very few exceptions, the younger ones had proved even more woefully experimental. 'This was always part of Diana's logic,' her friend Simon Berry said. 'Who else was he going to marry?'[58]

By 1980, if Diana hadn't existed they would have had to invent her. In fact, they did. Suzanne Lowry, the Living section editor of the *Observer*, found a classy-looking secretary called Sarah, had her interviewed, and then photographed in a tiara and an off-the-shoulder Hardy Amies evening dress. The *Observer* billed her as 'THE TRUE PRINCESS', complete with coat of arms. In a style reminiscent of the *Mirror* poll all those years ago on Princess Margaret, they urged, 'Take her, Charles, she's yours. And, of course, ours.' This princess 'loved animals, was a vegetarian, hated polo and blood sports, didn't suit her hair up and', wrote Lowry later, 'had that spotless purity that convinces the masses'.[59] It was a perfect description of the perfect generic princess. And, oddly enough, it perfectly matched the still unknown Lady Diana Spencer.

She had appeared on the Queen Mother's watch list at the grand society wedding at the Guards Chapel in April 1978 of her sister Jane Spencer to Robert Fellowes, now the Queen's assistant private secretary. Diana was one of three bridesmaids, and afterwards was noticed flirting and talking with artless appeal to the guests. There was a buzz later among the royal contingent about what a looker the young Spencer girl was turning into (despite James Whitaker's observation that she had an 'unlovely pink dress'). She was ebullient and fresh, but also elegant, with her long legs and impeccable manners. The Queen Mother had told a gratified Earl Spencer at the wedding reception at St James's Palace what an excellent job he had done in raising Diana. 'But now you have the most difficult part,' she said, with a knowing smile. 'You must think about her future settlement in life.' 'Perhaps,' Lord Spencer would later reflect, 'her advice was not as uncomplicated as I had thought.'[60]

At Prince Charles's thirtieth birthday celebrations nine months later, the unpretentious charm of the seventeen-year-old Diana Spencer was noted again. The Queen Mother thought Diana's 'sweetness and modesty and willingness to fit in made her an ideal personality for the role of Princess of Wales', Lord Charteris recalled.[61] Moreover, the Spencers, as one of the leading aristocratic families in England, were, on paper, perfectly positioned to be royal in-laws. They had dollops of royal blood that could be traced back to various illegitimate offspring of Charles II and James II. Diana's father, for heaven's sake, had been equerry to both George VI and Elizabeth II. The girl's two grandmothers, Cynthia, and Ruth, and two of her Spencer great-aunts had served on the Queen Mother's staff. Lady Fermoy was still very much around as the Queen Mother's woman of the bedchamber and her valued cultural concierge. With her background as a trained concert pianist, she used to rustle up pleasing musical diversions for the Queen Mother at Royal Lodge and in private recitals at weekend house parties often perform herself (sometimes with a friend like Sir David Willcocks, the distinguished conductor, in an after-dinner duet from the Victorian age ending with their hands crossed on the keyboard).[62] After forty years in place, Ruth was thoroughly embedded in the Queen Mother's off-duty life, lending a quiet distinction to royal dinner parties with her nimbus of very white hair and discreetly snobbish smile. Diana's royal ascendance would indeed be a satisfying social vindication of the embarrassment of her daughter Frances 'bolting' from her marriage to Earl Spencer eleven years ago. 'All Ruth Fermoy wanted was that her granddaughter be the future Queen of England,' said Lady Edith Foxwell, a friend of Princess Margaret and some of the minor royals. In turn, the Queen Mother told her eligible grandson over lunch in the spring of 1980 'not to miss the chance of Diana Spencer'.

A trickle of invitations started to include Diana in theatre parties where the Prince of Wales was present. While Charles persisted in his affair with Camilla, those invitations now began to increase. Lady Fermoy, for instance, deftly included her granddaughter in an excursion with the Prince on 3 May 1980 to hear Verdi's *Requiem* at the Albert Hall.

It is one of the ironies of Diana's story that the more Prince Charles fell in love with his mistress, the more pressing it was for the Palace to produce somebody to replace her. The arc of Diana's ascendance in Charles's life was thus always entwined with the arc of Camilla's. What no one understood at the time, least of all the eighteen-year-old bride-to-be, was how much it suited Camilla too, for Diana to marry Charles. The likes of Anna Wallace were way too assertive, worldly and disruptive. In the words of Camilla's brother-in-law, Richard Parker Bowles, 'She [Camilla] initially encouraged the relationship between Charles and Diana because she thought Diana was gormless. She never saw Diana as a threat . . . Camilla knew that as a woman with a past she could never be accepted as Charles's wife. But she also thought that Diana was someone whom she could manipulate . . . She never wanted to marry Charles. She wanted to continue to be his paramour but her game plan was to stay married to Andrew . . . She wanted two things from her life: to retain her special relationship with the Prince of Wales, and a marriage to someone she was genuinely fond of.'[63] The youngest Spencer girl was such a sweet little thing. She was sure to be quiet, passive and obedient. How could she possibly be any trouble?

# Chapter 7

# The Hunter and the Hunted

'Now the area is buzzing with talk of Charles's midnight meetings.'
— *Sunday Mirror*, November 1980

While the House of Windsor was increasingly consumed with its need to pick a malleable bride for the heir to the throne, one who would suit their dynastic needs and consummate a pact with tradition, Lady Diana Spencer was living in her own movie, the ultimate chick flick. A prince was in love with her! And she had become a bonafide beauty, understated and thoroughly English, with those appealing blue eyes and that soft, peachy complexion. 'I didn't realise when she was a child that she was going to turn out so beautiful,' her elder sister Sarah said. 'But all my friends, male and female, were talking about – not exactly the ugly duckling – saying she's going to be stunning. They could see it. But you don't notice it in your siblings.'[1]

Oh really? Sarah had noticed it plenty, is the truth – not only when her little sister (and erstwhile cleaning lady) mysteriously got herself on the list for Charles's thirtieth birthday ball but also when she was added to the invitation to Sandringham in January the previous year. While Sarah had paid her social dues by going on a long, arduous ride across ice-rutted dirt tracks with the Queen, Diana had been busy pretending to be a shooting enthusiast and flirting like mad with the heir to the throne. As Charles was narrowing his sights on pheasants, she was narrowing her sights on him.

In July Diana received another surprise invitation, this time to a house party at New Grove, the Sussex home of Commander Robert and Philippa de Pass. Their son Philip made the apparently casual suggestion to 'come and stay for a couple of nights at Petworth because we've got the Prince of Wales staying'. Then, with appropriate offhand macho, he added, 'You're young blood, you might amuse him.'[2] How totally fab! Diana did not know that the invitation to stay in the same house party as the Prince of Wales was far from offhand. Commander Robert de Pass, the host, was a polo-playing friend of Prince Philip; his wife was a lady-in-waiting to the Queen. A senior Palace aide claimed the Queen Mother was behind Diana's unexpected social summons, but Prince Philip's reaction when he discovered that Sabrina Guinness – ex-flame of Prince Charles – was also a weekend guest suggests the Diana invitation originated closer to home.

Ms Guinness had been surprised herself to be asked to join Prince Charles at the de Pass party, since the Prince had dumped her nine months before for Anna Wallace. Despite a background as the well-connected daughter of a merchant banker, the twenty-six-year-old Guinness had not, to date, led a life of the utmost discretion. She had enjoyed an Almost Famous phase of travelling around in the entourage of the Rolling Stones. She had dated Jack Nicholson and, in a cooler, more jet-set interpretation of Sloanedom, she had held a party-central job as Tatum O'Neal's nanny in Los Angeles. As a self-styled 'rock chick', Guinness, on that visit to Balmoral, had felt the royal chill of disapproval from Charles's parents when she landed at Aberdeen airport and failed to evade the press. Arriving, rattled, at the castle, she remarked that the car that met her at the station looked like a Black Maria. 'You would know all about Black Marias,' Prince Philip responded.[3]

Nonetheless, the stylish Guinness was a little startled when the host advised her to arrive at 7 p.m. in order to not collide with Prince Philip, who was departing at 6 p.m. The French-farce strategy unfortunately misfired when the royal curmudgeon delayed his exit. And he looked thunderously annoyed when Ms Guinness sashayed into the drawing room. 'He took me on one side,' Guinness recalled, 'and said "What are you doing here? I don't want you seen in public with my son." I wish I had been the woman I am today as I would have answered back, but it shook my confidence.'[4] Prince Charles, apparently oblivious, asked Guinness if she was going to watch him play polo at Cowdray Park. She declined after Philip's broadside, knowing the grounds would be crawling with the press.

Lady Diana Spencer had no such inhibitions about joining the laughing group as it set off to Cowdray Park to marvel at the Prince of Wales on his horse. *Sun* reporter Harry Arnold and photographer Arthur Edwards spotted her there, a fresh-faced girl they vaguely recognised with a gold letter D hanging round her neck, who seemed to be included in the royal party. The resourceful Edwards took some pictures for his files, just in case.[5]

Women who have been later rejected by a man rarely admit how keen they were to attract him in the first place. Diana's account to Andrew Morton of Charles being 'all over her' that weekend in a way that was 'not very cool' does not match the memories of Guinness and others.[6] By their accounts it was Diana who was 'all over' Charles, not the other way round. 'She was flirting, she was giggling. In the evening at the barbecue she was sitting on his lap, looking up at him and saying, "I've got no fillings in my teeth and no O levels. Do you think that matters?"' Guinness remembered. 'She was furiously trying to make an impression, saying how much she loved riding.' Guinness had all the more reason to feel irritation about the relative positions of their bedrooms that night: hers, a very long way from Prince Charles's, Lady Diana Spencer's right next door to him, in the room where Sabrina herself had been berthed on her visit to the de Passes' house the year before.[7]

That night was one of the rare occasions when the agendas of Diana, the House of Windsor and the press were all aligned under the same hopeful star. The youngest Spencer girl may have had an academic record the size of an index card, but her emotional radar was at full power. On her first sight of Charles in the ploughed field at Althorp, despite the excitement that surrounded him, she had divined an inner melancholy. 'God, what a sad man!'[8] was how she recalled that encounter for Morton. It was an acute perception. She had sensed what Barbara Cartland would have called 'an unmistakable air of lonely vulnerability'. Sitting beside Charles on a bale of hay, and knowing that he had just finished with Anna Wallace, she played her ace. 'You looked so sad when you walked up the aisle at Mountbatten's funeral,' she told him soulfully. 'It was the most tragic thing I've ever seen. My heart bled for you when I watched. I thought, you're so lonely – you should be with somebody to look after you.'[9] She had rightly sensed that the way to puncture the royal reserve of the heir to the throne was to appeal to his deep reservoirs of sympathy for himself. Charles, she said later, 'practically leapt on me' – which is believable, but she was fibbing furiously when she claimed that she found his behaviour 'very strange' and wasn't 'quite sure how to cope with all this'.[10]

Diana coped with it just fine – especially the part where she turned down the Prince's leery suggestion that he drive her back to London. She was far too canny to fall for a line that promised Charles's usual dating scenario of speeding off in the Aston coupé for a one-night legover at the royal digs. Nor did his next idea get a response. 'I've got to work at Buckingham Palace,' he said. 'You must come to work with me.' No, she implied to the Prince, it would be frightfully bad manners for her to just disappear on her host and hostess like that. 'Frigid wasn't the word,' she recalled proudly. 'Big F when it comes to that.'[11] She had shown Charles that she could switch in a moment from girlish flirt to woman of empathy who felt his pain. Then she showed him that her heels weren't as round as he imagined. Now all she had to do was wait.

The summons came in early August. The course of Diana's budding romance with Charles was pinioned to the high points of the late-summer social season. Early August meant Cowes Week, the week-long annual yachting regatta that takes place out of Cowes, home to the Royal Yacht Squadron, on the Isle of Wight. Charles's assistant private secretary, Oliver Everett, drove Diana down to Portsmouth to join the Prince aboard *Britannia* for the jolly nautical festivities. The royal men, with their shared naval-officer backgrounds, were out in force. Prince Charles, Prince Philip (who used to race the 1930s classic racing yacht, the sixty-three-foot *Bloodhound*), Philip's cousin, the exiled King Constantine of Greece, and an influx of other seafaring German relations of the royals – Hons and Vons, as one Cowes regular described them.

Everett noted during the drive how young Diana seemed, with her cheerful banter and her comments on nice things in the windows of shops she passed. 'She was light-hearted all week,'[12] he says. Observers found her shy and confident at the same time, wonderfully good-looking, and popular with the crew, who loved her hanging out with them. Charles didn't seem to take any notice of her at the beginning, though her eyes followed him everywhere.[13] She was a blank canvas on whom everyone had begun to project their hopes. Diana was more cryptic. 'His friends were all over me like a bad rash.'[14]

Late August, the 'Glorious Twelfth', meant the whirr of baby grouse in the heathery moors of the Highlands of Scotland. At the same time that Diana was spending her days in Belgravia, throwing Mrs Robertson's toddler's romper suits in the tumble dryer, she was preparing to embark for Balmoral Castle at the invitation of the Queen.

The occasion was the Braemar Games, an opportunity for spectators to observe kilted Scotsmen with hairy legs hurl heavy objects, as they did for a few centuries when English knights coveted their peaty bogs. Diana had never before stayed at the castle itself. On other trips she had been billeted with her sister and brother-in-law in their house on the Balmoral estate. She had been there with the Felloweses in early August when Prince Charles also happened to be on hand at the Queen Mother's house, on the edge of the awesome Glen Muick about nine miles from the castle. Diana had scored some long, chatty walks with her hero and an auspicious invitation to one of the QM's grand picnics. 'Oh, this is the life for me! Where is the footman?' she chirped when the table napkins, silver cutlery and menu card were produced.[15]

To be asked back for the Braemar Games when the Queen was in residence was a big deal. Everything goes into high gear at Balmoral when the sovereign arrives for her annual summer holiday, which she has observed at the same place and time every year since the first summer of her life in 1926. The castle and its 50,000-acre estate are purged of tourists in readiness. Three days before she arrives, sixty bagpipers begin rehearsing an ear-splitting welcome. As Her Majesty's dark green Rover sweeps into the long majestic drive, the entire staff of the estate – including seventeen gardeners, five cooks and four scullery maids – line up like the cast of a Busby Berkeley musical to greet her behind the fence at the entrance. Every asparagus, gooseberry and tomato in the castle vegetable garden is geared to ripen for these two royal months when grouse can be bagged. Not every rustle in the heather is a bird. Within twenty-four hours of Her Majesty's arrival the moors and grounds are crawling with invisible security details, diplomatic police and soldiers from the Queen's Regiment, and to the cuck-cuck-cuck cry of grouse is added the yapping pack of royal corgis.

The Queen and her family used to do the first leg of the annual August journey to Balmoral on the royal yacht until the killjoy government confiscated the multimillion-pound upkeep of the *Britannia* in 2002. The Royals would cruise round the coast of the Western Isles of Scotland to Aberdeen, anchoring along the way in Caithness, at the sixteenth-century Castle of Mey, the Queen Mother's other home, for a multi-generational picnic lunch. A guest recalls seeing the draft of a ship's signal from the Queen Mother to *Britannia*: 'Dearest Lillibet, Bring lemons, have run out.'[16] (When everyone was still on speaking terms, *Britannia* would also do a circuit past the house of Diana's mother, Frances Shand Kydd, at Oban. The Queen, Prince Philip, Charles and Diana, and Princes William and Harry would all come out on deck and wave to Frances, who stood at the edge of her garden by the ocean. 'Look, they're waving to Granny!' Frances told a friend. 'Isn't that cosy!')[17]

Diana was terrified before her first Balmoral visit. The spirit of Queen Victoria still rules on the estate bought for her by Prince Albert. No one is allowed to sit in the deceased monarch's favourite chair, still positioned where she liked it in the drawing room. You can see Prince Albert's Ludwig influence in the castle's Ruritanian turrets and spires. It sits in the shadows of Lake Lochnagar like a little bit of Bavaria dropped into a Scottish forest amid puffs of cloud – Planet Zog, one of Prince Charles's aides calls it.

With the immediate royal family all in residence, the Queen's most private estate is the world's poshest commune. 'I wanted to get it right,' Diana told Andrew Morton.[18] For a first time visitor a weekend sojourn is a social minefield. It is not the easiest prospect on the way to a draughty bathroom to be suddenly confronted by the looming figure of Prince Philip in a swinging kilt. As the Prime Minister's wife, Cherie Blair found joining her husband's compulsory visits 'too unbelievably horrible for words'. She suffered an allergic reaction to the fur and feathers of the stuffed animals and hunting trophies which adorned Balmoral's walls and was deeply turned off by how when a corgi let out a yap a footman escorted it out to repair the problem with a pooper scoop. She also blew it immediately with the dour Princess Anne by suggesting that the Princess Royal call her 'Cherie'. 'Actually, let's not go that way. Let's stick to Mrs Blair, shall we?' Anne replied. The Queen, for her part, was said to be underwhelmed by Mrs Blair's 'hectoring legalistic tone' and her stout refusal to curtsy, a requirement of every guest.[19]

Everything about the Balmoral routine, from the bone-rattling blast of bagpipes for the 6 a.m. reveille to the choice of picnic sites, stays the same year after year. Castle life when the Queen is in residence is governed by the punctual observation of form, to which everyone must adhere. On Sabrina Guinness's ill-fated visit to see Prince Charles she had irritated the Queen almost immediately by sitting in Queen Victoria's sacred chair.[20] Regardless of age, there is a strictly enforced dress code, which outlaws trousers for women. (The Queen Mother was said to be 'mortified' when Cherie Blair wore a trouser suit to lunch on her first visit.) Guests are expected to perform a routine of constant costume changes, from informal breakfast attire to sporting clothing for going out with the guns to another change into afternoon wear for tea – and then it all comes off again in favour of something long and dressy for dinner. (It was even more high-intensity at Birkhall with the Queen Mother, who insisted on full-blown evening attire with jewellery, even when the company was just a few old friends.)

The irony is that this is the royal family at their most relaxed. This is the most uninhibitedly carefree they ever get to be. At least there are no official engagements, except church at Craithie on Sunday morning and such obligatory 'heavy furniture' dinner guests as the head of the Church of Scotland.

For Diana, Balmoral might have been daunting – 'I was shitting bricks!'[21] she told Morton – but she did have the precious gift of proximity to Charles. When he had an impulse to go for a walk and telephoned her room, she could join him in a jiffy. She could show her appreciation of the royal pantry by tucking into the sausage rolls and scones spread out every day for picnic teas and savouring the steaks emerging from a specially designed trailer to be grilled by Prince Philip himself, with the Queen bustling in attendance. Diana could show off her domestic skills and team spirit by pitching in to clean up and help with the dishes after the barbecues set up every day at a different keeper's croft. More important for Diana than the dishes was to join Charles on the banks of the River Dee for salmon fishing *à deux*. Casting a line in fly fishing is an art, of course, selecting the right fly is another, positioning it yet another. Diana sat for hours on the riverbank as if her life depended on penetrating these mysteries, admiring the nifty demonstrations from her patient tutor Prince Charles. Well hooked, sir!

It was a big plus to Diana's cause that she appeared so happy tramping over sodden moors. The Queen found her charming and appropriate. Without fresh-air credentials, Diana would have never got past round one with any of them – the Prince of Wales, his parents, or his ever-present circle of friends, that possessive clique of tweedy squirearchs and landed middle-aged traditionalists who'd known each other for ever. She would get to know them all, and all too well, in the months ahead: ski champion Charles Palmer-Tomkinson and his garrulous Anglo-Argentine wife Patti; Nicholas 'Fatty' Soames, grandson of Winston Churchill and the Prince's former equerry, who divides the people he dislikes into 'crashers' (crashing bores) and 'tossers' (those who practise self-abuse); the thumping snobs the van Cutsems, Hugh and his wife Emilie; Lord and Lady Tryon (he a 'crasher', and we know why she's there); Lord and Lady Tollemache, (endless plant talk from the wife, a landscape gardener); and always, always, the Parker Bowleses. All very 'grown up' (i.e. old) compared to Diana's friends. 'I was the youngest by a long way,' she said.[22] (Big yawn when it comes to that!) Charles seemed to ask their opinion about everything, unfortunately, so they had to be charmed.

She definitely pulled it off with one set of her fellow guests that weekend, the Palmer-Tomkinsons. 'We went stalking together,' remembered Patti. 'We got hot, we got tired, she fell into a bog, she got covered in mud, laughed her head off – she was a sort of wonderful English schoolgirl who was game for anything, naturally young but sweet and clearly determined and enthusiastic about him, very much wanted him.'[23]

It's an index of how crazy she was about Charles that Diana displayed such authentic-seeming devotion to huntin', shootin' and fishin' – prerequisites even to be a serious candidate for a mistress. Ask Dale Tryon, Charles's Aussie good-time girl. She knew all about standing for hours at a time up to her thighs in freezing water holding a fishing rod. Ditto Camilla with her hunting teas and designer dog-hairs. A guest at Balmoral remembers that even a sophisticate like Lord Snowdon felt it necessary to take himself off to shooting school before risking a weekend at Balmoral with Princess Margaret. Prince Philip, said the guest, was always asking Snowdon to go fishing. 'I am no good at it, sir,' Snowdon said, to which Philip replied, 'Don't be ridiculous. Go and practise on the lawn.' So he went and sat in the middle of the lawn at Balmoral and started casting on the greensward. Prince Charles came out and asked him with a puzzled look, 'Why are you casting on the lawn? You should do it in the cinema.'[24]

The adjectives every witness applied enthusiastically to Diana in these early days of her romance with Charles were 'uncomplicated', 'jolly', and 'easy-going'. The Queen's guests were as charmed as Prince Charles. Lord Charteris, Elizabeth II's former private secretary, was intrigued by what he saw as Diana's 'wonderful instincts' that week at Balmoral. 'She played the Prince perfectly. She kept herself in his line of vision as much as possible. Always looking pretty and being decorous. Always being jolly. She was canny by nature and understood that few men can resist a pretty girl who openly adores them, especially one who has a ready laugh and a witty retort . . . [and was] available and sent out very clear messages of worship. The Prince was flattered and enchanted.'[25]

What happened later to the Diana of these courtship months? Almost from the moment she got married, that Diana was missing in action. The cheerfulness, resilience and humour she showed amid pressures that had done in a regiment of girls before her – it couldn't all have been fake (except perhaps the needlepoint she was sighted working on diligently at the Queen Mother's house when she revisited Balmoral in October). Another of Charles's friends, Lady Romsey, the wife of Mountbatten's grandson, Norton Romsey, believed that Diana had fallen for the idea rather than the man. She recalled a conversation when Diana used the phrase 'If I am lucky enough to be the Princess of Wales'.[26] Palmer-Tomkinson, however, concurred with his wife about Diana and Charles. 'They got along like a house on fire,' he enthused. 'They were passionate about each other. They shared the same zany sense of humour. They had similar temperaments. They loved country life.' But Palmer-Tomkinson also instantly exhibited the revisionism that was to mark the attitudes of all of Charles's friends to Diana. 'Within weeks he was asking if we thought he ought to marry her,' Palmer-Tomkinson continued. 'We were all horror-stricken. They barely knew each other. It was obvious they had nothing in common.'[27] Huh? Were they not a moment ago two peas in a pod? Did Palmer-Tomkinson reverse himself in one breath because he knew a parallel truth? Yes, she was jolly, perfect, sweet, etc., but the friends were no doubt just as aware of other factors that might make the match with one so young less than advisable – especially his relationship with another guest at Balmoral that weekend, Mrs Andrew Parker Bowles.

Soon, though, the opinion of the friends was not as important as it might have been. There was another, stronger power base out there to be cultivated, if only the jolly country girl could learn how: the press.

This was treacherous ground. Premature exposure, and certainly any kind of publicity-seeking, would be worse than casting the wrong fly. On the other hand, people who show marked hostility to the ravenous band of royal correspondents invited nasty retaliation – images of one in ungainly postures, sarcastic headlines (an art form in the tabloid press), humiliating harassment at airports. A trio of royal watchers alert for any new royal liaison were in wait that weekend for the photo ops afforded by the Braemar Games: Arthur Edwards, still working at the *Sun*; James Whitaker, royal correspondent for the *Daily Star*; and the beady-eyed photographer Ken Lennox, also with the *Star*.

In hopes of catching Prince Charles in dalliance with a new blonde, they staked out HRH's favourite fishing spot on the River Dee. They were quickly rewarded with a glimpse of a tall girl in fishing gear on the banks. But she spotted the ambush, dodged behind a tree without showing her face and performed an expert manoeuvre for a youthful novice: she pulled out a compact mirror, watched the trio watching her without letting them see her face and then bolted for the Prince's nearby car. All the lensman Lennox got were pictures of her rear. Whitaker was impressed by her cunning. 'This one,' he said, 'is clearly going to give us trouble.'[28] But who was 'this one'? Edwards pumped his sources at the Games. He heard the name 'Diana', and deduced that this might be the girl at the polo match wearing the necklace with the D. Edwards called his office and told them to get out his polo picture of Lady Diana Spencer at Cowdray. His rival Whitaker found the name himself by chatting up a police contact, but was ill-rewarded for his enterprise by the news desk, which buried his story on page seven of the *Star*. But the 'soaraway *Sun*' recognised that Edwards had a scoop, and played it on the front page. The hunt was on!

James Whitaker was lying in waiting for Diana at Aberdeen airport when she flew back south to become a part-time nanny and nursery teacher again and await a call from a prince with a silver slipper. Whitaker sidled up and asked her how she had enjoyed herself with her little trick with the mirror. She blushed deep red, as a country girl should.[29] On 8 September the *Sun* played the story with a 'screamer': 'HE'S IN LOVE AGAIN. LADY DI IS THE NEW GIRLFRIEND FOR CHARLES', thus earning itself the honour of being the first newspaper to refer to Diana as 'Lady Di'. Then she became 'Shy Di', in response to her trademark giggle and lowered head.

When she first started to appear in the tabloids, peeping out from under her wispy fringe, Diana struck most of us as a place-saver for Charles's next Hot Girl. One picture, published in the *Evening Standard* on 17 September 1980, changed that. John Minihan knocked on the door of the Young England Kindergarten early that morning and asked for just one snap of Diana and he'd go away. The head teacher, Kay Seth-Smith, took him at his word and urged her to do it, in the futile hope it would make the posse of photographers depart. The sugary image of the young blonde teacher holding one child in her arms and one by the hand could have made just a fetching conventional moment if Diana hadn't been gifted with the luck of being memorable. As she posed outside the kindergarten with her infant charges, the sun came out from behind its cloud and backlit her light cotton skirt, clearly revealing the full extent of her amazing legs. It was one of those charmed, decisive moments that make a picture iconic. Kay Seth-Smith remembered Diana's reaction when she saw the photograph later that afternoon splashed on page one of the *Standard* under the headline: 'THE GIRL THE ROYAL "BUZZ" IS ABOUT'. 'She took one look at it, went bright red, and put her hands up to her face in absolute horror.'[30] Seth-Smith was worried that her urgings to pose had blown it for Diana. The reverse was true, because the picture was so obviously, and beguilingly, a show of inexperience. The British public was instantly enchanted by this delightful mixture of feminine messages – modesty, sexuality and affection for children. It was a story England, in its shabby complaining mood, wanted and needed. It didn't do Diana any harm with Prince Charles, either. 'I knew your legs were good, but I didn't realise they were *that* spectacular,' he commented.[31]

After the kindergarten shot, everyone wanted to know more about the boarding-school blonde from the shires with the short buffed nails, the low-heeled court shoes, and the shirt with a frill whom destiny seemed to be guiding towards a royal marriage. James Whitaker, on stake-out duty for the *Daily Star* outside her apartment block at Coleherne Court, asked the mystery girl, 'Is it true that you are in love with Prince Charles?'[32] Diana blushed, said nothing, and drove away as fast as she could in her mother's Renault.

Was all this reticence for real? The press went into overdrive to find a former boyfriend. Reporters vacuumed every inch of Diana's small life for indiscretion. All they got was a few chivalrous comments from some disappointed suitors. Wine merchant Simon Berry offered this shocker: 'Many tried to win her, sending her flowers and begging for a date, but she always politely declined.'[33] A youthful gardening writer named, appropriately enough, the Honourable George Plumptre, had bland memories of dinners after the theatre. The eligible deer farmer Adam Russell who came down from Oxford with a degree in languages in 1979 gave a maudlin confession about always having hoped for more than just friendship from Diana.

If Diana had had a girlish affair, there was a rhythm to the growing conspiracy of certainty that made any former paramours close ranks. *Tatler*'s reporter noted that when the name of James Boughey, an Old Etonian army lieutenant, was mentioned in an interview with her flatmates, an 'awkward hush' fell over Coleherne Court. 'I love a man in a uniform,' Diana used to say later, after she'd loosened up.[34] At first the newspapers had difficulty constructing a profile of Diana because she was such an upper-class archetype. The sheer uneventfulness of her world and the time-warp harmlessness of her circle of friends were a source of head-scratching to the sensation-seeking press. In the age of Sid Vicious and the fashion iconoclast Vivienne Westwood, every detail of Diana's sheltered life seemed like the sudden discovery of a secret society. Lady Di spent two nights a week at home with her flatmates, listening to records by groups like the Police! The naughtiest film she'd ever seen was *La Cage aux Folles*! She preferred hot vegetables to the fashionable *insalata di radicchio*!

At *Tatler* we were already wondering how someone as unworldly as Diana would fit into the more sophisticated world of Prince Charles. Coleherne Court dinner-party conversation concentrated on Benetton sale bargains, which friend was working at the fashionable boutique Parrots, and who'd just had their bicycle stolen. Chez Charles, the weighty topics were architecture, conservation, historical biography and the like, leavened by horse talk. 'Lady Diana will invariably find herself seated on the right of the chairman of the function, obliged to show, or at least feign, familiarity with its fund-raising activities, operations abroad or the strictures of international high finance,' *Tatler*'s commentator, Nicholas Coleridge, editorialised. 'How will she react to the tumbling French Bourse after the election of Mitterrand when the topic looms over the egg mayonnaise? How will she cope with excited discussion about the justness of the Suss Law when it breaks over the lamb cutlets?'[35]

Such pedantic concerns didn't bother the popular press. The pack now trailing the intriguingly uncontroversial Lady Di made her apparent shyness the story. In reality, Ken Lennox would recall, 'she's never been shy and she's never been coy and she's never been silly . . . The shy Di is a myth. That came about because she would put her head down and her hair would fall over her face and she would glance up every now and then to see where we were . . . But when the cameras would go down, she would chat, laugh, look at *Private Eye*, see what they're saying about her, sit in the cars, joke about how she'd lost us the day before and then she would talk about serious things . . . things that we'd got wrong and she didn't ever tell us a lie. If we'd ask her about something – were you at such-and-such, she would say, "No, I wasn't, Mr Whitaker, or I wasn't, Mr Lennox."'[36]

One by one, the hack pack fell in love with her. In James Whitaker's eyes she was 'delightful . . . immensely flirtatious. And she did definitely seduce the media that were with her. I took a decision, and I think some of my colleagues did, that . . . she was a pretty suitable person to become the Princess of Wales.'[37] The Diana charm was just as effective on women. The *Sun*'s junior royal watcher, Judy Wade said: 'We all fell in love with her. We really got behind Diana and pushed her towards him. I am absolutely convinced that we the media forced Charles to marry her.'[38] Feature writers were so eager to make Diana the perfect fit for

Charles that they ignored the ominous auguries of the gap in age, culture and education, and played down the searing drama of the Spencer marital rift in her background. In a *Sunday Mirror* article, 'Kissing Cousins and the Young Lady Di Calls the Queen her "Aunt Lillibet"',[39] royal correspondent Audrey Whiting trilled, 'For the heir to the throne, she really was the sort of kid sister he always yearned for – happy, jolly and full of fun, all the things Princess Anne never was when she was young,' adding, 'although the Spencer children were deeply distressed at the departure of their mother from Park House, they do not appear to have been unduly scarred.'[40]

What was remarkable about Diana was that she already seemed to have a cool understanding of the peril as well as the power of media attention. She could count off all the mistakes her sister Sarah had made in her own failed romance with the Prince – too eager, too available, too recklessly indiscreet. ('Sarah got frightfully excited about the whole thing,' she told Andrew Morton.)[41] Yet she also knew that boring stock denials would not fly, either. She was a natural at giving the press what they wanted. Diana's ease with the cameras and the press did not derive only from her father's obsession with amateur photography. She was herself an avid consumer of tabloid news. These were not just faceless snappers and hacks outside her flat. These were people whose stories she read. She even knew where they lived. The *Daily Express*'s Steve Wood had a flat round the corner from Coleherne Court and he was startled to see Diana outside his front door once, checking out his address.[42]

Diana may have grown up surrounded by treasures that most people see only in museums, but she was a tabloid girl in a tiara. She understood the popular press because she was their audience. She 'got' that audience's need to be fed with pictures and dreams, its requirement of novelty and surprise, its yearning to find a newcomer and crown her Queen. Forget *The Times* and the *Daily Telegraph*, the traditional house organs of the Establishment. Her favourite breakfast fare was the emotion-charged *Daily Mail*, with Dempster's sizzling daily reportage on all the people who touched the perimeters of her circle and that of her racy elder sister Sarah. When not engrossed in romantic fiction or TV soap operas, Diana was constructing a world view shaped by the narratives of the tabloids. Every day she inhaled their glorious mix of sentimentality, sensation, gossip and moralising, and she knew exactly how to hold their interest.

'She invited me up for a cup of cocoa one night as they were going to bed and she knew I was bedding down in the car outside,' Ken Lennox said. 'And I got up to the landing of the flat, the girls were standing in their jim-jams. And I just laughed, and she said, "Are you laughing 'cos it's funny seeing us all in our pyjamas?" And I said, "No, I thought you were gonna invite me in." She said, "What, and have a detailed description of the flat in the paper tomorrow? Do you think I'm stupid, Mr Lennox?"'[43]

It was a significant question from the girl who'd always maintained she was 'thick as a plank'.[44] Diana had at last found something that she was good at: media relations. Her gift first intrigued, then profoundly irritated Prince Charles's friends. They were busy weighing her up and rushing to patronise her, judging her terribly sweet or awfully shy, telling each other 'I do hope she will be able to cope', only to pick up the paper the next day and find the press more in love with her than ever.

She got a kick out of beating the newsies at their own game. The *Daily Express*'s Ashley Walton says that in the early days of the courtship she always gave him the slip. 'She was an extremely good and fast driver. Whenever I lost her I would have to return to Coleherne Court and sit and wait. When she came back you always got a little wave and a grin that said, "Catch me if you can."' Walton and *Express* photographer Steve Wood sat for hours in a heavy snowfall at Sandringham on one occasion, hoping to get the money shot – Diana with the Prince himself. 'She either had a great sense of humour and had been watching us, or perhaps it was just a coincidence, but just at the moment we both decided to take some much needed relief she suddenly popped up in her little VW. There we both were in full view, peeing on the Queen's land. She braked, stared and burst into hysterics. We could hear her laughter through the closed windows. She sped off with a wave and we scrambled in pursuit but lost her at the next crossroads.' When Diana saw the trespasser next at an official press function she mouthed at him mischievously, 'Sandringham.'[45]

Prince Charles, meanwhile, was impressed with the way his new girlfriend was acquitting herself with the enemy, which he saw as the press (and she saw as his friends). Diana had noticed a discomfiting subtext at the Parker Bowles house when they went to stay there – too often for her taste. 'I'd been staying at Bolehyde . . . an awful lot,' Diana told Andrew Morton. 'And I couldn't understand why [Camilla] kept saying to me, "Don't push him into doing this, don't do that." She knew so much about what he was doing privately . . . I couldn't understand it. Eventually I worked it all out.'[46]

Charles continued to offer her to his circle for their approval and give Diana a *tour d'horizon* of their future life. He took her to see Highgrove House, the 347-acre estate in Gloucestershire which he had just bought with £750,000 of his Duchy of Cornwall funds. 'The Royal Family are rather short of residences,' a Duchy of Cornwall Martian said when explaining the purchase to the press. 'And the Prince only has a set of rooms at Buckingham Palace and Windsor Castle that he can use.'[47] Highgrove not only saved Charles from the fate of sharing one of the royal family's four palaces, it was also near the Beaufort, his favourite hunt, his sister Princess Anne, who lived at nearby Gatcombe Park, and a forty-five-minute drive from the house of Camilla Parker Bowles. Sometimes the Prince invited Prince Andrew and his best friend Nicholas Soames to come with him and Diana for the weekend, and Diana stayed on at the house after Andrew and Soames left.

When they visited Highgrove, Diana used to wander round the empty, undecorated 'Georgian Gem' alone while she waited for Charles to return from hunting – a hologram, you might say, of later married life. Highgrove would become the base for everything she most disliked: horses, Camilla and 'heavy furniture' neighbours. Privately, the girl who'd spent her adolescence amid the splendours of Althorp wasn't much impressed by the nine-bedroom house in its raw state. Nor was she anxious to be drawn into doing it up, something the Prince rather cheekily assumed she'd love to do. His valet Stephen Barry recalls them having tea together and later a light supper on a card table in the sitting room before driving back to London in a shooting brake with a policeman in the back. A member of Charles's staff, Sonia Palmer, hints that it was more than tea. '[Stephen] used to say Diana always left with a glow and her hair freshly brushed. Why did she need to brush her hair if they were discoursing on philosophy?'[48]

That tired old virgin thing again: the investment in that aspect of the fairy story had become so intense that it developed a life of its own. On the night of 4 November 1980, Diana attended Princess Margaret's fiftieth birthday party at the Ritz in Piccadilly. What she did or did not do on two nights afterwards sent the Palace machine into near-hysterical overdrive.

The stimulus was a splash in the *Sunday Mirror* for 16 November 1980: 'ROYAL LOVE TRAIN' by Wensley Clarkson and Jim Newman.[49] They alleged that on 5 and 6 November, the nineteen-year-old Diana had two secret, late-night meetings with Prince Charles on the royal train as it stood in secluded sidings in Wiltshire, when Charles had been visiting the Duchy of Cornwall estates in Somerset. The Prince was noisily livid about the report, fuming to his valet, 'It's rubbish and it has put Lady Diana in such a bad light.'[50]

The royal train, nine carriages that can be individually joined up depending on how many are travelling, has always been an especially convenient – and sexy – place for royal assignations. Adorned with the claret livery of the royal household, each carriage has individual saloons on a private corridor with only one other compartment, that of the close-lipped police protection officer. The Queen's carriage is as grand and as comfortable inside as any room at the Palace – it has its own plushly appointed bedroom, bathroom and sitting room. The Duke of Edinburgh's features Scottish landscapes by Roy Penny and Victorian prints of earlier rail journeys. A boon as far as Charles was concerned was the train's freedom to stop and pick up a guest at any remote country siding he wished.

According to the Sunday Mirror, on the nights of 5 and 6 November, the royal train stopped at a well-established resting place near the village of Holt, on a track running next to a narrow country lane called Station Road. 'Under cover of darkness', said the Sunday Mirror, Diana arrived at a checkpoint manned by plain-clothes police near the end of the lane. She was ushered through. A detective accompanied her in her blue Renault car down to the deserted siding, then escorted her aboard the train. It went a short distance up the line to Bradford-on-Avon, near the village of Staverton. 'Then,' as the Mirror coyly put it, 'there followed hours alone together for the couple whose friendship has captured the country's imagination.'[51]

Diana later emerged from the coach, reported the paper, and drove back to London. These activities were reprised the next night. While Charles entertained Duchy tenants in Bath, the Sunday Mirror had Diana driving west again to the country home of his confidante Camilla Parker Bowles, where Diana got the phone call that sent her dashing back again to the same railway siding. Then, for the second evening running, she stayed with the Prince until the early hours. Reported the Mirror: 'A member of Mrs Parker Bowles's staff said yesterday, "Lady Diana stayed for a few hours and then went out very late. But I dare not say anything more about this." Now the area is buzzing with talk of Charles's midnight meetings.'[52]

Immediately after publication, Prince Charles's private secretary Edward Adeane asked Michael Shea, the Queen's press secretary, to fire up a protest letter to the Sunday Mirror's editor, Robert Edwards.

The only guests on board the train on either night, said Shea, were the Secretary of the Duchy of Cornwall, his successor and the local Duchy Land Steward. 'Grave exception has been taken to the implications of your story and I am writing to ask you for an apology which we would require to be printed in your newspaper in a prominent position, at the earliest possible opportunity.' The letter was marked 'Not for Publication'.[53]

The timing of the *Sunday Mirror* story was certainly sensitive. Diana had just spent a telling four-day weekend at Sandringham for a family-only thirty-second birthday party for Prince Charles. She had had to leave early after the press harassment ruined the Duke of Edinburgh's shooting. A plan was hatched to spirit her away. Prince Charles's Range Rover went one way as a decoy, while the Prince himself took Diana in a Land Rover in the other direction to meet up with a police car that took her to London. After such a meaningful endorsement as the family birthday party, the *Sunday Mirror* story could no longer be dismissed as the usual tale of princely sexual capers. This was the future Queen they were suggesting was being smuggled in and out of the royal train for a naughty romp – and if it wasn't, a very young girl's reputation had been severely compromised.

Robert Edwards was nonetheless surprised at the strong reaction from the Palace. He believed he had an impeccable source, and he did: it was one of the local policemen assigned to watch the royal train for security risks when it stopped at the siding. Edwards accordingly answered Michael Shea, 'Certainly we never knowingly print anything that is untrue . . . In view of your denial of our report, I am having further enquiries made and will get in touch with you shortly. In the meantime I note with some surprise that "grave exception" has been taken over the report. Certainly we did not intend to imply that anything improper had occurred, nor do we consider that the report carried any such implication.'[54] After further questioning of his source, Edwards could find no holes in the story. He refused to publish an apology. Instead he offered to print the correspondence (and get himself another headline for the *Sunday Mirror*) – a solution agreed on by the Palace. The splashed correspondence under the headline 'PRINCE CHARLES AND LADY DIANA' succeeded in killing any serious follow-up without forcing Edwards to eat humble pie.

Diana herself seemed unusually upset by the royal train story. 'I was *sooo* shocked,' she asserted to *Daily Mail* reporter Danae Brook on 24 November, after the storm had passed. 'I *simply* couldn't believe it. I've never been anywhere near the train, let alone in the middle of the night. Even though they rang me up first, they printed it anyway. Afterwards they rang up to apologise but that doesn't change people's minds about what they think when they read a story like that.'[55]

Six years later, when Edwards was awarded a CBE in the New Year's Honours list – he believes the train story cost him the expected knighthood – a card arrived from the veteran political insider Lord Wyatt of Weeford. It bore a cryptic message: 'I think you'll find it was Camilla.'[56] Ever since, Wyatt's nod has been the received wisdom of the event. The train, after all, was parked in a siding only about twenty-one miles from Camilla's house. Over the long years of her affair with Charles such resourceful trysts were her forte.

But for a number of reasons I have become convinced it was indeed Diana on the royal train. If it was Camilla, why didn't Diana include the incident in her remorseless narrative of marital torture and betrayal in any of her confessional gut-spilling for Andrew Morton or Martin Bashir? Her later discovery, before the wedding, that Charles was planning to give Camilla a bracelet, became an operatic incident in her long list of unforgivable hurts. For a girl on the verge of engagement it would have been devastating to find that her boyfriend was secretly two-timing her on the train while she was tucked up in bed at Coleherne Court. 'I had some supper and watched television before going to bed early. I had been at Princess Margaret's party at the Ritz the night before and I was feeling very frail and hungover,' was another curious alibi that Diana – who never drank – offered to James Whitaker on 27 November. 'I am not a liar. I have never been on that train. I have never even been near it.'[57]

The police source for the Mirror story, however, could not have been mistaken in his identification of Diana. In the unlikely event that he had confused the light-voiced nineteen-year-old girl of unusual height with a squat woman in her thirties who spoke in a distinctive baritone, the number of the car licence plate carrying Prince Charles's guest that night had been faxed through to him in advance. The Mirror reporter cross-checked it and discovered the at first alarming detail that it did not belong to Diana. But it did belong to her mother, Frances Shand Kydd, whose blue Renault Diana was in the habit of borrowing.[58]

Diana's stopover at the Parker Bowles house checked out, too. With the old reporter's trick of cold-calling the house to ask if Lady Diana Spencer was 'still' staying there, the Sunday Mirror's Wensley Clarkson confirmed Diana's presence at Bolehyde Manor on the date of the love-train rendezvous, just as the newspaper had said. 'Oh, no,' the maid, or whoever it was who answered the Parker Bowles phone, innocently replied. 'She's not here any more. She was here last week' – (the time of the train incident)[59] – thus illuminating the interesting *Liaisons Dangereuses* role Camilla was now playing, helping to promote Diana with Charles even as she subtly undermined her. (Surely, even one as determined as Camilla would not have sneaked off to see Charles while his soon-to-be fiancée was a guest in her house?)

One might ask why a police officer would leak the royal train info to the *Mirror*'s Wiltshire stringer in the first place. It was for an obscurely amusing reason. In those days, trains, even royal trains, did not have sanitary tanks. This proud member of Wiltshire's police force was outraged when he learned that if the royal train stopped in a siding overnight, two British Rail employees were required to stand by with mops to clean up any steaming emissions on to the tracks from the royal toilet chute. He decided to retaliate on their behalf by bestowing a burst of unwelcome publicity.[60]

It seems clear now that Diana, for reasons of panicked self-protection, colluded with the Palace machine to protect the anachronistic façade of virginity right up to the altar. She may or may not have been *intacta* for the Prince at the outset, but was it really necessary for her chastity to be wrapped in clingfilm to the bitter end? Diana clearly knew somehow that her assignations were about to be revealed by the *Sunday Mirror*, which took ten days to publish its story, and someone on the Queen's staff seems to have known, too – probably via a tip from an insider on the Prince's side. Without foreknowledge of the impending Love Train story, how can we explain the strange outburst of Diana's uncle Lord Fermoy on 10 November, five days after the train made its stop and six days *before* the *Mirror* published its scoop? 'Purity seems to be at a premium when it comes to discussing a possible bride for Prince Charles at the moment,' Fermoy told a startled James Whitaker in an interview for the *Daily Star*. 'And after one or two of his most recent girlfriends I am not surprised. Diana, I can assure you, has never had a lover.'[61]

Huh? Since when have uncles known such details of their nieces' private lives – and felt the need to offer them unsolicited to tabloid reporters? And why else would Diana go into such laborious detail about the whereabouts of her car on the crucial nights, and tell Danae Brook of the *Mail* on 24 November, 'They [the *Sunday Mirror*] rang up to apologise,' when both Robert Edwards and Wensley Clarkson tell me they most certainly did nothing of the kind?[62]

The compulsion to defend Diana's maidenhood was most likely impelled by the politics of privilege. The royal train was paid for by the British taxpayer through the Civil List. Politically, therefore, as a venue for assignations it was a potential train wreck. The Prince knew that the last thing the Palace needed on the eve of a royal engagement was a row about the abuse of publicly funded royal luxuries. Whoever was on the train, the Queen would have been livid with Charles for jeopardising a fragile perk. 'The Palace lied outrageously,'[63] a still annoyed Clarkson said, but so did Diana. In a sense the Love Train incident was the moment she first became a royal, supported in muffling the truth by a network of polished operators who had agendas of their own. Where she was not yet royal was in still remaining outside the physical protection of Palace walls.

Danae Brook, who was a resident of Coleherne Court, witnessed first-hand the media frenzy building around Diana. In the beginning Diana found it 'quite funny', but what became known as the Siege of Coleherne Court then began to frighten her. She and her neighbours, Stephen Vizinczey, the bestselling author of In Praise of Older Women, and the actor Corin Redgrave and his wife Deirdre, were 'completely horrified' at how unprotected she was. 'My sons got to know Diana as they were coming home from school at about the same time as she was returning from the nursery,' says Brook. 'She used to chat to them in the sweet shop at the end of the road. The media thing became quite insane with reporters pressing the bell at night saying they had an appointment with Diana. They would wait for her to get into her car and drive away, then they would cut in and drive in front of her. It was terribly dangerous and frightening.' Brook saw her on the stairs, very flushed and in tears about some incident outside. 'She thought they were taking an interest in her because she didn't have a wild past. It was like talking to a fourteen-year-old. She was a real ingénue in those days, very unsophisticated. She would blush when she talked to you. But she had these mesmerising eyes, almost violet blue.' Brook got used to hearing the same music playing over and over again from Diana's record player. It was the Three Degrees, the star turn at the thirtieth birthday of Prince Charles.[64]

The press became so wearing by December that Frances Shand Kydd took up the cudgels and wrote a letter to the editor of The Times, protesting about the 'lies and harassment' that Diana had endured since the romance became public and throwing in a gratuitous pounding of the Royal Love Train story: 'She [her daughter] has also denied, with justifiable indignation, her reported presence on the Royal Train.'[65] Diana – undoubtedly complicit in her mother's letter to *The Times* – kept her sweetheart status with the press by pretending to James Whitaker that she disagreed with what her mother had written. 'There are times when people upset me,' she said artfully, 'but that's rare, and I like to think I get on very well with most of you. The only thing that really annoys me is when my children [at the kindergarten] get frightened by things like flashguns.'[66] Even under so much pressure, she still had perfect pitch. Diana had now entered the zone of spin and would have to live there till the end of her life. But she was playing a dangerous game with the press. She had come to think she, and not they, would control the outcome.

## Chapter 8

# Whatever in Love Means

'I've got something to ask you.'
                    – Charles to Diana, February 1981

For a man whose spiritual age has always been somewhere north of sixty-five, it was difficult to see the smitten, romantic teenager, Diana Spencer, as a future wife, let alone the future Queen of England. Was Prince Charles ever in love with Diana? 'She is exquisitely pretty, a perfect poppet . . . but she is a child,' he told a woman friend.[1]

Steve Kroft of CBS's 60 *Minutes* told me that in his pre-interview research for a 2005 segment on Prince Charles he found that every American woman he spoke to unfailingly raised the response Prince Charles made to the question 'Are you in love?' on the day of his engagement to Diana as a reason why they had negative feelings about him.

The famous exchange on 24 February 1981 began, 'I am positively delighted and frankly amazed that Diana is prepared to take me on.' When pressed by the BBC interviewer, 'And in love?' Diana answered immediately, 'Of course,' with a girlish giggle. Then Charles said it: 'Whatever "in love" means.'[2]

It was a killing caveat that would haunt his life. At the time, however, this remark was not used in any of the newspaper reports of the broadcast. In a moment of collective amnesia, the print press literally erased 'whatever "in love" means' from their accounts. No one, it seems, wanted to break the spell. Three thousand people had showed up at Buckingham Palace for the Changing of the Guard hoping to hear the official confirmation of the engagement and, when it came through, the euphoria was captured by a band of the Coldstream Guards striking up 'Congratulations'. On the videotapes with voice coach Peter Settelen in 1991–2 Diana claims that she was 'absolutely traumatised' when her intended came out with the line but 'didn't dare' to ask him what he meant. Ever since, the words have served to symbolise the cold heartlessness of Diana's royal groom.

But was Charles's damning answer really a window on a chilly soul – or just that old reflexive upper-class instinct that quickly moves to negate any show of messy feeling? Self-deprecation is Charles's mode of expression, and it's never served him well as a means of mass communication. It could also have been a sudden burst of truth, from a painfully sincere man, which involuntarily broke through the fairy story and demanded to be heard; the Prince had briefly got confused and thought he was in a different movie, *cinéma-vérité* instead of Hollywood romance. As he said to the BBC reporter, after he made the remark, 'Put your own interpretation on it.'[3]

Ten years later his authorised biographer Jonathan Dimbleby stated, 'The Prince made it clear he was never in love with Diana and felt he had to propose after he came under pressure from his father' – a revelation that was duly splashed on the front page of the *News of the World* as: 'I WAS NEVER IN LOVE WITH DIANA'. The headline stung the Princess so much she prodded the *News of the World* the next day to release the photos of Charles and herself cavorting ecstatically on the beach in the Bahamas on their second honeymoon in 1982 in Eleuthera (The *News of the World* obliged, publishing the pictures under the headline 'THE LIAR KING'.) The interviews for Dimbleby's book were conducted in the bitter aftertaste of a broken marriage – and there is no more reason to trust that the feelings the Prince expressed were true than we should believe each of the miseries Diana recounted to Andrew Morton. All these later statements must be seen as the early salvoes of their divorce wars.

In 2005 Charles's marriage to Camilla cemented the received wisdom that his ties with her were always too deep to break. Their mellow romance became the new fairy story. But the Prince had shown that he was capable of at least infatuation with other women than Camilla. He was nuts about Anna Wallace; he loved being with Dale Tryon; and there is no doubt he was utterly charmed and beguiled by Diana in the early days of their relationship. Three days before the wedding, Diana was seen horsing around in the dining room at Broadlands, having grabbed Prince Charles's army cap after a visit to Tidworth Barracks. She whirled around with it on her head as Charles roared with laughter.[4] Mark Bolland, Prince Charles's communications guru in the nineties, has no doubt. 'He did love her in my view.'[5] A former member of the Waleses' staff remembers a romantic moment the Prince conjured up for Diana for their first wedding anniversary at an uninhabited royal residence. 'He took over Queen Charlotte's house in Kew and I sent over a cold dinner. They took the candelabras from Kensington Palace and had cold lobster.'[6] Years after her death, Charles would occasionally betray a lingering respect and affection. Once when the Prince was raking leaves at Highgrove, Bolland remarked on a sweater he was wearing and Charles said, 'Diana bought it for me. She had terribly good taste about those kind of things.' At an event in St James's Palace for Children of Courage, Charles scored a hit with his easy unpatronising manner with the children. 'Diana told me how to do that,' said Charles. 'She said you have to crouch down to their level and talk to them.' Even though Bolland owed his allegiance to Camilla, he thought on such occasions, 'Why the hell didn't you two sort it out?'[7] Three days after the funeral, a confidante of the Queen Mother, much trusted by Prince Charles, was moved by the sad sincerity of his admission, 'You know, whatever they say, when we got married we were very much in love.'[8]

So why was the courtship such a fraught affair? It was a collision of romantic expectations and inflexible certainties. Charles had waited so long to get married he had become the toxic bachelor, impaled on a life of public duty and private indulgence that left little room for anyone who hoped to share it. He was uncertain about Diana, yes, but perhaps more uncertain about marriage itself and how his bride would cope with 'La grand plonge', as he liked to call it in his flowery way.[9] A former aide later opined, 'What Diana could not understand was that duty rules his life. You can be sensitive but still come back to feeling that you will always do the thing that your mother has always done before you. It's a very German family, not open to embracing; Diana yearned for that.'[10]

On his tour of India, the press hounded Charles for a commitment, but they were asking him to make clear feelings that were not yet clear even to himself – something calculated to panic any bachelor. 'I can't live with a woman for two years, like you possibly could,' he ruminated aloud in an off-the-record aside. 'I've got to get it right first time because if I don't, you'll be the first to criticise me.' 'And then,' said Arthur Edwards of the *Sun*, 'we thought, "This is *the one*."'[11]

The One was furious that Charles did not call from India. Sarah Spencer, suspicious that her little sister had pulled off the romantic coup she had believed would be hers, wound Diana up further by probing the course of the romance. Diana confided to Mary Robertson, for whom she was still nannying two days a week, 'I will simply die if this doesn't work out. I won't be able to show my face.'[12] Robertson noted that since she and Charles had few meetings and almost none of them were private, her infatuation with him must have been based on her romantic image of him combined with his lofty position. But there was so much more to Diana's longing than personal ambition: there was a checklist of expectations – Daddy's pride in his little girl, Mummy's return from the cold as the mother of a royal bride, the Sarah contest settled, her rescue fantasies finally fulfilled, marriage to the Prince that could never, ever be broken. Everything she longed for, ironically, was everything Charles feared. The cornered Prince confided to a friend in a letter in January 1981, 'I do very much want to do the right thing for this country and for my family – but I am terrified sometimes of making a promise and then perhaps living to regret it.'[13]

The Prince was by now in such a tortured state of ambivalence it was several days after his return from an added-on trek in the Himalayas that he finally picked up the phone. Diana told Lady Colin Campbell, 'I was spitting with anger . . . I knew he'd call. So I took the receiver off the hook. And left it off for days. I did it to teach him a lesson. Let him chase me a little.'[14] Whitaker says that he was informed by the nattering royal valet, Stephen Barry, that on return from India, Prince Charles spent a couple of stolen days with Camilla.[15] Old habits die hard; there was no pressure there.

The Christmas of 1980 was a tense business with Diana en famille at Althorp and Charles with the royal family in Windsor. Diana's cousin, Robert Spencer, who came for the Althorp Christmas lunch, found her wandering the garden in tears. 'I rang up and spoke to Raine,' recalled Lady Bowker, who later became very close to the Princess. 'I said, "How is Diana?" Raine said, "She is very sad. She is in the park and she is walking alone, and she is crying because Charles is not proposing."'[16]

On New Year's Eve the most talked about girl in the world was without a date. At the turn of every year, Princess Margaret hosted a dinner at Kensington Palace for what she termed 'a few strays'. A novelist among the guests in 1980 was surprised to find Diana there, 'Why aren't you at Sandringham?' (The royals always moved there for New Year.) 'Haven't been asked,' Diana replied sullenly. She wore 'a coral-coloured organza dress of the dreariest kind,' the woman reports. She was 'quite large, and frightened, and very alarmed by all the paparazzi who pursued her non-stop. She could talk of nothing else. I felt a bit sorry for her. She was a gawky young English girl out of her depth.' The novelist's husband had Diana as a dinner partner and found the going hard – he forgot to bring up the subject of children, so they flogged on and on about skiing. In the spirit of her mood that night, Diana was 'killed' in an after-dinner game of Murder in the Dark.[17]

Mary Robertson sensed all was not well with the romance. She was packing up to go back to America, her husband having been relocated, and she wished she could stay longer to give Diana support. Since she had told her noble nanny they were leaving London, there had been a subtle shift in their relationship from employer to mother figure, something Diana sought again and again in her life. She wrote Robertson a typically thoughtful valedictory letter. 'I can never thank you enough, Mrs Robertson, for being so kind and understanding with the whole of Fleet Street following me. Never have I adored looking after a child [more] than Patrick and thank you for providing such happiness over the year for me.'[18] Diana showed how much the Robertson family meant to her when she learned Mary had fallen ill on the eve of the family's departure. At the height of the press pursuit of her, she rushed over to Belgravia to help Mary pack up Patrick's room and toys. 'We were just sobbing when we said goodbye,' recalled Robertson.[19]

The Diana frenzy was becoming seriously irritating to the Queen and Prince Philip, used to being left alone at appointed seasonal moments. The Duke of Edinburgh was so cranky about the invasive press attention, he wrote to his son advising him that Diana's 'honour' was at stake and that he should make up his mind forthwith. Any missive from Philip made Charles overreact. He carried the letter round in his pocket to show to family and friends as proof of his father's intolerable bullying, Patricia Mountbatten, who saw it, thought the letter actually very reasonable,[20] but family Rashomon meant that Charles understood only the pressure in his father's words and interpreted them as pushing him to marry Diana.[21] Prince George of Denmark, who was staying at Sandringham at the time, confirmed the thunderous parental mood. He says Prince Philip made Charles know that the press speculation couldn't drag on much longer . . . It was torture for all concerned.[22] Nicholas Soames, the Prince's closest friend, laid into the Duke's private secretary, Lord Rupert Nevill, for allowing the Duke to force the pace. 'Mismatch . . . doomed, utterly doomed,'[23] he groaned to Nevill. He thought Diana 'wasn't up to Charles's weight, to use a riding expression', said a friend of Soames. 'She was pretty childish and very unformed.'[24]

Charles ran away again, this time skiing for a week with his friends Patti and Charles Palmer-Tomkinson in their chalet in Klosters. He was still plagued with doubts about Diana, mostly on grounds of her youth. Mary Robertson believes that sexual incompatibility was one issue. 'Diana was probably clueless. She had been very sheltered and he showed his lack of interest.' One of his skiing companions on the Klosters trip was struck by Charles's visibly changing moods, also reflected in his letters. 'It is just a matter of taking an unusual plunge into some rather unknown circumstances that inevitably disturbs me but I expect it will be the right thing in the end,' Charles wrote wanly in his letter of 28 January 1981 to a friend.[25] There's an air of the wounded ensign picking up the regiment's fallen standard in his call to Diana from Klosters on 2 February 1981, 'I've got something to ask you.'[26]

Until Prince Charles publishes his diaries, the only account we have of the big moment when he popped the question comes from Diana via Andrew Morton, heavily scored for cello and bass. It has to be read accordingly. Diana arrives in a state of high excitement at Windsor Castle at 5 p.m. on 6 February, and the Prince sits her down in the nursery. He says, 'I've missed you so much.' Diana recalls there is 'nothing tactile' about the moment and she thinks it is a joke. ('I said, "yeah, ok,"' she told Morton). He tells her, 'You do realise you will one day be Queen,' and a voice inside her says 'You won't be Queen but you'll have a tough role.' She goes on to tell Morton, 'It was like a call of duty, really – to go and work with the people.'[27]

The whole scene reeks of rewrite. There is not a chance in hell that Diana was thinking about duty and working with the people in that emotionally charged moment. The truth is she was flat out over the moon when Charles asked her to marry him. 'She looked as happy as I have ever seen her look,' her brother Charles confirms when he saw her later at their mother's London apartment. 'It was genuine because nobody with insincere motives could look that happy. It wasn't the look of somebody who had won the jackpot but somebody who looked spiritually fulfilled as well.'[28]

'I love you so much,' she does admit to telling Charles, believing that 'he was very much in love with me', though she can't help recasting his expression as 'a sort of besotted look about him, but it wasn't the genuine sort'.[29] If she is accurate, it probably reflected

Charles's confused pleasure – if the nation, the press and his parents all wanted her so much then surely eventually he would want her too. The momentum of events never gave him a chance to locate whatever tenderness for her had awoken in him any more than it allowed her to discard her fantasy prince and appreciate the real man sitting on the chair next to her. By the time she talked to Morton in 1992, she did not like admitting that Charles's feelings eleven years before may have been just as real as hers, just different. The credible bit of her account is that when Diana got back to the Coleherne Court flat that night she sat on the bed to savour her triumph. '"Guess what?" They said, "He asked you. What did you say?" "Yes, please." Everybody screamed and howled and we went for a drive around London with our secret.'[30]

Only one member of Diana's circle expressed serious doubts – her mother. Before the news was announced, Frances Shand Kydd whisked Diana off to a remote hideout in Australia, to throw off the press and make her think more seriously about the momentous step. Contrary to what has been billed as her mother's untrammelled delight, a close friend of Frances[31] says she made every effort to dissuade Diana from marrying Charles, seeing the parallels between her daughter's relationship and her own disastrous first marriage to Johnnie Spencer – too young, too hasty, too incompatible, too great an age gap with too many responsibilities. 'Frances was against it because she felt it was a plot by her mother, Ruth Fermoy and as such unsound,' the friend said. Diana apparently responded, 'Mummy, you don't understand. I love him,' to which Frances replied, 'Love *him*, or love what he is.' And Diana said, 'What's the difference?'[32] After the match went wrong, her grandmother Lady Fermoy got busy denying the marriage had anything to do with her. The Queen's biographer Sarah Bradford has a 'courtier' saying that Lady Fermoy was 'always horrified at the prospect of an engagement', which smacks of backspin. 'Is it true?' Fermoy is alleged to have complained about the engagement. 'Nobody tells me anything,'[33] which sounds more true. It would have delighted Frances to exclude her mother from anything resembling pleasing news. Other family members were left out of the engagement loop too, in the excitement. On the tiny Caribbean island of Mustique where Princess Margaret was on holiday, Lord Glenconner was present when she got the telephone call and learned Lady Diana Spencer would become a member of the royal family. Princess Margaret's quickly adjusting response was, 'I know her. I like her. In fact I love her.'[34]

Diana's return from Australia was greeted by an extravagant bouquet to her from Charles. His horse, alas, had better instincts. On 20 February at Lambourn as Diana watched Charles exercising his eleven-year-old bay gelding Allibar – his first racehorse – the noble steed collapsed and died of a heart attack. Prince Charles cradled the dying Allibar's head in his arms. Diana wept copiously.[35] It was the first real emotional experience they shared, allowing Diana at last to do what she was so good at – offer comfort.

James Whitaker called Diana at home to talk to her about her Australian holiday and claims something about the tone in her voice told him this would be the last time she picked up her own phone, 'Goodbye, Mr Whitaker,' she said 'and thank you.'[36]

Now that the announcement of the engagement was imminent, Diana did the debby thing and went shopping with her mother at Harrods to buy the suit she would wear to face the world as a future queen. Their first stop was one of Diana's favourite boutiques, Bellville Sassoon, but neither of the designers were in. She was treated with such snotty disregard by the senior *vendeuse* who failed to recognise the schoolgirlish customer she went to Harrods instead.[37] The Cojana suit she picked off-the-rack was air-stewardess blue with a matronly print blouse tied by a large pussy-cat bow that made her look like a plump Sloane on the frontispiece of *Country Life*. The engagement ring was paid for by the Queen. Diana picked it from a tray of diamonds and sapphires presented to Charles, the Queen and Diana by Garrard, jewellers to the Crown, at Windsor Castle. Betty Battenberg (as some below-stairs wags like to call the Queen) raised her eyebrows as Diana chose the biggest rock in the batch, an enormous sapphire surrounded by eighteen diamonds set in eighteen-carat white gold, costing £28,500. It was a ring to show off with. Her choice created a profitable rage for sapphires instead of diamonds in the engagement market. Diana later claimed she didn't like it, realising perhaps that it didn't fit her youthful way of life. She was not wearing it when, shortly afterwards, she went with Charles to lunch at Broadlands. Lady Mountbatten tells a story of asking Diana if she might see the ring. 'Diana said it was in her bag in the sitting room,' Lady Mountbatten told Gyles Brandreth. '"Charles, go and fetch it," she said. And he did.'[38]

The night before the engagement, Johnnie Spencer, walking with difficulty after his stroke and helped by Raine in mink and pearls, joined Diana and Charles for a festive drink in the Prince's apartment at Buckingham Palace. It was the first time the Spencers had met the

Prince since the courtship began. They stayed only thirty minutes before the Prince left to have a celebratory dinner with the Queen[39] while Diana was escorted to sleep among the Fabergé eggs at the Queen Mother's official residence, Clarence House. Her bedroom looked out on the Mall where in a few months' time she would ride in a glass coach on her way to St Paul's. Her new Scotland Yard bodyguard, Chief Inspector Paul Officer, took a bit of the gloss off it all. 'I just want you to know,' he told her 'that this is the last night of freedom ever in your life, so make the most of it.'[40]

William Tallon, the Queen Mother's page, knew there would be an engagement between Charles and Diana when the Queen Mother told him conspiratorially, 'We must prepare to greet Lady Diana here. We are to give her refuge.' 'So I waited downstairs all day,' he said, 'but she didn't come. In the evening the Queen Mother said to me, "Oh did you wait all day? No, no, she is coming here under the cloak of night." Then I knew there would be an engagement.'[41]

Diana found an unsettling surprise awaiting her on the splendid four-poster bed – a letter from Camilla Parker Bowles. It showed her how closely in the loop her rival was because it was dated two days previously when no one was supposed to know the announcement was imminent, let alone that she would be sleeping at Clarence House. 'Such exciting news about the engagement,' Camilla wrote. 'Do let's have lunch soon when the Prince of Wales goes to Australia and New Zealand. He's going away to be away for three weeks. I'd love to see the ring, lots of love, Camilla.'[42]

Very early on the big day, a member of the Queen Mother's staff took Diana out to get her hair done by Kevin Shanley at Headlines in South Kensington in readiness for facing the world's media. 'We passed through the equerry room,' the staff member said, 'and she saw a copy of The Times which said "Lady Diana Engagement Today." She turned to me and said, "You see. Someone has betrayed me all already."'[43] The only flowers she took with her when she moved from Clarence House were her father's.

Diana started to shrink like Alice as soon as she went through the Buckingham Palace Looking Glass, her home for the next five months. She was now carrying the burden not only of her own childhood dream but the dreams of the British nation. The sceptred isle seemed to have forgotten all about the irony, alienation and class resentment that were hallmarks of the period and turned into a jubilant Shakespearean mob rolling in patriotic sentiment. In the 184 days between the February engagement and the July wedding, £400 million worth of royal wedding souvenirs overflowed into the red, white and blue windows of British stores.

With the eyes of the nation and half the world upon her, it's hardly to be wondered at that Diana grew obsessed with her appearance. The sight of herself in that accursed indigo engagement suit, and a 'a stray comment' from Charles about how 'chubby' she felt when he put his hand on her waist, sent Diana into a dieting binge that lost her fourteen pounds between March and July. It was the onset of a chronic bout of bulimia. 'The little thing got so thin,' her former flatmate Carolyn Pride said. 'I was so worried about her.'[44]

A lot of brides take off weight, but between the first and last fittings of her wedding dress Diana's waist shrank from twenty-nine inches to twenty-three and a half inches. It became an ongoing nightmare for Elizabeth Emanuel, who made the dress, and who didn't want to cut into the ivory taffeta fabric until she had some idea of what size her client was going to be.

Too much ink has been expended psychoanalysing the cause of Diana's bulimia. It's clear her affliction began as a counter-attack against three heavy meals a day and the addition of a cake-laden Windsor tea, the results of which were faithfully logged in 'fat girl' shots flashed round the world. Celebrity magazines today are filled with the sunken cheeks of formerly pneumatic starlets who are turned by round-the-clock exposure into tiny famished ghosts attached to hair weaves. Shy Di now had everyone looking at her and her blush was as crimson as the Palace carpet. Body abuse was second nature to the women in Diana's family – like writing thank-you letters. Bulimia in a way is the polite girl's hunger strike. First you please your host by eating with gusto, then you purge your sin by sneaking off and throwing up. After a time, it's the purging, not the eating, that's the craving. Diana always said it made her feel 'quieter', almost sedated afterwards. When her mother's marriage to Shand Kydd hit the rocks Frances often 'forgot' to eat and had a liquid lunch instead. Diana's sister Sarah's anorexia was so bad in Diana's impressionable early teen years that Lady Elizabeth Anson, herself a 'recovered' sufferer from bulimia, declined to hire Sarah for a job at her Party Planners agency. Lady Elizabeth believed that bulimia sufferers expend all their energy on secrecy and protective lies and did not want to be accused of exacerbating Sarah's already chronic condition.

Buckingham Palace was tailor-made for a bulimic outburst. It is suffocating and empty at the same time, and everyone is trained to look the other way. Inside it's the royal equivalent of that spooky movie, *The Village*. The Palace's occupants speak the same language as their neighbours, but they live in an astral plane of their own. The Palace houses the offices of the royal officials, secretaries, comptrollers and equerries, as well as the platoons of footmen, butlers, maids and so on, who have their own police station, twenty-four-hour fire brigade, post office, doctor's surgery, laundry, chapel and chaplain, electricians, carpenters, gilders and plumbers.

All this may make it sound as if Diana was surrounded by cheerful bustle, but nothing could be further from the truth. Most of the staff labours out of sight in rooms connected by a maze of underground corridors. You rarely run into people above ground in the labyrinth of interconnecting areas and hallways linking more than six hundred rooms. A wrong turn down a corridor can lead you into the middle of an atrophied cocktail reception or medal-flashing social ceremony. The averted eyes of so many scarcely breathing factotums make all who live there feel invisible. Paul Burrell, Diana's gossiping butler, describes the hushed world very well. Housemaids, he tells us, are not allowed to switch on vacuum cleaners before 9 a.m. to avoid disturbing the royal family. Instead, stiff brushes are used to sweep the deep red shagpile upright. Staff must never walk down the middle of the carpet because it is considered presumptuous: freshly brushed carpet is fit only for royal feet. Staff walk along its twelve-inch-wide border instead. Tea trays for members of the royal family all have their own personal map, showing the exact position of condiments, teapots and milk jugs.[45]

The best servant performs his duties without being seen at all, the ultimate act of self-effacement. This requirement leads to an army of maids or footmen scurrying to hide until the coast is clear. At Sandringham maids dart into a walk-in cupboard under the stairs so as not be seen when the Queen comes down into the main hall, a practice identical to the approach of the monarch in *The Madness of King George*. If a member of the royal family materialises in a corridor and it is too late to disappear, the protocol is to stop walking, stand to attention, turn with back against the wall and bow silently as the great one passes. The sense of isolation is increased by each member of the royal family – Prince Andrew, Princess Anne and Prince Edward – having their own separate apartment and staffs. They run separate fiefdoms and rarely mix. (When I visited Prince Andrew in his apartment there, it had the impersonal quality of a Harrods showroom, or a suite in the Berkeley hotel with better pictures. Even though he is tolerably tech savvy, the TV and video screens crop up in rooms almost accidentally as if someone had just dumped them and departed.) At weekends and holidays, the Palace is dead. It's like visiting a prep school when everyone's gone home.

Diana was quickly introduced to the odd dichotomy of her future life. Outside the Palace walls, she was the centre of attention. Inside, she was very much junior-fry in a system set up to revolve around the Queen. If Prince Philip wants to have lunch with his wife, he sends a message to her office via a page, and she sends one back to his with her reply. When the Queen is at Balmoral and Prince Charles wants to walk the grounds, he first makes sure his mother is alerted through her private secretary to ensure she would not prefer to have the grounds to herself. It is one of the sadder aspects of Diana's story that she nurtured the hope that the Queen, of all candidates, could become a supplementary mother and role model she could emulate. Diana was in tremendous awe of Elizabeth, a feeling that only increased when she saw the burdens of the sovereign's life up close. 'I just long to hug my mother-in-law, and tell her how deeply I understood what goes on inside her,' she wrote in a note to Paul Burrell in 1996. 'I understand the isolation . . .'[46] Diana yearned to please the Queen and be on relaxed terms. Once a week, as instructed, she sent a message to ask: 'Is the Queen dining alone tonight?'[47] The Queen often was – a tray on her lap in front of the television in her sitting room. More often than not she preferred to keep it that way, whacked out herself from a week of being sucked up to.

The suite Diana was given had once belonged to the royal governess, Miss Peebles, and was subsequently used by the sainted Mabel Anderson, Charles's nanny, who Camilla Parker Bowles was the spitting image of. Diana was allocated a bedroom, bathroom and adjoining kitchen, located, appropriately enough, on the royal nursery corridor. Prince Charles's vast bachelor apartment was on the same floor but acres away.

Diana desperately missed the giggly old Sloanes from Coleherne Court. She said afterwards how much she longed to go back there and sit and have fun and borrow clothes and chat about silly things. Before the engagement she had seen the privacy of the Palace as the ultimate haven, secluded from the relentless harassment of the press, but at least the raucous newsmen who drove her crazy were real. It was easy to imagine that their solicitous nocturnal phone calls to get a quote for the late edition meant they actually cared for her. Even a woman as self-possessed as Mary Robertson found it daunting to get through the new layers of official gatekeepers protecting Diana. When her old friends did come to see the bride-to-be there was always some pickled footman or eavesdropping flunkey hanging around. 'It was as though she had been whisked off to an ivory tower . . . never to be seen again,' Carolyn Pride said.[48] (Today, the Duchess of Cornwall, a woman thirty years older than Diana was then, finds the presence of all the royal servants so invasive she insists on retaining her own house in Wiltshire as an escape.)

The Coleherne Court friends could sense that Diana was pulling away and were hurt about it. But Diana was ashamed to tell her former flatmates that she now saw her old besieged apartment, not the Palace cocoon, as her 'safe shell'.[49] She spent her time practising ballet and writing letters to old friends in her rounded schoolgirl hand. 'I long for company my own age,' she wrote to Mary Robertson,[50] who was surprised and touched at how often she heard from her, feeling it should be her mother, not her old employer, whom she turned to for this kind of support. But Diana's family relations had always been, well, difficult. Sarah's rankling failure to land Prince Charles for herself precluded too much sisterly confiding of secret anxieties there. Her elder sister Jane, who lived in the grace-and-favour apartment at Kensington Palace with her husband Robert Fellowes, was helpful with navigating royal etiquette and often came to lunch, but she was the squarest of her siblings, fully at ease with the royal life that Diana didn't like to admit she now found so intimidating. Their mother was a whirlwind of efficiency when it came to buying the trousseau – 'so capable and elegant',[51] in the words of Sonia Palmer, one of the secretaries on the Prince's staff – but Frances had never been good at sustained emotional support. It didn't help that she had already made her views clear on the wisdom of the match.

As a wedding dress takes shape, most brides are accompanied on fittings by their mother or sister or a girlfriend. Frances went with Diana on the first appointment to the tiny Mayfair studio of the Emanuels to choose the wedding dress that would be seen by 750 million people, but after that the most famous fiancée in the world always came for fittings by herself. 'We bonded with her because she got no help or advice with the dress from the Palace,' said Elizabeth Emanuel. 'Nor did we. She was always alone.'[52]

Perhaps because their lives are bound by duty, a word Diana soon began to dread, the royals are singularly unable to detect when duty is not enough. The Queen herself learned the harsh protocols and isolation of Palace life during her childhood. For her its rigours and eccentricities were normal. Everything in royal circles is therefore always assumed and never asked about outright. To ask is to imply the possibility of a kind of weakness deemed unthinkable in the first place. It was assumed that since Lady Diana came from the nobility and was no stranger to large households, she would cope perfectly well with the transition. It was assumed that if she was lonely, or needed help, she would find a way to get on with it. It was assumed that when she started to shrink before their eyes, it had nothing to do with the pressures of the Palace experience. Prince Charles was desperately worried about how thin she was getting, but the Queen put the problem firmly down on the Spencer side of the ledger, judging it 'a psychological condition brought on by problems during Diana's difficult childhood',[53] as Elizabeth Longford heard it. It was altogether assumed that Diana would soon pull herself together.

To get her ready for princessly duties, the Queen did send over her closest lady-in-waiting, Lady Susan Hussey. This seasoned forty-two-year-old courtier later resented the folklore that Diana had been given no help by the Palace. She spent many hours putting Diana through her paces on such protocol as how to wave, where to hold her handbag, how to deftly end a conversation with a pressing admirer. (The Queen herself has an expert technique of disengaging her hand from sweaty grasping supplicants by an adroit little discarding manoeuvre.) But Diana's antennae told her that Hussey's loyalties would never be to her. Hussey was one of the clique of older women who adored Charles. She was an establishment insider and court politician whose direct links to the monarch made Diana uneasy. 'Susan would have been lady-in-waiting to all six of Henry VIII's wives,' said a writer in the court circle.[54] Hussey, for her part, became vexed, another friend told me, by the fact that Diana 'didn't seem to listen'.[55] It never occurred to Hussey – or to any of them – that the novice at the royal game had already begun to reinvent the rules.

Diana reverted to her childhood pattern at Althorp: seeking company below stairs. She was much more relaxed with the housemaids, pastry cooks and laundry ladies than she was with the courtiers and private secretaries. She sat on the beds and chatted with the chambermaids about their lives, befriending Maria Cosgrove, who would become Paul Burrell's wife. Accustomed to the ways of the Queen, who was hardly likely to drop in and raid the fridge, the kitchen staff felt at first discomfited by Diana's merry visits. Chumminess, after all, was a sackable offence. But Diana had no resources for being left on her own. She seemed to them like a child, one who required to be indulged, petted and amused, and eventually they got used to her visits and even looked forward to them.

What is clear now is that she barely knew her prospective bridegroom. By her own account, she only saw him a total of thirteen times from the beginning of their courtship to the day of their wedding. Her agonies to come stemmed from a frantic desire to find out who he actually was when prised from duty. The two were almost never on their own, which gave her little chance to learn – and now the elusive Prince was taking off for a five-week tour of New Zealand, Australia, Venezuela and Williamsburg, Virginia. To make matters worse, just before the Prince's departure he had taken a goodbye call from Camilla Parker Bowles, for which Diana had heroically left the room so he could speak to her in confidence. Diana's tears at the airport were not of grief but of rage.

The Charles lobby has always maintained that Diana's growing paranoia about Camilla at this time was neurotic fantasy – that Camilla was a back number, of little importance to Charles until five years into his collapsing marriage. According to Charles's biographer Jonathan Dimbleby, the Prince saw Camilla on only one occasion from the moment of his engagement to Diana until 1986, and that was to say farewell. Diana's obsessive jealousy of his ex-lover, they say, became a self-fulfilling prophecy.

Yet what are we to make of the girls' lunch, dripping with hissy subtext, that took place between fiancée and mistress while the Prince was away? As Diana recounted to Andrew Morton it was 'very tricky indeed. She [Camilla] said: "You are not going to hunt are you?" I [Diana] said: "On what?" She said: "Horse. You are not going to hunt when you go and live at Highgrove are you?" I said: "No." She said: "I just wanted to know," and I thought as far as she was concerned that was her communication route.'[56] Diana deduced, rightly, that Camilla was already manoeuvring for assignation times, 'working out what was going to be her territory and what was going to be mine'.[57]

But a shrewd director of this drama might play the scene with a different emphasis. Isn't it Camilla's insecurity, more than Diana's, that is on display here? The bride-to-be was too inexperienced in sexual war games to understand how much she had started to unnerve Prince Charles's favourite mistress. 'Camilla, in private, had a very patronising attitude towards Diana,' said her ex-brother-in-law Richard Parker Bowles, 'but . . . she massively under-estimated the Princess.'[58] The timing of the girls' lunch gives the game away. It was a few weeks after Diana's stunning appearance with Charles on their first public date, a musical recital at the Goldsmith's Hall, in the City of London, on 3 March 1981. Diana wore a drop-dead black décolleté number that had not been in the image of Camilla's casting at all. Diana had seized the super-sexy gown from the rack in the Emanuels' studio when the dress she had ordered wasn't ready, intent on convincing Charles that she was no longer a 'poppet' but a heat-seeking missile. 'Black to me was the smartest colour you could possibly have at the age of nineteen,' she said later. 'It was a real grown-up dress.'[59] Until this moment the public and the Prince – and Camilla – had seen Diana only as a demure English rose. When she stepped out of the limousine in that nipple-busting, black taffeta eye-popper it was the greatest moment of sexual theatre since Cinderella swapped her scuffed scullery clogs for Prince Charming's glass slippers. 'Wasn't that a mighty feast to set before a King!' the ancient beauty, Lady Diana Cooper remarked to a friend about the ingénue's sudden revelation of cleavage.[60]

The Emanuels' dress was all wrong, really. Royals were never supposed to wear black except to funerals, and as one fashion critic pointed out, décolleté for a concert is a disaster because it makes you look as if you are in a hip bath. But, as so often with Diana, one wrong made a right. The contrast with the subtly sophisticated air of Princess Grace of Monaco, who was also present, only charmingly emphasised the point. To the British public, Diana was every teenager announcing a sweet determination to be seen no longer as a child but as a grown-up, alluring woman. The transparency of intent made Diana vulnerable, not vulgar. Camilla could not know that, in the powder room, the glamorous new Diana opened up to Princess Grace about the stress and insecurity she felt. 'Don't worry,' said the unflappable Grace. 'It will get a lot worse.'[61]

I noticed a rare unease in Camilla at this time when, for *Tatler*, I went with the photographer Derry Moore to take a set of pictures of the Parker Bowleses at home. The mere fact that this private pair were opening the doors of Bolehyde Manor for the camera was out of character, suggesting a sudden need for glossy exposure. Many of the others in Prince Charles's circle were manifesting the same unusual new friendliness to the press, only to find themselves suddenly of no interest. Compared to the freshness of the emerging Diana, the legendarily sexually confident Camilla suddenly seemed a knocked-about blonde with too much back story. There was a sort of electric indifference between her and her husband Andrew as they posed for Derry Moore's portrait. Camilla had all Prince Charles's speech mannerisms. 'Stowell Park? Oh it's a brute of a *hice* but it has some *virry, virry* nice pictures.' Andrew, for his part, spent the whole shoot staring at my chest.

It was obvious that day that Camilla was still competitive with Charles's other blonde 'confidante', Lady 'Kanga' Tryon, who, uncoincidentally, had been featured in *Tatler* the month before. (My, how those ladies were scrambling.) 'All this stuff about Dale Tryon being such a friend of Charles,' Camilla said to me. 'She's never even *met* Diana Spencer.' It was clear that Camilla was intent on negotiating her place in Charles's life in a new world order that would have to contain a Princess of Wales – and not just any Princess of Wales, but one who was captivating the nation. On Charles's tour of Australia the press noticed that he was beginning to see his fiancée through their eyes. 'Wherever he went, he could see her image on the TV. James [Whitaker] and I think we saw him fall in love with the idea of her at a distance,' royal biographer Anthony Holden observed.[62] A letter from Charles dated 5 March 1981 – written soon after his engagement – to a trusted confidante – appears to back up Holden: 'I am very lucky that someone as special as Diana seems to love me so much,' wrote the Prince wonderingly.[63]

The changing status quo rattled Lady Tryon as much as it did Camilla. It surely contributed to Tryon suddenly giving up Kanga, her Knightsbridge dress business, and moving full-time to Wiltshire – 'for the sake of my marriage', she told me over lunch, but also no doubt as a run-for-cover measure. Marital and mistress dynamics alike were discombobulated by the prospect of a royal bride the media adored this much.

A more self-assured girl than Diana might have perceived that it was she who held all the cards in this contest. She could have seen Camilla off if she had chosen wiles instead of tears, sexual artfulness instead of sexual jealousy, but sadly, she was too young to know how. Instead she obsessed about a gift, destined for Camilla, she found on the desk of Michael Colborne, Prince Charles's personal secretary now co-opted to help with the avalanche of wedding gifts arriving in every post. Diana had a perch in his office at the Palace. Colborne was an Australian meritocrat who had been in the navy with Charles. The Prince had hired him over the objections of the Palace old boy network, and he had won Diana's trust for just that reason. He was outside the circle of self-regard. She preferred his gruff sincerity to the more courtly charm of her new private secretary, Oliver Everett, who had once been in the office of Prince Charles and had been plucked out of a promising career with the Foreign Office in Madrid to come and help with the numerous challenges of the wedding. Diana was an obedient student in Everett's efforts to school her, but she was secretly intimidated by him. He insisted on treating her like a grown-up, producing daunting memos for her to read and background notes to study.

Colborne had a blunter approach. A colleague says he once told Diana, 'After 29 July you are going to become a B-I-T-C-H. If you want six umbrellas you'll get them. If you want your car out in front, it will be there.' He was apparently touched by her repeated desires to 'help bring the royal family together more', always asking questions like 'Isn't it Princess Anne's birthday today?' to make sure she sent a card. If it weren't so sad, it would be comic that Diana actually thought she could turn the determinedly dysfunctional royal family into a warm and fuzzy replacement for her own fractured clan.[64]

What Diana loved was to sit and listen for hours to Colborne's stories of his time in the navy when he had nothing to do with royal life. It took her mind off the insistent refrain of *duty*, that once theoretical word that was beginning to develop associations of cold apprehension. Colborne told her, 'You could get a diary for three years from now and write in it the things that you are going to have to be doing – Trooping the Colour, Ascot, Order of the Garter – and you'll know where you'll be and what date.'[65] She experienced her own claustrophobic details daily. One weekend in Windsor at the Queen Mother's house, Royal Lodge, she went for a walk on her own and discovered on her return that a search party had been sent to find her.

Diana had developed an informal enough relationship with Colborne that she often rushed over to his side of the room to examine what new wedding present had arrived. He was out of the office talking to Edward Adeane, Prince Charles's private secretary, when she spied an incoming package that looked interesting. She discovered it was a gold chain bracelet with a blue enamel disc bearing the initials G.F. She knew 'Girl Friday' to be Charles's nickname for Camilla. (Because she did everything for him? Or because she only slept with him on weekends?) When Colborne came back to his office, Diana had disappeared and didn't come back that day. Later, says a witness to the scene, Adeane told Colborne he had seen Diana leaving the office in tears. 'What have you done?' Adeane said to Colborne in alarm.[66]

The bracelet issue has entered legend as one of Charles's most hurtful transgressions, but it could equally be seen as more backlit drama hyped for the Morton tape recorder. Charles was always known for thoughtful presents, as long as they didn't cost much. He sent out a ton of them to friends of both sexes before he took 'la grande plonge', usually accompanied by one of his voluminous, sensitive notes. What is harder to go along with is the assertion by Jonathan Dimbleby, Charles's official biographer, that Charles's insistence on delivering the gift to Camilla in person was an 'act of courtesy'.[67]

'Bollocks to that!' shouted Diana when told in 1994 about the gloss Dimbleby had put on the bracelet incident[68] – and what modern woman can disagree with her? But her response also underestimates the bollocks that happened to be the code the Prince of Wales lived by. Charles was about to do the equivalent of taking holy orders, put aside any residual doubts and, for the sake of the country, marry the girl picked by his parents. He may have viewed the maddening insensitivity of delivering the gift to Camilla himself as a last act of mistress appeasement.

Either way, it was bloody irritating. The sheer momentum with which these events were unfolding meant Diana had no time to process them. 'Well, bad luck, "Duch",' Diana's sister (for sure the salty Sarah) famously said when Diana confided her distress. 'Your face is on the tea towels so you're too late to chicken out.'[69] The effort of trying to understand it all was crushing Diana. Her romantic dream had always had only two people in it: Prince and Princess. Now there was not just a third – Camilla – but a cast of thousands. The intensity of the media participation in her fantasy was giving her heatstroke. In addition to the British press at fever pitch, London was now crawling with international reporters and photographers attempting madly to get up to speed on the baffling irrelevancies of royal detail.

The wedding did wonders for the sales of Tatler, for example. It put us on the map. England's tiny social magazine was suddenly in the middle of the biggest tabloid story in the world. I was hired, along with just about everyone else I knew, by an American network TV show – in my case NBC's Today programme, as their on-air royalty expert for the week. 'Excuse me,' asked one of ABC's producers at the solemn briefing by the BBC for all media covering the event, 'isn't Lady Diana's coach a major security risk?' 'It's not all glass and it's not all driven by mice,' replied the BBC representative with a superior smile.

At Diana's last public appearance with Charles before the wedding, to watch him wield the royal mallet in a polo match against Spain at Windsor Great Park, twenty thousand people showed up at Smith's lawn to gawk at her. The *Daily Mirror*'s front-page picture showed Diana pursing her lips and looking tense. 'Her face was pale grey as limestone and she hardly smiled,' the *Mirror*'s John Edwards reported in the kind of play-by-play coverage of her moods usually reserved for World Cup football matches. 'She ran out of Prince Charles's open Aston Martin before the car had actually stopped. She went straight to the shelter of the Queen's private chalet and stayed there twisting a white cardigan in her hands, peeping nervously from behind the door at the crowds and not wanting to join them.' She was pictured rubbing her forehead with both hands. 'A few days seemed to have changed her,' Edwards bore on. 'Her bounce had gone. The quips stayed buried. She had shed weight and was uneasy with the crush all around her.'[70] It never seemed to occur to Edwards that he and his colleagues were themselves the problem.

Yet what is striking about Diana is how with all these extraordinary pressures she could still appear calm about the things that send other brides over the edge. David and Elizabeth Emanuel were now working on what the press came to call 'The Dress' like atomic scientists in a top-secret laboratory. Diana's choice of the rising husband-and-wife designer team for the bridal gown had been her first act of rebellion. They were young and inexperienced and on no one's list for a dress this important. Yet in those secretive visits for her fittings, Diana was self-possessed. She always knew exactly what she was looking for down to the diamond-studded horseshoe sewn in the waistband for good luck. 'The Dress' was the fulfilment of her princess fantasy. She was insistent in her demand for its puffy sleeves and floating silk, its twenty-five-foot taffeta train, its nipped waist, and its antique lace embroidered with pearls and sequins. She would be a fairy bride for her father and her Prince. Those creamy ruffles and ivory frills would float her away from the agonies of the present to a future of certain love. By the 1990s, when she was a svelte power woman and girls were marrying in body-hugging tubes, the voluminous crinoline she had worn on 29 July 1981 embarrassed her. It hangs now in its glass case in Althorp like an artefact from Miss Havisham's attic, Exhibit A in the museum of a dead dream.

The guest list was more problematic for Diana than 'The Dress'. All the Hons and Vons of House of Windsor friends and relations had to be invited, leaving little space for the bride's side. The Queen was so desperate to know what to do with the influx of Germanic freeloaders she phoned Lady Anson and asked if she'd throw a post-wedding party at Claridge's to get them off her back.

The question of what to do about Barbara Cartland became a national cause célèbre. In the run-up to the big day, Alexander Chancellor, the editor of the *Spectator*, wrote an editorial in which he called for a special Act of Parliament to ban Raine and her mother from St Paul's Cathedral, adding, 'For it would be more than a little unfair on everybody if these two absurdly theatrical ladies were permitted to turn a moving national celebration into a pantomime.'[71] Diana was so afraid the pantomime might indeed take place, she pressed for stratagems to blackball Cartland. (The romantic novelist may have spun the dreams that got Diana into St Paul's, but the frantic feathered personage who wrote them was too much for her to bear.) Two versions circulate about how the nixing of Cartland was achieved: (a) Cartland was simply struck from the guest list, or (b) Cartland was invited but given a seat behind one of the cathedral's great pillars. According to one of Prince Charles's aides, 'Barbara was so humiliated she wanted to go abroad for the wedding day. But her sons said that it would make it look as if she was banished.'[72] To save face she made the canny move of throwing a party for the Volunteers of St John Ambulance to which she wore the tailored brown uniform of the Order of St John instead of her usual costume of pink ostrich feathers. (Fifteen years later the 'Queen of Romance' made a succinct judgement on the reasons for the marriage's failure. 'Of course, you know where it all went wrong. She wouldn't do oral sex.')[73]

On the eve of the wedding, the royal bride and groom sank awkwardly into canvas director's chairs for a television interview with the BBC's establishment anchorwoman Angela Rippon and ITN's Andrew Gardner that was broadcast on both channels. The interview, seen today with our awareness of what was to come, is a festival of body language. The couple give the appearance of having been propelled onto the air after arriving from two separate places. The thirty-two-year-old Charles looks young yet seems ancient compared to his childlike fiancée. The crisp, practised heir to the throne shoots solicitous glances at the almost inaudible Diana, who shrinks deeper and deeper into her director's chair. She wears a silvery grey young governess dress with a Peter Pan collar, pale tights and flat grey pumps, a look which at that moment was flooding British high streets with thousands of Lady Di lookalikes. Charles tells Gardner he hopes marriage will be calming. 'Getting interested in too many things and dashing *abite*, that's going to be my problem,' he says as if he rather hopes it will be. Asked which presents she's liked, Diana looks relieved to be on safe terrain at last: 'Anything that comes from children, really.'[74]

'Any personal touches for the service?' Rippon tries. Charles fiddles with his sleeve as soon as the word 'personal' is uttered. He turns to Diana for help. 'Any personal touches?' 'Just our friends really,' she replies but she seems distracted. Her expression is both wary and wistful as if she half knows already her dream is a thing of the past. Asked to enumerate the interests they share, she gives a list of things they did not: 'Music, opera and outdoor sports including fishing, walking, and' – the activity she hated most in the world – 'polo.' Charles truly comes alive only when he talks about the music for the service, which he has planned to the last detail. For the three-and-a-half-minute walk down the aisle he says he wants something 'very stirring, very dramatic and noisy, so ankles can't be heard creaking'.[75] For his hymn, he says he has chosen the musically sophisticated 'Let the Bright Seraphim' from Handel's *Samson*, and that he has flown Kiri Te Kanawa in from New Zealand to sing it. But it is Diana's choice that everyone remembers. When in her clipped, swallowed, cut-glass accent she says, '"I Vow to Thee My Country",' the Anglican hymn that carries the message of patriotic sacrifice of those who died during the First World War, it evokes the image of boarding-school girls singing in morning assembly.

'Are you worried?' Rippon asks Diana. 'No, I'll just go along with everyone else,'[76] she replies with a level, veiled, determined stare. Dale Tryon and Camilla Parker Bowles would discover what that meant: over the objections of Prince Charles, Diana banned them from the wedding breakfast. To keep her end up, Lady Tryon invited sixty-five friends and took over half of the fashionable San Lorenzo restaurant. She was quoted in Dempster's diary as saying: 'I was not invited to the Palace and I know Mrs Parker Bowles wasn't either . . . She is also holding a party for friends. Obviously I cannot comment on why I wasn't invited.'[77]

Stephen Barry, the valet to Charles, alleged that on the night of the pre-wedding ball at Buckingham Palace, Charles sneaked off for a last tryst with Camilla. The perilous logistics of such a subterfuge make it seem unlikely, even preposterous. Barry himself had written in his memoir, 'Buckingham Palace was totally unsuitable for anything secret to take place.'[78] There were eight hundred guests that night, including

Nancy Reagan, Margaret Thatcher and every head still crowned in Europe. The ball was a scene of such sparkle and joy only a priapic clod – which, whatever you think of him, Charles was not – would have jeopardised such a long-planned night of unforgettable national affirmation. Besides, his 'boffs' with Camilla rarely took place at Buckingham Palace. It was Mummy's territory, crawling with spies, and he was as yet far from the point at which he would no longer care if he humiliated Diana. Sally, Duchess of Westminster, noted to diarist James Lees-Milne that the Prince was absent from the festivities for a time. Her intelligence was that 'Charles left his bride for several hours to spend the time with the "Goons" in another room,' Lees-Milne recorded her words in his diary. 'The pathetic Lady Di was left alone without an escort, to make conversation to people she did not know. This confirms what I have heard from other sources that he is not in love with her.'[79] Is it possible Charles's mysterious disappearance from the party that night was actually to be entertained by his favourite court jesters Spike Milligan and Harry Secombe, his fellow 'Goons'?

He may have been in love with Camilla still, but he was as much in love with the Goons. If a conversation with the Prince of Wales flags one of the hazards is he will reach for one of his determined impersonations of one or other of the Goons. It would be a wonderful refutation of the conspiracy theory of life if it were not a sexual encounter with his mistress that lured Charles away from the festivities but impersonations of the surreal Ned Seagoon and Major Bloodnok. (For what it's worth, I would bet on gags over shags.)

Diana did not strike Mary Robertson as the pathetic figure Sally Westminster perceived. There is a palpable vein of envy in all the grander upper-class women towards this snip of a girl who was now garnering so much public adoration. The reason is obvious. Wedding guest Sir Charles Johnston noted in his diary: 'I have never seen such a strong charge of innocently provocative sex.'[80] To Mary Robertson, Diana was at her most ravishing that night in a fuchsia-pink taffeta Emanuel gown and a diamond and pearl necklace, and danced with all the former Tim Nice-but-Dims from the Coleherne Court days. Rory Scott remembers hitting the floor with Diana in front of PM Margaret Thatcher and embarrassing himself, by constantly stepping on Diana's toes, ho ho. Adam Russell has the joyous recall of 'everyone horribly drunk and then catching taxis in the early hours – a blur, a glorious, happy blur'.[81] Princess Margaret attached a balloon to her tiara; Prince Andrew tied another to the tails of his dinner jacket. Raine Spencer's son, William, now the Earl of Dartmouth, said, 'You had the feeling that everyone was thrilled to be there, that every guest was exactly where they wanted to be, at the A-list party of the year. I think the last time that an Englishwoman had married an heir to the throne was Anne Hyde to the future James II. It's funny, because when she was growing up, it was Sarah you noticed, not her.'[82]

Not quite everyone in England was feeling so festive. The run-down area of Toxteth, Liverpool, was still tense after a month of racial street riots. Unrest in areas of unemployment played out like a dark alternative TV show, one that no one wanted to watch. On the wedding eve itself, Prince Charles lit the first of a chain of beacons across the country. After the fireworks he stood at a window of Buckingham Palace with the ever-attentive Lady Susan Hussey, looking down at the flags and the barricades in the Mall that was already alive with joyful people and ruminating on the momentous change his life was about to undergo.[83] Diana was absent from the fireworks display. She had been returned to bridal purdah in the care of the Queen Mother at Clarence House. Charles sent her a gift – a signet ring engraved with the Prince of Wales feathers, and a fond message, 'I'm so proud of you and when you come up the aisle I'll be there at the altar for you tomorrow. Just look 'em in the eye and knock 'em dead.'[84]

When she was at last ushered into Clarence House, Diana was a girl already much changed from that winter night five months before when she had first been given refuge there, as the Queen Mother put it 'under the cloak of night'.[85]

Gone was the country mouse in the air-stewardess suit plucked from a Harrods rack. She was now the most famous ingénue of the century, her innocence a commodity of glamour. She dined with her sister Jane in her rooms upstairs while her grandmother, Lady Fermoy, kept the Queen Mother company below. According to Hugo Vickers, the Queen Mother was relieved to be watching the celebratory fireworks on television rather than on the scene with the rest of the family on account of the 'proliferation of German royal guests'.[86] The two venerable architects of the wedding enjoyed a victory dinner à deux, and watched a rerun of *Dad's Army* while upstairs Diana indulged in a bulimic splurge and was, in her own words, 'sick as a parrot'[87] after eating everything in sight.

That's how she described herself ending the evening, anyway, when she talked about it to Andrew Morton eleven years later. The sombre recollection denied the lightness of heart that others saw in her that night. The Queen Mother's elderly page William Tallon had a memorable encounter with her before she went to bed. When Clarence House was largely silent, Diana wandered downstairs in search of company. She seemed at such a loose end that Tallon invited her into his office for a chat with himself and an equerry. He remembers he asked her, 'Well, so shall we all have a drink?' And the equerry 'poured me a stiff one, and an orange juice for Lady Diana and she was very happy. Then she saw my bicycle standing against a wall and she got on it and started to ride round and round, ringing the bell and singing "I'm going to marry the Prince of Wales tomorrow." Ring, ring. "I'm going to marry the Prince of Wales tomorrow!" Ring, ring! I can hear that bicycle ringing now. She was just a child you know, just a little girl.'[88]

Diana's dream was reaching its crescendo. The wedding day's magic was so powerful that a mad unreasonable joy coursed through the nation. The symptoms of royal fever as noted by Tatler included extreme pulsations of patriotism at the sound of choral music, tears welling up involuntarily in eyes, shivers up spines, and intense envy of the bride and groom. The splendour and hopefulness of it all offered a vision of England that turned every hack into a troubadour, every Roundhead into a Cavalier. Even Princess Anne was transformed on the big day from gumbooted grouch to radiant Gibson girl, complete with four-string pearl choker, drop earrings and frothy chapeau. Diana said later that she felt like a, 'lamb to the slaughter', when she rose that morning, but as 'The Dress' was lowered on to her now skinny frame at Clarence House she burst into a joyous singalong of 'Just One Cornetto', that ice-cream ad to the tune of 'O Sole Mio', with her dressers and bridesmaids joining in.[89]

'The Dress', anticipation of which had now reached fever pitch, provoked a moment of national anxiety. When the fairy Princess alighted from the glass coach at St Paul's, it was suddenly obvious that the inexperienced Emanuels had miscalculated. They had failed to see that the eighteenth-century coach would be too small for a train that large, especially when crammed in beside the heavy figure of Earl Spencer. The first glimpse made it look like a bundle of old washing until the two designers leapt forward and unfurled it like a billowing, creamy flag.

Diana later said that as she advanced up the aisle on her proud father's arm she caught sight of Camilla (who, along with Dale Tryon, had at least made it into the service) 'wearing a pale grey, veiled pill box hat, her son Tom standing on a chair'.[90] But I suspect that the look

Diana shot in her direction was not to confirm her trepidation, as she claimed, but to register her triumph. Camilla was a mere mortal on that day, forced to watch the man she loved disappear behind a curtain of ceremony with a shining, nubile young princess. There should be little doubt who felt the winner at that moment. In truth, Diana, ever the carer, was more focused on her father's difficult journey up the aisle. Fear that he might pass out at any minute aroused considerably greater anxiety among his family than was apparent on television, causing his son-in-law, Robert Fellowes, to keep leaning worriedly forward. The Earl supported himself so heavily against Diana that father and daughter gently tacked and weaved as they advanced towards the waiting Prince.

When Diana lifted the demure cascade of the white veil to say her vows, the rustle inside the majestic church fell silent. The great and the good craned forward to listen. They heard the bride make a mistake, addressing Charles Philip Arthur George as Philip Charles Arthur George, but in her it was considered an adorable lapse. Even the sardonic critic Clive James called it in the *Observer* a 'blunderette that completed the enslavement of her future people by revealing that she shared their capacity to make a small balls-up on a big occasion'.[91] Diana would have us believe that, as she left behind the pealing bells of St Paul's on the arm of the Prince, she was thinking that while everyone was happy because they thought that she and her bridegroom were happy, her own mind was darkened by a 'big question mark'.[92] Perhaps so. But I return to the image of her at Clarence House the night before, riding round and round on the borrowed bicycle, ringing the bell, and singing like a jubilant schoolgirl, 'I'm going to marry the Prince of Wales tomorrow!'

## Chapter 9

## The Scream

'I sometimes wonder what on earth I have got myself into.'
— The Princess of Wales, 1981

Until the wedding, Diana's life had all been about the Dream. She is not the first bride to bury her rising doubts in the froth and fervour of planning the big day. In her case the entire British nation was a partner in a fantasy that made every media organisation in the world breathless with romance. But from the moment the honeymoon began it was as if she had awoken at last from an insulin coma. During the engagement her wish to preserve the delusion had become a wilful not-knowing. Her survival depended on its preservation. She had submerged herself so deeply in her escape scenario she had refused to see the warning signals that now rushed in on her from every side.

To Andrew Morton she itemised all the particular acts of rejection by Prince Charles that were the cause of her desolation – the photos of Camilla that fell out of his diary as they cruised the Mediterranean on *Britannia*, his retreat into his solitary, highbrow reading, the cufflinks from Camilla he wore in defiance of his new wife's feelings – but the really terrifying dimension to her grief was the sudden sharp understanding that all the things that had oppressed her during her engagement were now her life for ever. It was like an icy wave hitting her in the face. The oldness, the coldness, the deadness of royal life, its muffled misogyny, its whispering silence, its stifling social round confronting sycophantic strangers, this is how it would be until she died. Nothing else can explain the violence of her panic. As a former member of Prince Charles's staff put it: 'She saw she was going to become like the Queen, possibly the loneliest woman in the world.'[1]

'We have put her living in the tomb.' Edgar Allen Poe's line from 'The Fall of the House of Usher' is how the twenty-year-old Diana

Spencer experienced the days after the sound of trumpets in St Paul's Cathedral had faded. When I think of the young, beautiful, newly married Princess of Wales at this time I see her sitting up abruptly in the middle of the night in the spartan spaciousness of her bedroom at Balmoral and uttering a long, blood-curdling scream . . .

How could Prince Charles possibly understand? He had some glimmer of the awfulness of his own existence, but he'd never known anything else. It had shaped him and made him who he was, a man who had never been young.

Diana had had the beginnings of a life. It might have been small but it was free and full of promise, nipping around London at the wheel of her Metro, tenderly administering to other people's children at work, making spaghetti with her flatmates for dinner and flopping down for a night of TV and jokes over a tub of ice cream. Following the wedding of the century she was wound up to such a pitch after all the weeks and months of hype a dreadful comedown was inevitable. What she wanted was to sleep and make love and live for a while in a cocoon of unhurried intimacy with the husband she hardly knew. At Broadlands, the Mountbattens' splendid Palladian home in Hampshire where they were interred for three nights before they flew to Gibraltar to begin their cruise, the Prince spent most of the day trout fishing on the River Test. The newly-weds slept in the same small four-poster bed where the Queen and Prince Philip had passed their wedding night thirty-four years ago. Diana was intrigued by an eighteenth-century French print of a woman at her toilette with a suitor at her feet which hung above the fireplace in the bedroom. Her schoolgirl French required Charles to translate the French verse, '*Égard, tendresse, soins, tout s'épuisse en ce jour / Bientôt l'Hymen languit et voit s'enfuir l'amour.*' When he demurred she asked if it was 'rude'. 'No, but it isn't very hopeful,' he said. She persisted and he translated: 'Consideration, tenderness, courtesy, all flow from this day / But soon Hymen [the god of marriage] will languish and, behold, love will fly away.'[2] Great. She told Andrew Morton 'it was just . . . grim' and that her own 'tremendous hope was slashed by day two'.[3]

The Princess had believed that her Prince, cut off at last from his mistress, would find her alluring, but Diana seems to have been immediately aware that she had failed to please Charles. The Prince told a friend: 'That first night was nothing special. It was pleasant enough, of course. But she really was painfully naive.'[4] The trophy that had been fetishised in the lead-up to her marriage – her virginity – was now a source of ill-concealed sexual disappointment to the man she adored. Charles enjoyed women who led him, mastered him and mothered him. He was used to being served, not required to seduce. Diana was eager but uninventive. On honeymoon the sex only happened 'infrequently' and when it did 'it wasn't up to much'.[5] She later said he would give her only a 'roll on, roll off' performance.[6] The problems, she confided to James Colthurst, were 'geographical', suggesting either His Royal Highness had difficulty locating her erogenous zones or that his own erogenous zones were focused on somewhere she didn't want to go. In fairness to Charles, her throwing up all the time didn't help sexual relations. Her bulimia, she admitted to Morton, was 'rife'.[7] Whatever the technical issues, the twenty-year-old bride was entitled to long for the affection and intimacy that comes after a long session of good marital sex. The trouble was that Charles was married already. Those warm post-coital interludes Diana dreamed of belonged to Camilla Parker Bowles. Broadlands was full of memories of his ex-mistress. It was chief among the 'safe houses' where they first used to rendezvous twelve years before.

By the second day of their cruise on *Britannia* along the coast of North Africa heading for the Greek Islands, Charles was calling Camilla. He too was in a state of secret panic. The Prince could not live up to being a fantasy man. He needed Camilla to make him flesh and blood. He apparently sent his old mistress a three-page letter from the boat describing his confused feelings. 'The Prince simply had to be in constant contact with Camilla or he couldn't function properly,' Charles's valet Stephen Barry said. 'If he went without his daily phone call he would become tetchy and ill-tempered.'[8] For the Princess, *Britannia* only reinforced the well-populated loneliness that defines royal life. There were twenty-one naval officers, a crew of 256 men, a valet, a dresser, a private secretary and an equerry sharing their romantic getaway. A crew member, Philip Benjamin, says the staff wore rubber-soled slippers so as to make no noise that might disturb the couple. 'We were told to fade into the background. We were to act like air.'[9] Diana nonetheless knew the invisible flunkeys were always listening. There's a painful vignette from Benjamin who remembers her emerging from the royal suite one afternoon in a filmy white negligee with a pink satin bow at the bosom untied and open. 'Chulls,' he quotes her as saying to her husband in a teasing sing-song voice, 'come here and do your duty,' but her charms could not entice the Prince who was deep in his tome in a deckchair.[10]

The age gap between the couple now seemed not twelve years but forty. What Diana had to face at last was that no aristocratic thirty-two-year-olds were like Prince Charles any more. The royals are always at least twenty years behind everybody else because they are the last bastions of tradition. Charles was culturally more influenced by his grandmother, the Queen Mother, and his venerable 'honorary uncles', Lord Mountbatten and the octogenarian writer of mystical travel books, Laurens van der Post, than by his parents or anyone of his own age. Thanks to Prince Philip's spartan regimes and the Queen's arm's-length motherhood, he had had a childhood almost Edwardian in flavour. Who else since the Tsar of Russia's offspring had been paraded for the camera in those white-collar sailor suits or worn a parting that never strayed from the side of his head all through the flower-power era of his adolescence? Who else shot his cuffs at the age of fourteen or shook hands with his mother at the airport? His speaking voice, with its strangled tones, could no longer be heard except in historic recordings of Alfred, Lord Tennyson reading 'The Charge of the Light Brigade'. The Prince's pleasures were those of a man twice his age. Whether contemplative or sporting, they were routinised and ritualised. When he wrote from *Britannia* to friends he talked of his young wife like a grandfather about his teenage granddaughter 'Diana dashes about chatting up all the sailors and the cooks in the galley etc. while I remain hermit-like on the verandah deck, sunk with pure joy into one of Laurens van der Post's books.'[11]

Diana's below-stairs dashing *abite*, of course meant she was bored out of her mind with the company on A deck. And who can blame her? She loved the swimming and the sun but the only other thing to do on the boat was read and books had never been her long suit. At night the couple were liable to be joined for dinner by a phalanx of crisp, rippling *Britannia* senior officers on their best behaviour and serenaded by a mood-enhancing medley of the Royal Marines. There was no pulling into a port to hit the cafés and shops as they cruised past the seaside playgrounds of the Mediterranean. Aside from the complications of the press, *Britannia* showing up means the Crown is in Town. The royal yacht could not visit foreign soil without being met and feted by local dignitaries. In Port Said they had to welcome the President of Egypt, Anwar Sadat, and his wife aboard for dinner.

The voyage would have all been perfectly OK if Diana had felt a more passionate connection with her husband or had had some intellectual resources. As it was, she kept surprising the crew by gatecrashing their below-deck parties and picnics. The petty officers once found her playing the piano to a room full of cheering sailors. They quietly suggested she return upstairs.[12] The trouble was that in this shipwreck movie there was no stowaway Leonardo DiCaprio to ravish Diana under the tarpaulin of a lifeboat. Instead there was the Prince of Wales trawling his way through the complete works of Laurens van der Post. A memory that seems to have been especially painful to Diana was the Prince's insistence on analysing passages from his favourite author with her over lunch.

Boredom fed her jealousy of Camilla and climaxed with the Affair of the Cufflinks, one of the most notorious incidents of alleged heartlessness. The row happened after the Sadat dinner when Diana noticed the Prince sporting the telltale gold entwined Cs on his crisply ironed cuffs. Is it credible Charles could have been so flagrantly insensitive on his honeymoon that he deliberately chose to wear a gift from his former mistress? What causes me to be sceptical is that the Prince never chose his clothes himself. Ties, suits, shirts were always picked out every morning with cufflinks pre-inserted and offered to him like a choice of hors d'oeuvres by his faithful valet Stephen Barry. At Buckingham Palace, Windsor or Sandringham the valet opened his curtains in the morning and ran his bath. An orderly from the Welsh Guards arrived at dawn's light to shine his shoes. Even the Prince's toothbrush was prepared with pre-squeezed Macleans. According to Paul Burrell 'a silver key, bearing his feathers was attached to the end of a toothpaste tube like a sardine-tin key and turned to squeeze enough to fit on the brush.'[13] Paul Burrell also revealed the unedifying detail that Michael Fawcett, later promoted to the honoured post, even held Charles's specimen bottle when a sample was required.[14]

Diana mocked Charles's dependence on his valet to the historian Paul Johnson during one of his vain attempts to give her a tutorial on the British monarchy. After listening to an anecdote about how King George IV would pull the cord for his valet to know the time even when there was a clock over his bed, Diana exclaimed: 'That's just like him! [Charles] Once I was in his dressing room and the valet would put out his clothes, always giving him a choice of three shirts. I asked him which shirt he was going to wear and he told me he didn't like any of them. Across the room there were open racks and racks of endless shirts and all he needed to do was get up and choose one but instead he pressed the button and the valet would have to get more from the rack. So I said to him, "Why don't you cross the room and choose them yourself so the valet can get on with all the other things he needs to do?" But Charles just shouted, "He's paid to do it.'"[15]

Stephen Barry was 'paid to do it' on *Britannia* too, and he already had no love for the new Princess of Wales. He felt himself usurped. Until she came along master and servant had a comfortable well-worn complicity. Barry had been in on the rendezvous with Camilla, he had seen the girls come and go. He was the last person who spoke to Charles at night and the first in the morning. When the Prince first bought Highgrove, Barry had spent bachelor weekends with Charles setting the place up and helping him hang pictures. Now there was a moody and possessive young wife to deal with who did such unlovable things as replacing the formal lace-ups Barry always ordered handmade from John Lobb of St James's with unprincely off-the-rack loafers and picking out sweaters for him to wear in overly fashionable pastel colours the Prince actually seemed to like. Diana never trusted Barry. She found him too familiar with Charles. She actively resented him from the moment he refused her access to the Prince of Wales's rooms in Buckingham Palace during the engagement: 'HRH says no one is allowed in, Lady Diana, I'm sorry but orders are orders. I hope you understand.'[16] She didn't and gradually started to freeze him out.

Barry was in a simmering hissy fit about all this and it's perfectly in character for him to have paid Diana back by inserting Camilla's cufflinks in the royal shirtsleeves as the Prince absent-mindedly dressed for dinner with the Sadats. Perhaps Diana suspected his hand in it herself because by mid-October the frost on their relations was such that Barry handed in his resignation. When he discussed with her what employment he might do next, the Princess said, 'Why don't you read the weather? It only takes two minutes a day.'[17]

Things might have improved if Charles had not made the deadly mistake of taking Diana to Balmoral for the last leg of the honeymoon. Correction. Charles had spent the six weeks from the middle of August to early October at Balmoral every year of his life so it was unthinkable for him to have taken his wife anywhere else. The court was at Balmoral with the Queen and this is where they now had to be. But the Scottish retreat, scene of all the happy, gosh-I'm-all-muddy courting weekends became a toxic place for Diana. Six weeks with your in-laws and their entire extended family – in this case not just the Queen, Prince Philip and the Queen Mother but Princess Anne, Princes Andrew and Edward, Princess Margaret and her two children, Lord Linley and Lady Sarah Armstrong-Jones and all the attendant courtiers and house guests – is very different from faking it through one experimental long weekend. The formality of Balmoral's intractable routine made Diana desperate.

When it wasn't a forced march to a familial picnic barbecued by Prince Philip it was formal dinner with the Queen and whichever august, elderly visitors happened do be in Her Majesty's party. Prince Charles was used to it, always ready in kilt, jacket and frothing jabot ten minutes before they had to leave for the cocktail hour, but Diana was mutinous. Balmoral etiquette required she would not sit next to Charles. She had to take her place between a couple of courtly fogies and listen for two to three hours to the booming of Prince Philip about the evils of the trade unions, or Princess Anne barking on about her day's 'bag'. (Anne, like her brother, went out stalking five days a week. A guest recalls her falling downstairs once at Balmoral. 'She got up, swore horribly, dusted herself down' and headed out with the guns.)[18] Guests had to stay seated until the Queen's bagpipers wheezing traditional Scottish airs finished parading round the table and signalled the women had to leave the men to their port and cigars. Getaways could not be made afterwards until the Queen's exit allowed them (usually a little before midnight), though they could be trapped till 2 a.m. listening to Princess Margaret playing old show tunes on the piano.

Diana was so clearly bored with all this, the royals began to get the alarming realisation that for a girl of her pedigree she was somehow a social novice. They had not understood that she rarely had to contend with set-piece dinners as a teenage girl at Althorp. Perhaps because no one in the immediate royal family had brought a female commoner into the family since the Duke of York married Elizabeth Bowes Lyon in 1923 the older generation were hopelessly out of date with the informality with which aristocratic young women nowadays live their lives. Diana wasn't very different, for instance, to one of the daughters of the 6th Earl of Cawdor, who once showed me to my room at Glamis Castle eating a yogurt with a plastic spoon and wearing skintight black leggings and an oversized T-shirt. It is fair to say that some of the other girls Charles had dated would have handled the Balmoral boot camp better. If Charles had married, say, Lady Jane Wellesley or Amanda Knatchbull, a more sophisticated social proficiency could have been assumed. Lady Jane's parents, the Duke and Duchess of Wellington, entertained handsomely (the Queen herself on many occasions) at Stratfield Saye in Hampshire and Lord Mountbatten's granddaughter, Amanda Knatchbull, was no stranger to glittering company at Broadlands. The royals had expected, wrongly, that Earl Spencer's daughter had had a background too of acquitting herself with small talk to the local grandees. After all, when Stephen Barry first visited her family home he was struck by how much more impressive it was inside than the Queen's own home of Sandringham.[19] None of the royals had really registered what an isolated figure Johnnie Spencer was at Park House after his divorce until he married Raine, eating in solitary, depressed splendour while his children roamed the kitchens picking from the fridge with the staff. Nor did they know how the Spencer children boycotted Raine's soirées in favour of mulish retreats with a tray to their top-floor bedrooms. The reality was that Diana had had little exposure and no practice at the formal art of conversation. Besides, as she told Paul Johnson, she always felt she was 'too thick' to compete.[20]

Faced with the relentless need to be on her toes and social, Diana's intellectual inferiority complex kicked in with a vengeance. While Charles comported himself with his usual polished charm, Diana shrivelled into a silence not appreciated by the Queen. Her Majesty became increasingly tired of the glum face of her new daughter-in-law. A dinner guest recounts how the Queen cornered him one night and exploded: 'Look at her, sitting at the table glowering at us! The only time she bucks up is when Charles speaks to her.' The guest replied: 'Perhaps if you look around the table, ma'am – they're all so much older than her.' She said, 'I don't care. She'll just have to buck up.'[21]

Could any young, contemporary girl have subsumed herself as much as the royal lifestyle required? With her own friends Diana could be the life and soul of the party, lifting any gathering she was in with her wonderful smile and teasing wit. She later told Rosa Monckton that one of the hardest things to get used to was being addressed not as Diana but as Your Royal Highness with 'people hanging on [my] every word – only I had none!'[22] Even visitors three times her age found Balmoral daunting at times. Lord Glenconner, a regular guest of Princess Margaret, once found himself rebuked for failing to get up in time to be present at breakfast. Margaret herself, a divorced woman, often complained to friends of her loneliness when she was there. The Queen's sister was reduced to spending hours alone in her room sticking pictures in her photo albums, yet it would never have occurred to her to buck the royal routine and refuse to go. The Windsor rules were never rethought. 'You are either with them or dead,' the Duchess of Windsor once said to the actress Lilli Palmer.

With them AND dead, is how Diana felt. It rained and rained. The royals baulk at the price of turning the heating on and she always seemed to be cold. It got on her nerves that as soon as you left a room at Balmoral someone behind you would switch the light off.[23] To try to cheer her up Charles moved them out of the castle itself into Craigowan, one of the guest houses ('austere, cold, painted prep-school green' according to a guest who has also been accommodated there), which at least allowed Diana to run her own house. He was trying to be solicitous of his wife but he refused to take her back to London as she wished. His view was that this was basic royal rigour and if she was now a member of the Firm it was essential she learned to handle it. It also happened to be his favourite place on earth. He could not, would not believe that she wouldn't come to love it too, especially after the Oscar performance she had given tramping through the heather before the engagement. Had she not listed 'the country' as one of the things they had in common in the interview on their wedding eve? The Prince modified his own routines not at all, setting off at nine thirty every morning with the guns wearing the grey-green tweeds of the royal estate and absent all afternoon fishing on the banks of the River Dee with his grandmother. Every year his grandmother gave Charles a new fishing rod for Christmas. Diana refused to join the shooting parties for lunch. She no longer felt the need to pretend to enjoy the slaughtering of feathery baby grouse.

Left in the house with the big old-fashioned TV on legs and the kind of phone only seen these days in Agatha Christie's The Mousetrap, Diana pined for London. There were tables groaning with wedding gifts still on display at Buckingham Palace. She longed to have the fun of placing some of them in her new home at Kensington Palace. As one of the Prince's staff put it: 'She was a girl who loved shopping. She'd had a taste of glittering functions, parties and shops and all of the sudden a country girl had become a city girl.' Stuck in Balmoral with her Sony Walkman she was Emma Bovary in headphones. 'I feel totally out of place here,' she wrote to one of her former flatmates. 'I sometimes wonder what on earth I have got myself into. I feel so small, so lonely, so out of my depth.'[24]

She could not get away here with her usual trick of consorting with the servants for light relief. In this most traditional of the Queen's homes, below-stairs visits, or 'Scandinavian practices' as they were known after laxer European royal families, were not tolerated. After one such visitation from Diana, the Yeoman of the Glass and China approached her with a cheerful greeting as she walked into the kitchens. Gesturing towards the door, the yeoman told her firmly: 'Through there, ma'am, is your side of the house. Through here is our side of the house.'[25] Diana beat a blushing retreat.

The *News of the World* carried a picture of her looking tense walking ahead of Princess Margaret on a shopping excursion to the nearby village of Ballater. 'Diana in a baggy shirt, summery skirt and cardigan and Margaret in tweed skirt, blouse and cardigan, were accompanied by a detective and a lady-in-waiting. They spent half an hour in two shops looking at traditional Scottish woollens.'[26] Traditional woollens. A far cry from the Emanuels' chic and humming little studio in Mayfair.

It has always been puzzling to me that Diana didn't invite more of her own friends up to Balmoral for company. She did ask her sisters and her mother and two of her flatmates for a few days but she could have had a constant flow of distracting chums. It's not as if there wasn't room. Her former London circle would have been thrilled and honoured to visit. James Colthurst says he believes the reason was Diana was embarrassed. She didn't want to reveal to them how badly she coped. She'd last been seen leaving St Paul's Cathedral in an open-topped landau cheered through the streets of London by the British nation and the whole world. Now she was 'small' again, Diana the Dim. Her dashing new identity had collapsed. At Balmoral she was neither Daddy's indulged little girl as she had been before Raine arrived at Althorp, nor the adored media darling of the red tops. Balmoral was not her show, it was the Queen's, and after hers, the Queen Mother's. 'He [Charles] was in awe of his Mama,' she told Morton, 'and I was always the third person in the room. It was never "Darling, would you like a drink?" It was always "Mummy, would you like a drink? Granny, would you like a drink?" Fine, no problem. But I had to be told that was normal because I always thought it was the wife first – stupid thought.'[27] Stupid thought, yes, or maybe something worse: the onset of superstar entitlement. The Prince offering first a drink to his mother – even if she were not the sovereign – and then his eighty-five-year-old grandmother ahead of his twenty-year-old wife, was only basic good manners ('age before beauty'), something Charles never forgot. Six months of adulation from the press had begun to reshape Diana's world view.

In September Charles and Diana were sighted for the first time on an official engagement at the annual Braemar Gathering and Highland Games, a relief to Diana because even watching the whirling sporrans of Highland Dancing and Tossing the Caber were better than mooching around Craigowan waiting for Charles to return with a dead fish. When the national anthem struck up the Prince whispered to her, 'They're playing our song.' Diana started to giggle, causing the Prince to forget the discipline of a lifetime and silently crack up too. It could have been a delightful moment of new marital complicity but the filthy look the Queen sent across froze them both. A member of the Spencer family told James Whitaker: 'That was a definite faux pas. But though the Queen was annoyed with Diana she was furious with Charles. I can assure you neither will make that mistake again.'[28] Caught between his mother's requirement of duty and his wife's requirement of him, the Prince of Wales couldn't win.

By October things had got so bad, Charles requested that his aide, Michael Colborne, come up from London and 'sit with' Diana. Lady Romsey, wife of Charles's close friend, Mountbatten grandson Norton Romsey (and latterly a close confidante of Prince Philip), had been deputed to spend the day with Diana while Charles and Norton hunted deer, but Diana didn't want to be babysat with one of Charles's Camilla set. 'She couldn't relate to Lady Romsey anyway,' said a staff member, 'because she was indoctrinated into Charles's way of life.'[29] Diana asked instead for Charles's forthright Australian personal secretary who had provided his kindly paternal support during the engagement.

Colborne caught the night train to Craithie and was driven up the hill to Craigowan. He was appalled when he arrived to see how thin Diana had become. She had dropped from ten stone to eight stone twelve – alarmingly low for her five-foot-ten frame. Colborne had expected to stay with the Princess a couple of hours but ended up sitting with her for seven, often in silence listening to the ticking of the white clock on the wall while Diana sat with her head bowed or raged about her feelings of frustration, anger and abandonment. 'I can't stick it much longer,' was her tearful refrain.[30]

Charles too, was clearly at the end of his tether. According to a palace official, when Colborne picked up the Prince from Craigowan in the evening to take him to the royal train in Aberdeen from where they were leaving for a regimental engagement in Aldershot the next day, he could hear the Prince and Princess inside having a flaming row. The door burst open and Charles appeared, looking thunderous. 'Michael!' he said and threw something gold at him. It was Diana's Welsh gold wedding ring the British people had so recently seen being placed tenderly on her third finger before the Archbishop of Canterbury. 'Get it made smaller,' the Prince of Wales said.[31]

Prince and royal servant drove down the winding road in silence, until Charles suddenly turned on Colborne. He started to vent about, of all things, the carpets that had been installed against his wishes in his new Range Rover. He minded that when he slung the deer he'd shot in the back of the car it left blood all over the mat. The berated servant, who had already informed the Prince that the mats had press studs for removal for just this purpose, was nursing his hurt feelings on the train when the Prince summoned him to his private carriage. He offered Colborne a drink. 'Tonight, Michael,' he said, 'you displayed the best traditions of silent service. You didn't say a word.'[32] He then proceeded to reward Colborne by dumping his problems all over him again. For five hours the Prince ruminated aloud about Diana's baffling dislike of country pursuits, her possessive need to be in his company all the time, her lack of any sustaining hobbies. Penny Junor alleges that Diana had became so frustrated one night with the sight of Charles kneeling beside the bed saying his nightly prayers that she hit him over the head with the family Bible.[33] Perhaps Charles forgot to mention that domestic detail.

It seems he also forgot to mention another detail in his wife's 'irrationality' – Camilla. Or what he liked to call his wife's 'obsession with Camilla'.[34] The gloss his friends like to put on it now is that Diana's crazy jealousy of the past made Camilla ever-present. Their insistence that the Prince at this time had put his ex-mistress behind him is deliberately disingenuous and obfuscatingly literal. Charles was too decent a man to have been already contemplating adultery on his honeymoon, but his emotions were still deeply engaged there and for Diana that was worse. She was plagued with dreams about her rival and it's not surprising. Most brides would resent their husbands continuing to correspond with and making calls to a mistress as recent and long-lasting as Camilla Parker Bowles. Friendship takes much longer to replace love than a few paltry weeks. And Diana's unerring female antennae rightly told her that Camilla's 'friendship' was a strategy for deftly sustaining her control. If Diana was 'possessive' it was because she knew that when it came to his wife, Charles had never been possessed.

The fact that Charles, with the approval of the Queen, now took his wife down to London to seek professional help was a sign of how desperately worried he had become. The royals are very suspicious of psychiatric interventions and doctors in general for that matter. When Princess Margaret, after suffering a series of strokes, was seriously depressed towards the end of her life, a friend went to see the Queen to suggest they might bring in a therapist. 'Perhaps when she's better we could consider that,' said the Queen.[35]

Diana suggests to Andrew Morton that not just one but several psychoanalysts and pharmacologists 'came plodding in trying to sort me out. Put me on high doses of Valium and everything else.'[36] She rejected the medication, suspecting a plot to muzzle her spirit – she knew the Duke of Kent's wife, Katharine Worsley, had been through similar traumatic times after a miscarriage in 1977 and was now labelled 'poor mad Kate Kent' in their social circles. It was clearly a time of great disorientation because even ten years later when she talked about it to Andrew Morton she spoke about herself in the third person as if trying to hold on to the girl she was such a short time ago. 'The Diana that was still very much there had decided it was just time, patience and adapting were all that were needed.'[37] The consultations, anyway, had little chance to be effective. Diana withheld crucial medical information. If Charles wanted to nurture his secret then she would have a secret too. She never revealed the bulimia that was so pivotal to her mood swings.

It was not till mid-October that the Prince and Princess of Wales finally ended the honeymoon from hell. In a singularly bad piece of planning, neither Highgrove nor their apartment in Kensington Palace was ready to receive them, and they would spend seven months in Charles's old bachelor flat at Buckingham Palace. Among the royal family there was growing trepidation when they left about what appeared to be Diana's incipient nervous breakdown. They had seen nothing yet. For the next sixteen years the unacknowledged nervous breakdown was theirs.

## Chapter 10

# The Upstage Problem

'The Princess had everything going for her except the ability to not upstage the Prince.'

– Stephen Barry, Prince Charles's valet

The immensity of Diana's star quality was something the Firm could never fully comprehend. The Queen Mother was long accustomed to being a warm and fuzzy love object. Princess Margaret's paparazzi impact had had a movie-star dimension in its time. And the Queen herself, who has always been viewed with a respect verging on fondness, had possessed phenomenal appeal when she was young and beautiful.

Cynthia Gladwyn and her husband, the British Ambassador to France in the mid-fifties, entertained the Queen at the Paris embassy in 1957. Lady Gladwyn's diary reflects the awed fascination the monarch engendered in those days. 'To my mind she is almost perfect,' she wrote. 'She has dark hair, blue eyes and a lovely English skin. Her features are not classical but she is much prettier in real life than in photographs, she has an exceptionally charming soft clear voice, high-pitched and pitched just right like a singer and with an almost bell-like quality . . . To quote Cecil B in his letter "she scored a bull's eye every time she smiled."'[1] (The reference was to Beaton, though it could as easily have been de Mille.) At the young Queen's side, Prince Philip's commanding height and striking, virile good looks created 'an easy democratic atmosphere', Gladwyn noted, like a 'breezy sailor who has known what it is not to be a royalty'.[2]

In later years the Queen developed the turned-down Hanoverian mouth of her ancestors, but the smile that enchanted Beaton could still transform her features. Edward Mirzoeff, the BBC film-maker who spent many months studying her up close for his celebrated documentary *Elizabeth R*, avers that she has always been very attractive to men. 'It's something in the eyes and the smile. Martin Charteris [her former private secretary] was in love with her – you could see that.'[3]

Undeniably, the sovereign and her consort had crowd-pleasing charisma in the early years of their marriage. In a conversation with Gyles Brandreth, Philip talked about the days when he and the Queen were seen and talked about and written up as characters in a fairy tale. 'The level of adulation – you wouldn't believe it,' he said, with perhaps a touch of nostalgia. 'It could have been corroding. It would have been very easy to play to the gallery, but I took a conscious decision not to do that. *Safer not to be too popular.* You can't fall too far.'[4]

If the Duke of Edinburgh is making a veiled suggestion here that the only qualitative or quantitative difference between Diana's fame on the one hand and that of himself and his royal wife on the other was Diana's pushiness and their self-restraint, then he is kidding – and flattering – himself. It wasn't just that since the 1950s the mass media had multiplied its outlets and abandoned its reticence. There was also an order of magnitude's difference between the containable, appropriate, rather formal admiration bestowed on the young Queen and her consort and the incendiary star power of Princess Diana. Its wattage kept increasing every year Diana was alive rather than 'damping down' as the royal family had expected. By 1992 Diana's global magic was so intense that the bench she sat on at the Taj Mahal was renamed the Princess Diana Seat, blowing out 339 years of the historic karma surrounding the woman whose beauty had inspired the building, Mumatz Mahal. Diana would have always been a beautiful, warm and empathetic woman, but her tribulations gave her the incentive to become extraordinary. Pain made her luminous. And what made her so riveting to the British people is the way they saw this transformation happening before their eyes.

Diana's impact was confusing even to herself. Her self-image still carried strong traces of the 'big awkward girl' remarked on by Princess Margaret's guest on New Year's Eve only nine months before. Now she was rake-slim, her height gave her a natural elegance, and her rounded little girl's face had gained the refined contours of a beauty that was bred in the bone. Those changes would have made her a show-stopper anyway, but a bigger transformation than duckling into swan was under way. 'Diana had a similar relationship to the camera that Garbo had,' said Meredith Etherington-Smith, who curated the auction of Diana's dresses for Christie's in New York in 1997. 'They can almost feel the way the light hits them and react instinctively. It's not something you acquire.'[5]

Prince Charles himself had not truly begun to apprehend it until the screening of their wedding video for *Britannia*'s officers and crew in the royal yacht's private cinema. As the replay of that spectacular day unreeled, to the accompaniment of occasional cheers and whoops of delight from the audience, the magical charm of the new Princess of Wales, the sweet, human way she interacted with her young brides-maids, the tender *connection* she seemed to have mysteriously forged with the British people – all this was blindingly apparent. Stephen Barry noted a subdued vibration in the Prince that implied a dawning understanding of something ominous. 'The Princess had everything going for her except the ability to not upstage the Prince,' Barry said.[6] *Upstage*, however, implies a wilful effort to grab attention. That would come later. No one could accuse Diana of showboating on her wedding day. Nor was it the crowd appeal of Diana's beauty alone that discomfited Prince Charles. As a bachelor, Action Man had been used to being photographed with gorgeous girls. They made him look more dashing. No, what Charles had suddenly perceived was that unlike the Queen and Prince Philip, who presented a charming double act of grace and granite, Diana's strengths did not act as a foil to his. Instead they served to spotlight his shortcomings. It was as if for the first time in his life the Prince's own lack of naturalness, spontaneity and feeling were suddenly laid bare. Diana's instinctive nature called into question everything he had toiled to learn. All *she* had to do was be herself.

If Charles had had the self-assurance of a man like John F. Kennedy he might have figured out a way to channel this potential threat. But how could he have that kind of self-assurance? Yes, JFK was movie-star handsome and Broadway-star suave while Charles was awkward and jug-eared. (Of course, Gary Cooper was awkward, too, and Clark Gable had jug ears.) But there was more to it than that. To go with his looks, JFK had real power, and he knew how to use it. The American presidency and the British monarchy both come equipped with impressive façades. Indeed, compared to the monarchy, with its crowns and ermines and yacht and castles and gilded coaches and elaborately costumed guards, the 'republican' panoply of the presidency – the plain white columned mansion, the businesslike Oval Office, the jet with its presidential seal, the silent, wary secret service men – is actually rather modest. But behind the presidential façade is the power of life or death over the whole world. Behind the monarchical façade is . . . well, not much. A family, and a fairly dysfunctional one at that (though no more dysfunctional than a great many non-royal families). As a putative man of power, Charles was thrice mocked: by history (five hundred years ago the monarch's power was nearly absolute; a hundred years ago it was still considerable); by contemporary political reality (the monarch has no power, but must do whatever the politicians say); and by propinquity (Charles was not even the monarch, merely the heir). 'I am the man who accompanied Jacqueline Kennedy to Paris,'[7] the President said bemusedly at the end of a state visit to France, and everyone chuckled. He could get away with poking fun at himself as a slightly clueless, slightly hapless, almost anonymous husband – a sort of Denis Thatcher – precisely because he was nothing of the kind. When Prince Charles said in Wales, 'At least I know my place now. I'm nothing more than a carrier of flowers for my wife,'[8] all anyone could do was cringe and think – well, yes.

Shortly after their marriage the new dynamics of Charles and Diana's relationship could be seen at a black-tie dinner I attended at the American Embassy in London. It was an extraordinarily beguiling moment, when Diana's star quality was emerging but the schoolgirl was still there. She was a princess poised in transition between innocent impact and calculated effect. Wearing a dress of white organza and blue sequinned chiffon that revealed her pale shoulders, her neck circled by the glimmer of a triple pearl choker fastened with a diamond clip, she had the look of an uncertain fairy-tale wraith. We were asked to form up in groups of four to be introduced. The playwright Tom Stoppard was in my group. It was the first time I'd ever seen him at a loss for words. Diana came before Charles, pure and fresh and charmingly angular with her sixth-form looks, leading the small talk with a slightly pointed chin. I told her I had come back from a wonderful trip to Venice by train. 'I can never sleep on trains, can you?' she replied. When Charles joined her, his accomplished manner made Diana seem younger still. 'I've thought of a good idea for a play,' the Prince told Tom Stoppard. 'It's about a hotel which caters entirely for people with phobias. It was a small item in *The Times*.' 'We'll go halves on the take, sir,' said Stoppard kindly. 'Actually, I thought it was so amusing,' Prince Charles persisted, 'I telephoned Spike Milligan and told him. It's a most frightfully funny idea, don't you think?'[9] Naturally, everyone fell about until he moved on.

I was struck by how odd it must be to always be coming upon silent people who stand there waiting to be addressed. But even at this early stage Diana had evolved a perfect way to deal with it. In a light, airy way she broke through by offering a shared little experience of her own that immediately communicated she was human. She didn't really need to say anything. Every pair of eyes followed her hungrily as she bade the ambassador a slim, luminous goodnight.[10]

Diana's new poise was proof of how much she had already learned on the Wales tour, the three days in October which had been the first serious public exposure of the Prince and Princess as a married couple. It was a gruelling initiation into the art of the royal walkabout. Diana had discovered she was pregnant on the eve of the visit and was feeling like hell. It was cold and damp. When she talked about it to Morton all she remembered was how she had thrown up with morning sickness before each engagement and felt hopelessly out of her depth. 'Wrong clothes, wrong everything, wrong timing, feeling terribly sick carrying this child looking grey and gaunt and still being sick.'[11] That may have been how she saw herself, but it was hardly how she came across to the people of Wales. She had the star's natural ability to present the dazzling opposite of how she felt. The outfit was indeed tragic, a heavy red and green threaded sofa throw by the look of it, with a fringed stand-up collar and a dinky little John Boyd bowler hat on her head bobbing with three ludicrous ostrich feathers, but far from finding this ensemble all wrong, the crowd was wowed by the freshness of Diana's approach. 'She was enchanting,' said the writer Victoria Mather who was watching her that day. 'Her little red hat was so beguiling. Her youth and innocence were incandescently pretty.'[12] Charles told her lady-in-waiting Anne Beckwith-Smith, 'Stay close to her, she needs your support.'[13]

Despite the weather, thousands lined the streets to Caernarvon Castle. Charles walked down one side and Diana walked down the other. Jayne Fincher, a photographer covering the tour, was struck immediately by the difference between Diana and the other royal women, whose style was to extend a gloved hand to a crowd member and pass by with a polished remark. When the Queen is exposed to a crowd she is dignified and formal. She might walk to the edge of a barrier and take some flowers very gently and elegantly, but more often than not she does not risk the 'clutch' problem by shaking hands.[14] Princess Anne worked devotedly for the Save the Children Fund, but she had never been seen to pick up a child or kiss or even touch one on her numerous trips to Africa as the foundation's president. *Sun* photographer Arthur Edwards recalled that at a mass vaccination in Swaziland in 1982 he saw Princess Anne watch as five thousand crying babies in the arms of their fearful mothers were inoculated against childhood illnesses. 'Not a flicker of feeling passed over her face,' said Edwards. 'Trained, like the rest of her relatives, never to show her emotions, the Princess Royal failed to reveal what was obviously in her heart.'[15] With Diana it was all heart all the time. She had learned how to say the Welsh for 'thank you', 'Diolch yn fawr', when she was handed gifts and embraced a child with spina bifida.[16]

Said Judy Wade, the Australian journalist with the Sun, 'She would get down, bend down and talk to small children. She was just so different, so much closer to the people. It was brilliant for us – it provided good stories every single day.'[17] Her nursery-teacher days made her a natural at engaging with infants, offering hugs, hand squeezes and encouraging smiles. Her early touch as a school volunteer at a mental hospital was reprised with the sensitive way she reached out to the wheelchair-bound and the elderly. In Carmarthen it started to rain but despite her rampant nausea she kept smiling and continued to work the crowd without a coat. Jayne Fincher noticed how strained Diana looked when you got up close. 'She'd gone from this lovely, tanned, healthy, robust girl to looking really quite tired and thin and pale.'[18] Alighting from the car to see a jostling, craning crowd, all chanting her name, all wanting to touch her 'She can suddenly stop smiling,' recorded an observer, 'and look around with the purest terror in her eyes.'[19] But this only endeared her to the protective streak in the Welsh. An invalid woman near her in the crowd said: 'You must be cold.' Diana looked at her and said feelingly: 'Not as cold as you, I should think.'[20]

The Mayor of Brecon recalled what happened when Prince Charles spontaneously decided to switch with Diana and go over her side of the road. 'Every time this happened you had this huge "oooah" from the people that she was leaving. All the time people kept calling "Di, Di" to come to their side.'[21] Help! At first Charles beamed and collected all the flowers on behalf of his wife, and he was always solicitous of her, crossing the street once to shield her with an umbrella, but Jayne Fincher saw the Prince's face start to fall as the day wore on. 'It would be really embarrassing,' she said. 'On the other side of the road they'd all be going "Oh no!" because they'd got him. He'd just turn around and say, "I'm really sorry, she'll be here in a minute."'[22] When their Rolls approached an expectant village, the people yelled 'There she is!' not 'There they are!'[23] A Palace official noted Charles kicking a pebble around. The Prince told him: '"They don't want to see me." He was wobbly. He seemed schizophrenic, deeply caring followed by deeply selfish.'[24] The worst of it was that when Diana was resting, Charles would be off in other parts of Wales delivering speeches. Coverage for these the next day was nil.

It is impossible to overemphasise how devastating the Wales experience was for Prince Charles. He was the Prince of Wales, for God's sake, not the Prince of Scotland or Ulster or Devon. Caernarvon Castle had been the scene of his Coming of Age as the heir to the throne, televised twelve years before to a dazzled nation. This was his turf and he had never before had to share it with anyone. His brothers and sister didn't get equal billing. They may have been his immediate family but they were still treated as 'minor royals'. It would have been difficult enough for Charles to accept that he had an equal, let alone a spouse who left him in the dust.

Diana was clearly discomfited herself by the excessive attention directed at her. She kept prodding her handlers about how they could beef up response to his side of the crowd. She later asked Ronald Allison, a Buckingham Palace press secretary, if the publicity about her would go away soon. Allison saw the writing on the wall. 'I'm sorry, it won't,' he replied. 'And it never will. I wish I could tell you otherwise, but if I did I would be telling you a lie.'[25]

Like any woman who finds that the balance of power has suddenly shifted in her marriage, Diana clearly saw how this would ruffle the relationship. 'If you're a man, like my husband a proud man, you mind about that if you hear it every day for four weeks,' she told Martin Bashir in the BBC interview in November 1995. 'And you feel low about it, instead of feeling happy and sharing it.'[26] She had expected to be lavished with praise by the Palace for her heroic efforts, but no response was forthcoming and it ate at her. 'Diana couldn't understand why nobody said, "Well done,"' recalled a former Palace aide. 'The reason is that they all do their duty, and they wonder what is so unique.'[27] They wondered all right. She told James Colthurst that she 'really got it in the neck from Charles' after the Wales tour.[28]

A week later, on 4 November 1981, it was Her Majesty's turn to experience the Diana factor. The State Opening of Parliament is the starring moment of the Queen's year, when she gets to sit on a throne in the House of Lords wearing the Imperial State Crown with the Black Prince's ruby glinting in the centre and accept the fealty of her government in a blaze of pageantry and trumpets. The occasion offers reassurance to the monarch that, while her real power may be diminished, her job security – unlike the Prime Minister's – is rock solid.

Every so often there is speculation that the Queen of England, like some golden-parachuting CEO, will abdicate to 'make way' for a new generation. This fails to understand the true nature of the monarch. It's not an office, it's an incarnation. You don't run for it and (as the sad example of the Duke of Windsor cautions) you don't run away from it. You're born to it and therefore you die in it. 'All the days of my life,' was the Queen's coronation oath in Westminster Abbey. When she learned from Michael Shea on 30 April 1980 that Queen Juliana of the Netherlands had abdicated in favour of her daughter, Elizabeth II replied briskly, 'Typical Dutch.'[29]

But it's safe to say that between Diana's marriage to Charles on 29 July 1981 and their official separation on 9 December 1992, the State Opening of Parliament was never the Queen's (nor Mrs Thatcher's) show again. It became instead an annual showcase for Diana's latest look. This was clear from the moment that the Princess alighted from the glass coach in which she had travelled to Westminster next to Princess Anne. All eyes swivelled to Diana's side of the House of Lords when she and Prince Charles and their retinue of pages entered to sit on one side of the Queen and Prince Philip, while Princess Anne and her entourage sat on the other. Some peeresses even trained their opera glasses on Diana's glossy head. Desperate not to repeat the mistake of dressing too provocatively, Diana got it exactly right the first year in a simple, almost virginal, pure white V-necked chiffon gown worn with a tiara and a pearl choker. Her tall simplicity utterly eclipsed the short, jewel-upholstered figure of the fifty-five-year-old Queen Elizabeth II. Diana had no official role in the ceremonies; it was the drama of her look that stole the show.

But the fastidious director of the Victoria and Albert Museum, Roy Strong, was unimpressed by what she said, or might have said, when he met her that same night at the unveiling of the Splendours of the Gonzagas exhibition from Italy at the V&A. In his diary he raved about the Prince's 'easy charm and dignity' but was contemptuous of Diana's inexperienced awkwardness. His observation of how much she had to learn and how she was 'a typical product of an upper class girls' school' shows how fast Diana could be reduced to gaucheness in the presence of intellectuals or establishment bigwigs. To the humble Welsh crowds she was never stuck for something to say. 'Her accent is really rather awful, considering that she is an earl's daughter,' wrote the rather more awful Strong. 'Not an upper class drawl at all but rather tuneless and, dare I say it, a bit common, as though it were the fashion to learn to talk down.'[30]

It serves Strong right perhaps that the picture relayed round the globe the next day was one that caught Diana nodding off on the red velvet throne the Victoria and Albert provided her to sit on next to Charles. She was exhausted, poor girl, after the ordeal of being on display all day long. (Strong did at least have the sensitivity to note, 'I didn't think he – Charles – looked after her enough.') The irresistible image, captioned everywhere as 'The Sleeping Princess', swiftly prompted an announcement that proved Diana's lapse was not boredom but forgivable fatigue. The Princess of Wales was pregnant! More press hysteria and maudlin national festivity. Strangers broke out into strains of 'Congratulations' any time she was near a band. In the *Daily Express* her usually successfully muffled step-grandmother Barbara Cartland broke loose with one of her saccharine fatwas. 'The first baby should be conceived in the full bloom of romance!' she decreed. 'This baby will be a victory over the horrid modern practice of putting off a family until one or both partners' careers are established. It is a great mistake to delay a first child. It is interfering with nature and nature always knows best. I hope it will be a son because it's what every English man and woman wants.'[31]

Unfortunately, nature also made Diana violently sick every day. She kept cancelling joint appearances, wanting only to curl up in bed and sleep. This raised the eyebrows of the other royal women, for whom a pregnancy was supposed to be taken like a jump over a hedge. The Queen did not appreciate the press encomia about the sort of exemplary mother Diana was likely to be in contrast to the way Her Majesty had raised Prince Charles. 'There'll be no patent shoes, velvet collars and those knickerbockers which made Charles stand out like a sore, gloved thumb among ordinary children even twenty years ago,' blathered the *Daily Express*'s doyenne, Jean Rook. 'I can't see Diana shoving her child astride a pony just because royal children are traditionally pictured on their ponies, even if their little pink-scrubbed ears are laid back in terror.'[32]

One might ask why Diana had elected to get pregnant with her first child so quickly when she had so much else on her plate. A top consultant gynaecologist at a London hospital rued the decision in the *News of the World*. 'I always tell women that the two things they shouldn't do if they don't want things to go wrong is get themselves exhausted or under too much strain,' he wrote. 'The Princess is constantly on public view, which we already know creates stress in her because she collapsed in tears at a polo match just before her wedding.'[33] Prince Charles had not wanted to start a family so early himself, imagining three years when Diana could play herself in as a new member of the royal team and notch up a few tours like the one they now had to cancel to Australia and New Zealand. But Diana was steeped in her mother's turbulent maternal history. She knew that the way to regain instant familial approbation within the House of Windsor was to produce the heir and the spare, giving her husband, whether he was impatient for it or not, what 'every English man and woman wants'. The news of her pregnancy flabbergasted feminists who were already baffled by Diana's wilfully retro life choices. At twenty she would now add motherhood to her other rapidly assumed roles of Princess, national sweetheart and wife. It isolated her further from the friends of her old life, most of whom weren't even married, let alone *enceinte*. But getting pregnant fast gave Diana something real to do. The girl who loved busying herself with domestic chores now had everything done for her. The girl who loved being around the young now spent most of her time around the old. She needed the tenderness of a baby in her life or she would freeze to death.

Until May the couple were still living in Buckingham Palace, where Diana felt oppressed by the old routines of Charles's bachelor life. She was demoralised, too, by the feeling of being, not an empowered young wife, but an insignificant satellite of her royal mother-in-law. The more inadequate she felt the more she pored over the critiques and panegyrics of her press. Her success in the metropolitan sphere confirmed her rejection of Charles's passion for country pursuits. Her distaste for shooting and hunting was turning to outright hostility. No one expected her to indulge in blood sports which made her uncomfortable, but could she, to please her husband, not get up on a horse once in a while? It was a similar attitude of defeatism her teachers had noted at school. Knowing she couldn't excel like Camilla on horseback, Diana didn't want to try. And fishing was too contemplative a sport for a girl who longed only to escape her thoughts. No, her natural habitat now was London, where Camilla and her gumboots would never reign. The Princess's aides noticed that while Diana loved discussing the decor of their future apartment at Kensington Palace, she took almost zero interest in the planning of the Prince's new country retreat, Highgrove.

It's not surprising that Kensington Palace was more congenial to Diana. She was too young for all the chatelaine stuff that would have enthralled a sophisticated social wife in her mid-thirties. Like a schoolgirl who's just discovered the Big City, Diana was madly enamoured with London buzz. Not that living in KP, as it was known, was typical of the bright young thing urban experience. It was like having a luxurious triplex in the grandest of apartment buildings – except that all the other apartments are full of people to whom your husband is related or whom you want to avoid (in Diana's case often the same thing). Edward VII once described the place as an aunt heap.[34] It did, however, offer Diana more autonomy to run her own show. The Wales apartment occupied Numbers 8 and 9, secluded on the Palace's north side. The rooms were spacious and elegant but also compact and manageable in size. Diana had already declared her independence by having the three floors decorated not by David Hicks, the top-of-the-line decorator married to Mountbatten's daughter Pamela, whom everyone expected was a shoo-in for the job, but Dudley Poplak, a conventional, chintzy decorator friend of her mother's. Charles, never wild about Poplak's Sloaney taste, upgraded it with furniture and pictures from the Royal Collections. The apartment's Georgian windows overlooked a private walled garden of a peacefulness that made it hard to believe you were in the heart of a teeming metropolis. Diana used to sunbathe there in the summer months. The below-stairs pecking order of butler, housekeeper, valet, two chefs, two chauffeurs and a cleaner – with the addition of a ground-floor equerries room and the loitering presence of two police protection officers awaiting their orders for the day – gave Apartments 8 and 9 the feeling of a boutique hotel without the tourists.

There were four other royal households based in KP, creating a gossip channel that ran through the rooms like the low chatter of liveried mice. Apartment 1A housed the now fifty-one-year-old Princess Margaret, the Queen's fadingly glamorous younger sister, who had such a short time ago seemed almost fast-track, with her Caribbean tan and young hippyish boyfriend, Roddy Llewellyn. She now led a boring grand life, rising at 11 a.m. to go to her hairdresser's, David and Joseph in Berkeley Street, and emerging in full make-up for a boozy lunch with one of her gay walkers at the Ritz. Margo, as she was known by the family, was at first a cautiously sympathetic ally of Diana. They sometimes travelled to royal events together in the elder Princess's Rolls, with Margaret, a canny diva herself, guarding against the upstage problem by always exiting from the car first, shaking hands with her host and only then introducing the junior-in-status Princess of Wales.[35] Eventually they quarrelled, when Diana fired her butler Harold Brown for no apparent reason and promoted Paul Burrell. Margaret picked up Brown for her own household, but Diana, far from being glad that her former employee had found a job elsewhere, indulged one of her outbursts of focused spite demanding Brown get out of KP altogether – including out of his rent-free apartment. She made the mistake of telling Margaret so and felt the full force of the Queen's Sister Act. 'Just remember who owns the flat,' Princess Margaret told Diana icily, 'and who owns *yours*, too.'[36]

One useful legacy of the friendship was Diana's discovery that the approach to Margaret's front door in King's Court was the only one in the Palace not covered by closed-circuit TV. (Once upon a time Margaret, too, had had a juicy private life she wished to hide.) Better still, across the courtyard opposite Margaret's was a secret passage that led to the back entrance of the Waleses' Apartment 8.[37] Diana made full use of its secrecy. When the amorous Hasnat Khan was smuggled into the Palace courtyard under a blanket in the back of Diana's BMW driven by Paul Burrell, the butler drove him not to the Princess of Wales's front entrance but into the unpoliced King's Court and the back entrance.

One pair of curious eyes Diana sought to avoid belonged to the occupant of Number 10: the Austrian dynamo Princess Michael of Kent, aka Princess Pushy, who resided there with her husband, the Queen's cousin Prince Michael of Kent, a bearded Tsar Nicholas II lookalike, and their two small children, Ella and Freddie. Diana was convinced that 'the Führer', as she called Princess Michael, sometimes spied on her through her curtains and retaliated by spying back through her little opera glasses.[38] There was a lot of trench warfare between the Princesses Margaret and Michael, too. The latter accused Margaret of nearly poisoning the Kents' cat in a reckless campaign to annihilate the Palace squirrels.[39] Princess Michael's Valkyrie good looks, shortage of cash and serial snubbings from the rest of the family made her the gift that kept on giving to the media. An especially lively episode was the day the *Daily Mirror* discovered her father was a member of the SS. The Queen's press secretary, Michael Shea, had to put it to the Austrian princess. She said, recalls Shea, 'I don't know. I will have to ask my mother.' Then she called back and said, 'It appears to be true.'[40] The day the unmistakably tall Austrian blonde was caught emerging from an Eaton Square address in a red wig followed by Texas millionaire John Ward Hunt was a bigger ratings draw still.

The Duke and Duchess of Gloucester and the Duke and Duchess of (confusingly, also-named) Kent were lower-profile Palace neighbours. In Mrs Thatcher's abrasive times the writing was on the wall that these two ducal descendants of George V and their families were unlikely to hang on for long to their income from the Civil List. The axe finally fell under Tory Prime Minister John Major in 1992, leaving them wholly dependent on the Queen's generosity. Hence they never complained if the Queen's office dispatched them to open a fish-packing plant in Grimsby in the middle of the Christmas holidays.

The Gloucesters had a thirty-five-room Palace apartment while the Duke and Duchess of Kent were ensconced at Wren House, inside the royal compound. 'Eddie' Kent is a strangely elongated version of Prince Charles, with whom he is close. (The Duke looks even more like a hall-of-mirrors Wales at the Queen's annual garden parties when he wears a top hat.) He spends his time carrying out second-tier engagements the big royals have passed on, while the Duchess ('Nutty Norah' to the staff) has been known for her mysterious 'troubles' and conversion to Catholicism. Diana came to see her as a sweet saintly woman whose charity work was an inspiration. She sometimes accompanied her on her hospital rounds and watched in admiration as the Duchess gave patients bed baths and emptied bedpans. 'She was the only member of the Royal Family I ever saw doing anything like that,' Diana told Simone Simmons. 'Her values are humanitarian. Theirs [the other female royals'] are material.'[41]

There was very little neighbourly interaction between the separate fiefdoms of Kensington Palace. Each had their respective private secretaries, equerries, ladies-in-waiting, butlers, chauffeurs, maids and valets (a hundred people in all, including Robert Fellowes and Diana's sister Jane, who had their own apartment inside the compound). The Princess's mild friendship with 'Margo' did not extend to the older woman ever asking Diana to lunch or vice versa. And Diana considered Princess Michael 'a waste of space'.[42] She preferred the friendship of a new circle of glossy tastemakers. The fashionistas of *Vogue* started to fill the role of the Princess's support system. Diana had turned to the magazine that used to employ her sisters to provide a choice of outfits for her increasing number of engagements. *Vogue*'s fashion department was hers to explore. Anna Harvey, the senior fashion editor, became a major resource. 'When she got engaged we used to get this call from Anna Harvey asking to see things as samples,' the designer Jasper Conran said. 'Then a call back to send a size 10. We figured it out quickly but it was all Very Secret Squirrel.'[43] Against the background of a life that featured innumerable formal functions, Diana's trips to the hairdresser and excursions to designers' studios for fittings were the only real fun she had. In the past she had relied on romantic fiction to escape. Now she could summon the best of the nation's image-makers to help create her alternative reality. She saw the transformative power of the editorial wand when Harvey would turn an entire room at Vogue House in Hanover Square into an Aladdin's cave of called-in designer loot for her to try.

Diana was still a cautious dresser in the first year. Her fashion efforts reflected an eagerness to please the Firm, dressing the part of a princess as seen through a very young girl's eyes, with billowy meringue evening dresses or young matron ensembles splashed with polka dots, topped by huge white sailor collars. The need for chic maternity clothes brought her to Catherine Walker, a discreet and elegant couturier of French birth who became a major style guru for the next fifteen years. Bruce Oldfield, the lanky, half-Jamaican erstwhile foster-child, gave Diana evening glamour and a taste of café society. The elfin Conran, son of Terence, provided contemporary flash, pushing her away from the frou-frou of her earliest Princess days into a more streamlined look. He made Diana a favourite white mohair jacket which she often wore with her dresses at polo matches. 'No matter what you were making for her,' Conran told me 'the question was always, "Will my husband think I am sexy in this?"'[44]

The answer to that question, sadly, was not sexy enough. Charles's sexual interest in Diana decreased in exact ratio to how much more desirable she became to the world. The Prince wasn't brought up to be the backstage handler of a turbulent child star. He was used to being the one who got all the stroking himself. His princely *amour propre* was briefly restored by Diana's swift pregnancy (she had been right about that) but his happiness was marred by how madly volatile it made her. Combined with her bulimia, it left her in hormonal chaos much of the time. She threw a huge tantrum when she went through the wedding gifts and found an inoffensive small watercolour from the Prince's friends Lord and Lady Tryon. It depicted Iceland, where Charles used to love joining them for the fishing trips that gave him quality time with his confidante.[45] Dale Tryon herself was still on Diana's shit list, stewing in the shires.

There was an almighty row at Althorp in January when Charles and Diana paid a belated visit to receive the estate workers' wedding gifts.

The countryside in winter was always a danger zone for Diana, even in her father's home. Raine was all over the Prince of Wales with her grating charm and it aggravated her stepdaughter to see her successfully buttering up Charles. The row between Diana and Charles when they retired for the night got so ugly that an antique mirror was shattered, an eighteenth-century chair leg damaged and a pane of glass in the window broken. There was another blow-up that same month during a pheasant shoot at Sandringham when Diana tried to stop Charles going out with the guns. Eleven years later she told Andrew Morton that she threw herself down a staircase afterwards in a suicide attempt, but this was just material from her internal post-marital rewrite desk. The last thing she would ever have done was hurt her unborn child. One of Diana's aides at the time told me that she remembers Diana saying, 'Very embarrassing. I slipped down the stairs and landed at the Queen Mother's feet. I saw the gynaecologist but he said, "You'll be fine, stop worrying."'[46] In the version of the story she gave to Andrew Morton, Prince Charles was supposed to have gone straight out riding after the incident and when he came back it was, she told him, 'just dismissal, total dismissal.'[47]

Bollocks to that, as Diana would say. A member of the Sandringham staff who witnessed the scene told James Whitaker that Prince Charles had been desperately concerned when Diana took her tumble. It was he who called the doctor. Far from going out riding, the Prince stayed with his shaken wife for the day and took her out for a picnic lunch at the royal family's beach house on the Norfolk coast, near Wells-next-the-Sea.[48] In the light of this it's hard to know how much credence to give to the other suicide attempts Diana spoke of, such as slashing herself with a lemon slicer. 'How do you kill yourself with a lemon slicer?' said 'a relation to the Prince' interviewed by Lady Colin Campbell. 'Do you peel yourself to death?'[49]

Very funny – except it wasn't. Diana had plenty of reasons for feeling desperate. In 1967, two US Navy researchers, Dr Thomas Holmes, a psychiatrist, and Richard Rahe, a navy scientist, had devised the 'Social Readjustment Rating Scale'. According to the Holmes–Rahe formula, Diana scored an alarming 407 on a scale at which 150–299 points could lead to mental illness.[50] Her stress chart changes included marriage, pregnancy, career changes, change in work responsibilities, outstanding personal achievements, change in living conditions, revision of personal habits, change in work hours or conditions, change in church activities, change in residence, change in social activities, change in recreation, and change in family get-togethers, holidays and Christmas.[51]

Not all the tantrums were hers alone. Prince Charles was far from easy to live with himself. Indeed, if Princess Anne, had indulged in some of his shows of temper we would probably be reading she had borderline personality disorder. All his life the Prince of Wales had been surrounded by sycophants who leapt to assuage his moods. On a flight to visit the Gurkha regiment in Pirbright in Surrey, he was furious to discover that his Man Friday, Michael Fawcett, had forgotten to pack his aiguillettes; Fawcett, according to a witness, reacted by 'prostrating himself on the floor of the plane and crying like a child'. A member of Kensington staff recalls that, when frustrated by the Princess's grievances, the Prince was in the habit of throwing things, such as an antique Vuilliamy clock. 'The staff would get it off to the conservation workshop and it would come back good as new,' said this Palace alumnus.[52] Michael Shea once watched as the Prince fiddled with a button on his jacket sleeve and then get so angry when it came off that he threw the offending button at his valet, Stephen Barry.[53] Staff knew that a sure-fire way to excite the Prince's temper was an overheated room. A legacy of Gordonstoun was that he insisted on sleeping with all the windows open. This fact gives credence to a Palace staffer's theory that it was not Diana but Charles who broke the window at Althorp, supposedly by putting a chair through it.[54]

The Prince's persistent feelings for Camilla continued to haunt Diana. Professor Hubert Lacey, an expert on eating disorders, believes that Diana's defeatist obsession with Camilla was a replay of how she experienced her father's relationship with Raine, something she couldn't beat. It changed the focus of his attention. It was Charles's love Diana wanted, not his 'concern'. To be fair, her belief that it was Camilla who still stood between them wasn't just irrational retrospective jealousy. There was a sighting of Charles with his former mistress on 2 November, shortly after the Wales tour. The press spotted the Prince riding beside the tightly jodhpured Mrs Parker Bowles out with the Vale of the Horse Hunt at Ewen near Cirencester. (Flashback: Camilla 'Will you hunt?' Diana: 'On what?' Camilla: 'Horse!')[55] The Prince was clearly agitated about being seen; on catching sight of the snoopers he lost it. 'When are you bloody people going to leave me alone?'[56] he yelled. The press, still invested in the fairy-tale scenario, did not report the incident.

Diana looked increasingly to the press for the reassurance she wasn't getting at home. Its fascination with her mounted daily. She had a top-notch private secretary in Oliver Everett, and a sturdily no-nonsense lady-in-waiting in Anne Beckwith-Smith, the thirty-year-old daughter of Major and Mrs Peter Beckwith-Smith, the kind of Englishwoman who, a hundred years earlier, had kept the British Empire tidy. A lady-in-waiting is really an executive secretary with social access. While Beckwith-Smith handled all the logistics of Diana's public life, Everett's role was to sift the avalanche of requests for charity patronage, speaking engagements and ceremonial appearances. (Every regiment in the British Army seemed to want the Princess of Wales to be their Colonel-in-Chief.) Everett accompanied her on engagements when Charles could not. Diana was terrified of public speaking, but she generally did just fine, because all she had to do was show up and look sideways under her eyelashes and the crowds went crazy.

The trouble was that Diana's popularity was growing so intense that she needed something more. She needed the savvy handlers of a Hollywood PR machine. The Buckingham Palace press office, headed by the shrewd Michael Shea, who wrote crime thrillers in his spare time, had only one client: the Queen. Prince Charles's manly communications apparatus, led by Vic Chapman, was geared towards the needs of his bachelor days. Diana found that playing the part of affianced Sloane-next-door, with all its pressures, was easier for her to get right than the role of Princess in the Tower. Michael Shea disputes Diana's complaint that she got little media help from the Palace in the early days. He remembers taking her to newspaper offices and television newsrooms, establishing all the media contacts she would later artfully turn against them. Shea and his colleagues also had her rehearse her early speeches and answers to formal interview questions. Before the pre-wedding interview with Angela Rippon and Andrew Gardner, the Palace press office had coached her through the questions in advance.[57] This new professionalism meant Diana was required to negotiate a tricky new relationship with the press pack. Too accessible and she would be eaten alive; too aloof, too 'produced' and she would forfeit her wildly successful common touch and start to become a deadly traditional royal. Her best assets were native media sense and natural good manners. 'There was no indication of favouritism after she married Charles,' said the *Daily Express*'s Ashley Walton. 'We were all talked to and she would make a point of coming over and talking to us all.'[58]

She was rarely rewarded with good manners in return. In December

Diana went to pieces after an excursion from Highgrove to a village shop in Tetbury, where she emerged to buy a packet of wine gums and was caught in a ravening press onslaught. Her meltdown was such that the Queen broke the rules of a lifetime and asked Michael Shea to summon to Buckingham Palace the editors of all twenty-one national daily and Sunday newspapers and the key figures at the BBC and ITN. It was sleek staff work. Some of the hoariest of newsmen turn into wide-eyed little boys when treated as royal insiders, and Shea's performance showed that the Palace knew a thing or two about co-option. The briefing was staged in the Palace's white and gold 1844 Room, so named because of its occupation that year by Tsar Nicholas I of Russia. The only editor missing was Kelvin MacKenzie, Rupert Murdoch's freebooting ruffian at the *Sun*. MacKenzie had sent word, obviously under duress, to say that he was unable to attend because of a previously scheduled meeting with his employer. 'We had no reverence for the Royal Family,' *Sun* staffer Harry Arnold later said proudly. 'We didn't believe in following rules laid down by the old guard.'[59] (The ill feeling was mutual. Shea wrote in an article in *The Times* in December 1992 that a good page-one headline for the *Sun* might be 'FIND A FACT INSIDE AND WIN A MILLION'.)[60]

Shea's message to Fleet Street was that the Queen was worried about invasions of the privacy of the Princess of Wales. Diana, he said, was 'more than usually affected by morning sickness because of her age and build'.[61] He outlined how camouflaged photographers were bivouacked in the bushes, waiting in ambush in Tetbury High Street if she went out to buy a paper or some sweets, and he pleasantly begged for some restraint. Shea then invited the editors to join him next door for drinks. The representatives of the press were ushered into the even more splendid Caernarvon Room, hung with paintings of the Spanish guerrilla war against the armies of Napoleon. Then, in an unprecedented move for a sovereign who believes in never complaining or explaining, and to the astonishment of the assembled editorial eminences, in came the Queen, escorted by her younger son Prince Andrew, popular at the time as a dashing naval pilot. Monarch and Prince moved deftly from group to group, distributing cordiality to everyone present.[62] So snowed were these fearless news hounds that none of them brought up the Diana privacy question until the *News of the World*'s Barry Askew, aka the Beast of Bouverie Street, bucked etiquette by speaking to the monarch head on. 'If Lady Di wants to buy some wine gums without being photographed,' he growled, 'why doesn't she send a servant?' 'What an extremely pompous man you are,'[63] replied the monarch with a smile, a much guffawed-over riposte generally considered a palpable hit for Her Majesty. (Askew was relieved of his editorship a month later, presumably for having irritated Murdoch, though it was unclear whether his offence was making an ass of himself at the meeting or just attending it.)

The effect of the briefing was chastening. For a while, the papers turned down the heat on Diana, which helped her bear up more cheerfully.

In February 1982 the couple flew to the Bahamas for what amounted to a second honeymoon. They stayed at Windermere on Eleuthera, the home of Lord and Lady Brabourne. In this simple, secluded spot, infinitely more romantic than Broadlands could ever be, they were able to do real couple things for the first time. They took turns grilling barbecue suppers. They waterskied, windsurfed and sunbathed on their own. They were sighted standing in the sea with their arms around each other, kissing – proof positive that removed from the pressures of Palace life and the shadow of Camilla, their relationship might have seriously got off the ground.

That's right: sighted. Of course. It would have taken more than a sherry in the Caernarvon Room to stop the capos of the tabloid mafia, the *Daily Star*'s James Whitaker and his photographer sidekick Ken Lennox, from plying their awful trade. Equipped with jungle gear and binoculars, Whitaker and Lennox started crawling through a spit of land opposite the beach shortly before sunrise, carrying a long-distance lens the size of a howitzer. At 11.20 a.m. they were rewarded with the irresistible image of Diana in a bikini, her five-month-pregnant belly noticeably (though of course prettily) convex. The *Star* splashed the pictures on the front page, beating out the *Sun*'s Harry Arnold and Arthur Edwards, who got there shortly afterwards.

The Queen took it personally. She issued a statement calling the invasion of her daughter-in-law's privacy 'tasteless behaviour' that 'is in breach of normally accepted British Press standards'. The distance royal coverage had travelled can be gauged by how the Queen herself was treated during her own confinements. When she was pregnant with Prince Charles and Princess Anne, the Queen was merely said to be in 'an interesting condition' and all photographs of that 'condition' were prohibited.[64] Even in the early 1980s, in those pre-Demi Moore days, before it became routine for starlets to pose knocked up and naked for the covers of national and international magazines, a photograph of a beautiful pregnant woman, the bare skin of her swollen belly unmistakably proclaiming her sexual experience, bordered on the pornographic. If the woman was not only famous but also famously demure, private, 'innocent' and protected, and if she had been photographed against her will, then to the thrill of voyeurism was added the stronger kick of – the word is all too apt – violation. And this is the truth of how the pack increasingly viewed Diana. Whitaker at least had the candour to admit that he got off on – another too exact word – penetrating the Princess's modesty. 'I've never done anything as intrusive in my life,' he said. 'But it was a journalistic high.'[65] A high, for sure. But not a journalistic one.

## Chapter 11

# *Stardust*

'How can anyone, let alone a twenty-one-year-old, be expected to come out of all this obsessed and crazed attention unscathed?'
— Prince Charles, April 1983

The birth of William on 21 June 1982 at St Mary's Hospital, Paddington, was the fulfilment of Diana's destiny. Prince William Arthur Philip Louis would one day be the forty-second monarch since the Norman Conquest, and the sixth in descent from Queen Victoria. Diana had done what she was hired to do, produce the next heir to the throne speedily and with success. There had been so much hype about the impending royal birth the Princess felt the whole of England was in labour with her. Jingoistic excitement was at full throttle anyway after the week-old British triumph of ejecting the Argentines from the Falkland Islands after they rudely invaded the British territories without warning. 'STICK IT UP YOUR JUNTA' was one memorable headline in the *Sun*. The newly commissioned Prince Andrew found himself a national hero after courageously flying helicopter missions from the aircraft carrier HMS *Invincible* based in the South Atlantic, a terrific image-boost for the Firm that had become almost exclusively Diana-centric in the year since the wedding. The Falklands War was brief, victorious with many feats of British courage. Its success created the perfect Henry V flag-waving atmosphere in which to produce the next heir to the throne. The anti-monarchist Labour MP Willie Hamilton was the only royal spoiler when he declared that baby Wales's life would henceforth be 'one long story of nausea, deference and Land of Hope and Glory rubbish for many years'.[1]

Diana's dynastic efforts were rewarded with a forty-one-gun salute in Hyde Park, a carillon of bells in Westminster Abbey and a tsunami of tabloid sentiment. The Prince of Wales showed his gratitude to his wife by presenting her with a necklace of diamonds and cultured pearls with a sparkling heart at the centre and a new custom-built, apple-green Mini with a convertible foldaway roof and enough space for a collapsible cot. Frances Shand Kydd, with her usual style, organised a champagne toast to the baby with her eighty-four fellow passengers on the Glasgow–London British Airways shuttle. 'I love children I always have,' she told the *Daily Mail*. 'I had five of them in nine years.'[2] Etiquette prescribed that the Queen, rather than Diana's own mother, was her first visitor in hospital. The Princess of Wales was lucky not to come out of labour to find the owlish figure of Home Secretary Willie Whitelaw at her bedside. It was George VI in 1946 who abolished the arcane rule of having the Home Secretary present at the birth of a royal child to avoid a repetition of the 1688 Warming-Pan plot when a substitute baby was reportedly placed between the sheets with the wife of James II. Queen Elizabeth's first comment when she saw her new grandson was, 'Thank Heavens he hasn't got his father's ears.'[3]

Diana later told Morton that William's birth had been induced early to fit in with Charles's polo calendar, but this is the forked tongue of later bitterness speaking, not a reflection of the couple's joyous mood at the time. The Prince was present throughout all sixteen hours of Diana's difficult labour, a most un-Windsor thing of him to do. In fact, he was the first ever Prince of Wales to be in the room when his wife gave birth. Charles sounded like any besotted New Dad when he wrote to Patricia Mountbatten: 'The arrival of our small son has been an astonishing experience and one that has meant more to me than I could ever have imagined. I am SO thankful I was beside Diana's bedside the whole time because I really felt as though I'd shared deeply in the process of birth and as a result was rewarded by seeing a small creature which belonged to US even though he seemed to belong to everyone else as well.'[4]

It was Diana's wish that Charles had such an intimate participation in the birth. Her campaign to reverse all past patterns of royal parenting was the best she fought. She fended off Charles's lugubrious plan to invite his own former nanny Mabel Anderson to take charge of William, choosing instead the feisty Barbara Barnes, who'd worked in the unconventional household of Lady Glenconner. She wanted her boys raised as OshKosh kids not Little Lord Fauntleroys. Diana considered the photographs of the Prince of Wales as a child of six formally greeting the Queen on her return from a six-month Commonwealth Tour Exhibit A in a deprived childhood. She insisted, against the remonstrance of Charles's uptight private secretary Edward Adeane, on taking up then Australian PM Malcolm Fraser's suggestion of bringing William on their first big six-week visit to Australia and New Zealand. While the Prince and Princess toured every state in the Australian continent the nine-month-old William was based with his nanny on a sheep station at Woomargama in New South Wales. His presence added severe complications to the planning of the tour – every three or four days Charles and Diana would break off and visit the baby – but it also gave the beleaguered couple a taste of authentic family time. Charles acknowledged that in a letter home to his friends, the van Cutsems: 'The great joy was that we were totally alone together,'[5] he wrote, suggesting the hunger they both still had to forge a real bond after two turbulent years of marriage.

The months leading up to the Australia trip had been another nosedive into hell for the couple who had everything. Peace reigned for a mere two months until Diana's post-natal depression kicked in. The Prince cleared his diary and stayed home with mother and baby. 'Charles loved nursery life and couldn't wait to get back and do the bottle and everything,'[6] Diana told Morton, but the Glorious Twelfth of August descended on her psyche like the Highland mist. Charles still did not seem to get that his wife's aversion to the annual sojourn at Balmoral now bordered, like Cherie Blair's, on the allergic. The Prince remained bemused by what he saw as a lack of stamina in his wife that seemed to defy the hardy female ethic of her background. Had he been sold a bill of goods? Like most aristocratic wives schooled in country life, the royal women themselves are formidably tough. They are trained to a daily existence where they almost never do anything they really want to do or see anyone they really want to see. They are used to being on their feet all day shaking hands and never betraying a day's ill health. This means that their private life is conducted with the rigid intensity of borrowed time.

When the Queen Mother was at her Scottish home at Birkhall she thought nothing, at the age of eighty-two of presiding over an elaborate picnic lunch, standing in her waders in freezing water fishing all afternoon, and hosting a bibulous formal dinner until midnight. At eighty-nine she attended the forty-fifth anniversary of the Normandy landings at Bayeux, speaking fluent French to the veterans and returning to London by helicopter. Soon afterwards she breezed through five days of engagements during a heat wave in Toronto.[7] Hugo Vickers recounts how when the Queen Mother, at the age of a hundred, during a fire drill at Sandringham, the treasurer, Nicholas Assheton, asked if she was coming down, the reply came back: 'No, but she has put her pearls on.'[8] She rarely betrayed emotion or encouraged it in others. Prince Charles saw his grandmother as a model of warmth and compassion but when his beloved Jack Russell, Pooh, disappeared down a rabbit hole in 1994 during a walk across the moors surrounding Birkhall, never to be seen again, the Queen Mother's only comment to the distraught Prince was: 'Oh, I'm sorry to hear that. Anyway, have some tea.'[9]

Princess Anne is similarly stoic. She was the winner of the Individual European Three-Day Championship at age twenty-one and is still ready to clear a hedge on horseback in driving sleet for the hell of it. With a gun she's the Windsor version of Annie Oakley. On an official visit to Saughton Prison in Edinburgh, Anne thawed a bunch of sullen youth in the prison recreation room by picking up a billiard cue and potting the ball on the green baize with such crack marksmanship the juvenile offenders thought she was cool.[10] Athleticism underpins the prodigious stamina of the Queen herself. Elizabeth II is a horsewoman of international class. She rides at least four or five times a week, displaying toughness and mastery in the saddle. She brought her horse back under control within seconds in June 1981 when some seventeen-year-old fruitcake shot six blank cartridges directly at her as she turned down Horse Guards parade ground for Trooping the Colour. The Queen merely ducked, patted her horse, Burmese, and rode on. A more up-close and personal security breach that occurred in July 1982 left the Queen equally unfazed. A thirty-one-year-old unemployed labourer named Michael Fagan broke into the Queen's bedroom at Buckingham Palace at 7.15 a.m. by scaling a sixty-foot drainpipe. The Queen was still in bed at the time, awaiting her tea tray. When the intrusive Mr Fagan appeared at her side, the Queen got up, put on her dressing gown and slippers and told him sternly: 'Get out of here at once.' No security officer appearing, Her Majesty sat on the edge of the bed and chatted politely to Fagan for a long five minutes about his family problems until a policeman finally surfaced. 'Take him outside and give him a cigarette,' said the Queen.[11]

So rarely were the royal women discomposed or sick they almost considered it bad manners to be so. 'Maybe I was the first person ever to be in this family who ever had a depression or was ever openly tearful,' Diana said to BBC *Panorama*'s Martin Bashir. 'And obviously that was daunting, because if you've never seen it before, how do you support it?'[12] How do you acknowledge it, was more to the point. The Queen was extremely fond of her younger sister but she found it vexing, for instance, that when Princess Margaret was struck down by her third stroke she was unable to observe Sandringham's appointed mealtimes. The sovereign once complained to one of Margaret's companions over the Christmas holidays that her sister 'always insists on sleeping through lunch and when she wakes up the chef has gone off'. Margaret's companion suggested that perhaps a plate of scrambled eggs in bed might be a nice treat for the malingering Princess. 'Oh. I suppose so,' said the Queen. 'We never thought of that.'[13]

Diana had shown a royal ability of her own to withstand the stress and the weather on the tour of Wales, but the extended vacation in Balmoral surrounded again by the family en masse was another matter. At one point there she went for three nights without sleeping, spending most of the time locked in the bathroom throwing up after a bulimic junk-food binge. Bathrooms seemed to loom large in the Waleses' Balmoral holiday that year. Diana told Andrew Morton it was as her husband had a bath that she'd heard the Prince on the telephone furtively calling Camilla Parker Bowles signing off, under the disguising noise of pounding tap water, with the treacherous 'Whatever happens, I will always love you'.[14] Perhaps it was this incident that made the Prince take the classic guilty-husband action of insisting that his wife was in dire need of psychiatric help.

Diana might have said: 'There were three of us in this marriage. Charles, me and Laurens van der Post.' It was from none other than the venerable travel writer whose books dogged Diana on the honeymoon aboard *Britannia* that the Prince sought marital advice. He begged his mentor to come up to Balmoral to assess the Princess's state of mind. One would like to have been present at the interview between the disconsolate twenty-one-year-old uber-Sloane who pined for the boutiques of Beauchamp Place and the eighty-year-old explorer and Japanese prisoner-of-war camp survivor who had lived for months on end with the Kalahari Bushmen. Lucia van der Post, Laurens's daughter, insisted: 'My father had a quick sense of people's inner core. He was immensely human and tender with young people – he'd had problems with his father when he was growing up.' The discreet van der Post told Lucia only that 'Diana had shown "great paranoia" and had spent a lot of time "looking through keyholes".'[15] (Bathroom keyholes one would guess.) Van der Post recommended Diana visited a psychiatrist he knew in London, Jungian disciple Dr Alan McGlashan, which at least occasioned Charles and Diana making a joint trip to town. For Diana, the trouble with Dr McGlashan was he was almost as old as van der Post and his expertise was in analysing dreams. Since Diana's dreams were mostly about her husband's ex-mistress she saw no effective reason to parse them out with Dr McGlashan. 'I was fine until I got sucked into the royal way of life. That's my problem,'[16] Diana commented to Lady Colin Campbell, a remark whose pragmatism might have sounded, in other circumstances, like the Queen herself.

Diana dumped McGlashan in favour of Dr David Mitchell who saw her every evening at Kensington Palace, but he too made little headway. Mitchell was on the right track because he was more concerned about her relationship with her husband than investigating Diana's subconscious. In every session he would ask Diana to recount the details of her day, at which point, she told Andrew Morton, she would start howling and the talking would cease. Mitchell too was soon dumped, but it's unlikely he would have got very far as Diana again withheld the crucial facts about her bulimia. 'The thing about bulimia,' she said to Martin Bashir, 'is your weight always stays the same, whereas with anorexia you visibly shrink. So you can pretend the whole way through.'[17] Not entirely. The press had started to notice how unwell she seemed. *Daily Mirror* photographer Kent Gavin had a picture withheld by the paper which showed just how haunted she looked. Her behaviour towards the press was also less sunny and obliging. There was a bad moment on a ski slope in Liechtenstein in February when Diana reneged on a promise Prince Charles had made to press photographers to give them a joint photo op if they would cut the holidaying couple some slack. She shrieked: 'I can't stand it! I can't stand it!'[18] – a display of dramatics that didn't go over well with the usually adoring rat pack. 'If she wants to sulk inside a woolly hat she shouldn't have taken on the Crown,'[19] fulminated the *Daily Express*'s Jean Rook. Royal reporter Judy Wade recalled a photographer going to Kensington Palace to take official pictures. 'When he arrived, a highly placed official said, "If they start to fight and row, please try to ignore it." He was talking as if it was a regular occurrence.'[20]

Where was Diana's mother in all this *Sturm und Drang*? nowhere that was particularly helpful, is the answer. Frances Shand Kydd had created some aggravation of her own in the summer with an unexpected outburst in the press about her marriage to Diana's father. In Gordon Honeycombe's book, *A Royal Wedding*, which underwent a splashy serialisation in the *Daily Express*, Frances had decided at last to give her side of her divorce story and explode once and for all the widely held notion that she was a 'bolter' who had callously walked out on her four children. An outraged Johnnie called his ex-wife's account of the custody battle 'cheap and unkind', and Diana was hugely distressed by her parents' public feuding. 'She feels like the embarrassed poor cousin with too many skeletons in the family cupboard,' a friend of Diana's said.[21]

The truth was that Frances had complicated feelings about her youngest daughter's stardom and every so often shone the spotlight on herself. 'I have good long legs, like my daughter,' she told the press when she arrived back from Australia before the royal engagement.[22] In other words, I'm gorgeous too. Frances's marriage too was suffering under the publicity burden of Diana. Adam Shand Kydd remembered his father walking into the kitchen in the Isle of Seil and finding a TV camera crew setting up for sound bites about Diana. It did not please Peter Shand Kydd, any more than it did Frances, to find his identity entirely submerged in the fame of his wife's daughter. Marital rockiness of her own could be the only excuse for Frances being so little in evidence throughout Diana's post-natal tribulations. 'I'm a firm believer in maternal redundancy,' she told the *Daily Mail* in June 1982. 'When daughters marry they set up a new home, and they don't want mothers-in-law hanging around. They should be free to make their own decisions and maybe to make their own mistakes.'[23]

Unfortunately for Diana, all the women in her family on both sides seemed to hold the same view. True to form, her grandmother Lady Fermoy was already distancing herself from a match that was turning out to have embarrassing problems. At a dinner in March 1982 Fermoy told Sir Roy Strong primly 'how much the Princess of Wales had yet to learn'.[24] To her close friend Robert Runcie, Archbishop of Canterbury, Fermoy was more candid. She confided how 'distressed' she was by the behaviour of Diana whom she regarded 'as an actress, a schemer'. Runcie reflected that Ruth was 'totally and wholly a Charles person because she'd seen him grow up, loved him like all women of the court do'.[25] The Archbishop who, as the critic Clive James commented in his coverage of the royal wedding, could always be relied on to 'put unction in your function',[26] did not point out that, as Diana's grandmother, Lady Fermoy had seen the Princess grow up too. Given that it was Ruth's decisive testimony in the Spencer custody suit that ensured Diana was raised without her mother around, Granny Dearest was in a better position than most to understand the challenges Diana faced as a child. The Spencer and Fermoy women seem to have matched the Windsors round for round in self-absorption. Asked by James Whitaker about the evidence that Diana might have anorexia, her sister Sarah replied: 'We would like to have a chat with her about it but she does not take advice kindly.'[27] We would like to, yes. But who actually did?

No one at Balmoral, that's for sure. Diana was like a half-evolved butterfly, dragged kicking and screaming back into the chrysalis every time she was around the royals for any extended time. What is striking is how she was always able to pull herself out of her malaise when exactly the right opportunity to shine presented itself. Diana's star quality was increasingly a survival mechanism. The Queen was not in favour of any Windsor women going to Monaco for the funeral of Princess Grace, who died on 14 September 1982 from her injuries in a car crash that eerily prefigured Diana's own. 'We women don't go to funerals,' she said. 'Charles must go.' The Prince had no desire to do so.[28] Monaco is a tinpot kingdom as far as the British monarchy is concerned and Grace was a creature of Hollywood, albeit an elegant one. The Princess, however, knew instinctively that world-class glamour like hers thrived in the high-profile cosmopolitan settings the other royal women abhorred. It was clear that every fashionable celebrity and the world's press would be at Grace's funeral. Among the movie stars, crowned heads and First Ladies of America and France, the Princess of Wales knew she would stand out as the luminous real thing. Besides, she felt a genuine sisterhood with the deceased Princess. Grace, with her cool beauty, self-discipline and discretion, would have been an excellent mentor for Diana. 'We were psychically connected,' Diana told Grace's daughter Princess Caroline.[29] Actually, they were connected in more ways than Diana knew at the time – the Princess of Monaco never allowed her own façade to crack. Grace's distress about Prince Rainer's infidelity, her battle with the bottle and retaliatory love affairs were not exposed until some time after her death. Perhaps the keenly intuitive Diana sensed these painful undercurrents. She was so intent on attending the funeral she appealed over the heads of Charles and the Queen's private secretary, Sir Philip Moore, to the Queen herself, who decided in the end, since no one else wanted to, to let Diana go.

The funeral of Princess Grace was like a small-scale dress rehearsal for Diana's own. As many as 26,000 people filed past Grace's casket in the scented shadows of the cathedral.[30] The whole affair had the devout atmospherics surrounding a medieval saint. The streets of 'the sunny place for shady people' were awash in weeping women. Wearing a below-the-knee black dress with her diamond and pearl heart necklace and a black straw boater, Diana took her place between Nancy Reagan and Mme Mitterrand. Her youthful dignity and poise won her rave reviews. She impressed a member of the Prince of Wales's office, who noted that 'Everything went wrong. The Rolls broke down. We got stuck in a lift. My respect for her rose a hundredfold. She was very hassled but behaved brilliantly.'[31]

On the plane journey at the end of a long day she burst into tears of exhaustion. 'Will Charles be there to meet us?' one of her team remembers her asking as they prepared to land at Aberdeen.[32] It was an unrealistic expectation since Diana's arrival from Monaco coincided with Prince Andrew's victorious return from the Falkland Islands and the Prince of Wales had accompanied his parents to Portsmouth to meet him. The British Navy's role in the routing of Argentina had been an act of great skill, especially as the Ministry of Defence had equipped them with ships about as well suited to the task as camels in a polo match. The arrival of the HMS *Invincible* after 166 days at sea was therefore a major media event. The last great ship to return from the war was escorted into Portsmouth by a large flotilla of yachts and tugboats blowing their sirens. Not exactly an event the Prince of Wales could quietly skip. The homecoming hero, Prince Andrew, posed for a picture with the Queen at the quayside with a red rose clenched between his teeth. Charles's friends bitchily implied that Diana regarded the Falklands War as an intrusion on her press coverage.[33] More likely it simply didn't impinge at all. Real events like the Falklands occurred in a public world Diana was as yet too callow to comprehend. She was still engulfed in her Brigadoon mist. 'We looked at her big eyes looking out of the window in expectation,' a member of the entourage on the plane home from Monaco recalled. 'One police car,' Diana said, looking crestfallen. 'That means that Charles isn't coming.'[34] The next day she was equally crushed to receive no congratulations about her Monaco performance from the Palace. 'Look at the papers. They say you did brilliantly,' one of her team reassured her.[35] 'Good,' she replied, 'cos nobody mentioned it here.'[36]

Not mentioning it was the point. This was Monarchy 101 and she had better get used to it, was the Palace view. Diana, it seemed to them, was simply unable to come to grips with the double reality of being an international celebrity in the eyes of billions of people while simultaneously, in the Palaces and apartments where she actually spent most of her time, being treated as just a cog in the royal machine. That she struggled with that duality was the difference between being born and raised a royal and becoming one, as it were, by adoption. 'She wasn't born into our way of life,'[37] the Queen herself had said when she met the Fleet Street editors with Michael Shea. To the Windsors, public appearances were not personal performances. They were acts of state, symbolic assertions of national identity, *ex officio* rituals having nothing to do with individual characteristics and everything to do with impersonal roles assigned by tradition and birth. Their essence could not be affected by compliments or criticisms, by good reviews or bad ones. A favourite pejorative Elizabeth II likes to use to describe a certain kind of produced public appearance is 'stunt'. 'That's just a stunt, and I am not going to do it,' the Queen will say if asked by her press secretary to do anything remotely theatrical in gesture or tone.[38] Her goal has always been to exhibit museum-quality authenticity, whereas the world the Princess of Wales inhabited was applause.

Unluckily for Diana, the Prince of Wales was the member of the royal family most sensitive about his own image. Indeed, there are those who judge Charles's persistent desire to be appreciated as the most hopeless of his causes. Responding to publicly voiced resentment that he was interfering in areas beyond his expertise, Charles told an interviewer in the mid-1980s: 'There's no need for me to do all this, you know. If they'd rather I did nothing, I'll go off somewhere else.'[39] Prince Philip has done endless good works and fund-raising and doesn't expect people to appreciate him. This yields him the benefit of not having to appreciate people in return, which is probably the right course.

The six-week tour of Australia and New Zealand in March 1983 was a threatening experience for Charles's ego. It confirmed the Princess as a global superstar and it scared her husband to death. There were a hundred or more press on the tour from the UK alone, and seventy more photographers from France, Germany, America and Japan. *Daily Mirror* photographer Kent Gavin observed that out of every hundred pictures he took on this tour, ninety-two involved Diana and only eight showed Charles. 'She is so popular,' added Gavin at the time, 'that she is in my lens from the moment she arrives at a place until the moment she leaves.'[40]

The tour had a serious political goal – persuading the grumpy and increasingly republican Australian continent that it still wanted a monarchy in the first place. The Liberal Prime Minister Malcolm Fraser had just lost a landslide election to the Labour leader Robert James Lee

'Bob' Hawke who epitomised the churlish mood of the populace when he commented, 'I don't regard welcoming them [Charles and Diana] as the most important thing I'm going to have to do in my first nine months in office.' Regarding Prince Charles he added dismissively, 'I don't think we will be talking about Kings of Australia forever more.'[41]

Diana's magic turned the whole mood around. The crowds shouting her name were overwhelming, the tiara version of Beatlemania. In Brisbane alone, 400,000 turned out to scream for the Princess, bringing the city centre to a dead halt. 'I'd seen the crowds in Wales but the crowds in Australia were incredible,' Jayne Fincher said. 'We went to Sydney and wanted to photograph her with the Opera House but just when we got there it was like the whole of Sydney had come out. It was just a sea of people as far as you could see, not just on the land, the harbour was full of boats and people. And all you could see was the top of this little pink hat bobbing along.'[42] It was, as Diana put it herself, 'the hard end of being the Princess of Wales'.[43] She felt hot, jet-lagged and was still intermittently throwing up, but Diana wooed the Australians like a pro, hurtling with Charles between mob-scene walkabouts, glamour receptions, marathon dinners, making forty flights between Australia's eight states. Anne Beckwith-Smith, Diana's lady-in-waiting, realised that even though they had packed nearly two hundred outfits, some of which she had worn before, it wasn't enough. Nothing was enough. They were insatiable for Diana. The crowds and the press wanted to see their love object in something new every day. What the Australians adored was Diana's lack of pretension, the opposite of colonial arrogance. The Princess's own intellectual insecurity was an unexpected asset. It made her head immediately for the underdog in any room – the aged, the shy, the very young. 'She didn't speak to confident people half as easily as those who weren't,' her mother Frances Shand Kydd has said. 'And this was, in her case, a kind of battle that went on. She wasn't all that confident herself, she knew she had this gift with people and she used it wisely and generously. But in fact she felt going into a big room of people rather drawn to those who are feeling a bit nervous, rather as she was herself.'[44]

The excitement of it all lifted Diana's depression and gave the couple's relationship a renewed charge. The dynamic between them was complicated but it was alive. She was often in tears of exhaustion and fear, but she relied on Charles to help her get through it and he did. When they were driving through the crowds in an open car she discreetly clung to her husband for comfort.[45] In a letter home she even confessed to feeling a trifle ashamed of how volatile her behaviour had been before she left England.

Early in the tour there was a dance in Melbourne at the Southern Cross Hotel and the royal couple got lost in the lift trying to find the right floor. The AP photographer Ron Bell remembers the lift doors opening and Prince Charles stepping out with shining eyes: 'Ron, isn't she absolutely beautiful?' he said. 'I'm so proud of her.'[46] It was true – Charles was smart enough to see what a stunning political asset Diana had become – but he was also deeply disturbed by all the adoration coming his young wife's way. Its excess frightened him. You can see him still trying to figure out Diana's mystique in a letter from Australia to a friend dated 4 April. 'Maybe the wedding, because it was so well-done, and because it made such a wonderful, almost Hollywood-style film, has distorted people's view of things?'[47] There's a telling picture of Diana in a bright yellow dress at a school in Alice Springs, crouched down in a warm, natural way to the level of the kids who crowd around her in ecstasy while Charles stands stiffly by. Just like in Wales, the crowds that got him instead of her in their joint walkabouts openly groaned in disappointment. 'It's not fair is it? You'd better ask for your money back!'[48] the Prince would say with a rueful, sporting smile.

The lukewarm reception for himself was especially discomfiting for the Prince because it had once been his treasured dream to become Governor General of Australia, an idea first mooted in the sixties. Again, when Charles was especially tormented by the nagging of his father in the mid-seventies, the idea of escaping down-under for a few years surfaced, fuelled in his imagination by his Aussie confidante 'Kanga' Tryon. The Prince felt an affinity with Australia after spending his impressionable post-Gordonstoun year living in the outback. In his bachelor days, Bondi Beach was the scene of some of his most glamorous photo ops. Unfortunately, republican resentment still smouldered over the 1975 dismissal of Prime Minister Gough Whitlam by the Queen's representative (Sir John Kerr), for failing to get a budget through Parliament. The sacking was the most controversial act in Australian history and outraged the chippy national pride of the former colony. By the time of the visit by Charles and Diana, even outgoing Liberal PM Malcolm Fraser believed the resentment of Sir John Kerr's high-handed ways was still too strong to allow Prince Charles ever to be installed in Yarralumla (Government House). Now the Prince felt doubly snubbed by the euphoric reception the Australians were according to his wife. 'He took it out on me,' Diana told Andrew

Morton. 'He was jealous. I understood the jealousy but I couldn't explain that I didn't ask for it. I kept saying you've married someone and whoever you'd have married would have been of interest for the clothes, how she handles this, that, and the other, and you build the building block for your wife to stand on to make her own building block. He didn't see that at all.'[49]

Vic Chapman, the press secretary on the tour, got used to late-night phone calls from Charles complaining about the scant coverage of himself in the press compared to the hagiographic acres accorded his wife.[50] The Prince retreated into Jung's *Psychological Reflections* and wrote exasperated letters to his friends: 'I do feel *desperate* for Diana,' he wrote in his 4 April letter to a friend. 'There is no twitch she can make without these ghastly and I am quite convinced, mindless people photographing it . . . What has got into them all? How can anyone, let alone a twenty-one-year-old, be expected to come out of all this obsessed and crazed attention unscathed?'[51]

Stronger than ever, is the answer. In Australia and New Zealand, Diana graduated to being a seasoned, media sophisticate with the stamina and the charm repertoire of a big-time star. She mesmerised Bob Hawke and even extracted a curtsy from his wife, Hazel. By the end of Charles and Diana's tour a poll in Australia found that monarchists outnumbered republicans two to one and that was the point, wasn't it? The young Princess of Wales had proved she was a dazzling new PR weapon for the British Crown. She told Morton that she was 'a different person'[52] when she came home and for once she was telling him the truth.

During the tour she had become fascinated by the development of her own image in the pages of the British tabloids that were sent to her and reviewed them studiously on a daily basis. When she got home she would start the morning skimming the newspapers for pictures of herself, starting with the tabloids and going on to the broadsheets.

'She was a complete press addict,' *Daily Express* royal correspondent Ashley Walton alleges. 'She would read everything about herself right from the beginning and knew exactly who had written what. We know that because she would remark on a particular story to us. When she was living at Highgrove she would take some money and go into Tetbury where she would buy armfuls of newspapers and magazines. We used to doorstep the newsagents. If her picture was on the cover, she would buy the magazine.'[53]

Diana's ballooning star power strengthened her growing independence. At the end of the tour, the Princess was told by the Palace that the baby-in-tow format would not be allowed again. She responded by saying in that case, she would not go on long tours. 'Children cannot be left for that length of time at their age,'[54] said the Princess who knew all about being left. She later insisted that no trips away could be scheduled on the weekends the boys were home from boarding school. And she sent them both to Wetherby, an unpretentious nursery school in Notting Hill. The other mothers would turn up looking very dressed and eager to push their kids at Diana but she would just be wearing a tracksuit and trainers. Her personal protection officer Ken Wharfe remembers William standing in the school lobby in his cap and tie when a classmate asked him, 'Don't you know the Queen?' and William looked at him and replied, 'Don't you mean Granny?'[55] 'I used to pass her every day in that little corridor where the children were divided into swans and cygnets,' writer Andrew Barrow remembers. 'She had that wonderful vulnerable star quality.'[56]

When his wife stood up to the Palace on issues like carving out more time for his children, Charles admired Diana's spirit. He rarely took such a stance himself, especially when his father was involved. One of his aides once risked a friendly lecture about how the Prince should assert himself more often. As they walked around the grounds of Highgrove the Prince had said: 'You know, it's awkward between me and my father,' and the aide replied: 'You ought to stand up to him more.'[57] Charles shrugged. At a family business meeting at Sandringham, a member of the Prince's staff remembers Charles saying nothing in reply when the Duke of Edinburgh commented, 'Hah. You're here. I suppose the weather isn't good enough for hunting,' as Charles took his seat. 'Philip resented Charles,' the staff member said. 'He felt he had come from nowhere himself and yet his son had everything done for him.'[58]

Perhaps Diana was unafraid of Philip, first because she was a Spencer, raised at one of the most splendid country seats in England, Althorp, with the blood of the Stuarts running in her veins. (The Duke of Edinburgh's crustiness was nothing compared to her terrifying grandfather, the 7th Earl Spencer, Jack.) And second, because she was beautiful and she knew that the Duke of Edinburgh was deeply partial to young, alluring women. Diana was too shrewd to risk the sovereign's displeasure by flirting with her consort but it was a card her lowered lashes knew how to play.

Buckingham Palace was furiously competitive about the success of the Prince and Princess of Wales's Antipodean travels. The frostiness from members of the household towards Diana when she returned was obvious. No one said a word about how well she had coped, how superbly she had represented her country over six gruelling weeks and turned around the Australian attitude to the Crown. Alan Clark, the patrician Tory MP and acidic diarist who died in 1999, believed that the Queen was more directly threatened by Diana than has previously been supposed. In an unpublished interview I've seen, Clark opined that ever since the Princess of Wales's wedding day, 'When Diana said, "I will," a great roar went up – like the Middle Ages. This rang alarm bells for the Queen. Mrs Thatcher and Diana – these two women threatened her. Here clearly from the outset was a rival. Here was the embodiment of The Way Ahead. A walking icon who conformed to every convention that young people fantasised about.'[59] The Queen's men were especially irked by the BBC devoting a half-hour of Sunday prime time to the Waleses' Australia and New Zealand trip, unprecedented coverage for a royal tour.

This time, though, Diana didn't care that the Palace weren't appreciative. She was building a power base beyond the Palace walls that would give her the leverage to play by her own rules. The royal women had been dismayed at how lacking in toughness Diana was in the first two years of her marriage. Now, thanks to her personal ordeals, her media experience and her rigorous training on the road, Diana, just as the Queen feared, would become the most formidable of them all.

## Chapter 12

## Dynasty Di

'Did Joan Collins's wedding kick me off the front page?'
– Diana to Sir Nicholas Lloyd,
November 1985

England in the 1980s was defined to the rest of the world by three globe-girdling divas: Diana, Princess of Wales, Prime Minister Margaret Thatcher and Joan Collins, middling movie queen turned gigantic TV star. The British Isles have shrunk a little since they reverted to a culture curated by men.

Maggie force-fed her political medicine to the trade unions, the Tory 'wets' and the presumptuous Argentine generals like an avenging nanny administering castor oil. Joan ruled the airwaves as Alexis Carrington, the sexy, scheming, big-haired, magnificently mascaraed British bitchissima in America and worldwide hit night-time soap opera *Dynasty*. And Diana, vamping around in backless lamé dresses by Bruce Oldfield, unleashed the full force of her star power. 'She did enjoy the feeling of being a forties movie star,' Jasper Conran told me. 'It was all about the entrance, everyone clapping and cheering. She loved that.'[1] Big women ruled the runways, too. The first wave of anorexic waifs – Twiggy, Penelope Tree – had receded, and heroin-flavoured anorexia chic still lay in the future. Amazonian supermodels like Christie Brinkley, Naomi Campbell and Cindy Crawford ruled. And Diana – tall and athletic, like a supermodel herself – outshone them all.

The defining moment of her global metamorphosis came at the White House dinner hosted by Ronald and Nancy Reagan on 9 November 1985, when she was spun round the dance floor by John Travolta as the marine band played 'You're the One that I Want'. She always knew how to seize a moment for maximum exposure. The day before the dinner, at a morning press reception at the British Embassy in Washington, the Princess met Sir Nicholas Lloyd, then editor of the *Daily Express*. Her first words to him in the receiving line were 'Did Joan Collins's wedding kick me off the front page?'[2] If she did, it wasn't for long.

Dynasty Di. It was irresistible to not see the Princess's life in these years through the prism of Aaron Spelling's hit show, which epitomised Reagan-era *arriviste* glitz. In Britain, *Dynasty* was appreciated as an upmarket version of *Coronation Street*. Viewers were tickled that *Dynasty*'s female lead, Collins, with her gloriously campy manipulativeness and her glittery veneer of designer flash and clawing red fingernails, was one of their own. But the British press is the best in the world at constructing narratives of caricature which brand the weary protagonists for life. Even the Queen got caught up in the tabloid trope of catfights. Rarely do we know what Her Majesty thinks about a current prime minister, but gossip columns feasted on the displeasure the Queen was supposed to harbour towards an increasingly regal Mrs Thatcher. 'We have become a grandmother,' declared Maggie to waiting reporters when her son Mark's wife had a baby boy in March 1989.[3] On another occasion, she made the much-lampooned comment, 'We are in the fortunate position in Britain of being, as it were, the senior person in power.'[4]

Her Majesty was painted as unamused to be blown off the front page of *The Times*, no less, when Diana chose 6 November 1984, the day of the State Opening of Parliament, to experiment with a swept-back Vera Lynn coif held in place by combs. As Her Maj droned on about the government's legislative agenda – an agenda 'almost devoid', *The Times* wrote, of 'any striking initiatives except in the municipal line' – all eyes were on the Princess of Wales, who was sitting below the throne to the Queen's right, and her controversial updo. 'How dare she make a fool of you like that?' an incensed Princess Margaret is alleged to have complained to the Queen.[5]

Princess Anne's aversion to personality press did not protect her either from getting written into the feline storyline. Diana's omission to invite her to be a godmother to Prince Harry was supposed to have peeved Anne so much she declined to attend the christening. A statement put out by the Palace said that the Princess Royal and her husband, Captain Mark Phillips, had a shooting party at Gatcombe Park and could not leave their guests. It 'fooled no one', writes James Whitaker in his book, *Diana v. Charles*. 'There was no love lost between the two women. They had little in common and Anne was irritated by

Diana, the constant carry-on in the press about her clothes and her charm. When it was suggested to Diana that she might have Anne as a godmother for any daughter she might have, Diana retorted: "I just don't like her. She may be wonderful doing all that charity work for Save the Children and others, but I can do it as well."[6]

The scenarios of female conflict poured forth from both royal palaces like oil from a Carrington gusher. The same characters who for years had churned along with their low-boil royal lives were now seen in cartoon Technicolor for one reason only: the unforgiving spotlight following Diana, the glamour blonde whose presence was turning the monarchy's dull unchanging rhythms into a year-round peak season of vivid melodrama.

The themes were so persistent that even the members of the family themselves capitulated to tabloid characterisation. Diana herself likened Kensington Palace to *Coronation Street* when newsman Jeremy Paxman lunched with her there in 1996. 'As we go out you'll see all the curtains twitching,' she told him. Ten years later, when Paxman joined a royal house party at Sandringham, he asked Prince Charles what he thought the function of monarchy was. The heir to the throne replied, 'in a world weary way, "I think we're a soap opera."'[7] He did not mention that the opening scene of the soap opera had been a fairy-tale wedding at St Paul's Cathedral.

In the autumn of 1985, a year after I moved from London to New York to become editor-in-chief of *Vanity Fair*, I wrote a cover story updating the American public on the status of the relationship between the Prince and Princess of Wales. Published on the eve of their first official visit to the White House and headlined 'THE MOUSE THAT ROARED', the piece chronicled the full extent of the marital discord between Charles and Diana. It was hardly a scoop that all was not well with the couple, but the piece's narrative of role reversal – the thesis being that the girl who'd been picked to be the Royal Mouse of Windsor had turned into a hellacious ball-breaker in the space of four years – lent it a certain novelty.

Arriving in London in the summer of 1985 to research the report, I had found that backstairs gossip at Kensington Palace was reaching a crescendo. Forty members of the Wales's household had resigned, including his private secretary Edward Adeane, whose family had served the monarchy since Queen Victoria. Some of this was the inevitable staff fallout of a fusty bachelor finally getting a wife, some just the equally inevitable transition of the Princess's journey from freedom to royal purdah. Diana's clashes with two successive police protection officers, Paul Officer and David Robinson, fall into that category. Unlike Princess Anne, who'd put up with a police protection officer in her daily life ever since she was a child – and for whom Robinson went on to work most happily after his six-month bronco ride with the Princess of Wales – Diana wasn't used to the presence of a detective shadowing her around when she slipped off to have lunch with a friend or shopped surreptitiously for underwear in Marks & Spencer. Robinson, especially, was new to the job himself and hadn't yet mastered the art of melting into the background. He was nonetheless devastated when he was summoned by the Queen's personal protection officer, Commander Michael Trestrail, and told without warning that 'the chemistry didn't work'.[8] Other voluntary departures, including those of Diana's private secretary, Oliver Everett, yet another of the Prince's valets, Ken Stronach, and the butler Alan Fisher, were further signs of trouble. A scary new picture of the golden ingénue was emerging from Palace circles. A variety of well-placed sources – the Queen Mother's friend Woodrow Wyatt, the Queen's cousin and celebrity photographer the Earl of Lichfield, a lady-in-waiting, a former private secretary – were eager to fill my ear, lending plenty of credence to the below-stairs tattle.

All of them in one way or another portrayed the Princess as a temperamental fantasist and press hog and Prince Charles as an increasingly sad-sack, eccentric figure racked by self-doubt and appalled by the megastardom of his wife. 'She has banished all his old friends,' ran the summary of complaints I listed in *Vanity Fair*. 'She has made him give up shooting. She throws slippers at him when she can't get his attention. She spends all his money on clothes. She forces him to live on poached eggs and spinach. She keeps sacking his staff. The debonair Prince of Wales, His Royal Highness, Duke of Cornwall, heir to the throne, is, it seems, pussy-whipped from here to eternity.' The Princess, I reported, now spent hours in isolation dancing to Dire Straits and Wham! on her Sony Walkman while Charles talked to his plants and turned for solace to assorted gurus, quack philosophers and spiritualist mediums, through which he hoped to communicate with the spirit of his 'Uncle Dickie' Mountbatten. His new wimpishness had led to more tension with his father. 'When Prince Charles walks into a room,' I wrote, 'Prince Philip walks out of it.'[9]

Two days after 'The Mouse that Roared' hit the news-stands I was woken up in New York by the gravelly voice of a *Daily Mail* reporter called Rod. 'Is that 'Urricane Tina?' said the voice, alluding to the advent of Hurricane Gloria, said to be on its way. 'You've certainly caused a ruckus over here.'

The ruckus was all the tabloids in concert pretending that what I had written was a scandalous pack of lies in order to justify repeating every juicy detail. According to the *Daily Mirror*, I was 'a rat bag of gossip' who had traduced the sanctity of the royal marriage – *Now read on!* The *Daily Mail* kept up the bashing for a week, climaxing – with its usual demonic creativity – in a parody written anonymously by the editor Sir David English himself. The spread was titled 'How Would Tina and Harry's Marriage Stand up to the *Vanity Fair* Treatment?' It cast me as 'the Joan Crawford of journalism' in big shoulder pads, barking orders at cowering underlings while my husband, 'once known as the James Bond of journalism', moped at home, a ghost of his former self, longing to return to England and the safe comfort of the House of Lords. In *Tatler*, my alma mater, the polemicist and wit Auberon Waugh teasingly speculated, in a piece headlined 'Blue Wales', that 'The Mouse That Roared' was the revenge of the career woman (i.e. me) who had dreamed of becoming Princess of Wales herself on the shy girl with no O levels (i.e. Di) who had actually snagged the Prince.

If I harboured any doubts that my sources for 'The Mouse That Roared' had got it right, they were dispelled when the Prince and Princess of Wales used the occasion of an ITV interview with Sir Alastair Burnet to refute it. The Palace usually only bother to deny something that's true. To go to the unusual step of having the Prince and Princess address the content of a story in person – even obliquely, without reference – meant the facts in it were probably only a glimmer of what more was there.

One point on which I had defended Diana in the piece turned out to be mistaken: I claimed the Princess was not, in fact, to blame for the unhappy departure of Oliver Everett. I later learned she had in truth unfairly frozen him out. His crime was as follows. One day, after having been informed by the Princess that she could not meet with him because she was 'going over to see the Queen', Everett knocked and entered her rooms to leave papers to sign. The Princess turned out to be there after all, enjoying a moment of solitude. After that, Everett found himself reduced by Diana to a 'non-person' and felt he had no course but to resign, a disappointing career move for a man who had been a rising star in the Foreign Office and given it up at the request of Prince Charles.[10] I suspect the breakdown in relations occurred because the Princess had been caught out by Everett in a lie. Who else but Diana would use such an overstated excuse as an audience with the Queen to avoid dealing with a boring in-tray of official admin? Being caught heightened her sense that the brainy Everett was judging her all the time.

Diana's frantic desire to be seen as nothing short of perfect was apparent in an especially inauthentic moment in the ITV interview, in preparation for which she had gone so far as to be coached by Sir Richard Attenborough. When Alastair Burnet asked Charles a question about whether as a couple they had arguments, the Prince replied, truthfully, 'Most married couples do' – only for Diana to insist that no, never, they didn't argue at all. Still, when Sir Roy Strong's diaries, published in 1997, included an account of the state of play between Charles and Diana, written on 24 May 1984, it was almost identical in message to 'The Mouse That Roared', except this time quoted from the mouth of Diana's neighbour at Kensington Palace, Princess Michael of Kent. Strong recorded how at a concert for the Prince's Trust charity, at the Victoria and Albert Museum, Princess Michael had launched into a confidential after-dinner salvo about what Strong summarised as 'the catastrophe of the Princess of Wales: droves of the household were leaving and then there was the terrible mother, Mrs Shand Kydd, who was a baleful influence. Poor Prince Charles who had bought Highgrove to be near his former girlfriends. Nothing was happy. Diana was hard. There was no pulling together, no common objectives, and it was misery for him. How long can it last? And Diana has become a media queen which only makes it worse . . .' Diana, she had concluded, was 'a time bomb'.[11]

Princess Michael was right about that. Diana's tantrums, her bulimia, her whole crazy drama – it all feels today like a furious desire to repudiate not just her Windsor present but her Spencer past. All of it – the whole bill of goods she'd been sold as a female from the moment she'd been able to gaze up fetchingly at her father's camera, the ladylike education that continually assured her that she was stupid, the generations of beauties gazing down from the picture gallery at Althorp telling her to be pleasing and powerless, the fraudulent fairy-tale wedding, the force-feeding of mothball traditions and duplicitous double standards, all the women she didn't want to be, her mother, her grandmother, her stepmother, her old blushing, gullible, romantic self – she wanted to vomit it all up, tear it apart, hurl it into a pit of fire. That's what all the screaming and cutting and bingeing and starving was about. She would be her own Frankenstein's monster, and nobody else's.

Like most new identities forged in an inferno of suppressed emotion,

Diana's was at first exaggerated and unconvincing. She stopped dressing only to please and started dressing only for effect. Remember that Catherine Walker white suit with drum majorette gold frogging and asparagus-like epaulettes that she wore to meet King Fahd at Gatwick airport? Or the gondola-sized, bottle-green Emanuel hat and matching coat dress, upholstered in loud check like a Scottish club chair, that appeared on her gaunt frame on the waterways of Venice? In the first half of the eighties the times she got it wrong were as numerous as the times she got it right. She recognised it herself when the honed, streamlined nineties Diana cleaned out her wardrobe for the auction at Christie's in New York and marvelled at all the blunders she'd worn on her back. The curator of the show, Meredith Etherington-Smith, recalls Prince William commenting, 'Mummy, that's too awful to sell,' when they added one especially over-the-top bugle-beaded number to the pricey inventory of glittering duds.[12]

The Dynasty Di construct reflected the exact opposite of Diana's self-view at the time. The more emphatic the clothes got the more she was searching for inner definition. All she knew was that the Grand Sloane act had to go. It just encouraged acts of repression from a royal machine that took her *comme il faut* outfits to mean capitulation.

It wasn't such unreasonable paranoia. Diana was watched and informed on constantly by the old guard at Buckingham Palace. Patsy Puttnam remembers a dinner in 1984 that she and her husband, the film producer David Puttnam, attended with Diana and Charles at the London home of Lord Waldegrave and his wife Caroline. Just as the royal couple were leaving, Waldegrave's sister, Lady Susan Hussey, the Queen's lady-in-waiting, called to check with her brother on 'how it had gone' – an obvious code, Patsy sensed, for 'how the Princess had behaved', which clearly flustered Diana. 'She hated Susan Hussey,' said Patsy. 'She knew she was all about the crowd that were trying to control her. They couldn't even wait till the two of them were out the door. The network needs to know *tonight*. I would die under that sort of circus.'[13] In fact, it was Charles's bad behaviour, not Diana's that made an impression on the Puttnams that night. While Diana was solicitous and affectionate towards the Prince, he was openly dismissive towards her. 'He behaved as if she was an irritant,' said Patsy. 'He would have liked her to be invisible, and she knew it.'

It is worth noting that Camilla Parker Bowles, well over twice Diana's age and sophistication when she married Prince Charles in 2005, has sensed similar dismissiveness from the Prince's overhauled coterie since she graduated from mistress to Duchess of Cornwall. Richard Kay's report in the *Daily Mail* in October 2006 on the eve of Charles and Camilla's state visit to Pakistan reads like such a reprise of Diana in the eighties you can almost hear the theme music of Wham! come up from Diana's Sony Walkman.

'When Charles first brought Camilla home as his wife, the staff couldn't do enough for her, falling over themselves in their unctuous bowing and scraping,' reported Kay. 'The phrase "Camilla wants" became an incantation as members of the household strained and sweated to respond to the Duchess's every whim.' (Note: at the Palace, men have wishes. Women, except for one, have whims.)

'To their surprise, they found the easy-going countrywoman to be "quite sharp and demanding", and her liberal use of the phrase "I need" had similar magical properties to rubbing a magic lamp – things were done and problems solved with astonishing speed.' Now, says Kay, the unthought-out nature of Camilla's role in public life, combined with the Palace's determination not in any way to diminish the spotlight on the Prince of Wales as he closes in on the British throne, leaves Camilla feeling 'increasingly isolated'. 'She feels a general air of disapproval hangs over her,' one of Camilla's friends tells Kay. 'It's a very uncomfortable position for her to be in, and she doesn't know the way out of it.' Kay concludes that the overarching strategy is that nothing and no one should ever again be allowed to overshadow the Prince of Wales, 'and if this means keeping Camilla down, then so be it'.[14]

In the light of the Duchess's experience, perhaps Diana's turbulent rejection of numerous members of her own and her husband's staff looks less like tantrum and more like self-preservation. She sensed, correctly, that their loyalty was not to her but to the system. In May of 1983, an anonymous courtier told the *Daily Mirror*: 'The problem is it appears that Diana does not appreciate that the slightest alteration in her schedules involves an immense upheaval for those who have to accommodate the new arrangements. After a particular plan has been drawn up, Diana will pop her head round the door and announce at the last minute that she would rather prefer to add a walk-about to the programme or visit a kindergarten or whatever. As delightful as such "whims"' – that word again – 'are, they create a nightmare for those who serve her. A small demand could involve massive, heart-thumping mayhem, with courtiers scurrying hither and thither like Sandringham chickens with their heads chopped off.'[15]

What else, one might ask, did the headless chickens have to do that was so pressing? Diana's desire to rescue a marmoreal royal trudge through some comatose British institution with a more spontaneous act of human flair is the thing that made her visitations such a triumph. Plus, her understanding of the emotional dimension of Charles's commitments often made more of a difference to how the Prince was received than any amount of briefing and planning. Diana instinctively seemed to know that the only power royalty has left is the power to disappoint, and she never did, either with her physical presence or in her responsiveness to human detail. While the Prince's correspondence piled up for weeks, her thoughtful thank-you letters were not just round the next day to her host, they were often written the same night and delivered before breakfast the next morning. On the evening of the Waldegrave dinner, Lady Puttnam remembers that the Prince and Princess had been committed by Charles to go on to see an art exhibit at a gallery and it was getting late. 'Diana was concerned,' she said, 'because the host was holding the gallery open for them and they were keeping them waiting, something he didn't seem to care about at all.'[16]

Had their marriage worked, Diana could have been as politically useful to Charles as Nancy was to Ronald Reagan. Diana had a shrewd instinct for detecting the freeloaders, charlatans and sycophants for whom her husband had a fatal susceptibility. 'She used to say, "Why are we having these people to dinner?"' a member of the Prince's staff told Anthony Holden. 'She knew they had ulterior motives for sucking up, like being asked to shoot at Sandringham.'[17] The Prince's three mentors, Earl Mountbatten, Laurens van der Post and Armand Hammer had more than a whiff of fraudulence about each of them. Hammer, whom Charles tried to foist on Diana as a godfather to William (she rejected him as a 'rather reptilian old man'), turned out to be an outright crook whose money came from a slush fund established to pay bribes to the corrupt middlemen who had arranged his company's oil concession in Libya. He was also accused by investigative journalist Edward Jay Epstein of being 'a KGB stooge' who had 'long provided a convenient conduit for the laundering of Kremlin funds used to finance Soviet espionage activities'.[18] Since the Prince had been told all his life he was brilliant, it was hard for him to discern or admit it when he'd been taken for a ride.

This worrying trait was one of the tensions that underlay the departure of Edward Adeane. Diana's opposition to him as private secretary only accelerated what was an inevitable parting of the ways between Prince and royal servant. In Adeane's eyes, Charles, since his marriage, was changing as alarmingly as Diana was. In fact, in his own way the Prince was acting out as surely as if he, too, was wearing an outsize emerald-green Emanuel hat. The more attention his wife received, the more Charles sought attention for his ideas. Adeane, a barrister by profession, who'd been Charles's private secretary for six years, saw his role as guiding the Prince towards kingship. He was known to be appalled by Charles's increasingly controversial causes and serial public outbursts. Indeed, some of the Prince's choices of forums at which to sound off were either inspired or insane, depending on how you looked at it. Charles denounced modern architecture in general and a proposed steel-and-glass addition to the National Gallery in particular (he called it a 'monstrous carbuncle') at a dinner honouring architects. He inveighed against the evils of a technological approach to medicine when he was a guest of the professional body epitomising that approach, the British Medical Association. He delivered a radical assault on conventional farming methods to a large conference of conservative farmers at the Royal Agricultural College. Then there was the little matter of the Prince's desire, on his visit to Rome with Diana in April of 1985, to take communion with the Pope – an act which, had the Queen not intervened, would have violated the 1701 Act of Settlement, creating the unfortunate side effect of depriving the Windsors of their legal hold on the throne.

As noted, Adeane made it clear he was deeply opposed to the 'excessive' amount of time Charles now devoted to his children instead of to his princely duties, an issue on which Diana immediately had taken a stand. In fact, you could argue that all the things Adeane disapproved of were Charles's most redeeming features: his obsession with global warming, his 'hokey' fascination with alternative medicine, his interfaith initiatives, his most unroyal desire to be with his young sons. It turns out the issues the Prince was mocked for in the eighties and nineties were not just relevant but cutting edge. 'The degree of misunderstanding between the Islamic and Western worlds remains dangerously high,' he told a yawning audience in 1993, 'the need for the two to live and work together in our increasingly interdependent world has never been greater.'[19] It seems he even had some clever business ideas. The 'half-baked' concept everyone laughed at, of creating a Duchy Originals line of organic foods at Highgrove, raked in a million pounds for his charities in 2005. In his muddly, Eeyoreish way, Charles had come up with his own version of a project as novel as Paul Newman's salad dressing. Talking to plants no longer looks so wacky either. Four per cent of British farmland, following his Highgrove lead, has gone organic in recent years. In 2006, the new Tory Party leader, David Cameron, touted his green credentials by proposing to put a wind turbine and solar panels on the roof of his west London home. Prince Charles was way ahead of him, having installed eco-friendly insulation at Highgrove long before.

It was just bad luck for the Prince that while Diana's personal transformation synchronised perfectly with the zeitgeist, Charles's generation has never recognised him as its own – not because of what he does or what he thinks but how he seems. Who else but Prince Charles, at the age of thirty-six, would wear a navy blue suit while accompanying Diana to the July 1985 Live Aid concert at Wembley Stadium and refer to it afterwards as 'some pop concert jamboree my wife made me go to'?[20] It's not his fault that the body language bequeathed to him by his bizarre Edwardian upbringing was a vanishing tribal semiotic that modern Britain had almost lost the ability to decode. Diana, who was supposed to be so much in love with him, couldn't see past it either, so buried under the Windsor training and veneer was the Prince's own struggle for identity.

Instead, Charles's work, his 'hobby horses' and his country pursuits were another wedge between them when they should have been the glue. Diana, unlike Camilla, was not practised enough to flatter Charles as a man of ideas. (On the notorious Camillagate tape of 1989, the Prince's mistress shows what an old hand she is at the seduction game by begging, no, really, *begging* Charles to send her a copy of his latest riveting speech.) Nor was Diana able to keep up with him in 'grown-up' discussions. Andrew Neil, then editor of the *Sunday Times*, noted the intellectual disparity between the royal couple when he lunched with the two of them at Kensington Palace in 1984. 'Charles roamed far and wide on the issues of the day,' recalled Neil. 'He was particularly keen that Britain's armed forces developed a rapid reaction out-of-Nato-area capability to respond to threats to our interest outside Europe, a sensible view with which I concurred. Diana played little part in the conversation, talked about a rock concert she had been to the night before and piped up when President Reagan's imminent visit to London was mentioned. She said Reagan was "Horlicks" – apparently a Sloane Ranger expression for boring old fart – and claimed Nancy Reagan was only coming so she could have her photograph taken with the royal couple and the children. She was determined not to oblige the First Lady. She seemed to have the typical English upper-class distaste for supposedly vulgar Americans. Charles made no attempt to involve her.'[21]

Diana had keen emotional intelligence but her lack of education meant she struggled with the framework of public affairs. Nor did she grasp what underpinned the things that other people understood as their work. How could she? She had no experience of it. No men in her family did and the women were not expected to. She married virtually right out of school. Until her travels as a princess over the years exposed her to other cultures she was hopelessly class-bound and local. Her own star power made her underrate process. Her presence alone obviated the necessity for content, something that was not true for her husband who toiled for hours in his study on the speeches that were such a source of comic relief to the press. For her own public utterances Diana often tapped clever friends like Dr James Colthurst to come up with good lines or ventriloquise bright responses for visiting dignitaries rather than trek through briefing papers from her private secretary. 'I'm sitting next to Mitterrand at lunch in fifteen minutes,' she would tell Colthurst. 'Quick! Give me something to say.'[22] She knew her poise and beauty meant she could fake her way through. She saw Charles's earnest efforts to be 'substantive' mostly as a good visual foil to her own ability to dazzle.

On their tour of Italy together Diana, even with her repertoire of unfortunate hats, was so beguiling she had the Italians eating out of her hand. When Charles told her to mind her head under an arch in the garden of the famous aesthete Sir Harold Acton, she responded prettily, 'Why? There's nothing in it.'[23] In Rome she was mobbed like a rock star. A former private secretary on the British Embassy staff told Nigel Dempster, 'It was a huge success but not necessarily for Charles. He wore the horns. He was, as Florentines so delicately put it, *il vecchio cornuto* – the old cuckold. He was seriously boring. It corresponded exactly to the age-old Italian fantasy – old, rich, impotent husband . . . Beautiful young wife . . . They loved the way she would slip her shoes off beneath a restaurant table. They pitied the way he had to roll up his spaghetti with the help of a spoon.'[24]

'We'd have been such a great team,' Diana said to me regretfully about her ex-husband in New York in 1997. But a team in Diana's terms meant one that acknowledged something that would always be unacceptable to the heir to the throne: that the starring role was hers. She no more understood why Charles valued the earnest audiences he provided to architects, philosophers and environmentalists than she could later see why cardiologist Hasnat Khan spent such an unreasonable amount of time at the hospital. 'I just don't get him,' she told her friend Lucia Flecha de Lima about Khan in a phone call in 1997. 'He's always so busy and his work is so important to him. I keep telling him he doesn't need to work at the hospital. We would make a great team. *We could do my work together*. But he doesn't want to know.'[25]

All divas eventually subjugate the world around them to support the qualities and conditions that allow them to shine. Charles may have read more, but Diana was a swift, decisive executive in her own cause, as clear in what she wanted as Charles was confused. Her ballet dancer friend Wayne Sleep says he thinks Diana could have been an editor or a director, so clear was she on visual details that did or did not work. She *was* a director in a sense, of her own *mise en scène*. Even Edward Adeane was impressed by the speed with which she cleared her desk, compared to her husband, whose executive style one aide likened to 'nailing jelly to a wall'.[26] Only a year after her ditzy comments at lunch with Andrew Neil, she sat next to the former Goldman Sachs chairman John Whitehead at a National Gallery dinner in Washington and impressed him with her incisive questions about the American political system and the structure of Congress.[27] She was a work in progress while Charles was a work in aspic – that's how she saw it, anyway. Where the Prince of Wales had once cut such a dashing, accomplished figure in her eyes, she now considered most of Charles's public commitments, his dull, interminable round of seasonal royal rituals and treks to cheer on efforts of industry, philanthropy and commerce – what he termed on the eve of their wedding his 'dashing abite' – as 'a waste of space', to use another Diana term. After all, wasn't it she everyone wanted to see? Bruce Oldfield records a touching moment of marital disconnect when he went to fit Diana for one of her backless show-stopping dresses in her sitting room at Kensington Palace and Charles interrupted the fitting bearing a catalogue from the Tate Gallery exhibit of George Stubbs paintings. The Prince pointed at the image of a duchess astride a horse and asked Oldfield eagerly: 'Do you think my wife would look good in something like that?' 'A full seventeenth-century riding outfit?' thought Oldfield. 'It wasn't quite what we'd had in mind.'[28]

Stephen Fry, who was and is a friend of Charles, sensed in Diana what he calls 'an instinct of recruitment'.[29] She knew how to draw the people it was expedient to charm to her side of the aisle. Dread of this subtle guerrilla warfare of his wife's became Prince Charles's own special paranoia. While Diana saw his staff as oppositional, the Prince saw his staff as slowly but surely falling under her spell as well. It was too much to bear! According to one of them, he exploded with such vehemence about it at Michael Colborne on the tour of Canada in June of 1983 that it led, after nine happy years of service, to his personal secretary's resignation in 1984. Colborne's mistake had been to respond to Diana's request to join her on the quarterdeck of *Britannia* to advise her about upcoming events. When Charles returned from an engagement and found them in an animated planning session he asked Colborne to step into the cabin normally used by the Duke of Edinburgh for a 'private word'. He proceeded to go ballistic. 'I hired you away from the navy. You owe your loyalty to me!' His Royal Highness yelled. When Colborne emerged severely rattled from the cabin, he found Diana outside, where she'd been listening at the door, sobbing.[30]

It was futile, of course, for Charles to declare war on his wife's powers of seduction. It was an area where he could only meet with defeat. You could interpret Charles's resistance to Diana in the bedroom (once every three weeks, she told her voice coach Peter Settelen, was about as often as he sought her out)[31] as a necessary act of self-definition, a line in the sand against the one seduction his wife could not achieve.

'Somehow we had Harry,' Diana told Andrew Morton. Jasper Conran, who made many of her clothes during her second pregnancy, says it was clear she was striving hard to be a turn-on for her husband, eager for Conran to design outfits that would show off her fuller cleavage. 'She wanted to be sexy during her maternity,' he says. 'There is no doubt in my mind that she was madly in love with her husband and wanted to please him until after Harry was born.'[32] Diana herself told Andrew Morton that the last six weeks before Harry's birth were some of the closest times in her marriage but that their relationship effectively died as soon as the baby was born.[33] Conran observed that after the pregnancy Diana would often be weepy in her fittings. 'I didn't ask her what was the matter,' he says. 'With royalty you don't intrude. Her hormones were racing, coupled with her uncertainty, and she felt such immense pressure from the outside world. I'd sit her down and give her a cup of tea. One assumed that her family was helping her. She was really deeply alone.'[34]

Diana claimed to Morton that it was her husband's obvious disappointment that she had given birth to a second boy, rather than the girl he wanted, that plunged their marriage deeper into crisis. 'He's even got red hair!'[35] Charles is said by Diana to have cried in a hurtful voice of alarm when Harry emerged after nine hours of labour in St Mary's. If he did, it seems an unlikely source of incapacitating marital grievance. Charles could not have been that surprised to find that his son, in toff parlance, was a 'ginge'. Most of the Spencers were, including Diana's eldest sister, Sarah, and half the ancestors on the walls of Althorp, pre-eminently the so-called 'Red Earl' (1835–1910) with his resplendent orange beard. Charles's sharp exclamation about Harry's colouring seems no more than the kind of fascinated sense of otherness many parents feel when a baby only imagined for nine months suddenly appears in all its amazing refusal to conform. Diana's obsession with being perfect may well have made her misread her husband's reaction. The Windsors had had an uncanny knack of producing first a boy then a girl. Diana was so reluctant to be different that, even though she knew after her amniocentesis test in 1984 that she was carrying a boy, she had failed to share that information with her husband.

Two Diana biographers, Anthony Holden and James Whitaker, both allege that it was the re-emergence of Camilla that was to blame for the breakdown. They say that by 1983, the year before Harry's birth, Charles had gone back to his mistress physically as well as emotionally, and that Diana knew it. I accept this view, and I accept it in spite of – no, because of – the insistent testimony of Charles's friends and his official biographer Jonathan Dimbleby that the affair didn't recommence until three years later, in November 1986. The repeated assertion feels like talking points provided by St James's Palace. How can they or anyone claim to know the secrets of the bedroom with such vehement certainty? It's logical to conclude that they are repeating what they must have been told by the two people who shared a strong interest in looking as decorous as possible: Charles and Camilla. Gyles Brandreth, the Prince's more recent apologist, goes so far as to introduce a new reason why the date was 1986 or after: the sight of Diana dancing provocatively with her old boyfriend Philip Dunne at the wedding of Tracy Ward to the Marquess of Worcester in June 1987. According to Brandreth, Charles, seeing this, decided that Diana was probably pursuing extramarital affairs herself. But this version overlooks the provocative fact that Charles had already spent half the night dancing first with his former lover Anna Wallace and then with Camilla herself. He was sighted slipping away early as Dunne and Diana held the floor.[36]

There is other evidence, swept aside in the cleaned-up version, that the affair with Camilla resumed earlier than 1986. When Diana was in

London, Charles would join Camilla at the Beaufort Hunt, with all its opportunities for dusk assignations. A member of Highgrove's household told Anthony Holden that one weekend in November 1983 Diana pressed the recall button in Charles's study and it connected to Camilla. They had a 'monumental' row in front of the staff – Diana in tears; Charles striding off.[37] Diana herself told Andrew Morton she saw many more concrete signs of marital subterfuge: 'Nocturnal telephone calls, unexplained absences and small but significant changes in his usual routine.'[38] Marie Helvin, who began dating Camilla's brother Mark Shand in 1983 and often stayed with the Parker Bowleses at weekends, had the strong sense that Camilla was always in Prince Charles's life. 'There was a hint that [the ongoing relationship] was always there,' she told me. 'My feeling was that they were always together.'[39] The testimony of Stuart Higgins, the editor of the *Sun* (1994–8), who had formed a friendly relationship with Camilla when he was the *Sun*'s royal reporter, suggests the same conclusion. Higgins told one of Diana's biographers, Sally Bedell Smith, that from 1982 to 1992 Camilla briefed him about once a week on background about all that was going on in the Charles/Diana relationship. 'I never sensed that she was out of contact,' Higgins said, 'though I definitely believe there was a cessation in the relationship and that Charles put an effort into the marriage. Our relationship was two ways . . . she [Camilla] was really trying to gauge whether the press was on to her [and Charles] so it was a question of her keeping in touch too.'[40] Since making those remarks Higgins has gone silent. He says he now prefers not to discuss those habitual phone calls with Camilla, citing as his reason that he 'continues to work on projects for the Duchess of Cornwall'.[41]

At a loss to win Prince Charles's attention after the birth of Harry, Diana tried to dance her way into his heart. In private, she would put on sexy lingerie and low music and attempt to tantalise him with a striptease he is said to have only 'mildly enjoyed'.[42] And, in December of 1985, she made a painful public attempt to woo him.

The occasion was a performance for the Friends of Covent Garden, a VIP evening of skits and entertainment the Royal Opera House puts on every year for special patrons. Ballet dancers sing, singers appear in tutus, and there's often a surprise turn from a guest celebrity. Though a royal often shows up in the audience, no one that year was expecting the Princess of Wales. But for weeks, in secret, Diana rehearsed with the diminutive Wayne Sleep, devising and preparing a dance routine. Two numbers before the end of the show she slipped from the royal box, where she was seated with Charles. Minutes later, to his – and the audience's – utter astonishment, she emerged before the footlights to the rocking sounds of Billy Joel's 'Uptown Girl', wrapped in slinky white satin and dancing a lithe *pas de deux* with Sleep. 'I was worried she'd fall apart under the spotlight,' Sleep says now. 'But she totally carried it off. Not many people could handle being under such scrutiny in front of an insiderly audience on that huge Covent Garden stage. She showed natural star quality.'[43] Diana received a standing ovation and eight curtain calls – except from her husband. She had played all her moves to Charles up in the royal box. But afterwards, when she and Sleep joined the Prince for a small reception, he behaved coolly, even distantly. It was embarrassingly clear that he had not been ravished by the spectacle of his wife *en pointe*. His disappointing response, when it leaked, was interpreted as frigid disapproval of Diana's lapse in royal etiquette. She was, after all, the future Queen. Sleep, however, believes that what actually irritated the Prince was that he had been left out. The previous year, at the same occasion, Charles and Diana had performed a skit together – as Romeo and Juliet, in which the Prince's role was to sing the ad jingle, 'Just One Cornetto'. But this year Diana had chosen to appear without him. It made him uneasy. 'It was her first sign of independence and the Palace got worried. I think they thought she was going to be the dumb blonde and suddenly this thing started to grow,' Sleep said.[44]

The Prince was right. If Diana felt emboldened to an act of such sexy exhibitionism, it was because she had experienced seismic acclaim for another high-octane dance. A month earlier, *le tout* Washington had been mesmerised by her whirl across the East Room of the White House in the arms of the movie star and disco-dance icon John Travolta. That time, the occasion was the dinner for Charles and Diana, hosted by 'Horlicks' and Nancy Reagan. For the Reagans and Diana alike, it was a moment of what investors of that go-go era called synergy.

The finest facelifts from Bel Air and Georgetown floated above the pouffiest frocks from Oscar de la Renta, Valentino and Dior to rattle their rocks in honour of the Prince and (really) the Princess of Wales. Diana alighted from a silver Rolls-Royce in a midnight-blue velvet Victor Edelstein number with long dark blue gloves and demurely dazzling pearl and sapphire choker.

The Russian ballet star and choreographer Mikhail Baryshnikov, who was to be seated next to the Princess at dinner, was walking with a cane as he advanced along the receiving line to where Diana stood with Prince Charles next to the President and Mrs Reagan. 'You're a lucky man,' Prince Charles told him with practised urbanity. 'My wife has requested that you sit next to her tonight. She loves to make me jealous.' Baryshnikov warned the Princess that, sadly, an injury to his ankle meant he could not ask her to dance. 'My loss,' she blushed. He was struck by 'the extraordinary transparency of the Princess's skin against the tight blue dress, the deep blue eyes, so much more beautiful than any photographs or TV'.[45] John Travolta, also in line, thought Diana looked ten feet tall. 'She was so charismatic and full of presence, like a movie star,' the movie star recalled to me.[46]

Travolta had no idea he was going to end up with top billing that night. At the time, his career was idling. Two years had passed since his last big moneymaker, *Staying Alive*, and the film which would put him back on top, *Pulp Fiction*, was still nine years in the future. The marquee Hollywood guest at the White House was not the second-magnitude star of the now antique hit *Saturday Night Fever* but Clint Eastwood, who was soaking up Oscar buzz for his role as the sombre Preacher in *Pale Rider*. As Travolta donned his new Armani dinner jacket before the party, he mused to himself, 'Wow, I'm lucky to be asked! I may not be hot but I'm not forgotten!'

When he reached Diana in the receiving line, she asked him sweetly about the bigger star. 'Have you seen Mr Eastwood tonight?' 'No, I haven't,' he replied. 'You do suppose he will be here?' she said. 'Oh, yes,' Travolta said. 'Of course,' Diana said, smiling. 'Where else would he be?'

'I thought that was pretty clever and pretty neat,' Travolta told me two decades later. 'I thought, she not only knows who she is, she knows what this is – and how big this is. She was so savvy about the media impact of it all.'[47]

For the dinner of eighty guests, Diana was seated, as promised, between the President and the ballet legend. She established immediate intimacy with Baryshnikov by telling him about her children ('from the heart', the dancer recalled), showing him pictures of William and Harry, and asking him about his own family. 'She talked to me as if I were her girlfriend. She could create complicity straight away.' She giggled at the Californian kitsch of a white-chocolate biscuit with her profile stamped on it and asked him to point out who was who in 'such lovely mischievous way'.[48] Paul Burrell has reported that Baryshnikov asked for Diana's autograph, but that is not what happened. 'No, I asked her if I could keep her place card as a souvenir,' the dancer told me. 'She looked at me sideways, placed her finger to her lips, and said, "Only if I can keep yours."'[49]

Prince Charles's dinner partners were the First Lady and the opera singer Beverly Sills. 'I asked Nancy how I got so lucky,' Sills recalled, 'and she said, "Because he loves opera – and you're the only person in this room who knows anything about it."'[50] 'Sadly, there were no lovely actresses or singers,' Charles wrote in his diary the next day. 'I had been rather hoping that Diana Ross would be there.'[51]

About 9 p.m., right before the entrée, John Travolta, seated at another table, was interrupted by a tap on the shoulder from the First Lady. 'She said, "Look, there's only one wish that the Princess has,"' he recalled. 'And I said, "What's that?" And she said, "That's to dance with you." I said, "Really?" "Well, would you do the honours?" Mrs Reagan said. "Yes, where, how, when?" I asked. She said, "Around midnight. I will tap you on the shoulder and tell you it's time." It was clearly planned. I knew it would be an attention-grabbing moment, and I had three hours to sweat.'

Travolta relived for me what happened next. 'I try to recall Diana dancing with Charles. I'm six feet tall. I think with heels she's probably my height. Tall woman, and slender – so the illusion is tall. I go back in my mind to my formal ballroom-dancing schooldays. *Put hand in middle of back so you can guide her.* I'm remembering all the tricks. *Whatever you do, let her know you're in control.* The tap tap on the shoulder comes. My heart starts to race. Nancy takes me over. Princess not facing me, she's facing toward the president. I tap her on the shoulder and I say, "Would you care to dance?" Her head dips in the famous dip, she blushes a little and says, "Of course. I would love to." As soon as we get out there, the whole place clears for our encounter. I think I hear "Grease" and "Night Fever". I want it to go off well and show her I am in control and she doesn't need to worry and knows I'll lead. I bring her hand from a higher position and gracefully position it lower so she knows I can run the dance. No talking. Talking during a dance is difficult when seventy-five people are watching you. And I look her in the eyes and reassure her with my eyes, to say, "We're OK." We probably only dance ten minutes but it feels like twenty.'

Travolta said that up close he could feel how seductive Diana was. 'Absolutely I found her sexy, yes. People are either innately sexual or sensual or not. She had both. She was aware of me and I was aware of her. I didn't know anyone was taking pictures, to be honest – but I did know it had to look like a million dollars, because it was history being made. And it was my job to make it look as good as if it was in a movie.'[52]

All the guests I spoke to about that night sensed they were participating in an iconic moment. Washington was and is a dowdy town, a centre of power but not of fashion. The wives of heads of states trundle squatly through in their sparkly Lurex Escada knits. Among the 'cave dwellers' of Georgetown, the reigning bottle blondes from the network news bureaus are what pass for heat. The imported A-listers, B-listers and *Celebrity Squares* C-listers from the Reagans' Bel Air and Park Avenue circles added glitz but not tone. Diana's combination of beauty, refinement and youth made her exactly the corrective the Reagans needed. The glow she lent their little dinner-dance made up for roomfuls of Nancy's usual gnarled, air-kissing lunch-lady friends and fussy walkers. ('She was a baby,' marvelled Beverly Sills. 'That's what we were all thinking. Her skin was like peaches and cream.')[53] Baryshnikov was struck by the vision of Diana on the dance floor, 'so radiant and fresh, and John, so very dashing, this great American symbol of popular culture, and the White House marines in their dress uniforms looking on'.[54]

So what if Paul Burrell tells us now it was Baryshnikov himself whom Diana was really hoping to dance with that night? ('It was probably as well it was Travolta, not me, out there,' says the five-foot-seven Baryshnikov. 'My nose would have been round about at her bosom.')[55] So what if at the next morning's reception at the British Embassy Christopher Hitchens saw the Princess looking 'pale and ill' and the couple descending the stairs as if they'd just had 'a really, nasty, bitter, pointless row'?[56] The language of gesture is more powerful than any murky subtext. There was a Hollywood dimension now to Diana's glittering fable of the shy girl who married a dashing prince.

'You could feel the awe in the moment from people in the audience,' Travolta insists. 'It was dense with life, filled with life, and you'd have had to have been dead not to feel the joy around it. You had the sense that she'd seen *Grease* or *Saturday Night Fever* as a teenager. Clearly a princess's dream of a big magnitude that you could feel. She was a young woman watching those movies, she wasn't a princess back then, and now even a princess's dreams can come true. You got it – all you had to do was see the picture the next day and you got it. At the end she curtsied, and I bowed, and – well, I guess I turned back into a pumpkin.'[57]

## Chapter 13

# Cries and Whispers

'Charles thought he knew, but he never had any proof.'
– Diana to Peter Settelen, September 1992

While the world was thrilling to the spectacle of Diana's life as a Rodgers and Hammerstein musical, her home life was becoming more like something out of Hitchcock. Under a *King and I* façade lurked a *Rebecca*-like sinister melodrama. Highgrove, the Gloucestershire Manderley where the Princess spent her weekends with Prince Charles and the boys, had its own Mrs Danvers, Wendy Berry, who kept regular notes from 1985 to 1993. (It had its own Rebecca, too, living sixteen miles way away at Bolehyde Manor, near Chippenham, with her husband, Andrew Parker Bowles.) From the guests and visitors I've talked to, the authentic bleakness of Charles and Diana's life together in the late eighties seeps into the consciousness like the dampness of a November night.

It should have been idyllic. Highgrove House – in the hamlet of Doughton, near Tetbury – is and always was Prince Charles's beloved demesne. It was his deepest emotional connection, its garden his personal Xanadu. The house, with its grey neoclassical façade softened by an ancient cedar tree in the foreground and 340 acres of undulating farmland, was not a grand royal redoubt but a country gentleman's retreat. Here Charles could escape from being a prince and rake the leaves in baggy corduroy trousers and sweaters with patched elbows. This did not mean Highgrove was without its Ruritanian touches. When Paul Burrell was the butler there, every Friday afternoon had an Iwo Jima moment. Ten minutes before the Prince arrived Burrell was obliged to struggle up to the flagpole on the roof, sometimes in a towering wind, and improvise the Highgrove answer to the flying of the royal standard at Windsor.[1] It was Charles's boyish show of independence. Highgrove was one of the few things in the heir's life that his parents did not control. The garden expressed his inner life. Over the years he has turned it from a few scruffy thorn bushes, a dreary lawn and an unprepossessing square pond to something, magical, wild and surprising, alive with secret bowers and scented pathways. The romantic charm of the garden is actually the least part of the Prince's achievement. It is in his development of the farmlands that he has shown a rare vision and courage. Many farmers doubted whether it was possible to grow food and livestock naturally without using chemicals against weeds, insects and fungal attacks; snickers about the crankiness of natural organic farming were a commonplace of journalism. In fact, though he had to endure losses in the early years, natural farming has been not just a success at Highgrove, but possibly a model of healthy, sustainable natural farming for the twenty-first century. Lunch guests feast on such organic treats from the kitchen garden as Belgian carrots, green zebra tomatoes, and broad beans which are as delicious as their red flowers are beautiful.[2] 'All the things I have tried to do in this small corner of Gloucestershire,' Charles said to the author of a book about the Highgrove estate, 'have been the physical expression of a personal philosophy.'[3]

When these pastoral ruminations were read out to Diana by a friend, the two chums 'dissolved into peals of derisive laughter'.[4] The Princess felt she knew only too well what, or rather who, the Prince liked to do in that small corner of Gloucestershire. Diana's resistance to Highgrove's pleasures can be attributed to a single, or rather a married, factor: the propinquity of Camilla. Her rival's presence, real and imagined, invaded every aspect of Diana's experience of the serene beauty of the house. In 1986 she tried to persuade Charles to sell Highgrove and move 130 miles away from the dreaded Camilla set to Belton, former home of the 7th Lord Brownlow in Lincolnshire, but after pretending to consider the idea the Prince rejected Belton as too expensive to run and too far from the Duchy of Cornwall. Instead, in 1986, it was the Parker Bowleses who moved – but only three miles further away, buying Middlewick House, an eighteenth-century manor in the village of Pickwick, near Corsham in Wiltshire.

Camilla used to let herself into Highgrove from the terrace after arriving at the back entrance via Thyme Walk. There is a telling moment from the summer of 1990, two years before the Waleses separated, while Diana was still in residence. Camilla was observed poking her head out of Highgrove's French windows and catching

Charles by surprise. He was on the terrace in his sunglasses and stripped to the waist. 'Hello, darling,' she whispered. 'How is my favourite little Prince today?' Charles turned to see who it was, and laughed. 'Take off your glasses, Charles,' Camilla told him. 'I want to see your eyes.' 'I am frightened to let you see what my eyes reveal,' said Charles enigmatically. 'They might give too much away.'[5] Diana's relationship with her husband had nothing that could compete with this kind of loaded clandestine byplay. The Princess's youth and beauty were feeble weapons against Camilla's combination of cajoling intimacy and sexual imperiousness, which derived from a long, languid understanding of her man.

There is a creepy subtext to life at Highgrove that keeps reminding visitors that something is going on offstage. The gloom is enhanced by the fact that Gloucestershire has a very wet climate. Inside there are sounds of slamming doors and muffled sobs, the pleading voice of Charles asking what on earth has he done wrong now. There are times when the sound of retching can be heard from Diana's bathroom, and the Princess emerges looking flushed and secretive. In February 1986 the sharp wind seems to mirror Prince Charles's indifference to his wife.

On Sunday afternoons, Diana prepares to leave Highgrove for London to take the boys back to school, while her husband stays on in the country. She always seems to be in tears. Charles is baffled and exasperated. 'Why are you crying now?' is his marital refrain. It's as if what is welling up in Diana is not just her own sorrow but her mother's, all those years ago, when Frances Shand Kydd would weep inconsolably on Sunday evenings as the time neared for Diana and her brother to return to the custody of Earl Spencer.

Gloucestershire people have to be one of two things – hunters or gardeners. (Highgrove was nine miles away from the Duke of Beaufort's celebrated Beaufort Hunt on the Badminton estates.) Camilla and Charles were both, but Diana, displaying a determined marital death wish, elected to be neither, retreating ever further inside her bedroom in the house, as her husband retreated further and further out of it. On Saturdays, despite hysterical pleas from his wife, Charles would play polo or hunt for most of the day. The pastimes that made his wife nuts were the very things he thought kept him sane. She would awake to find him in full hunting drag, about to pull out of the drive in the Range Rover. According to the actress Minnie Driver's father, Ronnie, who was a guest at Highgrove in November 1983, 'Diana started screaming . . . accusing him of being selfish, a bastard, and a few four-letter words into the bargain.' Prince Charles, undeterred, left anyway.[6] In retaliation, she frequently refused to entertain his friends. The distinguished English country gardener Rosemary Verey, who died in 2001, often advised Charles on his plantings at Highgrove. On one of her visits there in the late 1980s, the Prince dispatched a servant to tell the Princess of Wales that their guest had arrived. The sash window from Diana's bedroom flew up and the Princess shrieked out of it, 'FUCK OFF!'[7] – whether at her husband or his guest was uncertain.

Yet midst the mayhem staff tell of interludes of domestic contentment. Prince Charles's exuberant warmth when he greets William and Harry on Friday afternoons, picking up William to whirl him around, the evenings of truce when the Prince and Princess dine together from a card table in the living room and chat like any civilised married couple about their respective engagements, Diana's surge of joy on their seventh wedding anniversary when she arrives at Highgrove to find an enormous bunch of wild roses from the garden on the piano – all hint at possibilities both have thrown away.

But the shadow of Rebecca is never far away. Ken Wharfe, Diana's police protection officer at the time, told me how only a few months after the happy mood of the seventh anniversary there was another tearful Sunday-afternoon departure. Diana suddenly turned to Wharfe in the car when they'd already been on the road to London for half an hour and said, 'Wait! I want to go back.'[8] They retraced their journey and pulled again into the drive of Highgrove. As Diana had suspected, Camilla's car was now parked outside.

The mistress had as much familiarity with the house as if it were her own. When the Prince used to visit Camilla at her own house, to cover his tracks he would eat an early dinner, dismiss the staff for the evening, and circle the Sunday TV shows he was supposedly going to watch in his copy of the *Radio Times*. Sometimes he would borrow the chef's car, because no one would recognise it. 'One time he smashed it up in a skid on the ice,' Mervyn Wycherley, said. 'The car had gone by 7 a.m. next morning and was returned all mended and nobody said anything.'[9]

The tenacious ghost of Mrs Parker Bowles, however, wasn't the only spectre haunting those Highgrove weekends. Diana had her secrets, too. There was the question of that ever-present shadow, her bodyguard, Barry Mannakee. William and Harry loved having him around but was there something too frank in his admiration for their mother? Personal protection officers – PPOs in Scotland Yard parlance – have to be cast to slip unobtrusively into the world of their 'principal', the term for their assigned VIP. If the principal is Prince Philip, the PPO can be an older man who blends in with the establishment and the guests at state occasions. If it's Prince Harry, the PPO is a young inspector who can sit all night in a raucous club looking cool and eyeball a drug pusher coming the principal's way. What kind of man do you cast to guard a beautiful and unhappy young princess? Someone very strong, very sane, and very married. Someone who could steer her out of trouble. 'You find you live their life one step ahead of them,' said Colin Tebbutt, a retired protection officer who has guarded Princesses Alexandra, Anne, Margaret, Michael of Kent and Diana. 'You often spot things that could wreck their lives if they take a particular direction. But you should never cross the line.'[10] The most obvious 'line' is personal intimacy with the principal. Less obvious is the temptation to succumb to the VIP's way of life. 'Red-carpet fever,' Ken Wharfe calls it – a common mistake because of the Pygmalion nature of a protection officer's training. Tebbutt, who coached many officers for the royal detail, recalled, 'I would send them off to Green's Oyster Bar and ask them what newspaper they read. If it was the Sun, I'd tell them to get the pink bit (the Financial section) of the Evening Standard. I'd show them how to put on a white tie in three minutes and tell them what to wear on various occasions. Basically, you have to dress the same as them. I would have everything from Barbour and green wellies for the country to white tie and tails for formal occasions.'[11] Ken Wharfe, who trained officers, too, says he used to 'tell the guys not to go home and tell their partners as they were opening a tin of beans in the kitchen they had just had caviar at the Ritz'.[12]

For a woman in a golden cage, bodyguards are an obvious candidate for romantic fixation. A bodyguard may be the only real man a princess meets. His strong shoulders clear the path ahead in the crowd. His firm hand on her elbow guides his principal to the refuge of a waiting car. His sharp eyes sweep deserted streets outside grand private houses at night and never peer at what's going on inside. Travelling in the front seat of the car to public events, he hears about the principal's nervousness and expectations. In the dark on the way home he is the recipient of her triumphs and disappointments. As the relationship deepens over time he's privy to her loneliness, too. With royal women, even when nothing is said, loneliness is mostly what he will hear in the silence. It's inevitable that such unspoken need will sometimes lead to an erotic charge. Even the well-defended Princess Anne, who'd lived with these boundaries since she was a child, was partial to her personal protection officer in 1986.

Sergeant Barry Mannakee, a cocky East Ender with kind eyes who had been a police dog handler, was assigned to the Royalty and Diplomatic Protection Group as a personal protection officer on the Wales backup team in September 1983.[13] He was moved closer in when Scotland Yard decided he'd got the hang of royal life. In April 1985, Mannakee took over as Diana's PPO from Chief Inspector Graham Smith, who would die of throat cancer in 1993. Diana, at twenty-four, had become less rebellious about the invigilating presence of a cop. In the first six months of her marriage, Mervyn Wycherley says, the Princess would worry the life out of Inspector Smith by getting into her car after a row with Charles and driving all night by herself.[14] She came to respect Smith's professionalism, however, and become deeply fond of him, visiting him regularly in the last days of his illness. She loved, too, the florid cockney Ken Wharfe who was Mannakee's successor. 'Wharfie', as she called him, is an inspired mimic, with an impersonation of Charles's strangled tones so hilariously exact he could take it on the road. He describes Princess Michael as 'your archetypal snob who had her husband's scrotal sac double-wrapped in cling film and buried in the cottage garden'.[15] He used to crack Diana up.

When Barry Mannakee became her bodyguard in 1985, the Princess was at her most vulnerable, still trying to live within the chafing confines of her marriage but increasingly unwilling to give up on her need for love. She was already familiar with him as a backup cop. He was dark and handsome in a blokey way, with a nice helping of spontaneous warmth. Their intimacy may have even begun earlier than accepted. The connection was forged, I am told, by a fishing accident when the royals were summering at Balmoral. Diana had accompanied Charles on an expedition to fish on the estate of Anne, Duchess of Westminster, at Lochmore in north-west Scotland, and as she glumly watched her husband at his favourite occupation, a salmon hook from a careless cast became embedded in her eyelid. Personal protection was radioed to take Diana back to the house to receive medical attention. It was Mannakee who drove the car, Mannakee, not her husband, who consoled her. Over the months that followed it was noted by other members of staff that when Mannakee was on duty Diana began to request the royal train for overnight journeys rather than fly. Diana had learned from her husband what a handy place the train was for assignations. In this case, handier than ever, since the police officer would be the only other person who slept on the corridor next to her saloon. A brother officer struggling to identify Mannakee's appeal came up with 'he was the kind of feller you felt would be good at do-it-yourself'[16] – a recommendation, it's safe to say, that would never be levelled at the Prince of Wales. Mannakee's sense of fun was a hit with her sons when he moved in closer to be her personal protection officer.

Mannakee accompanied Diana as PPO on the 1985 tours of Italy, Australia and America. The Princess relied heavily on his reassurance before public events. She used to tell him she couldn't go ahead with it, and Mannakee would hug her to stop her crying. What else could he have done? Asked for a new assignment should have been the answer, unless he wanted to sabotage his own career. Superintendent Colin Trimming, the senior officer who guarded Prince Charles, warned Mannakee about being 'over-friendly' and advised him to cool it, but Mannakee seems not to have taken his advice. 'He really had the hots for her,' said a former Highgrove staffer. 'He acquired all these cashmere sweaters. It went to his head.'[17]

Mannakee denied, perhaps to himself as well, that anything untoward was going on. Soon the reassurance Diana sought from her policeman was about being not just an adequate public performer but also a beautiful woman whose husband had lost interest. 'I was always wandering around trying to see him,' Diana admitted to her voice coach, Peter Settelen, on his videotapes. 'I was only happy when he was around . . . I was like a little girl in front of him the whole time, desperate for praise, desperate.'[18] Mannakee gave the little girl a wide-eyed owl to add to the collection of stuffed toys on her bed, later the first clue to James Hewitt that the police officer's relationship with her had been closer than a professional one. Diana loved to tease Mannakee when she was glammed up for a premiere or a public appearance, 'Barry, how do I look?' she would ask him coquettishly. Rank is an explosive element in sexual chemistry. It was hard to resist Diana when she had you in her sights. Being a princess conferred all the more allure on her beauty and vulnerability. The men she had her eye on were always bowled over by the flattery implicit in her willingness to show her need to be desired. 'I was told he was totally fixated on her,' Wharfe said of Mannakee. 'He broke the golden rule and stepped over the divide between the grey carpet to the red. He was a typical victim of red-carpet fever.'[19] But Wharfe and Colin Tebbutt both dismiss the rumours that Diana and Mannakee actually went so far as to become lovers. They believe it was below-stairs gossip, stoked by the jealousy of less favoured staff, that put round the rumour of an affair and did Mannakee in, 'People used to say he was a cocky bastard,' a police colleague explained.[20]

'He had tea with Diana in her private drawing room, which was unheard of,' Wharfe said. 'They' – the other staff – 'didn't like it.' Wharfe notes, too, that consoling Diana when she was in tears was not an unusual duty for her police protection officer. 'When her father died I sat on her bed for four hours with her crying in my arms,' he recalled. 'But that's not having an affair. It's a much easier role looking after the Queen. You know exactly where the boundaries are.'[21] Did Mannakee know where the boundaries were? On the videotapes recorded by Peter Settelen in the early 1990s, Diana talks about her warm feelings for her protection officer but stops short of confirming that theirs had been a physical relationship. She admits to dreaming of 'giving all this up just to go off and live with him', calls him 'one of the biggest crutches of my life', and laments, a little mysteriously, that 'I should never have played with fire, and I did'.[22]

Diana often said things like that, for effect, but I have become convinced that Mannakee was indeed Diana's first extramarital affair. One senses the male rivalry – and the collegial protectiveness, of course – that might make the other PPOs say it didn't happen. Diana's close friend Dr James Colthurst confirmed to me that she told him it was an affair.[23] A trusted senior Scotland Yard source who was in a position to know told me the same thing. There is the further testimony of James Hewitt, who says in his memoir *Love and War* that Diana told him she and Mannakee were lovers – a point on which Hewitt had no particular reason to lie.[24]

The change in the relationship between the Princess and the bodyguard is said to have deeply unsettled Mannakee himself. 'Once it began, Mannakee was very distraught about being caught up with her,' a friend of Prince Charles told Sally Bedell Smith. 'She was so intense and difficult to handle.'[25] Mannakee was now in a trap that became familiar to all Diana's admirers. Having become her fantasy man, he had no will to break the spell. The Princess's neediness, fuelled by secrecy and danger, was too insistent, too naked and too fragile to be denied, and yet the consequences for Sergeant Mannakee were potentially career-ending. A Highgrove colleague told Andrew Morton, 'Barry told me that Diana was quite forward with him. He was a frightened man, not because he was in fear of his life, but for his job.'[26] He did well to worry. Royal protection officers were required to keep notes on all official engagements and private visits, and these notes were logged. As Charles's senior protection officer, Superintendent Colin Trimming would have had enough access to have a strong idea of how much time Diana was spending in private with Mannakee. On the eve of Sarah Ferguson's marriage to Prince Andrew on 23 July 1986, the inevitable happened. Mannakee and Diana were allegedly discovered in a compromising position.[27] During the next day's ceremony, Andrew Morton watched Diana closely from the press gallery at Westminster Abbey. He noted that she seemed uncharacteristically distracted during the wedding of her then best friend.

Participants in the royal environment are never fired as the consequence of one act of bad faith. They are instantly transferred, then ignored, then dropped. 'It was all found out and they chucked him out,' Diana told Peter Settelen. One of Diana's staff confirmed, 'He was certainly moved very quickly.'[28] Immediately after the incident, Mannakee was drafted out of royal service into the Diplomatic Protection Squad. Nine months later he was dead.

The Princess never lost her belief that Barry Mannakee was murdered. 'I think he was bumped off,' she told Settelen.[29] Mannakee was killed in a motorcycle accident on 22 May 1987. He was riding pillion behind another cop when an inexperienced driver, a seventeen-year-old girl named Nicola Chopp, turned into the main road from a side road and collided with his Suzuki GS400 motorbike, smashing him against the side of her car.[30] In December 2004 the *Daily Express* ran a sensational interview with Nicola Chopp's mother under the banner headline 'WHY I BELIEVE DIANA'S LOVER WAS MURDERED', alleging that there were too many unanswered questions in the inquest. But when I spoke to Joy Chopp in 2006 she angrily disavowed the *Express* headline. Not only did it misrepresent her views, she said, but she had unequivocally asked the reporter to ensure her words were not twisted that way. When she protested, the reporter explained that 'she'd tried but it was what the editor wanted'.[31] Truth meets tabloid reality. 'IT WAS AN ACCIDENT!' is never going to move newspapers.

Prince Charles broke the news of Barry Mannakee's death to Diana on the way to a joint appearance at the 1987 Cannes Film Festival just as they were arriving at RAF Northolt to board their royal flight to Nice. She wept all the way there on the plane. 'That was the biggest blow of my life,' she told Peter Settelen.[32] Diana's torment was increased by having to conceal the extent of her grief from her husband. 'Charles thought he knew, but he never had any proof. And he just jumped on me like that. And I wasn't able to do anything.'[33] It is unlikely Charles did not know. There is little chance that Trimming would not have enlightened his boss on the reasons for the bodyguard's abrupt departure from the Princess's side. Charles may have requested the move himself. He apparently walked into Diana's bedroom once after they had had a row and heard her on the phone pouring out her miseries about himself and Camilla to Mannakee.[34] Perhaps the Prince now felt some satisfaction in seeing Diana having to pretend to be a carefree, globetrotting princess before the crowds at Cannes while underneath her heart was breaking. 'I just sat there all day going through this huge high-profile visit to Cannes, thousands of press, just devastated,' she confided to Settelen. 'Because, you know, I wasn't supposed to mind as much as I did, if you know what I mean.'[35] She told the voice coach that for a long time she had disturbing dreams about Mannakee that ended only when she went to the cemetery in Essex and laid flowers on his grave. Diana's ability to retain the mask of a radiant princess in Cannes when she was in such distress is a key moment in her evolution as the Princess of Wales: call it her initiation into the protocols of royal pain. Secrets and lies: Diana was getting good at them – almost as good as Prince Charles.

Who were Diana's confidantes? No one, was the trouble. A subterfuge as risky as Mannakee was too dangerous to discuss with a friend. Nor did Diana have that kind of closeness to her mothers or her elder sisters. The women in her family rarely revealed what they were feeling to the world and only occasionally to each other. 'I'm like my mother,' Diana once said. 'Even when I am feeling like hell I can pretend.'[36] When Frances's brother Edmund, Lord Fermoy, shot himself at the age of forty-five after a history of depression, Diana's grandmother Ruth Fermoy received the news of her son's death by telephone at Royal Lodge, where she was staying with the Queen Mother. Lady Fermoy took the call, and, saying nothing, returned to the drawing room with the assembled party to finish the evening before withdrawing to grieve.[37] Diana, too, had been raised to live her life in compartments – the world of Frances, the world of Johnnie, the world she would never share with Raine. She had hoped to escape all that when she married Prince Charles, but now she found herself in a web of secrets more dense than ever. 'Trust for her became so complex and labyrinthine,' said Jasper Conran. 'She got confused by it. There was a lot of not knowing whether people would betray her.'[38]

In such an atmosphere of suspicion, the arrival of Sarah Margaret Ferguson, aka Fergie, as Diana's prospective sister-in-law was a welcome blast of female complicity for the Princess of Wales. Woodrow

Wyatt records in his diary that at Fergie and Andrew's pre-wedding ball at Windsor Castle, Diana was overheard telling a dance partner how lovely it was to have Sarah as a 'mate' in the royal family. Wyatt observed: 'Now she doesn't feel so lonely.'[39] The two girls would burn up the telephone wires trading gossip and irreverent royal titbits they could share with no one else. It was Fergie whom Diana called as soon as she landed at Cannes to pour out her heart about the death of Mannakee.[40]

In the world in which Diana now lived, Fergie's girl talk was a tonic. With Prince Andrew in tow, Fergie would descend at weekends on haunted Highgrove like a ghostbuster, breezy, loud and mischievous. Throwing staff a suitcase of dishevelled clothes to press, she'd hug the children and rush outside for a refreshing walk. The Princess and the soon-to-be Duchess had known each other for at least six years through the polo circuit, where Charles's passion for the sport often condemned the Princess to hang around. She was actually Fergie's fourth cousin, and, coincidentally, their mothers, Susan Wright and Frances Roche, had been best friends at Downham School. Diana had been foiled in the appointment of Fergie as her lady-in-waiting by sceptical Palace influences, but she wangled her friend a prized invitation to the Queen's Ascot Week house party at Windsor Castle in June 1985. Better still, she connived to get Fergie seated at lunch next to the twenty-five-year-old Prince Andrew. It was a gift from heaven for Fergie to be thrown together with the Queen's second son. The redhead was emerging from a fruitless three-year attachment to Paddy McNally, a rich widower twenty-five years older than herself, with two teenage sons. He had recently declined to marry her and she was still nursing her chagrin. Andrew, now a self-confident, raucous naval officer with few of the hang-ups of his older brother, was also feeling the pressure to settle down. Before Fergie came along his penchant for female entertainment was a parade of stacked party girls with sprightly pasts whom he prevailed upon the Queen to be nice to at Balmoral. His only serious love affair was with the amiable soft-porn star Koo Stark, but in 1983 he was pushed to drop her, which he did most reluctantly. (His mother paid the bills, and he had no leverage to argue.) Within an hour of chatting her up, Andrew was flirtatiously coaxing a merry-eyed Ms Ferguson to eat every one of the chocolate profiteroles on her plate. A year later, on 23 July 1986, they were married at Westminster Abbey as the Duke and Duchess of York.

Diana was delighted. It was deeply cheering for her to have an ally inside the Firm. And more cheering still to have the Yorks' marriage playing alongside her own like the subplot in a sitcom. The Duchess was the perfect visual foil to the Princess of Wales. Fergie's buxom figure, hit-or-miss wardrobe and exploding mane of Titian hair provided a useful distraction for the press, which had begun to sour on Diana's fashionable ways and now embraced Fergie as a 'breath of fresh air'. Diana was a shrewd enough student of the press cycle to know that this would change – the Fergie boom was actually a boomerang that hadn't yet come back – but in the meantime it was a relief. With an arch look the Princess said to her friend, Wayne Sleep, 'Fergie lightens the load, Wayne.'[41] Besides, whenever she felt like reasserting herself it was easy to arrange. Shortly before Fergie and Andrew's wedding, when the Duchess to be was still in her press honeymoon, Diana upstaged her at a polo match by turning up wearing red and white spotted bobby socks and red high heels.[42]

Diana was now the royal pro who had to coach the novice Duchess of York. Fergie idolised her sister-in-law's elegance and poise and viewed Diana, her friends say, as a genius with the media, 'the best publicist in history'.[43] There was piquancy for Diana in watching the newly minted Duchess blunder through all the adjustments to royal life that she had had to cope with five years before. It reminded her of both what she had gone through herself and how far she had come. Fergie was enduring a lower wattage version of the Princess's fate, though with fewer of the rewards. While the Waleses lived independently on £1 million in disposable income from the Duchy of Cornwall and a further £2 million from investments,[44] Prince Andrew's navy salary was £35,000 a year and he depended for the rest on the largesse of the Queen, an irksome position for a grown man and his wife. Even the lavish spread the Yorks built at Sunninghill near Windsor (immediately christened South York by the press) was in the Queen's name, not theirs.

Fergie endured the same isolated pre-wedding night with the Queen Mother at Clarence House as Diana had, the same hostility from snotty Buckingham Palace courtiers, the same experience of the closing of the ranks when she eventually fell from grace. The difference was she was not from a grand family herself, and she was not the mother of the heir to the throne. She had little hope of winning the respect of the system because there was so little to back her up. Unlike the landed and endowed Spencers, the Fergusons were always strapped for cash. Her mother, Susan, was a baronet's niece, good-looking and well connected but without the trust fund of Diana's mother, Frances. Sarah's father, Ronald Ferguson, dubbed 'the Galloping Major' by *Private Eye* (like Andrew Parker Bowles, he was a former officer in the Household Cavalry), was the Prince of Wales's polo manager. That was a social position that placed him only on the fringes of royal circles, scoring him occasional invitations to shoot at Sandringham as a guest of the Queen. The Fergusons were possessed of some modest acreage in Hampshire, where Sarah was raised in a rambling Queen Anne house named, incredibly, Dummer Down Farm. From the age of sixteen she had had to fend for herself, living not in an apartment bought by her mother in genteel Coleherne Court but in a rented room in a flat near a graveyard south of the Thames, working her tail off as an assistant at an art gallery and a publishing house and taking backpacking holidays round South America. She described her clothes as 'upscale Salvation Army'.[45] For an impecunious, second-tier Sloane like herself, the brother of the heir to the throne was a spectacular catch.

The differences between the Princess and the Duchess, however, were never as great as the bonds. Later, they competed for positive press, they were rivals, they fell out, but they were the only two women on the planet under thirty who had had the peculiar experience of being absorbed into the British royal family. 'I loved all her funny mad ways,' Fergie often says.[46] Like Diana in the early days, the Duchess left alone for weeks on end in the chilly atmosphere of the Palace while Andrew was on naval duties, felt utterly at sea in the ordeal of how to become a fit wife for the Queen's second son. Her sudden sense of what she had lost began at her wedding when the moribund royal tradition of not toasting the bride and groom left her longing for a jolly, ribald speech from the best man or for her father to unload on the stuck-up guests some sweet embarrassing memories of her girlhood.[47] She shared with Diana a deep mistrust of the Queen Mother, whom she found an impossible snob, and a longing to kick over the traces with the rigid routine at Balmoral.

Fergie was more of an influence on Diana than is sometimes recognised. The power balance between the slim, incandescent Princess and the plump, rambunctious Duchess was by no means all weighted to Diana's side. As ascendant as the Princess was in her public life, she was less assertive than Fergie in private. The Duchess was more experienced with men, had lived a knockabout life in ski resorts and nightclubs, had travelled alone to exotic places. She gave jolly dinner parties in her apartment at Buckingham Palace. Diana envied Fergie's spontaneous sexuality, her free and easy manner, the genuine warmth of her relationship with Andrew, which had begun as a bona fide love affair and even after divorce remains an affectionate friendship. Starved of fun, Diana was encouraged by Fergie's presence to indulge in a delayed teenage rebellion. The Princess joined her on the boisterous prank Fergie choreographed on Prince Andrew's stag night before their wedding, dressing up in a policeman's costume and attempting to gatecrash the stag party at Annabel's in Berkeley Square.[48] In June 1987 she and Fergie ganged up together at Royal Ascot and were photographed poking a courtier in the behind with an umbrella. It was the kind of Hoorayish exhibitionism that wasn't Diana's style, but she liked toying with the new image of being a royal daredevil. Being a rebel was better than going under. The dyspeptic Woodrow Wyatt records that his wife saw Diana there, 'fooling about in the most childish manner, pulling people's hair and tweaking them. I'm not surprised that Prince Charles is bored with this backward girl who couldn't even pass any O levels.'[49] Their complicity resurfaced in the early nineties when Fergie's marriage hit the rocks like Diana's. Lord Glenconner, staying as a guest at Balmoral in 1990, remembers the two girls as 'thick as thieves. Fergie was always saying to Diana, "When we get in we'll change all this, all this stiff court behaviour."'[50] One summer night the following year, when they were staying at the castle, the two of them commandeered a tandem bike and raced around the golf course, wreaking havoc with the greens. They then 'liberated' the Queen Mother's Daimler and careened around the drive with Diana behind the wheel wearing a chauffeur's hat.[51] It was bizarre behaviour for two women hitting their thirties, smacking of desperation. Edward Mirzoeff, who made the famous BBC documentary about the Queen to commemorate the fortieth anniversary of her accession to the throne, recalls the Princess and the Duchess together at the state reception at Buckingham Palace for President Cossiga of Italy in October 1991. 'It was a big grand party. Everyone was in their best fig, Diana and Fergie both very glamorous. After about half an hour they must have got the sign it was OK to leave, and I got a glimpse of the two girls running down the corridor outside the state rooms in their ball gowns, shoes off – they'd been released and they were shrieking with laughter. They were kids, really, running away from it all.'[52]

It wasn't just high jinks these two royal women shared. Fergie carried psychic scars from her past that were uncannily similar to Diana's. Her family history has always got short shrift compared to her more famous sister-in-law's, but there was plenty of backstory in the Ferguson household waiting to undermine the equilibrium of the Duchess of York. She was a raw, overweight thirteen-year-old when her mother Susan abruptly left Ronald Ferguson to go and live with her lover, the polo player Hector Barrantes, two thousand miles away in Argentina. ('So glad there's another rotten apple at the bottom of the barrel with me,' Diana's mother wrote to Susan when Andrew and Fergie's engagement was announced.)[53] True, Mrs Ferguson had good reason to dump Ronnie – the Galloping Major was a serial womaniser whose goatishness was finally unmasked when the press caught him at a sleazy massage parlour in 1988 – but her exit from the family home was handled with as much sensitivity as Frances's departure for Peter Shand Kydd. In Fergie's 1996 memoir, *My Story*, she describes how, after an absence of many months, her mother returned to Dummer in 1973 to inform Major Ferguson of the finality of her decision to go and live with Hector Barrantes in Argentina. Without acknowledging her two teenage daughters, Susan Ferguson strode past them into their father's study, then emerged to tell them brusquely, 'I'm going, and I'm going to be with Hector.' Sarah said nothing, so Mrs Ferguson asked, 'So you don't mind, then?'[54]

*Mind?* That awful social word. It's as if these women of privilege were as ruthless about their pleasure as their mothers were about position. Fergie, with no apparent bitterness, recalls that she replied: 'No, no, it's perfect, that's great.' And then adds that she didn't 'mind' because 'Hector did love her and I got on well with him. Deep down, I was relieved that Mum was happy.'[55]

Poor Fergie. Even twenty-three years later, when she wrote her cheerful, unreflective memoir, she couldn't own up to the rejection she must have felt at her mother's decision to decamp to the other side of the world without her. She was left to the care of a series of mean-spirited housekeepers, and the usual tepid, low-calibre boarding school. (At house parties she said she'd pretend 'to be frightfully intelligent and digest the *Sunday Times* when you hadn't the foggiest idea of what you were reading'.)[56] She ate as compulsively as Diana without the desire to throw it back up. One holiday season both parents forgot the family tradition of a Christmas stocking, until her father, suddenly reminded she was there, took Fergie off to a garage and stuffed a pillowcase full of sponges and antifreeze and windscreen cleaner in honour of her having passed her driving test. The worst thing about this story is that Fergie recounts it as a touching anecdote about her father's rough affection.[57]

If Diana's childhood was *A Little Princess*, Fergie's was Roald Dahl, the fat girl raised as a boy, the dumb girl raised at Dummer. She and Diana shared such awful scenes in their pasts that, true to their backgrounds, the damage was too deep for them to acknowledge. Fergie told me once that the experience of being left by their mothers – one that I had assumed was paramount in their bond – was never a subject she and Diana more than passingly discussed. But it was there, unspoken, leaving both with a bedrock of insecurity they had sought to assuage by the imagined permanence of becoming royal.[58]

Their shared lack of confidence soon surfaced in neuroses of comparison. Fergie was obsessed with how thin, elegant and beautiful Diana was compared to her own weight struggles and lack of poise. The press fanned her inferiority complex. The narrative of a catfight was too irresistible for the tabloids to be charitable to Fergie for long. 'It became fat Fergie against wonderful Diana,' the *Sun*'s Harry Arnold said. 'Her dress was often compared – of course, she had nothing like the budget that Diana had.'[59] Diana meanwhile had not anticipated what a hit Fergie would be with the other members of the Firm. The Queen liked her new daughter-in-law because she was a country girl, a real one this time, with an unfeigned passion for riding derived from a childhood on the Hampshire horse-show circuit. A friend of the Queen's told her biographer Ben Pimlott: 'The Queen was very fond of Fergie. She liked the way she used to sit with her legs apart, making jokes.'[60] Diana was mortified to learn that when Prince Andrew was away, the 'Top Lady', as Diana called Her Majesty, often asked Fergie to dine at Buckingham Palace – something she rarely did with Diana. The Duchess even found favour with Prince Philip by learning to carriage drive, his favourite sport. Prince Charles was enchanted with Fergie's zest for field and stream. 'Why can't you be more like Fergie?'[61] was the Prince's new refrain as Fergie charged around in her wellies with her outdoor glow. When they all went on a skiing trip at Klosters, Fergie bombed down the slopes with Charles and Andrew like a pro while Diana wobbled along or sulked in the chalet.[62] 'I got terribly jealous and she got jealous of me,' Diana admitted to Morton. 'I couldn't understand it – she was actually enjoying being where she was, whereas I was fighting to survive.'[63]

Even worse was the ease which Fergie was able to deal with the annual sojourn in Balmoral. In August 1986 Diana was once again dreading the annual eight-week vacation. The interminable length of her incarceration there loomed like an iceberg in the chilly North

Atlantic of her marriage. She dreaded going to 'bloody Balmoral' as she called it. Her husband could not but be aware that Balmoral through Fergie's eyes was a very different place from Diana's castle from hell. The Duchess saw Balmoral as 'the perfect haven, a staunch fortress against the arrows . . . I loved the crackle of its morning frost and the smells of the heather and peaty soil, so delicious and earthy.'[64] Can this vision of bracing beauty really be the same as Diana's dank vomitorium? When Fergie speaks of Balmoral it's as if the Highland mist recedes and we behold for the first time the Scottish idyll as the other royals do. 'Here I could take my dogs out and walk for miles,' raves Fergie. 'Or we could trek up . . . [to] little huts built by Queen Victoria for her beloved Albert when he was out stalking. When I rode at Balmoral with the Queen, with our mounts willing and the air so sharp, I would almost feel at home.'[65] Grrrr. Diana was fully aware of the threat to herself in Fergie's robust example. She told Andrew Morton, 'Up in Scotland, she used to do everything that I never did. So I thought, "This can't last, the energy of this creature is unbelievable." Meanwhile, everybody looking at me – "it's a pity Diana has gone so introverted and quiet, she was so busy and trying to sort herself out, and then this holocaust arrived."'[66]

That Diana was so deeply hurt by Fergie's popularity with the family shows how much she still longed for their acceptance. While she was never intimidated by Prince Philip she was in awe of the infallibility of the Queen and craved her approval. She was always visibly energised in her duty after a visit to see her mother-in-law. Deprived of female role models in her past that she could ever truly admire, she still entertained wan hopes of becoming Her Majesty's favourite. The Queen, however, communicates best through the language of shared interest. Her lifelong closeness to the Queen Mum was expressed by daily calls to share racing tips, her liking for Fergie by friendly chats about dogs. She didn't have much in common with Diana except for her affection for her grandchildren. She found her mood swings tiresome and the Queen has a short attention span for problems she can do nothing about.

Diana's jealous obsession with Camilla was one such problem. The Queen did not approve of her son's refusal to give up his mistress – no one in the family did. In the late eighties, I am told by Michael Shea, Princess Anne even debated writing to her brother to remonstrate with the way Charles declined to stop humiliating his wife.[67] Charles's tenacious feelings baffled Prince Philip who later wrote to Diana that 'I cannot imagine anyone in their right mind leaving you for Camilla.'[68] But Charles was a grown man, not a child, and the Queen was of a generation and background that viewed infidelity in marriage as a regrettable weakness to be firmly ignored. In 1967 the British secret service quietly asked representatives of the management side of some of the more respectable London papers to do what they could to avert any publication of reports about Prince Philip's indiscretion that might embarrass the Queen. (Philip responded with a long, silent stare when Fiammetta Rocco of the *Independent* quizzed him about rumours of his having extramarital affairs. He finally erupted, 'Good God, woman, I don't know what sort of company you keep.')[69] Debo, Duchess of Devonshire (née Mitford, sibling of Jessica), who is six years older than the Queen, once said to her other celebrated sister Diana Mosley that it was such a relief when 'jealousy was gone'. All through Debo's sixty-three-year-marriage to Andrew Devonshire she had had to pretend not to see the Duke's serial infidelities – a task that was painful, but only until what she called 'the wonderful moment when you realise you are anaesthetised'.[70] What you were supposed to do, in short, is outlast your husband's distractions or, failing that, accept them. Faced herself with a problem in her marriage as persistent as the presence of Camilla, the monarch would have handled it by simply blanking it out.

Why couldn't Diana? Because she was a modern girl with modern expectations and a modern desire for romantic fulfilment. Her heartache was not that she had lost Charles to Camilla, but that she felt she had never had his love in the first place. It was her bad luck not to share the usual upper-class unease with intense emotion. Her love for Charles was embarrassingly intense and stubbornly uncompromising. She sought to blank out the pain in other ways than denial. Her bulimia was more pernicious than ever. Chef Mervyn Wycherley always had to leave a custard for her to binge on in the fridge when she came in from dinners.[71] 'It gives you a feeling of comfort. It's like having a pair of arms around you' is how she later tried to explain her bulimia.[72] In the summer of 1986 her sister Jane Fellowes noticed marks on Diana's chest when she was wearing a V-necked T-shirt. Diana admitted she had cut herself with a penknife on her chest and thighs after a row with Charles.[73] In a bloodless world perhaps she wanted to see the colour of her own blood. On an official visit with Charles to Canada's Expo 86 in May, Diana was so undernourished that she slid to the floor of the California Pavilion and fainted. 'Darling, I think I am going to disappear,' she whispered – earning a sharp rebuke from the Prince for not saving the theatrics till she was out of sight of the crowds.[74] On their tour of Germany together in November 1987, Brenda Polan of the *Guardian* saw the Prince and Princess at a fashion gala. 'They were surrounded by a crowd and as they were ushered away he wanted her to get into a lift with him, but she was still surrounded and said, "I'll go downstairs, darling." He went purple and shrieked "No! Come here this minute!" She didn't know her place, two paces behind him. He was out of control, intimate and inappropriate.'[75] Spurned by Charles, jostled by Fergie, out of favour with the family and deprived of the comforting arms of Barry Mannakee, Diana needed another romantic hero. On 2 September 1986, Woodrow Wyatt recorded in his diary a note about what he had heard went down at Fergie and Andrew's pre-wedding ball. The Princess, he wrote, had been seen dancing enthusiastically with the handsome husband of one of Wyatt's friends. 'I met the most marvellous man who dances divinely,' Diana was overheard saying to Fergie, 'but the first thing he did was introduce me to his wife.'

'She adores dancing, particularly with good-looking young men,' Wyatt recorded. 'This one was described to me as "a very pelvic dancer". There is trouble ahead.'[76]

## Chapter 14

# Two Kinds of Love

'I have lain awake at night loving you desperately and thanking
God for bringing you into my life.'
– Diana to Major Hewitt, August 1989

James Hewitt often asked himself in later years if it was really an
accident that had thrown him together with the Princess of Wales at a
courtiers' cocktail party in the autumn of 1986, when she was twenty-
five and he, just three years older, was a staff captain in the Life Guards,
a regiment of the Household Cavalry. He suspected that he had been
set up, Mannakee removed, and the whole thing engineered by
Buckingham Palace – that 'place of long corridors and quiet whispers',
as he called it. By the time he wrote those words, in his book *Love and
War*, published in 1999, Hewitt was infected with the paranoia that
engulfed everything to do with Diana after her death. It is nonetheless
noteworthy that during the five – or more – years of their secret affair
neither the Palace hierarchy nor Scotland Yard ever made a move to
stop him seeing the Princess. Hewitt, unlike Mannakee, seems to have
had the blessing of the Prince of Wales to be his wife's lover, and one
can see why. Unlike Mannakee, the young army officer knew how to
play by the rules. He hailed from an upper-middle-class army family,
was a graduate of a fancy boarding school, was comfortable moving on
the fringe of court circles, and was now a rising young captain based,
conveniently enough, at Knightsbridge Barracks. He was not unlike a
younger, cuter, less complicated and far less burdened version of Prince
Charles: cordial, mannerly and handsome in the tall, chiselled
storybook way that Diana always admired. Another plus: in a ploy to
spend time with him, Diana herself had enlisted him to give her riding
lessons. He was unlikely to want to rock any boats. 'Only one thing
went wrong,' Hewitt would write. 'We fell in love.'[1] Actually, a lot of

things went wrong – mostly because with Hewitt, as Diana later acknowledged, 'his head was inside his trousers'.[2] But at first, he was a heaven-sent solution for the frisky young Princess of Wales.

Diana needed this affair. Her sex life was non-existent. Charles was all but gone from her bed. Their miserable country weekends were made more excruciating by the fact that in between they were travelling the world together as a dazzling ambassadorial couple. The Prince and Princess's tour of the Arabian Gulf in November 1986 was hailed as the model of what they could achieve when they worked together as the perfect royal team: the future King – man of substance, well versed in Islamic tradition and history – and his poised, radiant Queen-to-be. Such was the local clamour to meet Diana that the royal couple were able to brush aside the desert kingdom's single-sex tradition and host a reception aboard *Britannia* for Saudi business leaders. Sir Jeremy Greenstock, then commercial counsellor at the British Embassy in Riyadh, watched the star-struck businessmen buzz like flies around the glittering vision of Diana in a long pale pink Jacques Azagury chiffon dress dotted with gold sequins. 'There was one prominent Saudi named Essam Kattan who didn't join the throng around her,' Greenstock recalls. 'I went over to where he was leaning on the rails of *Britannia* gazing pensively at the water and I said, "Why don't you join the others in the group round the Princess?" And he replied, "I prefer to worship from a distance. I could not trust myself to go any closer."'[3] This was the Princess of every man's fantasy, whose charisma you could 'surf on', as one admirer put it.

Under the façade, she was a wreck. James Hewitt describes her at the start of their affair, soon after she returned from the Gulf, as 'emotionally very fragile. The bulimia had taken its toll on her. She was painfully thin and her skin hung almost lifelessly on her bones. She was a woman deeply damaged by rejection.'[4] In turning to Hewitt, however, she was turning a corner. This was no accidental involvement like the Barry Mannakee liaison. Hewitt was set up – but by Diana herself, not by Buckingham Palace. He was on his way out of a meeting at the Palace on military ceremonies for Sarah Ferguson and Prince Andrew's wedding in July and, turning a corner, was entranced by the sight of the Princess standing at the bottom of the stairs, in a long summer skirt, barefoot with her shoes in her hand, giggling with friends. Diana registered the admiration in the gaze. 'Like the outfit,' she said with her trademark sexy sidling glance at his Guards uniform.[5] Later she asked her lady-in-waiting Hazel West to invite the officer to a drinks party, where she told him of her great desire to regain her confidence on horseback. Naturally, he offered to give her personal instruction.

The Princess's riding lessons with Captain Hewitt very soon became regular and frequent. When he was promoted to acting Major and given command of the Headquarters Squadron at Combermere Barracks in Windsor, she was so enamoured of his teaching style she would drive herself over from London to ride with him in Windsor Great Park. Dressed in tight jodhpurs, silk shirt, hacking jacket and boots, she would arrive for her lesson at 8 a.m. She made the first sexual overture by reaching to kiss him when they were alone in the officers' mess, telling him, 'I need you. You give me strength. I can't stand it when I'm away from you. I want to be with you. I've come to love you.'[6] Not exactly a message he could miss. Indeed, from beginning to end, it was Diana who ran this affair. She was as much in control of its pace and rhythms as she had been out of control in the pace and rhythms leading up to her marriage. This would be her romantic pattern from now on. Forget the modest blushing – she would do the initiating. There were few men bold enough to make the first move on the Princess of Wales. The affair took place on her schedule and on her turf: Kensington Palace and Highgrove when Charles was away.

Diana's cover for asking the army major to stay was that he was helping the boys with their horsemanship. It was an unusual arrangement for a riding instructor. The Princess covered her tracks by asking other guests to come along, too – Hazel West, the lady-in-waiting who had introduced them, and her old friends from Sloane days, William and Carolyn Bartholomew. Diana was now so practised that after Hewitt had spent the night in her bed she would ruffle up his sheets on his bed in the morning to make them look as if he had slept there. Then she took it on herself to formally notify her personal protection officer Ken Wharfe. In a businesslike fashion, the Princess summoned Wharfie in August 1987 to discuss the matter when she and the Prince were on a tense stay in Majorca as guests of the King and Queen of Spain. Wharfe's private assessment when he learned about Hewitt was as follows: 'He was a protest fuck.'[7] But Hewitt was more than that. He became such a familiar private guest whenever the Prince was away that William and Harry developed a fondness for him. Hewitt had little army uniforms made for them for their visits to Windsor Barracks. They loved playing on the Highgrove lawn with the army captain and his black Labrador. Sometimes Wharfe and Hewitt would join forces for pillow fights with the boys. One weekend the Lab ran amok and ripped up the new plantings round the edge of the pond. 'Wales went ballistic,' when he saw the damage, Mervyn Wycherley says, but he didn't stop Hewitt's visits.[8] Diana told her lover that her husband knew about the extent of the relationship. 'It was a tacit understanding between Diana and Charles,' Hewitt said, 'that I was a part of her life in the same way that Mrs Parker Bowles was a part of Prince Charles's life.'[9] Even so, Hewitt was always nervous at Highgrove. He could hardly fail to be, with staff like Berry watching every move and the presence of elaborate security systems, including an electric fence surrounding the property and a police box, fashioned out of Cotswold stone, that was home base for five cops. They watched the constantly switching television monitors which surveyed the gardens.

An index of how relaxed Hewitt made Diana feel was that she was able, for him, to be a country girl. For him she would go for country walks; for him she would conquer her fear and ride horses. 'She loved the countryside,' Hewitt said – a piece of news that would have astonished her husband. 'She liked shooting and the whole way of life, of countryside pursuits and living in the country. In my experience, she loved that.'[10] It is remarkable what a satisfying sex life will do.

Hewitt was said by Diana to be an accomplished lover. He helped Diana achieve orgasms of a reliability and intensity she had never enjoyed before. He soon came to see that loving Diana was a mission to save her life, and he stepped up to it admirably. For five years he was as available and attentive as a medieval troubadour. His attentions bolstered her confidence. The shy royal fiancée who had waited for her Prince to phone from India only six years ago was now a brazenly assertive lover. During the summer of 1988, Hewitt told her he wouldn't be able to see her over the weekend because he was playing in the inter-regimental championship at the Tidworth Polo Club in Hampshire. Hewitt was captain of the Life Guards team playing the 13/18 Hussars for the Captains and Subalterns Trophy. Diana replied by telling him she would be there, too. After all, didn't he recall that she was the honorary Colonel-in-Chief of the 13/18 Hussars? She called the Hussars' commanding officer and announced she was going to attend, then showed up and plonked herself down on the grass where Hewitt, his mother and his two sisters were enjoying a picnic. 'There's a stuffy lunch going on,' she told the flustered Hewitt, who asked her if she oughtn't to be with her troops. 'No,' she replied merrily, 'I said I was just coming over to give the opposition a bit of encouragement.'[11] In a crowning act of audacity, she presented Hewitt, captain of the victorious team, with the winners' cup. In an iconic photograph their eyes meet, locked in exuberant subterfuge.

It's remarkable that it took nearly five years for anyone in the press to cotton on to Hewitt and Diana. One can only marvel at the version put forth in 1993 by the *Mirror*'s James Whitaker, whose main beat was the Princess of Wales. In his book *Diana v. Charles*, he chronicles the course of Hewitt's charged friendship with the Princess – and then sonorously blows off any notion that the attraction between the two was actually consummated. 'Moralists may argue that infidelity takes place in the heart and head and needs no physical act to accompany it,' Whitaker intoned. 'But the fact remains that Diana maintained a psychological advantage over her husband by practising self-restraint.'[12] That Diana was able to hoodwink Whitaker proves how skilful an actress she had become. On 13 June 1987, the Waleses were among the guests at the wedding of the Duke of Beaufort's son, 'Bunter' Somerset (the Marquess of Worcester), to the model Tracy Ward, at Cornwell Manor in Oxfordshire. At the reception, Diana threw the press off the scent by blatantly flirting with a hunky old Etonian banker, Philip Dunne. Their very public monkeying around on the dance floor had the tactically gratifying result of setting press tongues wagging as far away as Australia, where the *Daily Telegraph* reported, 'During one smoochy number, saucy Di pecked Superman look-a-like Dunne on the cheek and ran her fingers through the 28-year-old city banker's dark hair.'[13] Later, a guest at the party went to his car to retrieve a packet of cigarettes. It was late, and as he walked back through the almost-empty tent in the garden, he had a tantalising glimpse of Diana in a private moment: as the band played its last set, the Princess of Wales was dancing alone, spinning and arching and whirling to the music as if in a euphoric, sensuous trance. 'It was the first time,' he said, 'that I realised what a sexual being Diana was.'[14]

Her husband, unfortunately, did not notice. Prince Charles spent most of that evening talking to his seductive old flame Anna Wallace and then was nose to nose with Camilla. At 2 a.m. the Prince suggested coolly to Diana that they take their leave. It was reported that she laughed in his face and partied on without him. James Fox, the journalist and biographer, who was a guest at the party, noticed the Princess's play-acting. 'I felt sorry for her that night,' he told me. 'She looked as if she was desperately wanting to have a good time. When I saw Charles slipping out on his own, I realised their relationship was just as bad as one had read about. Diana seemed really ready for it. I remember thinking, Wow – she's looking for fun. She's looking for a boyfriend. This is quite a dangerous situation.'[15] So it was, but the danger, of course, had already arrived.

The secrecy of her affair with Hewitt allowed her to harvest the fantasy of a different kind of married life. It was as unrealistic as her later fantasy of becoming the wife of the heart surgeon Hasnat Khan. 'I have lain awake at night loving you desperately and thanking God for bringing you into my life,' Diana wrote to Hewitt when he was in France in August 1989. 'I just long for the days when finally we will be together for always, as that is how it should be.'[16]

The two of them played at being regular country-weekenders. They would often take off to his mother, Shirley Hewitt's modest, cosy cottage in Devon for the weekend, where they walked by the seaside and Diana helped Mrs Hewitt do the dishes. Hewitt found Diana sexually voracious on these excursions, even demanding sex in a field. 'When we used to go to Devon there was considerable "activity",'[17] said Wharfe.

Hewitt's consoling embraces helped fortify Diana enough to maintain interludes of civilised cold war with her husband. There were no more public scenes with Charles for a time. The Waleses' double act was on show in their visit to Australia in January 1988 for the country's two hundredth anniversary. They put on such a sparkling display of marital unity at a dinner-dance in Melbourne that even Hewitt, watching it on TV, was impressed – and a little baffled. The sight of the Prince and Princess dancing together with every sign of mutual delight made Hewitt wonder how Diana could seem so happy with a man he believed 'she now hated with a vitriolic intensity'.[18] The public sense, as Georgina Howell wrote in the *Sunday Times* in September 1988, was that Diana had decided to go the time-honoured royal route and make the best of a cool marriage, instead of fighting it.[19]

Her insecurity was too great for that. Diana's relationships survived only as long as the fantasy could be sustained. In Hewitt's case it was of inexhaustible *cavalier servant*. There was always a toy-boy element in her attitude to the army captain. All the power was on her side. She showered him with gifts – a diamond-studded tiepin, a gold-and-silver clock from the royal jeweller Asprey, a cupboardful of shirts and ties and sweaters. At the time Hewitt was seeing Diana, an ex-girlfriend, Emma Stewardson, noted he was perhaps suffering a little from the red-carpet fever that afflicted personal protection officers. 'After one of his trips to Highgrove he came back raving about the solid-gold dinner service,' Stewardson said. 'He liked the high life. I was worried he might become a bit dazzled by it all.'[20] But when Hewitt told Diana in the summer of 1989 that he had been posted to Germany for two years to take charge of a tank squadron, she did not behave like a chipper army wife. She behaved like a spoilt society woman whose kept man has developed an annoying life of his own. She insisted that there was no need for Hewitt to go to Germany. She made the point that Andrew Parker Bowles was never sent abroad. She wanted to pull rank and 'fix things' by speaking to Major General Sir Christopher Airy, who commanded the Household Division. Hewitt existed for Diana only in so far as he would be there to serve her needs. Her greed for his support made her selfish. Her terror of rejection made her reject him first. 'You promised you'd always be here for me and now you've broken that promise,' she said icily.[21] She had begun to acknowledge to herself that the athletic army major wasn't the brightest bulb. ('About as interesting as a knitting pattern,' she said later.)[22]

Before he left with his unit for Germany, Hewitt watched the Princess swinging her legs beside the swimming pool at Highgrove and reflected how Diana was an entirely changed woman. 'In her bikini that afternoon, her skin fresh and tanned, her body in athletic shape thanks to her diet and her workouts, her expression so full of joy and free of worries, I reflected that she had come a long way – *we* had come a long way – from the bulimic girl I first encountered.'[23] The only thing wrong about that statement was 'we'. It was more than three months before he heard from her again.

After Hewitt went to Germany, Diana lived increasingly as a single woman about town. She protected her *amour propre* with a praetorian guard of distracting flirts, which she gathered around her in the second half of the 1980s. Many in this circle were drawn from her old Sloane life – admirers like the ever-attentive Philip Dunne, the army officers David Waterhouse and Rory Scott, and James Gilbey, an upmarket car dealer related to the Gilbey gin family. They took her to dinner at San Lorenzo (where the maternal Italian owner, Mara Berni, protected their privacy), made up bridge parties at the London houses of girlfriends like Kate Menzies and Julia Samuel, and escorted her to the ballet. To Ken Wharfe, all the 'Dianamen', as he called them, were interchangeable chinless wonders whose only talent was small talk and smart dressing – in Savile Row tailors' parlance, '42 Longs'. James Hewitt, James Gilbey, Philip Dunne, David Waterhouse (who was in the same regiment as Hewitt), Rory Scott – 'all', says Wharfe, 'were tall, of similar physique, dressed and spoke in the same manner, shared the same tastes and the same circle of friends, and often the same mannerisms . . . all had one other thing in common: they were nothing like her serious-minded husband, twelve years her senior, and by his own admission a man who acted older than his years'.[24]

Philip Dunne, at least, was actually better than Wharfe allows. He was bright, if conventional, and is now a Tory Member of Parliament. He was a perfect escort because, as a close friend said, he was constitutionally 'not a bad boy' – meaning, among other things, that he had too elevated a sense of decorum to try to sleep with the wife of the Prince of Wales. Dunne's father was Lord Lieutenant of Herefordshire and a good friend of the Queen and the Duke of Edinburgh, whom young Dunne had no desire to offend. But he was handsome and fun and good for Diana's morale.

The one who did begin an affair with Diana was James Gilbey. He was a classic 42 Long who used expressions like 'so-and-so has lots of pennies' (meaning rich). The piquant reassurance he offered Diana was unfinished business. He was the same Gilbey whom she had dated in her Coleherne Court years and whose car she had 'egged' when he dumped her in 1980. Now, in the summer of 1989, they reconnected at a thirtieth birthday party in Berkshire for their mutual friend Julia Samuel, the elder sister of Sabrina Guinness. Diana was sitting glumly at a table with her sister Jane Fellowes. Gilbey joined them and they ended up discussing their separate romantic failures.[25] He found Diana at twenty-eight to be a very different creature from the plump, self-effacing Sloane he had passed over nine years before. She was now the most glamorous woman in the world, and he was bowled over that she seemed to relish having him panting after her. If she had not met Prince Charles, she would probably have married Gilbey or one of these other lightweight charmers in her deck of cards and lived a satisfying, traditional family life in the country with four children riding ponies. She would not have been so sensationally beautiful – her desire to become extraordinary was enmeshed with her experience of suffering – but she might have been content. To the 'Dianamen' themselves, she was the opposite of contentment. She was the icon next door – a fabulous, electrifying status symbol to have as your friend, as long as you didn't get too close. The risk, as Gilbey would discover, was getting burned.

Fergie was a casualty. The Princess had garnered a rash of negative press for what the *Daily Mail* called Diana and Fergie's 'undignified' behaviour shoving around in the snow in Klosters followed by their bottom-poking antics at Ascot.[26] By the following year, the Princess had seen the light and she distanced herself from the Duchess. At Ascot in 1988 Diana strolled with ladylike poise through the crowds in a cool cut-away grey silk morning coat and white straw hat. Her twenty-seventh birthday on 1 July brought such press bouquets as 'star quality', 'the best thing to happen to the Royals', and 'the feminine ideal'.[27] Diana's powers to dazzle were changing her. She could try on a new identity every day, but what she longed for was a role. She had become interested in and excited by what her star power could achieve beyond the instant gratification of a flattering photograph. Mrs Thatcher's economic revolution was unleashing plenty of opportunities. London in the eighties was dancing to the beat of City money and a promotion-based social calendar that required new personalities and buzz. The social world was driven by marketing budgets now, not family trees, and by the tailwind from Reagan's America. The co-host of a party was more likely to be a car company or a perfume launch than a person. Sometimes there was no flesh-and-blood host at all, just some brand of champagne and an expensive shoe shop in association with a certain designer chocolate and a rising young cigar company. This sort of thing may be numbingly familiar now but it was new then. Public relations executives, not titled women, had become the gatekeepers of the hottest guest lists.

Mrs Thatcher's willingness to embrace high unemployment and her eagerness to crush the unions in order to make British industry competitive sharpened the divisions between rich and poor, especially after the miners' strike in 1984 and 1985, with its scenes of violence and rhetoric of class warfare. The social atmosphere in fashionable circles was a more mercantile, gayer, harder-edged edition of swinging London with a more aggressively high-low effect (and a drug regimen that favoured cocaine over cannabis). The sense that England was being commanded, not eased, into confronting its old complacencies generated a nervy consumer energy reminiscent of New York's – what the advertising guru and writer Peter York called a 'Let's buy ourselves a lifestyle feeling'.[28] In Kensington Palace Diana felt the vibrations emanating from the world of fashion and dance friends like Jasper Conran and Wayne Sleep.

The effect of Diana's glamour on café society in the 1980s was therefore twofold. First, she turbo-charged it. London felt stylish and sexy and fashionable for the first time since the late sixties. Second, she steered it to acknowledging something worthier than itself. There was a gaping hole of need left by the ruthlessness of the Thatcher era, and Diana instinctively knew she could help fill it. Americans had long taken the three-way marriage of commerce, society and philanthropy for granted, but in London the phenomenon was new and directly Diana-related. Since the Princess of Wales could not be expected to show up at a perfume launch or a car show, the way to secure her presence was to turn it into a philanthropic happening. Sponsoring a charity event with Diana present was a better buy than the expense of a conventional PR campaign. With company logo blazing, a gift bag stuffed with new product samples and a handsome photograph of the CEO next to the smiling Princess of Wales, commercial enterprises learned they could score not a few ignorable paragraphs of hype in the business pages, but front-page and TV coverage in every media outlet in the land. Call it the Diana synergy. Her star power, which everyone wanted a piece of, created an explosion of sponsored charity events. Here's an example of how it worked. The president of Tiffany & Co., the Hon Rosa Monckton, who did not know Diana at the time, sought the Princess's imprimatur in order to help reposition the company's snooty luxury-goods stores with a more youthful image. She called Marie Helvin, a supporter of the Aids Crisis Trust, and told Helvin that if she could secure the Princess's presence (and seat her – Monckton – at Diana's table), Tiffany's would underwrite an elaborate benefit for Diana's (and Helvin's) pet cause.[29] Diana did not hesitate. The Tiffany Ball, as it was christened, was held at the famous former Astor home, Cliveden House, in Buckinghamshire, to raise money for the Aids Crisis Trust. One item in the celebrity auction was a polo lesson with the father of Sarah, Duchess of York, Major Ronald Ferguson. It went for £2,500 – not bad at the time, given the notorious stinginess of the British upper class.

London got used to seeing the flash of Diana's red-carpet arrivals boosting causes that had once been consigned to dowdy do-gooding. Barnardo's was anxious to shed its lingering image as a dour Dickensian orphanage and reposition itself as a modern support network for troubled kids. The charity got the makeover of its life when Diana succeeded Princess Margaret as its president in 1984. While Margaret had showed up at one Barnardo's gala per year, Diana attended 110 events during her twelve-year tenure, including sixteen in 1986 alone. The charity's former chairman, Sir Roger Singleton, says Diana once came to three smaller Barnardo's functions in a single week. Her new blood encouraged one of her favourite designers, Bruce Oldfield, in a decision he'd been contemplating for a while: coming out about the buried sadness of his childhood in foster care. In March of 1985 Oldfield put together a gala fashion fund-raiser for Barnardo's, built round Diana as guest of honour. They charged what was then a whopping price for London, £100 a ticket, and still sold out, raising approximately £200,000. (The chief donor for the night, interestingly, was Mohamed Al Fayed, who supplied £75,000 worth of products from Harrods.) Diana arrived at the Grosvenor House in a blaze of halogen wearing a show-stopping backless pleated silvery-blue lamé creation – a PR coup for Barnardo's that put the charity (and Oldfield, who designed the dress) on the map. With a supporting cast that included Joan Collins, Barry Humphries in full drag as Edna Everage, and songstress Shirley Bassey in all her big-haired, spangled glory, it was a classic New London night. Oldfield sat beside the Princess at dinner. He would recall it as 'quite an extraordinary moment. There was the future Queen of England and there was me. I certainly can't imagine a scenario where Norman Hartnell would have sat next to the Queen. The fact it was allowed to happen marked a new age.'[30]

Diana's generosity of spirit to people and their concerns unleashed a gold rush. She had always been able to catch the need in others and respond with warmth, an echo of her grandmother Lady Cynthia Spencer rattling along in her little Morris Minor and dropping in food parcels on the Northamptonshire needy. Now anyone who reached her with a story of deprivation could be assured of those big blue eyes flooding with eager compassion, the hand on the arm, the leaning forward, and the longed-for words, 'Just tell me how I can help.' She knew she only had to smile at a Bond Street merchant or department store executive before they were ponying up the expenses for a black-tie dinner or charity premiere on behalf of a cause she cared about.

For Diana the flash of the galas was the least of it. Her relationship with the charities and their causes brought as much to her as to them. In the wards of hospitals, in the run-down homeless shelters where the people left behind by Thatcher's revolution cried out for help, she rediscovered her own big heart. Like a method actor, she plumbed the unhappiness of her own life and turned it into empathy. Her presence, her warmth, the way she interacted with patients – a visit from Diana was the ultimate placebo effect. 'I think it was a genuine gift she had, the power of being able to reach out and touch somebody,' observes one of her mentors, David Puttnam. 'She once said to me, "It's all about touching. The first time it happened to me it was like an electric shock."[31] Great Ormond Street Hospital for Children valued her ability to raise morale even more than the pulling power of her fundraising. The hospital's former chief executive, Vice Admiral Sir Anthony Tippett, saw her do this for the sick children and the people who worked with them 'year on year. Great Ormond Street was a place of great contrasts – great joy and great sadness . . . She always left the hospital in a better place than when she'd entered it, because of this lift she gave people.'[32] What distinguished Diana, Barnardo's Roger Singleton says, was her ability, when she met young offenders or disabled kids, to create 'pools of intimacy' as she talked to them. Even if a few feet away there were TV cameras and bigwigs like the Lord Mayor in his ceremonial chains ('the Chain Gang' Diana called them), her listening gaze held the parent or the child she talked to in a protective private circle.

Marjatta van Boeschoten was highly sceptical in May 1983 when she heard that Diana was to visit one of the facilities of the Paradise House Association, a learning centre for disabled adults, in Painswick, Gloucestershire, on her way out to Highgrove. Ms van Boeschoten, a lawyer and trustee of the Paradise House Association, and now a management consultant for, among others, the British Medical Association and the National Health Service, is unsentimental about royalty. She was glad that Diana was coming to the House because it would get it some welcome attention, but that was all she expected. She was stunned by what happened. It was an unseasonably cold and rainy morning, but by some divine stroke of luck the sun came out just as the Princess's car swept into the forecourt of the facility. A detective followed Diana around holding a pair of wellies but she didn't need them. 'She had something that lifted one,' said van Boeschoten. 'It had that effect on everybody. There was a radiance and a warmth about her as well as her beauty. One could sense her vulnerability. I noticed how she leaned over and listened so attentively to one of the caregivers, giving her full attention. A year later the caregiver was still moved by it. She saw it as a key experience in her life. It was as if everyone there that morning had been touched by light.' Attempting to analyse the nature of that light, van Boeschoten spoke of the direct way that Diana had looked in her eyes and said with an embarrassed smile, 'Please excuse my cold hands.'[33] The combination of great physical beauty, human accessibility and a magical sweetness was made all the more powerful by the refined poise that went with it. When you add the conferred mystique of royalty and a hint of her own unexpressed pain, Diana's smile was a laser that went straight to the heart.

Diana provided a different experience from that offered by other royal visits. All the members of the Firm did and do stalwart work for charity – especially Princess Anne, with her workhorse dedication to the Save the Children Fund. Prince Charles has a diffident charm when he steps out. After the riots in Toxteth in 1981 the Prince considered it his personal duty to respond actively to the ugly scenes of violence in the north of England. He refocused his philanthropic fund, the Prince of Wales Trust, into an imaginative and generous force providing, among many other initiatives, financing for the training and mentoring of lost, unemployed young people. And a visit from the Queen is always a credibility boost to the organisations she visits.

Being a member of the royal family is a purely gestural role whose only power is how well that gesture is made. Much of what royals do for their considerable perks is either desperately dull or supremely depressing. For most people it would be like thinking of the worst aspects of your job and only doing the bits that bore you the most – sucking up to clients, say, or attending soul-destroying sales dinners – with no prospect, ever, of retirement. One of Prince Charles's less endearing comments to his aides when he travels to such events is, 'Tell me again why I am doing this.'[34] ('Because you live in palaces, sir,' is the unspoken response.) It was one of his many resentments of Diana that she derived so much pleasure from the dutiful round.

In doing so, she brought something new: hope. Without reflecting on what she was doing, she established an idiom of philanthropy distinct from the aristocratic Lady Bountiful style of the past. As the feminist writer, Beatrix Campbell has noted, Diana's was 'a *humanitarian*, rather than *patrician*, orientation with which the public completely identified'.[35]

Some of Diana's strength came from an essentially practical nature that was thwarted by a royal life where everything is done for you. Diana got sick of perfectly arranged rooms and waiting cars and everyone fussing over her in a restaurant. She could be nurse-like in her lack of squeamishness. You can imagine her deftly dressing the wound of an amputated leg in some groaning ward in Amiens during the First World War. (*The English Patient* was her favourite film.) In November 1989, she stood in 94-degree heat in Jakarta, Indonesia, and shook hands with a hundred lepers. 'Faced with the horror of leprosy, Diana shook a little girl's hand and showed no hesitation as she grasped the gnarled, bent fingers of the patients, touched the bloody bandages of an old man and stroked a woman's arm,' wrote the *Sunday Mirror* on 5 November 1989.[36] In the geriatric wing of an east London hospital full of incontinent old people staring blankly at the wall, Patrick Jephson, her equerry who later became her private secretary, was knocked back by the smell of ammonia. Apart from the low murmuring of those occupants still awake, he remembers a 'room which I could literally describe as deathly'. The Princess did not shrink or make her performance more perfunctory when she saw that the patients were so comatose her presence was hardly registered. She 'metaphorically squared her shoulders and set to work', Jephson writes. 'I watched in admiration as she systematically quartered the room, an innocent-looking girl among so many ancient, wasting bodies. In her sharply tailored, bright red suit, radiating health and energy against such a background of age and infirmity, she was like living proof of some youthful wonder drug.'[37] This was Lady Cynthia Spencer on steroids.

No cause perhaps was more ready for the Diana effect in the 1980s than Aids. Its sufferers were not merely afflicted, they were pariahs. And like tuberculosis in the nineteenth century, it was also the romantic disease, slayer of artists, dancers, photographers and poets. Diana's fashion-world friends with their dying partners brought the spectre of sickness home to her every day, as did the numerous gay members of the Palace staff. The Prince's former valet, Stephen Barry, died of Aids. Gay men formed much of the support network of Diana's life. She loved their weightlessness, their resistance to passing judgement, the freedom they gave her to have young, modern fun without causing rumours in the papers. When she showed up for supper *à deux* at the cosy Kensington mews house of Wayne Sleep, the tiny, outrageous former principal dancer of the Royal Ballet, she could pretend to be just a larky, campy girl. 'Diana Wales here!' she would bellow down the phone at the dancer when she called to make a date. Jasper Conran feels his last sight of Diana in the summer of 1997 defines the playful nature of their relationship. He was driving along in central London in his old Bentley, and heard someone hooting wildly at him from behind. 'I turned and flicked a V-sign. Then I saw it was Diana, driving herself, and laughing hysterically.'[38] These irreverent playmates were her antidote to what Fergie used to call 'the little grey men of the Palace'. As Aids took its toll in the 1980s she couldn't bear to see her friends in such peril.

Diana was actually intensely nervous when, in April 1987, Middlesex Hospital invited her to attend the opening of the first Aids ward in the UK. It is easy to forget the superstition and ignorance that first surrounded the causes of HIV contagion, the aura of sexual seediness that gave it the name the 'Gay Plague'. Diana's decision to shake hands, without gloves, with twelve male Aids patients she met that morning was the shake felt around the world. Such was the stigma of the disease that only one of the patients she extended her hand to agreed to have his picture taken – with his back to the camera. 'You could almost feel the taboos being broken,' said the *Daily Mail*'s Richard Kay. 'I think of myself as a reasonably liberal, open-minded person, but nonetheless I was pretty amazed.'[39] Professor Michael Adler, then a doctor working with Aids patients at the Middlesex Hospital and later the government's chief adviser on sexual health matters, believes that Diana was crucial in dispelling prejudice towards Aids. He said that, before her involvement, 'people did not like the whole ambience. It was seen to be mainly occurring amongst gay men and it involved sex, all the things we are not good at handling but she actually cut through that. She gave it respectability and a profile.'[40] Adler and his wife, Baroness Jay, invited Diana to become a patron of the National Aids Trust, of which Adler was chairman. Two years later the Princess visited a hospital in Harlem, New York, and spontaneously hugged an HIV-positive seven-year-old boy.

It became hard at times to tear her away from these bedsides of the sick. The visit of the First Lady, Barbara Bush, to the Middlesex Hospital in 1991 was quite an occasion. The two got on well on their walkabout, though their styles were very different. Mrs Bush, while emitting genuine warmth, was more regal and royal; Diana, deploying what Jephson describes as 'the unbeatable mixture of charm, humour and controlled pathos', could not be contained from embracing a patient who was in tears.[41]

The first time one of her friends died of the disease was in August 1991. Adrian Ward-Jackson was a forty-one-year-old fine art consultant to some of the most prestigious collectors in Europe and chairman of the Ballet Rambert. He bought so many pictures for Basia Johnson, the Polish widow of Johnson & Johnson heir John Seward Johnson, his apartment was known as the Polish Corridor.[42] Diana had been introduced to Ward-Jackson by her friend, the former ballet dancer Angela Serota, and worked with him on the Aids Crisis Trust. The sick man had not been an especially close friend of the

Princess, but from the moment he became ill Diana paid him almost daily visits at his jewel-box flat in Mayfair, where the once cherubic Ward-Jackson, reclining on an Oscar Wildean sofa amid Renaissance bronzes and French engravings, received a parade of society friends, as well as High Church clergymen who sustained him in his faith. His sickbed, for a time, became the place to be. He invited Diana to be among the select few present when he drew his last breath, and she agreed. Perhaps Ward-Jackson saw the headlines this nineteenth-century scene would make as his final gift to the cause of fighting Aids; perhaps he had become genuinely dependent on the Princess's compassion; perhaps both. In any case, Diana instructed Patrick Jephson to get her a special pager so the dying man could buzz her in his last hours. When the call came on Monday 19 August it was her friend Serota to tell Diana he was near death. Diana was at the opposite end of the country, in Balmoral. She drove six hundred miles south through the night with her police protection officer.[43] Her abrupt departure did not go down well with the royal family, who were assembled in Scotland for the annual reunion. In her rush, Diana had failed to observe protocol and ask the Queen for the customary permission to leave. The Queen Mother in particular thought there was something unhealthily macabre about Diana's intense involvement with Ward-Jackson's decline. 'Why can't she take on less gloomy things?' she was heard to ask.[44] Diana seemed to have saved up the intensity of feeling from all the Aids wards she'd walked around in the 1980s. She broke with royal tradition again by attending the funeral of a commoner. At the memorial service at the Grosvenor Chapel in Mayfair on 29 August, populated with *le tout* London society like a scene from *La Traviata*, Diana shook with grief. It was as if the drama of other people's pain was the only thing sure to work in the assuaging of her own.

The increasing theatricality of Diana's mercy missions was suspect to some. If Diana's motives were mixed, they did not impinge on the sincerity of her response when she arrived at her appointed destination. There was little real satisfaction in her life. Does it really matter if the needs of the public also happened to serve her own need for applause? Nor were cameras always present. She had no accompanying press when, driven by Ken Wharfe, she would put in hours at the Passage, the homeless centre next to Westminster Cathedral. As William and Harry got older she occasionally took them along. 'She wanted them to see the reality of people sleeping on the floor,' Wharfe says. 'On the way in the car she would give them a good briefing. She would say, "They are human beings like us. They have a right to clothing and to be warm. It's an obligation of the welfare state." '[45] As Jasper Conran put it, 'She was just a very kind, thoughtful and generous woman who found herself in an unbelievable position and tried to make the very best of it.'[46] Diana's craving to make something pure out of all the tarnishing was the essence of her mystery and the source of her inspiration.

Was she also eager to score off the royal family? Some of the time, yes. Prince Charles's friends, noting how often her charitable photo ops were timed to upstage her husband, were increasingly impatient with Diana and what they called her Sisters of Mercy act. The Prince dealt with his own feelings of unhappiness by employing the opposite tactic. He sought solitude as much as she sought the comfort of strangers. In March 1987, he went off to the Kalahari Desert with his mentor Laurens van der Post to commune with a vast herd of wild zebras. In May he was alone again, walking and fishing at Birkhall, then took a solitary trip to the Outer Hebrides that did not play well against his wife's simultaneous walkabout at London's National Hospital for Nervous Diseases. The *Sun* headlined the Prince's contemplative tour 'A LOON AGAIN'.[47]

Even those times he was in a bad way himself, his friends complained, Diana displaced the focus to her own efforts. When the Prince broke his arm in a polo accident during a match at Cirencester Park, the Princess went to visit him after his surgery at the Queen's Medical Centre in Nottingham. She wound up not at his bedside but that of twenty-three-year-old Dean Woodward who was in a coma after a car crash. She sat at the young man's bedside every day for a week winning the headline in the *Sun* 'DI WEEPS AT BEDSIDE OF COMA DAD DEAN'. Dean's uncle tells the paper, 'She had been sent by God . . . she's an angel . . . We are all praying for a miracle.'[48] By late autumn, when Dean had recovered, Diana made his day with a call promising to visit him at home on New Year's Day. The *Sun* played the mercy mission against pictures of Charles riding at Sandringham. So who tipped off the *Sun*? her critics wanted to know. But what they omit to say is why Diana wound up in Dean's hospital room in the first place. She knew that the first visitor at Charles's bedside was not herself but Camilla Parker Bowles. Diana's staff were instructed to call as she approached the hospital so the mistress and the Princess would not collide in the ward. Diana was bitterly hurt that Charles seemed so indifferent to her desire to look after him. Dean Woodward seemed a more worthwhile patient for her to visit.

All fine and good, except there was a limit to how far extending love to strangers could satisfy a desirable woman of twenty-nine longing for love herself. In the summer of 1990, with the mounting drumbeat of a likely Gulf war, she fell back on the fantasy of an affair with a gallant soldier, a role for which James Hewitt could be recycled. He had been posted to the Gulf in September of that year, in command of a squadron of fourteen Royal Scots armoured personnel carriers of the 4th Armoured Brigade. She wasn't really in love with him any more, but it was an irresistible plotline to be involved with a soldier at the front. Diana bombarded him with letters, sometimes twice a day, rekindling dreams of a life spent together. To keep him going, she included in her comfort packages copies of *Playboy*, *Penthouse*, and *Mayfair* – and, ever the lady, *Horse & Hound*. She filled shampoo bottles with whisky for him to get round the Saudi regulations. He enclosed his own billets-doux in envelopes addressed to his mother to pass on. Hewitt distinguished himself in the war, receiving a mention in dispatches for his valour under fire in kill-or-be-killed confrontations with the Iraqi Republican Guard; his unit destroyed forty tanks and took a thousand prisoners. Diana was so involved with the fantasy of their wartime affair that she forsook her customary TV soap operas for all-night sessions glued to the news. 'I heard Bush, 5 in the morning our time,' she wrote when Kuwait was liberated, 'telling us of the ceasefire, and because of the ghastly time in the morning there was no one to celebrate with! The whole country is upside down with elation . . . I long to know when you're coming home.'[49]

But even as Diana wrote Hewitt passionate letters and agreed that one day they should be married, she told Ken Wharfe that Hewitt was getting 'too serious'. He was talking openly about spending the rest of their lives together and it was unnerving Diana. He was certainly getting indiscreet. Photographer Ken Lennox who was embedded with the 4th Armoured Brigade saw Hewitt standing in his tank, waving a 'bluie' (a blue airmail letter) shouting, 'Look what I have got in my hand – you would pay a fortune for it.'[50] The 'bluie' was a letter from Diana. It appalled Wharfe that Hewitt was reckless enough to borrow the *Daily Mail* satellite phone from Richard Kay, who was there supposedly to cover the Life Guards, to call Diana from the desert.[51]

Soon after the liberation of Kuwait, Kay's *Daily Mail* colleague Nigel Dempster picked up on Hewitt's closeness to Diana in an item on 15 March 1991, slugged 'Di's Dashing Pal to Tell of Desert Deeds'. He told the *News of the World*: 'Jamie can't wait to see Di again.' He reported that the relationship had blossomed from horse riding to 'picnics or tea at Windsor Castle when Prince Charles was away'.[52] When Hewitt's ex-girlfriend Emma Stewardson cashed in nine days later in the *News of the World* with the bombshell, 'I Lost my Lover to Di', Diana panicked. She had promised Hewitt in her letters that when he came home in June she would take him to hear Pavarotti sing at Covent Garden and dinner at Claridge's, but instead she kept her toy soldier under wraps at Highgrove during one of Prince Charles's absences. Soon after, when the Major returned to his unit in Germany, she kissed him off again with radio silence. No longer knowing Diana's private mobile phone number, he had to go through the Kensington Palace switchboard operators, who only once in a while were instructed to put him through. When they did, all he learned was that Diana was ever more concerned to keep their association quiet. Diana's financial adviser at the time, Joseph Sanders, said, 'She had great difficulty when she finished a relationship. Instead of meeting somebody and saying "I don't think we ought to see each other any more, this is goodbye," having a meal with them, or doing it in a pleasant way, she literally would not speak to them from one day to the next, so they didn't know where they were.'[53] The paradox is that the woman who was so genuinely compassionate with strangers was capable of being cruelly dismissive of people closest to her. She was programmed by parents who never explained emotional decisions and now she had the prerogatives of a princess behind a palace wall: she preferred to press the delete key and move on.

The spurned lover called Wharfe in desperation to find out why the Princess had gone silent. Wharfe met him and explained that it was not his place to interfere in such private matters. Still, sensing trouble, he hastened back to advise Diana to get her sixty-four radioactive letters back. Hewitt declined her request, saying he wished to keep the letters as a memento of their 'deep love for each other'.[54] Whether or not the emotion was genuine, the letters were a bomb with a delayed fuse. A reader of Jane Austen rather than Barbara Cartland might have seen that Hewitt was not a high-principled Mr Darcy but a morally flaky Captain Willoughby. Deprived of Diana's stardust he began to fall apart. The once exemplary officer was twice fined for disobeying orders in the autumn of that year and failed his promotion exams to make his acting position of Major a permanent one and essentially destroying his military career.

His affair with Diana, though rumoured, did not become undeniable until he finally blabbed to Anna Pasternak of the *Daily Express* in 1994.

The fact that it had eluded detection for so long only stimulated suspicion then that it had begun earlier than the year Hewitt gave Pasternak – 1986. Harry, recall, was born in September 1984. It was a leap, but not a giant one, to speculate that the red-haired Prince was a love child of the liaison with the red-haired Hewitt. In photographs taken at his eighteenth birthday in 2002, Harry does uncannily resemble Diana's lover at the same age 'like peas in a pod',[55] says the veteran royal reporter, Harry Arnold. But he also resembles all the Spencers on the walls of Althorp. 'Harry's the naughty one, just like me,' said Diana to a friend.[56] In 2005 the publicist and big-mouth Max Clifford sallied forth with a new carbon dating of the Diana–Hewitt affair that fanned the speculation further. In his book he alleged that Hewitt first sought his counsel about 'a clandestine relationship with a VIP' (who turned out to be Diana) as early as 1984. And in that meeting, says Clifford, Hewitt confided he and Diana had begun their sexual relationship well before Harry was conceived – indeed, had begun it a few months after the birth of William in 1982.[57]

This is not a proposition Wharfe accepts. 'Diana was not stupid,' he says today. 'She was in love with Charles and she knew her duty was to produce the heir and the spare. She even said something to me – that she didn't know how she and Charles managed to have Harry but they did' – an odd way to give your endorsement. Hewitt himself was for years unequivocal that he had no claims to be the father of Harry, but shortly after Clifford's assertion in 2005, he changed his mind. He recanted with the assistance of a 'past-life regressionist' named Tony Rae on Channel Five's Under Hypnosis. Rae put Hewitt into a deep hypnotic TV trance, under which Hewitt, in a hollow, zombie-like voice, confessed that he had indeed slept with Diana much earlier than he had ever previously admitted. He had lied, he said, to protect her.[58]

Yet Jasper Conran, designer of her maternity clothes during her pregnancy with Harry, insists that Diana's focus was all about Charles at this time. 'There's no shadow of a doubt there could be another man on the horizon.'[59] Indeed, Diana's tears during her fittings and her request to make her 'sexy for my husband' bolster evidence that it was Charles who strayed, returning to Camilla before, rather than after, the birth of Harry as he has always said. Whatever is the truth, there is no question either that Charles adores his brave, reckless, roistering second son and vice versa. Harry is said to be closer to his father than William is, the royal heir.

Perhaps paternity rumours are no more than a reflection of the primitive tribal significance which, even today, is attached to the birth of royal princes who are in the line of succession. When Prince Charles first learned that a newspaper was about to float a story about a possible Harry–Hewitt link, his immediate response was at once dismissive and surprising. 'Well, I don't know what she was doing at the time.'[60] If nothing else, it was a truer reflection of the couple's relations than Diana's gloss in the months before Harry was born.

Hewitt, meanwhile, having blabbed once about Diana, kept on blabbing every time he was offered a cheque to do so. His ultimate decline – and ultimate treachery – was to be a marker in the darkening atmosphere that would envelop Diana in the 1990s. Foul dust floated in the wake of all her romantic dreams.

# Chapter 15

# Sex, Lies and Audiotapes

'Inexorably, Diana's phone was bugged.'
— John Nelson, audio expert, 2006

From the moment that the monarchy changed from an institution of power to one of representative virtue, the thing that made it work was something that, for a time, survived the change: the Palace code of silence. It wasn't possible, of course, for fallible human beings to be infallible, as the royal family were required to be as totems of the nation's highest moral values. Even though they couldn't count on the press any more, they had the expectation that their inescapable personal failures would remain private, protected by the *omertà* of the court and the discretion of their friends. At the turn of the decade all those assumptions were abandoned. Escalating press competition and Diana's need to shatter her fairy story converged to make the 1990s an era of royal turbulence that threatened the very survival of the monarchy.

In the early days of Charles and Diana's marriage, the couple's PR was handled by Buckingham Palace press officers who, themselves aloof and rather grand, assumed that their *raison d'être* was simply to deny anything irregular or unannounced. 'No, Princess Anne is not in love with Captain Mark Phillips,' they told reporters a couple of days before the Princess announced her engagement. 'Fiction beginning to end' was their verdict on Anthony Holden's 1988 biography of Prince Charles depicting the Wales marriage in ruins.[1] Prince Andrew, in an endearing lapse, casually told a group of journalists he spoke to in Malta in 1998 that Palace officials had lied to the media about the royals for twenty years. (Buckingham Palace immediately issued a statement 'clarifying' his remarks.)[2] Naively, the Palace press officers genuinely believed that the media frenzy surrounding the Waleses would die down. They were totally unprepared for the enduring power of Diana's face on the cover

258

of every magazine and newspaper and increasingly baffled by their failure to control the swirl of negative rumours that surrounded the marriage. What they thought, though, didn't matter much, because the press simply bypassed denials that had come to be regarded as routine.

Kelvin MacKenzie, Murdoch's raucous editor at the *Sun*, set the tone for Palace coverage from 1981 to 1994. MacKenzie saw the royal family as a vaudeville show, a gallery of papier mâché gargoyles that existed purely for daily target practice. The *Sun*'s photographers referred to the royals as 'the Germans' and described taking their pictures as 'whacking the Germans'.[3] According to the media commentator Roy Greenslade, who was one of MacKenzie's features executives at the *Sun* in the early eighties, Kelvin would assume a shocked look and say, 'I'm afraid we've upset the Palace. How can we do it today?'[4] His gloves-off approach was one symptom of an increasingly uncontrollable British epidemic of lèse-majesté. Another was the success of the savagely satirical ITV puppet show *Spitting Image*. The awesome power of the programme could help wreck, and sometimes make, political careers. (The show's handbag-wielding figure of Margaret Thatcher bearing down on her wimpish male Cabinet colleagues rather enhanced her Iron Lady image.) The royal family were latexed into crude parodies of their physical selves – the Queen a frumpy suburban housewife, the Queen Mother de-sanctified for the first time as an absent-minded old boozer whose every utterance was accompanied by a shower of spittle. In one episode the Duchess of York was portrayed undergoing colonic irrigation. *Spitting Image*, I am told, was one of the Princess of Wales's favourite shows. 'If we hurry we can get back to Sandringham in time for *Spitting Image*,' she said over Christmas in 1988 to a Norfolk friend with a sly, inclusive smile that seemed to savour the risk of how bad such a disrespectful admission would look in a headline.[5]

The royals had played their own role in manoeuvring themselves into *Spitting Image*'s cross hairs. In 1987, the extent to which they had succumbed to the seduction of TV became disastrously clear when Prince Edward, secured the participation of Princess Anne and Prince Andrew in a cringingly undignified BBC celebrity game show, *It's a Royal Knockout*, to raise money for charity. The end was laudable enough, but the means were lamentable. On a muddy field in Staffordshire, royals competed with B-list celebrities such as Meatloaf, Tom Jones and Pamela Stephenson to pelt each other with fake hams, chase each other through tanks of water and play games dressed as enormous chess pieces and vegetables. The Palace somehow imagined that it could inoculate itself against press invasiveness by discarding royal mystery for TV's fake accessibility. Diana, of course, was far too canny to participate in such a vulgar display. But poor Princess Anne clearly realised that *It's a Royal Knockout* was a disaster as soon as the cameras started to roll. When the host, Stuart Hall, asked her, 'Do I have to call you the Princess Royal?' she replied icily, 'I don't know. It's nothing to do with me.'[6]

The reviews were merciless.

As the royals recognised too late, *It's a Royal Knockout* was the nadir of Palace image control. It dramatised the conundrum they blamed Diana for importing into their lives: how to be familiar without breeding contempt. (The Queen herself has always known how to do this. Said a former courtier, 'The Queen is not your friend. She is friendly.')[7] The House of Windsor's sense of itself had been rocked by the Princess who had crossed over to white-hot superstardom, and it had no idea how to protect itself from the media heat.

The paradox was that even as the monarchy was supposed to be emblematic of the nation's highest moral standards, the nation itself didn't seem to have any. Even though Maggie Thatcher herself was punctiliously polite in her observance of protocol with the Queen, the Thatcher economic revolution had driven a stake through the residue of the British culture of deference. New money meant new mobility. It wasn't just the media that were less respectful to royalty now. Diana herself had become shockingly casual with the Queen, leaving the room before Her Majesty and stipulating whom she did and did not want to sit next to at the formal Balmoral dinners. The late-eighties financial debacle of the insurance company Lloyd's of London, traditionally the safe repository of quiet upper-class fortunes, pushed many a strapped toff into ropy new lines of business, importing undesirable friends into their circles and eroding accepted codes of discretion. While the Queen and Prince Philip have always mixed with the ducal families and landed gentry, the young royals' friends were less narrowly screened. Fergie's circle, for instance, consisted of a couple of interior decorators, a wine merchant, a banker, an importer of ski clothes and a gift-shop proprietor.[8] Fergie also had a weakness for health gurus and sooth-sayers. One of her favourites was the Greek medium Madame Vasso in north London who provided a blue plastic pyramid in which Fergie sat to be cleansed and healed.[9] Diana's unfortunate habit of unburdening herself to the help became downright risky. Retainers who were as close-mouthed as they were servile grew voluble when Fleet Street's chequebooks were waved in their direction. 'It was really easy for the newspapers to get dirt on their private lives. Brown envelopes of used notes used to find their way to junior members of staff,' said the Queen's former press secretary Michael Shea. Sources in royal protection it was too risky to pay in cash were procured Cup Final tickets.[10] Diana's star power had raised the market value of gossip to the point that a whole industry of snitches, trivia cops and media peeping Toms rose to slake the media's appetite for royal dish. And there was plenty to feed on, not just the Waleses'.

The marriage of the Duke and Duchess of York had degenerated into farce. It didn't take Fergie long to fall from grace with the family and the press alike. The marriage unravelled mostly because Fergie could not stand being left alone at Buckingham Palace while Andrew was off in the navy. In 1990 the peripatetic young Prince spent only forty-two nights with his gregarious wife.[11] Prince Philip, was trying to be helpful when he pointed out to Fergie that Lady Mountbatten had been left at home by Uncle Dickie when the future First Sea Lord joined the navy.[12] But Edwina, after all, had bowled her way through the beds of half London society as well as having celebrated affairs with Douglas Fairbanks, Bill Paley and possibly even Pandit Nehru, but the only time she ever had to read about it afterwards was when the American press – but not the British – named her as the other woman in the Fairbanks divorce. Anyway, the Mountbattens' life together was a lot more exciting than the Duke of York wanted. On Andrew's rare home leaves the debonair Prince whom Fergie had married turned into a boorish couch potato. Moreover, he was cheap. Edwina Mountbatten had had a fortune of her own to supplement Mountbatten's frugal naval pay. Fergie was neither allowed to earn her living nor given the means to keep up with new public expectations of glamour; and she was saddled with her bolting mother Susan's debts when Hector Barrantes died.

The Duchess was so short of cash she was soon labelled the Freebie Queen of Buckingham Palace. Her first gaffe was accepting a fur coat on a tour of Canada in 1987, incurring the fury of the animal rights lobby. Worse was her sale to *Hello!* magazine in August 1990 of forty-eight pages of pictures of the York Family at Home for a quarter of a million pounds, paid into a trust fund for her mother. Then, on 15 January 1992, some cheesy two-year-old holiday snaps of Fergie holidaying in Morocco with the thirty-eight-year-old Texan playboy

Steve Wyatt were stolen by a snooping window cleaner from the top of a dusty wardrobe in Wyatt's flat in Cadogan Square. Inevitably, they were offered up to the *Daily Mail*. The stolen goods could not be published in the UK but after Scotland Yard took custody of them, the snaps mysteriously found their way to *Paris Match*. They depicted Fergie cavorting by the pool with her arm around Wyatt, and enjoying a candlelit dinner with her lover wearing a raised mask of a big-eyed green toad. The one of Wyatt with Princess Beatrice in his arms reportedly infuriated Prince Andrew. Fergie believed the pictures were a plant to discredit her.[13]

The cycle of tawdry global dissemination became a familiar feature of the nineties, the decade that left the royals with no place to hide. The stolen pictures hit the news just before Fergie and her father were due to travel to Palm Beach for a fund-raising polo match sponsored by Cartier. Fergie was representing the Motor Neurone Disease Association, of which she was the hard-working patron. The poor girl was so distraught that she had a meltdown coming home. A horde of snickering journalists trailed her on the flight from Miami and observed her knocking back champagne, throwing wet towels, peanuts and tissues around, and placing a sick bag over her head into which she reportedly made strange 'telephone noises'. (Buzz buzz? Ring ring? They do not enlighten us.) James Whitaker quoted her bodyguard's assessment – bodyguards, a hitherto silent fraternity, now offered assessments – that the Duchess was 'deeply troubled'.[14] The Queen does not seem to have put up much resistance when at Christmas 1991 Andrew and Fergie came to see her to discuss a separation. Her Majesty's only request was that the couple wait to go public until after the general election. She suggested a six-month period of reflection. 'I don't need any more time to think, Mother,' Andrew apparently replied. 'My mind is made up.'[15] After the Wyatt pictures were published the Queen could see Andrew's point.

If the Yorks were hurtling towards divorce, Princess Anne had already got there. Behind her horsey gravitas, the Princess Royal has always been catnip to equerries. She has a lithe body from all that riding, and especially good legs. Her dignified public presence and zealous fulfilment of her charitable commitments discountenanced gossip, but in April 1989 even she was enveloped in the noxious new climate. Four intimate letters to her were stolen from her handbag by a staffer who gave them to the *Sun*. Unable to identify the writer, the *Sun* ran a front-page story about the existence of the letters – without disclosing the contents – and then returned the letters to the Palace, fearing to be charged with receiving stolen property. A reporter from the *Mail on Sunday* rang the Palace to check out a name about to be published by the *People*, a rival Sunday tabloid. As if he had taken a truth serum, the spokesman politely revealed that the letter writer was really Commander Tim Laurence, one of the Queen's equerries. In the words of one of the royal hunters, 'Buckingham Palace found itself in a poker game it didn't know was taking place. The Palace was simply no match for the lizard-like tactics of a bunch of hacks.'[16] The Letters fiasco hastened the separation and divorce of Anne from her husband of nineteen years.

The secondary royals, though fun to torment, were a sideshow as far as the press were concerned. The one who sold papers in serious numbers was Diana. At the end of the eighties, few people except the couple's closest friends knew just how bad the Wales marriage had become. It was seen as Georgina Howell saw it in 1988 in the *Sunday Times*: a marriage that, however 'cool', was still workable.[17] It wasn't. All the things that would bring another couple together seemed to drive these two spoilt people apart – including tragedy. The accident in March 1988 that killed their friend Major Hugh Lindsay on a skiing expedition with Charles in Klosters served as a wedge, not a bridge. Diana had been back at the chalet with Fergie when the avalanche buried Lindsay and seriously injured Patti Palmer-Tomkinson, who was in the Prince's party, too. Diana blamed Charles for his recklessness in choosing such a hazardous run and fought with him about her determination that they accompany Lindsay's body home to his pregnant widow, Sarah. On their return, Charles retreated to Highgrove alone in a state of shock and guilt. When Paul Burrell brought him in a tray of dinner the devastated Prince didn't touch it. He was 'sitting there watching television with a completely blank look on his face', Burrell says.[18] Diana opted to stay in Kensington Palace consoling Sarah rather than her own husband. His loneliness was palpable.

Patrick Jephson, the Princess of Wales's private secretary, noted how Charles began to stick it to Diana during official tours. The Prince chose his most effective, most demoralising weapon: intellectual superiority. Now, rather than seek to include his wife in conversations with foreign dignitaries, he made it embarrassingly clear that she was fluff, he was IQ. On their tour of the Gulf States in March 1989, for example, Charles deliberately excluded Diana from the conversation with their royal hosts. Over coffee, one of the emirs eventually turned to Diana and asked what Her Royal Highness planned to be doing herself on the official visit. Diana, brightening, was about to answer with a list of the earnest programme of visits Jephson had planned for her – a tour of a day-care centre for mentally handicapped children, a visit to a clinic for immigrant women and a girls' business studies class – but before she could reply her husband blithely stepped all over her. 'Shopping, isn't it, darling?' he asked. 'The words dropped into the marble stillness like bricks into plate glass,' says Jephson. The Princess 'coloured, mumbled something inaudible, and lapsed into silence'.[19]

The Prince shafted her again on the April 1991 trip to Brazil in front of the Brazilian Ambassador to Britain, Paolo Tarso Flecha de Lima, and his wife Lucia (later a close friend), who on this first meeting noted how tense Diana was. On the plane out the Princess lightly referred to the briefings she was reading as her 'homework'. Charles promptly cut her down with, 'Oh, she doesn't know a thing about Brazil.'[20]

Diana was hungering to blow up the Golden Couple myth once and for all. She was tortured by its subterfuge, humiliated by its denial. Could there be anything more absurd than the elaborate royal dumb show for the press when the eight-year-old Prince William was delivered up to his first boarding school, Ludgrove in Berkshire in September of 1990? The handover of the boy had to be conducted like a prisoner exchange at the Berlin Wall: Diana and William travelling in her Jaguar XJS from Kensington Palace, Charles in his Bentley from Highgrove, both cars entering the Ludgrove grounds via the back entrance, Diana and William transferring from her car to Charles's behind the laurel bushes, the Prince and Princess driving away together from school in the Bentley, only to switch back again to two cars when they thought they were out of sight.[21] (They weren't, of course. James Whitaker witnessed the whole pantomime for the Daily Mirror.)

Diana's need to expel the lies she had gorged all through her married life started to manifest itself in ominous confrontations. In February of 1989 at Sir James and Lady Annabel Goldsmith's house in Richmond she had a showdown with Camilla at the fortieth birthday party of Camilla's sister Annabel Elliot. Charles had never expected Diana to attend what she had already referred to as a 'ghastly' party, surrounded as they would be by all the chortling brown-nosers from the Prince's Highgrove circle. Diana later became a close friend of Annabel Goldsmith too, but always underestimated how this bosomy charmer played both sides against the middle. Annabel, who had borne a child by the tycoon Sir James Goldsmith while still married and under the same roof as her husband Mark Birley, had lived a complicated life herself and was used to others doing the same. Even after she had a second child by Sir James and left Birley to live with and later marry Goldsmith, Sir James continued to spend half his time with his first wife in Paris and later a younger girlfriend in New York. (It was Jimmy Goldsmith who coined the famous epigram, 'When you marry your mistress you create a vacancy.')[22] Like Camilla, Annabel would have expected Diana to understand that the 'and Princess of Wales' on this particular invitation was strictly a matter of form and should be tactfully declined.

Diana, to Charles's great discomfort (and the other guests' amusement), refused to play the game. 'Why are you coming tonight?' Charles asked her testily on the way to the party. 'Because I am your wife, *sir*,' she might have replied. Ken Wharfe, who drove them there, says HRH 'needled' her all the way about her decision to go. It must have been thrilling for Diana: an act of rejection of all the suffocating social norms she had been raised with, of which the first is Spare Yourself Embarrassment. One can share her adrenalin rush as, heart racing, she mounted the steps of the Goldsmiths' large red-brick Queen Anne house, Ormeley Lodge, where lights blazed and music played. She later called it 'One of the bravest moments of my entire ten years'.[23]

As Diana, armoured in stunning décolletage, sailed into the buzzing throng, it was obvious – to Wharfe, among others – that many of the guests were surprised to see her. Dinner was not long over when she noticed that Prince Charles had disappeared. Other guests tried to distract her from going to look for him downstairs, she later told Morton, but she was not to be deterred. Descending as far as the basement, with an uneasy Ken Wharfe in tow, she found what she was looking for: Charles and Camilla huddled in intimate conversation on a sofa in the nursery. Ken Wharfe describes the guilty pair looking up, shocked, as Diana cried, '*Don't tell me I don't know what's going on!*'[24] In Diana's own version of the incident, which she related to Andrew Morton, she addressed Camilla, with deadly insouciance, 'Camilla, I'd love to have a word with you.' Charles immediately took refuge with an unnamed male guest who was present, and the two of them 'shot upstairs like chickens with no heads, and I could feel upstairs all hell breaking loose' – a sadly plausible description of masculine social cowardice. Diana, according to herself, sat down next to Camilla, and said calmly (though she was feeling 'terrified'), 'I would like you to know that I know exactly what is going on between you and Charles. I wasn't born yesterday.'[25] There's no record in this account of what the mistress said in reply, but in Wharfe's telling Camilla retorted, 'You've got everything!'[26] This seems unlikely to me. The sophisticated Mrs Parker Bowles is more likely to have maintained a dignified silence. Her stance would have been embarrassment for Diana, not for herself. It was, after all, yet more evidence that Charles's wife was 'unhinged'.

If she was, Diana loved the bitter taste of it. That night, she said, she 'cried and cried and cried. I cried like I had never cried before – it was anger, it was seven years' pent-up anger coming out.' The trouble was that like her night-time bulimic binges on white chocolate and custard, the catharsis left her wanting more heady bites of truth.

She got her chance seven months later, on the eve of the wedding of her brother Charles, Viscount Althorp, to the model Victoria Lockwood. Prince Harry was a page at the ceremony, dressed in a biscuit-coloured silk costume copied from one of Althorp's Joshua Reynolds paintings. Perhaps the high style of a big society wedding surfaced Diana's angst about her own 'lamb to the slaughter' moment. Or, perhaps, as she said later, it was her rage that after all these years out in the cold, her mother, who was also there, was still coldly ignored by both her father and his hated second wife. Or, perhaps, it was simply that there was no such thing as a gathering of the Spencer clan that was not blown apart by some outburst of buried fury. Whatever the subterranean currents, the wedding eve was the scene of an epic confrontation between Diana and the other woman in her life who had caused her nothing but grief: her stepmother, Raine Spencer.

The scene occurred in the afternoon. Since all the Spencer sisters' children were staying at Althorp (the youngest, like Harry, were pages at the wedding), Raine had organised a family tea party in the nursery at which Frances was also present. The atmosphere was uneasy. As Diana described it, 'My father and stepmother refused to even say hello to my mother. And it got me so angry, the behaviour of these grown-ups. I said it was very bad manners, they were just indulging themselves, this was Charles's day and Victoria's.' Diana then screamed, 'Do we have to live in the past every time Mummy walks into the house?' Clearly Diana did: she was twenty-nine, yet she referred to the other adults in the room as 'the grown-ups'. As Raine exited the nursery and was about to descend the staircase, Diana lurched forward and pushed her stepmother down the stairs. Raine arrived in a heap on the landing. 'It gave me enormous satisfaction,' Diana told Peter Settelen two years later. 'I was so angry. I wanted to throttle that stepmother of mine. She brought such grief. She kept saying to me, "Oh, but Diana, you're so unhappy in your own marriage. You're just jealous of Daddy's and my relationship." And jealousy was not high on the agenda. It was behaviour I was after. She said, "You know how much we've suffered because of Frances." I said, "Suffering, Raine? You don't know the word. I see suffering of such magnitude in my role that you would never even understand." I really spat it at her. I said, "We've always hated you. You've ruined our family life. You've done a great job there, Raine. Great job. Made us really unhappy. I hope you're pleased about that.'"[27]

Strong stuff from England's future Queen. Raine could have been forgiven if she had fled into exile to plot her revenge from some rival European court. As it was, she retained her stately poise. Raine's assistant, Sue Ingram, who witnessed the scene, describes her saying to her afterwards (and one can hear the vexed social tones of the Countess), '*What* has happened to Diana? *Why* such an occurrence? I just *don't* understand that girl.'[28] Afterwards, Earl Spencer did not speak to his daughter for six months.

Losing her father as a support isolated Diana further. He had always been a warm confidant in her marital problems. The Earl had warned her as early as 1985 that Camilla was winning the power battle and urged his daughter to do everything she could to revive her husband's interest. Still, it was hard for anyone of her father's age to understand just how intolerable she found her rival's hold over Charles. Johnnie Spencer would probably have lived with Frances's adultery if she hadn't demanded a separation. Diana's grandmother Lady Fermoy put up with Maurice's extramarital involvements. The Queen Mother, according to a member of her circle, was 'impatient' with Diana's blinkered view.[29] Are modern women less tough? Edwina Mountbatten's generation seemed to find it so much easier than Diana to set their faces against loss. The presence of Hewitt and all these other admirers in her life seemed to do nothing to make the Prince's mistress more tolerable to his wife. Charles and Camilla were now so solidly re-entwined that their friends in Gloucestershire regarded them as a couple. When Diana was absent Camilla was playing hostess at Highgrove as if the house were her own.[30]

The press knew of the affair, of course, but never suspected how deeply rooted it had become and how complicit his circle of friends was in nurturing it. We have a glimpse of the nature of the Camilla–Charles intimacy from the recording of the fateful telephone conversation in

December 1989, ever afterwards known as Camillagate. It was made fourteen days before Diana herself was taped speaking with embarrassing intimacy to her admirer James Gilbey. (The Squidgygate tape, as it was called, alludes to Gilbey's pet name for her.) The origin of these recordings and how they made their way to the public is a can of worms to be discussed later, but it was the contents rather than their provenance that riveted attention when they were first aired several years after they were recorded.

The Camillagate tapes are an extraordinary document. Even after many airings you feel uncomfortable listening in. The banal and grubby little vulnerabilities they reveal define what Hillary Clinton once hopefully called the Zone of Privacy. The script, delivered in the Prince's familiar mannered tones and Camilla's breathless basso, plays like a two-hander for Jeremy Irons and Emma Thompson at the National Theatre, so illuminating is it of adultery as performed at the top end of the class spectrum. Its existence in the audio ether for ever is an affidavit of the truth of Diana's worst imaginings as her fairy-tale marriage wound down to its sad conclusion.

From references in the call we can deduce that the time is late at night on 17 December 1989. We are in the waning years of Mrs Thatcher's reign, when a recession has set in and brought back the scowling social mood of the late 1970s. There's a strike of ambulance men and the army were called into help, apparently taking Camilla's husband Colonel Andrew Parker Bowles away from home. The Prince is making the call from Eaton Lodge, the home of the seventy-four-year-old Dowager Duchess of Westminster, known as Nancy, on the current Duke's estate, at Eccleston near Chester. The Dowager Duchess was yet another of the besotted surrogate grannies Charles cultivated to supplement the Queen Mother's attentions. Camilla is at home with the children and her Christmas tree at Middlewick House in Wiltshire. There is the implication that Camilla's marriage to Parker Bowles has taken a nosedive, finally corroded by their joint adultery. She refers to Andrew as 'it'. 'While you're rushing around doing things I shall be, you know, alone until *it* reappears . . . He won't be here till Thursday, pray God. Um, the ambulance strike, it's a terrible thing to say this: I suppose it won't have come to an end by Thursday?' There are wry lessons on the tape to Diana as a wife in the mistress's non-stop flattery of Charles's masculinity. She says he can trust Nancy Westminster as a confidante of their affair because the aged Duchess is in love with him.

CAMILLA: She'd do anything you asked. You know, those sort of people feel terribly strongly about you. You've got such a hold over her.

CHARLES (*the stage direction would say: 'With a purr of delight'*): Really?

CAMILLA: And I think, as usual, you're underestimating yourself.

Later on she makes the blatantly bootlicking request that the Prince send her a copy of his latest speech. In return he patronises her with 'Your greatest achievement is to love me.' The call had been taped from halfway through. In the first half, apparently, Charles had been reading the speech aloud to Camilla. (He did this often.) Even the radio ham couldn't bear to record that.

But it's the sex talk that is so mind-bending, given who these people are. The thirty-eight-year-old Camilla positions herself as lusting for Charles twenty-four/seven.

CAMILLA: You're awfully good at feeling your way along.

CHARLES: Oh stop! I want to feel my way along you, all over you and up and down you and in and out.

CAMILLA: Oh.

CHARLES: . . . particularly in and out.

CAMILLA: Oh, that's just what I need at the moment.

(*Man who recorded conversation speaks over couple to record date.*)

CAMILLA: . . . I can't bear a Sunday night without you.

CHARLES: Oh God.

CAMILLA: . . . I can't start the week without you.

CHARLES: What about me? The trouble is, I need you several times a week.

CAMILLA: Mmm. So do I. I need you all the week, all the time . . . Oh, darling, Oh! I just want you now.

CHARLES: Do you?

CAMILLA: Mmm.

CHARLES: So do I

CAMILLA: Desperately, desperately, desperately.

The clincher is Charles suggesting his permanent presence can only be achieved by 'living inside her trousers . . . Or, God forbid, a Tampax!' – an image he then riffs on, envisaging himself 'chucked down the lavatory' and 'forever swirling round the top'. In the Prince of Wales's world view he's unlucky even as a Tampax – and unlucky he certainly was that such a comment ever reached the public. There was a British health ad at the time encouraging condoms as a preventive to Aids with the slogan 'You can't die of embarrassment'. Camillagate proved that you can come pretty close, although Charles had to wait till 1992 – when the illicit tape found its way to the Australian magazine weekly *New Idea* and thence to fifty-three news outlets round the world.

The shock waves of embarrassment would slam into the lovers' friends, too. The phone talk proved that practically every high-born family in Gloucestershire and Wiltshire was colluding in making this extramarital affair possible. Most of the recorded discussion is a logistical debate about which house the lovers can next use for a sex venue, and it's a tour of the grand addresses listed in *Burke's Peerage*. Gyles Brandreth, in his biography of Charles and Camilla, has given an unimprovable parsing of the text of the call – to which we are indebted for, among other things, and for knowing whom the lovers are talking about.

CAMILLA: Darling, listen. I talked to David tonight again. It might not be any good. [*David is Leopold David Verney, known as David, 21st Baron Willoughby de Brooke, who lived at Ditchford farm near Moreton-in-Marsh, close to both Highgrove and Middlewick*]

CHARLES: Oh, no!

CAMILLA: I'll tell you why. He's got these children of one of those Crawley girls and their nanny staying. He's going – I'm going to ring him again tomorrow. He's going to try and hold them off till Friday. But as an alternative, perhaps I might ring up Charlie. [*Charles Petty-Fitzmaurice, Earl of Shelburne, since 1999 the 9th Marquess of Lansdowne, who'd been rumoured to have an affair with Camilla*]

CHARLES: Yes.

CAMILLA: . . . and see if we could do it there. I know he is back on Thursday . . .

CHARLES: It's quite a lot further away.

CAMILLA: Oh, is it?

CHARLES: Well, I'm just trying to think: coming from Newmarket . . .?

CAMILLA: Coming from Newmarket to me at that time of night, you could probably do it in two and three-quarters. It takes me three.

CHARLES: What to go to? Um, Bowood? [*Bowood: the family home of the Marquess of Lansdowne*]

CAMILLA: Northmore.[31] [*Northmore: a stud farm near Newmarket in Suffolk, at the time owned by Hugh and Emilie van Cutsem*]

They go on to canvass instead the possibility of staging the tryst at the house of – the treachery! – Patti and Charlie Palmer-Tomkinson, at Fergie's childhood stamping ground of Dummer in Hampshire. When the Princess of Wales finally heard the Camillagate tape played in full in January 1993, it was the complicity of so many friends, even more than the mortifying sexual intensity the lovers shared, that inflamed her. The reference on the tape to Hugh van Cutsem's wife Emilie being in on the secret after keeping her company so often at Balmoral was especially hard for Diana to take. Is it any wonder she had tried to purge those she saw as fawning, treacherous go-betweens from her husband's life? Since this was the reality Diana lived with, day in and day out, it is not surprising that she sought solace in the arms of other men. The fact that she did is made crystal clear by the Squidgygate tape, recorded just fourteen days later. That is what is so haunting about these parallel audio snapshots of a marriage. The texture of the relationship between Diana and James Gilbey, the man about town and car salesman whom she had taken up with during the summer, is registered on the Squidgygate tapes just as acutely as the Charles–Camilla liaison is on Camillagate. Indeed, after listening to the two recordings in succession you can find it at least plausible that the woman Diana has become in Squidgygate has been created by the cynical state of affairs depicted on the recording of her husband talking to Camilla.

From everything Diana and Gilbey say on the tape, it is clear that the call took place on New Year's Eve, in the waning hours of 1989. Diana is staying at Sandringham with the royal family. She is talking on a landline from her bedroom. Gilbey is on his Cellnet mobile phone, sitting in his parked car in a country lane in north Oxfordshire, some 150 miles away, en route to a dinner party for thirty. The time must be around 6 or 7 p.m., because at one point Diana is interrupted by a knock at her door from a member of the Sandringham staff, who asks for her dinner plans. 'Just some salad with yogurt,' she replies. 'Like when I was ill in bed. That would be wonderful – about eight o'clock.' Male voice: 'Bring it up on a tray?'

Not much fun for a princess to be supping from a tray on New Year's Eve. But then the whole ambience that Diana evokes is of a rainy Norfolk night. Like Camillagate, Squidgygate begins mid-conversation. Gilbey asks, 'And so, darling, what other lows today?' To which Diana replies. 'I was very bad at lunch and I nearly started blubbing . . . I thought: Bloody hell, the things I have done for this fucking family.'

Once again, there's a well-defined atmosphere to this high society radio play. It's a generation younger, with less intensity invested. Diana's flat, Sloane Ranger voice has a distracted edge. The royal cocoon applies to both calls. Gilbey, like pretty much everyone else the Prince and Princess meets, is as sycophantic to Diana as Camilla is to Charles. One senses that Diana's interest in him is a little desultory:

GILBEY: I cry when you cry.
DIANA: I know. So sweet.

She is playing with him, and the game isn't exactly the one he has in mind. In fact, when he tries to lead the conversation in a more promising direction she exhibits a detumescingly short attention span:

GILBEY: I haven't played with myself . . . for a full forty-eight hours. (*musingly*) Not for a full forty-eight hours . . .

DIANA (*sounding vague*): I watched *EastEnders* today.

He calls her 'darling' fifty-three times and 'Squidgy' fourteen times, but the sense one gets is that he's not so much serious as self-consciously smitten, congratulating himself on the charge he gets from a spicy late-night call with a woman as famous and glamorous as the Princess of Wales. There are moments when they seem more interested in her press coverage than they are in each other.

GILBEY: I get so possessive when I see all those pictures of you. I get so possessive – that's the least attractive aspect of me, really. I just see them and think, Oh God, if only . . .
DIANA (*pricking up at the mention of publicity*): There aren't that many pictures, are there? There haven't been that many.
GILBEY: Four or five today.
DIANA: Oh.
GILBEY: Various magazines. So, darling, I –
DIANA (*refusing to be diverted from the topic of herself*): I'm always smiling, aren't I?
GILBEY: Always.
Diana (*gloomily*): I thought that today.

The Diana we meet in this call, though a different creature from St Diana of the Public Prints, is recognisably the woman who was able to dispatch James Hewitt when he'd fulfilled his sexual obligation. She speaks with resentment of her royal husband – 'He makes my life real, real torture, I've decided'; she bitches about Fergie – 'the redhead' – getting help from the showbiz personality Jimmy Savile to compete with Diana's superior publicity; she chafes under the boredom of privilege – 'I can't stand the confines of this marriage'; and she makes a haughty reference to Hewitt, whose existence in her life the public didn't know about yet, as if he were her gigolo: 'I've decked people out in my time. James Hewitt – entirely dressed him from head to foot, that man. Cost me quite a bit.' The twenty-eight-year-old Princess of Wales is no longer the shy dupe in the bridal crinoline. She comes across as brittle, vain, worldly and well practised in subterfuge. She refuses to turn down the TV as they talk because, she explains, 'It's drowning my conversation.' (As the Prince Charles character comments in Stephen Frears's film, *The Queen*: '*Our* Diana and *their* Diana are nothing like each other.')

You don't much like her by the end of the call, but you do feel sorry for her. There are some pathetic clues to her shaky intellectual confidence. One is her odd misreading of a clearly well-intentioned conversational sally by the Bishop of Norwich – 'that Bloody bishop', as she calls him – which she caps off with an unlikely story of how she gave the eminent man of the cloth a rocket:

DIANA: He said, 'I want you to tell me how you talk to people who are ill or dying. How do you cope?'

GILBEY: He wanted to learn. He was so hopeless at it himself.

DIANA: I began to wonder after I'd spoken to him. I said, 'I'm just myself.'

GILBEY: They can't get to grips that, underneath, there is such a beautiful person in you. They can't think that it isn't cluttered up by this idea of untold riches.

DIANA: I know. He kept wittering about one must never think how good one is at one's job. There's always something you can learn around the next corner. I said, 'Well, if people knew me, they know I'm like that.'

GILBEY: So did you give him a hard time?

DIANA: I did, actually. In the end, I said, 'I know this sounds crazy but I've lived before.' He said, 'How do you know?' I said, 'Because

I'm a wise old thing.' . . . I said, 'Also, I'm aware that people I have loved and have died and are in the spirit world look after me.' He looked horrified, I thought, If he's the bishop, *he* should say that sort of thing.'

GILBEY : I don't really like many of those bishops especially.

DIANA: Well, I felt very uncomfortable . . . I said, 'I understand people's suffering, people's pain more than you will ever know.' And he said, 'That's obvious by what you are doing for the Aids.' I said, 'It's not only Aids, it's anyone who suffers. I can smell them a mile away.'

GILBEY: What did he say?

DIANA: Nothing. He just went quiet. He changed the subject to toys. And I thought, Ah! Defeated you!

Gilbey is suitably impressed, which is what he's there for: *'Marvellous, darling, did you chalk up a little victory?'* Nothing cheers Diana up more in her miserable marginality in the royal family than the pretence that she is a winged avenger of the establishment.

And then there is the story she tells Gilbey of how the day before their call she found herself on the edge of the Sandringham royal estate looking over a fence into the grounds of her old family home, Park House, which had been converted into a Cheshire Home for disabled people.

DIANA: I thought, Oh, what shall I do? Well, my friend would say, 'Go in and do it.' I thought, No, 'cause, I'm a bit shy, and there were hundreds of people in there. So I thought, Bugger that! So I went round to the front door and walked straight in.

GILBEY: Did you?

DIANA: It was just so exciting.

GILBEY: How long were you there for?

DIANA: An hour and a half . . . and they were so sweet. They wanted their photographs taken with me and they kept hugging me. They were very ill, some of them, some no legs and all sorts of things.

Is this the real Diana talking at last? I like to think so. It's a sad little vignette. This was her childhood home on the edge of a royal park where a sensitive little girl was taken to play with the royal children in the Big House. Now she is in the great house herself, a princess surrounded by rotten intrigue. The hugs she craves have to come from strangers or inconsequential diddlers like Gilbey. The story undercuts her attempts to come off as a confident power woman. So does the forlorn dependency she shows on the readings of astrologers. 'Anything you want you can get next year,' she repeats to Gilbey as one penetrating prediction. And when she talks about the Queen Mother it's clear that she still hankers for the senior royal's approval.

'His grandmother is always looking at me with a strange look in her eyes,' she tells Gilbey. 'It's not hatred, it's sort of interest and pity mixed into one. I am not quite sure. Every time I look up she's looking at me then smiles and looks away . . . I don't know what's going on.' It's piquant to speculate. The shrewd matriarch was probably thinking something on the lines of, 'Such a beauty, but so mixed up, poor girl. How on earth do we bring her under control?' Or, 'Charming, yes. Almost as good with the public as me. If only she were just a *little* less dim.' Or, 'What a shame she lets the mistress worry her. So *unnecessary*.' Later, Diana returns obsessively to the Queen Mother's scrutiny. With a sad hopefulness, she assures Gilbey that what she sees in the old lady's eyes is 'affection. Affection. It's definitely affection. She's sort of fascinated by me.' Which she probably was. She had no doubt heard that Diana had pushed her stepmother downstairs and wondered where the next explosion would come from. Because, assuredly, one was on the way.

Colder eyes than the Queen Mother's were taking stock of the Princess of Wales, for, as we know now, her suggestive relationship with James Gilbey was being observed and recorded. In the hue and cry that followed exposure of the Squidgygate tape, the fable was that it originated with a couple of people playing around with scanning receivers who just happened to tune in to one of 220 million mobile calls.

The apparent eavesdroppers were Cyril Reenan, a retired seventy-year-old bank manager, and Jane Norgrove, a twenty-five-year-old typist. They were in the same county, though unknown to each other. Reenan's home was in the rural town of Abingdon, Oxfordshire, and Norgrove's was seven miles up the road, in Oxford. Reenan, the first of the eavesdroppers to contact the press, has said he was highly nervous on hearing the voices, and his first impulse was to warn Diana. (He had received a small award from her Charities Trust for work with disabled children.) His second impulse, this being a story of almost universal bad faith, was to sell his tape for £6,000 to the *Sun*, a sum he later realised to be a rip-off.[32]

The tabloid responded to his call by dispatching Stuart Higgins, a royal correspondent, and subsequently editor of the paper. Higgins met Cyril Reenan at Didcot station, ten miles south of Oxford, on 8 January.

'We put the cassette in and listened to it almost mesmerised for twenty minutes,' Higgins said later. 'The content was so explosive we knew we had a major, major story.'[33] Higgins deduced that the James Diana was talking to was Gilbey, and confronted him outside his Lennox Gardens home. 'He went completely white, got in his car, and drove off. Clearly we had the right man.'[34] Gilbey immediately alerted the Princess. She was panicked. Evidence that she had been unfaithful to Charles was a hostage to fortune in any upcoming divorce wars, especially the explosive exchange that went:

DIANA: I don't want to get pregnant.
JAMES: Darling, that's not going to happen. All right?
DIANA: (chuckle) Yeah.
JAMES: Don't think like that. It's not going to happen, darling, you won't get pregnant.[35]

This was perilous indeed for the mother of a future king. Diana's leverage with the royal family depended on the adoration of the public and the widespread sentiment that she had been wronged. Notions of royal bastards and Gilbey chatting about a randy forthcoming reunion with Diana would shift public sympathy back to Charles. (Not long afterwards, the News of the World began receiving cut-and-paste notes alleging an affair between Charles and Camilla.)[36]

Strangely, after the Higgins–Gilbey confrontation, days passed, then weeks, then months – and the Squidgygate tapes did not appear. The Sun decided that Reenan's tape was too hot even for them. Scurrilous rumours are one thing, but hard evidence that the sweetheart of the British public was not all she seemed in the virtue department was thought to be a commercially risky proposition, one that might also expose the paper to prosecution for unlawful interception. Higgins hid the tape at home. Meanwhile, tales of its explosive content circulated as Fleet Street folklore. When Andrew Knight took over as chairman of the Murdoch newspaper group in mid-1990, he told me, he would occasionally get from Kelvin MacKenzie and Stuart Higgins 'knowing looks and half-remarks about dynamite evidence they had stashed away somewhere. I frankly never pushed to know more at that stage.'[37] Despite the absence of headlines through 1990 and into 1991, the Princess continued to be deeply uneasy – not least because, according to James Colthurst, she did not believe for a minute that the scanning of the call was accidental. She was right.

The analog mobile phone systems of the eighties were highly vulnerable to interception by amateur scanners. From analysis of the radio signals embedded in the Charles–Camilla tape, there is little doubt that it was genuinely recorded off air. In his memoir *Dogs and Lampposts*, Richard Stott, editor of the *Daily Mirror*, where the tape eventually was published, says it was made by a 'Scouser who had had a few pints of lager and a curry and decided he would test out his latest gadget, an electronic homing device that picks up cellnet signals'.[38] The Prince was very close to a cellular transmitting station just outside the country home in Cheshire where he was staying and his voice was immediately recognisable.

'This bloke was reading a speech,' said the lager-and-curry guy, 'and I didn't pay too much attention until I realised it sounded very like Prince Charles. That's when I decided to record it and straight away he started out with all this stuff. I couldn't believe it.'[39]

In short, the Camillagate tape, like a lot of things in Prince Charles's life, was just bad luck. The recording of Diana's conversation is altogether different. Cellnet said its base site in Abingdon, the only one from which Reenan might have picked up Gilbey's mobile signal, was not commissioned until 3 March 1990, six weeks after the conversations.[40] It is to be expected that Cellnet would be eager to defend the integrity of its service, but a detailed analysis of the tape itself, which the *Sunday Times* supplied to two communications experts – John Nelson, of Crew Green Consulting, Shrewsbury, and Martin Colloms, of Sony International – independently confirmed Cellnet's claim that Reenan could not have recorded the call. John Nelson told me he was so puzzled that he went to Reenan's home in Abingdon – and ended up even more bemused. 'I concluded his receiver could not have handled some of the frequency content on the recording,' he said.[41] Jane Norgrove, for her part, would not allow Nelson, or anyone else, to examine her bedroom scanning set-up, but Nelson's conclusion applies also to her: 'The recording could not have been made by Mr Reenan's receiver, or any other receiver, tuned to the output frequency of a cellular base station.'[42]

'Inexorably,' Nelson says today, 'the truth is, Diana's phone was bugged. That call had to have been recorded off a landline.'[43] This means a direct tap was made somewhere between her bedroom at Sandringham and the local exchange at Sandringham – i.e. within the royal house itself, since Sandringham, like all the royal houses, has its own exchange. Moreover, says Nelson, the tape showed it had been clumsily doctored to make it sound to the casual unprofessional ear like a mobile recording when distinctive hums detected showed it wasn't. Nelson finds it 'mildly surprising' that the media largely missed this point at the time: 'Perhaps the image of a retired bank manager huddled over a scanning receiver and listening in to royal misbehaviour was too appealing to abandon.'[44]

But who did the spying at Sandringham? Britain is not without its Philip Marlowe, private detectives ready and willing to intercept calls from local loops on behalf of high-rolling clients. All that is required is knowledge of the fixed target number, a listening position and a connection to a recorder.[45] The usual leaking brigade of below-stairs Palace trolls might have been able to do that, but none of them would have had the specialised technical knowledge or the sophisticated equipment required for doctoring the tape. Given the duty of the government's domestic intelligence agency MI5 to protect the royal family and the throne, it is plausible that MI5 officially, or elements within it quasi-officially, conducted a bugging operation on behalf of the monarchy – which is not the same thing as saying the bugging was done at the request of the royal family. Senior members of the Palace staff might well have seen the Princess as a loose cannon, imperilling the monarchy itself. Once it became known that the Camillagate tape existed and was being shopped to the tabloids, there was certainly a motive to get out a tape confirming that the Princess, too, had been unfaithful. Lord Rees-Mogg, the former editor of *The Times*, who knows his way around Whitehall and Westminster, told me he thinks that each of the leaks came from the supporters' clubs of the two parties within the intelligence community. ('But that was denied at the time,' he added, 'and I have no proof.')[46] On this conjecture, dissidents in MI5 who sympathised with Diana put Camillagate into circulation and supporters of Prince Charles released Squidgygate with or without his knowledge.

I am not all that impressed with any of the official denials in this rum business. The then Home Secretary, Kenneth Clarke, told reporters at the time that the idea of MI5's being involved was so wild it was akin to saying that 'the Archbishop of Canterbury was a mugger'.[47] In 2005, Gyles Brandreth, the author of *Charles and Camilla* who was formerly Whip and Lord Commissioner of the Treasury in John Major's government, tried to take it further. He raised the matter privately with Dame Stella Rimington, head of MI5 at the time of the tapings. She told him, 'As far as I know, the recordings of the calls – all, I think, made on mobile phones – were made by one or more private individuals using a fairly standard piece of kit then . . . Mobile phones are more secure now from casual eavesdropping. None of the British intelligence services routinely or in any other way spy on the Royal Family.'[48] Dame Stella's rebuttal is curiously worded: '*As far as I know . . . I think . . . more secure now . . . routinely . . . spy . . .*' Even this late in the day, she is apparently sticking to the amateur scanner fairy story, demolished by the two audio experts. Her language is a classic example of the importance of parsing statements from the security service. When Kim Philby of MI6 was finally exposed as a top Soviet spy, a Foreign Office man defended the denials that had previously been made: 'Oh dear, why does no one read our statements with the care with which we drafted them?'[49] When I went back to John Nelson, he commented: 'The simple fact is that what might be called the technical and forensic evidence [of bugging] is incontrovertible.'[50] There was no doubt among friends of Diana's that she was bugged. James Colthurst went so far as to buy her a scrambler for her phone. Liz Tilberis, the editor of *Harper's Bazaar* who died in 1999, told her husband Andrew she was often aware of 'intrusive click and seashell noise' on the line that suggested there was an eavesdropper. 'Diana would say it's the secret service don't worry. I heard examples of it myself,' said Andrew. 'I'd pick up the phone and hear the line being opened.'[51]

A James Bondian question remains unresolved: how did a doctored version of the landline Squidgy tape reach its disseminators, Reenan and Norgrove? The simplest explanation – or the least outlandish, since nothing in this mystery is simple – is that the eavesdropers-in-chief organised a rebroadcast or rebroadcasts of the tape. When I consulted Nelson about a rebroadcast, he was sceptical. 'From the technical point of view it would have been formidably difficult to arrange,' he said.[52] Yet if Squidgygate was not picked up from rebroadcasting, the scenarios get more and more bizarre. We have to imagine Reenan (in his pipe and slippers) padding to the front door in early January 1990, picking up a brown envelope with the tape inside, listening to it, deciding to sell it, and then spending the rest of his life lying about how he acquired it. To his dying day in September 2004, Reenan insisted that he recorded the conversation at 9.30 p.m. on 4 January 1990 – four days after the conversation's content shows it took place. 'I was not even home on New Year's Eve,' Reenan told the *Guardian*.[53] A delay of four days between a call and its interception cannot be attributed to any known atmospheric phenomenon. The story is so odd that it feels true. Having admitted to the nosy – and prurient – hobby of eavesdropping on other people's private phone calls, why would he then compound the embarrassment to himself by insisting that he recorded a conversation four days after it took place? None of this endeared him to neighbours. His wife commented at the time that all the publicity when the story broke in 1992 was making their life hell and they were ashamed even to go shopping.[54] Reenan later deeply regretted his whole involvement in the affair. In 1993, he said, 'I think I was set up . . . part of a sinister conspiracy.'[55]

What is clear in all this is that Diana's enemies were determined to expose her. Police sources have said that Squidgygate had been rebroadcast 'at least six times'.[56] A year after Reenan's meeting with Higgins, and still no story in the paper, Jane Norgrove, the other scanner, popped up to offer her own recording to the *Sun*. She said she had made it on New Year's Eve and explained the delay in coming forward this way: 'I didn't even listen to it. I just put the tape in a drawer. I didn't play it until weeks later, and then I suddenly realised who was speaking on the tape.'[57] But when she did realise it, a full year elapsed before she contacted the *Sun*, and the newspaper still held back from publication. In early 1991, the *Daily Mail*'s Richard Kay received a cassette in a plain brown envelope with a central London postmark. He consulted his editors and put it away, 'thinking it would never appear in a British newspaper'.[58] Another brown envelope with the tape showed up on the desk of Noel Botham, the London bureau chief of the *National Enquirer*, who finally broke the story in August 1992.

As the sleazy brew bubbled away for two and a half years Diana knew it had not gone away for good. She had two further anxieties: Hewitt's incriminating package of her love letters, still sitting out there, and the news that a scandal-mongering book revealing her love interests, *Diana in Private*, was on the way from Lady Colin Campbell. Campbell had an exotic personal history herself. A white Jamaican socialite, she had spent the first eight years of her life raised as a boy. Her brief marriage to Lord Colin Campbell, a younger son of the Duke of Argyll, had ended in a notorious 1975 divorce case in which he trashed her as a transsexual. (She vehemently denied it and has successfully sued anyone who suggests she is anything other than all woman.) Campbell, however, was an amusing dinner partner and retained enough connections to be scarily well informed about Diana's love life. Diana had made the mistake of canvassing Campbell as an official biographer and giving her a number of all too candid interviews but dropped her when she realised she was too much of a wild card to stick to the party line. Her impending book, Diana believed, was now sourced by a number of Charles's closest friends.

The Princess's thirtieth birthday in July 1991 triggered an onslaught of negative marital speculation. Some artful PR on her part, culminating in an especially well-informed piece by Andrew Morton in the *Sunday Times* suggested that she would be spending her milestone birthday alone at Kensington Palace. Charles's camp, furious, retaliated with a leak that the Prince had wanted to give his wife a bang-up party but she had refused the offer. 'This is the latest example whereby the Prince of Wales is being made to look bad through no fault of his own,' an unnamed Charles friend was quoted in the *Daily Mail*'s melodramatic black-bordered front-page take-out by Nigel Dempster.[59] (Diana, in turn, let it be known that Charles was going to invite only his stuffy Highgrove friends.) Diana appeared to win this round. She woke up at Kensington Palace on her birthday to the news that two opinion polls had voted her the most popular member of the royal family. This made Charles more angry still, and there was a sulky scuffle between the two of them over a special performance of Verdi's *Requiem* on 8 July at the Royal Albert Hall sponsored by the *Sunday Times* to commemorate the birthday itself. Diana was on the guest list to attend alone. Then, at the last minute, Andrew Neil, the paper's editor, got a call saying that Charles would be attending, too. They ignored each other all through the concert. As they left the royal box Diana turned back to wave at the audience and there was a burst of wild applause. Neil, who was sitting with them, says, 'Charles stormed out, looking miserable.'[60] Diana chalked up another win.

The Prince saw himself outmanoeuvred at every turn by what he saw as his wife's demonic mastery of public relations. He was correct, but much of her ability to score was owed to her natural sense of how to respond, as against his own jumbo-sized political tin ear. For example, in his ITV interview with Sir Alastair Burnet, Charles was given the option to cut from the broadcast the notorious segment in which he revealed that he talked encouragingly to plants. Despite the pleas of his advisers, he fought to keep it in – and then was puzzled that cartoonists depicted him for ever after in comical dialogues with flora and fauna. His determination to continue with his formal engagements after Prince William was hit on the head by a golf club at school in June 1991 looked like another display of cluelessness. William needed only a minor operation on his skull, and Charles's absence from his bedside that night would have been excused by the public if he had been consoling a hospital ward full of wounded soldiers or even other suffering small boys. But hosting a party of European environmentalists and British ministers at a performance of *Tosca* at the Royal Opera House? That was unfortunate, to say the least. And the next morning's headlines let him have it, 'WHAT SORT OF A DAD ARE YOU?' rampaged the *Daily Mirror*.[61]

Diana should have been well pleased by her domination of the image battlefield, but, typically, she was not. She wanted more than momentary public triumph. She was sure that unless people knew the full outrage of what she had had to put up with from Charles, she would get the blame when the marriage inevitably dissolved. She'd be labelled a bolter, like her mother. As it was, she was regularly infuriated by articles about what Helen Fielding, writing in the *Sunday Times* for 26 May 1991, called Charles's 'extramarital chummery' with Camilla Parker Bowles – as if the relationship was merely a flirtatious fondness for an old flame which Diana had a tiresome problem with. She was convinced that the *Daily Mail* front-page story giving Charles's side of the birthday party incident – that he had indeed offered a party and she had rejected it – meant, as she told James Colthurst, 'the mistress is running the show'.[62] Moreover, Lady Colin Campbell's hatchet job was on the way, and there still loomed the ever-present possibility that one day soon the Squidgygate tape would surface and blow up the Princess's hard-won state of grace. Diana's private secretary, Patrick Jephson, who knew nothing of the Squidgygate recording, recalls that he had heard 'a vague rumour about some tapes but dismissed it as just another among so many ghastly whisperings, gobbets of disinformation, and black propaganda that were by then my daily diet'.[63] Diana could not afford to dismiss it; she knew the 'ghastly whisperings' were true. When you consider how many newsmen were delivered anonymous copies of the Squidgygate tape, it's hard to deny her fear that the establishment was gearing up for a campaign to bring her down.

By the summer of 1991 the Princess of Wales saw the need for a pre-emptive strike. Newspapers alone were too discredited a forum. She must get her side of the marriage out in the form of a book that seemed to come from other sources than herself. Her decision to cooperate with Andrew Morton gave her, I suspect, the same rush of excitement as the night she confronted Charles's mistress at Lady Annabel Goldsmith's party. What mayhem would ensue! What cleansing, purging, bloody murder! In a letter to James Colthurst at the beginning of 1992, Diana wrote, 'Obviously we are preparing for the volcano to erupt and I do feel better equipped for whatever comes our way.'[64] She was about to break the last great royal taboo. She was about to talk.

## Chapter 16

## Rending the Veil

'The last thing I want to do is get up in the morning and read what my bloody crazy wife has been doing.'
– Prince Charles to a dinner partner at Sandringham, early 1990s

There were good days and bad days at Highgrove, but for Prince Charles the worst of the bad might have been Sunday 7 June 1992, the date that the first extract from *Diana: Her True Story*, by Andrew Morton appeared in the *Sunday Times*. The Prince descended for his habitual breakfast of birdseed muesli and home-grown fruits to find the shocking headlines carefully folded at his place at the head of the table where Diana and their house guests were already seated. 'DIANA DRIVEN TO FIVE SUICIDE BIDS BY "UNCARING" CHARLES' – that was the banner across the top of page one. And the subhead: 'Marriage Collapse Led to Illness; Princess Says She Will Not Be Queen.'

In our era, when media is king and celebrity-hunting is the sport of media kings, this is truly what royal training is for: to absorb the most public possible revelation of the most private possible revelations without showing any emotion at all. Diana, this time, could not perform that feat; it was too obvious that she was the source. She made her excuses and beat a retreat from the breakfast table to her room. Charles stayed where he was, impassively reading all the way through the sensational account of his own marital miseries. Then he chatted amicably with his guests and took them for a stroll around Highgrove's garden. Only then did he mount the stairs to his wife's room with the newspaper in his hand. Diana dashed downstairs with a scarlet face and brimming eyes and fled back to London.

The Prince had spent the night before the publication at Stratford-upon-Avon watching the Royal Shakespeare Company's production of *The Taming of the Shrew*. But how to tame this one? All the Highgrove staff agreed that the Morton extracts were much, much worse than they expected. The most damning quotes – about Diana's suicide attempts, her feelings of abandonment, her bulimia – were from the Princess's closest friends, Carolyn Bartholomew (née Pride, of Coleherne Court days), James Gilbey and Angela Serota. Their willingness to be named, Charles knew perfectly well, meant that Diana had sanctioned their indiscretions. 'I could hear my wife talking as I read those words in the paper,'[1] the Prince later told a friend. He passed the afternoon hammering a polo ball for his Tramontana team at Cowdray Park in Sussex and got home late from an unspecified destination having had a few drinks.

In a memo left for Paul Burrell, the Prince banned the *Sunday Times* henceforth from Highgrove's breakfast table. 'I never want to see that paper in this house again! As for the tabloids, I don't want to see any of them either. If anyone wants them, they will have to find them themselves – and that includes Her Royal Highness.'[2] He seems to have stuck to that policy. A literary guest at one of his Sandringham house parties in the mid-nineties says that the Prince apologised at dinner for any disturbance his radio may have caused her in the next bedroom. He had been listening, he said, to a tape of the actor Timothy West reading Trollope. 'I never listen to the radio news or read the newspaper,' he added. 'The last thing I want to do is get up in the morning and read what my bloody crazy wife has been doing.'[3] Diana's grandmother, Lady Fermoy, showed where her loyalties lay by coming to visit Prince Charles at Highgrove. She looked frail and drawn and made no secret to friends that she was appalled by what she had read.

The irony is that the book was now coming out after a year in which Diana had cemented her reputation as an international diplomat for the United Kingdom. Patrick Jephson was toasting his efforts to switch the focus on the Princess of Wales from her glamour – his office had stopped sending out detailed descriptions of her outfits – to her good works. She had performed her royal duties flawlessly. In Hungary in March, she showed how she could combine export-boosting with humanitarian gestures, mixing meetings with dour Balkan businessmen with a visit in freezing drizzle to refugees in a camp on the borders of war-torn Croatia.[4] In India, on an official six-day tour with Charles, she went alone to Calcutta to Mother Teresa's hospice, where she sat on the beds of incurables and wept when they sang a hymn. At the same time, she had become as deft as a twenties movie star sending silent messages. In India, while Charles was in Delhi on a mission for British exports, Diana did not miss a trick. Apprised of the information that Charles had once visited the Taj Mahal and said he would one day bring his wife there, she posed alone in front of the monument to marital love. 'It's a very healing experience,' she told the journalist Judy Wade.[5] The Prince tried to repair this public relations fiasco during the stop in Jaipur. In front of a hundred cameramen and 30,000 spectators and officers of the 61st Cavalry, dressed, the Prince recalled later in his diary, in blue blazers and Hermès cravats, and regimental grooms looking like a 'Raffles painting',[6] at the end of a polo match – and on the eve of Valentine's Day – he advanced on the Princess to plant a gallant kiss on her lips. She moved her head from side to side so he wound up chasing her lips around and kissing her just above her earring.[7] Three months later, on a solo trip to Egypt, she made sure the press got some good snaps of her looking wistful against the backdrop of the Pyramids. It was a lot of fun. Wrong-footing Charles had become her private-public parlour game. Did she really want to endanger a role that gave her such scope for her acting abilities?

There were bad auguries for what a break with the royal family looked like in the fate of the Duchess of York. The two girls had once giggled and schemed about leaping from their royal marriages together. Diana had soon bailed out of that pact, leaving Fergie stranded. The Princess realised her sister-in-law was more useful as the 'canary down the mineshaft',[8] as she put it. The canary was now swaying on its perch. As soon as the Yorks' separation was announced in March 1992, the Duchess was instantly dropped from all royal engagements and eaten alive by the press. Fergie later wrote that her 'public vivisection' was a warning the Palace sent to Diana. *This is what happens if you cross us.*[9] The Duchess's financial future didn't look too bright, either. Her predicament gave Diana misgivings, even before publication of Morton's book. At a dinner for media honchos at Claridge's, with David Puttnam, the Princess confided, 'I've done a really stupid thing. I have allowed a book to be written. I felt it was a good idea, a way of clearing the air, but now I think it was a very stupid thing that will cause all kinds of terrible trouble. I would like to reel the movie back. It's the daftest thing I have ever done.'[10] Puttnam could only agree, but it was too late.

This is always the snag about choosing books as an avenue for revenge. By the time it comes out, the anger that fuelled it rarely feels as it did when first committed to paper or tape. The culture of sound bites makes the fallout more hazardous still. But in the case of *Diana:*

*Her True Story*, it wasn't just sound bites. It was 150 pages of pay dirt that no one could say was a project she was suckered into. From day one, she and Andrew Morton were accomplished co-conspirators.

Why Morton? He arouses such jealousy among royal journalists that even today they tend to describe him with two adjectives: 'lucky' and/or 'dumb'. Ten years after her death, when the heat of newspaper competition has cooled, there is still a reluctance to admit that it was more than dumb luck that caused the Princess of Wales to hand a minor player in the Rat Pack with no exalted connections (his father was a small businessman in Yorkshire) a publishing scoop that sold seven million copies in eighty countries and earned him an estimated £5 million. It wasn't as if Morton's British publisher was much of a lure, either. The imprint he chose was the fly-by-night O'Mara Books, founded in 1985 as a back-bedroom operation in the Clapham home of a renegade American expat, Michael O'Mara, and his wife Leslie. In O'Mara's office today, now pretty much a Diana shrine, the publisher's coffee table sports such choice backlist items as books on boy bands, serial killers and farting. O'Mara, however, was the man for the job. He was nervy enough not to care about enraging the establishment. And so was his author.

Morton was always a loner. Unlike most of the royal reporters, who were monarchist groupies at heart, Morton approached the Crown as his personal cash cow, cranking out softie potboilers like *Diana's Diary*, a hagiographical dash through her day. He travelled with the pack on assignment for the *Daily Mail* and the *Daily Star* but showed a maverick readiness to break the rules of the club. At a royal reporters' holiday lunch, Michael Cole mentioned some of the details of the Queen's embargoed annual Christmas Day broadcast. While the others made merry, Morton snuck off to the office of the *Star* and wrote the snippets up as an exclusive. An embarrassed Cole had to resign.[11]

Morton was not a showboat personality like the *Mirror*'s portly James Whitaker or the *Sun*'s Harry Arnold, he of the hidalgo whiskers. But, at six foot four, he was hard to overlook. Physically, he was almost Diana's type. His boyish face suggested openness until you noticed his eyes, the wary grey eyes of a cop. There is something unsettlingly tough and withholding about Morton. The hero of Watergate might not like the comparison, but the journalist Morton most reminds me of is Bob Woodward. Morton's cultivation of Dr James Colthurst as a source from the day they first met in the canteen at St Thomas's Hospital in October 1986 had some of the strategic patience and cunning of the way young Lieutenant Robert Upshur 'Bob' Woodward, USN, befriended the powerful assistant director of the FBI, Mark Felt – aka Deep Throat – in a White House waiting room in 1970. A further similarity was Morton's occasional practice of withholding a scoop from his papers and saving it for his book. Morton went even further in putting rivals off the scent. In an article published shortly after the Princess's discordant thirtieth birthday, he gave the impression that everything was peaceful and quiet inside the Wales household.[12]

Morton met Diana in 1986 at St Thomas's Hospital on a routine assignment. The Princess was there to open a new CT scanner in the X-ray department, a humble gig for a Royal as wildly in demand as Princess Diana. Morton discovered what really brought her there when he sat down to chat in the hospital canteen with the thirty-five-year-old radiology specialist who had escorted the Princess round the wards. He learned that Dr Colthurst, the affable son of an Irish baronet, was one of Diana's oldest friends from her teens. Colthurst was already aware that Diana was unhappy in her marriage. Their friendship had lapsed from their ski chalet days, but Colthurst reached out to her early in her trials at the Palace. He invited her to an informal lunch in late 1981 with Carolyn Bartholomew at a Chinese restaurant, Mr Wing, near her old South Ken flat, with the sole agenda of cheering her up. 'We sensed she wasn't doing well and that it would do her good,' he recalled to me. 'We found her very subdued. It was sad, the sense that the dream had turned out to be no fun. Her dream had been so powerful.' His doctor's eye immediately deduced at lunch that there was a problem. 'I knew she was bulimic. She absented herself from the table after eating.'[13] Colthurst was one of the circle of friends, eventually led by Carolyn, who would gently steer her towards professional medical help in 1988. 'She was so vulnerable then,' he said. 'You couldn't mention it till she did.'[14]

Colthurst gave not the slightest hint of what he knew about the Princess's state of mind to Andrew Morton, but on meeting him for this first time, Morton immediately began ingratiating himself. The journalist and the doctor took to playing squash on the hospital courts and then retiring afterwards for convivial lunches at a nearby Italian restaurant.[15] At these get-togethers, Morton picked up on Colthurst's message not to fish for information about the Princess, but he took care to water his source against the day he might. In the meantime, he wrote beat-sweetening pieces that were negative about Charles and took her side.

In due course, Diana learned that her defender in the press was a friend of the trusted Colthurst. And she knew that Morton was planning to write another book about her anyway. So it made sense for her to co-opt him to do *her* book – for that's what it would be, down to her having complete approval of the text and making revisions in the margins of the manuscript in her own hand. The beauty of it was that no one outside the publishing team would know the extent of her involvement, because all the quotes would come not from herself but from 'friends'. She wouldn't even speak to Morton himself. All the interviewing would be done by Colthurst who would relay both Morton's questions and his queries when the journalist received her taped response.

It is puzzling why Colthurst, after being so discreet for so long, agreed to become the go-between. It was a dangerous assignment for a minor member of the aristocracy who knew that the book would offend not just Prince Charles but the Queen. Still, he sealed his pact with the journalist over bacon and eggs at a transport café in Ruislip, where he told Morton the extraordinary details of Diana's despair. The mission required Colthurst and the Princess to be so secretive over the course of the next six months that the cheerful doctor arrived at Kensington Palace for their taping sessions on a bicycle and ferried the smoking tapes back to Morton's apartment. Whenever Diana heard a knock on the door of her private sitting room as they talked, she hid the mike among the plump sofa cushions. Given how many hours Colthurst put in on her behalf over the next ten months, some might assume that he was in love with Diana. He even wound up writing speeches for her and advising her on PR strategy. It was Colthurst who, with Morton's help, wrote what Morton likes to call the 'famous hugging speech', in which the Princess told a psychiatry symposium of eight hundred doctors that 'a hug is cheap, environmentally friendly and needs minimal instruction'.[16] But Colthurst's ability to retain Diana's esteem over time very likely depended on their *not* becoming sexually involved. With exuberant eyebrows supporting a brainy forehead, he was hardly a typical Dianaman. His qualification for consigliere was not just his intelligence but also the protective fondness he felt for the trapped Princess whom he had known as a girl.

Diana needed one final reassurance before she took the plunge with Morton: she wanted to consult an astrologer. Felix Lyle was helpfully provided by Colthurst's wife Dominique, who happened to be an astrologer herself. Lyle read Diana's chart in the upstairs bedroom of the Colthursts' house in Fulham. No prizes for what he saw in her future during their two-hour seance. 'I said, "Well, there's scandal here,"' Lyle told film-maker Philip Craig. 'Neptune was playing a devious game and also Pluto was playing a very strong role . . . if this is what's happening anyhow, I might as well facilitate it. And we smiled and said, "Well, that's it, then. The book is going ahead."'[17] When Lyle got home, Colthurst called him to find out how it went. 'I've got the whole thing rolling,' Lyle told him.[18] Neptune's game may have been devious indeed, but it had nothing on Lyle's.

Colthurst feels there was an unmistakable sense of relief in Diana's unburdening.[19] Early in their conversations he asked Diana to let him know if there was something she didn't want to talk about, but that was never the case. Indeed, he says today, his role was mostly that of censor. She wanted to say more rather than less: 'She was one very cross lady.'[20] He dissuaded her from bitterly attacking members of her own family – her mother, her sisters, her brother, and her brother-in-law, Robert Fellowes – whom she believed had done little to help. What she insisted on keeping in was inflammatory enough. On her wedding day she was 'a lamb to the slaughter',[21] crying her eyes out on her honeymoon. Charles's obsession with Camilla had caused her bulimia. The royal family were 'cold and unfeeling'. Between William's birth and Harry's was 'total darkness'. After Harry was born her marriage 'just went bang'.[22] Camilla had 'always, always been there'. 'Rage Rage Rage'[23] when she even thought of her. She punched up the story with extra dashes of drama.

In 1997, three months after Diana's death in a book entitled *Diana: Her True Story – In Her Own Words*, Morton and O'Mara published the full transcripts of the tape-recorded interviews Colthurst had conducted with Diana from 1991–2. Here Morton revealed that Diana had asked for only a small number of revisions in the earlier manuscript before its publication in 1992. One of the few she requested involved an important detail about that incident in January 1982 when, pregnant with William, she supposedly tried to commit suicide by throwing herself downstairs at Sandringham. In her initial version, Diana said it was 'the Queen' who found her lying at the foot of the stairs. Later, she asked that the word 'Mother' be inserted after 'Queen'. The purpose of the change, she told Morton, was to protect Her Majesty.[24] Not so. Although the fall downstairs was real enough, the 'suicide attempt' was a fantasy, a fairy tale – in short, a lie. As noted, a member of Diana's staff confirmed to me, the fall at Sandringham was simply an accidental stumble and tumble, which left the Princess shaking more with embarrassment than anxiety. Diana changed the Queen's name because even she could see it was a bit dicey to include the sovereign of the realm in a made-up story. Given that the Queen Mother (a) had not spoken to the press since 1923 and (b) was of an age when people begin to forget things anyway, it was a reasonable risk that no contradicting statement would follow.

Parsing Morton was a dinner-party obsession for months. The author describes Diana feeling ill and left out by the rest of the royal family at the christening of William at Buckingham Palace on 4 August 1982. On the verbatim transcript of the tape she tells Colthurst, 'I was treated like nobody else's business. Nobody asked me when it was suitable for William – 11 o'clock could not have been worse. Endless pictures of the Queen Mother, Charles, and William. I was excluded totally that day.'[25] This is nonsense. There was an annual luncheon planned for the Queen Mother's eighty-second birthday which clearly took precedent over baby William's pressing itinerary of naps and bottles. The christening was a dynastic ceremony involving all the royal family, not a 'Mums and Tots' group. Sorting out what was true and what was dramatic licence provided an interesting new parlour game.

Diana was thrown into a panic when she learned that Lady Colin Campbell's tell-all book, *Diana in Private*, was due to come out shortly before Morton's and might steal her thunder. At just the right moment, however, a story came along that blew the rival book off the front pages. On 18 March, Morton and Richard Kay broke the news of the separation of Prince Andrew and Sarah Ferguson as an exclusive in the *Daily Mail*. The story was ruinous for Fergie's relations with the Palace. The Queen was personally infuriated by the leak, which later did not help Fergie's financial negotiations. The Grey Men of the Palace were convinced the Duchess had handed out the information herself, accusing her of hiring a PR company to give it to the *Mail*. The Queen's press secretary, Charles Anson, has been described as a man so polite he has a difficult time putting an end to a phone call. It was therefore doubly surprising that he gave a vengeful off-the-record briefing, stating that Fergie was unfit for royal life. The tenor of his comments was so strong the BBC radio and court correspondent summarised the content as, 'The knives are out for Fergie at the Palace.'[26] The Galloping Major was so outraged on his daughter's behalf that he called Robert Fellowes, the Queen's private secretary, and demanded a retraction. 'There were prompt apologies but the damage had been done.' Fergie wrote in *My*

*Story*, 'I had been tagged "unsuitable" for royal life and the charge stuck. I was frozen out and not just in the Palace; the wind from all the doors slamming in my face might have knocked me over.'[27] After Diana's death, Morton finally revealed that it was the Princess of Wales who had served up her erstwhile best friend to provide the necessary press distraction. The Duchess never suspected Diana as the source of the leak.[28]

Up to the moment of publication, Diana was involved in every detail of Morton's book. 'If she's so unhappy, why's she always smiling in the photographs?'[29] Morton's publisher, Michael O'Mara, wanted to know when he heard Colthurst's Diana tapes. He asked for proof besides Diana's word that Camilla was Charles's lover. Diana stole a cache of Camilla's love letters to Charles from the Prince's briefcase at Balmoral and allowed her publishers to peruse them as evidence. The team was instantly persuaded that the affair was real. And something else the letters showed – as became clear after Diana's death, when Morton offered remembered quotes from them for his later book – they suggested why Diana could never break the spell. Charles wanted more laughter and less agony in his life and he got that, as much as sex, from his mistress. In one letter Camilla apologised for breaking into gibberish when her husband, Andrew Parker Bowles, interrupted a secret phone call she was on with Prince Charles. 'The erstwhile Silver Stick appeared through the door looking like a furious stoat – pity they did not stuff him,'[30] she wrote. And at forty-five she signs herself 'your devoted old bag',[31] which is pretty endearing when your lover's wife is one of the most celebrated beauties in the world. The letters show a private understanding that sounds as if it was a lot more fun for Charles than his relationship with the woman depicted in such earnest Mortonisms as 'Diana went for colonic irrigation to deal with her inner rage', or the quote from Oonagh Shanley-Toffolo, who once nursed the Duke of Windsor and regularly visited Diana for sessions of acupuncture and meditation, 'She is a prisoner of the system just as surely as any woman incarcerated in Holloway jail.'[32]

Diana's mythomania was so infectious she could sweep along not only naive souls like Mrs Toffolo but also such traditionally button-lipped types as Bartholomew, Gilbey and Colthurst. Even Earl Spencer was persuaded by his daughter to supply some of his precious photographs of her as a child. Her brother filled in the words about her early years. The seduction of Diana's presence and position was such that the desire to please her overwhelmed all other considerations.

'When she wanted something, it was hard to talk her out of it,' says Colthurst.[33]

Diana's friends cooperated because they believed that she faced a choice – explode or implode. They were right, sadly. There is a vitality of survival in Diana's reckless act that eclipses its narcissism. Her mad courage blasted the Palace out of its frozen presumptions and institutionalised lying. She told the truth as she saw it. Her own lies of exaggeration were still not as great as theirs of withholding. Even today when cranked-up confessionals are the currency of every celebrity cover story, it is still amazing to consider what brass balls Diana possessed. Once upon a time, the royal family had despaired of her fragility, her thin skin, her lack of endurance. That day was over.

In Egypt, the *Daily Mirror*'s photographer, Kent Gavin, asked her outright if she had cooperated with Andrew Morton's forthcoming book and she lied through her teeth. 'Absolutely not.'[34] At this point she was already deeply involved in the serial arrangements. Andrew Neil, the editor of the *Sunday Times*, her first choice, did not believe publisher O'Mara's claims of the book's authenticity. Neil thought it 'fantastical' that the Princess would have authorised her friends to talk, and oddly he could not believe that a woman who cared so much about her appearance would inflict herself with bulimia.[35] So passionately did Diana want the imprimatur of the *Sunday Times*, rather than the flashy treatment of her favourite tabloid, the *Daily Mail*, she asked her friend Angela Serota to volunteer assurances of authenticity to Andrew Knight, the chief executive of News International, the newspaper's parent group. Andrew Neil (who had no idea of the extent of Diana's collaboration) put on a team to check it all out as far as possible and, when satisfied, won the rights for £250,000. (Ironically, the *Mail* and its editor, David English, decided, essentially, that they didn't want the aggravation. They made a nominal bid – what Morton calls a 'fuck-off offer' – of only £70,000.) As the day of publication approached, Neil got a call from Rupert Murdoch, warning him of the coming flak from the establishment. Murdoch – as republican in British terms as he is republican in American – didn't care much whether Neil published Morton or not, or whether the royal family would like it or not. But he knew from his early days as a Fleet Street press baron in the 1970s, when he trashed the sanctified former MP John Profumo, what it was like to get on the wrong side of the establishment. 'They will try to destroy you,' he told Neil on the phone from New York. 'Be careful:

they are not nice people and you are about to become their number one enemy.'[36]

Not quite. That privilege was reserved for HRH the Princess of Wales. It is worth reflecting that the girl taking the monarchy on in such outrageous fashion was not a starlet or a socialist but the descendant of a long line of courtiers, including her father. In 1953, the Palace had sent Johnnie Spencer, in his capacity as the Queen's equerry, to Kingston, Jamaica, to help with preparations for the visit of the young Queen Elizabeth II and the Duke of Edinburgh on their tour of the British Commonwealth. One of the Earl's tasks was to give lessons in royal etiquette to the staff of the Captain General and Governor-in-Chief of Jamaica, Sir Hugh Foot. Sir Hugh's son Oliver remembers those lessons well. Earl Spencer taught staff and children alike never to finish eating before the Queen, never to address Her Majesty first, and always to bow with a small nod of the head rather than a vulgar full genuflection. His daughter's decision to blow her stack to Morton was stupefying not just to the Prince of Wales and the court but because of all the ancient believers in the codes of loyalty to the monarch. No wonder the collective imagination of a people whose King beheaded Anne Boleyn persists in believing there is a reason Diana ended up dead.

Earl Spencer was so fond of his youngest daughter he would have supported her to the bitter end. Perhaps it's just as well he didn't have to. On 29 March 1992, one day before he was due to give an interview to Morton (and four months before the book's publication), the Earl died of a heart attack at age sixty-eight. Diana was skiing with the boys and Prince Charles in Lech in Austria. Her attitude to her husband was so hostile by this time that the Prince cravenly assigned the role of breaking the news to her to Ken Wharfe. Wharfe nursed the saddest of misgivings about the forthcoming scene, which he felt belonged within the intimacy of married partners. He found the Princess in her suite at the Arlberg hotel. Gently, he sat her down, told her that her father was gone, and held her in his arms while she wept. 'Oh my God, Ken,' she sobbed. 'Oh my God, what am I to do?'

At that moment, wrote Wharfe, 'she looked like a lost little girl who has suddenly been made to realise that she is alone in the world'.[37] Those were dangerous feelings for Diana to have: the lost little girl only knew one way to behave. She fought furiously with Charles about his insistence on adhering to the formality of returning home at her side for the Earl's funeral – a gesture of decency, imperative for the Prince, which she saw only as rank hypocrisy, as fake togetherness for the cameras. The service in the Church of St Mary the Virgin in Great Brington, near Althorp, had, noted *The Times*, 'a sense of the feudal',[38] a reminder that Diana's aristocratic lineage was longer than that of the resented Prince who sat next to her. Her father's ashes, placed in the family vault, represented the twentieth generation to lie there beneath four hundred Spencer coats of arms and a ceiling resplendent with banners. Lord St John of Fawsley, the former Tory Arts Minister and a friend of Raine's, delivered the eulogy: 'He was in many ways not a twentieth-century figure, not even a nineteenth-century one, but an illegal immigrant from the eighteenth century, when the aristocracy lived fully and at ease with their neighbours. He was the perfect gentleman, but one never afraid to speak openly about his emotions. The words of love were on his lips.'[39] In what must have been for Diana a bitter-sweet evocation of her wedding at St Paul's Cathedral, the oak coffin, surmounted by a spray of daffodils, was borne out to the familiar strains of 'I Vow to Thee My Country'. Her bouquet of lilies and sweet peas bore the invocation 'I miss you dreadfully, darling daddy, but will love you forever. Diana.'[40]

It had taken a final word from the Queen herself for Diana to accept Charles at her side, the clincher to Wharfe's persuasive point that it was what her father would have wished.[41] No one was empowered to make the opposite point on the late Johnnie Spencer's behalf, however, when Diana and her brother Charles, now the 9th Earl Spencer, wreaked their revenge on their father's beloved second wife. The Princess and Raine, who had sat on opposite sides of the church at the funeral, walked out supporting each other, but this was just for appearances. On 31 March 1992, a mere two days after her husband's death, Raine had been thrown out of Althorp by the new Earl. The Dowager Countess Spencer was forbidden to remove a single object from the house unless she could provide proof of purchase, and all her personal staff members were immediately fired. For Diana, the suppressed hurts of her childhood merged with those of her marriage. Johnnie and Raine's biographer Angela Levin tells us how the Princess kept vigil in the master bedroom as Raine's maid, Pauline Shaw, packed the Countess's clothes in four Louis Vuitton suitcases. Alas for Raine, the embossed S on the luggage caused Diana to determine that the suitcases, too, were Spencer possessions. She ordered that Raine's voluminous designer wardrobe be hastily unpacked and stuffed instead into black plastic bin bags. Her brother Charles then helpfully kicked the bags down the stairs. A member of staff who witnessed this appalling scene told Levin that Diana's brother 'had kept his anger pent up for so long that he grabbed possession after possession and threw them down. I think it made him feel much better.'[42] How intemperate these Spencers were under their easeful charm, how steeped in fury!

The Morton book was Diana's most elaborately mounted expression of choreographed rage. She made everyone sweat as the deadline approached. The Queen's press spokesman assigned to the Prince of Wales, Dickie Arbiter, the Prince's private secretary, Richard Aylard, the Queen's private secretary, Robert Fellowes, and her assistant private secretary, Robin Janvrin, and even the Princess's own private secretary, Patrick Jephson, dreaded what was about to break. Vivienne Parry, Diana's friend from the Birthright Trust, was with her at an event a couple of days before publication and found her twitchy and distracted. But even then Diana showed her redeeming gifts. 'You could see that she was unhappy,' Parry says, 'and yet I always remember on that day she met a lady who'd had an enormous amount of miscarriages who burst into tears, overwhelmed by the whole experience, and all her sadness just came pouring out, and Diana suddenly switched from being that person who was worried about her own future to being a person who was incredibly compassionate. She was able to home in on them and get to the core of them in a way which was extraordinary.'[43]

It was especially extraordinary, given what her actions had orchestrated at the Palace and at Highgrove. Transcripts of an interview *Sunday Times* editor Neil gave promoting Morton's book – 'Diana believes she will never be Queen' – spewed out of the fax machine at Highgrove under Paul Burrell's desk in the butler's pantry. They had been sent to Charles by one of his alarmed friends, Lord Romsey, from his house, Broadlands, in Hampshire. Burrell's memoir states, 'I saw the word *Broadlands* first. Thought, Romsey. Thought, Trouble.'[44] Twice in the last weeks before the Morton publication, Romsey had come to Highgrove for intense private discussions with the Prince over dinner. The Saturday before newspaper publication was a day of near panic. The phones at Highgrove rang all day. Richard Aylard felt that the Palace had to put out a pre-emptive statement formally disassociating Diana from Morton's book. Patrick Jephson read a draft to her. She refused to sign it. Robert Fellowes placed a call to the *Sunday Times* demanding to know the book's contents. He was blown off. Aylard did some briefing of the increasingly frenzied royal pack, trying to cool down the rumours with the Palace's traditional condescension.

'You know Morton – a bit of insight, a bit of invention, and the colour of a tablecloth,' he said.[45]

The storm, when it broke, did more than make the teacups dance. It blew through the House of Windsor and every assumption of establishment consensus – discretion, deference and mutual protection. Its assertion was that Diana wouldn't settle for the system of structural infidelity that maintained royal marital façades of the past. Prince Philip wasn't joking when he called Diana a 'fifth columnist'.[46] The royal curtain was ripped aside, and it had been done by the daughter of a long line of loyal servants of the Crown. Her revelations stirred a leap in republican sentiment that grew throughout the year. If the royal family was as imperfect as every other family in the kingdom it might as well be treated as such – an idea that had implications beyond the soap opera of the moment.

In passing, Diana also outwitted the august body set up to monitor the conduct of the press. Lord McGregor, chairman of the Press Complaints Commission, prepared a denunciation of the 'odious exhibition of journalists dabbling their fingers in the stuff of other people's souls in a manner which adds nothing to legitimate public interest in the situation of the heir to the throne'.[47] He checked what he was about to say with Sir Robert Fellowes, who in turn asked Diana for assurances she had not cooperated with Morton. Diana kept her cool. She lied to Fellowes, ardently denying her collusion. Lord McGregor unleashed his thunderbolt – and then was made to feel a bloody fool when Diana in the same week publicly visited the Fulham home of the book's oft-quoted source, Carolyn Bartholomew, to show support for the content. The press was tipped off, by Diana via Morton, to send a photographer to capture her being greeted by Carolyn at the door of the house. Fellowes – who juggled the impossible dual role of being Diana's brother-in-law as well as the Queen's private secretary – was so mortified after the tongue-lashing he got from McGregor for misleading him, he immediately offered his resignation to the Queen.[48] (Her Majesty would not hear of it.)

While the tabloids feasted on the sensation, the serious press got busy shooting the messengers. The abuse visited on Diana's publishing troika – editor Andrew Neil, publisher Michael O'Mara and writer Andrew Morton – was such that a more lily-livered team would have headed for the hills. The charge was led by what Neil calls the establishment bovver boys of the Tory press: the editors and columnists, past, present and future, of Conrad Black's *Daily* and

*Sunday Telegraph* and his weekly *Spectator* magazine. On the one hand, they said *Diana: Her True Story* was fiction. On the other, if there was a fact in there somewhere, it shouldn't be there because reporting it was grossly intrusive. Tory indignation plus sales competition were a potent mix. Morton sweated bullets for Diana's deniability. The *Daily Telegraph*'s patrician editor, Sir Max Hastings, denounced Morton as unfit to 'play the piano in a bordello' and dismissed the *Sunday Times*'s first extract as 'a deluge of rubbish and a farrago of invention. It lacked a single reliable fact.' Sir Peregrine Worsthorne, the bow-tied columnist and former editor of the *Sunday Telegraph*, whose shock of white hair is easily mistaken for a powdered wig, declared himself of the opinion that Neil should be horsewhipped for running Morton at all. The tweedy historian Charles Moore, editor of the *Spectator* (and later of the *Sunday Telegraph* and *Daily Telegraph*), revised the definition of journalism on *Newsnight* by decreeing that when writing about the royal family 'journalists should use hypocrisy and concealment'. This was a gift to an editor as pugnacious as Andrew Neil. He could cast himself as a defender of the freedom of the press with the riposte that he did not think it was his job to be a propagandist for the establishment. While he was about it, Neil, on an ITN news debate, ripped the fruity face off the disbelieving royal apologist and Raine friend, Lord St John of Fawsley, by flourishing a corroborating statement from James Gilbey: 'The Princess discussed with me, on numerous occasions, her attempted suicides, as she has done with other close friends.'[49]

Providentially for Diana, the debate over her story had been hijacked by pompous men. Many were moved to her side of the aisle by the condescending smugness of the Tory bovver boys' dismissals. With unseemly speed, because this is England, it all became about class. Hugh Montgomery-Massingberd dismissed Andrew Morton as a 'tabloid vulgarian from Leeds'. Old Etonian Philip Zeigler called the six-foot-four author 'a little hack'.[50] In the *Spectator*, Henry Porter described Morton as 'a man who is more interested in money than the survival of the Royal Family. As they say in Yorkshire, he is "hard on a penny" and is remembered by friends on the Mirror Group training scheme and at Sussex University as being a socialist with unsophisticated tastes.'[51] Even though Max Hastings, in his 2002 memoir *Editor*, had the grace to admit that his accusations of invasiveness turned out to be wrong, it's clear that even now snobbery plays a determining role in his judgement of Morton's credibility. 'I dismissed without serious thought,' he writes, 'the notion that the Princess of Wales might have trafficked with such a man, far less told him her secrets.'[52]

With her flawless sense of timing, the Princess cried at just the right moment to deflate the hot-air balloons. On a visit to Merseyside on 12 June, she was greeted by thousands of sympathetic fans: a woman reached out to stroke her face in solidarity. The gentleness of the gesture was Diana's cue to break down and weep. The tears, when they flowed, were genuine. Could no one see that this was not about media ethics or royal umbrage – it was about *her pain*? Diana was so lost in her own drama that she honestly believed – as James Colthurst confirmed to me – that once Charles (and the Queen and Prince Philip) was forced to read the naked truth, his overriding feelings would be not rage, but remorse. She had been so long in her private panic room she thought this deafening public scream would solve the matter once and for all. It was her pattern, the belief that a single volcanic act could fix everything. Diana was not a strategist. She was a tactician. She did not plan for the day after.

As it was, Diana had crossed a Rubicon with the Morton book. Her husband was the future King, not a guest on a touchy-feely talk show. Until he read the extracts, the Prince had hung on to the forlorn hope that Diana's friends, rather than Diana herself, had been out of line.[53] After the debacle in Jaipur, when she turned away from the kiss of the Prince, he had become so worried about his marriage that he had consulted the legal eagle Lord Goodman, the grand panjandrum of establishment secrets, about a possible separation. He had also talked to the Queen, who advised him to persevere for six months. Morton's revelations derailed that notion. In the Prince's world, infidelity, especially his own, was one of marriage's forgivable crimes. Talking to the press was not. The extent of Morton's knowledge forced him to recognise that the betrayal was his wife's. Their marriage was effectively over.

Diana met with Charles at Kensington Palace on 8 June to have the first real conversation about the state of their marriage. 'He's agreed, he's agreed!' she told Colthurst immediately after the meeting, referring to a separation. 'I've never heard her so ebullient,' he wrote in his journal. 'She was out of control with excitement.'[54]

But was separation what she really wanted? Diana had not really looked beyond her overwhelming desire to have her pain acknowledged. The trouble was that Diana never really thought about *process*. She had the girlish assumption that complex realignments could be achieved by simply making your wishes known. She thought of separation as freedom with her HRH and royal privileges intact, as being allowed to date without hiding, as keeping the good bits of being a princess and doing her own global thing without Charles around to cramp her style. She did not factor in the power of royal disapproval and its consequences.

On 15 June, the day after the *Sunday Times*'s second extract (headline: 'I DID MY BEST'), Diana experienced an ominous confrontation with the Queen, Prince Philip and Prince Charles together at Windsor Castle. It left Diana, Colthurst wrote in his diary, 'shaken rigid'.[55] It was one thing notionally to take on the heir to the throne and the Palace hierarchy, another to be ushered into the Monarch's presence and be made to feel the full gravity of what she had done. The Duke of Edinburgh charged her with lying all along about collusion with Morton. 'Philip angry, raging, and unpleasant,' Colthurst recorded in his journal after a call from Diana. 'Charles wouldn't raise with Diana about a "parting of the ways," even when she urged him to. He just stood there absolutely stum . . . He couldn't speak for himself when his parents were present. His physical proximity leaves her cold.'[56] The Princess told Paul Burrell: 'Mama' – as she sometimes called the Queen – 'despaired as she listened to me. I think she aged at that time because all I seemed to be doing was relaying to her my anguish.'[57] In truth, her copious weeping was puzzling to the Queen. Philip asked Charles to explain what was upsetting Diana now, to which Charles showed how suspicious he had become towards his wife by replying in exasperation: 'What? And read it all in the newspapers tomorrow? No, thank you.'[58]

According to Burrell, Diana told the Queen and Prince Philip that she had tried to be civil to Charles but 'she had come up against a stone wall and, regrettably, she felt separation was the only answer . . . A trial separation. Not a divorce,' says Burrell. 'She wanted freedom. Not a severance of ties.'[59] She also made it crystal clear how much she detested Camilla Parker Bowles.

The Queen recycled her favourite remedy, a six-month cooling-off period. A split at this stage would not be countenanced. According to Burrell, 'Both the Prince and Princess were told that they must learn to compromise, be less selfish and try to work through their difficulties, for the sake of the monarchy, their children, the country and its people.'[60] Philip, still fuming, told Diana he knew about her treachery because tapes existed of her phone discussions with the *Sunday Times* regarding where to place the serial rights. And if she didn't believe him, the recording would be sent to her the next day.[61]

Diana was rattled. Was Philip bluffing that she was under surveillance or, in his fury, was he revealing more than he meant to? In any event, a tape was never produced. Fellowes told Diana the next day that the matter had been dropped.[62] It's not hard to imagine that Prince Philip was reasoned out of it. ('*Sir, may I remind you it is in fact illegal to tape another person without their consent?*' '*So bloody what? Did any of us give our consent to Morton?*' '*I see your point, sir, but she is, well, rather unpredictable at this point and if she decided to, well, take it further . . .*' '*Ah, yes, yes, I see.*') The Princess agreed to have a second marital counselling session with the Queen and Philip and Charles at Windsor the next day. But, flouting every known tenet of etiquette, royal or otherwise, she did not show up.[63]

No wonder the temperature was icy in the royal enclosure at Ascot that same week. Inexorably, Diana was expected to attend. What is remarkable about her sangfroid is that the Palace were still not sure what her role in the book had been – and never would be until Morton revealed it after her death. Diana even rode beside the Queen Mother in a horse-drawn carriage in the royal procession up the racecourse. Princess Anne added to the raging subtext by inviting as her guest her ex-lover, a studiedly convivial Andrew Parker Bowles.

'The atmosphere was dreadful,' another guest told Robert Lacey. 'Absolutely no one in the family was speaking to Diana. They were blanking her completely. She curled up at the back of the royal box in floods of tears.'[64] She was better off than the Duchess of York. Still starring in the comic parody of the main action as surely as Bottom's theatricals in *A Midsummer Night's Dream*, Fergie was not invited to Ascot at all. Instead, she treated the press to a sideshow by appearing in the crowd as an ordinary spectator, hand in hand with her two young daughters, Princess Beatrice and Princess Eugenie, to wave at 'Granny' when the Queen rode implacably by in her carriage. It was a graphic parable of what it looked like to be on the royal outlist.

Diana, however, had consolations unavailable to Fergie. While the royal family withdrew into refrigerated umbrage, there was a surge of support for Diana from the British public. Outside the royal enclosure it was a love fest. Far from rejecting their new sad Princess, they found her a more sympathetic figure than ever. Her struggles dramatised a journey the British people felt they had shared – from romantic naivety to bitter experience. They recognised her courage.

Admitting her chronic eating disorder in a culture and a class schooled from the cradle in denial was Diana's single bravest act. 'Her involvements affected my patients dramatically,' said Dr Jill Wellbourne, psychiatrist and patron of the Eating Disorders Association and author of *The Eating Sickness*. 'One mother had refused to speak about her child's bulimia. She was so ashamed because she saw it as a self-inflicted disease. Once Di had gone public, the mother said to the child, "Oh, look, you've got the Princess Diana disease. No, in fact, Princess Diana's got *your* disease."'[65] A 2006 study by the Institute of Psychiatry in London showed that reported cases of the illness rose to 60,000 in the year after the Princess's revelation in 1994. Since that initial spike, the number has almost halved – a trend attributed to a 'Diana effect' that persuaded sufferers to seek treatment. The letters arrived at Kensington Palace by the sackful, saluting her stand or pouring out a stranger's answering pain.

Her own deadly battle with food ceased, too, for a time. Purging the decayed sweetness of the old fairy story gave Diana a taste of psychic relief. In the days after publication of *Diana: Her True Story*, she told Colthurst that she slept through the night for the first time in ten years.

The same could not be said of the royal family. The impact of the book could no longer be played as a personal issue by the Windsors. The stature of the Prince of Wales and the popularity of the monarchy itself were at risk. A cartoon in the *Sun* by Tom Johnson after Ascot showed the Princess and the Queen Mother driving past a crowd of people, all waving copies of *Diana: Her True Story*. The caption read, 'I can remember when they used to wave flags!'[66]

To help with damage control, the family's most confrontational figure cast himself in the role of marriage counsellor. When Diana did not show up for the second marital summit, the Duke of Edinburgh initiated a tough-love correspondence written by hand that found its way into Burrell's hands. 'Can you honestly look into your heart,' Philip kicked off, 'and say that Charles's relationship with Camilla has nothing to do with your behaviour towards him in your marriage?' Hardly a conciliatory start. Philip meant well but he betrayed hopeless masculine prejudice in telling Diana she should have been grateful (thank you, my liege!) that her husband had, initially at least, given up his mistress. Charles, Philip told her, 'had made a considerable sacrifice' in cutting ties with Camilla, and the Princess 'had not appreciated what he had done'.[67] Diana was so outraged she immediately sought advice from a lawyer. Her friends Rosa Monckton and Lucia Flecha de Lima helped her draft letters back defending herself from being seen as the root cause of her marital problems. Philip's reply – 'Phew! I thought I might have gone a bit too far with the last letter!'[68] – suggests that he respected her spirited defence. The correspondence mellowed and he must have thought he was getting somewhere. Some of the eight letters ran to four pages and ended 'With fondest love – Pa'. One paragraph gladdened her heart: 'Charles was silly to risk everything for a man in his position. We never dreamed he might feel like leaving you for her. I cannot imagine anyone in their right mind leaving you for Camilla. Such a prospect never entered our heads.' It pleased her, too, that for the first time he acknowledged that her bulimia was the source of 'behavioural patterns' for which she was not to blame.[69]

There's a hint of static in his connection with Diana in the letters. If Philip had been thirty years younger, he and Diana might have had something more than a fraught father-in-law/daughter-in-law relationship. Philip was as manly as the Princess was feminine and matched her in daring. Were some of the sparks that flew between them unacknowledged sexual chemistry? The Duke was a fabulous dancer, an attentive flirt, a renegade thinker. Women who work at the Palace, even now, admit to finding him devastatingly attractive. Staffers at Sandringham and Balmoral know that the guest list for house parties must reflect at least one woman he finds pleasing on the eye, and the Princess of Wales, though somewhat on the thin side, was certainly that. An understanding with Philip – undetectable, dangerous and fun – would have been the perfect payback for Charles's subterfuge with Camilla.

The Duke could have taught Diana a lot if she had wanted to listen. At a minimum, Philip had a sense of how hard it had been for Diana to enter the royal family. He had experienced some of the same frustrations. Like Diana, Philip too had once battled the Grey Men of the Palace. He was said to have been very badly treated by the Queen's then private secretaries, Sir Alan Lascelles and Sir Michael Adeane. A Palace insider told Graham Turner, 'The old establishment was also privately and publicly contemptuous of his background. "Is he Greek? Is he Danish? Is he German?"'[70] But it was the German in Philip that was uppermost in Diana's recoil. She had seen enough of his casual Teutonic brutality in his relations with Charles. The gulf – generational, cultural and behavioural – was too wide to span. The Duke believed that the items he listed to Diana – children, a love of opera and an interest in philanthropy – could make up for the profound emotional deficiencies in her marriage.

For Diana, however, Philip was simply the Firm's enforcer. And what the Firm wanted was her to shut up and disappear. Diana could not do that, even if she had been willing to; the press would not let her. Diana knew she was risking the disapproval of the royal family when she collaborated with Morton, but she severely underestimated what it would do to her relationship with the reporters who had covered her for years. The rat pack felt jilted. Their pin-up girl had bestowed her favours elsewhere, handed the ingrate freelance Andrew Morton access his colleagues had been denied. As Amanda Platell, former editor of the *Sunday Express* and the *Sunday Mirror* says: 'When we realised that she had collaborated with the Andrew Morton book we felt betrayed. They were going to get divorced anyway and she was always saying how she wanted to protect her boys, but this would only damage the boys. She was incredibly Machiavellian.'[71]

In another, darker way, though, the pack was jubilant. *Diana: Her True Story* was the tabloid press's Get Out of Jail Free Card. The rumours and gossip round the Waleses became self-perpetuating. After Morton, the war between the couple fed the press and the press fed the war. It engulfed the monarchy. 'The Morton book was cataclysmic for the royal family because it confirmed virtually ten years of the reporting of the kind that James Whitaker, Harry Arnold and others, and Morton himself, had been doing,' said Richard Stott, editor of the *Daily Mirror* (1991–2). 'It vindicated what had been going on in terms of the tabloid papers.'[72]

Beginning in the summer of 1992, Fleet Street declared open season on the Windsors. On 20 August, the *Mirror* splashed the paparazzi snaps of Fergie topless, having her toes sucked by her latest Texan, 'business manager' John Bryan, at a villa in the South of France. The Duchess had been tracked there by a French paparazzo who received a tip she was arriving at Nice airport on her way to a remote farmhouse near St Tropez. The *Mirror*'s James Whitaker was so beside himself with excitement when he saw the 117 photographs of Fergie being nuzzled by a bald American all spread out on the editor's kitchen table that he ate a breakfast intended for five.[73] The front-page headline – 'FERGIE'S STOLEN KISSES' – was splashed in what the Duchess of York calls 'hydrogen bomb type'.[74] The print run sold out so fast that the paper went back on press for another 400,000 copies at eight o'clock the next morning.[75] Poor Fergie was staying at Balmoral when the story broke. She was summoned upstairs to the Queen's sitting room, where Her Majesty sat like a thundercloud with the morning's papers. The ritual of working her way through a rustling pile of diverting reading matter from all sides of the political spectrum with a pot of tea had become a daily torment for the Queen of England. When Fergie backed out of the Presence in a deep curtsy she knew her life as a royal was well and truly over. She flew back to London with her two daughters. 'She faces a long, lonely exile,' a courtier told the *Daily Express* that day, 'and it is cold out there.'[76]

Who tipped off the paparazzo that Fergie would be in that secluded French villa with Bryan? Is there any coincidence in the timing? The intimate eavesdropped conversation between James Gilbey and Diana finally hit the media within three days of Fergie's news bomb. Today, I am told, Fergie believes it was the Princess of Wales who leaked the Duchess of York's whereabouts in France. Except for Fergie's police protection officer, the only person who knew where she was going was Diana – whom, despite all that had gone down, Fergie still thought of as her partner in crime. It makes sense that Diana would leak the information. As we know, she had done such things before.

How the Squidgygate tapes finally made it into print is as murky as its origins. On 23 June 1992, Lord Wyatt noted in his diary a conversation he'd had on the steps of the House of Lords with Lord Hesketh, the government Chief Whip. 'He said, "Charles has been bonking away like mad with Camilla Parker Bowles." I said, "Is there any evidence?" He said, "Yes, plenty." I said, "What about her [Diana's] relations with Gilbey and others?" He said, "Yes, but there is no evidence."'[77] That problem was solved for the establishment on 20 August 1992, when the invisible hand that had been peddling the tape all along pitched it over the receptive transom of Noel Botham, London bureau chief of the Florida-based *National Enquirer*, the closest American equivalent to the Fleet Street tabloids. Once the *Enquirer* had flooded America's supermarkets with the explosive extracts, the *Sun*'s editor, Kelvin MacKenzie, had all the cover he needed to dispatch his deputy, Stuart Higgins, to dig out the tape that had been mouldering for two years in his cupboard at home. The full transcript took up six full pages of *Sun* newsprint – column after column of grey type in a paper not noted for taxing its readers' attention spans. 'We just went for broke and published every word of the tape that we had,'[78] said Higgins. (Actually, there was one notable excision: Gilbey's fugue about playing with himself.) To hear the Princess's own ladylike tones, the public had only to call the Squidgygate phone line, helpfully provided by the *Sun* for thirty-six pence a minute.

Diana was shattered. Marooned like Fergie in Balmoral, she had to listen to the holidaying Patrick Jephson reading out all the embarassing and prurient press coverage from a payphone in Devon. But it damaged her less than she feared. Since the public already knew from Morton that she was a wounded wife (and that Fergie was up to much worse), one boyfriend more or less did not damn the Princess in their eyes. Jephson busied himself ramping up a busy schedule of rehabilitative charity events. The red tops affectionately rebranded the Princess of Wales's Royal Regiment (Queen's and Royal Hampshires), as 'Squidgy's Own'.

Diana was as lucky with the press as Charles was not. The 'Scouser' who had kept the Camillagate tape to himself for the last two years as a party piece suddenly realised, after the Squidgygate sensation in the *Sun* on 24, 25 and 26 August, that he was sitting on serious cash. He presented the Camilla tape to the Manchester office of the *Daily Mirror* in return for a fee of £30,000. The paper's editor, Richard Stott, was so startled by its risqué content he thought at first it was a sketch from *Spitting Image*.[79] He did not publish it immediately, because he was reluctant to throw the Tampax firecracker into the diplomatic round on the eve of Charles and Diana's trip to South Korea in October. The tour was being billed by the Palace as a reconciliation, but it became a prolonged exercise in animosity. Press spokesman Dickie Arbiter, who had gone ahead of the royal couple to Seoul, recalls, 'The door of the plane opened, and they stood there, and I thought, Oh God, we've lost it. There was no contact between them. It was as if an aisle curtain had descended between them.' The images of the Prince and Princess were so expressive of mutual loathing they earned the tabloid nickname 'The Glums'. 'At the military war memorial in the national cemetery Charles's face was creased like a sharpie dog and Diana's had a frozen-statue expression,' Arbiter told me. 'They all used that picture, of course.'[80]

On 11 and 13 November, the *Daily Mirror* ran a teasy two-parter slugged 'Camilla Confidential', using quotes from the tapes as unexplained dialogue. The headlines were bad enough. 'CHARLES'S SECRET BEDTIME PHONE CALL' and 'CHARLES AND THE TAPE RECORDING OF LOVE'. Another World Exclusive.

On 20 November a great fire at Windsor Castle burned down nine state apartments and a hundred rooms. For the Queen, who was in residence at the time with Prince Andrew, it must have seemed much more than a terrible accident caused by a spotlight igniting a curtain in a private chapel on the first floor of the north-east wing. Windsor was her childhood home, her favourite family rallying point. Prince Andrew helped organise the rescue effort as his mother forlornly watched the fire rage through eight hundred years of irreplaceable history. The TV cameras caught the unforgettable image of the sovereign's small figure in her raincoat and wellington boots etched against the eerie red glow of the gutted castle.

It was an index of waning affection that national outrage, not respectful acquiescence, followed the Heritage Secretary's announcement that the nation would bear the castle's estimated repair cost of between £20 million and £40 million. 'While the castle stands it is theirs,' wrote Janet Daley in *The Times*. 'But when it burns down, it is ours.'[81] In an editorial on 19 December 1992, the *Daily Telegraph*, no less, actually asked if the monarchy had a future. 'The most serious threat . . . stems not from the few who are directly hostile to it, but from the growing number who are indifferent.'[82] The weeks of uproar culminated in the Crown's agreement, for the first time, to pay income tax. In fact, the idea had been in the works already, a response to the republican scent in the air, but now the Queen was made to appear to fold under another demeaning press lynching. She betrayed a rare moment of feeling (and even then it was in Latin) on 24 November in her speech at the Guildhall lunch when she admitted that 1992 had been her '*annus horribilis*'. ('One's Bum Year', jeered the *Sun*.) Emotion for a woman raised to express none is rarely attached to the incident that causes it. One of the Queen's closest advisers at the time tells me that her greatest visible distress in the *annus horribilis* was neither the burning of the castle nor the breakdown of her eldest son's marriage but the day the *Sun* broke with tradition and published two days early the entire text of the Queen's embargoed Christmas Day broadcast. 'It was the last straw,' the adviser said. 'There was nothing especially sensitive in it, but you just thought – there's no barrier there. It was like taking a child's Christmas present and opening it in front of him three days before.'[83] The Queen's solicitor Matthew Farrer was authorised to sue for breach of copyright, but the *Sun*'s proprietor, Rupert Murdoch, shrewdly made a fast offer to pay £200,000 to charity. Her Majesty was advised to settle. Royalists felt that a great opportunity for humbling the press had been missed.

As for Diana, who had been the spark for much of the year's conflagration, she did not spend Christmas at Sandringham as usual. Nor did she go to Highgrove. On 9 December 1992, nineteen days after the Great Fire at Windsor, Prime Minister John Major announced the formal separation of the Waleses in the House of Commons. 'Their Royal Highnesses have no plans to divorce,' he said, 'and their constitutional positions are unaffected. This decision has been reached amicably and they will both continue to participate fully in the upbringing of their children. Their Royal Highnesses will continue to carry out full and separate programmes of public engagements and will, from time to time, attend family occasions and national events together.'[84]

The staff of Highgrove were shell-shocked. They watched the Prime Minister's announcement on television. After that, Jane Strathclyde from St James's Palace arrived and told each member of the household to which of the two principals he or she had been allocated. Paul and Maria Burrell, much to Maria's distress, were told they would be moving to London with the Princess of Wales. Burrell didn't want to leave Highgrove either, though that is not how 'the Rock' likes to position things in his book A Royal Duty. 'He didn't want to work for Diana,' Dickie Arbiter says. 'He told Richard Aylard he wanted to work for Prince Charles. Aylard told him that Charles didn't want him. That night there was the annual Christmas charity bash and I walked in and there was Burrell crying into his whisky. He said, "I've been told I have to work for the Princess!"'[85] Wendy Berry lost her job and the house that went with it and was given six months' severance. Diana's private secretary, Patrick Jephson, would continue to work out of the Waleses' joint office in St James's Palace, while the Queen's deputy press secretary, Geoffrey Crawford, would have Diana's PR under royal control from Buckingham Palace. The Princess would be encouraged to develop a public role under the royal aegis – i.e. only with the Queen's consent. She would travel abroad on official visits, but not as a representative of the Queen. As far as Diana was concerned this sounded all right. She had what mattered most, shared custody of the boys. She had fought for and retained the title of Princess of Wales. She did not see then that the agreement was laced with tripwire. Major's statement, for a start, that the Waleses' decision to separate had no constitutional implications brought a sharp intake of breath in the House of Commons. The notion that a princess who now so publicly hated her husband could, in the age of wall-to-wall media, be crowned as Queen consort was palpably untenable. Even George IV locked his despised wife, Queen Caroline, out of Westminster Abbey for the coronation rather than inflict such a charade on himself and the nation. Besides, the last time anyone checked, Prince Charles was due to be head of the Church of England. His marital issues could hardly be thought to be irrelevant to that sacred role. The former Bishop of Birmingham, the Right Reverend Hugh Montefiore, put the boot in right away. 'It would be abhorrent to a large proportion of the English people,' he opined in a statement put out by the Church. 'The question is bound to arise whether the Archbishop would in good conscience be able to crown her.'[86]

And then there was Diana's so-called independence. Did the Princess really expect the Palace to let her develop a rival court, a rival global mission, a rival power centre of influence to the heir to the throne? How things would really work was already writ large in the Christmas arrangements. While Diana spent the holiday with her brother and his wife at Althorp, Princes William and Harry went to Sandringham for Christmas and New Year, with their father and the Queen. Still oddly delusional about the terminal state of her marriage, Diana was mortified to learn that Camilla Parker Bowles was earmarked to receive for Christmas a diamond necklace from Prince Charles, while Diana would get a collection of cheap paste jewels.

Not long afterwards, in the mysterious unstoppable samizdat of scandal, the more intimate extracts of the Camillagate tapes showed up on the desks of news editors around the world. Even today, the Duchess of Cornwall tells friends that Sunday 17 January 1993, when the full transcript was published in the UK, in the *Sunday People* and the *Sunday Mirror*, was one of the worst days of her life. Under siege at her Wiltshire home, she felt abandoned. The Prince was abroad and Andrew Parker Bowles was nowhere to be seen. Camilla had to crawl through the undergrowth at times to get to her front door undetected by the media. There is a picture of her outside Middlewick House in a huge headscarf, holding a shopping bag and looking as if she'd like to put her head in it.

For Prince Charles it was more than embarrassing. It was annihilating. A close friend who spoke to him the weekend the final details of the tape broke said, 'It was a terrible moment. He wanted to be taken seriously, to be given respect as a man. He sincerely believed he had important things to say. He wanted to be thought profound. And in six minutes of private conversation that was nobody's business his reputation was ruined.' Almost worse, he was a fool in the eyes of his father. It didn't matter that Charles had a mistress, but an inability to hush up that he had a mistress was bad form and bad management. Prince Charles started to talk darkly of Mayerling. Only the Queen Mother could talk him off the ledge, encouraging him to show moral courage. 'She is a wonderful restorer of crumbling backbone,' said one of her circle.[87]

Diana pondered her new life as a semi-detached Princess of Wales. She determined to improve her speaking skills for her solo role on the world stage. Peter Settelen, a former soap-opera actor turned 'communications consultant', had been introduced to her as a speech coach by her exercise trainer Carolan Brown. In private sessions at Kensington Palace, he had told Diana that she should 'find her true passion' and talk to him about it. In September 1992, Diana plopped down on the same couch in her sitting room where Colthurst had sat with his tape recorder for Morton – and began all over again for Settelen's video camcorder. As the camera rolled, and kept rolling until the winter of 1993, the Princess unloaded again about the infrequency of her erstwhile marital sex life ('There was never a requirement for it from his case'), her feelings of isolation and, yes, the disruption of her eating disorder. (Settelen made a deal with NBC in the U.S. to air the juicier extracts in 2004.) It's as if Diana had become addicted to her own story and didn't care to whom she told it now.

In January 1993 Diana moved out of Highgrove for good. She descended on the house one evening with her sister Sarah and packed up her personal possessions (and little else) to be sent on to Kensington Palace. The young mother of two owned no property of her own. Her Spencer jewels belonged to her brother, those she had worn as Princess of Wales to the Crown. The two joined Kensington Palace apartments where she had lived with Charles, and from which she refused to move when the Palace tried to fob her off with a smaller one, were the property of the Queen.[88] All she took from Highgrove, aside from her photographs and knick-knacks, were a few charcoal drawings and cushions and the cheap furniture she had brought from her flat in Coleherne Court. The Prince had already begun to redecorate, importing Robert Kimes to remove Diana's cheery chintz furnishings in favour of the rosewood and mahogany of his preferred Edwardian womb. As Paul Burrell served the Princess coffee in January in her Kensington Palace sitting room, Diana wrote a booster memo to herself. As he tells it:

'"Self esteem,"' she scrawled. Ticked it. "Confidence." Ticked it. "Happiness." Ticked it.'

The last item on her list had unforeseen consequences. The Princess had decided she would no longer tolerate being spied on, which meant, except when she travelled with her sons, giving up the safeguard of royal protection.

'Then she wrote, "police" – and put a cross beside it.'[89]

# Chapter 17

## Saint and Sinner

'Stand by for a mood swing, boys.'
      – Diana to her private secretary, Patrick Jephson

Newly separated from her husband, the Princess of Wales set about administering her celebrity like a global brand. Her life was now devoted to tending, promoting and conserving the Diana franchise.

Her office at St James's Palace was like the vestibule of an ad agency, with two huge clip frames filled with magazine photo spreads, all of them showing her triumphs as a princess. Patrick Jephson managed her portfolio of charities with an eye to mixing the contemporary with the traditional, the cultural with the humanitarian. A former lieutenant commander in the Royal Navy, five years older than the Princess, Jephson had been moved from equerry to private secretary in 1991. He was astute and unflappable, and he thought about her commitments strategically, aiming to expunge any lingering perceptions of the Sloane Princess or Dynasty Di or Fergie's gal pal. His admiration for his new boss was not untinged with scepticism. He recognised how canny Diana had become at using philanthropy to enhance her standing with the public and thus her power over the rest of the Firm. 'Royalty is the most amazing conjunction of the idealistic and the self-indulgent,' he told me. 'But I still think Diana represented the better side of the equation.'[1] Sometimes he found himself heading off her more indulgent bids to make an image statement, but if you could get past Jephson into eye contact with the Princess she rarely said no. She was naturally responsive if her heartstrings were tugged and the asker had a link to someone or something she needed. The Dowager Duchess of Norfolk, chairman of the Hospice Movement, said that Diana was so involved with patients that when they eventually died, she would often privately invite their mourning relatives to Kensington Palace. Jephson described the 'mission statement' of the Princess's office as being 'like Disney – to bring happiness to people'.[2]

Diana's lean team of four eager beavers coexisted uneasily in the same suite at St James's Palace as the Prince's voluminous entourage of thirty-five. For privacy, she received her high-powered supplicants at her unofficial HQ at Kensington Palace. A cavalcade of show-business personalities, heads of philanthropic trusts, media leaders and politicians filed in and out of her sunny, flower-filled sitting room. People like Elton John, Gianni Versace and Hillary Clinton were her peer group now. If she was to meet a foreign dignitary and needed a briefing, she could call Henry Kissinger rather than James Colthurst. For financial advice it was not the Comptroller of the Royal Household but banker and taste baron Lord Rothschild. The Princess ran her schedule of public appearances like a brisk CEO whose distinctive marketing concept is the personal touch. Unlike many top people who are directly lobbied, she did not deploy her private secretary to politely renege a week later with a 'remembered' clashing commitment. A former Palace official remarked how she was 'very quick on the uptake. She was very practical when planning something. She would ask realistic questions, like "Where can I change?" She'd remember details and do it well. In stark contrast to her husband, a deal was a deal. She'd ask practical questions, then she'd say, "OK," and she'd remember it. We all adored working for her. Very professional.'[3]

The inspiration for her going global can be traced to an epiphany. After that first visit alone to Mother Teresa's hospice in Calcutta in February 1992, she wrote a note to herself on blue-embossed Kensington Palace writing paper: 'Today . . . [I] found the direction I've been searching for all these years. The sisters sang to me on arrival, a deeply spiritual experience, and I soared to such great heights in spirit . . . The emotion running through that hospice was very strong and the effect it had on me was how much I wanted and longed to be part of all this on a global scale.'[4] When she eventually met Mother Teresa herself in Rome a few days later, the saintly nun showed her pragmatic side, telling Diana, 'You couldn't do what I do, and I couldn't do what you do.'[5]

What Diana did do paved the way for the galvanising celebrity philanthropists of recent years – big-tent humanitarians like Bono, Angelina Jolie, Madonna and George Clooney. Celebrities who work these particular veins are always having to prove something to their beneficiaries: that they're not merely pretty faces yearning to spruce up their images on the backs of downtrodden Africans and Asians. Diana had no such problem. Her princesshood had given her that right from the moment she made her vows at St Paul's Cathedral. What better explanation could there be for her charity than the most obvious one: that she meant it?

She brought something else to her efforts: her own story. 'It wouldn't have worked if she'd just been a grand woman going round doing good works,' was the way her lawyer Anthony Julius put it. 'The pathos of her own position added to it: the extraordinary paradox of this very beautiful woman who had at the same time been rejected.'[6] Diana instinctively understood that in the media age invading your own privacy is a rite of passage.

Sharing = caring: the Diana equation. With the Morton revelations she had forged a visceral connection with millions. She had a fan base, a sisterhood. She had become the Oprah Princess without ever appearing on the rising electronic diva's show. 'Well, ladies, we all know what men can be like, don't we?' That was how she kicked off a discussion group with a circle of battered wives in March of 1993 at a family refuge in London. Her talk in April at Britain's first conference on eating disorders, at Kensington Town Hall, did something revolutionary in royal terms: it drew on the speaker's personal experience. Diana did not actually say she suffered from bulimia, but everyone understood that it was why she was there. When she spoke of the eating disorder as a 'shameful friend' and talked of how feelings of 'guilt, self-revulsion and low personal esteem' could create 'a compulsion to dissolve like a Disprin and disappear',[7] a dry medical meeting became a sensation. Her experiences as a mother brought new potency to the cause of post-natal depression. At a conference on women and mental health organised by Turning Point, she acknowledged the 'terrible torment' of women who are 'continually disabled by the belief that they should exist only for the benefit of others'.[8] The public – acquainted, through Morton, with her troughs of despair after the birth of William – knew that here, too, was something their Princess had endured.

Travel overseas was critical to her strategy of creating an identity not dependent on the Firm. To the chagrin of the Prince of Wales's office, foreign leaders and heads of states all wanted to meet the solo Diana. When she had visited Cairo in May 1992 without Charles, President Hosni Mubarak was eating out of her hand. In Paris six months later, she captivated not only the French public but also the discerning

President François Mitterrand and his wife Danielle, obliterating differences of age and language in an animated, laughing tea party at the Elysée Palace. The Diana team was not wholly displeased that when Prince Charles followed his estranged wife to Paris two weeks later, he made a speech that flopped at home. Sensitive trade talks happened to be going on at the time, and Charles, innocently extolling the merits of French farming methods, was deemed to be siding with the froggy foreigner.[9]

To help her own overseas push, Diana was shrewd in her courtesies to government ministers who could help. Arriving a few days after the Princess in Cairo, the Foreign Secretary, Douglas Hurd, was charmed to find on his dressing table at the embassy a long letter in the Princess's hand telling him what she'd been up to.[10] The rectitudinous Hurd offered a gushing account in his memoirs of the Princess at a banquet two days after the announcement of her separation in December 1992. She bestowed, he wrote, 'that special mixture of beauty and charm which melted men's bones. Presidents, prime ministers and foreign ministers as they dined could make no sense of what was happening in our Royal Family but were content to bask for an hour or two in an extraordinary radiance.'[11] The smitten minister had no inclination to cut off his own or the Foreign Office's links with Her Royal Radiance. He found the Princess not the least interested in politics but 'almost painfully anxious to continue overseas visits with our blessing . . . I was glad, or more accurately, enchanted to give it.'[12]

And help her he did. In March 1993, while the press was relaying images of Prince Charles blithely skiing at Klosters, Diana was on her way to the poverty-stricken mountain kingdom of Nepal, accompanied by Baroness Chalker, Britain's Overseas Development Minister. John Major's Tory government was clearly acknowledging the pulling power of the Diana brand, which was forging helpful new coalitions between charities. As well as visiting lepers and families in remote ramshackle huts, Diana was to join policy discussions with the Nepalese Prime Minister! (She had an especially charming guide, too: the Eton-educated, twenty-two-year-old Crown Prince Dipendra, who in 2001 would express his dissatisfaction with court protocol by killing nine members of his royal family and himself at a state banquet.)

In July, she took off for Zimbabwe for the Red Cross. The Queen blessed the trip in return for Diana's agreeing to put on a show of unity with Charles at a memorial service for World War II veterans at Liverpool's Anglican cathedral. Diana was happy to make the trade.

Zimbabwe was another triumph. President Robert Mugabe, monster in training, was so elated on meeting the Princess he announced, 'She brings a little light into your life.' The ever-intuitive Diana told Ken Wharfe that she found Mugabe 'a frightening little man' who had not stopped sweating throughout their entire meeting.[13] What made the front pages back home were pictures of the Princess in the bush doling out food to children from an iron pot at the Mazerera Feeding Centre. 'Di the Dinner Lady' applauded the *Daily Mail*.[14] Even the cynical Ken Wharfe was touched: 'Those who believe that Diana's work is nothing more than a series of photo opportunities in glamorous locations around the world should have seen this drained, exhausted woman sitting in the back of the helicopter that day and heard her speak of the heart-breaking scenes she had just witnessed.'[15]

Jephson's efforts steadily airbrushed the airhead out of Diana's public persona. The serious broadsheets were beginning to come round. The *Daily Telegraph* hailed the trip as a triumph: 'Africa, until now the undisputed realm of the Princess Royal, has a new champion.'[16] To Lord Rees Mogg, Diana's emergence as a power in her own right was expressed in her features. She was no longer just a beautiful woman. Her nose, he suggested, was 'expressive of powerful will, commanding eyes in strong sockets – a face like Margaret Thatcher's, not of prettiness, but of command'.[17] Diana's magic of course, was that she looked nothing like Mrs Thatcher, nor any of the cardiganned do-gooders who toiled without notice on the same charitable causes. Her thirties were her most seductive years. Lord Rothschild, for one, stood ready to educate her on more than her financial portfolio. 'I wish I could have some luck there,' Rothschild told Woodrow Wyatt. 'Well, you try hard enough,' replied Wyatt, 'but she doesn't like sex.'[18] (Wyatt couldn't have been more wrong about that.)

Diana's charisma and her renewed relevance to the British people scared her estranged husband and her in-laws to death all over again. Without Charles, Diana was supposed to deflate, downsize and turn back into a pumpkin. She was dropped from the Court Circular listing the day's royal engagements and no longer invited to Royal Ascot. The Prince's private secretary, Richard Aylard, told Patrick Jephson that 'ways have to be found' to 'put her in a safe box in which she could dash around doing what she wanted'.[19]

The blonde descendant of those bolshy red-haired Whigs had no intention of obliging him. Still, she was finding it more challenging than she had imagined in her pre-separation bravado. The reality was that for all her global acclaim Diana was frighteningly exposed. She felt the chill winds of disapproval in old-guard court circles and spiteful gossip wafting through the shires. She brooded that bad vibes emanated from Robert Fellowes' office, as well as from Charles's people. The Prince's team was committed to sabotaging anything that might upstage him. Patrick Jephson spent much of his time making lemonade out of lemons. When Diana lost her access for overseas trips to the Queen's Flight, he brokered a deal with Richard Branson, the founder of the Virgin Group, for the Princess to become Virgin Atlantic's first royal customer and get the PR bang of naming their first Airbus 'Lady in Red'.[20]

The opposition never gave up trying to 'put her in a box'. The BBC saw the Princess of Wales as a strong candidate to deliver that year's prestigious Dimbleby Lecture, but the project suddenly evaporated, in Jephson's words, 'to the accompaniment of suitably scathing and suspiciously well-placed comment in establishment newspapers'.[21] Talk of a tour to follow up on the success in Zimbabwe was summarily quashed, along with a projected Red Cross trip to Bangladesh. 'Someone, somewhere was determined that the Princess of Wales would no longer outshine "the rest of the Royals",' the photographer Arthur Edwards, noted darkly.[22] In March 1993, the IRA killed two children in a bomb attack in the Lancashire town of Warrington. Diana was eager to leave immediately to reinforce her sympathetic connections with the suffering on all sides of the Irish imbroglio, first established on her acclaimed walkabout in 1992 in the war zone of Belfast's Falls Road. Buckingham Palace vetoed it.[23] The Prince of Wales was sent instead. The pattern was to continue. In May 1994, Diana wanted to go the funeral service of the leader of the opposition Labour Party, John Smith, who had died suddenly of a heart attack at the age of fifty-five. The Palace said no.

None of this should have been surprising. The Morton book had been a Molotov cocktail hurled at the House of Windsor. Now the Palace was taking its revenge with a thousand cuts of quotidian smallness. Diana started to understand what it was she had lost along with the automatic protection and respect of the well-oiled Palace machine; whatever its shortcomings, she saw how nasty it could be when turned against her. It stoked her anger with Prince Charles. His failure to love her had not only ruined her private happiness, it was threatening her job satisfaction. Damn it, she would have been a wonderful queen. Now she was a princess without a realm, as toilsome a job as running an Internet start-up when you were once co-chairman of IBM.

Her own family didn't help, or that's how Diana saw it anyway. She had been looking forward to doing up the four-bedroom Garden House on the Althorp estate as a weekend retreat; her decorator Dudley Poplak had chosen a colour scheme. The boys loved their rural weekends shooting and riding with their father. Until the Althorp idea occurred to her, it made her uneasy that she couldn't offer them the same country pursuits. The Garden House would have had the added advantage of exposing William and Harry to their Spencer heritage. But in April 1993, her baby brother, now rejoicing in the title of the 9th Earl Spencer of Althorp and the rights of primogeniture that went with it, reneged on the arrangement. He had his reasons. The Garden House was too exposed to provide the right security and he had no desire for his young family to be disturbed by invasive gawkers.[24] He offered her other houses on the estate but her heart was set on the Garden House, a Palladian jewel that had been rented for a time to Peter O'Toole. 'If you are interested in renting a farmhouse [outside the park],' the Earl wrote to his beleaguered sister, 'then that would be wonderful.'[25] She dispatched a furiously hurt reply. It was returned unopened. Later, when relations did not improve, her brother asked her to return the Spencer tiara she had worn at the wedding.

Ranks had begun to close among the creepy-crawlies who vied for the favour of the Crown. Her husband had something more durable than media stardom: he was the next King of England.

'You were either in one camp or you were in the other,' said Lord Palumbo. 'You couldn't really be in both . . . And the tendency clearly was to drive the two people at the very centre of the drama apart . . . and the warfare is total, in such circumstances . . . very nasty and very deep and very bitter.'[26] Palumbo, a cultural power-broker and property developer, had been a polo-playing pal of the Prince until, in one of Charles's more forthright architectural salvoes, the Prince called Palumbo's prized postmodern City of London building 'a great glass stump'. Palumbo's wife, Hayat, elegant in an Audrey Hepburnish way, was a friend of the Princess in her own right, inviting her to cruise on their yacht, *Drumbeat*, and spend country weekends at their estate in Newbury. 'Diana was definitely ostracised by a great many social people after the marriage went publicly wrong,' she told me. 'One morning we were window shopping in Walton Street and bumped into a female friend of Prince Charles's. We were both face to face at the window of a shop and the woman had to curtsy and say hallo, and Diana said, "That was good. She hasn't spoken to me for seven months."[27]

Women who have had to crack London society from the outset are less mired in establishment loyalties. Lady Palumbo is the daughter of a Lebanese newspaper publisher and educated at the American University in Beirut and the Sorbonne. She was only one of a clutch of sophisticated friends and mother substitutes, all with one distinction: they were not British-born. The most durable of these was their mutual friend Lucia Flecha de Lima, the petite, raven-haired wife of the Brazilian Ambassador in London whom Diana had met during the royal tour of Brazil in 1991 – warm, social, loyal, a grandmother of three. She had the time and the patience to listen to Diana's long laments.

There was greater colour to these foreign-born women of the world than the pinched female courtiers who inhabited Palace circles. Diana was a woman of the world herself now, a veteran of at least three extramarital affairs, travelled, seasoned, a mother of two. Hayat Palumbo and Lucia Flecha de Lima were always pushing Diana to get more of an education. Like Jephson, they felt that she could have summoned any brain in academia to help furnish her with intellectual self-confidence. 'She was an intelligent girl, but it was a raw intelligence,' Lady Palumbo said. 'Lucia was always suggesting she get more schooling. Diana would say, "I will, I will." But she never wanted to give it the time.'[28]

It was a pity. With no intellectual resources to fall back on Diana was lonely. Ladies who lunch were no replacement for love. She began to feel paranoid that she had become an object of trophy lust. Her financial adviser, Joseph Sanders, even remarked that Diana worried – without any cause – that even Richard Branson's friendship with her was partly because he might fancy her. It is not surprising.[29] Even Prince Charles's camp acknowledged her allure. Dickie Arbiter told me with wistful candour, 'We would all have loved to rip her knickers off.'[30] To keep her company there was always what she called 'Le Gaget', the tiny vibrator one of the staff bought for her in Paris as a joke.[31]

Diana would come home high from one of her glittering galas or saddened by a draining exchange with the terminally ill and there would be no one to share it with. When she did not have an official invitation she was often spinning her wheels, as the American socialite and fund-raiser Marguerite Littman came to recognise. 'One night Diana called me and said, "What are you doing?" "I am doing a screening of *Philadelphia* for a few close friends." She said, "You didn't ask me." I said, "It's just a tiny screening at a Soho screening room."'[32]

Diana jumped at the chance to join her. Ken Wharfe reinforced the point. 'People have this image of Kensington Palace that there are flunkies and court jesters all over the place and it's buzzing all the time,' he said. 'But at 5.30 the butler, the cleaner, and the dresser go home. It's the most lonely place in the world.'[33]

It was especially lonely now. Prince Harry had joined William as a boarder at Ludgrove in Berkshire in 1992, and Diana was a preposterously young empty-nester. She missed the solace of her children's daily news and unconditional love. For years her schedule had been built around theirs; without them, she was horribly free. 'I hate the silence of this home,' she told Paul Burrell, now transplanted from Highgrove as her butler.[34] Sandra Horley, the chief executive of Refuge, remembers Diana bursting into tears when a child at the shelter gave her a card for Harry's birthday. 'She would sometimes break off a visit to rush up to Ludgrove – "an excuse to see them", she said.' When Diana had to hand over William and Harry to Charles on Christmas Day 1993 and leave them at Sandringham with the assembled royal family, the parting reinforced the reality that her boys first and foremost would always be Windsors. Their mother went back to Kensington Palace and had Christmas lunch alone. Then she cried in the plane all the way to Washington to stay at the Brazilian Embassy with the Flecha de Limas. 'I felt so sorry for myself,' she said later. 'She lived and breathed for those children,' said Mrs Horley. 'They meant everything to her. They were her life.'

But what if she lost them? Her mother's fate haunted her. Sharing weekend access when the boys were home from boarding school meant she saw even less of them than before. It gave her a taste of the emptiness Frances had endured. Despite everything, Diana remained tenaciously in love with Charles – more precisely, in love with the idea of being in love with Charles. The old unfulfilled dream haunted her. She saw it more clearly now that she had grown up. She understood better the pressures of his ceremonial life. She had learned to care about their country, not their country houses. She had more appreciation of what he had achieved with his Prince's Trust. Most of all, there was the love they shared for William and Harry. Diana desperately wanted more children – with him. Patrick Jephson believes that, but for Camilla's refusal to back off, the marriage could have been saved by a workable truce which might have eventually become a permanent negotiated peace. When the Prince and Princess put on that show of unity in Liverpool to please the Queen, Diana made a genuine effort and Charles cautiously responded. The sight of the royal couple smiling and laughing in the blustery wind was an affecting glimpse of a civilised ceasefire.[35]

Diana now realised, however, that by outing Camilla to Morton she had unwittingly done her rival a favour. The revelation locked Camilla further into the Prince's life. The two felt free to be less furtive about a known relationship. As the Camillagate tapes showed, many years of practice had made Charles and his mistress ruthlessly efficient in organising a network of friends who could be trusted to provide them cover. In theory, Diana could do the same, but she was under remorseless scrutiny. And there was the age-old double standard: as a woman, she was even now expected to maintain her aura of virtue.

In a conversation with the Princess, the historian Paul Johnson offered her an avuncular list of dos and don'ts for her post-separation life. Second on Johnson's list, after 'Stop talking to the press', was 'No sex'. That, Johnson told her, was something she needed to come to terms with: 'Other women kept their legs together, she owed it to her public.' However much he sympathised with her view that she had been treated badly, he said, sex was not good for her. 'And it's not good for her image and so forth, and I told her if she thought that was deprivation – well, hard cheese.' Diana, says Johnson, replied gloomily, 'I have to get used to hard cheese.'[36]

But why should she? It was a big issue for the Queen Mother's buttoned-up generation, but wasn't it different for a stunning, soon-to-be-divorced blonde of the 1990s? Not entirely, alas. 'Her celebrity was such baggage,' said Lady Palumbo. 'She could never look at problems evenly as we might. She had to think about them from every angle: what the royals might think, how it affected her fame, her press, her war with Charles. You and I just decide to do things. She had to weigh the consequences with the Queen, with Charles, all of it.'[37] Under the prying eyes of her husband's court and the glare of press coverage, there was little likelihood of Diana finding a new incarnation of her Prince. As usual, she turned to the wrong guy.

It was insanely self-destructive. Diana had begun to fall for the forty-seven-year-old, very married Oliver Hoare in the autumn of 1992. Six feet tall, sexually alert and tousle-haired, he was a dealer in Islamic art and intellectually a cut above the other Dianamen, a graduate of the Sorbonne as well as Eton. Some of his transgressive appeal was that he was a good friend of the Prince of Wales. The romance started when

Hoare offered to act as a go-between for a possible Wales reconciliation, but in a sly rewrite of *Der Rosenkavalier* he himself ended up in bed with the Princess. The complication was not just that Hoare was married with two children but that his wife was rich. Diane de Waldner Hoare, a French aristocrat and heiress to an oil fortune, helped underwrite Oliver's art gallery. This meant that, despite regular dalliances and many promises to the contrary, Hoare was never going to leave home. 'Oliver was naughty,' another friend said. 'He led her on.'[38]

Hoare's chauffeur, Barry Hodge, claimed that the Princess would phone her married lover as often as twenty times a day in his car, with Hoare furtively switching off the phone whenever Mrs Hoare joined him in the back seat. 'It was like a war zone. Diane Hoare is no fool, and she can smell another woman a mile off.'[39] The Princess was dreaming of marrying Hoare, moving to Italy and raising a second family. Her determination to make him leave his wife was as intense as the campaigns she waged against Raine and Camilla. 'Diana had wonderful qualities of heart, but she was terribly possessive,' said Lady Bowker. 'If she loved someone he had to leave everything, including children. Her possessiveness frightened men. Everything became drama.'[40] You can say that again. The Hoare household began to be plagued by scores of phone calls, some as late as midnight, which, when answered, yielded a long, yearning silence and then the dial tone. Mrs Hoare worried (or pretended she did) that the calls were coming from Islamist terrorists who had found Oliver through his gallery. To his supreme discomfort, she insisted he report them to the police. In January 1994, a Scotland Yard call tracer duly tracked the 'terrorist' to four landlines, three from Kensington Palace 'rented by the office of HRH the Prince of Wales' and one from the home of Diana's sister, Sarah McCorquodale; to Diana's mobile phone; and to public payphones in Kensington and Notting Hill. Scotland Yard privately alerted the head of the Royal Protection Squad. Diana was warned to stop. The Princess admitted to her confidant Joseph Sanders that she had been going out at night to make the payphone calls, wearing various disguises and gloves to cover her fingerprints. Sanders exploded. 'You know you're a very silly girl to behave like this and you shouldn't think you can get away with it,' he told her. He called the next day to apologise for his impertinence. Diana laughed. 'Oh, don't worry, the Palace are shouting at me the whole time.'[41] But she did think she had got away with it.

Diana was living in a world of secrets again. Perhaps they were the necessary corollary to her life in a strobe light show. Her disregard for her own security appalled Ken Wharfe. On a March 1993 ski holiday with her boys at the Arlberg hotel, in Lech, she evaded the night's bodyguard by jumping into a snow bank from her twenty-foot-high balcony. Undetected, she stayed out all night, most likely with Hoare, though Ken Wharfe was never quite certain.[42] It was scary stuff. Diana was becoming physically – and sexually – reckless.

Thanks to her daily workout with Carolan Brown, her figure had never looked better, the vestigial tall-girl slouch replaced by a sculpted, broad-shouldered pride. She loved showing off her new shape. At the Chelsea Harbour Club, where she worked out every morning, she flirted outrageously with England's macho rugby captain, Will Carling, even though in three months he was due to marry TV presenter Julia Smith. After Carling and Julia married in June 1994, the Princess continued to seek his advice about her workout regime. It was take two of Hewitt and the riding lessons, except Diana was a big girl now and wasted less time. William and Harry were toted along to Twickenham, the headquarters of English rugby, to watch Carling train, just as they had been dressed up in army uniform to visit Hewitt at Kensington Barracks. In 1994 Carling was happily nonplussed to be invited for a drink at Kensington Palace that ended in more than cocktails. 'I kept looking up and seeing all the family photographs,' he told a friend. 'It was mind-blowing.' To avoid detection by the press and Carling's wife, they sometimes adjourned for the afternoon to Eleven Cadogan Gardens, a small private hotel tucked behind Sloane Street in Chelsea, where Diana arrived through the kitchen entrance and was shown upstairs to find Carling awaiting her.[43]

To take such risks when she knew she was under intense scrutiny amounted to a game of truth or dare with the media. Her relationship with the image-makers who had helped create her had become a love affair in its nasty death throes, a cycle of dependency and combat. On the one hand, she was a master at providing striking images to dramatise the success of her philanthropic missions or to make a point to (and frequently against) Charles. Photographers would be tipped off when there was a prospect of heart-warming pictures of Diana with the kids at Disney World in Florida or at the amusement parks of Thorpe Park and Alton Towers, showing what a great mother she was.

On the other hand, she could not accept the repercussions of exposure. Diana wanted to dictate boundaries to photographers who recognised none. From the moment she was separated from Charles, the nearly all-male corps of paparazzi began to treat her as

disrespectfully as any starlet. The 'paps', as the representatives of this
new breed of freelancers called themselves, were ready to do things that
horrified even the old rat pack: ambush, abuse, bribe, heckle, lie, and
speed through red lights at eighty miles an hour in car chases
reminiscent of *The French Connection*. The more you look at the reality
of what she had to put up with from the paps, the more their argument
– 'she asked for it' – looks like the shopworn rationale for rape.

That reality is well represented in a little-noticed picture book,
*Dicing With Di*, by two in-your-face British paparazzi, Mark Saunders
and Glenn Harvey. They show a shocking reflexive cruelty towards the
Princess they stalked, branding the Princess's futile counter-aggressions
as Di's '"Loon" attacks'.[44]

'Sometimes a Loon attack would entail Diana sprinting towards a
photographer, forcing him to leap out of her way. At other times she
would run at full pelt away from snappers, creating a mad charge as they
desperately tried to catch up with her. But a worse kind of Loon attack
was when Diana just stood dead still, eyes welling with tears, head
down, giving the silent treatment.'[45]

The heroes of *Dicing With Di* gleefully describe the afternoon they
ambushed Diana in August 1993, when she had taken her boys to see
*Jurassic Park* at the Odeon Leicester Square. They had no care for the
fact that Diana had only recently attended with Prince Charles the
funeral of her grandmother Ruth, Lady Fermoy, at St Margaret's
Church, King's Lynn, an event full of emotion and painful memories.
Ruth had never really recovered from the Morton book or spoken to
Diana since, but in the weeks before she died, Diana made her peace
with the woman she had so bitterly disappointed and asked for her
forgiveness. On a day of melancholy summer rain, the Queen Mother
walked slowly and steadily to her seat in the church to mourn the
passing of a woman who had been one of her oldest friends. Now
Diana's daily existence was losing all the accordance of royal dignity
that Ruth had striven so hard to attain. The contrast must have been
unendurable to Diana when the paparazzi got in her face as she tried to
relax with her sons at the movies. She turned on the photographers
with wild anger, says Glenn Harvey. 'Her eyes were fixed on us and then
she let out a scream like a wild animal . . . "You make my life hell," she
screamed. "You make my life hell" . . . the veins on her neck protruding
and her face contorted with anger . . . She then ran to the waiting car
still crying with rage.' The *Daily Mirror* joined in the fun the next day
with a cartoon of Diana as a Jurassic dinosaur, bearing down with

extended talons on two cowering lensmen, watched by her supposedly amused sons. 'Wow, mum,' read the caption, 'You're better than the movie.'[46]

Di in distress was always a big seller. The paps waited like hyenas outside the Hampstead house of the American feminist and psycho-therapist Susie Orbach, author of a fashionable tract entitled *Fat is a Feminist Issue*, who had begun to see Diana in the spring of 1993 for a recurrence of bulimia. If the Princess kept her head down on coming out, they'd yell 'Bitch!' to make her cry and get a newsier shot.[47] When she covered her head getting into a taxi, a Spanish photographer shouted: 'Why don't you put your head up and start acting like a fucking Princess?'[48]

The paps are unapologetic in their admissions that they treated her entreaties and protests as a joke. Glenn Harvey recounts how Diana appealed for privacy for William and Harry: 'Your lenses are very daunting, very daunting . . . the children find them so daunting.' Then he sniggers: 'Daunting. Diana had learnt a new word that day.'[49] Harvey and Saunders preface all this by saying: 'We do not accept any accusation of harassment, intrusion, or invasion of privacy.'[50] But their book is full of proud descriptions of precisely that. Harvey notes that he had no idea that Diana had just learned of her father's death on the day in 1992 when he photographed her coming on to her hotel balcony in Lech. She ran out distraught, sobbing, 'NO, NO, NO, NO, NO, NO, NO, NO NOT NOW!' Harvey admits to 'pangs of guilt' when told why Diana was so upset. He dealt with the 'pangs' by selling every single frame.[51]

If the paps's conduct was inexcusable, some of Diana's behaviour was inexplicable in someone who cherished her personal privacy. The paradox was that the privacy she sought was also imprisoning. Whenever she wasn't out being the People's Princess, she was inside her cage, wondering what to do with all that energy and charisma, which could find outlet only in the adulation of others. This may explain why she would sometimes do things that seemed to court disaster – such as changing the venue of her daily workout from the discreet and handy Chelsea Harbour Club to a gym called LA Fitness, located all the way out in Twickenham and described by *Time Out* magazine as 'the least private gym in London'. Its slogan was 'No hiding place'. Perhaps what drew her there was its boast that patrons could 'get down and cardio funk', whatever that might mean. Diana could have had any number of exercise machines installed in Kensington Palace, or she could have worked out in the gym at Buckingham Palace, which was rarely used except by a handful of sweating footmen. Geoffrey Robertson, who represented the gym in the subsequent lawsuit, believes Diana wanted to 'wow the ordinary people – the dream of kings. Also, there was a palpable frisson when she was there.'[52] The Cybex leg-press machine the Princess favoured was not tucked away in the back of the gym; it was in front of a vast glass wall exposed to a forecourt. Kids who pressed their noses against it like a shop window could gaze on HRH the Princess of Wales working out in a vibrant array of crop tops, thong knickers, hot pants and cut-out leotards.

Nobody bothered her for a time, but the owner of LA Fitness, a dubious New Zealander named Bryce Taylor, soon put paid to that. Pictures of Diana arriving and departing were not enough. Like any sleazy bit player of the celebrity servant class, he saw in the Princess's patronage the opportunity to turn frisson into cash. With a little help from the Sunday Mirror and the promise of a cheque for a quarter of a million pounds, Taylor bought a Leica camera with a non-clicking shutter, hid it behind the false ceiling above the leg press Diana used, then sat in his office pressing a rubber bulb to send a charge of air through an eighty-foot pneumatic cable to get the crotch shot of the century.

How things had changed. Once upon a time a young kindergarten teacher had gazed with a burning face at photos of herself caught with the light behind a cotton skirt that showed off the outline of her legs. Now she – and 2.7 million readers of the Sunday Mirror – saw images of the Princess of Wales with thighs akimbo splashed over nine pages with the headline 'DI SPY SENSATION'.[53] Diana was so appalled she immediately took the rare royal step of suing for invasion of privacy, an area of law whose opacity was designed to enrich the legal profession. If she was reckless, her folly was always redeemed by the coolness of her courage when things went awry. In this instance she was making a smart gamble. Just by suing she would win points with the Queen and with Prince Philip who was especially gung-ho about punishing 'the scum', as he called the yellow press. And if she lost she would have given momentum to the calls for Parliament to remedy the loopholes in the law. She now saw herself as the La Pasionaria of a privacy bill.

Diana's lawyer, Anthony Julius, won a 'peeping Tom' injunction in the High Court against further publication.[54] Editors feared that such an egregious incident would indeed be the trigger for the long-resisted privacy law. But when Bryce Taylor, under legal aid, was given the services of the redoubtable Geoffrey Robertson, Diana was exposed to the risks of a cross-examination that threatened to be discomfiting about the role she had played in enabling Andrew Morton to thoroughly invade her husband's privacy. The Queen herself became concerned at the developing media frenzy over a member of the royal family standing in the witness box. In a deft manoeuvre, a group of friends, reportedly headed by Lord Palumbo, arranged to pay Taylor £600,000 on condition that he hand over the negatives, apologise and keep quiet about the payment. It was spun as a Di victory, although it was the first time in legal history that a defendant left court with more money than the plaintiff. No matter, the headlines were good.[55]

When she was staying on Martha's Vineyard in August 1994, a friend of *Washington Post* publisher Katharine Graham asked Diana if she had ever gambled. 'Not with cards,' she answered, 'but with life.'[56] She raised the stakes every day. She thought that separating with Charles would return her to some romantic notion of normalcy. Now she could see she had swapped the isolation of the Princess in the Tower for the gated community of fame. The dissonance between her private and her public life was destabilising in the extreme. To be as famous for being famous as Diana was invites an uneasy grip on identity. While the world applauded her fabulousness, she still felt 'thick as a plank', with no particular aptitudes, and unable to attract her own husband.

The American deal-maker Teddy Forstmann, founding partner of a private equity fund, was one who was always ready to offer reassurance. She was seated next to him at a black-tie dinner hosted by Lord Rothschild during Wimbledon week in 1994. At fifty-seven, he was unmarried and self-assured, with an athletic build, a baritone voice and an impressive pompadour of tweed hair, attributes which landed him in the 'Hopeless, but Hey You Never Know' section of a list of bachelors compiled by *Quest* magazine in 1995.[57] He sent Diana flowers every week for three years.

'She was so unhappy,' says Forstmann, 'I can tell you this. Diana definitely wanted a guy in her life. She really did. She was still very emotionally involved with the royal family. She lived with such a sense of rejection that when it came to guys she would add up two and two and make six. Oliver Hoare didn't treat her well . . . these smooth guys used her. If I had to give a one-sentence summary I'd say, she was a great mother and very bad to herself.'[58]

For their first date, Forstmann drove Diana to Marlow, near Windsor, for an intimate dinner at the Compleat Angler overlooking the River Thames. 'We were sitting looking out at the water, and I said, "What would you like to eat?" She said, "You choose." So I have to pick a dish for her, and I reach into my pocket for my glasses, and there are no glasses. So I'm looking to my right and holding the menu way out, and she's talking and I'm looking, and she said, "Can we order?" I said, "You hungry?" She said, "No, I'm afraid you are going to set fire to the restaurant." I was so mesmerised by her beauty, the menu was in the candle.'[59] Diana built an escape narrative around Forstmann for a time. 'It's a true story,' he told me, 'that Diana had the idea that we should get married, that I should run for president and she would be First Lady.'[60]

But dreams of being Queen in another country ignored the fact that a man like Forstmann could never be her Captain Wonderful. Diana was looking for a husband who would be confident, affluent and powerful enough to protect her from the press and the Palace, but power players like Forstmann are looking for a wife with the female version of the same – a gorgeous, brilliant, sexually gifted, high-achieving woman who is pliant, undemanding and entirely available for foreign travel. 'The romance never really got off the ground,' he told me. 'We ended up in the right place – friends – for three years.' Even so, Forstmann got a whiff of what it was like to be around Diana's singeing fame the very first weekend he took her out. He was closing one of his biggest deals, the acquisition of the Ziff Davis computer magazine empire, for $1.4 billion, and was immediately plagued by unwelcome publicity. 'I work my ass off all week and what does the *Evening Standard* say about me but "Friend of Di Has a Busy Week" he told Marcie Brenner at the time. How do I get this gossip to stop?'[61]

Forstmann found Diana obsessed with being watched and listened to. 'She had all kinds of theories about who was trying to do the tapping who was listening to her. There were few people she could trust.'[62] She became increasingly paranoid. She even began to suspect the loyalty of the devoted Ken Wharfe. Their relations soured after the LA Fitness episode. Wharfe had always been opposed to her going there and suspected that Diana had colluded in the pictures to contrive a high-profile confrontation with the press. 'Why,' he asked me, 'was Diana wearing full make-up at 6.50 in the morning for a workout?' He had found the way she jeopardised her own safety more and more vexing. He had learned to live with her volatility. 'Stand by for a mood swing, boys,' she'd say.[63] But Wharfe was not standing by any more. She had let fly at him on a shopping expedition when he protested that she had illegally parked in Kensington High Street. 'You're a policeman. You sort it out,' she told him, heading off to buy some CDs.[64] Wharfe adored Diana but he had seen too many of his colleagues put in the deep freeze. He resigned in November 1993 and was moved to other duties. The Princess, as so often when she was called to account, was deeply upset. But as Jephson writes, 'Once gone, always gone' was her motto.

She exiled everyone associated with helping her produce the Morton book. So rattled was she by the controversy, she now denied her participation even to herself. First to be cut off was Andrew Morton himself. To replace him as a conduit for spin she befriended a journalist who was part of the rat pack on the trip to Nepal and had the boyish good looks of a standard Dianaman – the *Daily Mail*'s Richard Kay. Per Diana's briefing, Kay wrote that she had dropped her old friends James Gilbey, Carolyn Bartholomew and Angela Serota because she was 'incensed . . . at what she perceived as a massive show of disloyalty' in having cooperated with Andrew Morton.'[65] Diana's castaways grew more numerous by the day. 'Never has the phrase "strike someone off the Christmas card list" had more pertinence,' said one exiled acquaintance.[66]

Vivienne Parry, who had worked closely with her at Birthright, confirms: 'There wasn't one friend that she hadn't fallen out with at one time or another. I think part of it was that she felt rather difficult in the company of people who were very close to her, particularly if they started to criticise.'[67] James Colthurst survived till late 1995, finally throwing in the towel after a row with Diana about William, who had enrolled at Eton in September. He told Diana she was showing up at the school too much and embarrassing her thirteen-year-old son, a tough thing for a mother to hear. 'Unless a mother was a widow, it wasn't done for them to go up without fathers or instead of fathers,' Colthurst told me. 'I was at Eton myself, and I told her she shouldn't be going up there as much as three times a week. She got very angry with me and hung up. And then I thought that's it, that's enough. I had been swamped with calls for three years and it was too much.'[68]

Diana's reliance on her friends' perennial availability on the phone was a kind of addiction in itself. She carried around as many as four mobiles at a time, allocating new numbers to the people she wanted to reach her. She was an addict of those multiple ringtones. Friendships were terminated by the sudden switching to a new number. Forstmann became one of her telephonic wailing walls. 'I used to get calls from her on Christmas Eve and she was alone,' he says. 'Whenever we talked it was all about tactics. What to do next. She was unhappy about Camilla. There was this war with the royal family, and she had to do this or that about it. She hated Prince Philip.'[69]

When friends were not available there was always the menagerie of New Age therapists and professional soothers. A garrulous procession of astrologers, psychics, palm readers and graphologists toted their charts and crystal balls into Kensington Palace. 'Diana was in the thrall of all these mad psychics,' Ken Wharfe told me. 'Mara Berni would look at her dolefully and say – in her Italian accent – "Oh, Diana, my dear, I had this strange dream about you last night. You must be careful today."'[70]

It all made for great lyrics for the Loony Princess theme song played by the Prince's camp, but the irony of their ridicule was captured by a tabloid cartoon that showed the Prince of Wales solemnly saying to his potted plants, 'I need hardly tell you how worried I am about my wife's state of mind.' Old school royalty just goes bonkers in quieter, more decorous ways. A member of Prince Charles's staff said they dreaded Charles's annual cruise to talk with the Eastern Orthodox monks of Mount Athos in northern Greece. He was liable to come back opposed to stem cell research or nanotechnology because they 'interfere with the natural order of things'.[71] (Having been born on top, Charles has a soft spot for the natural order of things.)

The Princess was at least as promiscuous a spiritual seeker as her husband, except in her case it wasn't the monks of Mount Athos, Carl Jung and Laurens van der Post. It was Simone Simmons, the raspy-voiced, chain-smoking electromagnetic energy healer from Hendon. Or it was Stephen Twigg, the former tax accountant and used-car sales-man, who claimed to have cured her of bulimia and now offered 'holistic therapy' and deep massage.[72] Or, later in the nineties, it was Jack Temple, self-styled homeopathic 'dowser healer'. (Dowsing consisted of swinging a pendulum over the body to detect 'energy blockages'.[73]) Temple's contribution to princessly peace of mind was to take Diana out of the twentieth century back in time through fossils taped to her body, or make her sit and renew her energy in a stone circle.[74]

'Was she always nutty or nutty because of the situation?' David Puttnam asked rhetorically. 'She became nutty because Prince Charles didn't love her, simple as that.'[75]

By December, for all the therapy – or, some would say, because of it – Diana made one of those emotional decisions she believed would be a transformative act. Still feeling betrayed by the gym photographs, and egged on by Peter Settelen, who wanted to see his drama student in action, she proposed to Jephson that she make a grand speech announcing her withdrawal from much of her public life. She fancied she could go dark like a theatre until she was ready for the next show. The fact that she wanted to announce it publicly was in itself a contradiction, one that the Queen herself, when apprised of Diana's intention, was said to have found ridiculous. It was proof positive to Her Majesty that Diana had never absorbed Royalty's first rule of thumb, that you get out there and wield your handbag to the day you die. Could the Princess not just take her commitments down a notch with a little carefully choreographed diary shuffling? Was it really necessary to put on some weepy swansong? But the truth was Diana really was burned out, overextended with engagements, exhausted by trying to keep her end up in the face of the obstructions from Charles's office, distraught about her miserable affair with Oliver Hoare, upset about the parting with Ken Wharfe, and at her wits' end not just with the deadly duel she fought with the media but her own addiction to it – as strong a negative force as her recurring bulimia.

Jephson wanted Diana's grand speech to be a Truth and Recon-ciliation aria that would secure the moral advantage by forgiving her husband. But Diana's reservoirs of hurt were too full for that. On the contrary, half the fun of her 'retirement' speech would be, as she later admitted, that 'I am a great believer that you should always confuse the enemy . . . The enemy was my husband's department.'[76] She plunged ahead on 3 December 1993, at a luncheon at the Hilton hotel to benefit the Headway National Injuries Association: 'Over the next few months, I will be seeking a more suitable way of combining a meaningful public role with, hopefully, a more private life . . . I hope you can find it in your hearts to understand and to give me the time and space that has been lacking in recent years . . .'[77] She wept copiously when she sat down.

In this year of turmoil, Charles had the consoling embraces of Camilla. Diana found solace in the kindness of her girlfriends and the support of strangers. Even as her own problems multiplied, people did not forget her many acts of compassion and continued to see her as the answer to problems of their own. In May 1994 – at the height of her painful romance with Hoare – she went on a private trip to Paris that would end up encouraging her to re-enter public life more fully. Her companions were her two close friends, Lucia Flecha de Lima and

Hayat Palumbo. It was a Sunday morning, Lady Palumbo told me, and Diana, who was returning to London after a diverting weekend, was not in a good mood. She had a depressing evening ahead: on the drive in to London from the airport she was going to visit a friend in hospital, and then, in the evening, she would arrive at her empty apartment in Kensington Palace (the children were with Charles at Highgrove). To cheer up Diana before she left, the two women friends had planned an interesting morning – a day of sightseeing and a late lunch at Dalloyou in the Rue du Faubourg Saint-Honoré. On the way, however, Lucia decided she wanted to stop and say a prayer at the Sainte Rita Church on the Left Bank in the 15th arrondissement. 'Diana didn't want to do that and neither did I,' said Lady Palumbo, 'but Lucia was desperate to do it. So we said, "OK, we will sit in the car while you go in." But Lucia was in there for ever, so we decided to sneak in and pull her out. It was packed with Filipinos and Spanish concierges taking their vows. Lucia was right at the front, oblivious, deep in prayer. Diana said, "Let's get out," but then as she left, the women suddenly caught on to who she was and flooded out on to the pavement. It was the first Sunday in May and the women all rushed to Diana saying, "Madame, Madame we support you." And what was amazing was the way she changed. This girl who had been in a foul mood a few minutes before suddenly projected total empathy. And she was so charming to the women with her little bit of French. She was just *shining*, as she was surrounded by the old women of the church. Outside the gates, we stood by the car with the bodyguard. She was wearing very simple clothes, a pair of trousers, very simple jewellery. I was first surprised and then moved by the welling up of love for her, the way the women tried to touch her as if she was the Virgin Mary. She slipped into this natural communication with them. It took about fifteen minutes. She held their hands, and looked into their eyes very carefully, and tried to reply in French. They started to hand her flowers and she gathered them all up. In the car, she was very quiet, very pensive.'[78]

When the three friends moved on to Notre-Dame, once again Diana was spotted and mobbed. But this was a different crowd – not humble women seeking sustenance but gawking tourists whose cameras objectified her as celebrity prey. 'It was a scary experience,' said Lady Palumbo, 'and we got out fast.'[70] The serenity of Diana's mood was shattered.

## Chapter 18

# The Return of the Beast

'Get on TV and tell the world she's a liar.'
    – Rupert Murdoch to Piers Morgan, editor of the *News of the*
*World*, August 1994

No single factor shaped the divorce of the Prince and Princess of Wales more than the decisions they made to involve the media. Newspapers witnessed the royal marriage; television brokered the celebrity divorce. Without Andrew Morton and the *Sunday Times*, Prince Charles would have never decided to give a disastrously revealing interview to Jonathan Dimbleby of the BBC. Without Dimbleby, Diana would have never have planned her retaliation by agreeing to give an incendiary, irrevocable interview to Martin Bashir on *Panorama*. And together, the interviews locked the royal protagonists into a course of no return.

Why did Charles agree to the Dimbleby interview? For the same reason public figures always fall into this sort of trap: a belief that they can somehow clear things up once and for all. In Charles's case it was an irresistible urge to explain himself after all the smears he had had to sit through from Diana – an eagerness to be 'repositioned'. He could have – and should have – simply sat it out. He was, after all, the future King. His was one of the few jobs in a media-driven age that allowed for taking the 'long view' in the matter of popularity. His sister's example should have been instructive. The fewer interviews Princess Anne gave, the more credibility she accrued – by seeming not to need public approval, the Princess Royal slowly but surely acquired it. Charles's weakness has always been a desire to be 'understood', and he assumed that, once understood, he would also be loved. The Dimbleby project – a two-pronged effort, involving both a film and an authorised biography by one of the BBC's most distinguished journalists – would be the cornerstone of a public relations offensive that would coincide with the twenty-fifth anniversary of Charles's investiture as Prince of Wales. It bolstered a new policy of the Prince's: making himself available for engagements at short notice, as a way of showing the world that he was as sensitive as his estranged wife. He announced he was giving up polo (a good excuse, too, for the dispatch of his polo manager, Fergie's father, whose imbroglio in a call-girl scandal had been adding to bad royal karma). A friend of the Prince's strategically leaked it to the *Sun* that Charles would use the time formerly spent on polo to see more of the boys during their summer holidays.[1] Nice.

It's easy to see why Charles became enamoured of the idea of the rumpled, serious Dimbleby. The decision had its own mad integrity. Charles liked Dimbleby for precisely the reason he was dangerous. No one could say he was a toady. As an interviewer he is prosecutorial and anti-establishment. Yet he is also a son of Richard Dimbleby. Jonathan Dimbleby is a member of a media dynasty just as Charles is heir to a royal one. Dimbleby, like Charles, is a holder of green views; in fact, he runs an organic farm of his own, near Bath. Charles began discussions with him in the summer of 1992 when he was still reeling from the Morton business. The two men bonded over long, philosophical talks as they tramped around Highgrove. The Prince, sceptical at first, was persuaded by these talks to provide what Dimbleby tells us are 'many thousands of the letters which he has written assiduously since childhood'[2] – pages of his voluminous diaries. Charles also green-lighted cooperation from his closest friends and 'some relatives'. In short, too much information – way too much. Here was something else the Prince and Princess shared: the blindness of privilege, an inability to see a decision from any perspective but their own.

Dickie Arbiter, the savvy voice in the press office at Buckingham Palace, had originally seen the twenty-fifth anniversary film idea as something bland and harmless. He was in the process of setting up such a project, when the Prince's private secretary, Commander Richard Aylard, told him, 'The Prince has decided he wants to do something different: Dimbleby! What do you think?' Arbiter told him, 'I think it sucks. It's going to be warts and all.' But Aylard, a yes man to his shiny shoes, replied, 'That's what he wants.' 'It still sucks,' Arbiter retorted.[3]

A close aide to the Prince also sounded out Max Hastings, a rural friend of Charles's as well as the editor of the royal-friendly *Daily Telegraph*, about the Dimbleby idea. 'Absolute madness,' Hastings told him. 'There's only one thing anybody's going to want to hear about it, and that's the marriage and the consequences will be disastrous.' 'But we've got to do *something*,' the aide said, and Hastings replied, 'But this is the fundamental huge mistake at the heart of all your thinking – that this is a sort of public war which can be waged by public relations means.'[4]

The June TV interview would precede the book. This was another mistake, because any corrective nuances in the six-hundred-page volume would be too late to have any salutary impact by the time it lumbered out in October. Diana, for her part, awaited the release of both in trepidation. She knew this would be Charles's statement as much as Morton's had been hers.

*Charles: The Private Man, The Public Role* aired on 29 June 1994, heralded by a metaphor for its reception: a few hours earlier, a Queen's Flight jet with Charles at the controls had overshot the runway on the Hebridean island of Islay and landed nose down in a bog.[5]

Just as Dimbleby had promised, he gave plenty of airtime for the Prince's philanthropy and diplomacy. He captured something touching about Charles by showing his awkward attempts to communicate with a bunch of underprivileged kids his Trust had sent to a holiday camp and his struggle to get on the wavelength of the residents of a decrepit public housing project in Birmingham. In a Bedouin tent on the edge of the Arabian Desert, the Prince of Wales was pictured sipping camel's milk from a plastic cup; in Mexico, he faced down a plate of mushy lamb. 'I always dread having something like that in case it is laced with chillis, which then rather ruins the rest of your day,' the Prince remarked. He was seen roaming the Scottish hills with William and Harry, a fair redress of the popular alternative picture of the heartless cad and deficient father of the Morton/Diana concoction.

Dimbleby's 'Charles' was the Prince his friends know: a slightly scatty, well-meaning chap with a self-deprecating sense of humour and some oddball ideas. His offhand suggestion on the programme that Britain's armed forces should become international mercenaries was one of several that made you glad we have seen the end of the Divine Right of Kings. And his statement that contrary to the small matter of his Coronation Oath he wanted to be 'Defender of Faith, not *the* Faith',[6] created an ecclesiastical shit storm in the Church of England that continued for many weeks. But few really cared about any of that.

What almost everybody cared about was what Dickie Arbiter had feared. Most of the programme was dominated by questions about the Prince's marriage. Three-quarters of the way through the interview, on a chintz-covered sofa at Highgrove, Dimbleby asked Charles whether after he married Lady Diana Spencer in 1981 he had tried to be 'faithful and honourable' to his wife. 'Yes, absolutely,' replied the Prince. Then he added the killer kicker: 'Until it became irretrievably broken down, us having both tried.'

Wham! There it was: CHARLES: I CHEATED ON DIANA – the official confirmation, right from the royal horse's mouth, contradicting years of Palace lies to the press.

Dimbleby bore ahead with a possible reason for this 'breakdown'. 'You were, because of your relationship with Camilla Parker Bowles from the beginning, persistently unfaithful to your wife and thus caused the breakdown?'

Hours of media training and preparation with Aylard and Arbiter elicited this portrait of a conscience on the march:

Well I, the trouble is, you see, that these things – again, as I was saying earlier – are so personal, that it's difficult to know quite how to, you know, to talk about these things in front of everybody, and obviously I don't think many people would want to. But I mean, all I can say is, there's been so much of this speculation and feeding on every other kind of speculation so it all becomes bigger and bigger. But all I can say is, um, that, I mean, there is no truth in, in so much of this speculation. And Mrs Parker Bowles is a great friend of mine, and I have a large number of friends. I am terribly lucky to have so many friends who I think are wonderful and make the whole difference to my life, which would become intolerable otherwise. And she has been a friend of mine for a very long time and, along with other friends, and will be continue to be a friend for a very long time. And I think also most people, probably, would, would, realise that when your marriages break down, awful and miserable as that is, that, so often you know, it is your friends who are the most important and helpful and understanding and encouraging – otherwise you would go stark, raving mad. And that's what friends are for.[7]

'It's so difficult to know how to play the media,' Charles said to Dimbleby. 'I'm not very good at being a performing monkey.'[8]

I'll say.

Blundering candour and tortured obfuscation are a lethal combination. Dickie Arbiter did not know which was worse, the sound bite about adultery or the scene where Charles and Dimbleby are sitting among the choir stools of Westminster Abbey and Dimbleby asks,

'Are you going to be King and the heir to the throne?' – *and Charles dithers*.

The Queen's response to Dimbleby, according to Gyles Brandreth, was to sigh, purse her lips and murmur, 'So it's come to this.'[9] Sir Robert Fellowes was said to be so appalled he was 'fit to be tied'.[10] It is an index of the changed moral climate in Britain since the abdication that, while the pompous commentariat went to town lecturing Charles about his morals, much of the public's overwhelmingly negative reaction was based not on the adultery itself but on the Prince's dumb naivety in admitting it. 'He is not the first royal to be unfaithful,' said the *Daily Mirror*. 'But he is the first to appear before 25 million of his subjects to confess.'[11]

The Prince's blunder was the best thing that had happened to Diana in a year. Things had not been going well since she bowed out with her famous 'retirement' speech in December 1993. Far from the paps respecting her decision and leaving her alone, she was now not just a princess, she was the ultimate forbidden fruit.

By formally withdrawing from public life, the Princess had increased the price of a Diana photograph by 25 per cent. A set of pictures of Diana out shopping might bring up to £2,000. Diana in a bathing suit was worth £10,000, and that was only for UK rights – a good set of pictures of Garbo Di would command three times as much abroad as it did at home.[12] She was top of the list as a cash cow.

A new breed of celebrity magazines pushed demand even higher. I call them 'fabloids', because they combine the tabloid hunger for sensation with the requirement to always look fabulous. The softer angled *OK!* and *Hello!* were now competing with raunchier newcomers and the innumerable magazines that came with an exploding market of weekend newspapers. In the nineties, a picture of Diana on the front page of a glossy magazine guaranteed a sales lift of at least 10 per cent. The fact that in the second half of the first decade of the twenty-first century the sales-hungry tabloid *Daily Express* still features Diana pictures and stories almost every Monday (Sunday is often a quiet day for news) is evidence of the amazing endurance of the Diana factor. The irony was that by cutting back on her charitable commitments, Diana had put her halo in hock – and thereby had made intrusion more defensible. By refusing to replace Ken Wharfe with another police protection officer unless she was with the boys – on the grounds that all the cops were spies – she multiplied the risks. There was no one now between the pursuers and the pursued.

'Once she stopped having a police guard it was much more difficult for her,' acknowledges the *Daily Mail*'s Richard Kay, who became her new media champion. 'She ran a daily gauntlet. They were parked in Kensington Court with their two-way radios and scanners monitoring her mobile phone calls.'[13]

The language got worse, too. Jasper Conran recalls: 'I had lunch with her once at San Lorenzo and I said, "How do you put up with it? This is unbearable." She would go out, they used to say awful things to get a reaction, "Diana, you are a cunt," horrible things. It would make her cry.'[14]

The burly Wharfe had once wrestled an especially intrusive French photo hound to the ground in an incident on a skiing holiday known as the 'Battle of Lech'. But without Wharfe, Diana's trip there in 1994 was ruined by a pap who snagged invasive pictures of her in a bikini, sunbathing on her balcony. She was sighted with her boys weeping in the streets of Zurs.[15]

In contrast, at a social event in California in the months following the Dimbleby broadcast, I was struck by how remote Charles seemed from any real conflict. It was a reception in Cerritos, Los Angeles, for the touring Royal Shakespeare Company, of which the Prince is patron. As the editor of the *New Yorker* at the time, I was listed as a host of the first-night dinner. Except for the fact that the Prince cracked his knuckles all through the performance of *Henry VI*, he seemed almost preternaturally serene. 'Is it disconcerting watching your ancestors murdering each other, sir?' I asked during the interval. 'They're only distant relations,' was his typically Charlesian reply. 'As a matter of fact,' he said, consulting his programme notes, 'I think I am descended from Vlad the Impaler, that appalling Balkan horror.'[16]

To be around Prince Charles is to see that very little is allowed to penetrate the royal shell. His life is swaddled round the clock by a squadron of brisk, officer-class apparatchiks whose job is to answer his whims and keep his spirits up. 'I get the most terrific people,' he said to me. 'They flake out after two years but they miss it, don't they?' he added, turning to the crisp, attentive figure of his deputy private secretary, Sir Stephen Lamport. 'Definitely, sir,' replied Lamport. 'I mean all the excitement,' said Charles. 'The excitement, sir, yes,' said Lamport.

At one point I found myself with the Prince in one of those unpredictable eddies of silence that happen at a big social event. 'They're strange, aren't they, in LA?' the Prince mused, cracking his knuckles again. 'I mean, they all want to go to bed at nine. At the premiere of *Frankenstein* they made me say something, so I was all prepared, you know, to wax on about the British film industry. But they made me do it before dinner because everyone just pushed off in their cars.' I explained that Hollywood, like New York, is all about work. The glamour is the myth. 'Surreal, isn't it?' he said.[17] No, I wanted to say to the Prince who fell to earth, you are the surreal one.

It's possible, since he declined to read the newspapers any more, that Charles didn't even notice that Diana thoroughly upstaged him the night of the Dimbleby broadcast. But everybody else did. At about the moment the Prince of Wales was confessing his adultery on national TV, his wife was stepping out of a limo at *Vanity Fair*'s annual June fund-raising event for the Serpentine Gallery in Kensington Gardens, wearing what fashion editors later called among themselves 'her fuck-you dress', a short, sexy, off-the-shoulder black chiffon number with a scarf panel wafting from the waist and black silk high-heeled Manolo Blahnik shoes. *Come and get it!* She had declined the invitation until two days before the event until news of the adultery quote began to leak in promotions for the broadcast. That's when one of the gala's organisers, an old family friend of Diana's, got a surprise phone call: 'She said she wanted to come after all. I said, "What are you up to?" And she said, '"You'll see."'[18] All became clear when the friend realised the gala was the same night as Dimbleby.

The three-deep photographers went crazy as Diana deftly paused before each of them on *Vanity Fair*'s red carpet. The dress's previously obscure Greek designer, Christina Strombolian, told the fashion commentator Georgina Howell that the Princess 'chose not to play the scene like Odette, innocent in white. She was clearly angry. She played it like Odile, in black. She wore bright red nail enamel, which we had never seen her do before. She was saying, "Let's be wicked tonight!"'[19] The pictures of her that blew Charles off the front pages the next morning provided the perfect context for discussing the only line in the Dimbleby broadcast that anyone remembered – the one about adultery. Here was, as the *Sun* put it, 'The Thrilla He Left to Woo Camilla.'[20]

What a shame Diana couldn't have left it that way. At that golden moment she was so far up on the high ground she might as well have been on Mount Olympus. As Charles floundered in a mess of his own making, Diana was proud that she was the only member of the royal family who understood the black arts of PR. And she was impatient with the Palace's lack of understanding, as she liked to say, of how to 'use' her. Nothing would have pleased her more than to be consulted by the Palace about the royal family's imagery. It would have been smart, for instance, if Prince Philip had brought her into the discussions he chaired twice a year, known as the Way Ahead Group, which were set up in the early nineties as a task force to ensure the monarchy's survival and reshape its agenda for the twenty-first century.

Diana had made it her business to know every editor and chairman of every important media outlet – just as, back when she was a single girl, she had got to know the members of the royal rat pack who stalked her. She solidified her influence at the *Mail* by cultivating not just Kay but a separate relationship with his boss, David English, editor and chief executive of Associated Newspapers. When Mark Bolland joined Charles's staff in 1996 to help rescue the Prince's image from the Dimbleby debacle, calling on David English was one of the first things he did. How on earth, Bolland wanted to know, could he reposition the Prince more favourably with the *Daily Mail*'s readers? English corrected him. 'One of your jobs is to teach the Prince of Wales that we were never against him, we were just for Diana . . . It was a commercial decision. Diana sells newspapers. Charles doesn't.'[21]

'The Prince found the Bolland–English exchange totally depressing,' Bolland says. 'He felt he was always doing this – remarketing himself to the press, doing the rounds of the newspaper editors to try and ingratiate himself. He said, "When I was young I did all this, but what's the point? They still believe all the terrible things Diana says about me."'[22]

The Princess had no such reticence about her own media campaign. She used the lure of lunch *à deux* at Kensington Palace to arrange strategic meetings with key newspaper editors. An encounter with the Princess on her own turf became a full-on, multimedia experience combining all she had learned and wanted to project. 'Everything went into the performance of Being Diana,' says *Tatler* editor Geordie Greig, whose sister Laura was one of the original Coleherne courtiers. 'When you met her you never felt more seduced, more glamorous, more famous, more intoxicated. Before she was famous she was an uninteresting schoolgirl – nice, polite, unenquiring, uninspiring. What made her change was being royal, rich, famous, watched, desired.'[23] The most effective device in her seduction armoury was to flatter the person she wished to manipulate with an indiscretion that made him or her feel (a) favoured and (b) protective, as if her fragile privacy was suddenly in his or her (usually his) hands. That 'instinct for co-option' again. 'What's it like, being Diana?' *News of the World* editor Piers Morgan asked her over their first KP lunch in 1996. 'Oh, God,' she replied. 'Let's face it, even I have had enough of Diana now – and I *am* Diana.'[24] Then, says Morgan, she nestled into the sofa, 'radiating a surprisingly high degree of sexual allure'.[25]

Diana never really understood that the willingness of the *Daily Mail*'s David English or the *News of the World*'s Piers Morgan to 'back her' did not include any willingness to withhold a sexy story when they had one. Our heroine was not a strategist, as we have noted. Each battle she fought was seen as a discrete incident of any given day's guerrilla warfare. *I will do this picture to annoy that paper that did the mean one of me yesterday. I will give this story to that journalist to stave off the one that's coming on Wednesday.* She was better informed than the highest paid spin doctor on the machinery of her coverage on any hour of any day, but lacked the concentration to find its compass. And her belief that somehow the press were 'hers' made every foreseeable revelation a nerve-racking ordeal.

Having laughed off the warning of her financial adviser Joseph Sanders about her obsessive pursuit of Oliver Hoare, she kept on phoning her elusive lover. The police were discreet about the harassment for months, but in the media climate of the nineties it was too good a story to stay leak-proof for long. Towards the end of August 1994, eight months after the police warning, she was alarmed to be told by (the other) Lord Stevens, the owner of the group that published the *Express* newspapers that the *Sunday Express* had heard about the calls to Hoare. Lord Stevens, whose Italian-Russian wife Maritza was one of Diana's circle of glamorous foreigners, killed the story in his newspaper, but Diana knew it would be shopped around. She always believed the tipster came from 'my husband's side', as she liked to call Charles's aides.[26]

On Saturday, 20 August, shortly after Stevens suppressed the story in the *Express*, the *News of the World*'s chief reporter had news for Piers Morgan. 'Got a rather big one here, boss,' Gary Jones told Morgan. 'Diana's a phone sex pest.'[27] The paper called Hoare for a comment for next day's story. He was panicked into admitting 'consoling conversations' with the Princess. He must have called Diana right away, since she immediately summoned her white knight, the *Daily Mail*'s Richard Kay, to give him her side of the story. Their friendliness had reached the point of inviting gossip about a closer relationship than source and journalist. Kay's tips from Kensington Palace came so thick and fast the rest of the press took to staking him out for leads to Diana's

# THE DIANA CHRONICLES

whereabouts. Kay admits today that Paul Dacre, who succeeded David
English as editor of the *Mail* in 1992, told him to take care. 'I was in
danger of becoming the story,' he says.[28] On Saturday afternoon, just as
Morgan was getting ready to break the phone pest scandal in Sunday's
*News of the World*, Kay picked up the Princess at a rendezvous point
near Paddington Station[29] and drove her around for three hours while
simultaneously absorbing her creative narrative about a boy at the
Hoares' son's school who was the real 'source' of the nuisance calls.[30]

A page-one story headlined 'WHAT HAVE I DONE TO DESERVE THIS?'
appeared under Kay's byline in Monday's *Daily Mail* as the instant
rebuttal of Morgan's 'DI'S CRANKY CALLS TO MARRIED TYCOON' salvo
in the *News of the World*.[31] The best line in Kay's story was Diana's 'I
don't even know how to use a parking meter, let alone a phone box'[32]
– an artful bit of dumb-blonde positioning. She had produced a slew of
fake diary dates to prove she was otherwise engaged when she was said
to be talking to Hoare. (Her former chef Mervyn Wycherley tells me he
has the menu books which show that when she said she was out, she
was actually home.)

At first, the counteroffensive seemed to be working. News bulletins
instantly started switching from the substance of the *News of the World*
scoop to Diana's furious *Daily Mail* denunciation. Morgan admits in his
diary he was in 'a cold sweat'. 'I got up at 6 a.m. and read the *Mail*. It's
hideous, a full denial in every way and so gut wrenchingly emotive I can
see no way of surviving this if we've got it wrong.'[33]

What had Paul Johnson advised Diana? No. 1: STOP TALKING
TO THE PRESS.[34] Only a fool, he might have added, has herself as her
own spin doctor. Her going to Kay and the *Daily Mail* had the effect,
after the initial shock, of sending the pugnacious Morgan into
overdrive. Worse, she had stirred his boss into taking an interest.
Morgan was in the shower when Rupert Murdoch called him. On the
phone from New York, the media mogul told his editor, 'The poor girl
is cracking up. Give her a bit of peace.'

Just kidding.

What Murdoch actually said was, 'Hi, Piers. I can't really talk for
long but I just wanted you to know your story is one hundred per cent
bang on. Can't tell you how I know . . . So get on TV and tell the
world she's a liar!'[35] Right, thought Morgan, she's going to get it now.
As Oliver Hoare and his wife retreated into dignified silence, the
story played all summer in a dreadful point-counterpoint of tabloid
warfare.

The net result was that the radiant Diana of the Serpentine was rendered as a nutcase who preyed on other women's husbands. The episode had one benefit. She was so furious that Hoare hadn't been willing to lie on her behalf that she finally cut him off. Richard Kay dropped the guillotine in the *Mail* in February 1995: 'The truth is she views Hoare as a pretty spineless creature. Ever since his failure to help her over the nuisance calls business, the friendship has been a one-way street. He is very much more besotted with her than she is with him.'[36]

Stuff happens. The other man in her life could not be disposed of so easily. James Hewitt, like Rasputin, surfaced again – and again. Now that the Waleses were on a clear path to divorce, Diana didn't need any more stories that impugned her image as a scorned wife. The once chivalrous Major Hewitt was not as clever as Rasputin. That was part of the trouble. He was not so much malicious as gullible. Given the treacheries, big and small, that followed in the wake of Diana's failed marriage, you could argue that Hewitt was remarkably restrained until he was broke. From the moment he became Diana's suspected lover in 1991, he had been trailed, taped and photographed wherever he went, fending off tabloid offers of up to half a million pounds to tell his story. Diana seems to have forgotten how upsetting it is to be pursued by the media without PR machinery. In a sense, she had thrown Hewitt to the wolves, just as she had been thrown to the wolves in the siege of Coleherne Court. In 1994, when he was dumped out of the army with an estimated £40,000 in severance pay and a £6,600-a-year pension, he was an easy mark for a smiling woman with a good line. He succumbed to the reportorial wiles of Anna Pasternak of the *Daily Express* in February, giving her a series of interviews that hinted at an affair without going so far as to confirm it. Pasternak then secured Hewitt's cooperation to rush out her book, *Princess in Love* based on Diana's letters giving all the torrid, explicit details and written with unintentional irony as a Barbara Cartland-style romance. For his dumb part in it, Hewitt received a not so dumb £300,000.[37]

The news of Hewitt's betrayal and the announcement of publication of *Princess in Love* in October 1994 was something Diana did not need. She was already in a state of anxiety about the imminent six-hundred-page tome by Dimbleby, also to be published in October. (Among the book's many grenades would be Charles's hurtful assertion that he had never loved her.) She feared Pasternak's portrayal of her as a persistent adulteress would sully her reputation just when she was trying to build her defences. On the day *Princess in Love* arrived in bookshops, in the first week of October, Diana came red-eyed to Simone Simmons's healing session. 'I hope his cock shrivels up!' she shouted.[38] Hewitt's wounding perfidy was added to her list of constant laments, but she was frightened, too. One of her terrors was how the Queen would react to the tell-all. It was a fear that Hewitt shared. Like some throwback to the lover of Anne Boleyn, he became obsessed by the fact that his affair with the wife of the heir to the throne made him guilty under the Treason Act of 1351 (still in force at the time and carrying the death penalty). He hid out from the press at the lawyer Geoffrey Robertson's house and babbled his fears that like Barry Mannakee he might end up dead.

Four hundred years ago Hewitt would surely have been beheaded by the royal axeman; today the press has taken over that duty. In a peculiarly vicious long-playing onslaught, the tabloids branded Hewitt the Love Rat, a shaming moniker that would stick to him even after he reclaimed a secondary notoriety ten years later in the twilight zone of reality TV.

Hewitt's revelations caused the Queen less grief than Diana had feared; Major Hewitt and his silly book was a detail to Her Majesty in the melée of family secrets going down. She was too preoccupied with her son's folly in giving Dimbleby such access to his diaries and private life. Charles had even allowed Dimbleby to see a number of official documents without consulting the Queen. She was so irate when she learned of it that she demanded their return forthwith.[39]

It was the first time the Queen had been dragged into the unseemly confessional culture that seemed to have engulfed everybody, including the heir to the throne. It was well known that Charles, like Diana with Morton, had confirmed all Dimbleby's facts for accuracy. The Queen did not appreciate the portrayal of herself as 'detached', of Prince Philip as 'inexplicably harsh' and both of them as 'unable or unwilling' to bestow on Charles 'the affection and appreciation he required'. Dimbleby's representation of Charles's childhood left them winded with annoyance. 'I've never discussed private matters,' snapped Prince Philip, questioned at the start of a historic visit to Russia with the sovereign. 'I don't think the Queen has either. Very few members of the family have.'[40]

In all the fallout, one consequence of Dimbleby's efforts that is often overlooked was the demise of the marriage of Andrew and Camilla Parker Bowles. For reasons of habit, face, money and religion (Andrew was Roman Catholic), the Parker Bowleses would have preferred to go on being married. The Brigadier had endured provocation over the years about his wife's entanglement with the Prince of Wales. At Ascot after the Morton book came out, Parker Bowles was ribbed by the Duke of Marlborough's brother, Lord Charles Spencer-Churchill, with the jocular cry of 'Ernest Simpson, Ernest Simpson, why don't you join us over here, Ernest?'[41] It was a reference to Mrs Simpson's cuckolded husband, but at least such mockery had been confined to his own circle. There had always been what one friend of Andrew's calls 'a cigarette paper's width of doubt' about the Parker Bowleses' marital arrangement.[42] Not any more. He filed for a divorce. In doing so, he accelerated the emotional momentum that undermined any wan hopes Diana had to retrieve her own marriage.

'The great birthday party of Sarah Keswick has taken place at the Ritz,' Woodrow Wyatt wrote in his diary on 22 October 1995. 'Camilla came to be with Prince Charles there . . . She is now acknowledged publicly as his mistress.'[43]

At the end of the month Diana was summoned to a meeting with the Queen and Prince Philip to discuss her future. A close adviser of the Princess tells me that the following exchange took place between Diana and her father-in-law. 'If you don't behave, *my girl*,' Philip told her, 'we'll take your title away.' 'My title is a lot older than yours, Philip,' Earl Spencer's daughter replied.[44]

The divorce war had begun in earnest. Two weeks later, the Princess of Wales sat down at Kensington Palace to record an interview with Martin Bashir of the BBC's flagship news programme, *Panorama*. The date, as it happened, was 5 November – Guy Fawkes Day, when bonfires and fireworks commemorate the Gunpowder Plot of 1605, a thwarted attempt to blow up the Houses of Parliament and the King of England.

# Chapter 19

# Deal or No Deal

'No woman ever leaves the House of Windsor with her head.'
                                    – The Duchess of York to a friend

On the crisp Sunday morning of 19 November 1995, the Princess of Wales headed for the M4 at the wheel of her blue BMW. It was the day before the BBC aired her interview with Martin Bashir, and she was on a difficult personal mission – to Eton College where her elder son, the thirteen-year-old Prince William, was in his first year. She parked opposite the spires of the fifteenth-century Gothic chapel and waited for the boys, dressed in their black tailcoats and white ties for Sunday services, to come streaming out. William was one of the last to emerge, walking with his head down, just as his mother did when she was trying to avoid the press. Diana called out to him but, looking up, the boy did not cross the road to greet her. Instead he glanced sullenly back. The non-stop coverage of his mother's private life had become increasingly difficult for William. Unlike Harry, who, aged eleven and still at Ludgrove, was more insulated from the tabloid onslaught, William could not even go out for a bar of chocolate without seeing some new sensational splash about his mother's latest boyfriend or the ugliness of his parents' marital war.

The photographer Mark Saunders, the inevitable pair of eyes recording this scene, saw Diana cross the road to William and seem to be pleading with her son. She took him by the shoulder and guided him behind a small hedge that ran along one side of the forecourt to talk to him privately – no doubt preparing him for the coming Bashir interview. Sanders climbed on to the roof of a Ford Escort to get a better view – and a better picture. 'Diana seemed to be trying to explain something to him which he just couldn't grasp. As my camera fired, William appeared close to tears. After a few more moments he walked away from Diana, making no attempt to kiss her or say goodbye. I watched in amazement as she got into her car and drove off, leaving a sad William watching her from the doorway.'[1]

Exposing her beloved sons to more turmoil was the last thing Diana ever wanted to do, and the fact that she was willing to do exactly that was a sign of desperation. Charles's revelations to Dimbleby had hurt Diana to the core. It was one thing to blow up the fairy story on which she had based her life, another to let his biographer tell the world – and their children – that even its tender beginnings had been a sham. Ever since Diana was a small girl she had been dangerous when hurt. The wound of Charles's claim that he had never really loved her elicited an electronic thunderbolt the careless Prince would never forget.

There were pragmatic reasons, too, that the Bashir interview had to be done. The Duke of Edinburgh was Her Majesty's enforcer; the Queen's men took their cue from him, and his threat to take away her title meant the gloves were off. The Palace machine was gearing up to write her out of the script.

Similarly, it was clear from the atmosphere at St James's Palace, where Charles's court was based, that there was no lover she could take, no public role she could conceive that would not be leaked, briefed against, or sabotaged by the Prince of Wales's team. The Highgrove set, led by Camilla, was spreading the word that she was 'bonkers', and the notion was gaining traction in elite London circles. (Dimbleby's biography had originally contained a chapter, sourced by the Prince's closest friends, making the case that Diana suffered from the psychiatric condition known as borderline personality disorder. At the last moment, the Prince asked him to excise it.)

The Princess knew her leverage in the battle with her husband was eroding. The Hoare telephone saga, Hewitt's book and, most recently, Will Carling's wife Julia blowing the whistle on her husband's affair with the Princess had tarnished Diana's image as a wronged wife and made it hard for her to undertake an affair. (Julia surprised Diana by noisily suing Carling for divorce. 'She picked the wrong couple this time,' Julia told the press.)[2] Under the circumstances, Diana desperately wanted to re-establish her sense of herself (and the public's sense of her) as a woman who had suffered, a beleaguered woman who, far from crazy, had kept her head in the face of massive provocation and had never sought divorce. For a message this important Diana needed the dramatising power of television. She arranged for a press release announcing the upcoming broadcast to go out on 14 November 1995 – Prince Charles's forty-seventh birthday.

The night of the *Panorama* broadcast the streets of London were deserted. Twenty-three million viewers were tuned to the heavily promoted programme. Diana herself was not watching. She was the guest of honour at a black-tie cancer benefit, accompanied by her private secretary Patrick Jephson and her lady-in-waiting Anne Beckwith-Smith. The host was Sir Ronald Grierson, chairman of General Electric International, who found Diana at her most sparkling as she moved among the guests, but Anouska Hempel, who created the fashion show for the night, remembers an undercurrent of tension in the room. She noticed that Diana had an air of excitement, 'a tiny bit of triumph', as if she had 'just cracked something she had meant to do for a long time'.[3] At 9 p.m. Grierson turned to the Princess and said, 'Ma'am, your broadcast is going out right now. Why aren't you nervous?' 'Professionalism,' she answered. 'You will be proud of me, Ronnie.'[4]

Pride, however, was not what Patrick Jephson felt two hours later, when, a glass of whisky in his hand, he sat on a sofa at Anne Beckwith-Smith's flat to watch a videotape of the interview. What he saw and heard made him feel ill, and he took refuge from his employer's out-pouring of candour by dropping to the floor behind the sofa.[5] Jephson's careful planning and repositioning of the Princess in the last five years was going up in smoke. There could not be a greater contrast between the sophisticated and crisply confident woman who had worked the room at the gala that night and the sad wraith with supplicating eyes reciting her grievances as a royal captive. Jephson had dreamed of slowly bringing Diana back into the Palace fold, eventually persuading the Queen to see her errant daughter-in-law as a royal asset. Fat chance of that now.

In a measured, more-sorrowful-than-angry voice, Diana told the British nation that the monarchy needed to change in order to survive.

I understand that change is frightening for people, especially if there's nothing to go to. It's best to stay where you are. I understand that. But I do think that there are a few things that could change, that would alleviate this doubt, and sometimes complicated relation-ship between monarchy and public. I think they could walk hand in hand, as opposed to being so distant.[6]

Doubt? Distant? Her comments were deeply disrespectful to the Queen. How dare the thirty-four-year-old Princess of Wales imply that the monarch was out of touch? How dare she question the strength of the forty-year bond the Queen and her consort had forged with the British people?

More unforgivable still, Diana went on to question the suitability of Prince Charles to be heir to the throne.

> There was always conflict on that subject with him when we discussed it and I understood that conflict, because it's a very demanding role, being Prince of Wales . . . being King would be a little bit more suffocating. And because I know the character I would think the top job, as I call it, would bring enormous limitations to him, and I don't know whether he could adapt to that.[7]

Or how about the temerity of this:

> BASHIR: But you really believe that it was out of jealousy that they wanted to undermine you?
> DIANA: I think it was out of fear, because here was a strong woman doing her bit, and where was she getting her strength from to continue?[8]

Could Diana actually be suggesting that the Prince of Wales or anyone in the royal family was jealous? Had she perhaps forgotten there was another 'strong woman' who was 'doing her bit' for the nation, one who happened to be sitting on the throne?

In the words of Dickie Arbiter, at Buckingham Palace, the *Panorama* broadcast went over 'like a cup of cold sick. We were gobsmacked, frankly. No one had seen it coming.'[9] Jephson, as much in the dark as everyone else about what his boss was going to say, had only been told by the Princess that she had done an interview and 'everything will be all right'.[10] As the videotape of the interview wound to its conclusion, Jephson writes, 'Anne switched off the TV and the ghostly face with the smudged dark eyes faded from the screen . . . "That's it," I said.'[11] He resigned two months later, along with the Queen's deputy press secretary Geoffrey Crawford, whose impossible brief had been to supervise Diana's exchanges with the press.

The whole escapade was Morton redux, a garish tapestry of carefully weaved conspiracies. For example, take the circumstances of the interview itself. It was taped on a Sunday in Diana's sitting room at Kensington Palace when all the staff had gone home. Security guards had been told to expect the delivery of a new hi-fi system in boxes. Once the cameras, microphones and other equipment had been smuggled in, Bashir and his two-man crew could walk straight up.

Such schemes to avoid detection by Charles's camp and Buckingham Palace were mirrored by skulduggery at the BBC, where the executives of *Panorama* and their superiors, right up to the office of Director General, made sure that the BBC Board of Governors knew nothing of what was afoot. An awkward fact was that the board's chairman was the one-legged war hero Marmaduke Hussey – Baron Hussey of North Bradley. Strictly speaking, Director General John Birt had a duty to tell his chairman about a programme that was certain to be not only controversial but also positively offensive to the sovereign. But Hussey was married to none other than Lady Susan Hussey, the Queen's woman of the bedchamber and closest confidante. If 'Dukie', as the formidable chairman was known, got so much as a whisper of what Diana and Bashir had planned, Birt feared, the broadcast might never see the light of day or be discredited in advance by the Palace.[12] Either of these possibilities could create a constitutional crisis concerning the BBC's editorial independence sanctified by royal charter.

This time Diana's 'instinct for co-option' had ensnared the institution that for the last half-century had not only punctiliously negotiated its access to the royal family through official channels but had also been the television partner of the monarchy for every state occasion since the Queen's coronation. For his part, John Birt had developed a trusting personal relationship with Sir Robert Fellowes and Robin Janvrin from the Queen's private office. 'I was sorry to hurt such good people,' wrote Birt in his memoir, 'but we were not only recognising the need to report the breakdown of the marriage of the heir to the throne and of the future head of the Church of England, we were also recognising a shift in realities in a more democratic age . . . In effect, the Diana interview marked the end of the BBC's institutional reverence – though not its respect – for the monarchy.'[13]

Diana was a siren of subversion. Even an anti-establishment figure like David Puttnam – who had advised Diana not to do the broadcast – questioned the BBC's judgement. 'I will never forgive John Birt,' Puttnam says today, 'for not explaining to Diana the implications of what she was doing and for not alerting Duke Hussey.'[14] In *The Times*, Lord Rees-Mogg, a friend and neighbour of Hussey, wrote: 'John Birt will have to apologise for his conduct or he will have to go.'[15] A group of MPs and peers huffed and puffed about revoking the BBC's royal charter.

Duke Hussey was made aware of what Diana and the BBC had done only after the interview, already safely in the can, had been viewed by the *Panorama* producers in a secret screening room set up at a hotel in Eastbourne and approved by the BBC's head of news, head of current affairs and its editorial policy adviser. Birt notified Hussey at the same moment Diana formally notified the Queen. She told Her Majesty that she had done a TV interview with the BBC, contents undisclosed. The Queen said nothing. On the day of the broadcast she hosted a lunch at Buckingham Palace for King Hussein's sixtieth birthday. 'I am very worried about the children,' the Queen said to one of the lunch guests as Prince Charles stared miserably at his plate.[16]

In Bashir, Diana had chosen as shrewdly as she had with Andrew Morton. She seemed to have an instinct for people who would break all the rules. Of Pakistani birth, from a lower-middle-class south London background, and a graduate of Southampton and London universities, Bashir was a loner who seemed to owe allegiance to no one. His persuasive powers derive less from any obviously discernible charm (he is brooding and hypnotic) than from a gift for manipulation. He can identify exactly which buttons to press to secure what in American TV parlance is known as The Big Get. 'Neverland is an extraordinary, a breathtaking, a stupendous, an exhilarating and amazing place, I can't put together words to describe Neverland,' he wrote to Michael Jackson in a successful effort to land an interview (which he then cut so incriminatingly it got Jackson arrested as a paedophile).[17]

Bashir is famously tenacious in his seductions. He had spent months wooing Diana, using her brother Earl Spencer, with whom she was now reconciled, as a conduit. He initially characterised the project as an investigation of Diana's oft-expressed beliefs that she was bugged and spied on.

To win her confidence, Bashir perpetrated a stunning act of journalistic manipulation. He had a *Panorama* graphics artist dummy up two fake bank statements which purported to show payments from News International, publishers of the *News of the World*, to a former employee of Earl Spencer. In this way Bashir simultaneously established his trustworthiness and credibility with the Spencers and strengthened Diana's resolve to keep everything she was doing secret from people who might try to dissuade her. Actually, it's hard to imagine anything dissuading her. Everyone she had canvassed in general terms about doing a TV interview – not just Puttnam but also Sir Richard Attenborough, the TV host and literary critic Clive James and her friend Lord Palumbo – advised her against it. James warned her that she ran the risk of Prince Charles and the Palace 'going nuclear' and continuing until there was nothing left. 'She would be on the run forever and there would be nowhere to go . . . She seemed convinced but of course she was pretending. She had already decided.'[18] Diana often did that, seeming to seek advice for a foregone conclusion. Panorama, in her mind, had gone from an idea to an imperative. She was determined to tell her story without any interpretation but hers. It was her ultimate psychic striptease for the British public.

Leaks soon began to percolate from within the BBC about Bashir's murky behaviour in securing the interview. Executives there were terrified that their broadcasting coup would be tarnished. Diana came to the rescue by sending round a handwritten note to the BBC, saying her decision to give the interview to Bashir had not been influenced by any documents. A haze of doubt nonetheless hung around Bashir after the interview. The BBC made no mention of the controversy in the 2005 documentary celebrating the historic interview's tenth anniversary. 'I did not regard it as a tragedy when Bashir left the BBC,'[19] said a senior BBC manager after their star interviewer departed for a current affairs show on ITV and later joined ABC's Nightline in the U.S.

Whatever his methods, Bashir had pulled off something extraordinary. Piers Morgan marvelled in his diary, 'It was utterly sensational, the most outrageous celebrity interview I have ever seen.'[20] With Bashir, Diana had finally divested herself of the smokescreen of monarchy. 'Here was a Royal talking like a real human being with all the traumas of a real person's life,' said the BBC's managing director of news, Tony Hall, recalling how stunned he was by the tape. 'I was bowled over by the frankness of it.'[21] Most people (apart from those who, having paid thirty-six pence a minute, had listened to the Squidgygate tapes) had not heard Diana speak at all since the early days of her marriage, when she was still a clipped, blushing Sloane Ranger.

Now, after a year of increasingly scurrilous tabloid caricature, the woman who sat opposite Martin Bashir displayed a dignity, composure and heartbreaking earnestness that bore no resemblance to the tawdry creature depicted in the media. Her face filled the screen in a melancholy close-up. 'Never having heard her speak before, I imagined she would be like a silly debutante,' wrote the usually spiky literary

diarist James Lees-Milne. 'On the contrary, she was adult and articulate
... Very beautiful, cocking her head to the left, lovely mouth, enormous
clear eyes.'[22]

Even today, to read the transcript of that interview is to be struck by
the blunt force of much of what the interviewee had to say:

> I'd like to be a queen of people's hearts ...
> There were three of us in the marriage ...
> The establishment that I married into – they have decided that I'm
> a non-starter ...
> The enemy was my husband's department ...
> Yes, I adored him [Hewitt]. Yes, I was in love with him. But I was
> very let down.[23]

The affair with Hewitt was treacherous terrain for Diana, but it was
a safe admission because he had already let that cat out of the bag in
*Princess in Love*. In the interview, Diana shifted quickly from confessing
the indiscretion with the army officer to enlisting one of her sons to
render it a forgivable lapse. Asked about how she felt in the days after
Hewitt's book came out, the Princess said: 'William produced a box of
chocolates and said, "Mummy, I think you've been hurt. These are to
make you smile again."'[24] Luckily for Oliver Hoare and Will Carling,
Bashir conveniently forbore to ask about them.

Towards the end of the interview, Diana threw down a gauntlet to
Charles's lawyers.

> I don't want a divorce, but obviously we need clarity on a situation
> that has been of enormous discussion over the last three years in
> particular. So all I say to that is that I await my husband's decision of
> which way we are all going to go.[25]

Could such brilliant sound bites have rolled out spontaneously? Of
course not. Diana knew which areas would be covered and had been
practising her lines for weeks. Hewitt remembered Diana using the
'three of us in this marriage' line a lot during their romance. What
struck him most was how utterly different the Diana in the broadcast
was from the 'confident, flirtatious, wickedly humorous' Diana he
knew. 'When she did look up through dark eye liner (which she never
usually wore) she spoke like a witness giving evidence,' Hewitt wrote in
his memoir *Love and War*.[26] He was stunned when she admitted their

affair on camera, noting how deftly she turned Bashir's question from
the physical to the emotional – 'Yes, I adored him', not 'Yes, I had an
affair with him'. But then Diana knew exactly how she wished to come
across to the audience.

'She was like an additional producer on the shoot,' one of the BBC
team commented.[27] Diana did her own make-up, applying her own
panda eyes and washed-out pallor. Behind the upward look from
beneath her eyelashes her bottom line was, Watch out!

I was the separated wife of the Prince of Wales. I was a problem, full
stop. Never happened before. What do we do with her? She won't go
quietly, that's the problem. I'll fight to the end, because I believe that
I have a role to fulfil, and I've got two children to bring up.[28]

The harassment beneath the charm was immediately apparent to
Charles's camp, if not the public. 'This psychopath, schizophrenic
creature is as mad as a hatter,' wrote Woodrow Wyatt in his diary,
channelling most of the establishment.[29]

Camilla felt vindicated. Diana had proved once and for all that she
was 'loopy, pretty half-witted, and possibly ought to be locked up', as
Richard Parker Bowles told it.[30] Frances Shand Kydd was so aghast that
she pretended to be on the other line when her daughter called her in
Scotland the next morning. 'It was so frightful I – literally – was
thinking I'm never going to be able to stand up for her again, because
it's so frightful, this *Panorama* thing.'[31] Nicholas Soames, Charles's best
friend, expostulated on the BBC's *Newsnight* after the *Panorama*
programme that Diana was in 'the advanced stages of paranoia'.[32]
Speaking for all her more prominent royal relatives, the normally mild
and reserved Princess Alexandra told Woodrow Wyatt at a private
dinner that she thought Diana was 'not only mad but evil wickedness
incarnate'.[33]

The public did not. They loved it. Diana had won her bet. The
Wednesday after the interview aired, the *Daily Mirror*'s opinion poll
showed 92 per cent support for the Princess's appearance on
*Panorama*.[34] A less proletarian national opinion poll commissioned by
the *Sunday Times* and published on 3 December, two weeks after the
broadcast, showed 67 per cent of the British public believing Diana was
right to give the interview, 70 per cent believing she should be given a
goodwill ambassadorial role abroad, and only 25 per cent saying she
should play a less active role in public life.[35]

'Never again,' wrote Brian Hoey, 'will anybody accuse her of being "thick as a plank."'[36] Soames, whose day job was Armed Forces Minister in the Tory government, came to regret blowing his stack about Diana's 'paranoia'. All it achieved was to confirm Diana's (and much of the public's) view that the grand friends of Charles were plotting to bring her down. When John Major bumped into Soames in the House of Commons, the Prime Minister, eager to keep his government out of the Wales domestic war, told Soames to 'shut up'.[37]

Diana went off on a low-intensity tour of Argentina that put the adulation of foreigners between her and the reaction of the establishment. She knew it was a false lull. There had not yet been any formal reaction from the Queen but only because Her Majesty was getting her constitutional ducks in a row with John Major and the Church of England. Jephson was still with Diana, but she knew not for long (to show she knew, she seated him in business class on the way back from Buenos Aires while her hairdresser travelled beside her in first class).[38] Like a heat-seeking missile, Diana went on to New York, where, alongside fellow honoree General Colin Powell, she was to receive a Humanitarian of the Year award from the United Cerebral Palsy of New York Foundation. As she left for the dinner from the Carlyle hotel where she was staying, a crowd of about two hundred fans were waiting on the pavement to applaud. The street was ablaze with TV lamps and the flashbulbs of thirty photographers waiting to get the front-page shot of the Princess in her clinging black evening dress with its plunging scoop neckline.

Diana had entered the zone of the big-time Manhattan warhorses, Donald and Marla Trump, TV star Barbara Walters and Henry Kissinger and all the other well-heeled citizens from the land of the $1,000-a-plate honorees.

From the podium at the Hilton she told the crowd, 'Today is the day of compassion.'[39] When a heckler dared to challenge, 'Where are your children, Diana?' she replied serenely, 'At school' – and got a standing ovation ('DI WOWS BIG APPLE' was the *New York Post* headline).[40] The ecstatic reviews of Diana as 'An American Saint'[41] obliterated Charles's press at home for an address to his Business Leaders Forum, which his office had touted as 'the first speech by HRH to be carried on the Internet'.[42]

Kissinger, who presented the award to Diana, tells me that during the dinner Diana confided her difficulty in finding a purpose. 'I advised her to do things that had a humanitarian appeal that didn't look like protest groups,' he recalls. 'Not to do things that she was against but things that she was *for*. She was shrewd. She had an emerging sense of how she wanted to define her life that she couldn't fully articulate.'[43]

What she did know was that the *Panorama* interview had given her the popular support she needed for a divorce on something like her own terms. She was, as she had told the British people, 'waiting'. She didn't have to wait long, and she herself pushed the button on the ejector seat from the House of Windsor. The occasion was the annual St James's Palace staff Christmas party.

After a month of foreign acclaim Diana suddenly cracked. Perhaps it was the strain of living such a weird double life, despised by the Palace and adored by everybody else. Perhaps it was a desire to speed things along by throwing another squib into Charles's domestic hearth. Or perhaps it was because she had just learned that only the day before Prince Charles had met with John Major to discuss the constitutional issues surrounding his wish for a divorce. Whatever it was, Diana chose this festive moment to insult Charles's personal assistant, who also happened to double as William and Harry's part-time nanny – the thirty-year-old Alexandra 'Tiggy' Legge-Bourke.

Legge-Bourke – a boisterous, unreconstructed Sloane from the shires, nicknamed after Mrs Tiggy-Winkle for her childhood love of Beatrix Potter's stories – had been appointed in 1993 by Charles to help him amuse the boys when they were visiting their father at Highgrove. Tiggy was naturally positioned to become a hate figure to Diana. Raised on a six-thousand-acre Welsh estate by a mother who was lady-in-waiting to Princess Anne and a father who was a rich merchant banker, Tiggy was poised, as Diana saw it, to move in on Prince Charles. Her threat lay less in her hearty brunette attractions than in the unexpected affection in which she was held by William and Harry. They adored her gung-ho personality. 'I give them what they need at this stage – fresh air, a rifle, and a horse. She [Diana] gives them a tennis racket and a bucket of popcorn at the movies,' said Tiggy in one of her irritating (and shrewd) reported comments.[44] Mark Bolland remembers getting into Tiggy's Vauxhall Frontera and finding three dead rabbits in the back seat. Tiggy took the young Princes abseiling without protective headgear, wore a hat with twinkling lights on at holiday parties, and was considered an exuberant addition to Klosters skiing parties. She was probably the only subject on which Camilla and Diana were united. They both wanted her out. Diana was convinced that Charles was having an affair with the nanny after she saw her wearing a diamond

Fleur de Lys brooch – a gift that Charles regularly used to bestow on his mistresses in the old days. Diana owned one herself.

There is no evidence of an affair, but Diana's fears about Tiggy were not entirely groundless. Tiggy was trouble. She proved it after Diana's death when she organised Charles's fiftieth birthday party at Highgrove on behalf of the boys and failed to invite Camilla. She claimed, implausibly, that it was the boys' decision, which only made the PR for Camilla worse. During the dark days of 1995 there was a growing Palace lobby to promote Tiggy as a second wife to Charles, augmented, surprisingly enough, by Diana's brother-in-law Sir Robert Fellowes. The Princess had become so fixated on Tiggy that sometime that year she wrote a bizarre note to Paul Burrell voicing her fears that someone on the Palace side was 'planning an accident in my car, brake failure and serious head injury in order to make the path clear for Charles to marry'.[45] (Diana's friend Lucia Flecha de Lima believes Burrell wrote it himself – he often helped Diana out with her Christmas cards, she said.)[46] Burrell seems to have fished out all manner of communications from the waste-paper baskets at Kensington Palace in his ongoing quest to finance his pension. The name of the person Charles was planning to marry was not mentioned in the Burrell book, but there was a collective tabloid gasp in December 2006 when, following Lord Stevens's Operation Paget Inquiry, the name long assumed to be that of Camilla, was filled in at last with Tiggy.[47]

On Thursday 14 December 1995, fresh from her triumph in New York, the Princess arrived at the Lanesborough hotel in Hyde Park Corner for the St James's Palace staff Christmas party. 'Keep standing by me and just watch,' she told Burrell. Then she bore down on the unsuspecting Tiggy with her most compassionate Diana smile. 'Hello, Tiggy, how are you?' she purred. '*So sorry* to hear about the baby.'[48] The insulted nanny fled the room in tears, accompanied by the Prince's flunkey-in-chief Michael Fawcett. The report of what the Princess had said raced round the party in horrified whispers. Was Diana out of her mind? The implication that Tiggy had aborted a child fathered by HRH the Prince of Wales was seriously nutty behaviour.

'Did you see the look on her face, Paul?' Diana screeched at Burrell. 'She almost fainted!'[49] But just as in Julia Carling's case, the Princess had messed with the wrong girl. Tiggy had had enough.

All hell broke loose. Tiggy's father encouraged her to hire Britain's ace libel lawyer, Peter Carter-Ruck, to fire off a letter to the Princess's law firm, Mishcon de Reya, accusing her of circulating 'malicious lies . . .

which are a gross reflection on our client's moral character'.[50] Robert
Fellowes, in his capacity as the Queen's private secretary, dispatched his
own letter to Diana, telling her that her allegations against Tiggy were
'completely unfounded. On the date of the supposed abortion she was at
Highgrove with William and Harry. It is in your own best interests that
you withdraw these allegations.' Added to his letter was a personal note
to Diana from the man who was also her brother-in-law: 'This letter is
sent from one who really believes that you've got this whole thing
dreadfully wrong, and that you must realise it – please.'[51] Diana took the
advice of her lawyer Anthony Julius and hastily settled.

Prince Charles was appalled, but not as appalled as the Queen. For
Her Majesty, this latest act of aggression by her daughter-in-law was
the final straw. It was compounded by Diana now reneging on the
Queen's invitation to join the boys for Christmas at Sandringham, an
olive branch from Her Majesty that also happened to be a command.
Downing Street agreed with the Queen's now irrevocable decision
that the marriage of the Prince and Princess of Wales must be
terminated forthwith. Ever since the Bashir interview, Tory ministers
– not just Nicholas Soames – had concluded that the official line that
the Princess could still be Queen was preposterous. In the words of a
Whitehall source of the *Daily Telegraph*, '*Panorama* presented the
Queen and Mr Major with the "impetus" and "opportunity" to seek a
peaceful solution.'[52]

On 20 December 1995, a uniformed courier from Windsor Castle
delivered a handwritten letter from the Queen to her daughter-in-law.
'Dearest Diana,' it began, and went on to request that she agree to an
early divorce from Charles 'in the best interests of the country'.[53] It was
signed 'Love from Mama'. The Queen let Diana know she had
discussed the matter with the Archbishop of Canterbury and the Prime
Minister and that both 'agreed you must divorce'. Her intervention
effectively got Charles off the hook: it was the Queen's decision to end
the marriage, not the Prince of Wales's. A letter came the same day
from Charles. It told the Princess that the marriage was now beyond
repair and that this represented a 'personal and national tragedy'.[54]

Diana placed the two letters on the desk and asked Paul Burrell,
'What do you see?' As Burrell tells it, her finger pointed to a sentence
in both letters 'referring to the "sad and complicated situation".' 'They
must think I am stupid,' said Diana, who promptly fired off a missive to
her husband. 'Your request has utterly perplexed me. I do not consent
to an immediate divorce.'[55]

The bravado was a sham. Diana was in meltdown now the reality was finally before her. She curled up on the sofa and sobbed. Her torment lay in understanding too late the deeper complexities of what she had lost – not just the man whose love she could never win but the invisible cloak of royalty that conferred so much dignity and protection. She was on her own now. But at least there was clarity: she had to have her wits about her or she would wind up in the same predicament as Fergie.

'No woman,' the Duchess of York observed wryly once, 'leaves the Royal Family with her head.'[56] Fergie was negotiating her own divorce just as Diana approached hers. The estranged friends had become close again since the summer, united by their marital problems. These days Diana often showed up for Sunday lunch at Fergie's rented house in Surrey. The Princess of Wales and the sister-in-law she liked to call 'the redhead' joked that they would end their days in the Tower of London.

'Sarah Ferguson was a very, very useful friend to the Princess during the months before the divorce,' said Jane Atkinson, who later joined Diana as her media adviser. 'If she hadn't had her house to go to she would have gone mad.'[57] Diana used her sister-in-law as a constant source of intelligence on Windsor tactics and saw the way that Fergie was being bested.

As the wife of the Queen's second son and mother of two princesses, Fergie exited her ten-year marriage to Prince Andrew with debts of £5 million and no house of her own – the settlement of £600,000 from the Queen to buy one stipulated it had to be in the names of her daughters, Beatrice and Eugenie, and could not be sold to raise capital. The Queen also provided £1.4 million in trust for the children. Andrew's contribution was to pay their school fees.[58] 'Even the most robust litigants fold at the first whiff of the Crown,' one of Fergie's business associates commented.[59]

Not if Diana was your client. Never once did the Princess let herself be intimidated. As soon as the Queen declared the casino officially open, Diana's steady nerves in the negotiations profoundly impressed her legal team – starting with her cleverness in choosing them in the first place. The Prince, naturally, enlisted the Queen's attorneys, Farrer & Co. Fiona Shackleton there, was a loud, large-boned bridge enthusiast and crack matrimonial specialist who had authored *The Divorce Handbook*.

Diana, instead of going to a similarly patrician firm, plumped for the more commercial Mishcon de Reya, distinguished by the strong Labour Party connections of its founding partner, Lord Mishcon. Diana's trusted man there was Anthony Julius, aged thirty-nine, built his reputation there not on matrimonial law but on the intelligence of his media litigation. As the son of a draper from the London suburbs, a literary scholar and combative intellectual (he caused a stir with a book about T. S. Eliot's anti-Semitism), Julius was notably free of the kind of establishment baggage that might make him vulnerable to Palace pressure. Indeed, Lord Mishcon, now elevated in old age to the ranks of the great and the good, was very unhappy that Julius insisted on handling Diana's divorce. The Princess understood, as Charles did not, that their final split would be as much a public relations battle as a legal exercise. When she called Julius to ask him to represent her he advised Diana that this was his first divorce case. 'That's all right,' she replied. 'This is my first divorce.'[60]

Julius told Diana that if she wanted him to handle her divorce she must behave as a regular client. Their meetings would not take place at Kensington Palace but at his office. 'We are not going to behave as if we are in a fairy story,' he told her, according to a colleague. He also refused to follow Lord Mishcon's own practice of representing Diana for nothing, as the firm had done in the past. To help Diana meet his fees, Julius secured her a bank loan.

When the letter from the Queen arrived, it was Julius who advised Diana to play for time and not agree yet to divorce. She must refuse to be stampeded into any rash decision, like Fergie had been. As expected, Diana's refusal to immediately capitulate made the other side nervous. The Queen telephoned Diana several times to enquire politely how negotiations were coming along. The Princess told Her Majesty that she was still considering her position. As the weeks of January and February ticked by, Charles's camp became increasingly restive, anxious to know what Diana was plotting. They suspected that her silence connoted a desire for an unacceptable sum of money. And they were right. Julius and Diana were busy working out exactly what the budget of a divorced celebrity princess would be.

This was a new process for Diana. In David Hare's play Licking Hitler, there is a character so aristocratic she thinks electricity is free. Diana was in that genre. She once asked her financial adviser, Joseph Sanders, 'How do you put petrol in a car?' She was raised to be oblivious to the value of money. The Prince of Wales himself had never possessed a credit card or carried money or a chequebook and neither had his wife. Her personal protection officer always carried the plastic. She once removed a large oval sapphire from a necklace she didn't like, given to her by the Saudi royal family, and declared that she was going to bury it in the walled garden of Kensington Palace.[61] In the nineties Diana's mobile phone account often ran to between five and ten thousand pounds a month. Her bills, even after the separation, were still sent directly to be paid by the office of the Prince of Wales, who regularly raised his eyebrows at his wife's £3,000-a-week 'grooming budget'.[62] Her divorce was a wake-up call but, as always, she was a fast learner. Her legal team found that though she may have been a little casual about spending Prince Charles's money she was no fool about how to hang on to it. The sum they came up with to maintain her status and security was not a penny less than £17 million.

On 15 February, when Diana had still not agreed to a divorce, the Queen invited her to the Palace to speed things along. On the agenda were the big issues that had to be decided before any money settlement: whether she could continue to live at Kensington Palace, the arrangement for the boys, and a thorny issue that had bedevilled the American divorcee Wallis Simpson before her: whether or not she would still be entitled to be called 'Her Royal Highness'.[63]

The children were never an issue, although decisions about William's education and career choices would always be in the monarch's purview. The Queen was sympathetic to Diana's concerns about seeing her boys as much as before and assured her, as Diana recounted to Burrell, that 'nothing will change the fact that you are the mother of both William and Harry. My concern is only that those children have been in the battleground of a marriage that has broken down.'[64] Nor was Kensington Palace a problem for the Queen – it was already an anthill of feuding royals. Keeping Diana on wouldn't make much difference, and, after all, it was the boys' home.

The HRH was a different matter. To many of us, it might not seem to count for much. Wasn't the important thing that Diana would still be a Princess? Did it really matter whether she was Your Royal Highness or Your Grace or Your Magnificence or Your Holiness or just plain My Lady? But HRH, though it has no constitutional meaning and no statutory basis, does denote a direct family connection to the Crown. It is awarded or withdrawn purely at the will of the monarch. Its lustre carries with it a knock-on effect of magic royal palaver, commanding a bow or a curtsy from everybody else. Without the protection of her HRH, Diana would be expected to bend the knee in the corridor of Kensington Palace every time she bumped into the Austrian neighbour she referred to as the U-Boat Commander – HRH Princess Michael of Kent.[65]

Tough luck. The Queen was never going to let Diana keep the title for the same reason the Queen Mother had been adamant about Wallis Simpson. Who knew where Diana's private life would take her in her second act and what kind of unforeseen difficulties might be caused by some ghastly second husband? The sovereign was mightily relieved, therefore, when in their conversation Diana appeared to not be making a fuss about the title, indeed seemed to accede before she was asked.

In truth, though, Diana left the Palace as deeply ambivalent about losing the title as she was about the divorce itself. She brooded on how Fergie's prospects in the outside world were plummeting now it was clear her royal initials would be confiscated. Diana had a dread of descending into her sister-in-law's freebie world, leveraging her tiara to pay for her highlights. Fergie would soon go from offices at Buckingham Palace to running her life out of a guest cubicle in Chelsea at the office of something called Sputnik Communications, hustling up deals to write more sequels to her children's books about a helicopter-flying budgerigar and to make infomercials as the spokes-duchess of Weight Watchers. Diana wanted no part of such horrors. Retaining the HRH title would assure her that she would always be included in state occasions and properly acknowledged as the future King's mother. The Queen may have regarded their talks on the matter of HRH as conclusive, but Diana did not.

Meanwhile, Charles was getting so nervous that nothing was moving that he sought a meeting without the lawyers. 'Let's move forward and not look back and stop upsetting one another,' he wrote to his wife.[66] They got together over tea at St James's Palace. It was an emotional forty-five-minute meeting that did not seem to banish their mutual mistrust. Diana agreed to divorce, but only on the understanding that her lawyers' conditions would be met. She walked the few yards to her own office and from there issued an immediate statement through her media adviser, Jane Atkinson. It said the Princess had agreed to her husband's request for divorce, would continue to be involved in all decisions relating to the children, would remain at Kensington Palace with offices in St James's Palace and would continue to be known as Diana, Princess of Wales. Her unilateral announcement infuriated the Palace. They briefed the press that Diana had asked Prince Charles to say nothing of the substance of their meeting, only, without consultation, then to divulge it herself. 'The Queen,' said the Palace, 'was most interested to hear that the Princess of Wales has agreed to the divorce . . . All the details on these matters including titles remain to be discussed and settled. This will take time.'[67] There was one ameliorating aspect to Diana's breach of trust. She had clearly agreed in the way she listed her title to surrender the HRH. But relief at the Palace was short-lived. Diana was already briefing her friend Richard Kay of the *Daily Mail* that 'the Princess wanted to remain HRH the Princess of Wales, but the other side refused and that had been the sticking point for the last two weeks'.[68] It was the usual Diana dance that concealed a serious purpose. Leaking the terms she wanted, she put the Palace on the defensive. Planting the HRH story with Kay created a good burst of populist feeling against the Palace meanies. It might just pressure the Queen to have a change of heart. Failing that, though it was a useful feint, gearing up the Palace for a fight about the title – when the real fight was going to be about money.

Squelching Kay's version of the HRH imbroglio, Charles Anson, the Queen's press secretary, told the media, 'The decision to drop the title is the Princess's and the Princess's alone. It is wrong [to say] that the Queen or the Prince asked her. I am saying categorically that this is not true.'[69] The title hare was off to a good start. Tally-ho! Press hounds of every persuasion spent the next three months barking about the merits or not of the Princess and her HRH. Once more Diana was igniting a debate about England's traditional self-obsessions that dramatised how redundant they had become. As the commentator and novelist Robert Harris noted, 'A nation's preoccupation with titles and protocol is in inverse proportion to the importance of the country concerned.'[70]

Having hurled her grenades, Diana retreated behind Anthony Julius. The Prince was first stunned, then outraged when, in April, Julius presented Shackleton with Diana's final £17 million term. Charles's annual income from the Duchy of Cornwall in 1996 was in the region of £4.5 million and he wasn't allowed to sell any of the assets.[71] There was worse news for the Queen; Diana's team had taken additional counsel, which confirmed that for her settlement Diana could look through Charles's personal wealth from the Duchy of Cornwall to the considerable Windsor wealth beyond. Who knew how far her demands might escalate? The Spencer gel was in danger of walking off with the Crown jewels.

Another thunderous silence ensued, this time from St James's Palace. They expected they could stare Diana down. In effect the royals wanted to do two contradictory things: to reject Diana and to control her. It was not possible to do both. The Princess held a high card: while Prince Charles was desperate by now to be rid of her, she could wait.

The editors of the *Daily Telegraph* had been clear throughout the divorce that they sided with Charles, which was fair enough, but on 13 July they inadvertently laid bare the sensitive nerve of establishment anti-Semitism. In an article comparing Julius unfavourably to the 'conciliatory, softly-softly Fiona Shackleton', they wrote that 'his background could not be further from the upper-class world inhabited by his opposite number. He is a Jewish intellectual and Labour supporter and less likely to be restrained by considerations of fair play. "I'd be very worried if I were the Royal Family," says a Cambridge don who taught him. "He'll get lots of money out of them."'[72] There were so many complaints from readers appalled by this casual interpretation of Julius as Shylock that the paper had to offer an apology.

In May, Diana went to the Queen and told her that unless her terms were met she would withdraw her consent to divorce. Without it, Charles would have to wait another two years until the obligatory five had been reached for a non-consenting divorce.[73] If she ran out of money, she would sell her jewels in order to live and that would be a great embarrassment. She left Buckingham Palace with the firm belief that the Queen was her ally in swift resolution, but it was the monarch's turn for mischief now. In response to Diana's ultimatum she phoned Prince Charles's lawyers and advised them to take all the time they needed.

The games continued. At Prince William's annual parents' day at Eton, Diana was cold-shouldered by the Knatchbulls and the Romseys and not seated beside her husband at the evening concert, until she insisted to the Provost's wife that she be moved to be near him. As they emerged she planted a kiss on Charles's cheek in front of the waiting cameras. 'Now Camilla knows what it feels like to be on the receiving end,' she said to Burrell at breakfast the next day as she surveyed the rash of front-page photographs.[74]

The Prince of Wales asked the senior partners at Farrer & Co. to try to break the impasse and reduce Diana's demands by going over Anthony Julius's head direct to Lord Mishcon. According to one of his associates, Mishcon agreed to a meeting, until it was pointed out that to allow the Palace to drive a wedge would jeopardise negotiations. With great reluctance Mishcon cancelled the meeting and the other side folded. On 13 July the divorce deal was sealed on the terms Diana asked. It was a sweet clear victory. She may have lost her title but she had won financial independence for the first time in her life.

The Prince hated being obliged to borrow from his mother to meet Diana's terms. Those terms included: the lump sum of £17 million;

£400,000 annually for Diana's office; and Diana to be known as Diana, Princess of Wales, without the style HRH. ('The form of address "Ma'am" is perfectly acceptable to the Princess,' said Buckingham Palace.) Diana had made one last attempt to salvage the HRH on the eve of the decree, appealing to Sir Robert Fellowes. On behalf of the sovereign, he declined the request. This brought forth a gesture of unexpected support from a usually competitive member of the family: Princess Michael of Kent, who sent Diana a note that said on no account must she think of curtsying to her when they met. 'If only Charles had loved you,' she wrote, 'this situation would never have happened. You will always have my support.'[75]

For Diana, William's response was the one that mattered. 'Don't worry, Mummy,' he told her when he learned that she no longer had the title. 'I will give it back to you one day when I am King.'[76]

Diana was still a princess, though, and would be a princess till the day she died – unless she remarried. She got to keep her residence and have her office at Kensington Palace. She was not prohibited from a public role – that would be 'for her to decide', though her foreign trips, unless they were private holidays, would have to be signed off on by the Foreign Office and the Queen. Oh, and by the way: she was no longer Colonel-in-Chief of the Light Dragoons, honorary Air Commodore of the Harrier jump jet base at RAF Wittering, or anything to do with HMS *Vanguard*, the first Trident ballistic missile nuclear submarine – perks, it must be said, that Diana could live without. A more underhand shaft was that no more was she allowed to pollute the Buckingham Palace swimming pool.

Diana wanted to do a joint TV announcement informing the world of the formal agreement to divorce. The Prince unequivocally refused. He was done with Diana's media circus. All he wanted back was a couple of watercolours of distant German relations, a pair of Regency chairs and his George III silver, and that would be that.

On 15 July 1996, in a shabby little room at Court Number 1, Somerset House, it took all of three minutes to dissolve the marriage of the century. HRH the Prince of Wales v. HRH the Princess of Wales, neither of whom were present, were listed as couple number 31.[77] Somerset House is just under two miles from St Paul's Cathedral, where, on another July day, a dashing Prince waited at the altar for the shyly smiling twenty-year-old bride in the billowing ivory taffeta wedding dress. Now that the marriage was formally over, both parties were profoundly sad. 'I want so much to be Charles's best friend,' Diana wrote in a forlorn note to Paul Burrell. 'I understand more than anyone what he is about and what makes him tick.'[78] Two weeks before – on July 1, Diana's thirty-fifth birthday – Charles had surprised her by dropping in to see her at Kensington Palace. 'I suppose you've come to take the furniture away, then, Charles?'[79] Diana asked, with her old sparkle, and as they laughed together and drank Earl Grey tea, Burrell reflected, as Jephson had done before him, on the marital friendship that might have been achieved without the shadow of Camilla.

There was regret in Charles's circle, too, reflected in the comments of his friends who had known Diana since the early days of the courtship. 'She was lovely. She was English. She was cheery,' said one to the *Sunday Times* (it sounds like Patti Palmer-Tomkinson). 'This darling girl was going to have ten children, and stroke his hair . . . and say, "You did awfully well today, dear." I just saw it as a lovely warm thing for him. But, as you know, she changed.'[80]

She changed, all right. But it's hard to stay a lovely warm thing when your husband has always been in love with someone else. Diana would have adored ten children too, but unfortunately her husband didn't want to sleep with her.

On Wednesday 28 August 1996, Diana kept a luncheon engagement at the English National Ballet to meet the season's troupe of new dancers. Actually she wasn't originally scheduled to be there that day. Close to the occasion she wrote to confirm that she would be there as planned 'on Wednesday.' The ballet's representative called to say that it had always been down in their diary for the Tuesday of that week. No, no, said the Princess, in her understanding it had always been Wednesday. So the whole luncheon was pushed forward a day. When an executive at the company saw no fewer than four hundred photographers outside their offices in Kensington, he suddenly understood the truth behind the 'mix-up'.[81] Wednesday 28 August 1996 was the day of the decree absolute, when Diana became a free woman at last.

She arrived for lunch wearing a chic eggshell-blue suit and deliberately got out of the left side of the car – where the photographers could get the best view. She held her bag with the ring finger of her left hand towards their lenses. On it was not just her wedding band, but her diamond and sapphire engagement ring. It reminded the world not only of the sad dissolution of their marriage that morning at Somerset House, but the joyous day of promises at St Paul's Cathedral fifteen years before.

'Good luck for this difficult day ahead,' Robert Fellowes had told her on the phone that morning. 'It's a tragic end to a wonderful story.'

'Oh, no,' she replied. 'It's the beginning of a new chapter.'[82]

## Chapter 20

# The Last Picture Show

'Is she an angel?'
   – Helena Ussova, aged seven, landmine victim in Angola,
                                                           January 1997

Diana never looked better than in the days after her divorce. Divestment was the name of the game, in her life and in her looks. The downsizing started with her Kensington Palace staff which she reduced to cleaner, cook and dresser. The assiduous Paul Burrell became maître d' of her private life, combining the roles of PA, Man Friday, driver, delivery boy, confidant and crying towel. 'He used to pad around listening to all,' says a friend of Diana's mother. 'I was quite sure his ear was pressed firmly to the keyhole when I went to Kensington Palace for lunch.'[1]

Diana reinforced her break with married life by stuffing a heavy-duty bin bag with her entire set of Prince of Wales china and then smashing it with a hammer.[2] 'Make a list of everything we need,' she told Burrell. 'Let's spend a bit more of *his* money while we can.'[3]

Diana now used police protection only when she attended a public event. Her favourite officer was Colin Tebbutt, who had retired from the Royal Protection Squad. He was a tall grey-haired matinee idol who was also a Class One driver, trained by the SAS. Tebbutt knew that by going to work for Diana he was effectively shutting the door to any future work with the Prince of Wales, but he had a soft spot for the Princess. 'There was always a buzz when she was at home. I thought she was beginning to enjoy life. She was a different lady, maturing.' Tebbutt says she would always sit in the front of the car, unlike the other royals, such as Princess Margaret who called him by his surname and, without looking up from her newspaper, barked, 'Wireless!'[4] when she wanted Tebbutt to turn on the radio.

'I drive looking in all three mirrors, so I'd say to Diana, "I'm not looking at your legs, Ma'am," and she'd laugh.' The press knew the faces of Diana's drivers, so to shake them off Tebbutt sometimes wore disguises. 'She wanted to go to the hairdresser one day, shortly before she died. I had an old Toyota MRT which she called the "tart trap", so I drove her in that. I went to the boot and got out a big baseball hat and glasses. When she came out I was dripping with sweat, and she said, "What on earth are you doing?" I said, "I'm in disguise." She said, "It may have slipped your notice, but *I'm* the Princess of Wales."'[5]

Every Tuesday night, the Princess sat at her desk in her study at Kensington Palace, writing her steady stream of heartfelt thank-you letters and listening to a piano playing Rachmaninov's Piano Concerto No. 2 and – her favourite – Manning Sherwin's 'A Nightingale Sang in Berkeley Square'.[6] In the living room, Maureen Stevens, a clerk from the Prince of Wales's office, who also happened to be a talented pianist, gave Diana a weekly private recital as she worked. You can almost hear Stevens piano rippling in the background as Diana writes a fulsome note to her close friend, *Harper's Bazaar* editor Liz Tilberis: 'Dearest Liz, How proud I was to be at your side on Monday evening . . . so deeply moved by your personal touch – the presents for the boys, candles at the hotel and flowers to name but few but most of all your beaming smile, your loving heart. I am always here for you, Liz.'[7] Sometimes Diana would stop and telephone Richard Kay – 'Ricardo', she called him – to help her with the phraseology of a letter. KP was her fortress. On warm summer afternoons, she vanished into its walled garden in shorts and T-shirt and her Versace sunglasses, carrying a bag of books and CDs for her Walkman. On weekends, when William and Harry were home, Burrell would see her in a flowing cotton skirt on her bicycle with the basket in front, speeding down the Palace drive with the boys pedalling furiously behind her.[8] On her thirty-sixth birthday, in July, she received ninety bouquets of flowers and Harry gathered a group of classmates to sing 'Happy Birthday' to her over the telephone.

Diana's charity commitments were pared down from around a hundred to the six she most cared about: Centrepoint, the Royal Marsden Hospital, the Great Ormond Street Hospital for Children, the English National Ballet, the Leprosy Mission and the National Aids Trust. The public announcement she insisted on reaped her unnecessary flak and the resignation of her media adviser Jane Atkinson. But Diana had a reason for being explicit. She wanted to avoid situations where she was just a letterhead. 'If I'm going to talk on behalf of any cause, I want to go and see the problem for myself and learn about it,'⁹ she told the chairman of the Washington Post Company Katharine Graham at that time.

There was a round of social purging. Lord and Lady Palumbo were excised after Peter's candid warnings about Martin Bashir. Elton John was in the deep freeze after acting as a go-between with Diana and Gianni Versace for the fashion designer's coffee-table book, *Rock and Royalty*. (The pictures of the Princess and the boys appeared amid a portfolio of semi-nude male models, and Diana feared it would further annoy the Queen.) Sir Ronald Grierson was bounced after he made the mistake of offering a job to one of the many secretaries Diana froze out. And Fergie was back in Siberia, this time for good. The divorced Duchess had cashed in with an anodyne memoir, which was full of nice comments about her sister-in-law – except for one fatal line. She wrote that when she borrowed a pair of Diana's shoes she had caught a verruca from them. Goddesses don't get warts. Despite Fergie's pleading apologies, Diana never spoke to her again. In 1997, the Princess gave a birthday party for her friend David Tang and told him he could ask anyone he wanted.

'Anyone?' he asked.

'Anyone.'

'All right, then – Fergie.'

'Absolutely not,' Diana replied, and would not be moved.¹⁰

A new and unexpected ally was Raine. In 1993, Diana had finally made her peace with her formidable stepmother. The painful years of separation and divorce from Charles made the Princess see her old adversary in a different light. Still grieving for Daddy, her greatest support, Diana was at last able to recognise that Raine had loved him, too. She invited her stepmother for a weepy reconciliation over lunch at Kensington Palace. For moral support, Raine brought along her fiancé, the French Count Jean François de Chambrun. The precaution turned out to be unnecessary. Afterwards, the Princess and the Countess were often sighted deep in a tête-à-tête at the Connaught Grill. One of Raine's cautions was to try to stay on friendly terms with Charles for the sake of the children. She told Diana that both she – Raine – and her mother, Barbara Cartland, had maintained warm relations with all their former husbands and lovers.¹¹

Diana also made an improbable friend of Katharine 'Kay' Graham. They had met in the summer of 1994, when Lucia Flecha de Lima had brought Diana to Kay's beachfront house on Martha's Vineyard. Not long after that Kay gave a luncheon for Diana and Hillary Clinton at her Washington home. At a British Embassy lunch on the same visit, Diana met Colin Powell again. He told her he had been nominated to lead her in the dancing at the gala that night to raise money for the Nina Hyde Breast Cancer Foundation. Scotland Yard had been worried that at a ball in Chicago earlier in the year a stranger had cut in on Diana's dancing partner. The General was deemed able to handle such an eventuality, but the Princess suggested she do a few practice spins with him in the embassy drawing room. 'She was easy with any melody, and we did all right in our rehearsal,' says Powell. 'She told me, "There's only one thing you ought to know. I'll be wearing a backless dress tonight. Can you cope with that?"'[12] Flirting with the big boys – what bliss!

Diana thrived in America. 'There is no "Establishment" there,' she told her fashion friend Roberto Devorik[13] – wrongly, of course, but correct in the sense that America had no establishment whose rules or members could possibly hurt her feelings. Richard Kay says she thought of America as 'a country so brimming over with glittery people and celebrities that she would be able to disappear'.[14]

Like her life, Diana's taste in fashion became pared down and emphatic after her divorce. 'English style refracted through an un-English sensibility' was how *Vogue*'s Hamish Bowles defined it.[15] Her new evening dresses were minimalist and sexy, a look that had been taboo when she was an in-house royal. 'She knew she had great legs and she wanted to show them off,' said the designer Jacques Azagury.[16] She wore his stunning red bugle-bead tunic over a short pencil skirt in Venice in 1995 and his blue crystal-beaded cocktail dress six inches above the knee to another Serpentine gallery evening. Diana actually looked her best at her most informal. Jumping rangily out of her car for lunch with Rosa Monckton at Le Caprice, wearing stone-washed jeans, a white T-shirt, a beautifully cut navy blue blazer and bare feet in flats (she was usually shod in Jimmy Choo's black grosgrain 'Diana' loafers), she was spectacular. *Vanity Fair* assigned the Peruvian-born photographer Mario Testino to capture her as she now wanted to be seen: a modern woman, active on the world stage – 'vivid, energetic, and fascinating', in the words of Meredith Etherington-Smith, the former fashion editor who introduced Diana to Testino. When Meredith first saw Diana at Kensington Palace, she was astonished at how different she was from the formal, public Princess of old. Now she was 'a tall, electrifying figure', wearing no make-up and 'revealing the truest English rose complexion. Her hair, no longer a stiff helmet, free of lacquer and back combing, flew around her head like a dandelion in the wind.'[17] With her unerring sense of the dramatic, Diana timed Mario Testino's stunning shots to come out on the cover of *Vanity Fair* the same week as her decree absolute.

Diana purged her cupboards of the past. She hated the sight of the frou-frou'd and sequinned relics of her roles as Princess Bride and Windsor Wife and Dynasty Di, embalmed in their suit bags. It was William's brainwave for her to auction off her old gowns for charity in New York, and Diana loved her son's creative notion. It would be at once a glorious psychic gesture to her new life and a boon to the charities she chose, the Aids Crisis Trust and the Royal Marsden Hospital Cancer Fund. A royal rummage sale had never happened before. Most of the Windsor women, including the Queen, consign their old private-occasion items to a discreetly respectable resale shop in London's West End. Diana's auction would be a first.

Old clothes are often suffused with the emotions of the wearer. Meredith Etherington-Smith, who also worked as creative marketing director of Christie's, was assigned by the auction house to help Diana choose and catalogue the items. They sorted through Diana's gowns every morning for a month while Diana relived the occasions when she had worn them. 'Out! Out!' she would cry, pointing at some star-spangled throwback, or 'No! I can't bear to give up this one!' In and out of the catalogue flew Victor Edelstein's oyster dinner dress with a strapless bodice encrusted with white bugle beads and matching bolero, which she had worn that elegant night at the Elysée Palace in Paris with President and Madame Mitterrand. 'It was such a happy evening,' she dithered.[18] She had been afraid of the French being so chic but she felt she had really pulled it off. She sighed over another Edelstein gown, an ink-blue silk velvet creation. This was the dress in which she had wowed the world with John Travolta at the White House. She relinquished it in the end, knowing it would get the auction's top dollar. (An anonymous bidder snapped it up for $222,500.)[19] In retrospect, wrote the fashion maven Suzy Menkes in the *International Herald Tribune*, all the high-glamour outfits of Diana's past looked 'like a dress rehearsal for the little black number worn on the evening Prince Charles confessed his adultery on prime-time television'.[20]

But now, in the year after her divorce, relations with Prince Charles were on a nicely even keel, starting with that tea in July. The arrival in 1996 of Mark Bolland as Charles's assistant private secretary inaugurated an era of glasnost between the offices of the Princess and the Prince. Bolland was a shrewd operator with a marketing background and a useful four years' experience as director of the Press Complaints Commission. He lived in the real world, not the Palace bubble. He owed his job to Camilla; he had come to Charles at the recommendation of her divorce lawyer, Hilary Browne-Wilkinson. In spite of that – or more likely because of it – part of his writ was to end the War between the Waleses. It got in the way, he believed, of the necessary rebuilding of Prince Charles's image. Bolland's first act was to persuade Charles to fire his private secretary, Richard Aylard, the facilitator of the Dimbleby fiasco, and rid the Prince's office of hold-overs from the bitter years of marital competition. Nor was Bolland a fan of the undislodgeable Tiggy Legge-Bourke, sharing Camilla's belief that Tiggy had the ability to wind Charles up.[21] Another positive augury, surely.

Better than all of the above, however, was that Diana's love life had simplified in a wonderful way. In the autumn of 1995, she had at last fallen for a man who was worthy of her affections, who wasn't married and who reciprocated her feelings: the thirty-six-year-old Pakistani heart surgeon Hasnat Khan.

'The One,' as she called him, was the oldest of four children from an affluent, closely knit upper-middle-class family in Jhelum, north of Lahore. Diana first met him at the Royal Brompton Hospital, where she had gone to visit the husband of her soother-in-chief, the Irish nurse-cum-acupuncturist Oonagh Shanley-Toffolo. Joseph Toffolo had suffered a massive haemorrhage during a triple bypass operation. Khan, the senior registrar working with the distinguished surgeon Professor Sir Magdi Yacoub, was in attendance. A grave Omar Sharif figure in a white coat, he arrived with his retinue of assistants when Diana was at the patient's bedside. The doctor was entirely absorbed in Toffolo's condition and took no notice of the Princess – which, for a woman used to everyone fawning over her, was almost unbearably sexy. So was the blood on his tennis shoes, and so were his caring, expressive eyes. 'Oonagh, isn't he drop-dead gorgeous!'[22] Diana hissed at Mrs Shanley-Toffolo after Khan left the room. So gorgeous, in fact, that the bemused Joseph had Diana fussing over him at his bedside for eighteen days straight. In no time, the Kensington Palace apartment was fragrant with the scent of burning joss sticks. The Princess became as keen a student of cardiology as she had been of riding and Islamic art. Her bedside table groaned under a fat copy of *Gray's Anatomy* and piles of surgical reports. She watched *Casualty*, the hospital soap, every Saturday night.[23] Her wardrobe filled up with a colourful selection of shalwar kameez, the bright silk tunic and trousers worn by Pakistani women. She considered converting to Islam. It impressed her that Khan, on religious grounds, refused to fully consummate their affair until the evening of her decree absolute.

Diana took to spending nights with Khan in his small overnight room at the Royal Brompton Hospital and sneaking home to the Palace at dawn. She asked if she could watch him perform open-heart surgery. 'Anybody with courage enough to watch a heart operation can come in,' Khan told her.[24] He couldn't keep her away after that. Sky TV had arranged to film Sir Magdi Yacoub operate at the Harefield Hospital on a seven-year-old African boy, flown to the UK by the Chain of Hope charity. The organisation asked Diana if she would attend to boost the viewership. The footage of her Bambi eyes in black eyeliner peering over the top of a white surgical mask in the operating theatre was the focus of much satiric commentary. Awkwardly, in late November 1995, a photographer from the News of the World caught Diana arriving at the hospital at midnight. She was due to meet Khan coming off his shift, but borrowing the photographer's mobile phone, she promptly dialled through to the paper's royal correspondent, Clive Goodman (nicknamed 'The Eternal Flame' by his colleagues because he never left the office – a habit interrupted when he was sent to jail for four months for tapping into the Clarence House voicemail). She told Goodman that yes, it was true, she was at the hospital comforting terminally ill patients. She did it, she told him, up to four hours a night three times a week. 'I try to be there for them. I seem to draw strength from them. They all need someone, I hold their hands, talk to them, whatever helps.'[25]

Goodman bit. 'MY SECRET NIGHTS AS AN ANGEL' was the News of the World's headline three days later.[26] The story gave birth to an eerie new image of Diana as a compulsive ambulance-chaser and death groupie. Private Eye came up with a 'Di-no card,' 'I, the undersigned, wish to make it clear that in the event of any injury, mental breakdown, life-threatening disease, or other such personal tragedy, I do not wish under any circumstances to be visited by the Princess of Wales.'[27] But better to be the butt of jokes than to be busted for sexy sleepovers with a young Muslim doctor.

It was worth it. The relationship with Hasnat Khan was the most fulfilling she had ever had. 'I found my peace!' she confessed to Lady Bowker. 'He has given me all the things I need!'[28] The doctor didn't want anything from her. She offered to buy him a new car, and he proudly refused. He had a dread of personal publicity. He was not interested in high life or fashionability. His one-bedroom flat in Chelsea was a mess and there was a bit of a paunch under the old T-shirts he wore when he was off duty. He loved what was best about Diana – her compassionate nature, her desire to embrace humanitarian causes. Diana turned the former equerries room in her apartment at Kensington Palace into a basement den for 'Natty', as he was known, so he could pop open a can of Heineken and sit around watching football. At weekends when the staff was off, she would try her hand at cooking him dinner. 'Marks & Spencer have got these very clever little meals that you just put in the microwave and you put the timer on and press the button and it's done for you!' she marvelled to Simone Simmons.[29]

She sometimes disappeared for a whole day to Khan's flat, where she contentedly vacuumed, did the dishes and ironed his shirts – a reprise of her old days with the Jif and dusters. On the night of her birthday, she went out to meet Khan wearing her best sapphire and diamond earrings, a fur coat and, underneath, nothing. Burrell helped run the affair behind the scenes. If there was a lovers' quarrel he would deliver a message to the pub near the hospital where Khan hung out.[30] Diana was practised at keeping things secret. The press rarely found out about the men she was seeing if she didn't want them to.

She made trips to Pakistan whenever she could to bone up on Hasnat's heritage. Her new best friend was Jemima Khan, the beautiful twenty-two-year-old daughter of Annabel and Jimmy Goldsmith. Jemima was married to the Pakistani cricket legend Imran Khan. The two women sat up talking late into the night about how to handle marriage to a traditional-minded Muslim.[31] Diana asked Paul Burrell to talk to a priest about the possibility of a secret marriage to Hasnat. The butler had a meeting with Father Tony Parsons at the Roman Catholic Carmelite church in Kensington High Street where Burrell's son was an altar boy.[32] The priest told him it was impossible to marry a couple without notifying the authorities – or without notifying the fiancé, as it turned out. Hasnat Khan was aghast when he learned of Burrell's consultation and said to Diana, 'Do you honestly think you can just bring a priest here and get married?'[33]

In February 1996, Diana went to Pakistan with Annabel and Annabel's niece Cosima Somerset, to stay with Jemima and Imran at their house in Lahore. The ostensible purpose of the visit was to raise funds for the Shaukat Khanum Memorial Cancer Hospital, founded by Imran in memory of his mother, who had died from the disease. But the real purpose was to flood the zone with images that would wow Hasnat's family.

Diana's desire to impress Khan gave her new purpose. He was a serious man for whom she wanted to do serious things. She was looking for a cause that would passionately involve her, something in which her presence could produce a transformative result, as it had done in the mid-eighties with Aids. 'She felt very strongly about getting involved with something that wasn't a ballet charity,' said a friend. Mike Whitlam, then Director General of the British Red Cross, had the answer. The Red Cross was among the charities Diana had dropped right after the divorce, but Whitlam knew better than to sulk. He understood her value and her temperament. He had seen how effective she was in ladling out soup to children in the Zimbabwe bush, but he had also taken note of why an attempt to recruit her to a special advisory committee of the International Red Cross in 1994 had failed. Diana couldn't cope with long, detail-oriented briefings on the Rwandan refugee problem. In committee meetings she had the attention span of a fruit fly. Whitlam knew that this skittish thoroughbred had to be led to missions delicately, or she would veer off on some impulsive detour of her own. The Red Cross was in the network of global organisations campaigning for a ban on the use of landmines, for their clearance, and for help for their victims. He began sending Diana photographs and reports about the devastating effects of mines that had been left uncleared after wars. He saw this as the right cause for Diana at the right time.

On Monday 13 January 1997, wearing blue denim jeans and a blazer, Diana stepped into the throbbing heat of Luanda, the capital of Angola, after an eleven-hour commercial flight to southern Africa with Whitlam and Lord Deedes, the grand old man of the *Daily Telegraph*. The country was reeling from a twenty-year civil war. Fifteen million mines had been scattered during that war among a population of twelve million, and clearance had barely begun. The streets were populated with men, women and children without legs, few of whom had wheelchairs or even crutches. Some 70,000 innocents had stepped on a landmine; every 334th citizen was an amputee, but only a few hundred false limbs were fitted every month.[34] Diana was galvanised by what she saw. In the wreck of Huambo, still a disputed and heavily mined area, she and her party had to walk in single file behind an anti-mine engineer to reach a small, godforsaken hospital that had no electricity and not enough beds. There was sixteen-year-old Rosaline, who had lost her right leg, and the baby in her womb. And there was seven-year-old Helena, who had gone out to fetch water and stepped on a mine. It had blown out her intestines. A saline drip was keeping her alive. Flies buzzed about her. Arthur Edwards, who was covering the expedition for the *Sun*, says the child was lying exposed on her back when Diana got to her. 'The first thing she did was something instinctive. She made the child decent, covered her up. It was the thing a mother would do. She was concerned for the child's dignity.'[35] The rightness of her gesture was something he never forgot, nor was the way she talked softly to the child and stroked her hand. After she moved on, Christina Lamb, the *Sunday Times* foreign correspondent, who speaks Portuguese, stayed with the dying child. 'She said to me, "Who was that?" It was quite hard trying to explain Princess Diana to somebody who didn't know. And I said: "She's a princess from England, from far away." And she said to me, "Is she an angel?"'[36]

The child died soon afterwards. 'The last thing she saw,' reflected Lamb, was this 'beautiful lady that she thought was an angel.'[37]

Diana had no celestial qualities in the eyes of various Tory MPs and ministers in the government in London. She was a 'self-publicist', a 'loose cannon', briefed Lord Howe, an Under-Secretary of State in the Ministry of Defence. Howe was offended that Diana's support for a ban on landmines was out of line with Tory policy, which was to oppose a unilateral ban while working for a worldwide ban which would exempt 'smartmines' that are effective only for a short time. Peter Viggers, a Tory member of the Commons Select Defence Committee, popped a vein. Why, she was just like Brigitte Bardot banging on about saving cats! 'It doesn't add much to the sum of human knowledge. This is an important and sophisticated argument. It doesn't help . . . for a very ill-informed Princess . . . to point at the amputees and say how terrible it is.'[38]

Actually, it did help. It helped enormously. The 'very ill-informed' Princess was backed by Tony Blair's Labour Opposition, by the Liberal Democrats, by Deedes, and by military figures no less imposing than the two Gulf War Generals, Norman Schwarzkopf and Sir Peter de la Billière. She had landed herself in the middle of exactly the kind of controversy Henry Kissinger had warned her to avoid. Well, too bad. Angola was a snapshot of the woman Diana was about to be. 'I never saw someone as much a project under construction as Diana,' said one of her friends from this period. 'We usually do that stuff in the wings of our personalities, but with Diana you could almost see the plumbing and the wires as she was changing in front of you.'[39]

Diana's landmine commitment was not, to use one of the Queen's favourite pejoratives, a 'stunt'. It drew forth everything that was best about her in the service of a cause that was heart-rending, under-publicised, and controversial. Chased in Angola by the press the day after the Tory smoke bombs went off in London, Diana did not engage in argument. 'It's an unnecessary distraction . . . It's sad . . . I'm a humanitarian, not a politician.'[40]

And indeed, few politicians would have had the courage to do what she did next. The Red Cross had decided that it was too dangerous to go to Cuito, Africa's most heavily mined town, laced with booby traps. Seven children had just been killed playing football in an area that was supposed to have been cleared. But Diana would not hear of cancelling. She pressed Whitlam, who was anxious for her safety. She lobbied the wife of the President of Angola. And the next day she was in Cuito, in visor, body armour over white cotton shirt and khaki trousers, ready to be delicately guided through another allegedly cleared area – even though exposed and half-extracted mines were visible. The volunteers in the Halo Trust, a British charity clearing mines, warned her to stay close to them. 'I think by the end of the briefing she was beginning to wonder if this was a good idea,' says Whitlam. 'But she did it.'[41]

Bringing to bear all the reckless bravery she'd once used to defy the royal family – but in a much better cause – she walked through a half-cleared minefield. 'One or two of the journalists,' said Whitlam, 'hadn't quite got the shot they wanted and jokingly asked if she'd mind doing it again.' To everyone's astonishment, she agreed. 'She realised that this was one of the shots that was really going to make a big impact around the world,' said Whitlam. 'So she did the walk a second time.'[42] This second walk was Diana's purest synthesis of courage, calculation and brilliantly directed media power.

The Tory government, having badly lost the public relations battle, smoothed it over as a 'misunderstanding' and promised support for 'progress towards' a worldwide ban.[43] Too late. It was just another symptom they were out of step with popular feeling. A few months later the Tories lost the general election by a landslide. Tony Blair, her new supporter, was Prime Minister at the age of forty-four. His victory, on a brilliant day in May after eighteen long years of Tory dominance, was welcomed with the euphoria of a new dawn. A young, modernising and empathetic Prime Minister and his independent, high-powered wife were pledging to end the corrupt, uptight ways of the crusty old establishment. High five! Diana stayed up all night watching the results coming in on

TV. She saw New Labour's England as a place that would have all the best things about America – classlessness, freshness and freedom from stifling tradition. And above all, of course, an appreciation of her.

'How dare anyone criticise Diana Princess of Wales for taking up this heartrending cause?' wrote Clare Short, who was Tony Blair's Secretary of State for International Development, in a July 1997 issue of the *Spectator*, referring to the landmine campaign. 'Diana's stand on the issue deserves the utmost praise. Her public profile is able to give hope to millions of victims and campaigners that once and for all there may be a global ban on the manufacture and use of anti-personnel landmines.'[44]

I wish we could leave Diana's story there. I wish we could leave her as I saw her that summer's day in New York in her mint-green suit and early tan when she came for the wildly successful auction of her dresses. She was a woman of substance then, who had found her future. But Diana was always fragile in her new roles. Love, or the lack of it, always dragged her down. With that descent came an emotion that never bedevilled her pioneer efforts on behalf of landmine victims or Aids patients: fear.

Hasnat Khan was slipping away for good. His refusal to go public effectively meant that he didn't want to marry her. He told friends he couldn't face the onslaught of becoming Di's New Guy in every tabloid newspaper. He recoiled from the prospect of his work at the hospital being invaded by reporters. There had been a nasty foretaste when the first story of a rumoured affair between the two appeared in the *Sunday Mirror*.[45] Panicked when she heard that it was about to run, Diana turned to Richard Kay for a red-herring counter-story.

'It' – the *Mirror*'s story – 'is bull****,' Kay quoted Diana in the *Mail*, which was always happy to rubbish the competition. The Princess, wrote Kay, 'is understood to be deeply upset at the allegations because of the hurt they will do William and Harry. Diana told friends, "It has given me a lot of laughs. In fact, we are laughing ourselves silly."'[46] Khan did not share the purported mirth. He was as wounded by Diana's silly denial as he was irritated by the exposure in the first place. He got on fine with William and Harry – especially William, who had had a long session with him one weekend asking career advice – so that reference annoyed him, too. He was starting to receive racist threats in the mail, which he found stressful.[47] For three weeks after Richard Kay's story Khan refused all contact with Diana, rendering her predictably hysterical. The secrecy of his affair with Diana actually suited Khan, who had no desire to arouse the wrath of his own relations.

Diana was better qualified than anyone to know that you don't just marry a man, you marry his family. Hasnat Khan was a Pathan, a group of peoples between Pakistan and Afghanistan, descended from warriors and notable for their fierce attachment to their cultural traditions. His parents had tried twice, in 1987 and then in 1992, to marry him off to a suitable Muslim bride with equivalent social standing, and by 1996 they were impatient to try again. It is one of the ironies of Diana's life that she was always searching to replace her own dysfunctional family with one that didn't want her. This time, as usual, the situation was doomed, but for a novel reason. With the Windsors, she was suitable but not desired. With the Khans, she was desired but not suitable. After Diana had spent eighteen months misleading the press, a *Daily Express* reporter landed an interview with Hasnat's father, Dr Rashid Khan, who offered a bruising assessment of Diana as a bridal prospect for his son. 'He is not going to marry her,' the elder Khan said. 'We are looking for a bride for him. She must belong to a respectable family. She should be rich, belonging to the upper middle class. Preferably to our relations or tribe, which is Pathan. But if we do not find her in our own tribe, we can try outside it. But preferably she should be at least a Pakistani Muslim girl.'[48] This was the first time a Spencer had been disdained as 'not quite our tribe', and it only challenged Diana to try even harder to nail Hasnat down.

It was a hopeless assignment. In May 1997, Diana's lover was deeply upset when, without forewarning him, she used the cover of a three-day trip to Pakistan to raise funds for Imran Khan's cancer hospital to descend without notice on Hasnat's sprawling family in an upscale suburb of Lahore. They clustered round and took her picture and served her English tea until a simultaneous power and water cut drove them outside to sit in a circle in the garden of their walled compound, making pleasant, if stilted, conversation with the charming stranger from the United Kingdom. It was a surreal scene, especially when one considers that Diana pictured herself moving in with them as their new daughter-in-law. The Khans were all perfectly charmed by Diana, who ended the evening lying on the floor watching cartoons with the youngest kids, but charm was irrelevant.[49] Hasnat's mother had no intention of letting the union happen, and Hasnat had doubts of his own.

He loved Diana, yes. How could he not? This beautiful, radiant creature, adored by the world, had chosen him, an obscure Pakistani doctor, when she could have had the pick of every billionaire on earth.

But Khan was troubled that the love he gave her never seemed to be enough. Was anyone's? 'Diana needed more love than any Englishman can give,' observes Diana's girlhood friend and later Tory MP Hugo Swire.[50] But there may have been no man alive who could have answered the clamorous needs of Diana's early abandonment. Like Hoare's, Hasnat's pager would go off twenty times a day on his medical rounds. For a woman so sensitive to the needs of others, she was strangely blind when it came to those of the people closest to her. She wanted to own his future, arrange his life. With Hewitt, she had wanted to call his superiors and get the order to send him to Germany countermanded. With Khan she wanted to rearrange his surgical schedule so he could travel with her. 'Diana believed, against all the evidence,' opined the essayist Clive James, 'that there was some kind of enchanted place called Abroad, where she could be understood and where she could lead a more normal life.'[51] James saw this place as a recurring theme in the last years of Diana's life. Her dream was a marriage between two globe-trotting humanitarians, rushing to trouble spots with her compassion and his doctor's bag. An overdose of public adoration had made her almost delusional. She told me over lunch that she thought she could resolve the conflicts of Northern Ireland. 'I'm very good at sorting people's heads out.'[52] She wanted to lift Hasnat out of the annoying grind and insane hours of the Brompton Hospital into some medical habitat where they could live together in sunny exile with a swimming pool – in Australia or South Africa. At an international think-tank dinner in Rimini, Italy, she found herself next to Professor Christiaan Barnard, the septuagenarian heart transplant pioneer. She lobbied him hard to get Hasnat a position in South Africa and twice gave him dinner at Kensington Palace to discuss Hasnat's future. The proud Mr Khan went ballistic when, on finally meeting Barnard, he was asked to submit his CV.[53]

In June, the Khans arrived en masse in Stratford-upon-Avon for their annual holiday. Their presence must have deepened Hasnat's doubts that a superstar princess could ever be absorbed into his close-knit Muslim family. It was clear to his relations that he was wrestling between his love for Diana and what he knew he had to do if he wished to pursue a serious medical career. A bad augury for Khan was a *Sunday Mirror* story on 29 June alleging that Diana and Hasnat had become 'unofficially engaged after the amazing summit with his family' in Pakistan in May.[54] Unbeknown to Diana, Simone Simmons, her therapist and confidante, had, for months, been selling stories to the newspaper about her, including details of her affair with Khan. Its news editor, Chris Boffey, authorised payments to Simmons of up to about a thousand pounds a week in cash, until he left the paper in February of that year. Over that twelve-month period the *Sunday Mirror* paid out about £20,000 to Simmons.[55] Is it possible that Diana was behind the leak herself? Simmons denied planting the Hasnat story, but Diana did not believe her – and never spoke to her again.

Khan, forced into the open, confided his agony about what to do to a trusted Pakistani confidant. His friend's advice was unequivocal: 'End the affair, and get on with your life.'[56]

When the Khan family, returning to Lahore in early August, gave Hasnat gifts for the beautiful Princess who had visited them, he told them to post them to her instead. He wouldn't be seeing Diana any more.[57] Knowing this rejection was coming, Diana took to reproaching him with scalding words and tears. She could not accept that her dream of marriage to Khan was over. But the serious young doctor was not a man who played games.

Diana began to sink. She felt she had nowhere to go, no one to share her miseries. She had cut off Simone Simmons. She was not on speaking terms with her mother. Frances, sadly, had become a drunk. She had lost her driver's licence in 1996 after failing a breathalyser test. She told her friend Barbara Gilmour that she cycled to a friend's funeral and, when it rained, hitched a ride home in the hearse. She was increasingly indiscreet about the royal family, referring to them as 'German dwarves' and said the Queen's outfits looked like they came from the Red Cross.[58] Frances infuriated Diana by giving a paid interview to *Hello!* magazine in May 1997 in which she had innocently remarked that Diana's loss of her HRH title was 'absolutely wonderful' since it allowed her to find her own identity.[59] More seriously, she angered the Princess with the ferocity of her objection to her daughter's relationship with 'Muslim men'.[60] Diana cut her off after that. Frances's letters apologising to Diana were returned unopened.

Increasingly lonely, Diana became unhealthily dependent on Paul Burrell. His busybody influence only fuelled her various paranoias. 'He didn't like anybody he thought was closer or had more access to her,' says Diana's former chef, Mervyn Wycherley. Wycherley believes he may have been 'stitched up' by Burrell.[61] There were false rumours that he tried to hawk the Kensington Palace menu books to Fleet Street when in fact he was made redundant after the Wales' separation, received a handsome settlement and parted amicably with both parties. (At his exit interview with Diana a colleague recalls she told the chef, 'You always hurt the one you love,' and handed him a carriage clock.)[62] Burrell had hardened her attitude to Fergie too, whispering to Diana that the Duchess, on her book tour in the US, was using her relationship with the Princess to get publicity. In fairness, it was the TV interviewers, not Fergie herself, who kept bringing Diana's name up.

In bad periods like this, the insecure Diana felt watched, and spied on. In the past she had twice had her rooms at Kensington Palace swept for bugs. On a trip to Rome with her Argentinian friend Roberto Devorik, she had startled him with her violent suspicions. A portrait of Prince Philip hanging on the wall evoked an outburst: 'He hates me. He really hates me and would like to see me disappear.' She would wind up dead in a fake accident, she told Devorik. 'I am a threat in their eyes. They only use me when they need me for official functions and then they drop me again in the darkness . . . they are not going to kill me by poisoning me or in a big plane where others will get hurt. They will do it when I am in a small plane, in a car when I am driving or in a helicopter.'[63] Devorik asked her why anyone should want to kill her. If she was so afraid, why didn't she travel with a bodyguard, still available to her from the Royal Protection Squad? She told him she thought they spied on her. She was fed up with being followed around.

'She saw the protectors as assailants,' Clive James noted. 'It seemed she would rather have gone down in a hail of broken glass than live in fear.'[64] Diana did live in fear, but it wasn't death she was afraid of. It was the thought of being 'dropped again in the darkness', as she put it to Devorik. She had carried that darkness inside her since she was a child. She had always fought it with her dazzle. Now, more than ever, she feared being left alone in the dark.

'Roberto, you are so naive,' she told him. 'Don't you see, they took my HRH title and now they are slowly taking my kids? They are now letting me know when I can have the children.'[65]

Diana's feeling of being marginalised was most intense as August approached. The boys disappeared into the heathery wilds of Balmoral and they loved it. After her appearance on *Panorama* and her divorce from the Prince of Wales, invitations to similar secluded aristocratic estates with shooting for the boys did not gush forth, and she was not inclined to ask her brother for help again. With her, William and Harry were stuck in London or harassed at Disney World or having to behave themselves at some nouveau riche billionaire's country mansion. She told Jasper Conran's mother, the writer Shirley Conran, that she felt that nothing she could offer William and Harry as a holiday could compete with Balmoral. 'They do all those manly, killing things,' she sighed, 'and there's that wonderful go-cart track.'[66]

The propinquity of Eton to Windsor meant William had forged a close bond with the Queen and the Duke of Edinburgh. Sometimes in the evenings he went for walks in Windsor Great Park with Prince Philip, responding to his grandfather's tough code and sense of humour with an eagerness Prince Charles had always scorned. Having failed with his own son, Philip saw William as the boy he always wished he'd had. They shared a passion for military history. It pleased Diana but it also made her jealous. William was her closest confidant. 'She told me she had very private and very profound conversations with him,' Roberto Devorik said, 'and he was an extraordinary moral support.'[67] Her son was older than his years, burdened as much by his mother's confidences as by his future responsibilities; she had taken him through the divorce terms before she agreed to them. She began including him in some of her lunches at Kensington Palace with the press.

'All my hopes are on William now,' she told me. 'I am hoping he will grow up to be as smart about handling the media as John Kennedy, Jr.'[68] But William was not John F. Kennedy's son. He was the heir to the British throne. However much William might look like her and smile like her, he belonged as surely to Prince Charles and the Crown as to Lady Diana Spencer – perhaps more. Inevitably, William would have to become, 'Windsorised'. As England's future King it was his destiny.

Diana's fear of exclusion was aggravated by the deterioration of her relationship with Charles. The promising thaw, in which she had invested hopes, did a straight nosedive once she perceived the key issue in Mark Bolland's agenda. She had not reckoned that Bolland's rehab plan for her husband's image would be focused so intently on the selling of Camilla to the public. The Prince's mistress would not have sponsored Bolland for the job if his agenda had not tallied with hers. Much of Bolland's day was spent figuring out who was opposed to this agenda and making sure they left the employ of the Prince of Wales. As for Camilla herself, from not wanting to marry Charles because the status quo suited her, she had taken the opposite position. The divorce from Andrew had left her short of money. When a friend went to have lunch with her at her house in Wiltshire after her divorce, he was startled when the doorbell ran and she rushed off to hide. 'God, it's the fishmonger – I haven't paid him,' she exclaimed. 'We have to hide until he's gone.'[69]

Camilla, however, received good financial counsel to rescue her from the predicament created by Charles. After all, if not for his confession to Jonathan Dimbleby, Camilla would not have been divorced in the first place. The crux of the advice was that with her million-pound half-share of the Parker Bowles marital assets, she should buy a house suitable to her position. Then, on the grounds that the Prince of Wales must be entertained in the style to which he was entitled, the Prince would be prevailed upon to meet the associated costs. Camilla had to be made 'cash poor', said one of her friends, 'to trigger in Charles not so much his sympathy as his responsibility towards the woman in his life'.[70]

In May 1995, for £850,000, Camilla purchased Ray Mill House, a seventeen-acre estate on the banks of the River Avon in Wiltshire, and began a campaign of expansion.

The new residence slowly but surely acquired a staff of two housekeepers, two gardeners, a chauffeur and car from Prince Charles's fleet, a separately built security cottage complete with Scotland Yard protection office, and stabling privileges at Highgrove. Bernie Flannery, the Highgrove butler, was instructed to do Camilla's grocery shopping at the local Sainsbury's whenever she wished – and to charge it to the Prince's bill. Arguing, truthfully, that a more visible royal mistress has to look good, Camilla was granted an annual dress allowance from the Wales war chest. Eventually Charles covered her debt of around £130,000 at Coutts bank. Eventually he granted Camilla her own stipend of £120,000 a year, rising to £180,000.[71] Eventually Camilla Parker Bowles became HRH the Duchess of Cornwall. Eventually – at least, my money's on it – HRH the Duchess of Cornwall will be the Queen. Now that Camilla's image reversal is complete, former St James's Palace staffers are amused that the favoured storyline in the press is of the patience and fortitude of the 'woman who waited'. From the inside it sure didn't look that way. 'It was Bolland who invented that fiction,' said a former colleague of his. 'And, I can tell you, it was quite an aggressive campaign.'[72]

Camilla's rise hit Diana with blunt force when Charles chose Highgrove as the venue for his mistress's upcoming fiftieth birthday celebration on 17 July 1997. The flagrant use of their former marital home was an unnecessary blow for Diana. It plunged her more deeply into her 'darkness'. She was deeply envious as well as deeply hurt: while Charles had found his love, Diana had lost hers. Salt was rubbed in the wound by a flattering television documentary about Camilla – another plank in Bolland's relentless campaign. Shirley Conran advised her not to watch it but Diana couldn't resist. After all this time she still wanted one question answered: Why? Why was it *this woman* who had taken it all – her Prince, her emotional security, her destiny as Queen? After watching the programme, Diana called her astrologer Debbie Frank in anguish. 'All the grief in my past is resurfacing,' Diana told her. 'I feel terrible . . . so frightened and needy.' She sounded, Frank said, 'breathy, childlike, again'.[73]

She needed to get out of town. She had toyed for a bit with spending the summer in the US, and asked Teddy Forstmann to find her a house near his in Southampton. 'I found her something but five days later she called back and said the security people had said the openness of the Hamptons wasn't safe.'[74] It was a boon when the importunate bullfrog Mohamed Al Fayed asked her to bring the boys to stay at his villa in the South of France. At Al Fayed's palatial villa, the Castel Hélène she would be fully protected, not just by the royal protection cops who always accompanied the royal boys but by Al Fayed's own prodigious security. It was a good place to nurse her disappointment. When her hairdresser Natalie Symons arrived on the morning of 11 July, after Diana's break-up with Khan, she was packing for the holiday and sobbing her heart out. Hasnat had spent what would be his last night with her at Kensington Palace and apparently an upsetting scene had taken place, 'I could tell she was totally distraught because she didn't have any mascara on, and she always put her mascara on before she did anything else,' Symons recalled.[75]

The spiral had begun. As she used to say to Patrick Jephson: 'Stand by for a mood swing, boys.' But her last oscillations spun so fast the contrasts seem more shocking. Dodi appeared three days into her holiday in the South of France, summoned by his father, and the now intensely vulnerable Diana fell for the bait. Within weeks, she was on a cruise alone with Dodi. The woman whose feet disappeared into the green pile carpet covered in Pharaoh's heads aboard Mohamed Al Fayed's private plane and squealed over Dodi's gifts in Bulgari boxes was the same woman who drove in sombre silence up Sniper's Alley in the shattered city of Sarajevo to comfort landmine victims.[76] The woman who posed for a boatload of French paparazzi in a tiger-striped swimsuit and called the gossip columnist Nigel Dempster at the *Daily Mail* to cackle, 'Nigel, what does everyone expect? That I spend the whole summer cooped up in Kensington Palace?'[77] was the same woman who, only weeks before had encountered a woman tending her son's grave in a Sarajevo cemetery and tenderly embraced her.

'God, we heard some terrible stories,' said Lord Deedes, who went with her into Sarajevo. 'She very often interviewed somebody without an interpreter and she would take some time over it. There was a widow who had lost her young husband. He had gone fishing and had hit a mine. When we went there the lady was absolutely brain-dead but when we left she was revived. I really did think there that Diana had a healing touch. There is really no doubt.'[78]

There is no doubt either that the press really preferred the Princess Di of the past. In Angola, Christina Lamb talked to the royal hacks in the bar of Luanda's Hotel Presidente and heard them 'wistfully recalling previous jaunts to Klosters and Barbuda, and longing for the Diana of old who went to balls and banquets and wore Versace instead of flak jackets'.[79] They found that Diana again only a few months later, when the *Jonikal* docked in Porto Cervo in Sardinia and Diana and Dodi went shopping. Diana came back to the boat with armfuls of cashmere sweaters because Dodi bought her every colour they had.[80] She told Rosa Monckton she found his conspicuous consumption embarrassing, but that did not prevent her from making herself demeaningly complicit.[81] Her mother became frantic at being unable to communicate her deep feelings of unease at the pictures appearing at home. Frances made repeated calls to the Queen Mother's page, William Tallon, a favourite of Diana's, begging him to try to talk her daughter, when she got back, into breaking her silence. Tallon had no success. Frances told an old family friend at this time, 'I cannot see the sun shining on my daughter's head again.'[82]

The murder of the flamboyant fashion star Gianni Versace in South Beach on 15 July, while Diana was afloat on Al Fayed's yacht, was a meteor shower in the exploding sky of her final summer. Versace had bridged the gap between fashion and celebrity, just as Diana had bridged the gap between royalty and celebrity. Versace had turned hooker-style into high fashion, adopted by movie stars and rock icons in the eighties and nineties. Even a princess could feel exciting in his clothes. He sent Diana trunkloads of his slinky gowns for nights when she wanted to make a splash. 'He was killed,' wrote *La Repubblica*, 'like a prince laid low in his own blood, with one hand outstretched toward his oil paintings, his tapestries, his gold.'[83] Diana at first assumed that the killing (which turned out to be the work of a gay psychopath) was a terrorist assassination. Dodi's bodyguard, Lee Sansum, found her on the deck of the *Jonikal* very early the next morning gazing sadly out to sea. 'Do you think they'll do that to me?' she asked him.[84] She made up with Elton John at Versace's funeral in Milan, sitting beside him and Sting and patting Elton's hand comfortingly – a preview of even sadder things to come.

Back and forth she swung that last summer until the pendulum took her to Paris. And yet in the days in between her boat trips with Dodi she seemed to have such a clear new future outlined in London. She plotted with Shirley Conran something she'd never had: a career. 'She wanted professional fulfilment,' said Conran. 'She wanted to do something herself that would show she wasn't an idiot.'[85] The something was a great idea – to produce documentaries like the well-received film she had made with the BBC of her trip to Angola. She was all excited about the project – a film every two years, each one the centrepiece of a discrete humanitarian campaign. First, she told Conran, she would raise awareness of the issue, then produce a documentary in partnership with one of the television channels, and ultimately leave a structure in place to maintain her involvement with the cause. It was Diana's version of a Clinton global initiative – and she had the idea first. The issue she wanted to start with was illiteracy.

'Thick as a plank' Diana was getting herself an education after all. The Red Cross's Mike Whitlam reminded her during their time in Angola, 'Don't forget there are ten million landmines left by the British in the deserts of North Africa.' She replied, 'Mike, I think you'll find it's twenty-three million.'[86] And she was right. 'We had a public meeting on landmines,' says Lord Deedes, 'and she really knew what she was doing. She wasn't just a royal overseer.'[87]

She wasn't just a royal anything. That was the beauty of it. Had she lived, losing her HRH might have turned out to be the best thing that had ever happened to her, just like her mother said. Yes, she was losing most of the perks and protections of the royal cocoon. But the power of her magic touch with the media and the public was something no one could take from her. And what she was gaining was freedom – the freedom to act without the constraints and limitations of Palace and political bureaucrats, the freedom to embrace causes of her own choosing regardless of their potential for controversy, the freedom to make a difference to the things that mattered and to see results.

In Ottawa, not so long after her walk through the minefields, 122 governments agreed on a treaty banning the use of anti-personnel landmines. The Nobel committee awarded the campaign the Nobel Peace Prize, it was coupled with the name of the leading American campaigner, Jodie Williams. In the House of Commons, during the second reading of the Landmines Bill 1998, the Foreign Secretary, Robin Cook, paid handsome tribute to Diana, Princess of Wales, for her 'immense contribution . . . to bringing home to many of our constituents the human costs of landmines'.[88]

Diana was not there to hear it. She was alone on an island, in her grave at Althorp.

## Chapter 21

# Crash

'Listen, mate, Diana's possibly been killed by the bloody paparazzi and you're trying to flog me pictures of her still warm corpse.'
— Piers Morgan's diary, Sunday 31 August 1997

Silent Sunday.

The people of England went to bed on Saturday night, having just seen happy television images of a playgirl princess leaving Sardinia with her racy new boyfriend. They rose to sombre bulletins about the return of her coffin. Some were awakened by ringing telephones while it was still dark: insomniacs and night workers, who first heard the news, were calling friends and family with the cry, 'I just have to talk to someone.' There was a power surge beginning at around 4 a.m. as millions of kettles were turned on to make pots of tea for the TV marathon.[1] The national anthem played every half-hour. There was no precedent for such a gesture – Diana was no longer a member of the royal family – but then there was no precedent for anything that was to happen in the coming week. The cancellation of the day's football coverage was bravely borne. On railways stations and in airports, the reticent British turned and hugged each other for comfort. The stiff upper lip was trembling. Soon it broke into the most astonishing collective weeping the nation has ever seen.

With the grief came a compulsion to blame. The loss of one so special and so young in circumstances so violent yet so mundane required a culprit or a conspiracy, an explanation commensurate with the scale of the shock. Diana's brother, Earl Spencer, got the tumbril rattling within hours of her death. Standing outside his leafy Cape Town home, where he was on holiday with his children, he issued a fiery denunciation: 'I always believed the press would kill her in the end. But not even I could imagine that they would take such a direct hand in her death as seems to be the case. It would appear that every proprietor and editor of every publication that has paid for intrusive and exploitative photographs of her, encouraging greedy and ruthless individuals to risk everything in pursuit of Diana's image, has blood on their hands today.'[2]

The paparazzi were truly in the cross hairs. If any representative of that nasty, foreign-sounding breed had showed his face that day in any of the shires or suburbs of England, he would have been drawn and quartered. It could hardly have looked worse for them. Of the pack pursuing Diana from the Ritz – five cars, three motorbikes and two scooters – the first to reach the crash had a name tailored for a public lynching: Romuald Rat, aged twenty-five. It didn't help that he was the same burly photographer who had shoved against Dodi and Diana as they entered Dodi's apartment on the Rue Arsène-Houssaye earlier that night. The Honda 650 on which Rat was riding pillion screeched to a halt twenty yards past the crash. The photographer jumped off and raced back towards the wreck. As he ran, he snapped off one picture, then two more. How could he not? The scene in the ghastly fluorescent-lit tunnel under the Place d'Alma was one of such hell it demanded to be recorded. The luxury Mercedes from the Ritz was now a bundle of twisted metal facing the direction it had come from. Grey smoke from its engine mingled with petrol fumes and a metallic smell of burning. Its horn blared ceaselessly, jammed by the dead body of the driver, Henri Paul, pinioned on the steering column by the impact of a direct collision with the thirteenth of the tunnel's concrete pillars at sixty-eight miles an hour.

The Princess of Wales, Dodi Fayed and their bodyguard Trevor Rees-Jones had been flung violently around as the car rebounded from the impact and hurtled spinning across two lanes into the right tunnel wall. Diana lay crumpled on the floor of the wreck, doubled up with her head wedged between the two front seats and facing the back. Her jewellery – a bracelet with six rows of pearls, a gold watch decorated with white stones – was scattered about.[3]

Rat prided himself on knowing first aid and resuscitation techniques. He opened the rear door of the Mercedes. He saw Dodi Fayed mangled, obviously dead, his jeans ripped apart, and Diana still breathing and apparently unmarked, her body covered by a floor mat. He lifted the mat and used it to cover Dodi's exposed genitals, then took Diana's hand to feel her pulse. She moaned. 'Be cool, doctor is coming,' Rat said to her in French-accented English.[4] He uttered the same reassuring words to Rees-Jones, semi-conscious in the front seat. The bodyguard's nose and eye sockets had been smashed back so far that, in profile, his bloodied face looked almost completely flat.[5]

Within two minutes of the crash, more camera flashes punctuated the eerie glow. In the car doorway, Rat was jostled by a rival French photographer, Christian Martinez, forty-three, taking pictures of Diana over Rat's shoulder, 'Get back, don't take any more pictures inside the car,' Rat shouted. 'Va te faire foûtre!' Martinez snarled. 'Go fuck yourself! Get out of the way! I'm doing the same job as you!'[6]

The first doctor appeared in little more than a minute after the crash. The photographers made way for him. Dr Frédéric Mailliez, thirty-six years old, worked for the emergency call service SOS Médicins, but it was by luck he was on his way from a birthday party when he entered the tunnel, in the opposite direction to Henri Paul, saw the smouldering wreck and called the emergency services on his mobile. 'The back door was already open when I reached the car . . . I began examining the young woman in the back. I could see she was beautiful, but at that stage, had no idea who she was.'[7] Diana was having difficulty breathing. Mailliez ran back to his car, rang the emergency services, grabbed an oxygen mask and tank from his boot, raced back to lift her head and gently fit the mask. She resisted, 'moaning and gesturing in all directions'.[8] When she cried out he knew she was English. 'She kept saying how much she hurt.' She had no obvious external injuries, beyond a gash on her forehead, and a weak and rapid pulse. Dr Mailliez thought she had a fair chance of surviving.[9]

A policeman fought his way to the car through at least a dozen excited paparazzi, whose flashes were going off like machine guns.[10] Officer Sébastien Dorzee and his partner, Lino Gagliardone, heading towards Place d'Alma along Cours Albert Premier in response to a radio alert, had seen people frantically pointing in the direction of the tunnel. 'There's been a crash – get down there – it's in the tunnel – a terrible noise like a bomb explosion – hurry up!'[11] Gagliardone radioed for backup from the patrol car while Dorzee ran to the Mercedes, reached the rear door, and took over briefly from Dr Mailliez. It was exactly 12.30 a.m. Dorzee recognised the Princess of Wales. Her eyes were open. She uttered something 'in a foreign language' – he thought it was 'My God', in English. She turned her head, and saw the lifeless Dodi just in front of her, and then turned her head again towards the front where the bodyguard was writhing and Henri Paul lay dead. She became agitated, then lowered her head and closed her eyes.[12]

At 12.33 a.m. Dorzee and Mailliez stepped aside for the *sapeurs-pompiers* – the Paris Fire and Rescue Service. Ten of them appeared in the tunnel in T-shirts and dark blue trousers, led by Sergeant Xavier Gourmelon. Two *pompiers* – firemen – lifted out Dodi and began, futilely, to administer cardiac massage. As for Rees-Jones, it was impossible to extricate him right away. The car roof would have to be cut off under floodlights by a *camion de désincarcération* – a truck outfitted as a kind of mobile tin-opener – and the disturbance was considered dangerous to Diana. They lifted the bodyguard's head so he could breathe and put him in a cervical collar. Sergeant Philippe Boyer, attending Diana, gave her a new oxygen mask and covered her with an isothermal blanket. Gourmelon heard Diana murmur, 'My God, what's happened?'[13]

The scene around the crash was now chaotic. Blocked cars were honking, people were yelling, the Mercedes horn was still blaring. There was the 'pin-pon' sound of sirens as police and fire brigades converged. The constant camera flashes, fast and strobe-like, made movement look jerky. Some in the gathering crowd shouted insults at the paparazzi. Dorzee tried to halt the frenzy of picture-taking but Christian Martinez pushed back. 'Piss off, let me do my work!' he yelled. 'In Sarajevo, the cops don't stand in our way!'[14] (Later, Dorzee asserted that 'at no time did a photographer come to lend a hand.')[15] Into the mélée in the tunnel roared a BMW motorcycle with a young woman, clad in black leather, riding pillion. It was Mme Maud Coujard, the deputy public prosecutor. Numerous photographers had fled on the arrival of police reinforcements; Mme Coujard had the rest rounded up and driven off in a van for interrogation.

While the French took their time investigating nine photographers and a motorcycle messenger on suspicion of 'involuntary homicide' and failing to assist people in danger, the focus of the blame in some quarters shifted to the supposedly poor French medical care. If only Diana had been tended by the superior British or American systems! She could have been saved! Five months later, two reporters for *Time* magazine, Thomas Sancton and Scott MacLeod, would give transatlantic weight to this xenophobic thesis, quoting American doctors in their 1998 book *Death of a Princess*.[16] In 2001 Professor Christiaan Barnard, Diana's big hope for a job for Hasnat Khan, fertilised another round of 'DIANA COULD HAVE LIVED' headlines.[17]

These 'what if?' scenarios boil down to an argument about emergency systems. In Britain and the US, the priority is to scoop up the victim and race to a hospital. The French have opted for a different system. They are proud of it, and of their emergency medical service, known as SAMU (for Services d'Aide Médicale d'Urgente), which is directly tied to the state-run hospitals. They believe that recovery is more likely if a patient in trauma is stabilised on the spot and then taken with all reasonable speed to a hospital already alerted to have appropriate teams ready to act. Their ambulances, which are equipped with state-of-the-art cardiac resuscitation equipment superior to what is found in conventional ambulances in the US and the UK, carry a doctor trained in emergency services. A supervisor on the spot liaises with SAMU Control and with the selected hospital.

French theory and practice were put to a tough test when SAMU's coordinator Dr Jean Marc Martino, a resuscitation expert, took charge of Diana at 12.40a.m. and was joined by Dr Arnaud Derossi at 12.50a.m. Derossi consulted with SAMU Control on the best way of treating Diana while Dr Martino examined her. He found her conscious but incoherent and confused. Indeed she was so agitated she pulled out the drip Martino had inserted in her arm. Her right arm was bent and dislocated, making her removal from the car a delicate operation. By 1 a.m. he had her blood pressure and breathing stabilised and, very gently, he and the firemen extracted her from between the seats and maneuvered her onto a stretcher. Alas, no sooner was she removed from the car when her heart stopped beating. This fact, overlooked or unknown to the critics, is inconvenient for the 'rush to hospital' school. Had the French doctors precipitously removed Diana from the car, she would very likely have died on the spot. When I asked the opinion of Dr Isadore Rosenfeld, the distinguished Professor of Clinical Medicine and Cardiology at Weill Medical College, Cornell University, he commented, 'Given the internal injuries reported, she might have been saved only if the seventy-mile-an-hour crash had been straight into an operating room.'[18] As it was, it took a full eighteen minutes of CPR for her to be stabilised enough to be moved.[19]

Inside the ambulance, Dr Martino put Diana on a respirator. Her blood pressure dropped so he gave her a line of dopamine to raise it. His examination revealed a right-side chest wound that had not been obvious initially. He worried that there might be internal bleeding. He was most certainly anxious to get her to the well-equipped hospital alerted by SAMU Control without delay, but he had a cruel dilemma. If the ambulance jolted Diana, he risked a repeat of the cardiac arrest.

At 1.41 a.m. Dr Martino directed the ambulance to head for the

Pitié-Salpêtrière Hospital, situated on the Left Bank beyond the cathedral of Notre-Dame and next to the Gare d'Austerlitz. It was a journey of 3.8 miles – ten minutes in normal traffic. Again, there has been criticism that she is not taken to the nearest hospital, the Hôtel-Dieu. But the Hôtel Dieu hospital does not have heart or neurosurgery teams and is not equipped to handle multiple injuries. Dr Derossi and SAMU Control agreed that Diana's best chance was in the Pitié-Salpêtrière. It had the key staff and on duty that night was a doctor particularly skilled in treating Diana's apparent injuries – Dr Bruno Riou, a professor of anaesthesiology and resuscitation,[20] who had quickly assembled the hospital's entire recovery team.

The police cleared all the roads. This time the motorcycle outriders that accompanied Diana were her guardians, not her aggressors. But the progress of the ambulance was agonisingly slow because of Dr Martino's conviction that Diana's heart could not tolerate the slightest jolt. His fears were confirmed. Just as they reached the Botanical Gardens, within sight of the hospital, Diana's blood pressure dropped dangerously low. Dr Martino stopped the ambulance at 2 a.m. He increased the level of dopamine to stabilise her again.[21] At last, they crawled into the cobbled courtyard of the Pitié-Salpêtrière.

It was a sadly appropriate destination for Diana's last journey alive. If the history of the Ritz hotel represents the acme of society's glamour, the history of the Pitié-Salpêtrière represents the nadir of society's outcasts, the sorry people that Diana had tried to embrace in her life's charitable work. The hospital was built in the seventeenth century to house homeless women and prostitutes who were rounded up and ordered arrested by King Louis XIV. It was designed by Louis Le Vau, the master architect of Les Invalides, and is walled off from the street by an extensive square courtyard. The hospital's imposing façade has the austere, grey dignity of four centuries of suffering. Today it houses some of the best medical expertise in Paris. Beyond the great, wrought-iron gates Diana was lifted out by two stretcher-bearers, with the help of the French Minister of the Interior, Jean-Pierre Chevènement and his aide Sami Nair.

As she was carried into the Pavilion Cordier housing the Accident and Emergency Department, Nair gazed down at Diana for the first time. 'She had a breathing apparatus on her face and swellings on her eyes, but she still looked beautiful,' he said later. 'Her face was extremely lovely, very fresh, very serene, very young. It was very moving. She had this blond hair which made her look Raphaelesque, and the Minister said to me, "She's beautiful, isn't she? She's beautiful.'"[22]

Inside the Pavilion Cordier, the battle for Diana's life was frantic but controlled. X-rays revealed she was bleeding in the chest cavity, compressing her heart and right lung. They drained the blood and gave her a massive transfusion, but at 2.10 a.m. her heart stopped again. Dr Riou summoned Professor Alain Pavie, the on-call cardiothoracic surgeon, but Riou and Moncef Dahman, the duty general surgeon, began at once to open Diana's chest to find out the cause of the bleeding. Professor Pavie arrived within twelve minutes and the Princess was transferred to the operating theatre. Pavie enlarged the opening. Now they found a tear in the upper left pulmonary vein caused when the velocity of the crash had displaced her heart from left to right. They stitched the tear. The bleeding stopped, but Diana's heart gave up again. For an hour they tried direct massage, adrenalin, direct stimulation and several microvolted defibrillations.[23]

But this time Diana's broken heart would never mend.

She was pronounced dead at 4 a.m. but was not taken to a mortuary. After the autopsy, she was moved to a secluded room on the first floor of the Pavilion Cordier, a white cotton sheet pulled up to her neck. She would remain there for the next twelve hours.

In London, Colin Tebbutt had been wakened at 2 a.m. by a royal protection officer at Balmoral who had heard that Diana's driver had been killed in a crash and thought it might be Tebbutt. He hastened to the office at Kensington Palace. There, Michael Gibbins, the comptroller of the Princess's household, and a few of her retainers, including Paul Burrell, were gathered round the television waiting for news from Paris. They were watching the Foreign Secretary, Robin Cook, tell the world from Manila that the Princess had been injured in an accident at the same moment that the phone call came to Gibbins that the Princess had just died. Burrell began to sob. Everyone was in tears and in shock – everyone except Tebbutt. He tells me that he could not allow himself to be emotional: 'I went back into policeman's mode.'[24] He escorted the weeping Burrell to Diana's apartment to seal it from intruders. The butler removed from a miniature marble statue the ivory rosary beads that Mother Teresa had given her, a lipstick and a powder compact, and put them in Diana's Gladstone bag.[25] There would be no more effusive thank-you notes from Diana's writing desk with the propped-up memo sheet of words she found difficult to spell. He drew the curtains and placed Diana's jewellery in the safe. Tebbutt shut the doors to the sitting room, the bedroom and the dressing room, and sealed them with thick parcel tape, adding a sticky label, which both men signed. Then the Princess's two closest retainers left for Paris to secure her possessions and take care of arrangements. Tebbutt borrowed a black tie from another cop in order to make the flight in time.[26]

In Paris, Tebbutt and Burrell were driven straight to the British Embassy on the Rue du Faubourg Saint-Honoré. As they sped through the early-morning streets, Tebbutt saw the incongruity of their situation. 'There we were, a chauffeur/minder and a butler with no authority. I said to Burrell, "They won't be expecting a chauffeur and butler, they'll be expecting a major general and ladies-in-waiting."'[27] But that was in the days when Diana was still HRH.

The British Ambassador to Paris, Sir Michael Jay, greeted them at the embassy. He was calm and collected despite his harrowing night at the Pitié-Salpêtrière. One of his staff had fainted in the hospital corridor when the doctors, their faces etched with defeat, emerged all at once from the operating room. The Princess who was the muse of every designer in the world had nothing to wear for her own death. From Lady Jay's own wardrobe, Burrell and the ambassador's wife selected a black woollen three-quarter-length cocktail dress with a shawl collar and black shoes.[28]

At the Pitié-Salpêtrière, a small, neat head nurse escorted the unlikely protectors of Diana's effects through the corridors to the wing where she was housed. Outside the door of her resting place, two gendarmes stood guard. Standing upright against the wall like friezes on an Egyptian tomb, were two undertakers. A sliver of daylight filtered through the slits in the venetian blinds and one wall light provided illumination. Beside Diana's bed stood a bouquet of roses from the former French President Valéry Giscard d'Estaing and his wife. The only sound was the whirring of a large fan. The room was stuffy, and Tebbutt asked for an air-conditioning unit. When he raised the blind a little Tebbutt could see members of the press across the way trying to get pictures. He put blankets up at the windows before he looked at Diana.

Her eyes were closed but her unblemished face was so beautiful. Just as in life, she had sustained injuries that showed nothing on the surface. 'I looked at the Boss lying there and her eyelids were fluttering [from the fan],' Tebbutt told me. 'For a minute I thought she was alive.'[29] 'She had that "I don't want to be here look"' he told the Coroner's inquests.[30] Burrell was so distressed he had to be held up by Tebbutt and the nurse. He handed the undertakers Lady Jay's clothes, the shoes and the make-up, and asked them to put the rosary in Diana's hands.[31]

Outside the hospital gates, the world's media was making camp. The hardy core of photographers who had managed to avoid arrest were multiplying like a virus. The vans of news crews were parked in an ever escalating electronic vigil.

'Assassin! Assassin!' That's how the amiable *Sun* photographer Arthur Edwards was greeted by the taxi driver he flagged down at the hospital, in haste to wire his pictures of the coffin leaving the Pitié-Salpêtrière's side entrance, led by the royal undertakers and flanked by soldiers of the presidential guard.[32] The insult to Edwards was wounding, given the warmth of his memories of covering the Princess since her days as Lady Di. 'I was hurting, too,' he told me. 'I had been sixteen years photographing Diana and now she was dead.'[33] Other pressmen at the Pitié-Salpêtrière found themselves hissed at and spat on. A hospital official had to come out and plead with the crowd: 'Behave like human beings. These gentlemen are only doing their jobs.'[34]

In the dreadful fable of her hunted death, the band of mercenaries on Diana's tail were lumped together. But the reality was they were by no means all the same species. Edwards, of course, was not in this category. He was from the old school of Fleet Street staff photographers – relentless, yes, but dependent on access for such bread-and-butter royal work as the tours and the state ceremonies. And even among those to whom the title 'paparazzi' unquestionably applied, there were many differences, as a canvass of even three of them reveals.

Rat was no mouse, but he behaved with tolerable decency at the crash scene. He did not take any photos of the car's interior, though he was abused as 'the fat photographer'[35] when someone in the crowd saw him lean into the wreck to take Diana's hand. He was checking her pulse, but the image of defilement tallied with the slimy image of the excesses of his trade. In truth, the excitable Rat was more of a glossy magazine 'people' photographer than a hard-edged paparazzo. For that honour you would nominate Martinez, a stocky, crew-cut fifteen-year veteran of the game described by one French reporter as 'a truculent, mean-spirited guy, always ready to punch it out'. He was a master of the kind of ambush photography that had harassed Diana without mercy.[36] Martinez (who despite his taunt to the police had never been anywhere near Sarajevo) later offered a surprisingly introspective explanation for his conduct: 'Being behind a camera helps. It's a screen and allows one to keep one's distance.'[37]

The career of another in the pack, Jacques Langevin, forty-three, the Sygma agency's tough guy, was the antithesis of Martinez's. Like the other six photographers arrested because they did not scatter with the arrival of the police, Langevin had spent half a lifetime courting danger in the pursuit of hard news. He had risked his life for his prize-winning pictures from Rwanda, Lebanon and the Gulf War. Covering the Romanian revolution in 1989, he had taken a bullet in the leg.[38] His photojournalism once got top whack at magazines like *Paris Match*, *Bunte*, *Stern*, *Gala* and the colour magazine of the *Sunday Times*, but by the late 1990s there was little call for the kind of gritty foreign coverage at which he – and many of his colleagues in Paris that night – excelled. The outlets they serviced now cared only about celebrities. Langevin felt demeaned by much of this work. He had been relaxing at a dinner party in the 15th arrondissement when the call came from Sygma for him to 'do the Diana job' at the Ritz. As he left for the assignment, he muttered, '*Scoumoune*' – Arabic for 'bad luck'.[39] He showed up at the hotel in time to snap the picture of her in the car leaving the Rue Cambon entrance. Seven minutes later, he was on his way back to the dinner party, driving through the underpass, when he happened on the accident.[40]

What all the fifteen or so photographers in that Paris tunnel had in common was the reality of the new marketplace. Subjects and photographers alike had been degraded by the media's inexhaustible appetite for celebrity images. Ken Lennox, by then promoted to picture editor of the *Sun* was woken up at 1.10a.m. French time with a muffled call from a papparazzo in Paris. 'He said he wanted £300,000 for the picture of Diana in the car taken twenty feet away. I could have the picture exclusively for one day. I said yes then and there, got dressed, and rushed into the office.' The caller – whom he misidentified as Romuald Rat – 'didn't sound upset,' says Lennox. 'He sounded as if he was eager to get a job over with.'[41] Even as Diana struggled for life, she was being sold as an exclusive.

In the subsequent police investigation, Martinez admitted, 'It's true, we didn't help the wounded. Maybe it was through a sense of modesty. It shows a lot of arrogance, going to help the people that we were following just a few minutes earlier.' But he broke down during the questioning. Under the French 'Good Samaritan' law it is an offence not to assist accident victims. 'I was paralysed,' he said in the same police interview, 'by the relationship between myself and the people in that car.'[41] Some relationship. Many of these photographers had spent years effectively dehumanising Diana. She was the 'Loon' – a commodity, a paycheque. Yet it is one of the paradoxes of her fate that the people who had hounded her the most were later the most bereft. Most of their careers went south in the aftermath of her death. After two years, all of them were cleared of causing the crash – none of them had been near the Mercedes – but in dismissing all the charges Judge Hervé Stéphan said that their behaviour 'raised moral and ethical questions . . . The continuous and insistent presence of the photographers had led Dodi to make decisions that, however imprudent, were a response to being hounded.'[43] All of them were tainted by events in the tunnel, and few ever earned big money again. Serge Benamou, forty-three, told the police he didn't want to see the shots he got that night. 'Because I took pictures and now I know the people are dead. It's a horrible memory.'[44] What none of the paparazzi expected was that the convergence of the most famous woman of the century and the horrific car crash that killed her would render their pictures unpublishable in mainstream media to this day.

The public shed no tears for the paparazzi's hard times. Nor were people in the mood to draw fine distinctions between the cowboys and the newspaper staff photographers. The empirical evidence of Diana's coffin escorted by her ex-husband and two older sisters and draped with the royal standard slowly emerging from the hold of the plane at RAF Northolt brought a collective gasp of disbelief from a nation that still had not really accepted her death. The soft whirr and click of cameras seemed already muted by shame. Edwards was soon abused again just taking pictures of the people holding vigil outside Kensington Palace. His paper, like the others, was assailed by angry readers the next day. The message: 'You killed her, you bastards.'[45]

The panic in the newsrooms was palpable. Grief and fear were in equal parts entwined. The royal reporters had all been in love with Diana to a greater or lesser degree. They had to put their human emotions on hold to write their reports while also believing in their hearts that they were the reason she died. A reeling Richard Kay locked himself in his office at the *Mail* to begin writing non-stop memories for an early edition on the streets and the next day's entire Diana paper. James Whitaker, on a South Pacific island holiday with his wife, spent the next seven hours on an open line to the *Mirror* pouring out ten thousand words straight to the copytaker for a twelve-page supplement headlined 'END OF A FAIRYTALE'. 'Diana is dead,' began his report. 'I can't believe I've written those words, but as I do so I am crying.'[46] The newspaper's art director, Simon Cosyns, on a driving holiday in France, was so stunned when he got the news that he drove into a wall.[47] Piers Morgan, who had left the *News of the World* to edit the *Mirror*, was 'sweating and bursting with tension' – and not only on account of the journalistic adrenalin that had made him rush to the office. On the picture editor's computer screen, he wrote in his diary, 'I have never seen more sensational news images,'[48] and all he wanted to do was black them out. His diary records him telling the representative of the issuing agency: 'Listen, mate, Diana's possibly been killed by the bloody paparazzi and you're trying to flog me pictures of her still warm corpse. Think about it, for fuck's sake . . . Ring everyone and say there's been a terrible mistake and these photographs are not for publication . . . Then if I were you, I'd turn your machines off and leave the country until it all blows over. Because if people find out what you were doing they will come and get you.'[49] At 6.00a.m. at the *Sun*, Ken Lennox looked at the £300,000 exclusive he'd bought sight unseen and ordered that every frame be deleted from the system.[50]

There was a real fear that the vengeful spirit in the air would end up shackling the press with a privacy law, one that would not only quash photographing public figures but also hinder legitimate investigations. The fact that France's strict privacy laws had made no difference to the fate of Diana was brushed aside by politicians baring their legislative teeth. Earl Spencer's demand for parliamentary action elicited 80,000 letters of support. Around the world, editorial confessions of guilt tried to keep one step ahead of the denunciations. 'FORGIVE US, PRINCESS' was the front-page headline in Italy's leftist *L'Unità*. 'We feel ashamed,' said Rome's *Il Messaggero*. 'Sick greed,' said a German editorial. 'Nothing to do with real journalism,' fumed Spain's conservative *ABC* newspaper in a call for privacy laws. 'Reporter-murderers' was the judgement of Moscow's most popular daily, *Komsomolskaya Pravda*.[51]

Watching the British press organise its defence was like watching an infantry square re-form under musket fire at Waterloo. The broadcast media framed the outcries as directed at the print media; the broadsheets as directed at the tabloids; the 'regular' tabloids as directed at the racier red tops; the red tops as directed at the foreign press. Papers that had been boasting their Di picture scoops professed never to use paparazzi pictures. Earl Spencer's fusillade against the press barons was treated to sly rewrites, characterised as being just an attack on paparazzi and not on the press paymasters. And of course the paps, you understand, weren't British. They were 'foreign celebrity snappers' (*Sun*); 'ruthless foreign paparazzi' and 'yobs with cameras masquerading as photo-journalists' (*News of the World*) 'the equivalent of cowboy mini-cab drivers' (*Daily Mail*). The relief felt by the tabloids when the lab tests reported Henri Paul had three times the French legal limit of alcohol in his blood (and twice the British) was like Christmas coming early. Piers Morgan celebrated in his diary with 'There is a God.'[52] 'DI DRIVER DRUNK AS A PIG' was the happy headline in the *Star*.[53]

The notion that Diana had been allowed to get into a car with a driver who was drunk was an even more unpalatable truth to the British public. In fact, Henri Paul had not appeared drunk in any obvious way. If he had been rolling about and slurring his speech, any number of people would have stopped him getting into the Mercedes as the last-minute recruit to drive Diana and Dodi. He appeared normal to most (though not all) of those who saw him that night, but the truth was that he had combined his drinks with pharmaceuticals – Prozac and Tiapride – whose labels carry warnings that taking them with alcohol can make it dangerous to drive or operate machinery.[54]

Royal drivers are expressly required to avoid alcohol for ten hours before getting behind the wheel. Yet Henri Paul's blood alcohol reading showed that he must have been drinking even before he was unexpectedly recalled to stand by at the Ritz at ten o'clock. He joined the bodyguards at the hotel bar and had a couple of glasses of what looked like a fruit juice, and made a joke about it being '*ananas*' (pineapple).[55] But the 'yellow liquid' was actually a Ricard *pastis*, the anise-flavoured aperitif, which is considerably stronger than wine. Robert Forrest, Professor of Forensic Toxicology at the University of Sheffield, has testified for Paget that before those two drinks Paul may have had 'something of the order of four to six extra 5cl Ricards' between 7 p.m., when he officially went off duty, and his recall at 10 p.m.[56] He was in no state to go hurtling at breakneck speed into a tunnel that had been the scene of thirty-four crashes and eight deaths in the previous fifteen years. 'I have never seen anyone take off like that,' one of the photographers told a German TV station of Henri Paul's departure from the Ritz. 'He was driving like a gangster.'[57]

The irony was that even in the Coleherne Court years Diana herself rarely panicked when she was in chases with photographers. Her friend Cosima Somerset remembers a James Bond-like pursuit by a motorbike when they went on holiday together in Majorca in May 1996. 'The man on the pillion had a camera which he pointed right up against the car window. I felt as if Diana had almost been assaulted, but she remained ice cool.'[58] It was Dodi and Henri Paul, not Diana, who couldn't handle it. 'Why were they driving so fast to get away from photographers?' Tebbutt asks today. 'A camera never killed anyone.'[59] Ken Wharfe rehearsed the same bitter thoughts when he watched the first bulletins about Diana's injuries. 'Trevor Rees-Jones was totally focused on getting her away from the paparazzi. But that wasn't his job. His job was to stop her taking a bullet.'[60] The evidence is that both Diana and Dodi would have survived had they been wearing seat belts; Trevor Rees-Jones, who did survive, suffered his dreadful injuries because, though cushioned on impact by the front air bag, his failure to buckle up allowed him to be hurled sideways against the interior.

Henri Paul should never have been the driver of that car on the fatal night of 31 August – if Diana had not refused police protection from Scotland Yard he never would have been. And if she had told the British Embassy she was in Paris, Sir Michael Jay would have arranged for the French police services to provide an escort car. Paul was not even a qualified limousine driver. His former boss Jean-Henri Hocquet, who retired in June 1997 as head of security at the Ritz, said that on one occasion he had actually forbidden Paul to drive a guest who was in danger of missing his plane because he did not have the necessary qualifications.[61] Of the night of the crash, Hocquet told Operation Paget that it was not surprising Paul agreed to work that night when he was off duty, because 'Monsieur Paul was simply nice, and as an act of friendship and because of his good nature, he could not say "no" [to the boss's son] and would agree to drive a vehicle'.[62] The last shot of Diana gazing out of the back of the Mercedes before the crash is telling not for what it shows of the Princess but for what it says about Henri Paul. The chauffeur's grimly smiling mouth, his bright, staring eyes are those of a man vibrating with alcoholic excitement. The testimony of the Ritz barman Alain Willaumez matches the photograph, 'I could see [he was drunk] first through his eyes and also the way he talked. But more especially in his eyes. [They] were brilliant, wide-open and he was visibly in an abnormal condition.'[63]

In the years since Diana's death, conspiracy theorists have woven Henri Paul's off-duty life into a web of inexplicable clues – his multiple bank accounts, his alleged habitual sobriety, his link to the French secret service, his 'missing hours' on the evening of her death. But, in reality, all the supposed clues point to a dour and unexceptional truth: Paul was a depressed, lonely man – what the French call a *vieux garçon*, a fusty, ageing bachelor who drank on his own, topped up his bank accounts with cash 'bungs' from Ritz clients for whom he did favours, and, in common with half the maître d's and security personnel of the world's five-star hotels, was paid by low-level intelligence agents and police services to inform on VIP clients whose movements were of interest. (The other half is paid by gossip columns.) The job of a security man is an isolating position. Few people want to pal around with a guy whose role includes keeping tabs on the other personnel. Paul was Mohamed Al Fayed's on-the-ground fixer. With little private life to interfere with his job, he was always ready to run interference. His nickname at work was 'la fouine' – the snooper.[64]

The most compelling interest of his story is the window it provides into the life of a bourgeois, balding, bespectacled Frenchman in solitary middle age whose daily routine intersects with the lives of rich and powerful people who spare him not a moment's thought. There is pathos to the sterility of Paul's two-bedroom bachelor apartment in the middle-class Rue des Petits-Champs. There is pathos, too, in the sorrow he apparently felt at the end of an affair with a former secretary in the Ritz personnel department – not so much because he missed the girlfriend but because he had grown fond of her two-and-a-half-year-old daughter. He needed a drink, the ex-girlfriend said, to lighten him up. 'Il avait le vin gai' – 'wine made him joyful.'[65] On his way home at night he used to park his car near a lesbian bar in the Rue de Chabanais at the corner of his street, not for some weird sexual voyeurism but because the owner, Josiane le Tellier, was a close woman friend. It was a good place for a lonely man to sit and nurse a drink.

Henri Paul's exposure as unfit to drive the Mercedes was as much a disaster for Mohamed Al Fayed as it was a relief for the press. Broken by loss, Al Fayed mixed his rage with the gods with the bitterness he felt for a lifetime of exclusion. Now he had to confront not only the fact that he had lost his eldest son, but that his dreams of ascendance to the pinnacle of the establishment were finished.

As soon as he learned of Dodi's death, Al Fayed flew to Paris on the Harrods helicopter. Muslim law required burial before sunset and since Al Fayed wanted the funeral in England he had to move fast. On his way in to Paris from Le Bourget airport, he received a phone call from Raine Spencer telling him that the Princess too had died. Stunned, he arrived at the Pitié-Salpêtrière, only to be told that his son was not there. He was redirected to the morgue on the Right Bank. Kez Wingfield, the bodyguard who travelled with Al Fayed, recalls him waiting forlornly at dawn in front of the morgue while someone searched for the keys. 'He just stood there in shock, looking at the doors,' said Wingfield.[66] It was a metaphor for a life of being shut out. While the world's attention was focused on the fate of a golden princess, Al Fayed was just some sad forgotten foreigner come to claim his dead son.

Al Fayed's relationship with Dodi had been complicated. By turns he had dominated and spoiled him, but all his hopes had been sunk in him, too. Dodi was a generous soul, his faults mostly those of good nature. He wanted everyone to have a good time and to like him. He would never have aspired to be the lover of the Princess of Wales if his father had not pushed. Now he was body No. 2146 in a French morgue.[67] 'I could see Dodi was at peace,' Al Fayed said later. 'He looked like a little boy again. For a moment I thought that his soul had come back in his body and he would live again but the injuries to the back of his head were too severe.'[68]

Mohamed Al Fayed's mourning was incendiary. The need to appoint a culprit became a lifetime's unholy war. Like everybody else, his public relations executive, Michael Cole, initially pinned blame on the paparazzi – 'Gallic kamikaze, a load of disgusting creeps' – and described Henri Paul as a 'sober, model employee' who was perfectly qualified to drive the Mercedes as a chauffeur.[69] If Paul was none of the above, then Mohamed Al Fayed himself risked having to share in the moral responsibility for the deaths of Dodi and Diana. Henri Paul was Al Fayed's employee from Al Fayed's hotel, driving a car arranged by Al Fayed's people. It was an agonising prospect for a grieving father, and on top of the unbearable pain there had to be the fear that he would be blamed and that no one would ever forgive him for taking the adored Princess from them.

With Michael Cole as Al Fayed's mouthpiece, a campaign of obnoxious brilliance began. Its aim was to convince the world that the simple explanation of a drunken driver going too fast was a sinister cover-up. Henri Paul's blood tests were swapped! The 'accident' was set up by British intelligence agents! MI6 rode in disguise with the paparazzi! Diana was embalmed to conceal her pregnancy! Someone had flashed a bright strobe light in the tunnel to blind Paul! Two SAS soldiers on the roof of the tunnel had fired frangible bullets at the front tyres! A Fiat Uno car had forced Paul into the columns! The Fiat had raced to the British Embassy! Or it was a motorcyclist! Sir Robert Fellowes was in Paris an hour before to organise the murder!

Sparing no expense, treating no reputation as inviolate, Mohamed Al Fayed's well-financed PR machine created nothing less than an alternative universe in which fantasy was fact, doubt was certainty, suspicion was conviction, absence of evidence was proof of its suppression, and anyone sceptical of the plot was either part of it or – his words – an 'arse licker'.[70] Diana was going to marry Dodi, she was already two to six weeks pregnant, and the marriage had to be stopped to save the future King of England from having a Muslim half-brother and an Egyptian Muslim as a stepfather. Who would do this? In Al Fayed's words: 'Prince Philip is the one responsible for giving the order. He is very racist. He is of German blood, and I'm sure he is a Nazi sympathiser. Also Robert Fellowes was key. He is the Rasputin of the British monarchy.'[71]

Al Fayed has been relentless in his vendetta against photographers who had nothing to do with the night of her death. Jason Fraser, the celebrity snapper and syndicator, was Diana's most trusted tip-off recipient. It was Fraser – acting on a lead he has never revealed, but certainly at the behest of Diana – who dispatched the big-time Italian glitz hunter Mario Brenna to get the celebrated 'Kiss' picture of Diana and Dodi on her first cruise aboard the *Jonikal*. When Fraser first began pursuing Diana and Dodi, Mohamed Al Fayed was only too pleased to see the pictures of his son's romance splashed around the world, and waved cheerily at Fraser's camera from the deck of the *Jonikal*. Yet he is still pursuing Fraser through the French civil and criminal courts for invasion of his son's privacy.

Al Fayed's campaign has been unceasing through a decade of rebuttal and documentation in France and Britain. It has seeded innumerable conspiracy theories – enough to provide fodder, at one time, for 35,000 websites – assisted by credulous journalism, led in recent years by the *Daily Express*, whose publisher, Richard Desmond, is a close friend of Al Fayed's. In February 1998, the *Mirror* splashed an Al Fayed interview headlined 'IT WAS NO ACCIDENT'. More than twelve million viewers watched Al Fayed's wild theories dramatised in a distorted 1998 ITV special, *Diana: Secrets Behind the Crash*; a poll the next day found 97 per cent were convinced by Al Fayed.[72] No doubt in his torment he convinced himself. In tribute to Dodi on the first Saturday after Diana's funeral, he walked alone across the pitch of his Fulham soccer club to the lament of a Scottish piper. The crowd stood in respectful silence. No doubt Al Fayed was emboldened by these scenes of popular support.

Near the tenth anniversary of the crash, the three-year British inquiry into Al Fayed's charges, Operation Paget, rigorously conducted by former chief of the Metropolitan police, Lord Stevens, disposed of every substantive allegation. So did the official French inquiry. And so did independent investigations, notably Martyn Gregory's book *Diana: The Last Days*. In any sequence of events of such complexity, speed and drama, there are bound to be confusions and discrepancies. But the evidence is overwhelming that this was a traffic accident – full stop. Paget's DNA tests showed that the only blood that tested positively for excessive alcohol was Paul's and Paul's alone.[73] No flash in the tunnel caused him to ram the pillar; Paget's meticulous reconstruction using 3-D lasers and computer models show that Paul lost control before he entered the tunnel. The 'flash before crash' story was the invention of alleged witness François (Levistre) Levi, a pathological liar with a criminal record.[74] The most valid of Al Fayed's questions on the case was the mysterious Fiat Uno seen in the tunnel with a muzzled dog in the back on which a sub-genre of conspiracy theories has been built. The Fiat, gaining access from a slip road, was on Henri Paul's right as he careened into the tunnel at a speed in excess of seventy-five miles an hour. Paul was already on a doomed trajectory, having encountered the notorious dip and slight bend in the road at this point. He swerved to the left to avoid the Fiat, brushed its left rear light, scraped the third column, swerved to the right and back again into the thirteenth pillar. The Fiat had by then driven on. It vanished. French police eventually interviewed a Vietnamese plumber and nightwatchman Le Van Thanh whom they thought might be the Fiat's owner, but it took the detective work of Paget nine years later to conclude that the French had indeed got their man – and he was not a conspirator. Thanh's failure to own up and the swift repainting of his car in red was not for any sinister reason. It was simply an immigrant's fear of getting entangled in French law which punishes a driver who fails to stop at the scene of an accident.[75] The Fiat was a complication for Henri Paul but only because he was driving too fast, the Mercedes already locked in its fatal momentum.[76]

The most tenacious of Mohamed Al Fayed's assertions was that Diana was pregnant. Paget's medical evidence was conclusive: she was not. The photograph Al Fayed said showed a suggestive swelling was taken *before* she met Dodi. Moreover, the French nurse who entrusted Al Fayed with Diana's dying words did not, according to the hospital spokesman, Thierry Meresse actually exist.[77] Therefore, nor, except in Al Fayed's mind, did the message: 'I would like all my possessions in Dodi's apartment to be given to my sister Sarah, including my jewellery and my personal clothes, and please tell her to take care of my boys.' For good measure, Al Fayed added: 'For me, to have a message from a mother through a nurse to her children was so important because Diana lived for nearly two hours in the operating theatre. She felt she was going…I was the first person there.'[78]

As for sinister forces organising the crash of the Mercedes, a conspiracy would have been beyond the capacities of all the intelligence agencies and royal masterminds in the grassy knoll of Al Fayed's imagination: pre-knowledge that Dodi would make the last-minute decisions he did; that Henri Paul would be the driver; that Paul would be drunk and drugged; that he would not follow the most obvious route to Dodi's apartment; that the argumentative group of paparazzi and the supposed intervening car or motorbikes were coordinated to the last split second in their movements; that Dodi and Diana would not wear seat belts – and on and on through an infinity of variables. One understands why Mohamed Al Fayed will continue to inhabit the alternative universe; it liberates him from any possibility of blame. But that doesn't make it real.

Prince Charles more rationally believed he knew where the finger-pointing would lead. 'They're all going to blame me,' he told his private secretary, Stephen Lamport. 'The world's going to go completely mad.'[79] The Prince and his mother anxiously conferred in their dressing gowns in the Queen's sitting room. They had been awakened just before 1 a.m. by Her Majesty's assistant private secretary, Sir Robin Janvrin, who was staying in a house on the Balmoral estate. One of the first people Charles talked to in those two hours between 1 a.m and 3 a.m. when it was still not clear how badly the Princess had been hurt was Mark Bolland in London. The Prince was anxious to know if his assistant private secretary had learned from the press anything more than he and the Queen had just been told. Charles was trying to digest the possibility that the mother of his children would return to England brain-damaged or paralysed. 'I always thought that Diana would come back to me, needing to be cared for,' Prince Charles brooded to Bolland.[80]

*Come back to me, needing, cared for.* The sad tenderness of the comment reveals the complexity of Charles's feelings. For the Prince, there could be something redeeming in having his ex-wife return to him in a condition of dependence. Until the birthday party for Camilla at Highgrove in July, things had improved between them. When Charles's mentor Laurens van der Post died in December 1996, Diana, immediately aware of how devastated Charles would be, dashed him off a sympathetic letter saying she knew how it felt to lose someone close. It moved him enough to call her to thank her for her understanding.[81]

No one can say what Charles would have done with respect to Camilla if Diana's powers to bewitch, and with them her independence, had been curtailed by physical or mental impairment. His line had always been that Camilla was 'non-negotiable', but there is no doubt that if Diana had come home broken, Charles would have done everything he could do to try to make her whole.

At 3.15 a.m. UK time, Sir Michael Jay called from Paris to confirm Diana's death. The Prince went into meltdown. He was seized by a tumult of emotions – concern for the children, guilt, a terrible certainty about how crazy the public response would become. 'He was in deep shock,' a friend of Camilla's told biographer Caroline Graham. 'His main concern was for the children. They were at such a vulnerable age to lose their mother. Charles is a very sensitive man and even though Diana was rebuilding her life, he kept asking himself, if he had handled things differently, she might not have ended up in the arms of a playboy, a decision which ultimately led to her death.'[82] For Camilla, too, the news was devastating. She had just begun to come out of the shadows. Now she was cast back into them, condemned for the foreseeable future to continue uncertainly as the Prince's mistress in private. The boys had not even met her yet and would certainly not want to meet her now. She would be even more of a hate figure to the British public. In the days ahead, she would stay well hidden at her house in Wiltshire, guarded by two officers from Scotland Yard.[83]

At 7.15 a.m, after walking the grounds of Balmoral alone, Charles went to the boys' rooms to perform the most awful task of his life. He woke William first. The young Prince had had a troubled night perhaps because of harsh words with his mother about Dodi. Now this terrible news meant they would never hug each other again. Father and son went to break the news together to Harry. For the younger boy, the blow was as frightening as it was sad. At twelve he was still a small boy beneath his manly façade. His favourite thing to do on nights in was huddle on a sofa with his mother and watch videos, just the two of them. He could not comprehend the awfulness of what had happened. He passionately wanted to go with his father to Paris to collect his mother. Charles decided it was best not to put him through it.

In situations of great distress, long-standing custom often prevails over emotional impulse – form over content – because it is sanctioned by the wisdom of precedent. For the young Princes, it meant getting dressed as usual and accompanying the rest of the royal family to church. For Charles and the Queen it meant focusing on the manner of Diana's return. Knowing how much the British people would blame him, Charles wanted every royal courtesy and ceremony to be extended to his former wife. The Queen did not see it that way. As the night turned to day Charles was increasingly at loggerheads with his mother. Better to wrangle over the logistics of Diana's journey home than bring to the surface all the anger, jealousy, regret and guilt the royals felt towards Diana when she was alive. Charles was determined that Diana should be brought back from Paris with royal ceremony to lie in the Chapel Royal at St James's Palace before a public funeral. The Queen strongly believed that they should accede to the Spencers' request that Diana's body should be returned to her family straight from the morgue in Fulham. The Queen's position was that Diana, after all, was Charles's ex-wife, not the future Queen. Her death was a private matter in which royal palaces, planes and ceremony could have no part, a position reinforced by Prince Philip. It looked as though Charles would have to get to Paris on a commercial flight from Aberdeen. For once, the Prince of Wales fought for Diana – harder than he had ever done in her lifetime. Faced with the unanswerable truth that Diana, HRH or not, was William and Harry's mother, the Queen by breakfast had granted Charles an RAF flight and permission to hold Diana's coffin on his own turf in the Chapel Royal at St James's Palace.

In all the discussion of what was and was not appropriate to a dead ex-wife's rank, little consideration from the Palace was given to Diana's mother. When Frances Shand Kydd was roused by a ringing telephone in her bungalow on the Isle of Seil, her first hopeful thought was that it might be Diana herself, a call that would signify the end of their cold war. But it was a friend, Janey Milne, who had seen an early newsflash about the accident. Frances began to throw clothes into a suitcase to go to Paris. 'It seemed quite natural to go to my wounded child,' she later told her biographers, Max Riddington and Gavan Naden.[84] But before she could leave, her middle daughter, Jane, phoned with word of Diana's death. Jane had heard the news from her husband, Sir Robert Fellowes, who was in close touch with Paris on behalf of the Queen from their home in Norfolk. Frances waited in vain for details from the Palace about when she would travel to bring her daughter home; in the meantime she was forbidden by Fellowes, via Jane, to talk to anyone until the death was public. The Queen never sent any message nor made any phone call of condolence to the woman who had brought Diana into the world. Frances was left out of the loop, just as she had been thirty-eight years before by Earl Spencer when their baby son John died. 'It really seems somewhat ironic to me that having buried two children, for entirely different reasons, I did not see or touch or hold them when they were dead,' she said bitterly.[85] She was not invited to retrieve Diana's body from Paris with Prince Charles and her two elder daughters (the youngest of Diana's siblings, Earl Spencer, still in South Africa, was unable to get to Paris in time.)

Prince Charles's composure at the Pitié-Salpêtrière was held together at first by the formality of the reception awaiting the royal party. They were greeted with the grave condolences of Sir Michael Jay; the French President Jacques Chirac and Madame Chirac; the Foreign Minister, Robert Védrine; the Interior Minister Jean-Pierre Chevènement; and the Health Minister, Bernard Kouchner. Charles thanked them all, in touchingly correct French, for their assistance. 'I was moved by his humanity and by how responsive he was,' the hospital spokesman, Thierry Meresse, recalled. 'His entire attitude from start to finish was one of concern for the Princess of Wales.'[86]

The Prince went into the room alone to view his former wife in death. Meresse says that at the moment Charles entered Diana's chamber he was still 'calm and collected', but it was 'another man who emerged . . . a man utterly shattered by what was happening'. Trained all his life, like the Queen, to transfer the expression of emotion to something other than its cause, the Prince became agitated about a detail – the loss in the crash of one of Diana's gold earrings (found two months later under the dashboard of the Mercedes). 'No, she can't go without her second earring!' he kept repeating distractedly.[87] He later told Camilla that seeing Diana's lifeless body was 'the worst sight I have ever had to bear witness to. I could only think of the girl I had first met, not the woman she became, and not the problems we had been through. I wept for her – and I wept for our boys.'[88] His face in the car leaving the hospital, with Diana's grieving sisters beside him, is the face of a man in torment. It was suggested to Charles that the Princess could be flown from the roof of the Accident and Emergency wing, where there is a helipad. ' No,' he replied firmly. 'There are people who love her waiting outside.'[89]

# Chapter 22

# Remember Me

'Is it true that Mummy is dead?'
                                    – Prince Harry, 31 August 1997

Where did it come from, the immense reach of this sorrow? In some mysterious transfusion of glamour, suffering and exposure, Diana had exchanged her identity as a daughter of privilege for that of an idol of the masses. For sixteen years, millions of Britons had felt themselves to be not spectators of but participants in her evolution and her struggles; the shy teenager who became a fairy princess and a mother; the wronged wife who searched for love and was always betrayed; the compassionate crusader who seemed to become more beautiful the more she shared the miseries of others.

Now she was gone, and they streamed into London to mourn her at the rate of six thousand an hour. The gates to Kensington Palace became a gigantic floral snowdrift bobbing with pictures of Diana. There were flowers strewn even on the trees and shrubs like the detritus of an exotic summer ball. The mountains of bouquets, clipped-out photographs, teddy bears, poems, messages, rosaries, queen of hearts playing cards and children's drawings; the sounds amid the crowd not simply of quiet crying but deep, gasping sobs; the lines to sign the condolence books at St James's Palace stretching away to vanishing point – it was amazing, and a little scary. The diversity of the crowd, as much as its numbers, was what made it a miracle: young, old, black, white, South Asian and East Asian, in shorts and saris and denim and pinstripes and baseball caps and hijabs. The death of an aristocratic girl who became a princess but refused to let palace walls enclose her had somehow triggered a historic celebration of inclusion.[1] Later chairman of the Commission for Equality and Human Rights, Trevor Phillips spoke for them all when he hailed her as 'a heroine who embraced the modern, multicultural, multi-ethnic Britain without reservation'.[2]

The then London bureau chief of the *New York Times*, Warren Hoge, was transfixed by the sight and sound of a country discovering itself. Britain, he says, 'had no idea it was this racially mixed, this driven by women, this aspirational until it asked itself: Who were all these people in the green spaces of London coming out for Diana?'[3]

Part of it, no doubt, was that she was the first great glamour icon to live and die in the age of round-the-world, round-the-clock multimedia. The loss of her dazzle happened all at once and everywhere on television and radio and the Internet, in newspapers and magazines, via mobile phone and email, creating the first great grief-a-thon. Her death came, too, at a moment of political transition. The British people in mid-1997 had had enough of stone-faced authority figures giving them castor oil and telling them to sit up straight. It's why Tony Blair won the election for Labour in May with the biggest landslide of the twentieth century, after eleven years of Margaret Thatcher as Nurse Ratched in Downing Street, seven years of John Major as a furled umbrella, sixteen years of the royal family failing to understand that the warm, golden, flesh-and-blood girl in their midst was the best thing to happen to them since the restoration of King Charles II. Now the British people's pent-up desire to *feel* found its release in the death of a princess who always gave permission.

People were turning to each other in the crowd to share confessional stories about their own depressions, their own eating disorders, and their own grief when their father/mother/brother/sister/child had died. 'Dear Diana, thank you for treating us like human beings, not criminals,' read one note pinned up on the Kensington Gardens notice-board. 'You were one in a million. From David Hayes and all the lads in HM Prison, Dartmoor.'[4] America's NBC commentator John Hockenberry recalls the reaction to Diana's death from a patient at an Aids hospice outside London to which Diana had once brought William and Harry. 'I was sitting at the table with a very gay gentleman in his early sixties. In the hospice cafeteria was a picture of him and Diana with another man and Diana was laughing hard in the picture. I said to him, "What the heck was going on that she was laughing at so hard?" And he said, "Well, I was so nervous and my lover, who was very sick – he has since died – was sitting beside me, and it was all very strange, and I didn't know what to say. I looked at her and I suddenly said, 'You're a princess and I – I'm a queen!'" And he started to cry as he said it, and it suddenly connected to me, that she was a symbol of letting it all go, letting all the bridges down. Even in the midst of being royal and being a celebrity royal, she was the symbol of saying fuck it, none of it matters.'[5]

Some of it did matter, of course. Tony Blair understood that part of his role in the weeks ahead would be to analyse the national psyche and distinguish what mattered from what didn't. He was in his Sedgefield constituency in County Durham when he was reached by Sir Michael Jay in the small hours of Sunday morning and apprised of Diana's death. Blair, like Prince Charles, foresaw that the nation, as Charles had put it, would 'go mad'. 'This is going to be absolutely enormous,' the Prime Minister told his press spokesman, Alastair Campbell, 'probably bigger than any of us can imagine.' He immediately set himself the task, says Campbell, of 'helping to get the Queen through it'.[6]

Blair solidified his reputation as master surfer of the zeitgeist by pausing to pay emotional tribute to Diana on his way to church with his family in the mining village of Trimdon in County Durham. In yoking Diana's death to the New Labour ethos of people power, Blair had incidentally effected a political hole in one. His voice cracking, Blair said: 'With just a look or a gesture that spoke so much more than words, she would reveal to all of us the depth of her compassion and her humanity . . . She was the People's Princess and that is how she will stay, how she will remain in our hearts and our memories for ever.'[7]

So what if the populist phrase had been swiped from Di biographer Anthony Holden by Alastair Campbell for Blair? So what if to some it had the rank odour of demagoguery? ('The people's heroine, why did we need one?' asks the writer James Fox today, in exasperation: 'It was celebrity culture meets the democratisation of monarchy.')[8] The catchy phrase was everybody's headline the next day and became the dominant slogan on the flurry of improvised posters tacked to the noticeboards outside Kensington Palace.

Not everyone was moved to tears. 'The grieving over Princess is beyond all belief,' groused Gloucestershire aesthete James Lees-Milne to his diary. Her death, he wrote, 'would be recognised as a mercy in the long run'.[9] Princess Margaret, who had cut short a holiday in Italy to return to her apartment in Kensington Palace, was more upset about the smell of rotting flowers outside her window. 'She didn't like any of the emotionalism one bit,' her lady-in-waiting, Lady Glenconner, explains. 'She said the hysteria was rather like Diana herself. It was as if she got everyone to be as hysterical as she was when she died.'[10] But Margaret and her ilk were in retreat, and they knew it. Wrong about a lot of things, Diana was right about this: that it was time the monarchy showed a more compassionate, more contemporary face. The people of England were demanding it, too. Flower power, the *New York Times* called it.[11] Floral fascism, Diana's detractors called it.[12] *Defy her if you dared.*

Every TV set in the country was tuned to the royal family's appearance at the 11 a.m. service at Craithie church, near Balmoral. There was first bafflement, then resentment that the royal response to the death of the most beloved member of their family was, in a word, nothing. The tableau before the cameras as the Firm disembarked en masse for Sunday morning worship was devoid of any discernible emotion. When you look at the pictures today, with the scared faces of the boys in the back seat of the black Daimler, it is clear they are all numb, frozen in a tragedy so awful that the only thing standing between them and a howl of agony is habitual routine. But that's not how it came across.

The young Princes were heartbreaking in their grown-up jackets and black ties, but Charles and Philip were wearing, for God's sake, kilts. Worse, as far as the public was concerned, Craithie parish church must have been the only house of worship in the country where there was no reference to Diana in the morning's prayers. Nor had there been since the day she lost her HRH, an excision, said Diana's friend Oonagh Shanley-Toffolo in 1998, that the Princess minded bitterly. 'She thought it was so hurtful to William and Harry.'[13] Even more discordantly, the sermon, by visiting preacher Adrian Varwell, a Church of Scotland minister, was about the unsettling experience of moving house, illustrated by jokes drawn from the ribald Scottish comedian Billy Connolly. (The regular minister at Craithie, Robert Sloan, later defended the sermon by saying, 'Everybody in the world knew what had happened. Our business was to conduct a normal service of worship'[14] – an explanation about as welcome to the British public, in Billy Connolly parlance, as a fart in a spacesuit.)

Perhaps it was the surreal public avoidance of the family's loss that provoked Prince Harry to ask his father, 'Is it true that Mummy is dead?' With so few tangible acknowledgements that Diana was gone no wonder her younger son had his heart set on going to 'bring Mummy home'.[15]

The Queen's detachment from her people was compounded by what her staff think of as 'the Balmoral effect', the unique sense of seclusion at their Scottish retreat. The castle exists in a Walter Scott novel, not in real time. When the royal family is there they are not just physically far away, they have retreated into a past they control. The feeling was intensified by a decision the Queen made to protect William and Harry. She ordered all the TV sets and radios in Balmoral to be moved or hidden so the boys could not see or hear any of the broadcasts about Diana's death. The sovereign and Prince Philip monitored the developments themselves through the only set available, sequestered in her private sitting room. Throughout the week the Balmoral staff followed the news surreptitiously from rogue radios and TV sets concealed in cupboards or behind sofas.

It is one of the ironies of the anti-monarchist feelings that swept the country in the face of the Queen's 'callousness' about Diana's death that for the first time in fifty years the monarch was, by her lights, putting family before duty, her grandchildren before her subjects. The whole family rallied to assist in supporting William and Harry. A member of staff at Balmoral noted that Prince Philip, who effectively lost his own mother at the age of ten when she was committed for three years to an asylum in Switzerland, was brilliantly effective with his grandsons, offering them gruff tenderness and outdoor activities like stalking and hiking to tire them out. Princess Anne was especially kind to Harry, whose fragility was manifest. She took him alone with her exploring the Balmoral wilds on foot and on horseback. She enlisted her children by Mark Phillips, Peter, aged twenty and Zara, aged sixteen. More temperamentally suited than any of her brothers to be King, Anne had raised her children to be self-reliant and do without royal titles. Peter and Zara proved inspiring role models and friends for William and Harry. Prince Charles evoked the good times the family had together, turning through their old photo albums to dwell on pictures of them all together in happier moments. Tiggy Legge-Bourke was summoned to provide warmth and familiar outdoor distractions. Indeed, so concerted was the family effort to leave the boys no time alone with their feelings that they had little space to grieve at all. Such is the Windsor way.

None of this family pain, however, was the business of the public. In showing an impassive face, the Windsors were doing what royals had always done – refusing 'to wear private grief on a public sleeve', as Princess Alice of Athlone once put it.[16] But the British people were no longer willing to be excluded from the zone of privacy claimed by a family whose purpose, after all, was to symbolise the nation. Diana had schooled them to expect inclusion. The Queen did not grasp that in the media era communication is at least as much a core value as stoicism. Up to now, she had understood perfectly the importance of knowing when not to talk; indeed, much of the monarchical magic she had managed to preserve had stemmed from the dignity of her silence in a culture of babble. But there are also moments, just as important, when the instinct of silence fails and words are a necessary consolation. 'All week we wanted the Queen to say she was suffering with us, but she didn't do it,' said Sam Stark, forty-three, a mourner who, with his god-daughter in tow, had joined the milling crowd in front of Buckingham Palace. 'When your parents don't listen you rebel.'[17] The fact that no words were forthcoming only served to reinforce the absence of empathy the Princess had experienced from the royal family during her life. It conjured up the huge, sad blue eyes of the Princess on the *Panorama* programme – *You see*.

Tony Blair smelled the potential danger early. He offered to lend Alastair Campbell and another top Downing Street aide Anji Hunter to the Palace team handling the funeral arrangements.[18] They joined Lord Airlie, the Lord Chamberlain, Sir Robert Fellowes, Richard Aylard and all the Queen's men at Buckingham Palace. The sovereign was still hoping that there could be a private ceremony at Windsor and then a burial at Frogmore – just like that other awkward anomaly, the Duchess of Windsor.[19] From Sunday afternoon, however, it was clear to everyone except the Queen that there would have to be a full-blown memorial service at Westminster Abbey. Charles astutely co-opted Blair to help him get the idea past his mother. The planning meetings to rush through the arrangements took place in the Chinese room at Buckingham Palace, with representatives from the Spencer family, Charles's staff, the Queen's men, Downing Street, and the forces of law, order and street traffic. Sir Robin Janvrin was on speakerphone from Balmoral. 'There was an argument about the children's role,' one of the attendees told me. 'The Windsors opposed the children being involved much because they didn't think they could handle it. There was an amazing moment when we were on speaker with what we thought was Janvrin alone and Prince Philip came booming over the squawk box. The Spencer side had been saying what the role of the children had to be and Philip suddenly blasted, "Stop telling us what to do with those boys! They've lost their mother! You're talking about them as if they are commodities. Have you any idea what they are going through!" It was rather wonderful. His voice was full of emotion, a real voice of the grandfather speaking.' Later in the week, the Duke butted in on the conference call again. 'Our worry at the moment is William. He's run away up the hill and we can't find him. That's the only thing we are concerned with at the moment.'[20]

Ironically, it was a practical miscalculation that kicked the notorious flagpole controversy into high gear. The Palace had not allocated enough condolence books at St James's Palace. The endless standing in line to sign them focused the public eye on a glaring deficiency: the flagpole on top of Buckingham Palace was bare.

In protocol terms there was no reason why it should not have been empty. The Buckingham Palace flagpole is strictly for the royal standard, with its lyres and lions rampant, and it is flown there only when the monarch is in residence. It is not so much a flag as an office 'In/Out' sign. It is never flown at half-mast, not even to mark the passing of a monarch, because there will be a new monarch on the throne. Nor does the Palace ever raise a Union Jack, not even to mark the passing of a national hero like Winston Churchill. But procedures that had been good for the Britain of a hundred years earlier – or five days earlier – were suddenly archaic in the new Diana dawn.

The royal biographer Anthony Holden, who was based outside Buckingham Palace with American TV crews for most of the week, turned into the unlikely Robespierre for incipient republican sentiment. At one point he was engaged in the frustrating task of explaining the arcane traditions of the flag to an American audience. As the camera panned around, showing that every other building in Whitehall and Westminster had a flag at half-mast, voices from the crowd around the TV platform urged Holden to speak out on behalf of the people. Egged on by TV executives in New York saying, 'This is great! Do it! Do it!'[21] he became the electronic megaphone, expressing the rumbling of the crowd to an audience of millions. Picking up from Holden, TV reporters went up and down the line asking members of the public the disingenuous question, 'So what do you think of the fact there's no flag up there, flying at half-mast?' On his way to the second day's 10 a.m. meeting at the Palace, Alastair Campbell noticed that the mood on the streets was turning nasty. 'It reminded me of coming out of a football match and not being sure if someone was going to jump you,'[22] he told me.

It was the perfect Day Three distraction for the tabloids. Retrieved from their uncomfortable infamy by Henri Paul's exposé as a drunkard, the popular press had a new blood sport: going after the Queen. How dare she be 'Out' from her Palace in London? The cry went up that she should be there in her capital with her grieving people. The front pages were a Greek chorus: 'Show Us You Care' (*Express*), 'Where is Our Queen? Where is Her Flag?' (*Sun*), 'Your People Are Suffering – Speak to Us Ma'am' (*Mirror*).' A *Sun* editorial: 'That empty flagpole at the end of the Mall stands as a stark insult to Diana's memory. Who gives a damn about the stuffy rules of protocol?'[23] The paper opened a hotline on the issue, and 40,000 readers called to express their disgust.

It is fashionable to believe that without the persuasive bridge-building of Tony Blair, there would have been a convulsion in which Britain would have became a republic. In the end, I doubt it. There has never been a serious appetite among the British people for replacing the monarchy, however flawed, with a regime fronted by some official in a business suit. They tried a version of it after beheading Charles I and nobody much liked it then. For most Britons, the Crown is the golden thread that connects the people to the most glorious moments of their history, exercising a force for stability in an otherwise bewilderingly changing world. Not for nothing have the Elizabethan and Victorian ages been named after those two great queens. It is seen as reassuring that the Crown represents a constitutional force above politics, providing a bulwark against the egos of over-mighty politicians (who in other countries at other times have established dictatorships). There is something satisfying about Blair's otherwise obstreperous aide Alastair Campbell having to trudge from Downing Street to Buckingham Palace for planning meetings when the rest of the world had to come to him.

Even in the middle of the Diana hysteria, two-thirds of the British people polled said the country was better off for having a monarchy. Its abolition was certainly not the wish of Diana, whose awe of the institution seemed only to increase the more she alienated the family who embodied it. 'I so want the monarchy to survive,' she wrote in one of her lonely nocturnal notes to Paul Burrell, 'and realise the changes that [*sic*] will take to put "the show" on a new and healthy track. I too understand the fear the family have about change but we must, in order to reassure the public, as their indifference concerns me and should not be.'[24]

According to urban myth, the Queen's authority is so deeply rooted in the national subconscious that the majority of her subjects are said to have dreamed about her at some stage in their lives.

If anything, Diana's wedding and Diana's death both made the same point about monarchy. The fascination they engendered in the rest of the world set Britain consciously apart from the Europeans, who seem to have presidents put in place by procedures no one can understand, and Americans, who worship wealth and celebrity in ways Britons find unwholesome. In the words of the historian Andrew Roberts, 'It is difficult to imagine two billion people worldwide bothering to watch the funeral service of an ex-daughter-in-law of an elected head of the Republic of Britain.'[25]

Still, Diana's passing was a nasty moment of truth for the monarchy, forcing it to confront how out of touch it had become. It required a shock to the system, not from Diana alone but from the public, whose disfavour could not be ignored. The Crown had pettily stripped Diana of her HRH, but with one concession at a time, the public willed its dignity back to her. The rigidities of protocol the Princess now had defied in her life tumbled before the outpouring of raw feeling from the people. The Queen was forced out of Balmoral to London for a public walkabout amid the grief and the flowers outside Buckingham Palace; she was obliged to make her first ever live TV broadcast to the nation, expressing an empathy she almost certainly did not feel and accept the flying of the Union Jack over Buckingham Palace. And as the coffin passed the palace, the monarch, standing outside, did something she had only done before for a head of state. She bowed her head.

One of the many extraordinary things about the days after Diana's death was the way the ritual of preserving the monarchy and the necessity of modernising the monarchy simultaneously played out at Buckingham Palace. From the grave, Diana achieved something she could never quite manage in her lifetime: she made the Palace listen to her. 'The death of Diana made the institution look hard at itself,' Sir Robin Janvrin admits. 'It was an opportunity to lift stones that hadn't been lifted. Who does come into Buckingham Palace on the guest list? What kind of engagements do we do? The death was an opportunity to shake the system.'[26] 'It was managing change through disaster,' another Palace official said.[27]

And so, miraculously, in planning her funeral, all present at the Palace meetings came to see that while ceremony mattered, what mattered more was that it be a ceremony reflecting an absence of awe and a presence of love. Diana would be carried not on a hearse shielded from the public by glass, but on an open gun carriage. The procession behind her coffin would be not of soldiers and military bands but of hundreds of the volunteers and workers from the charities and campaigns she had supported. The music in Westminster Abbey would be not only Verdi and the patriotic Victorian hymn she had chosen for her wedding – 'I Vow to Thee My Country' – but also, from her friend Elton John, a pop elegy, 'Candle in the Wind', written first to Marilyn Monroe, the unhappy star with whom Diana most empathised. Everything would be televised, and all along the route up to the abbey would be video monitors allowing the crowd to participate in the service.

Diana's coffin spent its last night before the funeral at Kensington Palace. There were candles flickering at each end. A courtier tells how before it left the Chapel Royal at St James's Palace the Queen Mother asked her page William Tallon to place flowers on her behalf. Tallon had already paid his respects in the morning but in the early evening he went again to fulfil the Queen Mother's request. He placed his flowers below the coffin and the Queen Mother's on top. Then he noticed that the coffin was lower in its position than it had been earlier in the day and he asked the chaplain, why it was lower now than before. 'Oh, that's for the boys,' the chaplain said. 'They're waiting next door in the vestry till you've gone. They are going to view her then.' That, Tallon told friends, was when he felt the real force of it. He cried and cried.[28]

At 8 p.m, the coffin made the twenty-minute journey to Kensington Palace in a four-car procession down the Mall, along Constitution Hill, to Hyde Park Corner, and from there, to Kensington Palace. Fifty thousand mourners watched in silence as the hearse, filled with flowers, moved slowly past Hyde Park Corner in the hiss and splash of the summer rain. Once the Princess was on her own turf the Spencer family alone was allowed to keep vigil. The candlelit inner hallway where the coffin lay all night glimmered with Diana's favourite flowers – white lilies, white tulips and white roses.[29] For Frances Shand Kydd these hours were her real goodbye to Diana. The choice of Westminster Abbey for the service the next day was, for her, an unhappy one. She associated the abbey with her wedding there in June 1954 to Johnnie Spencer; the marriage had ultimately caused her much grief, and she had no wish to be a part of the Windsor pomp and ceremony. To ease her pain, she wandered outside the palace most of the night among the mourners.

The day of the funeral was bathed in bright sunshine. The coffin was draped in the royal standard and covered in lilies, a wreath of pink roses, and the single posy of cream roses that broke every mother's heart: the handwritten card from Harry read, simply, 'Mummy'. As the coffin on its gun carriage, drawn by six black horses, emerged at 9.08 a.m. through the gates of Kensington Palace, a shrill wail, a spine-chilling, haunting cry, rose from the crowd. When the coffin reached

St James's Palace, the royal men – Prince Charles, the Duke of Edinburgh, and the pale, determined figures of Princes William and Harry – stepped forward, along with Earl Spencer, to take their places behind the gun carriage. It was Prince Philip who got the boys ready for the trial of walking behind. 'I'm not going to march in any bloody parade,'[30] William had said. Philip had gently cajoled him: 'If I walk, will you walk with me?'[31] Earl Spencer vehemently objected, saying that Diana would not have wished them to go through such an ordeal. I think he was wrong. Diana's ethos, even at her most distressed, was to rise to every occasion. She never let the public down. To keep the boys from breaking down along the route Philip talked to them quietly about each of the historic landmarks of London they passed. How gravely dynastic the three generations of Windsors looked as they strode in formation up the Mall. Their collective masculinity was a reminder of continuity and strength in adversity.

The sombre procession, with the boys keeping their heads lowered, moved through the Horse Guards arch and down Whitehall towards Westminster Abbey. The scene was rich in extraordinary images, but it is the sounds that linger: the grinding of the gun carriage wheels; the clatter of hooves; the sibilant slap of thousands of bouquets thrown on to the tarmac; the voices from the crowd calling out 'God bless you, William', 'God bless you, Harry'; the thin snuffle of sobbing. The funeral cortège arrived at 11 a.m. by the Great West Door of the abbey. 'You felt you were in the heart of the body of the world that was grieving,' says Geordie Greig, one of the guests.[32]

Inside the abbey were more unforgettable sounds: the solemn chimes of the tenor bell; the squeak of the guardsmen's boots as the eight pallbearers from the 1st Battalion, the Welsh Guards, all of equal height, carried the seven-hundred-pound coffin to a catafalque before the high altar; and the long seconds of stunned silence that followed the thrilling impertinence of Earl Spencer's eulogy – a silence so deep, Meredith Etherington-Smith remembers, that 'it was like being wrapped in black velvet, an almost physical feeling'.[33]

In a clear rebuke to the Queen who had personally taken back Diana's right to be styled Her Royal Highness, Earl Spencer said of his sister: 'She proved she needed no royal title to continue to generate her particular brand of magic . . . I pledge that we, your blood family, will do all we can to continue the imaginative and loving way in which you were steering these two exceptional young men so that their souls are not simply immersed by duty and tradition, but can sing openly as you planned.'[34]

Blood family! It was the second time in twenty-two months the Queen had been publicly kicked in the teeth by this spawn of off-the-wall Whigs. (The first was Diana's salvo on *Panorama*.) Thrown as it was in the frozen faces not just of the monarch but of the entire House of Windsor, Earl Spencer's address – written in fluid longhand on his way back from South Africa on the plane – was the nearest thing you could get in the late twentieth century to an Act of Sedition. The silence in the abbey was broken by a sound that everyone, at first, thought was the patter of rain. It was actually a wild burst of applause from the crowd outside. It washed through the Great West Door and down the nave until, for the first time in the great church's history, everyone – except the royal family – was clapping, too. A few centuries earlier, Earl Spencer might have been dispatched to the Tower. As it was, the Queen, who is the Earl's godmother, just stared stonily ahead. Prince Charles was so angry he had to be restrained from issuing a statement afterwards. 'Very bold,' the Queen Mother said archly when asked about it later in Scotland.[35] Prince Philip considered the eulogy a matter of sufficient gravity that he later consulted his close friend Lord Brabourne, the film producer, about what he thought the royal response should be. Brabourne, sophisticate in the ways of the media, told him to do *absolutely nothing*, and urged him to restrain the instinct of impulsivity in Charles.[36] What the Queen herself thought is evinced by her comment to Earl Spencer at the opening of the Diana, Princess of Wales Memorial Fountain in Hyde Park in the summer of 2004. 'I hope you are satisfied now,' she was overheard to tell her godson before she drove away.[37]

Would Diana have approved of her brother's reckless eulogy? More to the point: would she have given it herself? The answer to that, of course, is yes (though later she would have sacked all the people who'd helped her write it). It had all the hallmarks of a dazzling Spencer mistake: perfectly of the moment, brilliantly conceived and executed, and freighted with disaster for the future. Frances Shand Kydd, repudiated by the Windsors from the day she left Johnnie Spencer, had no doubts herself about its rightness: 'Strange though it may seem, Diana's funeral was probably the proudest day of my life as a mother. Proud of her; my daughters, who were rock steady in their readings, and my son, who gave the ultimate tribute of brotherly love for her.'[38] Frances and Earl Spencer had together chosen the site for the burial, not with her father and ancestors in the family vault in the thirteenth-century church at Great Brington but at Althorp itself on a small island, known as the Oval, in the middle of an ornamental lake 250 yards north of the house. The grave's seclusion, reached only by rowing boat, protected Diana from the invasions of privacy that had marked her life: a temporary wooden bridge had been erected for the coffin to pass, borne on the shoulders of eight soldiers from the Princess of Wales Regiment.[39]

The gates of Althorp opened at 3.30 p.m. to admit the hearse, still scattered with flower petals from the crowds who had lined the seventy-seven-mile route from London to Northampton. Once inside the drive of the Spencer ancestral home, the royal officials escorting the coffin carefully unstitched the royal standard and replaced it with the white, red and gold flag of the Spencer family. Only intimate relatives, along with Paul Burrell and Colin Tebbutt, would attend the burial. The Spencers with Prince Charles and his sons had arrived an hour earlier on the royal train – a strained ninety-minute journey, given Earl Spencer's performance at the abbey. The exhausted party of family mourners were served coffee at the rosewood table in the drawing room, the young Princes sitting with the silently brooding Prince Charles. A butler entered and Earl Spencer left the room. He returned to declare simply, 'Diana is home.'[40]

And so Diana the hunted was laid to rest in the beauty and tranquillity of the Oval with Mother Teresa's rosary and cards from nieces, nephews and her two boys as eternal keepsakes.

I asked Tony Blair a decade after he became Prime Minister and was no longer the eager young moderniser he was in 1997, but a man tempered by the vicissitudes and loneliness of power – what, if anything, Diana's life had signified. A new way to be royal? 'No,' he replied, without hesitation. 'Diana taught us a new way to be British.'[41]

And so she did; but she taught, and learned, much more. When she came into the world, at the beginning of the 1960s, to be British meant, in almost all cases, to live a life without surprises, to follow a path laid out by the circumstances of birth and the folkways of class. The pattern was especially circumscribed for women, and perhaps most for all for women of Diana's background, as straitened as it was privileged. 'Diana is home,' her brother said. But in many ways he could hardly have been more wrong. Althorp had not been home to Diana for a long time, if it ever had been. It was what, without really intending to, she had escaped.

Like the heroine of a fairy tale, she became a princess. But her instinctive refusal to play her assigned role in the expected way, her insistence on living (as opposed to just living happily ever after), and her unplanned, unfinished search for happiness on her own terms enabled her to break free to become a citizen of the world, finding her place far from the moist-lipped charmers and grim periwigged operators of the Spencers' ancestral past or the encrusted traditions of the Windsors' stagnating present. The political power of the monarchy has been haemorrhaging for nearly four hundred years, and by a century ago it was effectively gone. Diana stumbled on a new kind of royal power. She showed what could be done with the old concept of royal bounty when the drama of humanitarian concern is connected with the electronic nervous system of global media.

You can see the Diana Effect today on the Queen herself. During the London terror bombings of 7 July 2005, the sovereign did something spontaneous the first time in her reign but reminiscent of the Queen Mother in the Blitz. She did not wait, as she would have done in the past, for her diary to open up for a planned visit to the injured. The very next day she travelled by helicopter from Windsor Castle to tour the wards of the Royal London Hospital in Whitechapel in the East End. Another first: the Queen made a speech in the informal setting of the hospital's canteen. 'Yesterday's bombings have deeply affected us all,' she told the hospital staff to cheers and applause. 'I know I speak for everyone in expressing my sympathy to those who have been caught up in these events and, above all, to the relatives and friends of those who have lost their lives.'[42] And when Britain observed two minutes of silence on the week's anniversary of the tragedy, the Queen again broke with royal custom. As Big Ben chimed its solemn midday across the silent city, she appeared in the forecourt of Buckingham Palace, flanked by staff ranging from junior footmen to senior aides.[43]

The understanding of the power of the inclusive gesture was Diana's gift to the monarchy and so much more. She played her innovative role while also fulfilling to perfection the most important, if most atavistic, family duty to which she was assigned: the production of male offspring. She gave the Windsors and England, and all the world's photographers, two tall, handsome Princes of the Blood. But then she raised them with a commoner's hands-on warmth and informality. When Prince Harry, now Second Lieutenant of the Blues and Royals, a Household Cavalry regiment, insisted on serving in Iraq, you could hear his mother's voice: 'There's no way I'm going to put myself through Sandhurst,' he said in a BBC interview to mark his twenty-first birthday, 'and then sit on my arse back home while my boys are out fighting for their country.'[44] As for Prince William, the heir to the throne, he was happy to attend, before Sandhurst, the University of St Andrews rather than pull strings for the expected Oxford or Cambridge and his first solo foray with the press was not conducted at St James's Palace but propping up the bar at the Hare and Hounds pub in Tetbury. He was wearing baggy jeans, a red sweatshirt, and a charming smile. He was relaxed and confident, but in ninety minutes' friendly chat the tabloid reporters invited to join him, while smitten, learned precisely – nothing. He is a prince who has learned from Diana's experience, a prince after Diana's heart. Her legacy is in good hands.

# Sequels

**Martin Bashir** brought about the downfall of Michael Jackson with the 2003 ITV interview that caused the star to be investigated for paedophilia. He secured the interview by promising Jackson he would introduce him to Kofi Annan, the Secretary General of the United Nations. In 2004 Bashir moved to the United States to become a reporter for ABC's 20/20 and later co-anchor of Nightline.

**Paul Burrell** was in the middle of his trial at the Old Bailey in 2002 for stealing personal items of the late Princess of Wales when the Queen suddenly remembered hearing him mention that he planned to hang on to some of Diana's items for 'safe-keeping'. The prosecution's case collapsed and the charges were dismissed. Burrell's two books about the Princess made him famous enough to qualify for an appearance in 2004 on the ITV reality show I'm a Celebrity, Get Me Out of Here! where he scored a popular success by rising to such challenges as eating a kangaroo's testicle. In 2007 he launched the Royal Butler Wine collection at the National Hall, Olympia, in London – 'affordable luxury for everybody in the home'. (See afterword)

**Dr James Colthurst** left mainstream hospital medicine after a career as an interventional radiologist at St Thomas's Hospital in London and a Surgical Fellow of the Edinburgh Royal College of Surgeons. He became a pioneer in the clinical applications of electric impulse systems, founding a company, Eumedic, to develop a treatment system using what was dubbed a Fenzian – a small hand-held digital device resembling a TV remote control – to rekindle the body's own repair mechanisms in a wide range of illnesses. In 2007 his system was in trials to validate formally his own results in reversing the consequences of hitherto intractable angina and asthma.

**Robert Fellowes** was the Queen's private secretary until 1999, when he was created Baron Fellowes of Shotesham, GCB, GCVO, QSO, PC. In 2000 he became chairman of Barclays Private Bank and he also chairs the Prison Reform Trust.

**James Hewitt** had no luck with his riding school, which went bust. In February 2003, the BBC reported that he was trying to sell Diana's love letters. They had been returned to him after an Italian adventuress seduced him on the Riviera, stole the letters out of his safe, and tried to sell them to the *Daily Mirror*, which rejected them as stolen property. In 2004, he was arrested at the Cactus Blue Bar in Chelsea on suspicion of being in possession of cocaine. In 2006, he had a brief resurgence on the TV reality show *The X Factor: Battle of the Stars*. He was last seen trying to set up a bar on the Costa del Sol in Spain. In February he appeared on *Al Murray's Happy Hour*.

**Patrick Jephson**, after leaving royal service in 1996, made a career as a writer and journalist for the *Spectator*, the *Sunday Telegraph* and *Newsweek*. He has worked as associate producer on TV documentaries about Hurricane Katrina, mental health and travel, and is currently to be seen as special royal correspondent on CBS's *The Early Show*. In the 30 December 2006 edition of the *Spectator* he offered advice his former boss might have given to Kate Middleton were she to become Princess of Wales. 'And when you have problems – as you undoubtedly will – share them with each other, not with the world.'

**Hasnat Khan** is Consultant Cardiothoracic Surgeon at the London Chest Hospital. In May 2006, he married Hadia Sher Ali, aged twenty-eight, who is descended from Afghan royalty, in a traditional Muslim ceremony near the family estate in Jhelum, Pakistan. His bride is the daughter of a close family friend. (See afterword)

**Tiggy Legge-Bourke** remained as Big Sister to Princes William and Harry despite such PR gaffes as incurring the wrath of anti-blood sport campaigners when she took the boys fox-hunting with the Beaufort and passed out cups of sloe gin. In October 1999 she married her childhood sweetheart Charles Pettifer, a former Coldstream Guards captain, at a wedding in the chapel of her parents' six-thousand-acre estate in Wales attended by a whooping William and Harry. She now has two sons. She was made a member of the Royal Victorian Order for services to the

Prince of Wales in the New Year's Honours List of 2000.

**Piers Morgan** was fired from the editorship of the *Daily Mirror* in 2004 after photographs he published of British soldiers abusing Iraqi prisoners turned out to be fake. He became a transatlantic TV personality, appearing as a judge on the NBC show *America's Got Talent* and the BBC series *You Can't Fire Me, I'm Famous*. A sequel to his diaries (*The Insider*, 2005) was published in April 2007 under the title *Don't You Know Who I Am?*. He appeared on NBC's *Celebrity Apprentice* with Donald Trump and won.

**Andrew Morton** followed up the success of his books about the Princess of Wales with a best-selling authorised biography of Monica Lewinsky and an unauthorised biography of the soccer hero David Beckham and his wife Victoria, the former Posh Spice. The only other author who has rivalled Morton in garnering sales of books about Diana has been Paul Burrell, of whom Morton says, 'he is very good at serving tea.' In January 2008, his book *Tom Cruise: An Unauthorised Biography* was published int he United States to mixed reviews.

**Camilla Parker Bowles** married Prince Charles in a civil ceremony at the Guildhall, Windsor, on 8 April 2005, with a blessing attended by the Queen in St George's Chapel at Windsor Castle. As the consort of the Prince of Wales, she is legally the Princess of Wales but is styled as HRH, the Duchess of Cornwall. It is said that when Prince Charles succeeds to the throne her title will be HRH the Princess Consort. In the Queen's toast at the wedding reception, Her Majesty likened the romance to that day's arduous Grand National steeplechase. 'Despite Becher's Brook and the Chair and all kinds of other terrible obstacles my son has come through . . .'

**Frances Shand Kydd**, sustained by her faith after conversion to Catholicism in 1994, lived alone on the Isle of Seil on the coast of Scotland until her death in 2004 at the age of sixty-eight. She made annual pilgrimages to Lourdes as a carer for groups of disabled people. In Oban, she was a legend for her personal involvement in a multiplicity of local charities. She drove long distances to comfort the families of fishermen lost at sea and mothers who had lost children. She embraced the parents of Henri Paul, saying they had suffered 'the sorest ache of all'. An executor of Diana's estate, she stayed close to William and Harry.

**Raine Spencer** divorced her third husband, Count Jean-François Pineton de Chambrun, a descendant of the Marquis de Lafayette, in 1996, and reverted to calling herself Countess Spencer. She remains on the payroll of Mohamed Al Fayed as a director of Harrods and of Harrods Estates and is a fixture on the London social scene.

**Colin Tebbutt** continued his relationship with Diana's family by driving Frances Shand Kydd when she was in London and often dining with her to share memories of Diana. He was being interviewed by the Operation Paget investigation when he got the news that Mrs Shand Kydd had died. He still drives the Duchess of York and her two daughters, Princesses Beatrice and Eugenie.

**Ken Wharfe** is on demand on the after-dinner speakers' circuit and has developed a one-man show, *An Evening With Ken Wharfe*, enriched by his gift for mimicking the voices of Prince Charles, the Duke of Edinburgh and Paul Burrell. He is a stalwart of the English Chamber Choir. He still puts his thirty-five years with the Metropolitan Police to use in commentaries on royal security and has been critical of the lack of protection for Kate Middleton.

**The Duchess of York** paid off all debts by her own commercial and literary enterprises in the United States. In 2007, she celebrated her tenth year as the spokesperson for Weight Watchers. She founded Hartmoor, a creative development company for products and lifestyle design. In 2008 comes her first historical romance novel, also called *Hartmoor* and set in 1812. Its heroine is a flame-haired earl's daughter with tribulations not unlike her own. The Duchess still has warm relations with Prince Andrew and sometimes accompanies him to engagements in the U.S. In 2008 she investigated obesity for a TV reality show *The Duchess in Hull*, a two part special for ITV.

# Afterword

The Coroner's Inquests into the Deaths of Diana, Princess of Wales and Emad El-Din Mohamed Abdel Moneim Fayed (Mr Dodi Al Fayed) looked at the start as if it would be everything the Royal Family dreaded. The Palace had ardently hoped that the long-delayed British proceedings would be all wrapped by August 2007, the tenth anniversary of Diana's death, in time for the memorial concert planned by her sons, Prince William and Prince Harry, and the memorial service at the Guards Chapel. The deep desire of the Princes after ten long years of Diana mythomania and debasement and Mohamed Al Fayed's wild allegations about assassination plots was to draw a line under all that. And no wonder: in the preceding ten years hardly a day had gone by when William and Harry were not treated to some agonising detail, angle or fabrication about the last hours and minutes of their mother's life.

The Inquests finally began on 2 October 2007, at Court 73 at the Royal Courts of Justice in the Strand. Al Fayed had been campaigning for this day for for a decade, but now that it had arrived, it posed daunting problems for the Harrods tycoon. How would he cope with the apparently irrefutable evidence of Accidental Death from the French Investigation into the car crash and the exhaustive Operation Paget Inquiry and Report, and the corroborative testimony that would emerge at the Inquests? How would he escape from the fact that the Ritz's acting head of security, Henri Paul, who did not even have a chauffeur's licence, drove a Mercedes at high speed into the thirteenth pillar of the Alma Tunnel in Paris simply because he had imbibed a powerful cocktail of medication and alcohol? How could he continue to maintain that Dodi had visited the Repossi jewellery store in order to purchase an 'engagement ring' for the Princess when the CCTV videotape would show how fleeting and perfunctory his visit actually was? How would he hold fast to the thesis that Diana was pregnant even after an autopsy had found that she was not, even though such close friends as the Hon. Rosa Monckton were ready to take the stand to give details of her last menstrual period – as late as 15th August – and even after Debbie Gribble, the stewardess on the *Jonikal*, would testify that she saw Diana's contraceptive pills in her cabin?[1]

How could he continue to insist that Diana's brother-in-law Lord Fellowes, the Queen's former Private Secretary, had commandeered the communications centre at the British Embassy in Paris on the night of the crash to mastermind the assassination of Dodi and Diana along with agents of the Secret Intelligence Service, also known as MI6? Hard to explain, was it not, when evidence at the inquest would be given that on the night in question Lord Fellowes was not in Paris at all but publicly visible in Norfolk with a house party of friends watching an entertainment at Burnham Market church put on by Sir John Mortimer – the creator, appropriately enough, of *Rumpole of the Bailey*.[2] How would Al Fayed, even with his brilliant team of legal eagles, convince the jury that Henri Paul had been blinded by a flashing light in a car driven by a secret agent masquerading as a paparazzo? How, pray, would he answer the question the coroner would be bound to ask, about the way the pursuing motorbikes and cars were so brilliantly orchestrated for the split-second manoeuvres and changes of plan required for Henri Paul successfully to drive the Mercedes into a fatal collision with passengers who chose not to wear seat belts? Whom could he finger as the genius who duped Henri Paul into changing the route from the Ritz and thus unwittingly committing suicide?

The Coroner, Lord Justice Scott Baker, 70, was perfectly equipped to deliver the *coup de grâce* to any surviving scintilla of doubt on the previous judgments. As a Justice of the Court of Appeals since 2002 he'd been widely recognised for his rigor and fairness. He was perfectly cast for the job. With a head of snowy hair and an ironic twinkle behind large, glaring glasses he's the kind of sound Englishman who blows his nose with unapologetic volume into a large white handkerchief. He'd presided over the Old Bailey trial in 1999 of the former Tory cabinet minister Jonathan Aitken on charges of perjury and perverting the course of justice, and hadn't hesitated to send him down for eighteen months with a crackling rebuke.

Court 73, where the Inquests were held at the Royal Courts of Justice, was approached through the chilly Gothic halls leading to Bell Yard North and up two flights of stairs to the end of a corridor. On the first day I attended in January 2008 the public seats were occupied by a few newspaper-reading retirees, a chatty accountant from Cheshire who said he was there because his 'mum is absolutely obsessed and [he] just wanted to take a look', and one eccentric representative of the Diana fanatics, John Loughrey, a fiftyish former chef who came each day with DIANA written in greasy marker across his head and DODI scrawled across his nose and cheeks. 'She's with me every day,' he confided.[3]

The jury, sitting to the left of the courtroom, was mostly young and racially mixed.

An especially erected court annexe for the press overflowed into Bell Yard. Depending on who was on the stand, the atmosphere in the annexe veered between gregarious excitement and unpopulated melancholy. On many days only a few dedicated scribblers straggled in to watch the inquiry unfold on TV monitors. When, for instance, evidence was being given by Operation Paget's toxicology adviser, Professor Robert Forrest, a balding, bearded droner whose eyes were glassy from peering at moribund organs (in this case those of the dead chauffeur Henri Paul), the annexe had the deserted, forlorn look of a hospitality tent at a wedding the morning after the grand bash is over.

Professor Forrest's recitation of the cocktail of Prozac, Tiapride and alcohol in Henri Paul's bloodstream precisely predicted the tragedy. Even though it was detail that went to the heart of the case, few in the media or the public wanted to hear the bright memory of the People's Princess being reduced to a chemical inventory.

To rebut such evidence, Al Fayed had assembled a triple-barrelled legal team led by the celebrated Michael Mansfield QC, one of the highest-paid criminal defence barristers in the land. The most valuable aspect of his reputation as far as Al Fayed was concerned was for being one of the best cross-examiners of police (i.e. the Paget Report's Lord Stevens). Plus he could be relied upon to put Al Fayed's anti-Establishment case as bluntly as possible. In the courtroom Mansfield's grey, flowing locks and restless bulky physique give him the battered charm of an ageing matinée idol but 'his style is attack, attack, attack,'[4] a fellow lawyer told the *Daily Mail*. Alongside Mansfield, to separately represent Al Fayed's Ritz Hotel, were Ian Croxford QC, a skilled expert in Professional Negligence and White Collar Crime, and for the family of Henri Paul, Richard Keen QC, a thin-nosed criminal defense barrister and Dean of the prestigious Faculty of Advocates in Scotland. Keen's stock in trade was to gnaw away at witnesses like a punctilious ferret. The monthly tab for these legal hotshots – who also included some forty additional lawyers around the world – is said to have reached three million dollars a month.

On the big days in court Mohamed Al Fayed mostly sat at the back of the courtroom, stone-faced and haggard beneath the expressive crescents of his heavy eyebrows. He was usually accompanied by his blow-dried mouthpiece, Michael Cole, and John Macnamara, the onetime Scotland Yard detective who worked on Al Fayed's own investigation into the crash. Like Al Fayed's legal team, however, they were clearly taken aback when on Monday 18 February 2008 Al Fayed finally took the stand.

His three-page statement, was stunning in its simplicity and audacity. He simply ignored the evidence. He drew gasps of disbelief in the courtroom – and even boos in the press tent – when he laced into 'stooge judges' and accused two former heads of the Metropolitan Police of having 'acted unprofessionally', and having 'no conscience'. He described Prince Philip as a 'Nazi' and a 'racist' who had ordered MI6 to commit the murder because he could not countenance Diana marrying a Muslim and bearing his child. 'You know his [Philip's] middle name? It sounds like Frankenstein.' Diana, he said, had 'suffered for twenty years in this Dracula family'.[5] He accused Diana's closest friend, Rosa Monckton, of establishing a friendship with her simply to pass information to MI6.[6] He painted the same picture of lurid improbables that he had disseminated for the previous eleven years, adding one new detail: that Prince Charles, too, was implicated in the 'assassination'.

'They murdered her. Now he [Charles] is happy with his crocodile wife.'[7] Moreover, not only the Royal Family but also the French police, the attending medical staff at La Pitié-Salpêtrière Hospital and the Prime Minister at the time, Tony Blair, were all, according to Al Fayed, part of the plot and the cover-up. 'Such a momentous and horrific action would have been directly sanctioned by the Prime Minister,' flailed Al Fayed.[8]

'You said a little earlier,' said Lord Justice Scott Baker, cordially, 'that you would expose the gangsters who killed Diana and your son. Would you like to explain who you believe that those gangsters were?'[9]

'The gangsters are the members of MI6,' Al Fayed offered.[10] He went on to throw the then British Ambassador in Paris, Lord Jay, into the plot, alleging that his promotion in the Foreign and Commonwealth Office as head of the diplomatic service had been a pay-off for complicity in the murder. Lord Justice Scott Baker glared at him over his impressive glasses.

'A lot of people were involved in the plot,' he commented, to much laughter in court.[11]

We waited through, altogether, six months of testimony for the John Grisham turnabout that Al Fayed's team surely had up its sleeve to justify the millions spent and the burden on the British taxpayer. But as the months wore on it was clear he would once again reject every testimony of the Inquests under oath by the parade of forensic experts, every bit of evidence from the most senior members of the royal household and heavyweights from Scotland Yard, every careful reflection by personal friends of the Princess. Al Fayed simply dismissed as liars witnesses who swore to speak the truth even after his resourceful legal team had failed to discredit their testimony. Witnesses from his own side crumbled on the stand. Under fierce cross-examination from Richard Horwell QC, representing the Commissioner of London Police, John Macnamara (Al Fayed's former security chief), was forced to admit he had lied when he told ABC's Cynthia McFadden ten days after the crash that there was no evidence that Henri Paul had been drinking when he already knew there was a bar tab showing that Paul had downed two Ricard pastis spirits shortly before they took off for Dodi's Rue Arsène-Houssaye apartment.[12]

It was increasingly discomfiting to see such distinguished Establishment figures as the former Scotland Yard chief Lord Stevens and Sir Richard Dearlove, the former head of MI6, subjected to a barrage of manipulative 'baloney' (to use Al Fayed's favourite word) from the Fayedeen. Their anger was apparent when the imposingly tall Lord Stevens, on finishing his testimony, looked straight across at Al Fayed and demanded an apology for these 'quite outrageous' charges: 'one, that we were either negligent; two, that we had not done the job properly; or three, which was the extraordinary accusation, that I had been got at in terms of how the report was going to be put forward.'[13] Meanwhile Sir Richard Dearlove, in a cold, clear voice, unequivocally denied any MI6 involvement in the imagined 'assassination' of Diana and Dodi – 'a mischievous and fanciful allegation,' he called it. 'I don't want to be flippant, but I'm tempted to say that I am flattered. Once again, this is such an absurd allegation. It is difficult to deal with an allegation that is so absurd that it is completely off the map.'[14]

What did Al Fayed hope to achieve with this demented farrago? Author and commentator David Pryce-Jones wondered on his *National Review* blog if Al Fayed's obsession with foul play was fuelled by his formative years in Egypt, where victims of power struggles frequently were dispatched and secret police regularly caused Islamist radicals to disappear. Was Al Fayed's fixation on conspiracy another example of his stubborn cultural misunderstanding, just as, on a trivial level, he never comprehended why generous Harrods sponsorship of the Royal Windsor Horse Show did not result in tête-à-têtes at Buckingham Palace, or why owning the Villa Windsor was exactly the wrong status symbol to impress the aristocracy? Al Fayed could not grasp that in a free and ancient democracy like England the 'ruling class' doesn't – in fact, can't – go around ordering the Secret Intelligence Service to bump off anyone who disturbs the Royal Family's peace of mind. As Pryce-Jones reminded us, 'There is no record of British secret services murdering anyone anywhere at any time. Brigadier Mason-Macfarlane was British military attaché in Berlin before the war, and in a memorandum in 1938 he offered to shoot Hitler. Horrified superiors had him transferred at once to be governor of Gibraltar.'[15]

The tabloids decided that the simplest answer was that Al Fayed had lost the plot. But Al Fayed's behaviour was more rational and therefore more disreputable than that. His vindictive grief for the loss of his son combined with his boiling desire to punish the Establishment shredded the last vestiges of Diana's privacy.

Sometimes shining through the dross of the Princess's last hours, we glimpsed the Diana of a different time. The testimony of the fashion company executive Roberto Devorik, the Princess's friend with whom she travelled to Rome and Buenos Aires, evoked the once more digni-fied image of the daughter of Earl Spencer and the wife of the heir to the British throne. Devorik recalled how sometime after their marital separation Diana sharply rounded on a guest at a lunch party who made the mistake of openly belittling Prince Charles.

'He is the father of my children and he is going to be the future King of England, and if I have a difference with him it's my problem with him,' she had said. 'But nobody should make mockery about him.'[16]

In the months of the Inquests such moments were rare.

Day after day the legal vaudeville show Al Fayed served up included a steady stream of gaudy bit players from the cast of hangers-on, sycophants, and what the ancient but still spry Raine, Countess Spencer, Diana's former stepmother, termed on the witness stand 'soothsayers' who peopled the last years of Princess Diana's life.[17] There was always some fresh intrusion of absurdity to keep the show rolling along.

One such tabloid moment was the unmasking under oath of Paul

Burrell. Since the Princess's death Diana's former butler has raked in twenty million pounds out of Diana's memory with two indiscreet memoirs, his 'royal' range of furniture, crockery, and cutlery, and his lucrative seminars about the finer points of pouring tea. He told an enterprising undercover operative of the *Sun* that he came back to testify only because 'people who do my merchandising brands in America said, "If you didn't go, it's not going to look good for you."'[18] Recorded by a herd of TV cameras, he arrived at court fresh off a plane from the US and dressed in an overstuffed designer suit. His vaunted final 'secrets' about Diana, hinted at in his books, were ridiculed as a sham after Lord Justice Scott Baker, dispatched him to his home in Cheshire to find the supposedly red-hot documents. After reading them privately, the coroner declared, 'I have read the documents. I have caused a list to be made of their description, and I have come to the conclusion that there is nothing relevant in any of them.'[19] It didn't help Burrell's image that on the *Sun*'s undercover tape, he told the reporter after the hearing, 'Quite frankly, Britain can fuck off' – and then boasted that he hadn't told the truth in court anyway.[20] He refused to return to the UK to answer to the coroner. Lord Justice Scott Baker left no doubt about what the jury should believe in his summing up, 'it was blindingly obvious, wasn't it, that the evidence that he gave in this courtroom was not the truth, the whole truth and nothing but the truth?'[21]

By contrast, Dodi's former girlfriend Kelly Ann Fisher, who has kept to herself all these years, enduring the casual defamations of her by Mohamed Al Fayed, came forward to vigorously dispute his story. Al Fayed's hostility to the former Calvin Klein lingerie model – afterwards he had the gall to refer to her as a 'hooker'[22] – derives from the awkward fact that she considered herself engaged to Dodi at the same time he was supposed to be in love solely with Diana. Fisher was magnificent in the robust way she fought off the Mansfield hit squad. 'Philippe Dorneau [Dodi's regular chauffeur in Paris] was treated like shit,' she insisted at one point. 'I am sorry, he was.' Dodi, she told the Inquests, always berated his chauffeurs to drive faster. 'They are saying that Henri Paul – it was all his fault . . . Why should he take all the blame?'[23]

She recounted how Dodi presented her with a huge sapphire and diamond engagement ring in February of 1997 at the Beverly Hills Hotel and how she understood from him that they were to be married on 9 August 1997. She told how she first learned of Dodi's romance with Diana when she saw 'The Kiss' picture in a newspaper; how she had called her once-beaming prospective father-in-law, Mohamed Al Fayed, in London – only to be brushed off with profanities. She said when she showed up in the first week of August at what she thought was to be her future home with Dodi in Malibu she was told 'it was not my house, it was Mohamed's'.[24] She produced a tape recording of the bitter row she subsequently had with Dodi on the phone in which she can be heard sobbing, 'You even flew me down to St Tropez to sit on a boat while you seduced Diana all day and fucked me all night!'[25]

This was the glamorous new world Diana had drifted into after she left the protective tower of royal approval.

It is saddening to see just how rotten a scene her last romantic Mediterranean idyll really was underneath. It was made more unsettling by contrast with the people from the world she left behind and the way they dealt with the assaults from Mansfield's cross-examination. There was, for instance, Brigadier Sir Miles Hunt-Davis, the upright old Palace factotum, who once commanded the Brigade of Ghurkas, and has since 1991 been Prince Philip's private secretary. Mansfield, working to establish royal motivation for the assassination plot, pressed him to describe the 'extreme concern to the Royal Family that the Princess of Wales was cavorting on a yacht in the Mediterranean with the son of somebody who was regarded as undesirable'.[26]

'Specifically what dates are you talking about?' Hunt-Davis asked in his deadpan voice, and on hearing it was July 1997, the year after the Prince and Princess's 1996 divorce, he responded with words that would have brought a blush of rage to Diana's face. 'Mr Mansfield, I think what you have failed to accept is that, actually, once the divorce had happened, what Princess Diana did was not relevant to the mainstream Royal Family.'[27]

Meanwhile the former Metropolitan Police Commissioner Lord Condon, a man celebrated for routing out corrupt elements in the police force, had to sit in court and listen to Mansfield accusing him of being a key player in a criminal conspiracy.[28]

Condon acknowledged that he had been apprised of a note taken after a meeting with the Princess in October 1994 by the Deputy Assistant Commissioner David N. Meynell, Head of the Royalty and Diplomatic Protection Department. The formal tone of the note as it was read out in court seemed charged with currents of foreboding for the Princess of Wales. Meynell wrote the aide-memoire at a time when Diana was, privately, deep in her turbulent affair with the married

Oliver Hoare and chafing to shed any spies who might inform the press or the Palace.

'HRH did not display any of the confrontational attitude which was evident during our last meeting,' Meynell's notes read. 'She was "friendly and bright" on the surface. She commenced by stating that as some ten months had now elapsed since she had requested the withdrawal of her protection, she would like to know how I viewed the position. I opened by saying that my worst fears had not been realised and that at one stage there was cause to be quietly optimistic that things would begin to settle down. However, recent events had again meant that she was the subject of some considerable media interest with its consequential effect upon her privacy. HRH responded by saying that she had not been shot or injured in any way as she had predicted to me . . . She stated that there were some 50 or 70 members of the media present recently but they were of no concern to her and that she was determined to continue her policy of no personal protection officer other than for high-profile functions.

'I then went on to indicate that I was retiring. She laughed and stated that it was her intention to continue her policy of not having protection for the private part of her life.'[29]

She laughed: Diana was nothing if not trouble. I think of her fateful exchange with Meynell as I sit in Court 73 in January of 2008 watching the testimony of the only survivor of the Paris car crash, the bodyguard Trevor Rees-Jones (today he goes by the name of Trevor Rees). He is now a bulky forty-year-old whose big open face has been reconstructed after it was smashed to a pulp on the night of 31 August 1997. On this rainy January day he was here to speak in public for the first time.

The *Daily Mail*, in a gambit to build interest in its coverage, suggested that the bodyguard's memory blackout was finally lifting.[30] The possibility drew a bursting press tent and the appearance of the former royal Rat Pack veteran James Whitaker, Diana's erstwhile 'big fat tomato'. These days he lives the good life in semi-retirement in Spain (with occasional guest appearances as Royal Correspondent for ITV's *This Morning*), Whitaker is grander and stouter than he once was and given to anecdotes about Fleet Street in its gossip glory days, when lunches were long and dinner jackets were many. 'The *Mail* better be right he's getting his memory back,' he was saying into his mobile. 'I just bloody well hope he gets it back by 4.30 because I've got a train to catch.'[31]

Diana's oldest sister Lady Sarah McCorquodale sits on the left side of the courtroom talking animatedly to a Palace official, Major Jamie Lowther-Pinkerton, part-time private secretary to Prince William and Prince Harry. (Palace sources tell me that Sarah seems eager to ingratiate herself back into the inner Palace circle.) At fifty-three she is still very good-looking, with fine bones, translucent skin, and that russet Spencer hair colouring shared by Prince Harry – the county permutation of the family genes, minus Diana's super gloss. Still, there is a whiff of their mother Frances's slightly sexy hauteur as she waits in the small, drab courtroom.

The legal teams in the front row look up at the coroner's bench. Michael Mansfield QC, easy to see on account of his impressive silver mane and easy to hear on account of his bombast, has so far met his match in the cooler, more forensic style of Ian Burnett QC. Burnett leads the opposing team that includes the pin-striped figure of Richard Horwell QC.

Trevor Rees looked pale and sombre when he approached the witness stand to take his seat in court. He made a wide detour around Mohamed Al Fayed, who watched him warily from behind hooded eyes. The ongoing circus since Diana's death has been a source of aggravation to Rees. Since his recovery, the former paratrooper has preferred to take security jobs far from media intrusions, in places like East Timor and Iraq. Grateful at first to Al Fayed for paying his hospital bills, he soon became uneasy at his sense of being pressured to do newspaper interviews and influence the French investigation. His ghostwritten account of the events leading up to the accident, The Bodyguard's Story, had given a highly credible picture of the chaos of Dodi's constantly changing security requirements. Rees's principled departure from Al Fayed's employment and his refusal to corroborate Al Fayed's fanciful version of events had made him a target for Al Fayed, who had since called him 'so ungrateful and so deceitful' and a pawn of MI6.[32]

Rees is not easy to discredit. He is a transparently regular bloke. His big, scarred face manifests a flicker of pain as he watches, for the first time, the CCTV footage of his activities on that last night at the Ritz in Paris. It is eerie for us all but must have been far more so for Rees after so much physical agony and tabloid myth. He looks again on the yellowy glare of that lamplit Paris street, the to-ing and fro-ing of the Ritz staffers up and down the grand blue carpeted staircase, the hurrying stick figures in summer cotton trousers and shirts who were his younger, unscarred self and his bodyguard colleague Kez Wingfield – jump-cut images of impending disaster.

Watching the tapes, we see Trevor slumped on a chair outside Diana and Dodi's Imperial Suite on the first floor, looking tired and distracted. We see the figure of Henri Paul gesticulating, telling Trevor something. Off camera, a person we can't see opens the door. According to Rees it is Dodi, telling him about a change of plans: they will leave by the back exit. Trevor has always maintained, as did Wingfield, that Dodi says of the change of plan, 'It's been okayed by Mr Mohamed . . .'[33] His account in *The Bodyguard's Story* to that effect is read aloud by Richard Horwell QC. ('He's a liar. Definitely a liar,' Al Fayed responded on 18 February 2008 when their recollection was put to him in court and the Coroner ultimately chose to give the benefit of the doubt to his denial of approving the decoy plan).

On the tape, Diana can be seen descending in the service elevator of the Hôtel Ritz. I want to implore her indistinct, black-and-white image: Stop! Please stop!

Rees gazes impassively at the TV screen. He says in his testimony that he and Kez remonstrated with Dodi and Henri Paul about the new plan and gave in only when they began to fear that an angry Dodi might leave without any security at all. They settled for what Rees keeps repeating was 'a workable compromise'[34] whereby one bodyguard, Trevor, would accompany Dodi and Diana from the service entrance on the Rue Cambon while Wingfield would go ahead from the front of the Ritz in a decoy two-car convoy, a black Mercedes and Dodi's black Range Rover. Beyond that, Rees says insistently, he remembers nothing – and to Mansfield's relentless, sceptical questioning that sought to blame him for the night's disaster he keeps intoning, 'a workable compromise was reached'.[35]

'You see it wasn't a workable compromise?' thunders Mansfield. He is skilfully trying to get Trevor to admit that he was really not in control at all that night. And, sure enough, the CCTV footage shows that it does indeed seem to be Henri Paul in charge. He is the one talking to the paparazzi outside; he is the one coming up to notify the two bodyguards at the suite of something they appear to listen to with resignation. As Mansfield proclaims, nowhere on the CCTV footage do you see a heated dispute between the bodyguards and Henri Paul about what they were about to do.

It is unlikely that any royal protection officer would have capitulated to this improvised scheme simply to avoid the paparazzi's cameras. Diana was, as her former bodyguard Ken Wharfe pointed out in his Inquests' testimony on 9 January 2008, 'the most photographed woman in the world,' well used to the flash and scuffle of the press pack.[36] But then no royal protection officer had to work for Mohamed Al Fayed. Henri Paul was one of Al Fayed's most trusted go-to guys. Trevor Rees was much lower down the pecking order. He knew that to keep arguing was fruitless. He couldn't labour this point in court, because it would have suggested that he had allowed himself to be emasculated in his duties. Thus, Trevor could only repeat the fragile formula he had by then internalized: 'A workable compromise was reached.'[37]

In any case, the chaos of the exit plan that sent Diana to her death in a tunnel was not the fault of poor, stunned Trevor Rees. It was the half-cocked plan dreamed up by a nervy and agitated Dodi Fayed that set in motion the night's events: Dodi's unexpected arrival with Diana at the Ritz; the ensuing paparazzi mayhem outside the hotel; the call by the anxious security officer in charge, Francois Tendil, to his off-duty superior Henri Paul to return immediately to the hotel;[38] Dodi's demand that the Ritz's night manager Thierry Rocher get a third car to drive the couple from the back entrance on the Rue Cambon,[39] Dodi's decision that the driver would be not his chauffeur, but Henri Paul, now knocking back the first of two Ricards in the Ritz bar. And all these frantic, scurrying figures were ultimately in the pay of Dodi's father, the autocratic tycoon whom all of them strove to please, Mohamed Al Fayed. ('God is calling,' Diana would say when she handed the mobile phone to Dodi whenever his father called.[40])

Lord Justice Scott Baker in his summing up left not a millimetre of wriggle room for Al Fayed's royal conspiracy theory while being sensitive to the stresses on a bereaved father. 'No one who has not lost a child or a very close loved one can perhaps ever truly comprehend the devastating effect of such a loss and how it gnaws away at one.'[41] At the same time, he reminded the jury of 'the straight forward unreality' of Mohamed Al Fayed's belief that the Duke of Edinburgh was involved in killing his daughter-in-law and Dodi. 'A belief expressed in legal proceedings which is unsupported by evidence is worthless. It is not evidence in itself. It is no more than unsupported opinion.'[42] Crushingly, Scott Baker pointed out that Mohamed Al Fayed's own legal team didn't ask key players about the conspiracy they were supposed to be involved in. Why? Because they were bound by professional rules of conduct which don't allow attorneys to make allegations of serious misconduct for which there is no evidence.

It was hardly a surprise after this devastating analysis that the Coroner should tell the jury they could not by law return a verdict of unlawful killing in a staged accident. The Coroners' Rules insist that any verdict that appears to suggest civil liability or criminal liability of a named person or persons can be returned only if the Coroner can identify the justifying evidence – and against the Duke of Edinburgh he could identify none. 'Speculation, surmise, belief are one thing; evidence is another.'[43] He gave the jury the choice of five verdicts: accidental death; three versions of 'unlawful killing' – tantamount to manslaughter – by Henri Paul, or unlawful killing by the paparazzi; or unlawful killing by the combination; or an open verdict that would have left the case in limbo.

The Coroner was careful in assessing how far the pursuing paparazzi could be blamed. Their own photographs at the crash made it 'plainly untrue' that helping the victims was a higher priority than taking pictures.[44] Romuald Rat's criticism of Henri Paul was turned against the photographer. Rat had said he didn't understand why Henri Paul drove so quickly. 'A normal chauffeur knows that it is not the way that you should shake someone off.' Rat had said. 'He took too many risks.'[45] The Coroner dryly noted that if M. Rat's assessment were correct, the jury would have to consider whether it must also apply to any chasing group.

Still, as with Henri Paul, the Coroner stressed the very high level of proof required to return the verdicts nine members of the jury did – unlawful killing by Henri Paul through impairment of judgment by alcohol – and unlawful killing by the 'following vehicles,' clearly meaning the paparazzi and not the phantom assassins of Mohamed Al Fayed's lurid imagination. 'Mere' negligence was one thing. It meant falling below the standard of driving expected of a reasonably competent driver. But the *gross* negligence determined by the jury required their concluding that the drivers 'were wholly indifferent to an obvious risk of death or actually foresaw that risk of death, but determined to run it nevertheless.'[46]

More than 250 witnesses came forward in the Inquests' six months. There were a handful of absentees. None of the paparazzi came, save one of their motor cycle drivers – Stéphan Darmon, who drove for Rat. There was no explanation for the missing French forensic experts, severely chastised by the Coroner for shortcomings in their procedures. 'There are question marks, therefore, about the conclusions to be drawn from the analysis of the blood samples said to have come from Henri Paul.'[47]

The witness missed most by the press was less concerned with the pathologies of death and more with the emotions of life.

Hasnat Khan, Diana's last deep love, who left England in 2007, refused to return from Pakistan, where he now lives. In the previous eleven years Khan had been tormented by the press every day of his life about Diana and had never broken his silence. It took him nine years after her death to finally marry, in May of 2006, the beautiful, twenty-eight-year-old Hadia Sher, a descendant of Afghan royalty and a daughter of a friend of his parents. But that attempt to forget the Princess ended in separation after eighteen months of marriage.

At the beginning of 2008 Dr. Khan made an uncharacteristic decision. He granted his first ever television interview, to Sir Trevor McDonald, of ITN News. It was broadcast on January 14, 2008 – the day Paul Burrell was centre stage at the High Court Inquests. No longer the heartthrob doctor with the soulful eyes who had won Diana's heart, he looked overweight and gloomy.

The interview offered nothing new, but the email he sent in answer to questions from the solicitor to the Inquests gave more surprising insights.

Khan related that it was Diana who, frustrated by his refusal to go public, put a final end to their relationship. It happened at the end of July 1997, at Kensington Palace after Diana's first trip to the South of France with the Al Fayeds and her dinner à deux with Dodi in Paris – the dinner at which Dodi pulled out all the stops to impress her and gave her a bracelet and a watch with pearls. A gushing thank-you letter from Diana to Dodi written on 27 July 1997 was read out in court. It said in part:

'Seldom has this particular lady ever been lost for words, but the events of the last twenty-four hours has left her speechless! Your organisation & sense of detail is enormously impressive and I thought I was the one with the vision.'[48]

At the time, Dr Khan had no idea that Dodi had been present at the Castel St Hélène on the Côte d'Azur when Diana visited the Al Fayeds with her boys. Though on her return he noticed a new distance in her manner, his suspicion was that she had met one of Al Fayed's circle – perhaps, in a flashback to her attraction to Barry Mannakee, 'it could have been a bodyguard'.[49]

'I remember saying to her at the time, "You are dead,"' Khan's statement reads, 'meaning that her reputation was dead. I said this because I was sure it was someone from Mohamed Al Fayed's group and that was how I felt about anyone involved with him . . . I tried to ring

Diana the night she died, but could not get through to her. I genuinely thought it was downhill now for Diana and I thought I would just sit on the sidelines and watch . . . I suppose it is possible that Diana was trying to make me jealous, but I do not believe that was the entire reason she was doing it. I think that when she had gone away on the boat she had felt protected and thought she would wait and see what happened with Dodi.'[50]

What these marathon hearings made clear was that Diana fell into the ultimate honey trap when she succumbed to the Al Fayeds. The new timelines of the Inquests show that even as Kelly Ann Fisher was banging on the door of the house in Malibu, Al Fayed was sending Harrods brochures of the Paradise Cove property for Diana to peruse as a holiday home he would make available to her.[51] It is hardly a coincidence that he purchased the California estate for Dodi in June, shortly before Diana's first trip to the South of France and within the same period he also bought his lavish yacht the *Jonikal*.[52]

'[Dodi] has all the toys,' Diana had said to Lady Bowker.[53] But she was fooled again, just as she had been fooled as a very young girl by the promise of permanence as a member of the monarchy. Diana always looked in the wrong places for safety. She had been deprived of emotional security for so long that she could no longer distinguish between protection and danger.

The Coroner's Inquests were not so much an inquiry as an exorcism of every lie and every myth surrounding the way the Princess died. Diana and Dodi lost their lives because Mohamed Al Fayed's drunken Henri Paul, pursued by paparazzi, struck the pillar in the Alma Tunnel rather than colliding with something else; and a contributing factor was that they were not wearing seat belts.

Mohamed Al Fayed's claim to have been vindicated is plainly as grotesque as his conspiracy theories. The words the Boston lawyer Joseph Welch addressed to Senator Joe McCarthy in the Army hearings are fitting: 'Have you no sense of decency, sir? At long last have you no sense of decency?'

For the rest of us now let us return Diana to a time when she was defined by more than the endless replay of her most tragic mistake. Instead we should be allowed to celebrate her life, vivid and meaningful, for all its imperfections.

# Bibliography

## Books

Barry, Stephen, *Royal Service: My Twelve Years as Valet to Prince Charles*, New York: Avon Books, 1983.

Bedell Smith, Sally, *Diana: In Search of Herself*, New York: Random House, 1999.

Birt, John, *The Harder Path: The Autobiography*, London: Time Warner Books, 2002.

Botham, Noel, *The Murder of Princess Diana*, New York: Pinnacle Books, 2004.

Bower, Tom, *Fayed: The Unauthorised Biography*, London: Macmillan, 1998.

Bradford, Sarah, *Elizabeth: A Biography of Her Majesty the Queen*, London: Heinemann, 1996.

Bradford, Sarah, *Diana*, London: Penguin, 2006.

Brandreth, Gyles, *Charles & Camilla: Portrait of a Love Affair*, London: Century, 2005.

Brown, Tina, *Loose Talk: Adventures on the Street of Shame*, London: Michael Joseph, 1979.

Burgess, Colin, *Behind Palace Doors: My Service as the Queen Mother's Equerry*, London: John Blake, 2006.

Burrell, Paul, *A Royal Duty*, London: Penguin, 2004.

Burrell, Paul, *The Way We Were: Remembering Diana*, London: HarperCollins, 2006.

Campbell, Beatrix, *Diana, Princess of Wales: How Sexual Politics Shook the Monarchy*, London: Women's Press, 1998.

Campbell, Lady Colin, *The Real Diana*, London: Arcadia Books, 2004.

Caradec'h, Jean-Michel, *Lady Diana: L'enquête criminelle*, Paris: Michel Lafon, 2006.

Clarke, Mary, *Diana: Once Upon a Time*, London: Sidgwick & Jackson, 1994.

Clayton, Tim, and Phil Craig, *Diana: Story of a Princess*, London: Hodder & Stoughton, 2001.

Clifford, Max, and Angela Levin, *Max Clifford: Read All About It*, London: Virgin Books, 2005.

Coward, Rosalind, *Diana: The Portrait*, London: HarperCollins, 2004.

Curtis, Sarah (ed.), *The Journals of Woodrow Wyatt*, Vol. 1, London: Macmillan, 1998.

Curtis, Sarah (ed.), *The Journals of Woodrow Wyatt*, Vol. 2, London: Macmillan, 1999.

Curtis, Sarah (ed.), *The Journals of Woodrow Wyatt*, Vol. 3, London: Pan Books, 2001.

Davies, Nicholas, *Diana: A Princess and Her Troubled Marriage*, New York: Birch Lane Press, 1992.

Dempster, Nigel, and Peter Evans, *Behind Palace Doors: Marriage and Divorce in the House of Windsor*, New York: G. P. Putnam's Sons, 1993.

Dempster, Nigel, and Peter Evans, *Behind Palace Doors*, London: Orion, 1993.

De Zengotita, Thomas, *Mediated: How the Media Shapes Your World and the Way You Live in It*, New York: Bloomsbury USA, 2005.

Dimbleby, Jonathan, *The Prince of Wales: A Biography*, London: Little, Brown, 1994.

Edwards, Arthur, *I'll Tell the Jokes Arthur. Diana, How I Saw Her Laughter Turn to Tears*, London: Blake Publishing, 1993.

Evans, Harold, *Good Times, Bad Times*, New York: Atheneum, 1984.

Graham, Caroline, *Camilla: Her True Story*, London: John Blake, 2003.

Greenslade, Roy, *Press Gang*, London: Macmillan, 2003.

Gregory, Martyn, *Diana: The Last Days*, London: Virgin Books, 2004.

Hastings, Max, *Editor: An Inside Story of Newspapers*, London: Macmillan, 2002.

Hewitt, James, *Love and War*, London: Blake Publishing, 1999.

Hoey, Brian, *At Home with the Queen: The Inside Story of the Royal Household*, London: HarperCollins, 2002.

Holden, Anthony, *The Tarnished Crown: Diana and the House of Windsor*, London: Bantam Press, 1993.

Holden, Anthony, *Charles: A Biography*, London: Bantam Press, 1998.

Howell, Georgina, *Diana: Her Life in Fashion*, London: Pavilion, 1998.

Hurd, Douglas, *Memoirs*, London: Little, Brown, 2003.

Jebb, Miles (ed.), *The Diaries of Cynthia Gladwyn*, London: Constable, 1995.

Jephson, P. D., *Shadows of a Princess: An Intimate Account by Her Private Secretary*, London: HarperCollins, 2000.

Junor, Penny, *The Firm: The Troubled Life of the House of Windsor*, London: HarperCollins, 2005.

Kelley, Kitty, *The Royals*, New York: Warner Books, 1998.

Lacey, Robert, *Royal: Her Majesty Queen Elizabeth II*, London: Little, Brown, 2002.

Lees-Milne, James, *Deep Romantic Chasm: Diaries 1979–1981*, London: John Murray, 2003.

Lees-Milne, James, *The Milk of Paradise: Diaries 1993–1997*, London: John Murray, 2005.

Levin, Angela, *Raine & Johnnie: The Spencers and the Scandal of Althorp*, London: Weidenfeld & Nicolson, 1993.

Lindley, Richard, *Panorama: Fifty Years of Pride and Paranoia*, London: Politico's Publishing, 2003.

Lowry, Suzanne, *Cult of Diana: The Princess in the Mirror*, Oxford: Clio Press, 1987.

MacArthur, Brian (ed.), *Requiem: Diana, Princess of Wales 1961–1997. Memories and Tributes*, New York: Arcade Publishing, 1997.

Martin, Ralph G., *Charles and Diana*, New York: Putnam, 1995.

Morgan, Piers, *The Insider: The Private Diaries of a Scandalous Decade*, London: Ebury Press, 2005.

Morrow, Ann, *Without Equal: H.M. Queen Elizabeth, the Queen Mother*, Thirsk: House of Stratus, 2002.

Morton, Andrew, *Diana: Her True Story*, New York: Simon & Schuster, 1992.

Morton, Andrew, *Diana: Her New Life*, London: Michael O'Mara Books, 1994.

Morton, Andrew, *Diana: Her True Story – In Her Own Words*, completely revised edition, London: Michael O'Mara Books, 1997.

Morton, Andrew, *Diana: In Pursuit of Love*, London: Michael O'Mara Books, 2004.

Naden, Gavan, and Maxine Riddington, *Lilac Days*, London: HarperCollins, 2005.

Neil, Andrew, *Full Disclosure*, London: Pan Books, 1997.

Oldfield, Bruce, with Fanny Blake, *Rootless: An Autobiography*, London: Arrow, 2005.

Paxman, Jeremy, *On Royalty*, London: Viking 2006.

Pimlott, Ben, *The Queen: A Biography of Elizabeth II*, London: HarperCollins, 1996.

Pontaut, Jean-Marie, and Jérôme Dupuis, *Enquête sur la mort de Diana*, Paris: Stock, 1998.

Rees-Jones, Trevor, with Moira Johnston, *The Bodyguard's Story: Diana, the Crash, and the Sole Survivor*, New York: Warner Books, 2000.

Riddington, Max, and Gavan Naden, *Frances: The Remarkable Story of Princess Diana's Mother*, London: Michael O'Mara Books, 2003.

Robertson, Geoffrey, *The Justice Game*, London: Vintage Books, 1999.

Robertson, Mary, *The Diana I Knew: The Story of my Son's Nanny who Became Princess of Wales*, New York: Cliff Street Books, 1998.

Sancton, Thomas, and Scott MacLeod, *Death of a Princess: An Investigation*, London: Weidenfeld & Nicolson, 1998.

Saunders, Mark, and Glenn Harvey, *Dicing With Di: The Amazing Adventures of Britain's Royal Chasers*, London: Blake Publishing, 1996.

Shea, Michael, *A View from the Sidelines*, Stroud: Sutton, 2003.

Simmons, Simone, with Susan Hill, *Diana: The Secret Years*, London: Michael O'Mara Books, 1998.

Simmons, Simone, with Ingrid Seward, *Diana: The Last Word*, London: Orion, 2006.

Snell, Kate, *Diana: Her Last Love*, London: Granada, 2002.

Spencer, Charles, *Althorp: The Story of an English House*, London: Viking, 1998.

# Bibliography

Stott, Richard, *Dogs and Lampposts*, London: Metro, 2002.

Strong, Roy, *The Roy Strong Diaries 1967–1987*, London: Weidenfeld & Nicolson, 1997.

Vickers, Hugo, *Elizabeth: The Queen Mother*, London: Hutchinson, 2005.

Wharfe, Ken, with Robert Jobson, *Diana: A Closely Guarded Secret*, London: Michael O'Mara Books, 2003.

Whitaker, James, *Diana v. Charles*, London: Signet, 1993.

Wilson, A. N., *The Rise and Fall of the House of Windsor*, New York: W. W. Norton & Company, 1993.

York, Sarah, the Duchess of, with Jeff Coplon, *My Story*, London: Pocket Books, 1997.

## Documents

'Operation Paget Inquiry' into the allegation of conspiracy to murder Diana, Princess of Wales and Emad El-Din Mohamed Abdel Moneim Fayed, Overview and Report, by Lord Stevens of Kirkwhelpington, 14 December 2006.

# Notes

## Chapter 1

1    Interview Arthur Edwards, 16 November 2005
2    Tina Brown, 'A Woman in Earnest', *New Yorker*, 15 September 1997
3    Kate Snell, *Diana: Her Last Love*, 120
4    Tim Clayton and Phil Craig, *Diana: Story of a Princess*, 333
5    Trevor Rees-Jones, *The Bodyguard's Story*, 19
6    *Daily Mirror*, 20 December 1997
7    'The Diana Files', *Sunday Mirror*, 13 December 1998
8    Baroness Jay in conversation with author
9    *Washington Post*, Tina Brown, 6 November 2003
10    Off the record interview
11    Interview Colin Tebbutt, 24 August 2006
12    Kate Snell, 98
13    *Daily Mirror*, 20 December 1997
14    Interview David Tang, 20 June 2006
15    Interview Lord Palumbo, 27 September 2005
16    Interview Lord Puttnam, 26 July 2005
17    Interview Marie Helvin, 18 September 2006
18    Interview Colin Tebbutt, 24 August 2006
19    Trevor Rees-Jones, 17
20    Trevor Rees-Jones, 33
21    *News of the World*, 31 August 1997
22    Tim Clayton and Phil Craig, 336
23    *Sunday Times*, Christina Lamb, 7 September 1997
24    Geoffrey Robertson, *The Justice Game*, 364
25    Tom Bower, *Fayed: The Unauthorised Biography*, 347
26    Martyn Gregory, *Diana: The Last Days*, 42 and 107
27    'Operation Paget Inquiry', 55
28    'Operation Paget Inquiry', 64
29    *Sunday Telegraph*, 15 February 1998
30    Martyn Gregory, 25
31    Sarah Bradford, *Diana*, 367
32    Thierry Rocher www.scott-baker-inquests.gov.uk
33    Trevor Rees-Jones, 79

34  Interview Hassan Yassin, 24 September 2006
35  Kate Snell, 212
36  Ibid., 193
37  'Operation Paget Inquiry', 14 December 2006, 30
38  Daily Mail, 21 December 2007
39  TJS36 Key Events www.scott-baker-inquests.gov.uk
40  'Operation Paget Inquiry', 14 December 2006, 254

## Chapter 2

1  Rosalind Coward, *Diana: The Portrait*, 37
2  Andrew Morton, *Diana: Her True Story – In Her Own Words*, 23
3  Interview Rosa Monckton, 2 August 2005

## Chapter 3

1  Official website of Barbara Cartland www.barbaracartland.com
2  Gyles Brandreth, *Charles & Camilla*, 225
3  Settelen tapes, NBC *Dateline*, 6 December 2004
4  Nicholas Davies, *Diana: A Princess and Her Troubled Marriage*, 36
5  Sarah Bradford, *Elizabeth: A Biography of Her Majesty the Queen*, 430
6  Interview Barbara Gilmour, 27 September 2005
7  Interview Lady Glenconner, 30 September 2005
8  Gavan Naden and Maxine Riddington, *Lilac Days*, 296–7
9  Max Riddington and Gavan Naden, *Frances*, 42
10  *Independent*, 24 September 2006
11  Interview David Cannadine, 27 June 2006
12  Off the record interview
13  Interview Lord Glenconner, 26 September 2005
14  Interview Lady Glenconner, 30 September 2005
15  *Evening Standard*, 22 May 1953
16  *Hello!*, 24 May 1997
17  Angela Levin, *Raine & Johnnie*, 29
18  Ibid., 17.
19  Interview Earl Spencer, 12 February 2007
20  Interview Lord Glenconner, 26 September 2005
21  Lady Colin Campbell, *The Real Diana*, 13–14
22  *Hello!*, 15 June 2004
23  *Daily Mail*, 7 October 2003
24  Max Riddington and Gavan Naden, *Frances*, 26
25  *The Times*, 3 July 1961
26  Ibid., 31 August 1961
27  Ibid., 15 July 1964
28  *Sunday Mirror*, 9 November 1980
29  James Whitaker, *Diana v. Charles*, 95
30  Off the record interview
31  *Hello!*, 24 May 1997
32  Lady Colin Campbell, 16

33  Angela Levin, 48
34  *Sunday Express*, 28 September 2003
35  Interview Lady Glenconner, 30 September 2005
36  Sally Bedell Smith, *Diana: In Search of Herself*, 19
37  Off the record interview
38  Andrew Morton, *Diana: Her True Story – In Her Own Words*, 70
39  Interview Barbara Gilmour, 27 September 2005
40  *Hello!*, 15 June 2004
41  Lady Colin Campbell, 16
42  Settelen tapes, NBC *Dateline*, 29 November 2004
43  *Evening Standard*, 15 April 1969
44  Interview Barbara Gilmour, 27 September 2005
45  Lady Colin Campbell, 18
46  Ibid.
47  Sarah Bradford, *Elizabeth*, 432
48  Andrew Morton, *Diana: Her True Story – In Her Own Words*, 25
49  Mary Clarke, *Diana: Once Upon a Time*, 151
50  *The Times*, 8 September 1997, Charles Spencer – Funeral Address, 6 September 1997
51  *Birmingham Evening Mail* Special, 'Diana – The Early Years', 1 September 1997
52  Interview Lord Glenconner, 26 September 2005
53  Andrew Morton, *Diana: Her True Story – In Her Own Words*, 75
54  *Birmingham Evening Mail* Special, 'Diana – The Early Years', 1 September 1997
55  Interview Robert Spencer, 14 January 2006
56  Andrew Morton, *Diana: Her True Story – In Her Own Words*, 80
57  *Sunday Herald*, 14 February 1993
58  Andrew Morton, *Diana: Her True Story – In Her Own Words*, 28
59  Interview Lord Glenconner, 26 September 2005
60  *Daily Telegraph*, 17 November 1954
61  Ibid., 27 November 1954
62  Off the record interview
63  Roy Strong, *Diaries 1967–1987*, 73
64  Interview Lord Glenconner, 26 September 2005
65  Off the record interview
66  Interview Kenneth Rose, 18 November 2005
67  Angela Levin, 131
68  Andrew Morton, *Diana: Her True Story – In Her Own Words*, 29
69  Ibid., 28
70  Mary Clarke, 192
71  Kitty Kelley, *The Royals*, 259
72  Settelen tapes, NBC *Dateline*, 29 November 2004
73  *Sunday Mirror*, 9 November 1980
74  Interview Kenneth Rose, 18 November 2005
75  Ibid.

76 Ibid.
77 Off the record interview.
78 Sally Bedell Smith, 50

## Chapter 4

1 *Woman's Own*, 8 April 1978
2 Sally Bedell Smith, *Diana: In Search of Herself*, 38
3 *Sunday Mirror*, Graham Dudman, 23 August 1998
4 Angela Levin, *Raine & Johnnie*, 131
5 Sally Bedell Smith, 54
6 Andrew Morton, *Diana: Her True Story – In Her Own Words*, 87
7 Ibid.
8 Sally Bedell Smith, 48
9 Andrew Morton, *Diana: Her True Story – In Her Own Words*, 28
10 Interview Geordie Greig, 16 November 2005
11 Tim Clayton and Phil Craig, *Diana: Story of a Princess*, 16
12 Andrew Morton, *Diana: Her True Story – In Her Own Words*, 75
13 Angela Levin, 138–9
14 Jonathan Dimbleby, *The Prince of Wales: A Biography*, 279
15 Nigel Dempster and Peter Evans, *Behind Palace Doors*, UK edn 98
16 Settelen tapes, NBC *Dateline*, 29 November 2004
17 Tim Clayton and Phil Craig, 22
18 Nigel Dempster and Peter Evans, *Behind Palace Doors*, UK edn, 101
19 Interview Paul Johnson, 1 August 2005
20 Rosalind Coward, *Diana: The Portrait*, 67–8
21 Tim Clayton and Phil Craig, 17
22 Rosalind Coward, 68
23 Tim Clayton and Phil Craig, 17–18
24 Ibid., 18
25 Ibid.
26 Ibid., 19
27 Simone Simmons, *Diana: The Last Word*, 15
28 Lord Glenconner in conversation with author
29 *Le Monde*, 27 August 1997
30 Sally Bedell Smith, 56
31 Kitty Kelley, *The Royals*, 258
32 Andrew Morton, *Diana: Her True Story – In Her Own Words*, 98
33 Ibid., 100
34 Ibid., 31
35 James Whitaker, *Diana v. Charles*, xi
36 Andrew Morton, *Diana: Her True Story – In Her Own Words*, 60
37 Sally Bedell Smith, 60
38 Andrew Morton, *Diana: Her True Story – In Her Own Words*, 127
39 Interview Mary Clarke, 11 March 2006
40 Interview Peter York, 28 September 2005

41    Ibid.

42    Ralph G. Martin, *Charles and Diana*, 89

43    Andrew Morton, *Diana: Her True Story – In Her Own Words*, 102

44    Interview Danae Brook, 14 June 2006

45    Interview Dmitri Kasterine, 24 April 2006

46    Andrew Morton, *Diana: Her True Story – In Her Own Words*, 103

47    *Daily Mirror*, 19 November 1980

48    Interview Mary Robertson, 11 April 2006

49    Ibid.

50    Ibid.

51    Mary Robertson, *The Diana I Knew*, 20–1

52    Interview Mary Robertson, 11 April 2006

53    Mary Robertson, 23–4

54    Interview Mary Robertson, 11 April 2006

55    Ibid.

56    Mary Robertson, 33

57    Interview Mary Robertson, 11 April 2006

58    Gabé Doppelt in conversation with author

59    *Tatler*, 'The Lady Di Set March', 1981

60    Ibid.

61    Interview Peter York, 19 June 2006

62    Sally Bedell Smith, 60

63    Andrew Morton, *Diana: Her True Story – In Her Own Words*, 105

64    Ibid., 104

65    Ibid., 188

66    Interview James Colthurst, 13 June 2006

67    Ibid.

68    Tim Clayton and Phil Craig, 26

69    Simon Berry email to author, 8 March 2007

70    Interview James Colthurst, 13 June 2006

71    Mary Robertson, 38

72    Ibid., 43

73    *Sun*, 4 December 1993

## Chapter 5

1    Interview Shaun Plunket, 4 February 2006

2    A. N. Wilson, *The Rise and Fall of the House of Windsor*, 71

3    PBS *Frontline*, 'The Princess and the Press', John Grigg, 16 November 1997

4    PBS *Frontline*, 'The Princess and the Press', the Royals and the Press Timeline

5    PBS *Frontline*, 'The Princess and the Press', Harry Arnold, 16 November 1997

6    Roy Greenslade, *Press Gang*, 85

7    Robert Lacey, *Royal*, 194

8    Ibid., 195

9    *Daily Mirror*, Emma Hibbs, 11 February 2002

10    Interview John Lahr, 2 June 2006
11    Interview Sir David Frost, 24 May 2006
12    PBS *Frontline*, 'The Princess and the Press', Harry Arnold, 16 November 1997
13    *Daily Mail* chart
14    Tina Brown, *Loose Talk*, 58
15    *Sunday Times*, 2 August 1998
16    Interview Peter McKay, 20 June 2006
17    Tina Brown, 58
18    Ibid., 77
19    Interview Hugo Vickers, 11 November 2005
20    PBS *Frontline*, 'The Princess and the Press', Richard Stott, 16 November 1997
21    Arthur Edwards, *I'll Tell the Jokes Arthur*, 276
22    Piers Morgan, *The Insider*, 178
23    *Woman's Own*, 8 April 1978
24    Ibid.
25    Sally Bedell Smith, *Diana: In Search of Herself*, 64

## Chapter 6

1    Andrew Morton, *Diana: Her True Story – In Her Own Words*, 105
2    Interview Stephen Fry, 21 September 2005
3    Duchy of Cornwall website: Income & Expenditure Account Year ended 31 March 2006
4    Anthony Holden, *Charles: A Biography*, 82
5    Nigel Dempster and Peter Evans, *Behind Palace Doors*, UK edn, 80
6    Ibid.
7    Off the record interview
8    Brian Hoey, *At Home with the Queen*, 21
9    Gyles Brandreth, *Charles & Camilla*, 114
10    Off the record interview
11    Off the record interview
12    *Daily Mail*, 8 May 1993
13    Interview Michael Shea, 19 September 2006
14    *Daily Telegraph*, 22 May 2001
15    Ann Morrow, *Without Equal*, 201
16    Jeremy Paxman, *On Royalty*, 4
17    Nigel Dempster and Peter Evans, UK edn, 98
18    Interview Sabrina Guinness, 26 September 2005
19    FDCH Political Transcripts, 2 November 2005
20    Nigel Dempster and Peter Evans, UK edn, 85
21    Interview Hugo Vickers, 11 November 2005
22    Ibid., 28 July 2005
23    *Sunday Telegraph*, Selina Hastings, 13 November 2005
24    Roy Strong, *Diaries 1967–1987*, 314
25    Hugo Vickers, *Elizabeth: The Queen Mother*, 485

26  Interview Douglas Keay, 15 February 2007
27  Jonathan Dimbleby, *The Prince of Wales: A Biography*, 205
28  Ibid., 190
29  Ibid., 261
30  Nigel Dempster and Peter Evans, US edn, 77
31  Jonathan Dimbleby, 261–2
32  Gyles Brandreth, 201
33  James Whitaker, *Diana v. Charles*, 30
34  Gyles Brandreth, 54
35  Interview Marie Helvin, 18 September 2006
36  Gyles Brandreth, 46
37  Ibid.
38  Kitty Kelley, *The Royals*, 289
39  Gyles Brandreth, 183–4
40  *Sunday Times*, Minette Marrin, 13 February 2005
41  Sarah Bradford, *Diana*, 56
42  Jonathan Dimbleby, 191
43  Nigel Dempster and Peter Evans, US edn, 69
44  Interview Marie Helvin, 18 September 2006
45  Off the record interview
46  Off the record interview
47  Nigel Dempster and Peter Evans, UK edn, 72
48  Jonathan Dimbleby, 266
49  India Hicks letter to her uncle, Lord Brabourne, 26 May 2005
50  Off the record interview
51  Nigel Dempster and Peter Evans, UK edn, 115
52  Anthony Holden, *Charles: A Biography*, 137
53  Off the record interview
54  Anthony Holden, *Charles: A Biography*, 132
55  *Daily Mail*, 10 June 1980
56  Anthony Holden, *Charles: A Biography*, 138–9
57  Ibid., 139
58  Simon Berry email to author, 8 March 2007
59  Suzanne Lowry, *Cult of Diana: The Princess in the Mirror*, 24
60  Nigel Dempster and Peter Evans, UK edn, 65
61  Lady Colin Campbell, *The Real Diana*, 60
62  Roy Strong, 316–17
63  PA News, Andrew Woodcock, 25 November 1995

## Chapter 7

1  Rosalind Coward, *Diana: The Portrait*, 72
2  Andrew Morton, *Diana: Her True Story – In Her Own Words*, 32
3  Gyles Brandreth, *Charles & Camilla*, 208
4  Interview Sabrina Guinness, 26 September 2005
5  Tim Clayton and Phil Craig, *Diana: Story of a Princess*, 32
6  Andrew Morton, *Diana: Her True Story – In Her Own Words*, 32

7   Interview Sabrina Guinness, 26 September 2005
8   Andrew Morton, *Diana: Her True Story – In Her Own Words*, 31
9   Ibid., 32
10  Ibid.
11  Ibid.
12  Interview Oliver Everett, 9 March 2006
13  Stephen Barry, *Royal Service*, 189–90
14  Andrew Morton, *Diana: Her True Story – In Her Own Words*, 32
15  Jonathan Dimbleby, *The Prince of Wales: A Biography*, 280
16  Interview Victoria Mather, 22 May 2006
17  Off the record interview
18  Andrew Morton, *Diana: Her True Story – In Her Own Words*, 32
19  *Daily Mail*, Gordon Rayner, 20 September 2005
20  Gyles Brandreth, 208
21  Andrew Morton, *Diana: Her True Story – In Her Own Words*, 32
22  Ibid., 33
23  Jonathan Dimbleby, 280
24  Off the record interview
25  Lady Colin Campbell, *The Real Diana*, 56
26  Jonathan Dimbleby, 282
27  Lady Colin Campbell, 61–2
28  Robert Lacey, *Royal*, 271
29  *Daily Star*, 8 September 1980
30  Tim Clayton and Phil Craig, 42
31  Ibid.
32  *Daily Star*, 11 September 1980
33  *Tatler*, 'Pretty Amazing', September 1981
34  Lady Colin Campbell, 41
35  *Tatler*, 'Pretty Amazing', September 1981
36  PBS *Frontline*, 'The Princess and the Press', Ken Lennox, 16 November 1997
37  PBS *Frontline*, 'The Princess and the Press', James Whitaker, 16 November 1997
38  Interview Judy Wade, 10 May 2006
39  *Sunday Mirror*, 16 November 1980
40  Ibid.
41  Andrew Morton, *Diana: Her True Story – In Her Own Words*, 31
42  Interview Steve Wood, 7 June 2006
43  Tim Clayton and Phil Craig, 47
44  *Telegraph*, 21 January 1987
45  Interview Ashley Walton, 15 December 2006
46  Andrew Morton, *Diana: Her True Story – In Her Own Words*, 33
47  *The Times*, 7 August 1980
48  Lady Colin Campbell, 62
49  *Sunday Mirror*, 16 November 1980
50  Stephen Barry, 223

51    *Sunday Mirror*, 16 November 1980
52    Ibid.
53    Ibid., 23 November 1980
54    Ibid.
55    *Daily Mail*, 24 November 1980
56    Anthony Holden, *Charles: A Biography*, 145
57    *Daily Star*, 28 November 1980
58    Interview Robert Edwards, 26 June 2006
59    Interview Wensley Clarkson, 26 June 2006
60    Ibid.
61    *Daily Star*, 10 November 1980
62    Interviews Robert Edwards and Wensley Clarkson, 26 June 2006
63    Interview Wensley Clarkson, 26 June 2006
64    Interview Danae Brook, 14 June 2006
65    *The Times*, 2 December 1980
66    James Whitaker, *Diana v. Charles*, 112

## Chapter 8

 1    Nigel Dempster and Peter Evans, *Behind Palace Doors*, UK edn, 29
 2    Tim Clayton and Phil Craig, *Diana: Story of a Princess*, 62
 3    Robert Lacey, *Royal*, 278
 4    United Press International, Gregory Jensen, 25 July 1981
 5    Interview Mark Bolland, 27 June 2006
 6    Off the record interview
 7    Interview Mark Bolland, 27 June 2006
 8    Off the record interview
 9    Jonathan Dimbleby, *The Prince of Wales: A Biography*, 284
10    Off the record interview
11    PBS *Frontline*, 'The Princess and the Press', Arthur Edwards, 16 November 1997
12    Mary Robertson, *The Diana I Knew*, 47
13    Jonathan Dimbleby, 283
14    Lady Colin Campbell, *The Real Diana*, 72
15    James Whitaker, *Diana v. Charles*, 113
16    Sally Bedell Smith, *Diana: In Search of Herself*, 95
17    Off the record interview
18    Mary Robertson, 53
19    Interview Mary Robertson, 11 April 2006
20    Gyles Brandreth, *Charles & Camilla*, 224
21    Penny Junor, *The Firm*, 69
22    Lady Colin Campbell, 72
23    Gyles Brandreth, 233
24    Sally Bedell Smith, 96
25    Jonathan Dimbleby, 283
26    Andrew Morton, *Diana: Her True Story – In Her Own Words*, 33
27    Ibid., 34

28    Ibid., 117
29    Ibid., 34
30    Ibid.
31    Off the record interview
32    Off the record interview
33    Sarah Bradford, *Elizabeth*, 436
34    Interview Lord Glenconner, 26 September 2005
35    James Whitaker, 116
36    Ibid.
37    Georgina Howell, *Diana: Her Life in Fashion*, 25
38    Gyles Brandreth, 238
39    Stephen Barry, *Royal Service*, 202
40    Andrew Morton, *Diana: Her True Story – In Her Own Words*, 36
41    Interview William Tallon, 11 March 2006
42    Andrew Morton, *Diana: Her True Story – In Her Own Words*, 38
43    Off the record interview
44    Andrew Morton, *Diana: Her True Story – In Her Own Words*, 119
45    Paul Burrell, *A Royal Duty*, 23–4
46    Ibid., 303
47    Off the record interview
48    Sally Bedell Smith, 104
49    Andrew Morton, *Diana: Her True Story – In Her Own Words*, 37
50    Interview Mary Robertson, 11 April 2006
51    Lady Colin Campbell, 81
52    Elizabeth Emanuel in conversation with author
53    Gyles Brandreth, 227
54    Off the record interview
55    Off the record interview
56    Andrew Morton, *Diana: Her True Story – In Her Own Words*, 38
57    Gyles Brandreth, 228
58    PA News, Andrew Woodcock, 24 November 1995
59    Andrew Morton, *Diana: Her True Story – In Her Own Words*, 37
60    Hugo Vickers, *Elizabeth: The Queen Mother*, 422
61    Andrew Morton, *Diana: Her True Story – In Her Own Words*, 121
62    Sally Bedell Smith, 98
63    Jonathan Dimbleby, 284
64    Off the record interview
65    Off the record interview
66    Off the record interview
67    Jonathan Dimbleby, 287
68    Gyles Brandreth, 229
69    Andrew Morton, *Diana: Her True Story – In Her Own Words*, 39
70    *Daily Mirror*, 27 July 1981
71    *Spectator*, 28 February 1981
72    Kitty Kelley, *The Royals*, 376
73    Gyles Brandreth, 236

74  BBC/ITV, pre-wedding interview with Prince Charles and Lady Diana
75  Ibid.
76  Ibid.
77  Dempster and Evans, UK edn, 135
78  Stephen Barry, 169
79  James Lees-Milne, *Diaries 1979–1981*, 164–5
80  Hugo Vickers, 426
81  Andrew Morton, *Diana: Her True Story – In Her Own Words*, 124
82  Interview William Dartmouth, March 2006
83  Jonathan Dimbleby, 288
84  Andrew Morton, *Diana: Her True Story – In Her Own Words*, 41
85  Interview William Tallon, 11 March 2006
86  Hugo Vickers, 426
87  Andrew Morton, *Diana: Her True Story – In Her Own Words*, 41
88  Interview William Tallon, 11 March 2006
89  Tim Clayton and Phil Craig, 81
90  Andrew Morton, *Diana: Her True Story – In Her Own Words*, 42
91  *Observer*, 2 August 1997
92  Andrew Morton, *Diana: Her True Story – In Her Own Words*, 42

## Chapter 9

1   Off the record interview
2   Nigel Dempster and Peter Evans, *Behind Palace Doors*, UK edn, 136
3   Andrew Morton, *Diana: Her True Story – In Her Own Words*, 42
4   Caroline Graham, *Camilla: Her True Story*, 85
5   Gyles Brandreth, *Charles & Camilla*, 236–7
6   Simone Simmons, *Diana: The Last Word*, 41
7   Andrew Morton, *Diana: Her True Story – In Her Own Words*, 42
8   Caroline Graham, 88
9   Kitty Kelley, *The Royals*, 288
10  Ibid.
11  Jonathan Dimbleby, *The Prince of Wales: A Biography*, 294
12  Stephen Barry, *Royal Service*, 220–1
13  Paul Burrell, *A Royal Duty*, 27
14  *Daily Mail*, 6 November 2002
15  Interview Paul Johnson, 1 August 2005
16  Lady Colin Campbell, *The Real Diana*, 117
17  Off the record interview
18  Off the record interview
19  Stephen Barry, 228
20  Interview Paul Johnson, 1 August 2005
21  Tim Clayton and Phil Craig, *Diana: Story of a Princess*, 91
22  Rosalind Coward, *Diana: The Portrait*, 109
23  Simone Simmons, *Diana: The Last Word*, 41
24  Nicholas Davies, *Diana: A Princess and Her Troubled Marriage*, 126
25  Ibid., 129

26  *News of the World*, 20 September 1981
27  Andrew Morton, *Diana: Her True Story – In Her Own Words*, 43
28  James Whitaker, *Diana v. Charles*, 122
29  Off the record interview
30  Off the record interview
31  Off the record interview
32  Penny Junor, *The Firm*, 78
33  Ibid., 77
34  Off the record interview
35  Off the record interview
36  Andrew Morton, *Diana: Her True Story – In Her Own Words*, 44
37  Ibid.

## Chapter 10

1   Myles Jebb (ed.), *The Diaries of Cynthia Gladwyn*, 206–7
2   Ibid., 207
3   Interview Edward Mirzoeff, 11 May 2005
4   Gyles Brandreth, *Charles & Camilla*, 245
5   Interview Meredith Etherington-Smith, 26 July 2005
6   Nigel Dempster and Peter Evans, *Behind Palace Doors*, UK edn, 139
7   *Time*, 9 June 1961
8   ITV *Diana: The Story of a Princess*, Part 2, June 2001
9   Tina Brown diary
10  *Vanity Fair*, 'The Mouse That Roared', October 1985
11  Andrew Morton, *Diana: Her True Story – In Her Own Words*, 44
12  Interview Victoria Mather, 17 November 2005
13  Jonathan Dimbleby, *The Prince of Wales: A Biography*, 295
14  Tim Clayton and Phil Craig, *Diana: Story of a Princess*, 94
15  Arthur Edwards, *I'll Tell the Jokes Arthur*, 10
16  Tim Clayton and Phil Craig, 94
17  Ibid., 95
18  Ibid., 94
19  Ralph G. Martin, *Charles and Diana*, 233
20  Ibid., 235
21  ITV *Diana: The Story of a Princess*, Part 2, June 2001
22  Tim Clayton and Phil Craig, 96
23  Ralph G. Martin, 234
24  Tim Clayton and Phil Craig, 96–7
25  ITV *Diana: The Story of a Princess*, Part 2, June 2001
26  BBC *Panorama*, interview, 20 November 1995
27  Sally Bedell Smith, *Diana: In Search of Herself*, 125
28  Interview James Colthurst, 13 June 2006
29  *Evening Standard*, 3 May 2002
30  Roy Strong, *Diaries 1967–1987*, 291
31  Ralph G. Martin, 243
32  *Daily Express*, 6 November 1981

33  *News of the World*, 15 November 1981
34  Simone Simmons, *Diana: The Secret Years*, 26
35  Interview David Griffin, 30 August 2006
36  Simone Simmons, *Diana: The Last Word*, 263
37  Paul Burrell, *The Way We Were*, 140
38  Simone Simmons, *Diana: The Last Word*, 33
39  Off the record interview
40  Interview Michael Shea, 19 September 2006
41  Simone Simmons, *Diana: The Last Word*, 224
42  Ibid., 219
43  Interview Jasper Conran, 9 October 2006
44  Ibid.
45  Dempster and Evans, UK edn, 146–7
46  Off the record interview
47  Andrew Morton, *Diana: Her True Story – In Her Own Words*, 45
48  James Whitaker, *Diana v. Charles*, 126
49  Tim Clayton and Phil Craig, 235
50  Ralph G. Martin, 313
51  Ibid.
52  Off the record interview
53  Interview Michael Shea, 19 September 2006
54  Off the record interview
55  Andrew Morton, *Diana: Her True Story – In Her Own Words*, 38
56  *Daily Mirror*, 3 November 1981
57  Michael Shea, *A View from the Sidelines*, 121
58  Interview Ashley Walton, 7 June 2006
59  Tim Clayton and Phil Craig, 101
60  *The Times*, 1 December 1992
61  Harold Evans, *Good Times, Bad Times*, 314
62  Ibid., 315–16
63  Ibid., 316
64  Ralph G. Martin, 282
65  Sally Bedell Smith, 130

## Chapter 11

1   Ralph G. Martin, *Charles and Diana*, 289
2   *Daily Mail*, 24 June 1982
3   Anthony Holden, *Charles: A Biography*, 174
4   Jonathan Dimbleby, *The Prince of Wales: A Biography*, 304
5   Ibid., 332
6   Andrew Morton, *Diana: Her True Story – In Her Own Words*, 53
7   Hugo Vickers, *Elizabeth: The Queen Mother*, 463
8   Ibid., 491
9   Colin Burgess, *Behind Palace Doors*, 138
10  Michael Shea, *A View from the Sidelines*, 110
11  Ralph G. Martin, 316

12     BBC *Panorama* interview, 20 November 1995
13     Off the record interview
14     Andrew Morton, *Diana: Her True Story – In Her Own Words*, 139
15     Interview Lucia van der Post, 13 March 2006
16     Lady Colin Campbell, *The Real Diana*, 110
17     BBC *Panorama* interview, 20 November 1995
18     *Daily Mirror*, 11 January 1983
19     *Daily Express*, 19 January 1983
20     Tim Clayton and Phil Craig, *Diana: Story of a Princess*, 121
21     *Sun*, 16 August 1982
22     *Daily Telegraph*, 27 February 1981
23     *Daily Mail*, 24 June 1982
24     Roy Strong, *Diaries 1967–1987*, 317
25     Sally Bedell Smith, *Diana: In Search of Herself*, 140
26     *Observer*, 2 August 1981
27     James Whitaker, *Diana v. Charles*, 129
28     Off the record interview
29     Kitty Kelley, *The Royals*, 308
30     *The Times*, 18 September 1982
31     Off the record interview
32     ITV *Diana: The Story of a Princess*, Part 2, June 2001
33     Jonathan Dimbleby, 303
34     ITV *Diana: The Story of a Princess*, Part 2, June 2001
35     Off the record interview
36     ITV *Diana: The Story of a Princess*, Part 2, June 2001
37     Sir Harold Evans' diary
38     Off the record interview
39     Anthony Holden, *Charles: A Biography*, 227
40     Ralph G. Martin, 329
41     Ibid., 323
42     Rosalind Coward, *Diana: The Portrait*, 110
43     Andrew Morton, *Diana: Her True Story – In Her Own Words*, 48
44     Rosalind Coward, 115
45     Jonathan Dimbleby, 332
46     James Whitaker, 37
47     Jonathan Dimbleby, 333
48     Ralph G. Martin, 328
49     Andrew Morton, *Diana: Her True Story – In Her Own Words*, 49
50     Kitty Kelley, 306
51     Jonathan Dimbleby, 332
52     Andrew Morton, *Diana: Her True Story – In Her Own Words*, 49
53     Interview Ashley Walton, 7 June 2006
54     James Whitaker, 132
55     Interview Ken Wharfe, 15 March 2006
56     Interview Andrew Barrow, 15 November 2005
57     Off the record interview

58  Off the record interview
59  Off the record interview

## Chapter 12

1   Interview Jasper Conran, 9 October 2006
2   Sir Nicholas Lloyd 21 June 2006 conversation with author
3   *Evening Standard*, 18 July 2006
4   A. N. Wilson, *The Rise and Fall of the House of Windsor*, 24
5   Gyles Brandreth, *Charles & Camilla*, 247
6   James Whitaker, *Diana v. Charles*, 138
7   Jeremy Paxman, *On Royalty*, 10
8   Off the record interview
9   *Vanity Fair*, 'The Mouse That Roared', October 1985
10  Off the record interview
11  Roy Strong, *Diaries 1967–1987*, 361
12  Interview Meredith Etherington-Smith, 26 July 2005
13  Interview Lady Puttnam, 26 July 2006
14  *Daily Mail*, 6 October 2006
15  *Daily Mirror*, 11 May 1983
16  Interview Lady Puttnam, 26 July 2005
17  Sarah Bradford, *Diana*, 140
18  Anthony Holden, *Charles: A Biography*, 196
19  The Prince of Wales website, http://www.princeofwales.gov.uk/speeches andarticles/a_speech_by_hrh_the_prince_of_wales_titled_islam_and_the_ wes_425873846.html
20  *Vanity Fair*, 'The Mouse That Roared', October 1985
21  Andrew Neil, *Full Disclosure*, 256
22  Interview James Colthurst, 13 June 2006
23  Nigel Dempster and Peter Evans, *Behind Palace Doors*, UK edn, 163
24  Ibid., 165
25  *Sunday Mirror*, 13 December 1998
26  Sarah Bradford, *Diana*, 131
27  John Whitehead 17 October 2006 conversation with author
28  Bruce Oldfield, *Rootless: An Autobiography*, 261
29  Interview Stephen Fry, 21 September 2005
30  Off the record interview
31  Settelen tapes, NBC *Dateline*, 29 November 2004
32  Interview Jasper Conran, 9 October 2006
33  Andrew Morton, *Diana: Her True Story – In Her Own Words*, 51
34  Interview Jasper Conran, 9 October 2006
35  Andrew Morton, *Diana: Her True Story – In Her Own Words*, 51
36  Gyles Brandreth, 249
37  Anthony Holden, *Charles: A Biography*, 180
38  Andrew Morton, *Diana: Her True Story – In Her Own Words*, 147
39  Interview Marie Helvin, 18 September 2006
40  Sally Bedell Smith, *Diana: In Search of Herself*, 134

41 Stuart Higgins office statement to the author
42 Off the record interview
43 Interview Wayne Sleep, 17 September 2006
44 *Evening Standard*, 28 April 2003
45 Interview Mikhail Baryshnikov, 18 October 2006
46 Interview John Travolta, 6 April 2006
47 Ibid.
48 Interview Mikhail Baryshnikov, 18 October 2006
49 Ibid.
50 Interview Beverly Sills, 16 October 2006
51 Jonathan Dimbleby, *The Prince of Wales: A Biography*, 384
52 Interview John Travolta, 6 April 2006
53 Interview Beverly Sills, 16 October 2006
54 Interview Mikhail Baryshnikov, 18 October 2006
55 Ibid.
56 Tim Clayton and Phil Craig, *Diana: Story of a Princess*, 140
57 Interview John Travolta, 6 April 2006.

## Chapter 13

1 Paul Burrell, *A Royal Duty*, 110
2 James Hewitt, *Love and War*, 33
3 *Daily Mail*, Anne de Courcy, 16 March 1993
4 Gyles Brandreth, *Charles & Camilla*, 215
5 Ibid., 268
6 Nigel Dempster and Peter Evans, *Behind Palace Doors*, UK edn, 148
7 Interview Anne de Courcy, 8 March 2006
8 Interview Ken Wharfe, 15 March 2006
9 Interview Mervyn Wycherley, 5 September 2006
10 Interview Colin Tebbutt, 24 August 2006
11 Ibid.
12 Interview Ken Wharfe, 3 August 2006
13 *West Essex Gazette*, 22 May 1987
14 Interview Mervyn Wycherley, 5 September 2006
15 Interview Ken Wharfe, 3 August 2006
16 Off the record interview
17 Off the record interview
18 Settelen tapes, NBC *Dateline*, 29 November 2004
19 Interview Ken Wharfe, 3 August 2006
20 Off the record interview
21 Interview Ken Wharfe, 3 August 2006
22 Settelen tapes, NBC *Dateline*, 29 November 2004
23 Interview James Colthurst, 13 June 2006
24 James Hewitt, 50
25 Sally Bedell Smith, *Diana: In Search of Herself*, 161
26 *Daily Express*, 8 December 2004
27 Simone Simmons, *Diana: The Last Word*, 62–3

28   Off the record interview
29   Settelen tapes, NBC *Dateline*, 29 November 2004
30   *Guardian & Gazette Newspapers* (Essex), 23 July 1987
31   Interview Joy Chopp, 22 July 2006
32   Settelen tapes, NBC *Dateline*, 29 November 2004
33   Ibid.
34   Kitty Kelley, *The Royals*, 346
35   Settelen tapes, NBC *Dateline*, 29 November 2004
36   Off the record interview
37   Off the record interview
38   Interview Jasper Conran, 9 October 2006
39   Sarah Curtis (ed.), *The Journals of Woodrow Wyatt*, Vol. 1, 189
40   Off the record interview
41   Interview Wayne Sleep, 17 September 2006
42   Off the record interview
43   Off the record interview
44   Sally Bedell Smith, 194–5
45   Sarah, Duchess of York, *My Story*, 58
46   Off the record interview
47   Sarah, Duchess of York, 92
48   Ibid., 85
49   Sarah Curtis (ed.), *The Journals of Woodrow Wyatt*, Vol. 1, 377
50   Interview Lord Glenconner, 26 September 2006
51   Sarah Bradford, *Diana*, 214
52   Interview Edward Mirzoeff, 11 May 2005
53   Max Riddington and Gavan Naden, *Frances*, 42
54   Sarah, Duchess of York, 43–4
55   Ibid., 44
56   Ibid., 60
57   Ibid.
58   Tina Brown diary
59   PBS *Frontline*, 'The Princess and the Press', Harry Arnold, 16 November 1997
60   Ben Pimlott, *The Queen*, 523
61   Anthony Holden, *Charles: A Biography*, 200
62   Sally Bedell Smith, 170
63   Andrew Morton, *Diana: Her True Story – In Her Own Words*, 58
64   Sarah, Duchess of York, 2
65   Ibid.
66   Andrew Morton, *Diana: Her True Story – In Her Own Words*, 59
67   Michael Shea email to author, 6 February 2007
68   Paul Burrell, *A Royal Duty*, 164
69   *Sunday Mirror*, 14 January 1996
70   Interview Selina Hastings, 14 March 2006
71   Interview Mervyn Wycherley, 5 September 2005
72   BBC *Panorama* interview, 20 November 1995

73   Andrew Morton, *Diana: Her True Story – In Her Own Words*, 55
74   Ibid.
75   Beatrix Campbell, *Diana, Princess of Wales*, 159
76   Sarah Curtis (ed.), *The Journals of Woodrow Wyatt*, Vol. 1, 189

## Chapter 14

1    James Hewitt, *Love and War*, 51
2    Simone Simmons, *Diana: The Last Word*, 68
3    Interview Sir Jeremy Greenstock, 27 September 2005
4    James Hewitt, 20
5    Ibid., 9
6    Ibid., 18
7    Interview Ken Wharfe, 15 March 2006
8    Interview Mervyn Wycherley, 5 September 2006
9    Tim Clayton and Phil Craig, *Diana: Story of a Princess*, 166
10   Ibid., 163
11   Ibid., 169
12   James Whitaker, *Diana v. Charles*, 47
13   *Daily Telegraph* (Australia), 22 June 1987
14   Off the record interview
15   Interview James Fox, 25 September 2005
16   James Hewitt, 175
17   Interview Ken Wharfe, 15 March 2006
18   Sally Bedell Smith, *Diana: In Search of Herself*, 183
19   *Sunday Times*, 18 September 1988
20   *News of the World*, 24 March 1991
21   James Hewitt, 65
22   Simone Simmons, *Diana: The Last Word*, 68
23   James Hewitt, 62
24   Ken Wharfe, *Diana: A Closely Guarded Secret*, 77
25   Andrew Morton, *Diana: Her True Story – In Her Own Words*, 188
26   *Daily Mail*, 18 February 1987
27   Sarah Bradford, *Diana*, 182
28   Interview Peter York, 19 June 2006
29   Interview Marie Helvin, 18 September 2006
30   Bruce Oldfield, *Rootless: An Autobiography*, 244
31   Interview Lord Puttnam, 26 July 2005
32   Rosalind Coward, *Diana: The Portrait*, 175
33   Interview Marjatta van Boeschoten, 15 September 2006
34   Off the record interview
35   Beatrix Campbell, *Diana, Princess of Wales*, 166
36   Sally Bedell Smith, 202
37   P. D. Jephson, *Shadows of a Princess*, 153
38   Interview Jasper Conran, 9 October 2006
39   Rosalind Coward, 179
40   Ibid.

41   P. D. Jephson, 145
42   Interview Nicky Haslam, 2 August 2005
43   Andrew Morton, *Diana: Her True Story – In Her Own Words*, 174
44   Off the record interview
45   Interview Ken Wharfe, 15 March 2006
46   Interview Jasper Conran, 9 October 2006
47   *Sun*, 15 May 1987
48   Tim Clayton and Phil Craig, 198–9
49   James Hewitt, 143
50   Interview Ken Lennox, 30 January 1997
51   Ken Wharfe, 139
52   *News of the World*, 17 March 1991
53   Tim Clayton and Phil Craig, 278
54   Ken Wharfe, 140
55   Interview Harry Arnold, 30 January 2007
56   *Daily Mail*, 30 June 1993
57   Max Clifford and Angela Levin, *Read All About It*, 171
58   *Daily Mirror*, 19 September 2005
59   Interview Jasper Conran, 9 October 2006
60   Off the record interview

## Chapter 15

1   Garrick Alder Research, 12
2   *Sunday Times*, 4 October 1998
3   John Cassidy, *New Yorker*, 15 September 1997
4   PBS *Frontline*, 'The Princess and the Press', Roy Greenslade, 16 November 1997
5   Off the record interview
6   *Advertiser*, Bruce Wilson, 26 June 1987
7   Off the record interview
8   *Sunday Times*, 18 September 1988
9   Simone Simmons, *Diana: The Last Word*, 23
10   Interview Judy Wade, 10 May 2006
11   Anthony Holden, *The Tarnished Crown*, 89
12   Sarah, Duchess of York, *My Story*, 165
13   Ibid., 192–3
14   James Whitaker, *Diana v. Charles*, 167
15   Nigel Dempster and Peter Evans, *Behind Palace Doors*, UK edn, 201
16   *Sunday Times*, 16 April 1989
17   Ibid., 18 September 1988
18   Paul Burrell, *A Royal Duty*
19   P. D. Jephson, *Shadow of a Princess*, 97
20   Sarah Bradford, *Diana*, 205
21   James Whitaker, 162
22   *The Times*, 12 March 1989
23   Andrew Morton, *Diana: Her True Story – In Her Own Words*, 62

24  Interview Ken Wharfe, 15 March 2006
25  Andrew Morton, *Diana: Her True Story – In Her Own Words*, 63
26  Interview Ken Wharfe, 15 March 2006
27  Settelen tapes, NBC *Dateline*, 6 December 2004
28  James Whitaker, 192
29  Off the record interview
30  Gyles Brandreth, *Charles & Camilla*, 268
31  Ibid., 260
32  *Oxford Mail*, 9 September 1992
33  Tim Clayton and Phil Craig, *Diana: Story of a Princess*, 188
34  Ibid., 189
35  Dempster and Evans, *Behind Palace Doors*, U.S. edition, 240–64
36  Tim Clayton and Phil Craig, 189
37  Andrew Knight email to author, 26 November 2006
38  Richard Stott, *Dogs and Lampposts*, 17
39  Ibid.
40  John Nelson, 'A Technical Analysis of the "Dianagate" Tape', 22 January 1993
41  John Nelson email to author, 24 November 2006
42  John Nelson, 'A Technical Analysis of the "Dianagate" Tape', 22 January 1993
43  Interview John Nelson, 20 November 2006
44  John Nelson email to author, 24 November 2006
45  Duncan Campbell email to author, 25 November 2006
46  Lord Rees-Mogg in conversation with author
47  *Daily Mail*, 13 May 1993
48  Gyles Brandreth, 253
49  Harold Evans, *Good Times, Bad Times*, 44
50  John Nelson email to author, 24 November 2006
51  Conversation with Andrew Tilberis, December 2006
52  John Nelson email to author, 24 November 2006
53  *Guardian*, 14 January 1993
54  Ibid.
55  Ibid.
56  Ibid.
57  *Sun*, 5 September 1992
58  Sally Bedell Smith, *Diana: In Search of Herself*, 204
59  *Sunday Times*, 7 July 1991
60  Andrew Neil, *Full Disclosure*, 260
61  James Whitaker, 165
62  Andrew Morton, *Diana: In Pursuit of Love*, 37
63  P. D. Jephson, 377
64  Andrew Morton, *Diana: In Pursuit of Love*, 49

## Chapter 16

1  Robert Lacey, *Royal*, 317

2  Paul Burrell, *A Royal Duty*, 112
3  Off the record interview
4  P. D. Jephson, *Shadows of a Princess*, 330–1
5  Tim Clayton and Phil Craig, *Diana: Story of a Princess*, 225
6  Jonathan Dimbleby, *The Prince of Wales: A Biography*, 486
7  *Sun*, 14 February 1992 – photographed by Arthur Edwards
8  Andrew Morton, *Diana: In Pursuit of Love*, 128
9  Sarah, Duchess of York with Jeff Coplon, *My Story*, 201
10  Sally Bedell Smith, *Diana: In Search of Herself*, 222
11  *Spectator*, 6 June 1992
12  *Sunday Times*, 7 July 1991
13  Interview James Colthurst, 13 June 2006
14  Ibid., 1 December 2006
15  Andrew Morton, *Diana: In Pursuit of Love*, 24
16  Ibid., 45
17  ITV *Diana: The Story of a Princess*, Part 3, Felix Lyle interview, June 2001
18  Ibid.
19  Andrew Morton, *Diana: In Pursuit of Love*, 35
20  Interview James Colthurst, 1 December 2006
21  Andrew Morton, *Diana: Her True Story – In Her Own Words*, 41
22  Ibid., 51
23  Ibid., 38
24  Ibid., 19
25  Ibid., 46
26  Sarah, Duchess of York, 199
27  Ibid., 4
28  Andrew Morton, *Diana: In Pursuit of Love*, 50
29  Ibid., 34
30  Ibid., 47
31  Ibid., 48
32  Andrew Morton, *Diana: Her True Story*, 5th edn
33  Interview James Colthurst, 27 November 2006
34  Tim Clayton and Phil Craig, 229
35  Andrew Neil, *Full Disclosure*, 261
36  Ibid., 265
37  Ken Wharfe, *Diana: A Closely Guarded Secret*, 162
38  *The Times*, 2 April 1992
39  Ibid.
40  Ibid.
41  Andrew Morton, *Diana: Her True Story – In Her Own Words*, 181
42  Angela Levin, *Raine & Johnnie*, 271
43  Interview with Vivienne Parry, 5 March 2007
44  Paul Burrell, *A Royal Duty*, 153
45  Andrew Morton, *Diana: In Pursuit of Love*, 54
46  *Mail on Sunday*, 30 August 1992
47  Jonathan Dimbleby, 479

48  Robert Lacey, 317
49  Andrew Neil, 267
50  *The Times*, 30 June 1992
51  *Spectator*, 6 June 1992
52  Max Hastings, *Editor*, 328
53  Jonathan Dimbleby, 477
54  Andrew Morton, *Diana: In Pursuit of Love*, 57
55  Andrew Morton, *Diana: Her New Life*, 33
56  Ibid.
57  Paul Burrell, *A Royal Duty*, 158
58  Robert Lacey, 319
59  Paul Burrell, *A Royal Duty*, 159
60  Ibid.
61  Andrew Morton, *Diana: Her New Life*, 33–4
62  Ibid., 34
63  Paul Burrell, *A Royal Duty*, 159
64  Robert Lacey, 317
65  Interview Dr Jill Wellbourne, 6 March 2007
66  *Sun*, 18 June 1992
67  Paul Burrell, *A Royal Duty*, 162
68  Ibid., 163
69  Ibid., 164
70  *Daily Telegraph*, 22 May 2001
71  Interview Amanda Platell, 31 October 2006
72  PBS *Frontline*, 'The Princess and the Press', Richard Stott, 16 November 1997
73  Richard Stott, *Dogs and Lampposts*, 23
74  Sarah, Duchess of York, 10
75  Richard Stott, 24
76  Sarah, Duchess of York, 14
77  Sarah Curtis (ed.), *The Journals of Woodrow Wyatt*, Vol. 3, 59
78  PBS *Frontline*, 'The Princess and the Press', Stuart Higgins, 16 November 1997
79  Tim Clayton and Phil Craig, 240
80  Interview Dickie Arbiter, 14 December 2006
81  *The Times*, 24 November 1992
82  *Daily Telegraph*, 19 December 1992
83  Off the record interview
84  Jonathan Dimbleby, 489
85  Interview Dickie Arbiter, 14 December 2006
86  Noel Botham, *The Murder of Princess Diana*, 111
87  Nigel Dempster and Peter Evans, *Behind Palace Doors*, UK edn, 23
88  Paul Burrell, *A Royal Duty*, 168
89  Ibid., 176

## Chapter 17

1   Patrick Jephson to author, 15 January 2007
2   Ibid.
3   Off the record interview
4   Paul Burrell, *The Way We Were*, 89–90
5   Rosalind Coward, *Diana: The Portrait*, 256
6   Ibid., 261
7   *Daily Mail*, 28 April 1993
8   Beatrix Campbell, *Diana, Princess of Wales*, 171
9   *The Times*, 9 December 1992
10  Douglas Hurd, *Memoirs*, 501
11  Ibid., 430
12  Ibid., 501
13  Ken Wharfe, *Diana: A Closely Guarded Secret*, 229
14  *Daily Mail*, 13 July 1993
15  Ken Wharfe, 231
16  P. D. Jephson, *Shadows of a Princess*, 438
17  Anthony Holden, *Vanity Fair*, February 1993
18  Sarah Curtis (ed.), *The Journals of Woodrow Wyatt*, Vol. 3, 389
19  Patrick Jephson to author, 17 January 2007
20  P. D. Jephson, 470
21  Ibid., 444
22  Arthur Edwards, *I'll Tell the Jokes Arthur*, 324
23  *Chatelaine*, September 1993
24  Charles Spencer, *Althorp: The Story of an English House*, 55
25  Paul Burrell, *A Royal Duty*, 183
26  Tim Clayton and Phil Craig, *Diana: Story of a Princess*, 261
27  Interview Lady Palumbo, 18 November 2005
28  Ibid.
29  Off the record interview
30  Interview Dickie Arbiter, 14 December 2006
31  Ken Wharfe, 212
32  Interview Marguerite Littman, 21 July 2005
33  Interview Ken Wharfe, 3 August 2006
34  Paul Burrell, *The Way We Were*, 51
35  Ken Wharfe, 227
36  Interview Paul Johnson, 1 August 2005
37  Interview Lady Palumbo, 18 November 2005
38  Sally Bedell Smith, *Diana: In Search of Herself*, 258
39  Ibid., 259
40  Ibid., 258
41  Tim Clayton and Phil Craig, 275
42  Interview Ken Wharfe, 3 August 2006
43  Off the record interview
44  Mark Saunders and Glenn Harvey, *Dicing with Di*, 6
45  Ibid.

46   Ibid., 7–8
47   Andrew Morton, *Diana: In Pursuit of Love*, 85
48   Tim Clayton and Phil Craig, 270
49   Mark Saunders and Glenn Harvey, 35
50   Ibid., vii
51   Ibid., 39
52   Geoffrey Robertson email to author, 31 January 2007
53   *Sunday Mirror*, 7 November 1993
54   *The Times*, 9 November 1993
55   Kitty Kelley, *The Royals*, 452
56   Sarah Bradford, *Diana*, 271
57   Marie Brenner, *New Yorker*, 9 June 1995
58   Interview Teddy Forstmann, 6 December 2006
59   Ibid.
60   Ibid.
61   Marie Brenner, *New Yorker*, 9 June 1995
62   Interview Teddy Forstmann, 6 December 2006
63   P. D. Jephson, 149
64   Ken Wharfe, 243
65   Sally Bedell Smith, 230
66   Off the record interview
67   Tim Clayton and Phil Craig, 250
68   Interview James Colthurst, 13 June 2006
69   Interview Teddy Forstmann, 6 December 2006
70   Interview Ken Wharfe, 3 August 2006
71   Off the record interview
72   Sarah Bradford, *Diana*, 190
73   Simone Simmons, *Diana: The Last Word*, 24
74   Ibid.
75   Interview Lord Puttnam, 26 July 2005
76   BBC *Panorama* interview, 20 November 1995
77   *The Times*, 4 December 1993
78   Interview Lady Palumbo, 18 November 2005
79   Ibid.

## Chapter 18

1   *Sun*, 1 March 1993
2   Jonathan Dimbleby, *The Prince of Wales: A Biography*, xviii
3   Interview Dickie Arbiter, 14 December 2006
4   PBS *Frontline*, 'The Princess and the Press', Max Hastings, 16 November 1997
5   *Sunday Times*, 3 July 1994
6   Jonathan Dimbleby, 528
7   *Daily Mail*, 30 June 1994
8   *Maclean's*, 11 July 1994
9   Gyles Brandreth, *Charles & Camilla*, 249

10   *Evening Standard*, 1 July 1994
11   *New York Times*, 30 June 1994
12   Tim Clayton and Phil Craig, *Diana: Story of a Princess*, 267
13   Interview Richard Kay, 3 November 2006
14   Interview Jasper Conran, 9 October 2006
15   *Daily Express*, 25 March 1994
16   Tina Brown diary
17   Ibid.
18   Off the record interview
19   Georgina Howell, *Diana: Her Life in Fashion*, 154, 156
20   *Sunday Times*, 3 July 1994
21   Interview Mark Bolland, 13 May 2005
22   Ibid.
23   Interview Geordie Greig, 16 November 2005
24   Piers Morgan, *The Insider*, 117
25   Ibid., 116
26   *Daily Mail*, 14 July 1993
27   Piers Morgan, 42
28   Interview Richard Kay, 3 November 2006
29   *Daily Mail*, 22 August 1994
30   Sally Bedell Smith, *Diana: In Search of Herself*, 262
31   *News of the World*, 21 August 1994
32   *Daily Mail*, 22 August 1994
33   Piers Morgan, 43
34   Interview Paul Johnson, 1 August 2005
35   Piers Morgan, 44
36   *Daily Mail*, 20 February 1995
37   *BBC News*, 10 January 2003
38   Simone Simmons, *Diana: The Last Word*, 70
39   Robert Lacey, *Royal*, 332
40   *The Times*, 17 October 1994
41   Nigel Dempster and Peter Evans, *Behind Palace Doors*, UK edn, 214
42   Off the record interview
43   Sarah Curtis (ed.), *The Journals of Woodrow Wyatt*, Vol. 3, 563
44   Off the record interview

## Chapter 19

1   Mark Saunders and Glenn Harvey, *Dicing With Di*, 216
2   Andrew Morton, *Diana: In Pursuit of Love*, 123
3   Interview Anouska Hempel [Lady Weinberg], 1 February 2007
4   Interview Sir Ronald Grierson, 8 May 2006
5   P. D. Jephson, *Shadows of a Princess*, 538
6   BBC *Panorama* interview, 20 November 1995
7   Ibid.
8   Ibid.
9   Interview Dickie Arbiter, 14 December 2006

10    P. D. Jephson, 536
11    Ibid., 538
12    John Birt, *The Harder Path*, 409
13    Ibid., 414
14    Interview Lord Puttnam, 25 May 2005
15    John Birt, 413
16    *Sunday Times*, 26 November 1995
17    Tina Brown, *Washington Post*, 10 March 2005
18    Clive James, 'Requiem', *New Yorker*, 15 September 1997
19    Richard Lindley, *Panorama*, 373
20    Piers Morgan, *The Insider*, 103
21    Richard Lindley, 368
22    James Lees-Milne, *Diaries 1993–1997*, 195
23    BBC *Panorama* interview, 20 November 1995
24    Ibid.
25    Ibid.
26    James Hewitt, *Love and War*, 4
27    Off the record interview
28    BBC *Panorama* interview, 20 November 1995
29    Sarah Curtis (ed.), *The Journals of Woodrow Wyatt*, Vol. 3, 576
30    PA News, Andrew Woodcock, 25 November 1995
31    Sarah Bradford, *Diana*, 296
32    *Sunday Times*, 26 November 1995
33    Sarah Curtis (ed.), *The Journals of Woodrow Wyatt*, Vol. 3, 596
34    *Sunday Times*, 26 November 1995
35    Ibid., 3 December 1995
36    *People*, 22 December 1995
37    *Sunday Times*, 26 November 1995
38    *The Times*, 23 January 1996
39    *Daily Mail*, 13 December 1995
40    *Daily Mirror*, 13 December 1995
41    *Daily Mail*, 13 December 1995
42    *Evening Standard*, 12 December 1995
43    Interview Dr Henry Kissinger, 27 June 2005
44    *Sunday Times*, 28 January 1996
45    Paul Burrell, *A Royal Duty*, 322
46    'Operation Paget Inquiry', 14 December 2006, 102
47    *Daily Mail*, 14 December 2006
48    Paul Burrell, *A Royal Duty*, 217
49    Ibid., 218
50    Ibid.
51    Ibid., 219
52    *Daily Telegraph*, 22 December 1995
53    Ibid.
54    Paul Burrell, *A Royal Duty*, 222.
55    Ibid.

56  Off the record interview
57  Sally Bedell Smith, *Diana: In Search of Herself*, 314
58  *Sunday Times*, 21 April 1996
59  Off the record interview
60  Off the record interview
61  Simone Simmons, *Diana: The Last Word*, 24
62  Georgina Howell, *Diana: Her Life in Fashion*, 139
63  Robert Lacey, *Royal*, 343
64  Paul Burrell, *A Royal Duty*, 226
65  Andrew Morton, *Diana: In Pursuit of Love*, 212
66  Ibid., 210
67  *The Times*, 29 February 1996
68  Robert Lacey, 343
69  Ibid.
70  *Sunday Times*, 21 July 1996
71  *CNN News*, 4 January 1996
72  *Daily Telegraph*, 13 July 1996
73  *The Times*, 11 May 1996
74  Paul Burrell, *A Royal Duty*, 232
75  Ibid., 237
76  Andrew Morton, *Diana: In Pursuit of Love*, 212
77  *Sunday Times*, 14 July 1996
78  Paul Burrell, *A Royal Duty*, 242
79  Ibid., 236
80  *Sunday Times*, 14 July 1996
81  Off the record interview
82  Paul Burrell, *A Royal Duty*, 239

## Chapter 20

1   Off the record interview
2   Paul Burrell, *The Way We Were*, 29
3   Ibid., 30
4   Interview Colin Tebbutt, 24 August 2006
5   Ibid.
6   Paul Burrell, *The Way We Were*, 51
7   Courtesy Andrew Tilberis
8   Paul Burrell, *The Way We Were*, 34
9   *Washington Post*, 7 September 1997
10  Interview David Tang, 20 June 2006
11  Simone Simmons, *Diana: The Last Word*, 154
12  Interview Colin Powell, 9 February 2007
13  'Operation Paget Inquiry', 109
14  Brian MacArthur (ed.), *Requiem*, 57
15  Interview Hamish Bowles, 22 September 2005
16  Interview Jacques Azagury, 4 September 2006
17  Introduction by Meredith Etherington-Smith, in Mario Testino, *Diana*

18    Interview Meredith Etherington-Smith, 26 July 2005
19    *People*, 7 July 1997
20    *International Herald Tribune*, 13 May 1997
21    Off the record interview
22    Kate Snell, *Diana: Her Last Love*, 85
23    Andrew Morton, *Diana: In Pursuit of Love*, 152
24    Off the record interview
25    Sally Bedell Smith, *Diana: In Search of Herself*, 289
26    *News of the World*, 3 December 1995
27    *Daily Mail*, 4 December 1995
28    Sally Bedell Smith, 316
29    Kate Snell, 99
30    Paul Burrell, *The Way We Were*, 153
31    Kate Snell, 122
32    Paul Burrell, *The Way We Were*, 152
33    'Operation Paget Inquiry', 122
34    *Sunday Times*, 19 January 1997
35    Interview Arthur Edwards, 16 November 2005
36    Tim Clayton and Phil Craig, *Diana: Story of a Princess*, 315
37    Ibid., 316
38    *The Times*, 16 January 1997
39    Off the record interview
40    *Sunday Times*, 19 January 1997
41    Tim Clayton and Phil Craig, 317
42    Ibid.
43    *The Times*, 16 January 1997
44    *Spectator*, 5 July 1997
45    Kate Snell, 137
46    Ibid., 138
47    'Operation Paget Inquiry', 123
48    *Daily Express*, 9 February 1997
49    Kate Snell, 168
50    Interview Hugo Swire, 10 May 2005
51    Clive James, 'Requiem', *New Yorker*, 15 September 1997
52    Tina Brown, 'A Woman in Earnest', *New Yorker*, 15 September 1997
53    Kate Snell, 136
54    Sally Bedell Smith, 336
55    Interview Chris Boffey, 8 March 2007
56    Kate Snell, 184
57    Kate Snell, 184
58    *Daily Mirror*, 29 August 2005
59    *Hello!*, 31 May 1997
60    'Operation Paget Inquiry', 134
61    Interview Mervyn Wycherley, 5 September 2006
62    Off the record interview
63    'Operation Paget Inquiry', 108–9

64  Clive James, 'Requiem', *New Yorker*, 15 September 1997
65  'Operation Paget Inquiry', 108
66  Interview Shirley Conran, 9 February 2007
67  Sally Bedell Smith, 312
68  Tina Brown, 'A Woman in Earnest', *New Yorker*, 15 September 1997
69  Off the record interview
70  *Daily Mail*, 29 October 2005
71  Ibid.
72  Off the record interview
73  Sally Bedell Smith, 335
74  Interview Teddy Forstmann, 12 December 2006
75  Sally Bedell Smith, 336
76  Brian MacArthur (ed.), 63–4
77  Sally Bedell Smith, 337
78  Interview Lord Deedes, 4 August 2005
79  Brian MacArthur (ed.), 126
80  *News of the World*, 7 December 1997
81  Brian MacArthur (ed.), 63
82  Off the record interview
83  *New Yorker*, 28 July 1997
84  'Operation Paget Inquiry', 111
85  Interview Shirley Conran, 9 February 2007
86  Tim Clayton and Phil Craig, 312
87  Interview Lord Deedes, 4 August 2005
88  House of Commons, 10 July 1998, *Hansard*, col. 1349–50

## Chapter 21

1   Ashley Walton email to author, 17 February 2007
2   *NBC News* bulletin, 31 August 1997
3   Jean-Marie Pontaut and Jérôme Dupuis, *Enquête sur la mort de Diana*, 97
4   Ibid., 91
5   Trevor Rees-Jones, *The Bodyguard's Story*, 106
6   Jean-Marie Pontaut and Jérôme Dupuis, 93
7   *The Times*, 22 November 1997
8   Ibid., 2 September 1997
9   Ibid., 22 November 1997
10  Jean-Michel Caradec'h, *Lady Diana: L'enquête criminelle*, 30
11  Ibid., 29
12  Jean-Marie Pontaut and Jérôme Dupuis, 97
13  'Operation Paget Inquiry', 513
14  Jean-Marie Pontaut and Jérôme Dupuis, 98
15  Jean-Marie Pontaut and Jérôme Dupuis, 97
16  Thomas Sancton and Scott MacLeod, *Death of a Princess*, 29–33
17  *Standard* (Ontario), 12 March 2001
18  Interview Dr Isadore Rosenfeld, 20 February 2007
19  'Operation Paget Inquiry', 514

20   Ibid., 517
21   Ibid., 514
22   Tim Clayton and Phil Craig, *Diana: Story of a Princess*, 351–2
23   'Operation Paget Inquiry', 512
24   Interview Colin Tebbutt, 24 August 2006
25   Paul Burrell, *A Royal Duty*, 286
26   Ibid.
27   Interview Colin Tebbutt, 24 August 2006
28   Tim Clayton and Phil Craig, 355
29   Interview Colin Tebbutt, 24 August 2006
30   Colin Tebbutt www.scott-baker-inquests.gov.uk
31   Paul Burrell, *A Royal Duty*, 288–9
32   Interview Arthur Edwards, 18 February 2007
33   Arthur Edwards email to author, 15 February 2007
34   Ashley Walton email to author, 17 February 2007
35   Jean-Marie Pontaut and Jérôme Dupuis, 89
36   Thomas Sancton and Scott MacLeod, 201
37   Jean-Michel Caradec'h, 110
38   Thomas Sancton and Scott MacLeod, 199
39   Off the record interview
40   Jean-Michel Caradec'h, 115–16
41   Ken Lennox email to author, 12 February 2007
42   Jean-Michel Caradec'h, 110
43   Trevor Rees-Jones, 310
44   Jean-Michel Caradec'h, 238–9
45   John Cassidy, *New Yorker*, 15 September 1997
46   James Whitaker email to author, 26 February 2007
47   Piers Morgan, *The Insider*, 172
48   Ibid., 170
49   Ibid.
50   Ken Lennox email to author, 12 February 2007
51   *The Times*, 2 September 1997
52   Piers Morgan, 171
53   Tom Bower, *Fayed: The Unauthorised Biography*, 432
54   'Operation Paget Inquiry', 309
55   Trevor Rees-Jones, 81
56   'Operation Paget Inquiry', 362
57   *CNN News*, 5 September 1997
58   Brian MacArthur (ed.), *Requiem*, 78
59   Interview Colin Tebbutt, 24 August 2006
60   Interview Ken Wharfe, 3 August 2006
61   'Operation Paget Inquiry', 163
62   Ibid.
63   Daily Mail, 21 December 2007
64   Interview Jean-Michel Caradec'h, 16 September 2006
65   Thomas Sancton and Scott MacLeod, 177

66   Trevor Rees-Jones, 117
67   Jean-Michel Caradec'h, 429
68   Tom Bower, 429
69   Ibid., 431
70   *National Post* (Canada), 20 December 2005
71   Gerald Posner, 'Al Fayed's Rage', *Talk Magazine*, September 1999
72   *Press Gazette*, 13 August 1999
73   'Operation Paget Inquiry', 356
74   *The Spectator*, 8 January 2000
75   *Daily Mail*, 23 December 2006
76   'Operation Paget Inquiry', 500
77   Martyn Gregory, 89
78   *Daily Mirror*, 12 February 1998
79   Robert Lacey, *Royal*, 352
80   Interview Mark Bolland, 27 June 2006
81   Kate Snell, *Diana: Her Last Love*, 211
82   Caroline Graham, *Camilla: Her True Story*, 303
83   Off the record interview
84   Max Riddington and Gavan Naden, *Frances*, 157
85   Ibid., 165
86   Tim Clayton and Phil Craig, 356
87   Ibid.
88   Caroline Graham, 301
89   Tim Clayton and Phil Craig, 356

## Chapter 22

1    Brian MacArthur (ed.), *Requiem*, 133
2    Thomas de Zengotita, *Mediated*, 151
3    Interview Warren Hoge, 18 February 2007
4    *Sunday Times*, 7 September 1997
5    Interview John Hockenberry, 10 February 2007
6    Interview Alastair Campbell, 21 September 2005
7    *The Times*, 1 September 1997
8    Interview James Fox, 25 September 2005
9    James Lees-Milne, *Diaries 1993–1997*, 288
10   Interview Lady Glenconner, 30 September 2005
11   *New York Times*, 8 September 1997
12   *Guardian*, 27 December 1997
13   Oonagh Shanley-Toffolo email to author, 17 March 2007
14   *The Times*, 1 September 1997
15   Off the record interview
16   Interview Dickie Arbiter, 14 December 2005
17   *Sunday Times*, 7 September 1997
18   Robert Lacey, *Royal*, 361
19   Sarah Bradford, *Diana*, 377
20   Off the record interview

21  Tim Clayton and Phil Craig, *Diana: Story of a Princess*, 364
22  Interview Alastair Campbell, 21 September 2005
23  *Sun*, 4 September 1997
24  Paul Burrell, *A Royal Duty*, 303
25  Interview Andrew Roberts, 22 February 2007
26  Interview Robin Janvrin, 11 November 2005
27  Off the record interview
28  Off the record interview
29  Paul Burrell, 296
30  Off the record interview
31  Robert Lacey, 374
32  Interview Geordie Greig, 16 November 2005
33  Interview Meredith Etherington-Smith, 26 July 2005
34  *Washington Post*, 7 September 1997
35  Interview Hugo Vickers, 28 July 2005
36  Off the record interview
37  Off the record interview
38  Max Riddington and Gavan Naden, *Frances*, 174
39  Paul Burrell, 305
40  *Daily Mail*, 9 November 2002
41  Interview Tony Blair, 20 June 2006
42  *Journal* (Newcastle), 9 July 2005
43  *Daily Express*, 15 July 2005
44  *New York Times*, 23 February 2007

## Afterword

1   Testimony: Deborah Gribble 19 December 2007
2   Testimony: Lord Fellowes 12 February 2008
3   John Loughrey to author January 2008
4   *Daily Mail* 4 October 2007
5   Testimony: Mohamed Al Fayed 18 February 2008
6   Testimony: The Hon. Rosa Monckton, 13 December 2007
7   Testimony: Mohamed Al Fayed 18 February 2008
8   Testimony: Mohamed Al Fayed 18 February 2008
9   Lord Justice Scott Baker 18 February 2008
10  Testimony: Mohamed Al Fayed 18 February 2008
11  Lord Justice Scott Baker 18 February 2008
12  Testimony: John Macnamara 14 February 2008
13  Testimony: Lord Stevens 14 February 2008
14  Testimony: Sir Richard Dearlove 20 February 2008
15  David Pryce-Jones Blog, *National Review*, 4 October 2007
16  Testimony: Roberto Devorik 17 January 2008
17  Testimony: Raine, Countess Spencer 12 December 2007
18  *The Sun* 18 February 2008
19  Lord Justice Scott Baker 15 February 2008
20  *The Sun* 18 February 2008

21  Summing up: Lord Justice Scott Baker, 1 April 2008

22  Testimony: Mohamed Al Fayed 18 February 2008

23  Testimony: Kelly Ann Fisher 14 December 2007

24  Testimony: Mohamed Al Fayed 18 February 2008

25  Evidence: Telephone call Kelly Ann Fisher & Dodi Al Fayed August 1997

26  Michael Mansfield QC 13 December 2007

27  Testimony: Brigadier Sir Miles Hunt-Davis 13 December 2007

28  Michael Mansfield QC 17 January 2008

29  Evidence: D.N. Meynell Meeting with HRH Princess of Wales 18 October 1994

30  *Daily Mail* 23 January 2008

31  Author's notes

32  Evidence: Mohamed Al Fayed to Lord Stevens 9 February 2006

33  Trevor Rees-Jones, *The Bodyguard's Story*, 83

34  Testimony: Trevor Rees 23 January 2008

35  Testimony: Trevor Rees 23 January 2008

36  Testimony: Ken Wharfe 9 January 2008

37  Testimony: Trevor Rees 23 January 2007

38  Testimony: François Tendil 3 December 2007

39  Testimony: Thierry Rocher 4 December 2008

40  Testimony: Myriah Daniels 18 December 2007

41  Summing up: Lord Justic Scott Baker 31 March 2008

42  Summing up: Lord Justic Scott Baker 31 March 2008

43  Summing up: Lord Justic Scott Baker 31 March 2008

44  Summing up: Lord Justic Scott Baker 31 March 2008

45  Statement: Romuald Rat to French Police 31 March 2008

46  Summing up: Lord Justic Scott Baker 31 March 2008

47  Summing up: Lord Justic Scott Baker 31 March 2008

48  Evidence: Diana, Princess of Wales to Dodi Al Fayed 27 July 1997

49  Statement: Operation Paget inquiry Hasnat Khan 24 September 2006

50  Statement: Operation Paget inquiry Hasnat Khan 24 September 2006

51  Testimony: Paul Burrell 14 January 2008

52  Operation Paget inquiry 14 December 2006, 24

53  Tim Clayton and Phil Craig: Diana: Story of a Princess, 333

# Index